EARLY JUDAISM AND ITS MODERN INTERPRETERS

THE SOCIETY OF BIBLICAL LITERATURE

The Bible and Its Modern Interpreters

Douglas A. Knight, General Editor

1. *The Hebrew Bible and Its Modern Interpreters*
   Edited by Douglas A. Knight and Gene M. Tucker
2. *Early Judaism and Its Modern Interpreters*
   Edited by Robert A. Kraft and George W. E. Nickelsburg
3. *The New Testament and Its Modern Interpreters*
   Edited by Eldon Jay Epp and † George W. MacRae

EARLY JUDAISM AND ITS MODERN INTERPRETERS

edited by

Robert A. Kraft
and
George W. E. Nickelsburg

FORTRESS PRESS
Philadelphia, Pennsylvania

SCHOLARS PRESS
Atlanta, Georgia

SOCIETY OF BIBLICAL LITERATURE

CENTENNIAL PUBLICATIONS

Editorial Board

The Society of Biblical Literature gratefully acknowledges a grant
from the National Endowment for the Humanities to underwrite
certain editorial and research expenses of the Centennial Publications Series. Published results and interpretations do not necessarily
represent the view of the Endowment.

Library of Congress Cataloging in Publication Data
Main entry under title:

Early Judaism and its modern interpreters.

(The Bible and its modern interpreters ; 2)
1. Judaism — History — Post-exilic period, 586 B.C.–
210 A.D. — Historiography — Addresses, essays, lectures.
2. Jews — History — 586 B.C.–70 A.D. — Historiography —
Addresses, essays, lectures. I. Kraft, Robert A.
II. Nickelsburg, George W. E., 1934–   . III. Series.
BM176.E18   1986   296'.09'014   83-20317

ISBN: SP hardback: 0-89130-669-2
ISBN: SP paperback: 0-89130-884-9
ISBN: Fortress hardback: 0-8006-0722-8

1778F86   Printed in the United States of America   1–722
on acid-free paper

CONTENTS

Editors and Contributors ix

Preface to the Series x

Editors' Preface xi

Abbreviations xiv

Introduction: The Modern Study of Early Judaism
   George W. E. Nickelsburg, with Robert A. Kraft 1
     The Modern Study of Early Judaism 2
     The Changing Portrait of Early Judaism 9
     Possibilities and Prospects for Future Study 21

Part One: Early Judaism in Its Historical Settings 31

  1. The Political and Social History of the Jews in
     Greco-Roman Antiquity: The State of the Question
     Shaye J. D. Cohen 33
       The Legacy of Nineteenth-century Historiography 34
       A Methodological Crisis 37
       The Greco-Roman Context 41
       Social History 46
       Conclusion 51

  2. Diversity in Postbiblical Judaism
     Gary G. Porton 57
       Hellenistic Judaism 57
       Scribes, Hasidim, Apocalyptic Jews 60
       Samaritans, Qumran, Therapeutae 63
       Sadducees (and Boethusians), Pharisees and Related Groups 66
       Zealots and Sicarii 72

  3. The Samaritans and Judaism
     James D. Purvis 81
       Major Contributions of Recent Studies 81
       The Problem of Samaritan Origins:
         Background of Present Research 83
       Recent Reconstructions of Early Samaritan History 85
       Samaritanism as a Variety of Judaism and
         Varieties of Samaritanism: Problems and Perspectives 90

4. Judaism as Seen by Outsiders
   John G. Gager 99
   Anti-Semitism and Anti-Judaism in Early Christianity:
      The Debate since World War II 100
   Jews and Judaism in Pagan Perspective 105

Part Two: Recent Discoveries 117

5. The Judean Desert
   Jerome Murphy-O'Connor, O.P. 119
   The Discoveries...119
   The Editorial Committee 121
   The Antiquity of the Scrolls 121
   The People of the Scrolls...................................124
   The Sectarian Documents....................................125
   Pseudepigrapha 137
   The History of the Sect.....................................139
   Conclusion 143

6. Other Manuscript Discoveries
   Sebastian P. Brock 157
   Jewish Biblical Texts 157
   Apocrypha and Pseudepigrapha................................162
   Liturgical and Subliterary Texts............................163
   Nonliterary Texts 164
   Some Relevant Non-Jewish Texts 167
   Conclusion 168

7. Archaeology, Iconography, and
   Nonliterary Written Remains
   Eric M. Meyers and A. Thomas Kraabel 175
   Archaeological Sites..177
   Iconography 189
   The Nonliterary Written Evidence 197
   General Conclusions 201

8. Jewish Numismatics
   Yaakov Meshorer 211
   Under the Persian Regime: Fourth Century B.C.E..............211
   Samaritan Coins? 211
   Under the Ptolemies...212
   Under the Hasmoneans 212
   The Herodians 213
   The Coins of the Bar Kokhba Revolt (132–135 C.E.) 215
   The Coins of the Roman Procurators 215
   List of Principal Coins 216

Part Three: The Literature 221

9. Jewish Greek Scriptures
   Emanuel Tov 223
   The LXX Proper 223
   Revisions of the LXX...................................229

10. Palestinian Adaptations of
    Biblical Narratives and Prophecies
    I. The Bible Rewritten (Narratives)
       Daniel J. Harrington, S.J. 239
       Biblical Texts 240
       Literary Character...................................242
       Theological Tendencies and Setting in Life 243

    II. The Bible Explained (Prophecies)
        Maurya P. Horgan 247
        Description of the Texts 248
        Pesharim and Other Interpretative Writings 250

    III. Future Research 253

11. Testaments
    I. The Literary Genre "Testament"
       Anitra Bingham Kolenkow 259
       Formal Characteristics Relating to Setting.....................259
       Ethics and Apocalyptic: Content and Structure 262
       Pseudepigraphy and Midrash: Beyond Ethics 264
       Relationship to Other Genres.............................266
       Conclusion 267

    II. The Testamentary Literature
        in Recent Scholarship
        John J. Collins 268
        The Testaments of the Twelve Patriarchs 268
        The Testament of Job 276
        The Testament of Moses 277
        The Testament of Abraham 277
        Conclusion 278

12. Narrative Literature
    Robert Doran 287
       Introduction 287
       The Testament of Abraham 287
       Joseph and Aseneth 290
       The Martyrdom of Isaiah 293
       The Rest of the Words of Jeremiah 294
       The Book of Tobit 296
       The Additions to Daniel 299
       Judith 302

13. Jewish Historiography
    Harold W. Attridge 311
    Fragmentary Greco-Jewish Historians.......................311
    The Maccabean Histories 316
    Philo 323
    Josephus 324
    Conclusion 328

14. Apocalyptic Literature
    John J. Collins 345
    The Scope of the Literature...............................345
    The Nature of the Literature..............................347
    The Place of Apocalyptic Literature in Judaism 356
    Conclusions and Prospects 361

15. Wisdom Literature
    Burton L. Mack and
      Roland E. Murphy, O. Carm. 371
    Ben Sira..373
    The Wisdom Poem in Baruch 3:9–4:4 377
    The Letter of Aristeas 378
    Aristobulus 379
    The Wisdom of Solomon 380
    Philo of Alexandria 387
    Pseudo-Phocylides 395
    4 Maccabees 396

16. Jewish Hymns, Odes, and Prayers
    (ca. 167 B.C.E.–135 C.E.)
    James H. Charlesworth 411
    Review 411
    Summary...421
    Critique..422
    Conclusion 425

17. Reconstructions of Rabbinic Judaism
    Anthony J. Saldarini 437
    Sources 438
    Biography 451
    History...454
    Rabbinic Thought 460
    Postscript..464

Maps..478

Appendix: Bibliographies and Text Editions
  for Early Jewish Source Materials 480

Index of Modern Authors 487

EDITORS AND CONTRIBUTORS

Harold W. Attridge, Department of Theology, University of Notre Dame, Notre Dame, Indiana

Sebastian P. Brock, The Oriental Institute, Oxford, England

James H. Charlesworth, Princeton Theological Seminary, Princeton, New Jersey

Shaye J. D. Cohen, Jewish Theological Seminary, New York, New York

John J. Collins, Department of Theology, University of Notre Dame, Notre Dame, Indiana

Robert Doran, Department of Religion, Amherst College, Amherst, Massachusetts

John G. Gager, Department of Religion, Princeton University, Princeton, New Jersey

Daniel J. Harrington, S.J., Weston School of Theology, Cambridge, Massachusetts

Maurya P. Horgan, The Scriptorium, Denver, Colorado

Anitra Bingham Kolenkow, Dominican School of Philosophy and Theology, Berkeley, California

A. Thomas Kraabel, Luther College, Decorah, Iowa

Robert A. Kraft, Department of Religious Studies, University of Pennsylvania, Philadelphia, Pennsylvania

Burton L. Mack, The Institute for Antiquity and Christianity, Claremont Graduate School, Claremont, California

Yaakov Meshorer, The Israel Museum, Jerusalem, Israel

Eric M. Meyers, Department of Religion, Duke University, Durham, North Carolina

Roland E. Murphy, O. Carm., The Divinity School, Duke University, Durham, North Carolina

Jerome Murphy-O'Connor, O.P., École biblique et archéologique française, Jerusalem, Israel

George W. E. Nickelsburg, School of Religion, The University of Iowa, Iowa City, Iowa

Gary G. Porton, Program in Religious Studies, University of Illinois, Urbana, Illinois

James D. Purvis, Department of Religion, Boston University, Boston, Massachusetts

Anthony J. Saldarini, Department of Theology, Boston College, Boston, Massachusetts

Emanuel Tov, Department of Bible, The Hebrew University, Jerusalem, Israel

PREFACE TO THE SERIES

The present volume is one part of a trilogy, The Bible and Its Modern Interpreters. Together with three other series—Biblical Scholarship in North America, Biblical Scholarship in Confessional Perspective, and The Bible in American Culture—it has been initiated by the Society of Biblical Literature to mark the 1980 centennial of its founding. As a whole, the Centennial Publications program aims to scrutinize the history of biblical scholarship as well as the very diverse roles that the Bible has played in North American culture. Approximately 150 scholars are contributing to about forty volumes planned for these four series—graphic witness to the current vitality of biblical studies.

Whereas the other three series are devoted primarily to North American phenomena, such as distinctive schools of thought, influential scholars, fields of special activity, various confessional contexts, and arenas of cultural impact, the three volumes that make up The Bible and Its Modern Interpreters encompass the international range of research on, respectively, the Hebrew Bible, Early Judaism, and the New Testament. Structured according to the usual subdisciplines and subject matter, each sets for itself the task of describing the course of scholarship since ca. 1945. The essays are intended as critical reviews, appraising the current state of affairs in each area of study and calling attention to issues that scholars should face in the years ahead.

Deep appreciation goes to each person who has been involved in the planning and producing of this trilogy, most especially to the authors themselves, who have joined in this common effort to reflect on the developments in their fields. We also acknowledge gratefully the cooperation of the two publishers, Scholars Press and Fortress Press, as well as the generous support of the National Endowment for the Humanities.

Douglas A. Knight
Vanderbilt University

EDITORS' PREFACE

This volume documents the major developments in the study of "early Judaism" (ca. 330 B.C.E. to ca. 138 C.E.) from about the mid-1940s. Because this field of investigation is not as clearly defined or as well established as the areas covered in the other volumes of this trilogy (Hebrew Bible and New Testament), we have included a lengthy introduction that discusses the field itself and current interest in it, new tools and approaches, major topics and problems, and the types of study we feel are needed in the future. The introductory essay was drafted primarily by George Nickelsburg and edited into its current form by Robert Kraft.

The bulk of the volume is organized into three major sections. The first deals with "synthetic approaches" to the political, social, and religious history of the period. The original plan was to include in this opening section a major essay on problems of definition, with a focus on Judaism as religion, but that was abandoned and comments on these issues are now included in the introduction. Part 2 focuses on the recent discoveries that have stimulated and enriched the renewed study of early Judaism, from the Dead Sea documents and other written materials to archaeological and numismatic data of relevance. As the introduction points out, the sheer bulk of new materials renders many aspects of the older synthetic treatments obsolete and justifies the need for careful descriptive analysis at various levels before comprehensive new syntheses are attempted. Part 3 surveys work on the literature of early Judaism organized according to different types (form and/or content) of material. The concern here is primarily with the Jewish apocrypha and pseudepigrapha and the writings of Philo and Josephus, although some attention is also given to literary aspects of the Qumran scrolls (which are treated as such in chapter 5). The final chapter of the third part differs somewhat from the earlier ones in that it addresses the question of how the Jewish rabbinic materials, which mostly postdate the chronological limits that we have set for early Judaism, have been used or can be used responsibly in the study of early Judaism. The chapter that had been planned to begin this part, on the languages used by Jews in the Greco-Roman world, had to be omitted (see the general comments in the introduction).

The authors who contributed to this volume were asked to write selective and critical surveys of scholarship for particular aspects of the field, focusing on significant trends, emphases, and conclusions while also noting gaps and impasses of scholarship and indicating prospects for future work.

The original assignments were made in 1978, with the target date of spring 1981 for final editing. Thus, most of the contributions were completed by 1981 and have not been systematically updated to cover the subsequent years. The reader should consider 1980 as a rough *terminus* for the literature surveyed herein, although there will be sporadic inclusion of more recent materials.

Not every user will be pleased with the fact that there is no comprehensive bibliography to the volume, but that each chapter has its own separate list of works cited. This was a difficult editorial decision to make, especially since some of the same works are referred to in several different chapters, but the present format was finally agreed upon for all the volumes in the trilogy. To supplement the general index of authors and the individual chapter bibliographies, we have added an appendix detailing bibliographic resources for study of the apocrypha and pseudepigrapha and listing recent texts and editions of the ancient writings. The list of abbreviations should be consulted also for special monograph series, periodicals, etc. Since the volume has been prepared on computer, the editors will create a cumulative machine-readable bibliography for further development and circulation as appropriate.

Finally, we express our sincere appreciation to all those who have helped with this volume. We apologize to the contributors for the frustrating delays, and we thank them for their patience and cooperation. Nor should we overlook the various individuals, too numerous to name separately, to whom we have turned for assistance and advice at various stages. Several graduate students and other university personnel deserve explicit mention: Benjamin Wright, Ellen Shevitz, and Monique Nebolon at the University of Pennsylvania; Philip Frank and Randal Argall at the University of Iowa. Paula McNutt of Vanderbilt drew the two maps (see also vol. 1). Maurya Horgan and Paul Kobelski of The Scriptorium prepared the materials for the press. Douglas Knight was patient, gentle, and, when necessary, firm in fulfilling his role as series editor. Scholars Press and Fortress Press are to be commended once again for cooperating in this project, and special thanks are due to the National Endowment for the Humanities for its financial assistance with certain editorial and research expenses for volumes in the SBL Centennial Publications Series.

This preface goes to press shortly after the untimely death of our colleague and friend George W. MacRae. His association with the planning and the subject matter of this book was long, close, and important. Although he is better known for his work on Christian origins, his knowledge of early Judaism was broad and incisive and is already clearly in evidence in his (unpublished) Cambridge University dissertation on the relationships between Jewish apocalypticism and Gnosticism. As a charter member of the steering committee of the SBL Pseudepigrapha Seminar (later "Group"), he shared his wisdom and counsel in the making of important decisions. During his tenure as Executive Secretary of the SBL he facilitated the work of the Group including the publication of several volumes in the series Septuagint and Cognate Studies, and he played an important role in the planning of the Society's Centennial Publications series. His many other commitments notwithstanding, he participated regularly in the seminar sessions of the Pseudepigrapha Group. Through his roles as professor, editor, executive, and scholarly colleague, he has influenced the pages of this book in many imperceptible and immeasurable ways. We and our colleagues in the Society were fortunate to have known him, to have worked with him in practical and scholarly matters, and to have learned from him.

ROBERT A. KRAFT
GEORGE W. E. NICKELSBURG

ABBREVIATIONS

AASF   Annales academiae scientarium fennicae
AB   Anchor Bible
AE   *Année Epigraphique*
AGJU   Arbeiten zur Geschichte des antiken Judentums und des Urchristentums
AGSU   Arbeiten zur Geschichte des Spätjudentums und Urchristentums
ALGHJ   Arbeiten zur Literatur und Geschichte des hellenistischen Judentums
ALUOS   *Annual of Leeds University Oriental Society*
AnBib   *Analecta Biblica*
ANRW   *Aufstieg und Niedergang der römischen Welt: Geschichte und Kultur Roms im Spiegel der neueren Forschung.* Ed. H. Temporini and W. Haase. Berlin and New York: de Gruyter
AOAT   Alter Orient und Altes Testament
AOT   *The Apocryphal Old Testament*, ed. H. F. D. Sparks. Oxford: Clarendon, 1984.
APAT   *Die Apocryphen und Pseudepigraphen des Alten Testaments.* Ed. E. Kautzsch. 2 vols. Tübingen: Mohr-Siebeck, 1900.
APOT   *The Apocrypha and Pseudepigrapha of the Old Testament.* Ed. R. H. Charles. 2 vols. Oxford: Clarendon Press, 1913.
ARW   *Archiv für Religionswissenschaft*
ASOR   American Schools of Oriental Research
ASTI   *Annual of the Swedish Theological Institute*
ATA   Alttestamentliche Abhandlungen
ATANT   Abhandlungen zur Theologie des Alten und Neuen Testaments
ATDan   Acta theologica danica

BA   *The Biblical Archaeologist*
BAC   Biblioteca de autores cristianos
BAR   *Biblical Archaeologist Reader*
BARev   *Biblical Archaeology Review*
BASOR   *Bulletin of the American Schools of Oriental Research*
BBB   Bonner Biblische Beiträge
BE   J. T. Milik, *The Books of Enoch: Aramaic Framents of Qumrân Cave 4.* Oxford: Clarendon Press, 1976.
BETL   Bibliotheca ephemeridum theologicarum lovaniensium
BHS   *Biblia Hebraica Stuttgartensia.* Ed K. Elliger and W. Rudolph. Stuttgart: Deutsche Bibelstiftung, 1976-77.
Bib   *Biblica*
BibOr   Biblica et orientalia
BJRL   *Bulletin of the John Rylands University Library of Manchester*
BHT   Beiträge zur historischen Theologie
BLE   *Bulletin de littérature ecclésiastique*
BO   *Bibliotheca orientalis*
BR   *Biblical Research*
BTB   *Biblical Theology Bulletin*

BWANT   Beiträge zur Wissenschaft vom Alten und Neuen Testament
    BZ   *Biblische Zeitschrift*
  BZAW   Beihefte zur *ZAW*
  BZNW   Beihefte zur *ZNW*

   CBA   Catholic Biblical Association
   CBC   Cambridge Bible Commentary
   CBQ   *Catholic Biblical Quarterly*
 CBQMS   Catholic Biblical Quarterly Monograph Series
   CII   J.-B. Frey, *Corpus inscriptionum iudaicarum.* 2 vols. Vatican City: Institute of Christian Archaeology, 1936, 1952. Vol. 1 rev. by Baruch Lifshitz. New York: Ktav, 1975.
   CJT   *Canadian Journal of Theology*
  CNRS   Centre National de la Recherche Scientifique
ConBNT   Coniectanea biblica, New Testament
ConBOT   Coniectanea biblica, Old Testament
    CQ   *Classical Quarterly*
CRAIBL   *Comptes rendus de l'académie des inscriptions et belles-lettres*
 CRINT   Compendia Rerum Iudaicarum ad Novum Testamentum
  CSCT   Columbia Studies in the Classical Tradition
  CSCO   Corpus scriptorum christianorum orientalium
   CTM   *Concordia Theological Monthly*

 DBSup   *Dictionnaire de la Bible, Supplément.* Ed. H. Cazelles and A. Feuillet. Paris: Letouzey et Ané, 1928–
   DJD   Discoveries in the Judaean Desert
   DTT   *Dansk teologisk tidsskrift*

EncJud   *Encyclopaedia Judaica.* Jerusalem: Encyclopaedia Judaica; New York: Macmillan, 1971.
EstBib   *Estudios bíblicos*
   ETL   *Ephemerides theologicae lovanienses*
   ETR   *Études théologiques et religieuses*
   EvQ   *Evangelical Quarterly*
ExpTim   *Expository Times*

FRLANT   Forschungen zur Religion und Literatur des Alten und Neuen Testaments

  GRBS   *Greek, Roman, and Byzantine Studies*

   HAT   Handbuch zum Alten Testament
  HBMI   *The Hebrew Bible and Its Modern Interpreters.* Ed. Douglas A. Knight and Gene M. Tucker. SBL Centennial Publications; The Bible and Its Modern Interpreters 1. Chico, CA: Scholars Press. Philadelphia: Fortress, 1985.
   HDR   Harvard Dissertations in Religion
  HeyJ   *Heythrop Journal*
   HNT   Handbuch zum Neuen Testament
    HR   *History of Religions*
   HSM   Harvard Semitic Monographs
   HTR   *Harvard Theological Review*
   HTS   Harvard Theological Studies
  HUCA   *Hebrew Union College Annual*

IDB	*The Interpreter's Dictionary of the Bible.* Ed. G. A. Buttrick. Nashville and New York: Abingdon, 1962.
IDBSup	*Interpreter's Dictionary of the Bible, Supplementary Volume.* Ed. K. Crim. Nashville: Abingdon, 1976.
IEJ	*Israel Exploration Journal*
IG	*Inscriptiones Graecae.* Editio Minor. Berlin: de Gruyter, 1924–
INJ	*Israel Numismatic Journal*
Int	*Interpretation*
IOSCS	International Organization for Septuagint and Cognate Studies
ITQ	*Irish Theological Quarterly*

JAL	Jewish Apocryphal Literature
JANESCU	*Journal of the Ancient Near Eastern Society of Columbia University*
JAOS	*Journal of the American Oriental Society*
JB	Jerusalem Bible
JBC	*Jerome Biblical Commentary.* Ed. R. E. Brown, J. A. Fitzmyer, and R. Murphy. Englewood Cliffs, NJ: Prentice-Hall, 1968.
JBL	*Journal of Biblical Literature*
JDS	Jewish Desert Studies
JES	*Journal of Ecumenical Studies*
JJS	*Journal of Jewish Studies*
JNES	*Journal of Near Eastern Studies*
JPOS	*Journal of the Palestine Oriental Society*
JQR	*Jewish Quarterly Review*
JQRMS	Jewish Quarterly Review Monograph Series
JR	*Journal of Religion*
JRS	*Journal of Roman Studies*
JSHRZ	Jüdische Schriften aus hellenistisch-römischer Zeit. Ed. W. G. Kümmel et al. Gütersloh: Mohn, 1973–
JSJ	*Journal for the Study of Judaism in the Persian, Hellenistic and Roman Periods*
JSNT	*Journal for the Study of the New Testament*
JSOT	*Journal for the Study of the Old Testament*
JSS	*Journal of Semitic Studies*
JTC	*Journal for Theology and the Church*
JTS	*Journal of Theological Studies*

LCL	Loeb Classical Library
LTK	*Lexikon für Theologie und Kirche.* Ed. J. Höfer and K. Rahner. 11 vols. 2d ed. Freiburg im B.: Herder, 1957–67.
LXX	Septuagint

MGWJ	*Monatsschrift für Geschichte und Wissenschaft des Judentums*
MSU	Mitteilungen des Septuaginta-Unternehmens
MT	Masoretic Text

NAB	New American Bible
NC	*The Numismatic Chronicle*
NCE	*New Catholic Encyclopedia.* Ed. M. R. P. McGuire et al. New York: McGraw-Hill, 1967–74
NEB	New English Bible
NovT	*Novum Testamentum*
NovTSup	Supplements to *NovT*

NRT	*La nouvelle revue théologique*
NTS	*New Testament Studies*
OBO	Orbis biblicus et orientalis
OCA	Orientalia Christiana Analecta
OG	Old Greek
OLP	Orientalia lovaniensia periodica
OTP	*The Old Testament Pseudepigrapha*. Ed. J. H. Charlesworth. 2 vols. Garden City, NY: Doubleday, 1983–85
OTS	*Oudtestamentische Studiën*
PAAJR	*Proceedings of the American Academy of Jewish Research*
PEQ	*Palestine Exploration Quarterly*
PVTG	Pseudepigrapha Veteris Testamenti graece
PW	See *RE*
PWSup	*Supplementbände* to *RE*
RAC	*Reallexikon für Antike und Christentum: Sachwörterbuch zur Auseinandersetzung des Christentums mit der antiken Welt*. Ed. T. Klauser. Stuttgart: Hiersemann, 1950–
RB	*Revue biblique*
RE	*Paulys Real-Encyclopädie der classischen Altertumswissenschaft*. Ed. G. Wissowa. Stuttgart: Metzler, 1893.
RechBib	Recherches bibliques
REJ	*Revue des études juives*
RelArts	Religion and the Arts
RelSRev	*Religious Studies Review*
RevQ	*Revue de Qumran*
RevScRel	*Revue des sciences religieuses*
RevThom	*Revue Thomiste*
RGG	*Die Religion in Geschichte und Gegenwart*. Ed. K. Galling. 3d ed. 7 vols. Tübingen: Mohr-Siebeck, 1957–65.
RHE	*Revue d'histoire ecclésiastique*
RHPR	*Revue d'histoire et de philosophie religieuses*
RHR	*Revue de l'histoire des religions*
RQ	*Römische Quartalschrift für christliche Altertumskunde und Kirchengeschichte*
RR	*Review of Religion*
RSPT	*Revue des sciences philosophiques et théologiques*
RSR	*Recherches de science religieuse*
RSV	Revised Standard Version
RTL	*Revue théologique de Louvain*
SANT	Studien zum Alten und Neuen Testament
SBFLA	*Studii biblici franciscani liber annuus*
SBL	Society of Biblical Literature
SBLDS	SBL Dissertation Series
SBLMasS	SBL Masoretic Studies
SBLMS	SBL Monograph Series
SBLSBS	SBL Sources for Biblical Study
SBLSCS	SBL Septuagint and Cognate Studies
SBLTT	SBL Texts and Translations
SBS	Stuttgarter Bibelstudien
SBT	Studies in Biblical Theology

SC	*Sources chrétiennes*
SEÅ	*Svensk exegetisk årsbok*
Sem	*Semitica*
SIG	*Sylloge Inscriptionum Graecarum.* 3d ed. Ed. W. Dittenberger. Leipzig: Hirzel, 1915–24.
SJ	Studia judaica
SJLA	Studies in Judaism in Late Antiquity
SNT	Studien zum Neuen Testament
SNTS	Society for New Testament Studies
SNTSMS	Society for New Testament Studies Monograph Series
SOTSMS	Society for Old Testament Study Monograph Series
SPB	Studia postbiblica
SPap	*Studia papyrologica*
ST	*Studia theologica*
STDJ	Studies on the Texts of the Desert of Judah
StudHell	Studia Hellenistica
SUNT	Studien zur Umwelt des Neuen Testaments
SVTP	Studia in Veteris Testamenti pseudepigrapha
TAPA	*Transactions of the American Philological Association*
TD	*Theology Digest*
TDNT	*Theological Dictionary of the New Testament.* Ed. G. Kittel and G. Friedrich. 10 vols. Grand Rapids: Eerdmans, 1964–76
TLG	Thesaurus Linguae Graecae
TLZ	*Theologische Literaturzeitung*
TRu	*Theologische Rundschau*
TS	*Theological Studies*
TS	Texts and Studies
TSAJ	Texte & Studien zum antiken Judentum
TTZ	*Trierer theologische Zeitschrift*
TU	Texte und Untersuchungen
TZ	*Theologische Zeitschrift*
UNDCSJCA	University of Notre Dame Center for the Study of Judaism and Christianity in Antiquity
VC	*Vigiliae christianae*
VD	*Verbum domini*
VT	*Vetus Testamentum*
VTSup	Supplements to *VT*
WHJP	*World History of the Jewish People*
WMANT	Wissenschaftliche Monographien zum Alten und Neuen Testament
WUNT	Wissenschaftliche Untersuchungen zum Neuen Testament
ZAW	*Zeitschrift für die alttestamentliche Wissenschaft*
ZDPV	*Zeitschrift des deutschen Palästina-Vereins*
ZNW	*Zeitschrift für die neutestamentliche Wissenschaft*
ZRGG	*Zeitschrift für Religions- und Geistesgeschichte*
ZTK	*Zeitschrift für Theologie und Kirche*

INTRODUCTION:
THE MODERN STUDY OF EARLY JUDAISM

George W. E. Nickelsburg, with Robert A. Kraft

The fact that a volume such as this is included in the SBL Centennial Series on The Bible and Its Modern Interpreters itself sheds light on modern scholarly approaches to biblical literature. From the perspective of classical Judaism or of the Protestant Christian tradition, this volume does not deal with "biblical" writings at all. It is, instead, a miscellany of what remains from Jewish sources not covered in the other two volumes—chronologically, from roughly the close of volume 1 (Hebrew Bible, "OT") to roughly the close of volume 3 ("NT"). It is true that some of the ancient writings discussed in this volume are included in the Roman Catholic and Eastern Orthodox Christian Bibles ("the apocrypha" in Protestant terminology), but that is not the primary reason why such a volume is appropriate to this series. Rather, it is because modern study of the biblical literature has insisted on examining the broad context of history and society within which the biblical materials appeared that the subject matter of this volume takes on such interest, both in relationship to the other volumes of the trilogy and as an area of study in and of itself.

Scholars have referred to this ragged-edged period by many names. From the perspective of the Judaism that developed into classical orthodoxy and is the historical parent of modern varieties of Judaism, this volume deals with "postbiblical," "prerabbinic" Judaism, "between the Bible and the Mishna," or perhaps better (if also less flexible with respect to the biblical canon), "Second Temple Judaism"—from the rebuilding of the temple in the late sixth century B.C.E. through the two revolts against Rome in 70 and 135 C.E. From a Protestant Christian perspective, this has often been dubbed "intertestamental Judaism," although it clearly extends through the NT period. German Protestant scholarship even invented the term "late Judaism" to cover this material, apparently with a view to distinguishing between the "early" form of the Judahite religious impetus as found in Ezra and his colleagues, after the demise of "the religion of Israel" and its institutions, and the "later" developments that occurred in the Greco-Roman period—with clear interest in shedding light on earliest Christianity.

But if the classical Judaism that emerged out of its Pharisaic-rabbinic roots and survived into the modern period is entitled to the unadorned and commonly accepted designation "Judaism," what preceded it must be described as "early" in terms of historical sequence. Thus, although "early Judaism" is not a particularly precise term, especially with reference to its beginning point and to its biblical-canonical connections, the term is used here somewhat by default for its simplicity and relative comprehensiveness. By "early Judaism" we intend to refer to the phenomena collectively designated "Judaism" in the period bounded approximately by Alexander the Great (330 B.C.E.) on the one end and the Roman Emperor Hadrian (138 C.E.) on the other.

The chronological limits are not unambiguous since, by the very nature of the assignment, they must be correlated with the religious concept of biblical canon. Although some of the latest writings in the Jewish Bible apparently come from the period of "early Judaism" as defined here, they are covered in volume 1 and have no special place in this volume. The vagueness of the designation "early Judaism" contrasts sharply with the concreteness of "rabbinic Judaism," which is widely used to refer to the relatively homogeneous Judaism forged by the Pharisees-rabbis subsequent to our period. Whereas rabbinic Judaism is dominated by an identifiable perspective that holds together many otherwise diverse elements, early Judaism appears to encompass almost unlimited diversity and variety— indeed, it might be more appropriate to speak of early Judaisms. Nor should it be surprising that the materials covered in this volume do not neatly cohere but resist organization into a unified package. They have not, as a unit, been preserved through the ages by any single self-interested community (unlike Jewish and Christian scriptures or rabbinic Jewish literature). Indeed, the majority of early Jewish writings were preserved by Christians, but not all by the same Christian groups or in the same languages. A few were preserved also, in one form or another, by rabbinic Judaism. Others were not transmitted by any surviving community but were recovered from their graves quite accidentally after their users had vanished. Given this state of affairs, it is not surprising that the remains of early Judaism should be both exciting and frustrating to scholarly researchers, constituting a veritable museum of data that cry out to be analyzed, classified, and, to whatever degree is still possible, understood.

THE MODERN STUDY OF EARLY JUDAISM

The intensive modern study of these materials began in the early and middle nineteenth century with the publication of first editions and annotated translations of a number of apocalypses. This wave of scholarship crested between 1880 and 1928 with the appearance of various editions, translations, and synthesizing handbooks associated with such names as

R. H. Charles (*APOT*), Emil Kautzsch (*APAT*), Emil Schürer, Wilhelm Bousset and Hugo Gressmann, George Foot Moore, and Paul Riessler. An *International Journal of the Apocrypha* (at first called *Deuterocanonica*) was even published from 1905 to 1917. Although a few significant new works appeared during the Depression and the Second World War, sustained progress in this area of scholarship did not resume until the late 1940s, when it reemerged with new vigor. This explosion of interest in the history and literatures of early Judaism is one of the most remarkable developments in biblical studies in the past forty years, for it has involved the rebirth and rapid growth of an entire subdiscipline.

Scholarly activity relating to these materials is now widely evident. The books of the apocrypha are regularly included in major editions of almost all English translations of the Bible (e.g., JB, NAB, RSV, and NEB). New translations and collections of the pseudepigrapha are appearing not only in English (*OTP*, ed. Charlesworth; *AOT*, ed. Sparks) but also in a number of other languages, including German (JSHRZ, ed. Kümmel), French, Dutch, Danish, and Japanese (Charlesworth, 1981:26–29, 239). New introductory treatments of this literature are also available to scholar and student, clergy and laity (see below). Monograph series such as AGJU, ALGHJ, SBLSCS, SJLA, SPB, STDJ, SUNT, and SVTP, and new periodicals like *RevQ* and *JSJ* have been created to handle the avalanche of studies in the area (see also the appropriate volumes of *ANRW*).

Several factors have contributed to this rise of interest in early Judaism and its literatures. Most important has been the discovery of new data, and the Qumran scrolls understandably have attracted the most attention. Because the Dead Sea documents provided manuscript evidence from the three centuries surrounding the turn of the era and stemmed from a relatively little known sector of Judaism that seemed to show impressive similarities to early Christianity, they quickly refocused attention on the Jewish religion and culture of the period. Although the Coptic texts from Nag Hammadi had less immediate relationship to the study of early Judaism, their discovery and publication reinforced the message that scholars were receiving from the Qumran scrolls: Judaism at the turn of the era was a variegated and complex phenomenon, and a close study of it promises rich rewards to the historian. Alongside these two groups of texts were other newly discovered nonliterary texts that shed light on early Judaism.

The new textual evidence, moreover, has continued to be supplemented by material evidence from archaeological excavations in Syro-Palestine and elsewhere (see Michael Stone's delightfully written and illustrated survey article in the 1973 *Scientific American*). The appearance of new data was accompanied by the popularization of new methods of research, which promised new conclusions even from the sources that had long been known. As each new approach was applied to the canonical scriptures (e.g., form criticism, new methods of literary analysis [see

Knight and Tucker: xvi]), it would in turn be applied to the deutero-canonical and other Jewish literatures. Most recently, analytic methods derived from the social sciences are being applied to the written and material remains of early Judaism.

Extrinsic factors also contributed to the emergence of the study of early Judaism as a field in its own right. In the English speaking world, the rise of departments of religious studies in private and state universities has catalyzed new interest in early Judaism, and the study of pre- and non-rabbinic materials has flourished especially in these departments and in university-affiliated divinity schools, where the constraints of canon are not a primary determiner of scholarly priorities. At the same time, the rapid growth and program innovation in scholarly societies such as SBL and SNTS gave new opportunities for organizing sections on such developing areas of research and for exchanging and testing ideas (see Knight and Tucker: xv; Saunders: 58–61).

Another extrinsic factor that has helped to create new interest in the study of early Judaism and has influenced the shape of the field is the historical fact of the Holocaust. Reflection on this modern tragedy has led many NT scholars to question early Christian portrayals of Judaism, as well as typically Protestant interpretations of the texts and the anti-Jewish presuppositions that sometimes underlie both the texts and their interpretation. As a result, there is emerging a new, more empathic view of early Judaism based primarily on Jewish texts.

New Texts, Editions, and Translations

The publication of new texts and editions has been a significant factor in the progress of the study of early Judaism. The caves of the Judean Desert (see chap. 5) have yielded texts hitherto unknown to us. In addition, scholars have identified among the scrolls fragments of some texts in their original languages of Hebrew and Aramaic, texts previously known only in translations once or twice removed from the originals, for example, *1 Enoch,* the *Testaments of the Twelve Patriarchs,* the book of *Jubilees,* and Tobit. Study of these newly discovered Semitic fragments is proving important for research on ancient texts in a variety of ways. For the first time, there are controlled criteria for judging the faithfulness and accuracy of primary and secondary versions. The situation varies from book to book. Aramaic fragments of a Levi apocryphon indicate that the compositional history of the Greek *Testaments of the Twelve Patriarchs* included the compression and redaction of Semitic sources. Hebrew fragments of *Jubilees* seem to indicate that the secondary Ethiopic translation is a relatively faithful representation of the original Semitic. The Aramaic fragments of the Enoch literature bear witness to a more complex picture of the translation and literary development of that corpus.

In addition to shedding light on the issue of the faithfulness of the translations, comparison of the Semitic fragments with the translations will also reveal techniques and principles of translation (on *1 Enoch*, see Barr). Finally, with reference to *1Enoch* and the *Testaments*, the appearance of the new texts has been directly or indirectly responsible for the publication of new critical editions of the versions (see the following works cited in the appendix: de Jonge, 1964, 1978; Milik; Knibb).

In addition to the Qumran materials, many new editions of early Jewish texts, both biblical (chap. 9) and nonbiblical (chap. 6) have been published in recent years (see the appendix). We have already noted above the growing number of new translations that are appearing, some of which are based on textual research that has not yet been published as such. Equally impressive and potentially of great significance are the many and sometimes voluminous editions of nonliterary texts (chap. 6) and the valuable collection of non-Jewish texts with translations (a new Reinach) edited by Menahem Stern (see also chap. 4).

Introductions, Commentaries, Series, and Bibliographies

Although the time is not yet ripe for massive new syntheses of the history of early Judaism, new introductions and handbooks provide entrée into the texts and the state of the field. Geza Vermes, Fergus Millar, and Matthew Black are editing in three volumes an extensively revised form of Emil Schürer's classic study (the "new-Schürer"). A different approach has been taken in the new Compendia Rerum Iudaicarum ad Novum Testamentum (CRINT). Its two-volume first section, *The Jewish People in the First Century* (1974), documents the history and institutions of Judaism, and its three-volume second section, *The Literature of the Jewish People in the Period of the Second Temple and the Talmud* (1984–), will provide critical introductions. As a cooperative effort by Jewish and Christian scholars, this work emphasizes matters of interest to students of both traditions, taking care to clarify aspects of early Judaism that have often been misinterpreted by scholars governed by a Christian agenda. Albert-Marie Denis has focused on the Greek pseudepigrapha in his useful French introduction (1970). In English, G. W. E. Nickelsburg's introduction to major works of the apocrypha, pseudepigrapha, and Qumran scrolls (1981) is directed primarily to students, and John J. Collins has written an introduction to the literature of the Hellenistic Diaspora (1983).

In our enthusiasm for incorporating recent discoveries and new understandings of previously known materials into the broader picture of early Judaism, we should also note that much solid synthetic work has been done in the recent past by a variety of scholars. Many of the most influential and useful general treatments published in the past four decades are discussed below in chapters 1 and 2: for example, those by Elias Bickerman, David S.

Russell, Bo Reicke, Joachim Jeremias, Abraham Schalit, Martin Hengel, Michael Avi-Yonah, and Donald Gowan. To that impressive group, we add reference to the compact and informative survey by Robert H. Pfeiffer, the foundational works of Ralph Marcus, and the handbook by W. Foerster.

Commentaries on early Jewish literature are also beginning to appear with some regularity. A number of commentaries on the major Qumran scrolls were published in the 1950s and 1960s in several languages (chap. 5). The Anchor Bible (AB) promises a full complement on the apocrypha. Commentaries on the pseudepigrapha are being published in the series Studia in Veteris Testamenti pseudepigrapha (SVTP), and several volumes on the apocrypha, pseudepigrapha, and scrolls are announced for the series Hermeneia.

The prolific scholarly activity in this field is attested also by the creation of new monograph series and periodicals noted earlier in this essay. A number of special bibliographical publications have arisen to monitor these developments, in addition to the standard bibliographical periodicals *Elenchus bibliographicus biblicus*, *Old Testament Abstracts* (which also covers the apocrypha), and *New Testament Abstracts* (which documents other material on Judaism relevant to the NT and early Christianity). For convenience, special bibliographical tools are listed together in the appendix.

New Approaches, Methodological Self-consciousness

In recent decades, students of the biblical and related materials have become especially self-conscious about the approaches they use in the literary, archaeological, and historical aspects of their discipline (Kraft, 1976; Kraabel; Smith, 1983). It no longer suffices to assert what is meant by a passage or what happened in antiquity without attending closely to the tools and methods used to arrive at such conclusions. This methodological awareness has been accompanied by a radical revolution in the formal "methods" adopted by such scholars.

New approaches to literary analysis have led the way. In the decades following the publication of the editions of the apocrypha and pseudepigrapha by Kautzsch (1900) and Charles (1913), form criticism began to overshadow source criticism as the scholar's primary tool for the analysis of texts. This method, along with new approaches to the history of tradition, has left indelible marks on the analysis of all texts. This is perhaps nowhere more evident than in the study of rabbinic materials (chap. 17). The severe problems involved in using rabbinic literature as a window through which to view Judaism at the turn of the era are magnified by the newer approaches. As a result, the position of the apocrypha, pseudepigrapha, and the Qumran scrolls as the primary literary witnesses to this period has become all the more central.

Within a decade after the publication of the first Qumran scrolls, students of biblical and related materials began to employ redaction criticism, which shifted the focus from the study of particular traditions contained in a text to an analysis of the whole text in its preserved, edited form. The methodological situation has continued to change. Redaction criticism has been overshadowed more recently by types of literary criticism drawn from nonhistorical disciplines, which interpret whole texts apart from the question of their sources and literary seams and without a central concern for their "theology." Thus, in a relatively short period of time, the literary interests of some scholars have turned from dissecting texts to discover their sources to the study of texts as coherent, independent wholes. An early example of such an approach is Earl Breech's article on 4 Ezra (1973). His holistic analysis was especially significant because he was attacking the time-honored source criticism that had traditionally dominated the study of the early Jewish apocalypses.

That the ancient documents need to be treated as literary wholes, at least in their preserved edited forms, is becoming axiomatic among scholars, although the methods for determining what constitutes the appropriate entity vary with the documents and their interpreters (see Kraft, 1976). Strictly speaking, one could start with the actual manuscripts that have been preserved and ask how their actual users viewed the texts they contain. For many early Jewish texts, this approach might shed considerable light on the Christian perspectives of those who perserved the texts. When text-critical analysis has used the actual manuscripts to recreate the earliest recoverable form of a text, the scholar can investigate that "whole" as well and can attempt to determine the broader situation in which it functioned. By various other means, even earlier recensions and ancestors of a given text may be uncovered, each of which deserves to be viewed as a whole in its own world. In the hands of some interpreters, then, "holistic" analysis may not differ essentially from old-style source criticism, depending on the developmental stage identified as the "whole." Indeed, emphasis on the literary unity of the ancient texts has not precluded an interest in the smaller units within the texts or in literary aspects of those units. The older method of form criticism continues to be a useful tool and, together with a more recent emphasis on rhetorical analysis, can be highly suggestive for exploring an author's purpose and an author's literary and cultural heritage.

A combination of form analysis and the more recent approaches has proved especially fruitful in the study of the apocalypses. Focus on the literary genre apocalypse has produced awareness of aspects of the contents of these works long ignored and raises significant questions regarding the human context in which the documents developed. The study of genre also helps to clarify the development of the popular testamentary form and raises interesting questions about evident hybrid forms, like the *Testament of Moses,* which is at once "biblical paraphrase," testament, and apocalypse (chap. 11a). Holistic literary analysis works from these insights to facilitate a better understanding of complex works like *2 Baruch* (Sayler) and helps to explain how a text such as the *Testament of Moses* could have been composed initially during the time of Antiochus Epiphanes and yet testify to conditions under Herod the Great (chap. 11b). Appropriately, though surprisingly "late in the game," scholars are also beginning to study the early Jewish narrative texts in a similar manner, although firm conclusions about the genres of these texts may still be a long way in the future (chap. 12). Although students of early Jewish literature have been using approaches that are at home in structuralist analysis and the "new criticism," in general the historical-critical training of these scholars has deterred them from a "purely" literary analysis of texts that would ignore their historical settings.

Another recent interdisciplinary influence on biblical studies has been the use of methods and models drawn from the social sciences, notably from sociology and social anthropology. These concerns are not new to the study of early Judaism. Social history has long been an aspect of the historiography of this period (chap. 1), and the form-critical concern with *Sitz im Leben* (setting in life) is fundamentally sociological. Nonetheless, a new interest in these matters is widely evident, especially in the self-conscious use of extradisciplinary methods and models. Concern with social analysis appears in some of the recent work on apocalypticism (on the study of Palestinian apocalyptic, see Nickelsburg, 1983). One section of the 1979 International Colloquium on Apocalypticism was entitled "The Sociology of Apocalypticism and the 'Sitz im Leben' of Apocalypses" (Hellholm: 641–768). Concern about the roots of anti-Judaism and anti-Semitism has stimulated investigation of Christian and non-Christian attitudes toward the Jews in antiquity (chap. 4). The roles of women in early Jewish society have also begun to attract more attention, although much less so than in the scholarship on the canonical scriptures (for a bibliographical treatment, see Kraemer).

The use of approaches developed largely in other disciplines presents its own set of problems. One must be cautious about taking over models developed from empirically repeatable data and employing them in the study of an ancient time and culture for which such data is not available. Nonetheless, the careful use of these methods and models as heuristic tools can provide a whole new dimension to a discipline often dominated by theological or even philological interests.

Methodological and technological innovations have revolutionized the science of "biblical archaeology" (Dever). The material remains of Mediterranean and Near Eastern antiquity have significance that extends far beyond their relationship to the study of biblical texts and events, and as the archaeologists have moved beyond a preoccupation with "biblical archaeology" they have begun to ask radically different questions of the materials they uncover. The archaeological results must ultimately be co-ordinated with the findings of scholars who focus more on textual data and with the insights drawn from interests in social history, but the time does not yet seem ripe for this grand synthesis.

A final example of major methodological refinement and advance-ment is in the area of Hebrew and Aramaic paleography. The discovery of voluminous manuscript remains in the caves of the Judean Desert, in archaeologically controllable contexts, has provided important new data to help fill extensive gaps in the paleographical sequences. This in turn helps to create new controls for editing, dating, and interpreting ancient texts and thus indirectly supplies new data for reconstructions of the history of the period.

THE CHANGING PORTRAIT
OF EARLY JUDAISM

The discovery and publication of new data and the intensive study of old and new materials, partly on the basis of new approaches, are con-tributing to a drastically revised picture of early Judaism. The fullness of that picture, with all its details and hues, is not yet in clear focus. Research on the various parts has not yet advanced sufficiently to encourage prepara-tion of a comprehensive synthetic social, political, or religious history of early Judaism. Nonetheless, some aspects of the old syntheses remain valid and new research is producing fresh details from which a new picture, or a more representative collage, will ultimately emerge (see Stone; Kraft, 1975, 1976; Smith).

What Constitutes Evidence?

The developing new picture of early Judaism rests on a different perception of what data can legitimately be used as evidence for its history. New materials provide evidence that is, as a whole, richer and more variegated than what previously was available. Some older data are no longer considered to be valid evidence for the period, or at least their validity is seriously questioned.

The new evidence includes, first of all, a mass of literary texts, non-literary materials, and inscriptions (chaps. 5–8). Second, archaeological finds have been especially rich in the recent decades (chap. 7). The number of excavations yielding evidence for Judaism of the Greco-Roman period is in itself noteworthy. In addition to those treated in chapter 7 are the excavations at such Hellenistic sites as Beth Zur, Gibeah, and Araq el-Emir, Nabatean sites in Tannur and Petra, Samaritan sites at Shechem and Mount Gerizim, and other significant sites such as Qumran, the caves of the Judean Desert, and the Wadi ed-Daliyeh (see chaps. 5–6). The list could be extended. The more sensational aspects of archaeological discovery should not overshadow the important subdiscipline of numismatics (chap. 8). Large numbers of new coins have been found, and there have been significant changes in the interpretation of the evidence.

The information drawn from nonliterary texts, inscriptions, and archaeological projects promises to enrich and balance our picture of early Judaism. We are much more in touch with the realia of Jewish life in Palestine and the Diaspora and with the domestic, social, economic, and legal factors of that life. From material remains we can see more clearly where Jews lived and traded and met to worship. And new models of social description and analysis may enable scholars to extract further valuable information from these data. Although much remains to be done, it is a mark of the growth of the field that some of the evidence is already finding its way into the handbooks, e.g., the new Schürer, the volumes of CRINT, and especially Martin Hengel's *Judaism and Hellenism.*

Other aspects of the previously accepted data have become less significant for historical reconstruction or have come under suspicion. As indicated above, the rabbinic texts are of much less use as testimonies to the life and religious orientation of the early period. Moreover, some of the classical texts of the pseudepigrapha have come under suspicion. No longer can it be assumed that any given passage in the *Testaments of the Twelve Patriarchs* offers certain evidence of Jewish thought in Hellenistic or Roman times (chap. 11b). The Parables of Enoch (*1 Enoch* 37–71) also have come under suspicion, if not with regard to their Jewish origin, at least with regard to their traditional dating in the Herodian period (see chap. 5; Suter). In addition, we have learned to be very suspicious of tendentious statements about the Jews, notably the Pharisees, whether in the NT or in Jewish sources such as Josephus (see chap. 13).

A New Point of View

A central constitutive factor in the new scholarship on early Judaism has been a radical change in the point of view of the scholars themselves. During the century between the early 1800s and the Second World War, the study of these texts was largely in the hands of Christian scholars. It was rare to find a person who did not approach the texts with Christian presuppositions and prejudices. Consequently, a portrayal of Judaism emerged that was characterized by stereotypes that appeared in NT polemics, were developed further in patristic interpretations, and came to fruition in Reformation law/gospel theology. The details of this anti-Jewish interpretation of Judaism have been convincingly documented by G. F. Moore (1921), Charlotte Klein, and E. P. Sanders (33–59). According to this view, postexilic Judaism as a whole was a sterile mutant of the earlier, vital prophetic religion. The rabbis were legalistic nitpickers concerned with the form rather than the essence of religion. The Pharisees were self-righteous hypocrites. Christianity, on the other hand, was the true blossoming of the faith of Israel, based on events that were the fulfillment of ancient prophecy. Thus, Judaism in the Greco-Roman period could be called *Spätjudentum* ("late Judaism"); with the rise of Christianity, Judaism that did not accept the messianic status of Jesus had come to a dead end with respect to religious significance.

Since the end of World War II the situation has changed drastically. Hitler's Holocaust provides a grim reminder of the social and political anti-Judaism that is, in part, a function of the theological anti-Judaism already evidenced in the NT literature. Partly as a consequence of this reminder, Gentile interpreters of early Judaism have worked more empathically and inductively from the Jewish sources, attempting to be conscious of the anti-Jewish hermeneutic in their intellectual heritage. The result has been the beginning of a more balanced and historically responsible interpretation of early Judaism. Moreover, in another change from the prewar situation, Jewish scholars have shown new interest in the nonrabbinic literary sources of postbiblical Judaism. Their scholarly activity has tended to concentrate on the history of the period (e.g., Bickerman, Lieberman, Marcus) or on the Qumran scrolls, but they have made important contributions also to the literary and historical interpretation of the apocrypha and pseudepigrapha. The prewar study of early Judaism was marked not only by Christian stereotypes and schematizations but also by a variety of other oversimplifications, many of which were functions of the philosophical (primarily Hegelian) presuppositions that governed much of nineteenth-century continental historiography and theology. A fresh study of the sources has revealed that culturally, socially, and theologically, early Judaism was a complex and variegated phenomenon. In the sections that follow, aspects of this variety and complexity will be outlined.

Judaism and Its Environment

One of the most damaging oversimplifications of earlier scholarship has been the dichotomy drawn between "Palestinian" and "Hellenistic" Judaism (chap. 2). According to this scheme, Palestinian Judaism was free of the "pagan" (often philosophical) influences that had transformed Greek Diaspora Judaism for the worse. One of the foundations of this division was linguistic: Palestinian Judaism spoke and wrote in Aramaic or Hebrew; Hellenistic Judaism in Greek. Closer investigation of the older data (e.g., Lieberman), combined with new information and approaches, has called for a reorientation of attitudes. It is now clear that even as an independent Maccabean/Hasmonean kingdom, Jewish Palestine is best viewed as part of the larger "hellenized" world, whether its representatives were speaking and writing in Greek or in a Semitic dialect (Aramaic or Hebrew). That there were different Jewish responses to that world is also clear, but they are not defined primarily along linguistic or geographical lines. To state the issue more generally, the relation of Jews and Judaism to the Hellenistic environment was similar to that of other identifiable "subcultures" (e.g., in Egypt or Syria) and is treated most satisfactorily by accepting Hellenism as the norm against which to judge similarities and differences, rather than by positing some "pure" form of (Palestinian) Judaism as the norm. Hellenization, whether in Palestine or in the Diaspora, was a complex and variegated phenomenon that involved the syncretistic use of Greek myth, philosophy, literary forms, historiography, iconography, ideals of kingship, and the like.

The Languages of the Jews

Continued study of the languages of the Jews has been an important feature of the field in the past few decades. Although we have not been able to include a separate article on the subject in this volume, a few summary comments are appropriate here, in addition to the observations in chap. 7. The new manuscript discoveries and fresh nonliterary and inscriptional materials provide a wealth of new data of great value to philologians, linguistic historians, and exegetes. A survey of the linguistic data from Palestine is provided by Joseph A. Fitzmyer (1970; see also H. B. Rosen), who cites Aramaic, Hebrew, Greek, and Latin evidence.

The Qumran texts offer fresh data on the history of the Hebrew language. Not only do they supply a missing link between the Hebrew of the late biblical books and the language of the Mishna; they also show irrefutably that Hebrew was alive and functional in Palestine around the turn of the era, at least in some literate circles. Of equal significance are the Aramaic texts from Qumran and the other caves of the Judean Desert. Joseph A. Fitzmyer and Daniel J. Harrington (1978) have gathered these and other nonliterary and inscriptional materials, together with translations, into a sizable manual of Palestinian Aramaic texts from the last two centuries B.C.E. and the first two centuries C.E. Some of the implications of the new data for the history of the Aramaic language have been developed by E. Y. Kutscher, Fitzmyer (1971), and Jonas C. Greenfield (on Hebrew and Aramaic see also Naveh and Greenfield), and a comprehensive Aramaic lexicon project involving Fitzmyer, D. R. Hillers, and S. A. Kaufman has recently been announced (1985). These materials provide a broader base for the continued study of two large bodies of early Jewish literature: Greek Jewish texts that were supposedly composed in Aramaic, including the sayings of Jesus and similar early Semitic-Christian traditions, and the language of the major Targums, the antiquity and provenance of which are now being vigorously debated.

The use of Greek even among Jews in Palestine is well attested by the discoveries in the Judean Desert (chaps. 5–6), although it is less clear whether such Jews were predominantly multilingual and also knew Aramaic and/or Hebrew, or whether Greek was the primary or only language of large numbers of Jews in Palestine. Similarly, little work has been done on the question of the use of Semitic in non-Palestinian Hellenistic areas (e.g., Alexandria, Antioch) and less still on the possible Jewish use of other non-Semitic languages such as Latin and Coptic (see chap. 7 for evidence from Jewish inscriptions).

Who Is a Jew? Parties, Sects, and Social Structure

The division of early Judaism into parties and sects is a traditional topic in all of the older histories of the period (chap. 2). The customary schematization follows the description of Josephus, who claims that there were four Palestinian groups: Pharisees, Sadducees, Essenes, and the "Fourth Philosophy." He also mentions Samaritans as vacillating about their connections to Judaism. Other ancient sources refer as well to other "Jewish" groups (Therapeutae, Nazoreans, Hemerobaptists, Menistae, Genistae, etc.; see Simon), and some modern scholarship has created "Hellenistic Jews" as a group represented especially by Philo. The extent to which the named groups may have been influential outside of Palestine has not yet received extensive discussion.

What do such groups have in common? What makes them "Jewish"— or in the case of Samaritans, ambivalently Jewish? Whether ancient authors such as Josephus ever thought of these questions in just such terms is doubtful. Probably then, as now, a major consideration was how a person or group identified itself, a factor alluded to by Josephus in his treatment of the Samaritans. When Josephus casts doubt on the Jewishness of Herod the Great or of Philo's nephew Tiberius Alexander, how should we treat that information? When Paul refers vociferously to his Jewish credentials, should we listen? When a "magical" text claims to be by and for "Hebrews," what conclusions are to be drawn? How widely should the modern scholar's net be spread in attempting to bring together appropriate evidence for early Judaism in all of its multiplicity? The problems and pitfalls of these definitional issues continue to haunt the study of early Judaism and call for detailed discussion at the general as well as the specific level. An excellent example of the importance of this issue is the relative difference it makes whether Paul is to be treated as a first century (Pharisaic!) "Jewish" representative or not. Few students of early Judaism have faced such issues squarely (see further Kraft, 1975:188–99).

At the level of Josephus's four Jewish sects, progress is being made. The discovery of the Qumran scrolls (chap. 5) and recent work on the rabbinic texts have helped in challenging the rigid manner in which this schematization has often been applied (chap. 2). If the scrolls derived from an Essene community, as most scholars hold, they attest that the Essenes were not a monolithic sect or religious movement. (If they are not from Essenes, Josephus's list is itself flawed.) These writings show theological development over a period of time and reveal not only similarities to Josephus's descriptions of Essenes but also significant differences. Comparison of the scrolls with various pseudepigrapha results in the same ambiguity. Although there are close parallels between some of the scrolls and certain of the pseudepigrapha, none of the latter is indisputably a product of the community that wrote any one of the sectarian documents unique to the Qumran caves (excluding the *Damascus Document*). With regard to the Pharisees, prolific modern discussion leaves unanswered many questions about this group, their history and practice, and the validity of the sources that refer to them (chap. 2). Thus, for two of Josephus's four groups, the situation seems far more complex than earlier scholarship recognized, and the evidence suggests that other groups, or significant variations of those mentioned, also existed.

Similarly complicated is discussion of the Hasidim mentioned in 1 and 2 Maccabees. At least since Otto Plöger (7–9, 17, 23–24), it has been common to describe the Hasidim as the apocalyptic bearers of the prophetic tradition, and many commentators on the scrolls have posited close ties between the Essene authors of the scrolls and the Hasidim. However, more recent studies have argued that we actually know very little about a specific "Hasidim" party, its history, its beliefs, and its relationship to the Pharisees and the Essenes of Qumran (Nickelsburg, 1983:647–48).

In short, the discovery of the scrolls has forced us to revise drastically our religious and social map of early Judaism in Palestine. That there were more than four Jewish religious groups in Palestine is neither a new nor a surprising observation. From the scrolls we now know relatively more about the Essenes, or a certain Essene subgroup or sister group. About the others and the interrelationships among all of them we know much less than we once thought.

A discussion of the sects and groups of early Judaism must mention also the Samaritans (chap. 3). Although it is debated whether they should be considered an offshoot of Judaism, they also were heirs of the Israelite religious tradition in Greco-Roman Palestine. Here again, archaeological excavation and renewed study of the literary and inscriptional materials have led scholars to revise old theories and to move toward some new consensuses.

Many question marks remain in the recent discussions of social structures in early Judaism (chap. 1). The role of women at various times and places is beginning to receive close attention, but research is primarily at the data-gathering stage; and it is difficult to anticipate what adjustments to the existing conventional (male) wisdom—or to treatments of Jewish women in the context of early Christianity (e.g., Fiorenza)—will be necessitated (see Brooten; Kraemer). Another topic about which earlier studies

asserted firm conclusions, the relationship between the rabbis and the
"people of the land" (*'ammê hā'āreṣ*), also is deservedly receiving closer
examination. Many studies by NT students notwithstanding, it is questionable whether we should even talk about formal rabbis prior to the close of
the first revolt in the first century c.e., and it is uncertain what entity or
"office" (if any) in the early period corresponded to that of the later rabbis.

Jewish Literature

Literary texts are the major source for our knowledge of early Judaism. The appearance of new texts, editions, and tools has generated new
discussions of this literature. These discussions are characterized by two
major factors. The texts are being interpreted not simply as containers of
ideas but as literature with generic shape and purpose. Where possible, the
attempt is being made to place this literature in its historical context. In
both instances, however, much uncertainty and ambiguity remain.

An interest in form and genre has been central to the discussion. This
is partly due to the use of new literary-critical tools, but it is also related
to the nature of the new evidence. First, new genres have been uncovered
such as the Qumran commentaries (*pĕšārîm*) on scripture (chap. 10),
which prompt new questions about diversity in early Jewish interpretations of scripture. Second, we have new parallels to known genres. The
Genesis Apocryphon and the fragments of the Enochic Book of the Giants
not only shed new light on the history of specific traditions but may also
provide new evidence of a literary genre that interprets scripture by para-
phrasing it (see also *Jubilees,* Pseudo-Philo *Liber Antiquitatum Biblicarum*). But there is a danger here. Scholars must avoid begging the question
concerning whether such paraphrases are consciously based on materials
considered scriptural at that time, or whether these sources may independently attest the same traditions that became embodied also in the biblical
texts. Finally, the expanded corpus includes evolved examples of literary
forms found in the Bible. In content, structure, and prosody, if not in
genre, the Qumran *Hymns* and noncanonical psalms look very different
from their canonical counterparts (see chap. 16).

Tentativeness tends to characterize most scholarship on early Judaism
with regard to the precise background and origins of particular writings
contained in the apocrypha and pseudepigrapha, largely because of methodological caution or as a result of uncertainty about the religious map of
early Judaism (see above and Nickelsburg, 1973:7). For example, works
once identified confidently with the Pharisees are no longer so labeled, and
even Essene affinities are treated relatively cautiously. Also with regard to
more general issues concerning the social setting and function of these
writings, firm conclusions appear less frequently in the literature, except
perhaps with reference to the antagonists envisioned in a particular

writing. Such questions are not deemed invalid, but the answers are seen as more difficult.

Religion and Religious Thought

New perspectives on the culture, social structure, and literature of early Judaism have led to a new understanding of some early Jewish religious expressions and their conceptual frameworks (e.g., Qumran and Pauline apocalypticism). Essential to the discussion has been the recognition that theological conceptions are not disembodied entities, but that they arise, develop, and change in response to constantly changing historical circumstances. It is crucial that the study of early Jewish religious thought acknowledges historical change and complexity and admits the uncertainty and ambiguity that result from the gaps in our knowledge of that history.

The Bible and Scriptural Interpretation

It is not particularly useful to speak of a Jewish Bible in this period without asking: Whose Bible? The question touches on a number of issues. (1) Textual: As the biblical scrolls from Qumran indicate, the Hebrew text of the biblical books was in flux at this time. (2) The language of the Bible: Some Greek speaking Jews ascribed authority to the Greek translation(s) of the Semitic texts, and here, too, there were a variety of textual traditions (chap. 9). Concerning the use, function, and authority of Aramaic targums in this period we are, at present, ill informed. (3) Canonical consciousness: At what point and under what circumstances did Jews in our period come to consider certain writings to have special authority, beyond that of other writings? Did those who perpetuated the apocalyptic materials have the same attitude to the authority of fixed biblical texts as did Philo? (4) Extent of the canon: Which writings were accorded what authority by whom and when? Did Jews in the Greek Diaspora have different canonical lists from what was common in Palestine (on these problems, see Sundberg)? Although we cannot discuss these issues in detail here, their importance for a satisfactory understanding of early Judaism is crucial.

The heart of the Jewish Bible was the Torah, the five books of Moses. Classical Judaism's concern with the law (tôrâ) contained in Moses' Torah, its interpretation and observance, has often led Christian theologians and historians of Judaism to describe early Judaism as legalistic. Recent studies by Christian scholars have contradicted this view. K. Baltzer showed that already in the scriptures tôrâ was associated with the recitation of the exodus event. E. P. Sanders has also stressed the covenantal context of tôrâ, even if he has inappropriately universalized the pattern of "covenantal nomism" (see below). Earlier studies drew their evidence from rabbinic texts whose concern was primarily to expound the content of tôrâ in a given situation. The texts of the apocrypha, pseudepigrapha, and Qumran scrolls provide narrative, liturgical, and exhortative contexts that help to reveal the motivation and dynamics for *tôrâ* observance in various early Jewish settings.

Early Jewish biblical interpretation is a broad topic worthy of numerous volumes yet to be written. Here we will mention only four issues.

1. Jews in our period used a variety of genres to transmit and interpret their scriptures. They translated scriptures more or less faithfully into Greek and Aramaic, and perhaps other languages. They produced *pĕšārîm* and other types of commentary, in which portions of scripture are explicitly quoted and then interpreted. They collected specific scriptural texts and organized them as "testimonies" to elucidate particular interests. They paraphrased scripture or expanded it for specific purposes (e.g., Philo on Moses).

2. Nevertheless, it is not clear whether every apparent parallel to scriptural material in early Judaism should be interpreted as a self-conscious use of scripture in the senses listed above. Apart from formulaic references to scripture, when is it legitimate to identify a text as an intentional interpretation of scripture? Was the book of Daniel considered canonical when the interpolations and additions preserved in the Greek versions were inserted? Are the earliest narrative strata in *1 Enoch* 6–11 simply interpretations and expansions of a biblical text (Gen 6:1–4), or do they reflect very early traditions that have been abbreviated in Genesis? How do the sapiential materials in the Wisdom of Joshua ben Sira relate to those in Proverbs, and was Proverbs accepted by ben Sira and his predecessors as scripture? It would be unfortunate if, in our desire to know more about biblical interpretation, we neglected the possiblity that some of our sources may preserve pre- or nonscriptural formulations of certain scriptural traditions.

3. Variety of interpretation of the same scriptural passages is especially apparent in the interpretation of Torah. As the Qumran scrolls demonstrate in a number of ways, Essenic legal interpretations varied from later rabbinic, just as in rabbinic literature, Pharisaic interpretations sometimes vary from Sadducean or even among themselves. Pseudepigrapha such as *Jubilees* and *1 Enoch* indicate further variety in early Jewish interpretations of Torah. Interpretations of the nonlegal parts of scripture also varied. An important aspect of research in this field has been to trace the historical events and conditions that gave rise to this manifold interpretation of scripture.

4. In some instances an interpretation of scripture is offered as one interesting possibility, whereas elsewhere an interpretation may be presented as authoritative. The laws in *Jubilees* are said to be the authoritative exposition of laws recorded in scripture. The *Testament of Moses* finds the revealed fulfillment of Deuteronomy 28–32 in the events of the author's

own time. The Qumran *pĕšārîm* espouse a similar viewpoint. This assertion of revealed authority relates to the topic of our next section.

Apocalypticism

The most prolific and intensive area in the renewed study of early Judaism has been the reexamination of the phenomenon of apocalypticism (chap. 14). Both in its debt to new sources and its use of new methods, this activity often represents a microcosm of the field as a whole.

Social scientific models have called attention to the socio-historical contexts that gave rise to apocalyptic movements. Literary-critical methods have suggested and facilitated the analysis of the genre apocalypse, and have provided tools for the holistic study of the extensive and complex major apocalypses. Scholars are less concerned with compiling lists of theological themes in a given document and more interested in the literary indicators of emphasis, setting, and purpose. These indicators have shown many of the texts to be more complex than earlier scholarship had recognized. Apocalypticism, far from being preoccupied with eschatology, was encyclopedic in its interests and represented a fusion of elements that were at home also in prophetic and sapiential contexts. Paleographic analysis of the Qumran *Enoch* fragments and literary considerations point to the third century B.C.E. and earlier for the composition of substantial parts of *1 Enoch*. Judaism at this time was a broader and more diverse religious phenomenon than the contents of the Hebrew canon and the rabbinic writings have suggested (Stone, 1978).

Central to the apocalyptic phenomenon is a claim of revelation, whether of the future or of the heavenly world or both. This imbues the apocalyptic literature with an authority parallel to that of scripture. The Enochic corpus, for example, appears to be modeled, in part, on the book of Deuteronomy, but it claims more ancient origin. The appeal to revelation plays an important role in some of the scriptural interpretation referred to in the previous section. The teachings about the solar calendar contained in the *Enoch* corpus were revealed by an angel during a celestial journey. The author of *Jubilees* cites the heavenly tablets as the source of his halakah. The Qumran group believed that its interpretations of the Torah and its teacher's understanding of prophecy were revealed by God. In such instances, differences in interpretation and disputes about law are raised to the level of absolute truth and falsehood and have as their consequences salvation and damnation. We see at work here one of the essential characteristics by which sectarian division can be identified.

Eschatology

Eschatology has always been recognized as an important component in early Jewish religious thought, though its importance has been emphasized more by Christian than by Jewish scholars. Contemporary study, fed primarily by the discovery of new texts, has stressed the wide diversity in Jewish eschatology.

Messianism is a prime example. As the Qumran texts show, all Jews did not hold to the same expectation regarding a Messiah. Indeed, the term does not permeate the Jewish eschatological literature. Some Jews awaited a Davidic ruler, but for others a future anointed priest was central. Other expectations included an eschatological prophet, and a heavenly deliverer identified with Michael or Melchizedek or seen as a combination of the Danielic son of man, the anointed one, and the servant of Lord described in Second Isaiah. For still other Jews, God would be the eschatological deliverer.

Diversity also characterized Jewish speculations about the afterlife (Nickelsburg, 1972; Cavallin). The popular scholarly distinction between the Hebraic belief in a resurrection of the body and the Greek idea of the immortality of the soul is not substantiated by careful analysis of the primary sources. Early Jewish texts testify to a variety of beliefs including resurrection of the body, immortality of the soul, resurrection of the spirit, assumption to heaven immediately after death, and participation in the blessings of eternal life here and now.

Sanctuaries and Priesthood

It is an explicit teaching in much of the Hebrew scriptures that there is only one true temple, in Jerusalem. Critical and questioning attitudes about that Temple are, however, widely evident in the NT, in the Gospel accounts of Jesus' "cleansing" of the Temple, in the Stephen episode of Acts, in Pauline and deutero-Pauline spiritualizing of Temple language, and perhaps in the idea of the heavenly temple set forth in the Epistle to the Hebrews. The recent study of Judaism has shown, however, that the centrality and indispensability of the Jerusalem Temple were not axiomatic for all Jews, nor were the spiritualizing of the Temple and the idea of a heavenly temple Christian innovations.

Jewish temples were built in Egypt (Elephantine, Leontopolis) and at Araq el-Emir (Tyros) in Transjordan. Sacred status continued to be accorded to the area around Dan long after Jeroboam's sanctuary was destroyed. The Samaritans had their temple at Gerizim and their critique of the Jerusalem cult. The Qumranites and probably others before them criticized the Jerusalem Temple and priesthood. They spoke of their community as a temple with cultic functions and used liturgies that integrated their worship with that of the angelic choruses in the heavenly temple.

Iconography

It used to be axiomatic that early Jewish religion was anti-iconic. The discovery of the Dura Europos synagogue seriously challenged that viewpoint. The large murals depicting scenes from biblical events showed that at least some Jews around 245 c.e. could make such representations without compunction. Mosaic decorations in Palestinian synagogues of a later period indicate not only a lively iconographic tradition but also syncretistic influence. How far back these traditions can be traced and exactly how they fit with attitudes about the commandment prohibiting images remain open questions. But in any event, new evidence has overthrown an old stereotype (chap. 7).

Diversity and the Problem of Definition

Historians have often sought principles by which to systematize and synthesize what they thought to be the essence of Judaism. Writers such as Charles (APOT: xi; 1913) and Bousset and Gressmann made heavy use of the apocrypha and pseudepigrapha and emphasized eschatolology, the aspect of Judaism that became so important for the early church. Moreover, like Schürer before them, they criticized rabbinic Judaism as a sterile and legalistic perversion of preexilic prophetic religion. In reaction to this view, Moore maintained that rabbinic Judaism was "normative," and he relegated the apocalyptists to the fringe of his discussion (1927: 2.126–27). Most recently, E. P. Sanders has attempted a synthesis of both corpora of literature, arguing that the authors of the apocrypha, pseudepigrapha (except 4 Ezra), and the Qumran scrolls, as well as the rabbis, espoused the religious viewpoint of "covenantal nomism."

The study of Judaism in the past three decades has created serious difficulties for any attempt to distill an essence of early Judaism, normative or otherwise. In a multitude of ways we have come to find a previously unsuspected religious, cultural, and social diversity among the Jewish people of the Greco-Roman period. Judaism during this period was dynamic rather than static, pluralistic rather than homogeneous. It was transitional between what went before in the Persian period and what would follow with the rabbis, and was itself in transition, often in different ways at different times and places. Surely there were norms and boundaries, but they differed from time to time and place to place and among groups that were contemporaneous and contiguous.

Because Sanders's is the most recent synthesis and one that is often cited, it is appropriate to consider it briefly in the light of the issues discussed in this essay. Clearly Sanders is justified in criticizing the interpretation that early Judaism was legalistic and, given the history of research, his critique is salutary. Nonetheless, like all harmonizing approaches, his own synthesis obscures the dynamic variety in the documents and material remains that have been preserved for us. It may well be that, asked the question, any of the authors or rabbis that he cites would have said, "Of course, Torah stands in the context of covenant." Nonetheless, many of them chose not to express themselves in these terms in the texts that are at our disposal.

Remarkable in these documents is a wide variety of religious expression and emphases. Two examples will suffice. For Joshua ben Sira, the priestly covenant is a more central concern than the Sinaitic (compare the respective discussions of Moses and Aaron in 45:1–5 and 45:6–22). As Sirach 24 indicates, his emphasis is not on Torah as a gift bestowed at the historical event of Sinai; he stresses Torah as the perennial repository of divine wisdom, which both reveals God's will and enables obedience to it. At many points in the apocalyptic corpus, the Mosaic Torah is taken for granted, but the emphasis is on the revealed interpretations of that Torah and on the revelation of other laws, obedience to which is also necessary for salvation. In these and other texts, historical inquiry must listen to what the authors chose to emphasize and not stress what we think they took for granted.

Is it possible, then, to identify any elements common to the different individuals and groups lumped together under our collective descriptive category "early Judaism"? The following emphases seem to be present in many of the texts, and the silence of other writings on one or another of these does not necessarily imply divergence of perspective: (1) There is a pervading, though not always dominating consciousness of connection to the history of Israel. Even Ben Sira and the author of the Wisdom of Solomon make reference to it in their idiosyncratic catalogues of heroes and villains, and the Animal Apocalypse in *1 Enoch* even surveys it in some detail. (2) There is a pervading belief that God has revealed his will and that it is to be obeyed, although authors differ on the content of divine law and the manner of its revelation. (3) Finally, there is the conviction that God rewards those who obey his law and punishes those who disobey it.

Although the presence of these elements is not inconsistent with Sanders's theory of "covenantal nomism" as the focus of early Judaism, it is important that diversity of perspectives in the sources also be noted. God's activity in history is not always the focus. Law is construed in many different ways. Writers differ widely as to how, when, why, and to what extent divine justice is enacted. 1 Maccabees looks very different from *1 Enoch*, and many of the wisdom elements in the latter have little in common with the writing of the sage, Joshua ben Sira (see chap. 15). At the present stage of research, it would seem best to defer the construction of comprehensive syntheses until we understand better the elements that need to be synthesized.

POSSIBILITIES AND PROSPECTS FOR FUTURE STUDY

In many ways, the revival of research on early Judaism finds itself in a paradoxical situation. On the one hand, new discoveries and the intensified research they have stimulated are producing a revolutionized view of early Judaism. But at the same time, this activity has raised almost as many questions as it has answered. In what follows we will attempt to sketch some significant areas for continued research.

Textual Research

The study of early Judaism is dependent largely on analysis of the preserved literary texts. Critical editions of and critical commentaries on many of these texts are still needed. Thanks to new technologies (e.g., computer processing and printing), it will be easier to prepare, publish, and search such materials, and new approaches to writing commentaries will increase the scholarly value of the needed new productions.

Form-critical analysis is especially important in this field because studies of early Judaism have often tended to catalogue and synthesize particular ideas with little attention to the form and purpose of the larger texts that embody the ideas. Study of genre has been focused primarily on apocalypses and, to some extent, testaments. More of this type of analysis will benefit research on these two groups of literature, as well as the corpora of narrative, historical, exegetical, and hymnic texts.

Certain aspects of the study of early Judaism have tended to become compartmentalized. Although the Dead Sea scroll materials began to be available in quantity nearly three decades ago, Qumranic studies have tended to develop as a separate minidiscipline. Much more integrative work needs to be done with the scrolls and other early Jewish materials, giving close attention to literary, conceptual, and historical matters. The Qumranians may have isolated themselves from surrounding society, but they were still a constitutive part of the Judaism preceding, contemporary with, and following them. A similar kind of scholarly segregation has sometimes characterized the study of Philo and Josephus. Nevertheless, students of other early Jewish materials will often recognize in Philo and Josephus familiar ideas, traditions, and genres, and, of course, find especially in Josephus information about the historical contexts of the other materials.

The study of the Old Greek scriptures needs to be more closely integrated with the general study of early Judaism. The "Septuagint" texts are not simply tools for discussing the state of the Hebrew Bible text or philological aids in the study of early Christian Greek. They constitute a major surviving monument to Hellenistic Jewish thought and biblical exegesis and, as such, should be studied as an integral part of the corpus of early Jewish religious literature. This goal will be facilitated by the computerized data bank currently being prepared for this material under the joint direction of Robert Kraft and Emanuel Tov.

Since texts need to be examined in their contexts, more attention must be paid to the late Roman, Byzantine, and early medieval milieux in which many of the early Jewish writings were transmitted (Kraft, 1976:131–37). Study of these works has understandably proceeded primarily from the Jewish contexts in which many of them are presumed to have originated. But the fact remains that in their preserved manuscript form, such texts are products of Christian efforts. In some instances, it remains to be seen to what extent the present *literary* forms of these texts are also the products of Christian redaction. There is perhaps a fine line that separates such study from the analysis of texts that employ traditional Jewish genres and Christian pseudonyms. Martha Himmelfarb has begun such work on early Christian apocalypses.

Intellectual and Social History

Recent study has paved the way for new probes into the relationships between diverse conceptual orientations in early Judaism. Using the Greek scriptural translations along with other early sources, we can study the history of early Jewish biblical interpretation. New texts provide a wider range of data on the history of halakic (legal) development. Such materials, combined with new and old narrative texts and the Qumran scrolls provide points of contact for comparative study with the rabbinic corpora. Recognition that the "theology" of the apocalypses did not begin and end with eschatology bodes well. Interesting questions can be posed about significant points of contact between sapiential and apocalyptic texts. The nature and place of the eschatology, often called "apocalyptic," which is found in works that are not formally apocalypses can be assessed. Relationships between early Jewish apocalypses and later mystical traditions also need to be restudied, although this will require much text-critical and tradition-critical work on the mystical texts as well.

The study of cultural and conceptual orientations in early Jewish materials must begin with the recognition that a major characteristic of the Hellenistic world was its ability to embrace variety and encourage its incorporation into the new synthesis. To exist in the synthesis is, by definition, to be part of the synthesis. The varieties of Judaism in the Greco-Roman world are, in a very real sense, representatives of the Hellenistic synthesis. It is not helpful historically to protect "authentic Judaism" from "Hellenism" as though Judaism somehow presented a special case. What is needed is careful and consistent analysis of the relationship of Jews and Judaism(s) to other groups in that world and to the dynamic synthesis that bound them all together. Although some impressive and fruitful spade work has been done from this perspective, the hard questions need to be pursued with greater vigor. What contributions do the Jewish materials make to the Hellenistic synthesis? How are older Jewish perspectives affected by other streams that also flow into the synthesis (e.g., Egyptian,

Babylonian-Persian, Greek, Roman) as they become parts of the new situation (Nickelsburg, 1975)? How does the cultural situation in the Eastern areas (Parthia, etc.) relate to and interact with that in the Greco-Roman world proper? How are questions of language (Semitic, Greek, Latin, Egyptian, etc.) related to the larger issues of thought and culture?

Although the concerns and approaches of the anthropological and social sciences, and of folklore research, have made a mark in the study of early Judaism, additional careful work is needed in these areas. Unfortunately, there seem to be significant, if not irreconcilable, problems obstructing an easy appropriation of these approaches by the student of early Judaism. Models based on living cultures and their traditions may not be easily transferable to the bits and fragments of antiquity preserved for us in written texts and archaeological remains. It is not always possible to determine whether sufficient similarities are present between the modern models and the ancient evidence to give hope of fruitful results. The problems indigenous to the early materials are not necessarily analogous to those of the available models. Nevertheless, judicious exploration of such approaches should be encouraged, along with constant critical evaluation of the results.

Early Judaism in Relation to Its Broader Contexts

The study of early Judaism is, of course, part of several larger pictures, whether in terms of its own historical setting (the ancient world), its relationship to the living Jewish religious and cultural traditions (ancient Israel, Samaritans, classical Judaism, Karaites), its relationship to its "daughter religions" (Christianity, Islam) and their offspring, or its place in the history of (Western) human thought and life. Although it may be legitimate and even professionally necessary for a scholar to focus attention on early Judaism as such, its broader connections and relevance should not be neglected.

The study of early Judaism is, then, a segment of a larger scholarly task relating especially to the broader context of the history of the "Judeo-Christian" religious traditions. Its findings should be of interest to the scholar of the Hebrew scriptures. In the early Jewish texts one sees how the people who flourished at the time those scriptures were becoming authoritative interpreted them. One also encounters the next stages of development of the ideas found in the scriptures and of the literary forms that embodied these conceptions. Prophecy and wisdom contribute to the rise of apocalypticism, mysticism, and new wisdom forms. Narrative approaches are reshaped, and historiography records new events in new ways. Hymnic and liturgical expression serve new purposes. And through it all, the "people of Israel" maintain a dynamic tension between their present historical circumstances and their received traditions.

The study of early Judaism is also highly important for the student of the rabbinic writings. The new interest that rabbinic scholars are showing in these materials will benefit everyone concerned. Knowledge of the rabbinic corpus and its development of the earlier traditions helps our interpretation of both corpora. A knowledge of Judaism in the Greco-Roman period is indispensable to a proper interpretation of the rabbinic material.

Earlier in this essay, it was noted that Christian scholars often allowed Christian presuppositions to govern their interpretation of Judaism. This kind of historical and theological flaw notwithstanding, responsible study of early Christianity requires knowledge of its Jewish roots and context. And if the air has been cleared for the study of early Judaism to proceed as a recognized field, then the origins of Christianity can properly be studied also as part of that Jewish context.

A renewed study of early Judaism has many implications for students of NT and early Christianity. The following are a few examples: (1) Early Judaism research is in a state of flux; much is uncertain and still under discussion. Unqualified statements about, for example, apocalyptic or midrash are not helpful while the precise definition of such categories is still being debated. (2) As the variety and complexity of early Judaism continue to unfold, historians of early Christianity must be cautious in their claims about the kind of Judaism to which a particular figure or writer is supposedly responding. Since the variety extends to Jewish messianism and eschatology, much circumspection is needed in statements about the self-consciousness of Jesus, the nature of his teaching, the nuances of early Christologies, and reactions to Jesus and to early Christian preaching by Jews of that period. (3) Since so little is known about the types of Jewish teachers and preachers in first-century Palestine, special caution is required in relating Jesus to such models. (4) Responsible study of Paul and his thought must eschew the stereotype that early Judaism means legalism. It must be recognized that for many Jews in this period Torah obedience presumed divine grace and that at the same time salvation and damnation (or life and death) were construed as rewards and punishments relating to a person's deeds. (5) Early Christian statements about salvation and damnation, both in Paul and elsewhere, must recognize this Jewish context and not be treated a priori as if they represented some special Christian theology of grace.

A revised understanding of early Judaism also has implications for the broader study of Christianity, since Christians preserved earlier Jewish texts and continued to use literary genres inherited from Judaism (e.g., apocalypses). A better knowledge of the Jewish prototypes may shed light on the circles that generated their Christian counterparts. Study of these Christian texts and the Jewish texts preserved by Christians should facilitate a more rounded view of Christianity in Roman, Byzantine, and early medieval times.

A concern for the broad contours of Judeo-Christian tradition cannot afford to ignore its important and variegated Hellenistic and Roman intellectual, cultural, and religious environments. The history of Jewish and Christian religion is a crucial part of the general history of Western civilization as well as of the overall history of religions.

This volume attempts to describe a somewhat artificially defined but highly important field of study within the history and thought of the Jewish and Christian traditions. Much detailed work remains to be done within this field, and the results of such detailed study need to be incorporated into broader surveys of the pertinent subjects (Judaism, Christianity, Western civilization, history of religions, etc.). The latter task requires the cooperative enterprise of many scholars who are experts in their respective fields and are aware of the expertise of others in other areas. The knowledge explosion helps make such a panoramic view possible, within the limits of the available data and reliable conclusions. But it also can increase the scholarly tendency to isolation and fragmentation of knowledge. Means must be sought within institutions of higher learning and learned societies to prevent such fragmentation without discouraging the detailed research and to encourage and facilitate the ongoing task of refining and updating the broader syntheses.

BIBLIOGRAPHY

Baltzer, Klaus
    1971   *The Covenant Formulary.* Trans. D. E. Green. Philadelphia: Fortress. German original, 1964.

Barr, James
    1978–79   "Aramaic-Greek Notes on the Book of Enoch (I, II)." *JJS* 23: 184–98, 24: 179–92.

Bickerman, Elias
    1962   *From Ezra to the Last of the Maccabees: The Historical Foundations of Post Biblical Judaism.* New York: Schocken Books.

Bousset, Wilhelm, and Hugo Gressmann
    1926   *Die Religion des Judentums im späthellenistischen Zeitalter.* 3d ed. by Hugo Gressmann. HNT 21. Tübingen: Mohr- Siebeck.

Breech, Earl
    1973   "These Fragments I Have Shored Against my Ruins: The Form and Function of 4 Ezra." *JBL* 92: 267–74.

Brooten, Bernadette
    1982   *Women Leaders in the Ancient Synagogue: Inscriptional Evidence and Background Issues.* Brown Judaic Studies 36. Chico, CA: Scholars Press.

Cavallin, H. C. C.
1974   *Life after Death: Paul's Argument for the Resurrection of the Dead
          in I Cor 15.* Part 1, *An Enquiry into the Jewish Background.*
          ConBNT 7.1. Lund: Gleerup.

Charles, R. H. [See also *APOT.*]
1913   *Eschatology: The Doctrine of a Future Life in Israel, Judaism, and
          Christianity: A Critical History.* New York: Schocken Books.
          Reprint, 1963.

Charlesworth, James H. [See *OTP* and Appendix.]
1981   *The Pseudepigrapha and Modern Research, with a Supplement.*
          SBLSCS 7S. Chico, CA: Scholars Press.

Collins, John J.
1983   *Between Athens and Jerusalem: Jewish Identity in the Hellenistic
          Diaspora.* New York: Crossroad.

Denis, Albert-Marie
1970   *Introduction aux pseudépigraphes grecs d'Ancien Testament.* SVTP
          1. Leiden: Brill.

Dever, William G.
1985   "Syro-Palestinian and Biblical Archaeology." Pp. 31–74 in *HBMI.*

Fiorenza, Elisabeth Schüssler
1985   *In Memory of Her: A Feminist Theological Reconstruction of
          Christian Origins.* New York: Crossroad.

Fitzmyer, Joseph A.
1970   "The Languages of Palestine in the First Century A.D." *CBQ* 22:
          501–31.
1971   *The Genesis Apocryphon of Qumran Cave 1.* 2d ed. BibOr 18A.
          Rome: Biblical Institute Press.

Fitzmyer, Joseph A., and Daniel J. Harrington
1978   *A Manual of Palestinian Aramaic Texts.* BibOr 34. Rome: Biblical
          Institute Press.

Foerster, W.
1964   *From the Exile to Christ: An Historical Introduction to Palestinian
          Judaism.* Philadelphia: Fortress.

Gowan, D. [See the bibliography of chap. 1.]

Greenfield, Jonas C.
1976   "Aramaic." *IDBSup,* 39–44.

Hellholm, David, ed.
1983   *Apocalypticism in the Mediterranean World and the Near East:
          Proceedings of the International Colloquium on Apocalypticism,
          Uppsala, August 12–17, 1979.* Tübingen: Mohr-Siebeck.

Hengel, Martin [See the bibliographies of chaps. 1 and 2.]

Himmelfarb, Martha
1983   *Tours of Hell: An Apocalyptic Form in Jewish and Christian
          Literature.* Philadelphia: University of Pennsylvania Press.

Jeremias, Joachim [See the bibliographies of chaps. 1 and 2.]

De Jonge, M., and S. Safrai [See CRINT.]

Kautzsch, Emil [See *APAT.*]

Klein, Charlotte
  1978   *Anti-Judaism in Christian Theology.* Trans. Edward Quinn. Philadelphia: Fortress.

Knight, Douglas A., and Gene M. Tucker
  1985   "Editors' Preface." Pp. xiii–xxi in *HBMI.*

Kraabel, A. Thomas
  1982   "The Roman Diaspora: Six Questionable Assumptions." Pp. 445–64 in *Essays in Honor of Y. Yadin.* Ed. G. Vermes and J. Neusner. *JJS* Vol. 33, nos. 1, 2.

Kraemer, Ross S.
  1983   "Women in the Religions of the Greco-Roman World." *RelSRev* 9: 127–39.

Kraft, Robert A.
  1975   "The Multiform Jewish Heritage of Early Christianity." Pp. 174–99 in *Christianity, Judaism and Other Greco-Roman Cults: Studies for Morton Smith at Sixty,* Vol. 3. Ed. J. Neusner. Leiden: Brill.
  1976   "Reassessing the 'Recensional Problem' in Testament of Abraham." Pp. 121–37 in *Studies on the Testament of Abraham.* Ed. George W. E. Nickelsburg. SBLSCS 6. Missoula, MT: Scholars Press.

Kümmel, Werner Georg [See JSHRZ.]

Kutscher, E. Y.
  1972   "Aramaic." *EncJud* 3: 259–87.

Lieberman, Saul
  1942   *Greek in Jewish Palestine.* New York: Jewish Theological Seminary.
  1950   *Hellenism in Jewish Palestine.* New York: Jewish Theological Seminary.

Marcus, Ralph
  1948   "Hellenistic Jewish Literature." Pp. 745–83 in *The Jews: Their History, Culture and Religion* Vol. 2. Ed. L. Finkelstein. New York: Harper.
  1956   "The Hellenistic Age." Pp. 93–139 in *Great Ages and Ideas of the Jewish People.* Ed. L. W. Schwarz. New York: Random House.

Moore, George Foot
  1921   "Christian Writers on Judaism." *HTR* 14: 197–254.
  1927–30   *Judaism in the First Centuries of the Christian Era: The Age of the Tannaim.* Cambridge, MA: Harvard University Press.

Naveh, Joseph, and Jonas C. Greenfield
  1984   "Hebrew and Aramaic in the Persian Period." Pp. 115–29 in *The Cambridge History of Judaism: Volume 1, The Persian Period.* Ed. W. D. Davies and L. Finkelstein. Cambridge: University Press, 1984.

Nickelsburg, George W. E.
  1972   *Resurrection, Immortality and Eternal Life in Intertestamental Judaism.* HTS 26. Cambridge, MA: Harvard University Press.
  1981   *Jewish Literature Between the Bible and the Mishnah.* Philadelphia: Fortress.
  1983   "Social Aspects of Palestinian Jewish Apocalypticism." Pp. 641–54 in Hellholm, ed.

Nickelsburg, G. W. E., ed.
1973 *Studies on the Testament of Moses*. SBLSCS 4. Missoula, MT: Scholars Press.
1975 *Studies on the Testament of Joseph*. SBLSCS 5. Missoula, MT: Scholars Press.
1976 *Studies on the Testament of Abraham*. SBLSCS 6. Missoula, MT: Scholars Press.

Pfeiffer, Robert H.
1949 *A History of New Testament Times with an Introduction to the Apocrypha*. New York: Harper & Row.

Plöger, Otto
1968 *Theocracy and Eschatology*. Trans. S. Rudman. Richmond: John Knox.

Reicke, Bo [See the bibliography of chap. 1.]

Reinach, Theodor
1895 *Textes d'auteurs grecs et romains relatifs au Judaisme*. Paris: Leroux. Reprinted, 1963.

Riessler, Paul
1928 *Altjüdisches Schrifttum ausserhalb der Bibel*. Heidelberg: Kerle. Reprinted, 1966.

Rosen, Haiim B.
1980 "Die Sprachsituation im römischen Palästina." Pp. 215–39 in *Die Sprachen im römischen Reich der Kaiserzeit*. Beihefte der Bonner Jahrbücher 40. Cologne: Rheinland-Verlag.

Russell, David S. [See the bibliography of chap. 1.]

Safrai, S. [See CRINT and the bibliography of chap. 1.]

Sanders, E. P.
1977 *Paul and Palestinian Judaism*. Philadelphia: Fortress.

Saunders, Ernest W.
1982 *Searching the Scriptures: A History of the Society of Biblical Literature, 1880–1980*. SBL Biblical Scholarship in North America 8. Chico, CA: Scholars Press.

Sayler, Gwendolyn B.
1983 *Have the Promises Failed?: A Literary Analysis of 2 Baruch*. SBLDS 72. Chico, CA: Scholars Press.

Schalit, Abraham [See the bibliography of chap. 1.]

Schürer, Emil [See the bibliography of chap. 1.]

Simon, Marcel
1967 *Jewish Sects in the Time of Jesus Christ*. Philadelphia: Fortress. French original, 1960.

Smith, Morton
1956 "Palestinian Judaism in the First Century." Pp. 67–81 in *Israel: Its Role in Civilization*. Ed. M. Davis. New York: Harper.
1983 "Terminological Boobytraps and Real Problems in Second-Temple Judaeo-Christian Studies." Pp. 295–306 in *Traditions in Contact and Change: Proceedings of the 14th Congress IAHR*. Ed. P. Slater and D. Wiebe. Waterloo, Ont.: Wilfrid Laurier University Press.

Sparks, H. F. D. [See *AOT*.]

Stern, Menahem [See *GLAJJ*.]

Stone, Michael E. [See CRINT.]
   1973   "Judaism in the Time of Jesus Christ." *Scientific American* (January): 80–87.
   1978   "The Book of Enoch and Judaism in the Third Century B.C.E." *CBQ* 40: 479–92.
Sundberg, Albert
   1964   *The Old Testament of the Early Church*. HTS 20. Cambridge, MA: Harvard University Press.
Suter, David Winston
   1981   "Weighed in the Balance: The Similitudes of Enoch in Recent Discussion." *RelSRev* 7: 217–20.
Vermes, Geza, Fergus Millar, and Matthew Black, eds. [See the bibliography of chap. 1 under Schürer.]

Part One

Early Judaism
in Its Historical Settings

1

THE POLITICAL AND SOCIAL HISTORY OF THE JEWS IN GRECO-ROMAN ANTIQUITY: THE STATE OF THE QUESTION

Shaye J. D. Cohen

One Hellenistic sage remarked that "there is no end to the making of many books." This famous aphorism applies to the post-1945 scholarship on the political and social history of the Jews of Greco-Roman antiquity. In recent years we have been treated to a revision of a nineteenth-century classic (Schürer-Vermes-Millar), no fewer than two multivolume series (*The Jewish People in the First Century* [hereafter *JPFC*]; *The World History of the Jewish People* [hereafter *WHJP*], volumes 6–8), several large-scale specialized works (e.g., Hengel, 1961, 1974; Schalit, 1969; Tcherikover, 1957, 1959), and many surveys, both for the specialist (e.g., Abel; Avi-Yonah, 1973, 1976; Smallwood) and for the general reader (e.g., Baron; Ben-Sasson; Gowan; Reicke; Russell). When we consider too the number of articles devoted to aspects of our theme, we might conclude that the study of ancient Judaism is advancing mightily in robust good health. Such a conclusion, however, is unwarranted.

In this essay I do not intend to summarize and annotate these near-innumerable articles and books or to survey ancient Jewish history century by century and problem by problem. Such an attempt would serve little purpose when good bibliographical tools are available already (e.g., the survey articles by P. Schäfer and A. R. C. Leaney in Hayes and Miller). I am interested rather in modern historiographical trends. What methods and presuppositions have recent scholars brought to the study of the political and social history of the Jews of Palestine in antiquity? What subjects remain uninvestigated or underinvestigated? (For the sake of brevity and coherence I shall concentrate on Palestinian history from 200 B.C.E. to 200 C.E.) All in all, my assessment is that the basic scholarly issues and techniques, problems and methods, are the same now as they were one hundred years ago when Schürer completed the first edition of his famous history (1874). The study of the religious history of ancient Judaism has been revolutionized in the postwar period by the Dead Sea Scrolls, archaeological discoveries, and new methodologies in the interpretation of rabbinic texts, but no such revolution has occurred in the study of the topics that concern us here. As that previously quoted Hellenistic sage remarked, "There is nothing new under the sun."

THE LEGACY OF
NINETEENTH-CENTURY HISTORIOGRAPHY

In nineteenth-century Germany the history and culture of ancient Greece and Rome were the domain of classicists, the history and culture of ancient Israel the domain of theologians. The effects of this division still endure. Classical scholarship proceeded to its agenda without malice or favoritism. The fact that Theodor Mommsen's portrait of Caesar may have been intended to serve as a program for Bismarck and the new German empire proves only that even the greatest historians, no matter what their speciality, are influenced by their environment. Theologians, however, had their outlook determined by their theological tenets. As good Christians they were fundamentally unsympathetic to a subject they had to treat, the history of the Jews. Thus Schürer, in spite of his tremendous erudition, unparalleled bibliographical control, and prodigious good sense, was unwilling or unable to adopt a neutral perspective on his subject. The title of his magnum opus boldly declares his Christian orientation (im Zeitalter Jesu Christi). This Christian perspective—animus is not too strong a term—manifested itself in several areas:

1. Schürer's history begins with the Maccabees and ends with Bar Kokhba. Schürer justified these termini by appeal to two criteria, the one "political" and the other "inner." According to the former, the Maccabees and Bar Kokhba mark the beginning and the end of Jewish political aspirations. This seems fair enough (although see below), but why the age of Jesus Christ should begin with a political triumph and end with a political failure is not very clear. The connection between the title and the periodization is explained by the criterion of "inner" Jewish development. In Schürer's opinion the Maccabean triumph was the triumph of the legalism of the scribes and ultimately of the Pharisees; the failure of Bar Kokhba meant that Pharisaic legalism could dominate the people without the distraction of political adventures. It was this domination, of course, that Jesus in good Lutheran fashion sought to destroy.

2. Schürer had only disparaging remarks about Jewish legalism, religious sterility, and pedantry, all of which he considered synonymous with Pharisaic and rabbinic piety.

3. Schürer emphasized that the Pharisees and their successors, the rabbis, were not men of this world but maintained an autonomous and apolitical existence. Neither Pharisees nor rabbis were interested in the affairs of state so long as they were able to pursue their religious program without interference. These Jews had no political life. Similarly, both Pharisees and rabbis attempted to shut out the cultural life of antiquity;

they were not "Hellenistic Jews." As part of Schürer's system these sentiments had two important implications, one contemporary and the other
historical. First, that the rabbinic Jews of Schürer's Germany followed a
religion that blocked their acceptance of contemporary culture.

4. The second implication of the previous paragraph is that rabbinic
sources have little value for the reconstruction of the political history of the
Second Commonwealth. In addition to the fact that the rabbis simply were
not interested in political matters, Schürer buttressed his skepticism by
appeal to the relative lateness of the rabbinic texts and to their fantastic
literary character. The latter argument did not prevent Schürer from
basing his reconstruction of the religious life of the ancient Jews (i.e., their
legalism, pettiness, lack of spirituality, etc.) upon those very same rabbinic
texts. This illogical procedure Schürer defended on the grounds that the
Pharisees-rabbis dominated the Jewish religious scene, as Josephus and the
rabbis assert, and that the chronological limits of the subject could be
broadened without affecting the argument. Some theologians, however,
notably W. Bousset, refused to follow the rabbinic sources even here and
reconstructed the religious life of Second Temple Jews without utilizing
rabbinic texts.

Jewish history written from such a Christian perspective did not go
unopposed. Jewish theologians reacted by emphasizing the high spiritual
values of rabbinic Judaism and the high historical value of rabbinic texts.
Like Schürer, they accepted, on the basis of the joint testimony of Josephus
and the rabbis, the centrality of the Pharisees-rabbis, but they emphasized
that these Jewish leaders were in fact quite "cultured" and "hellenized."

The influence of these late-nineteenth-century theologians upon post-
1945 historiography has been enormous. Aside from the obvious fact that
all modern accounts of ancient Jewish history depend, at least to some
extent, on the work of Schürer and his colleagues—witness the fact that the
1973 revision of Schürer's first volume retained almost everything that
Schürer wrote—the fundamental issues raised by Schürer and his opponents remain on the scholarly agenda. While many scholars can be regarded as the heirs of Schürer in one respect or another, it is clear that the
legacy of Schürer's Jewish opponents has devolved chiefly upon the so-
called Israeli school of historiography. The works produced by this school,
although hardly uniform in style or content, share several characteristics,
among them a negative attitude toward Schürer and his fellow theologians. I shall illustrate these generalizations by referring to the four points
discussed above.

1. Schürer's periodization, professedly Christian, did not, as far as I
know, provoke any serious Jewish response in the nineteenth century. Nor
has it provoked any response in the postwar period. The question has
simply been ignored. This is the area in which Schürer has had least influence. What are the logical termini of a survey of ancient Jewish history?

From Alexander to Herod (Russell)? From 500 B.C.E. to 100 C.E. (Reicke)? From Alexander the Great to the Arab conquest (Abel)? Or, as Schürer said, from the Maccabees to Bar Kokhba? I suspect that it was Schürer who influenced John Bright to end his *History of Israel* with the Maccabees and Michael Avi-Yonah to begin his *The Jews of Palestine* with the defeat of Bar Kokhba. For the most part, I detect no Christian (or anti-Christian) bias among these modern authors. Occasionally, however, we may still find a Christian interpretation of history masquerading as unbiased scholarship. I refer, for example, to Martin Noth, who fails to explain why he regards 135 C.E. as "the end of Israel," and to G. Ricciotti, who at least has the merit of stating forthrightly why his *History of Israel* closes with Bar Kokhba: "Having served its purpose in the plan of divine Providence, an era of glorious history comes to a close" (2:vi). All in all, periodization was not an important issue for Schürer and his contemporaries, and it has remained unimportant for modern scholars as well. I have chosen 200 B.C.E. and 200 C.E. as the chronological limits of this essay not because they can necessarily be justified by philosophical or historical considerations but because they are dictated by our documentation. Josephus's knowledge of Jewish history before 200 B.C.E. is largely episodic and inconsequential, whereas after that date it is rich and reasonably coherent. Tannaitic literature begins where Josephus stops (70–100 C.E.) and is codified about 200 C.E.

2. After the holocaust it has become much less fashionable to denigrate the spiritual values of Pharisaic and rabbinic Judaism, although attitudes like Schürer's persist (e.g., M. Black in *IDB*, s.v. Pharisees). Israeli scholars have published many works that emphasize the spiritual worth of rabbinic Judaism. But this topic is not germane to our essay.

3. The notion that the Pharisees were hostile to Greek culture and indifferent to the state is found not only in the new Schürer but also in many other modern works. The hellenization of Judaism is not our concern here but the attitude of Pharisees and Jews toward politics is. One of the hallmarks of the Israeli school is its stress on the "political" and "nationalistic" aspects of Jewish history. Hasidism, Pharisees, and rabbis were always in the forefront of the Jewish struggles against their foreign oppressors—the Israeli school likes to emphasize, if not exaggerate, the oppression suffered by the Jews. For Tcherikover (1959) the Hasidim were not the quietistic pietists pictured by Schürer but religiously inspired revolutionaries who began the "Maccabean" revolt even before Antiochus proscribed Judaism. (Tcherikover had a considerable task defending this theory, since not a single ancient source reveals this crucial fact.) Similarly, G. Alon (1977:1–47) and Y. Ephron (1962) regard the Pharisees and rabbis not as political hermits but as opponents of Roman and Herodian rule and as supporters and admirers of the Maccabees. This reconstruction has some truth to it—Alon and Ephron correctly point out that those Jews who requested from the Romans the abolition of Maccabean (*Ant.* 14.3.2 §41)

and Herodian (*Ant.* 17.11.1f. §§299ff.) rule are not characterized as Pharisees—but it is as simplistic and biased as the Christian theory it was meant to replace. According to Alon (1977:269–313), R. Yoḥanan ben Zakkai's flight from Jerusalem during the great revolt was not a flight at all but a capture followed by detention in a paleo-Nazi (i.e., Roman) concentration camp. Tcherikover (1957) greatly magnifies the scope and consequence of the Jewish revolt in Egypt in 115–117 c.e. No one will deny that the war was serious and consequential, but did it mark the end of Egyptian Jewry? Paucity of papyri proves little (Turner: 45ff.), and by the Christian period there was a large and vigorous Jewish community in the land of the Copts. And as for the rebellion of Bar Kokhba, what Israeli historian would deny that this false messiah was supported by the rabbis? But such support is questionable on several grounds, not least of which is continued Roman support for the rabbinic establishment after the war (see Aleksandrov). These characteristics of Israeli historiography—a fundamentalist acceptance of rabbinic texts and a strong "nationalist" reading of Jewish history—are united in Avi-Yonah's *Jews of Palestine*. The central thesis of this work is that Schürer is wrong: Jewish political ambitions persisted even after the fall of Betar. Avi-Yonah, relying to a great extent on the work of Alon (1953–55), sees the patriarchate as the focal point of Jewish political aspirations, and rabbinic messianic speculations as the expression of a frustrated nationalism. In Avi-Yonah's hands the riots of 353 c.e. become virtually another war. Avi-Yonah's interpretations may in fact be correct, but his biases are evident.

4. Schürer argued that rabbinic texts were useful for the reconstruction of the religious life of the Second Temple period but not for much else. This ambivalent attitude toward the historical utility of rabbinic literature now predominates, but the Israeli school, inspired by Schürer's Jewish opponents, regularly assumes that these religious texts inerrantly transmit historical data. Occasionally even a German Christian scholar might share this fundamentalism (e.g., J. Jeremias). This issue deserves a full discussion.

A METHODOLOGICAL CRISIS

The study of Jewish history in the Greco-Roman period is now undergoing a crisis of method. The crisis centers on the following questions: Which sources are reliable? How are the sources to be used? What assumptions can we make? How can we determine which questions are answerable and which unanswerable? The major literary sources, 1 Maccabees, 2 Maccabees, Josephus's *Jewish War* and *Jewish Antiquities*, Philo's *Legation to Gaius* and *Against Flaccus*, and rabbinic literature, either are not interested in answering our historical questions or answer them in a manner that is unsatisfactory to us. 2 Maccabees and the two treatises of Philo are not "historical" works at all but theological reflections on sin, *hybris*, reward and punishment, the divine protection of Israel, and the like. 1 Maccabees and the two works of Josephus do attempt to recount the history of the Jews in the Greco-Roman world, but they are dominated by motives and methods that frequently distort the accuracy of the narrative. How then can we write ancient Jewish history at all? In posing this question I am advocating not historical nihilism but serious attention to historiographic problems. Once again Schürer and Schürer-Vermes-Millar can serve as convenient examples. The book opens with an analysis of each of the sources, but this historiographic introduction is forgotten when the story commences. 1 Maccabees and 2 Maccabees, the *Jewish War* and the *Jewish Antiquities*, the *Jewish Antiquities* and the *Legation*, the *Jewish War* and Josephus's *Life*—the data of each of these pairs are homogenized and blended to become "history," although the separate halves of these pairs frequently contradict each other. Without a careful perusal of the notes it is nearly impossible to discover from Schürer's narrative that the *Legation* is not always reconcilable with the *Antiquities*, that the *War* and the *Antiquities* give radically different assessments of the tenure of the procurator Albinus, that the *Life* contradicts the *War* in many points, and that Josephus's description of the beginnings of the great revolt in 66 c.e. is tendentious and obfuscating (Cohen: 97–100, 182–87).

Similarly, those who would use rabbinic texts as sources for the history of the Second Commonwealth must explain why these texts, none of them compiled before 200 c.e., should be regarded as reliable. No one denies that rabbinic texts preserve traditions that originated many centuries before the documents in which they appear, but how are we to separate these traditions from those of more recent date, and how are we to assess their reliability? We lack analyses of rabbinic historiography. The rabbis wrote no work comparable to the *Jewish War* and I suppose that the word "historiography" is a bit grandiose in this context, but the rabbis did tell anecdotes about their own times and about the period of the Second Temple. It is the reliability of these anecdotes that is in question. For example, rabbinic accounts tell us that Shimon b. Shetah, a rabbinic hero, was present at the court of Alexander Jannaeus when a delegation arrived from Persia, but this is something that cannot be verified, no matter how many times we read Josephus; similarly, the rabbis describe the gruesome suicide of Yakim of Zerurot, identified by moderns with the high priest Alcimus, but neither 1 Maccabees nor Josephus has a similar description. Since these anecdotes are not verifiable and since they cannot be assumed to be true merely because they are plausible, we must pose historiographical questions. What is the aim of these anecdotes? Who transmitted them and why? By what literary criteria were they shaped and transmitted? These questions may seem obvious, but they were not consistently asked with reference to rabbinic material until Jacob Neusner asked them. Much work remains to be done, but Neusner's researches have already made it clear that rabbinic historiography should be understood by analogy not with Thucydides and Polybius but with the popular historiography of the Roman Empire, of the sort known to us through Lucian's *How to Write History* and Christian hagiography (Delehaye). Without this historiographical introduction, the appeal of Schürer-Vermes-Millar, the *WHJP*, and Avi-Yonah (1976) to rabbinic anecdotes is not a bit more reliable or useful than that of J. Derenbourg over a century ago. (The enucleation of history from legal materials is another matter, which is outside the scope of this essay.)

Our methodological dilemma is heightened when we confront a contradiction between rabbinic and nonrabbinic sources. The most prominent example of this sort of difficulty is the nature and composition of the sanhedrin. Rabbinic texts, both legal and anecdotal, regard the sanhedrin as a supreme court *cum* senate, populated by rabbis and chaired by two rabbinic figures. Josephus refers to a *koinon* and *boulē* as well as a *synedrion*. From Josephus we do not know whether these are all one and the same institution and whether these are permanent or ad hoc bodies, but we see that aristocrats and high priests as well as Pharisees figure prominently in the discussion of these matters. The testimony of the NT matches that of Josephus (except that the NT does not use *koinon* and *boulē* to refer to a supreme council in Jerusalem). How do we resolve this contradiction? Should we conclude that the composition and leadership of the Jewish supreme council changed over the centuries and that the rabbinic and Greek sources reflect different stages in this development? Or should we conclude that Josephus and the NT present a basically accurate picture which the rabbis have "corrected" and improved either through wishful thinking or intentional distortion? Or should we conclude that two different institutions existed simultaneously in Jerusalem, the one described by the Greek sources and the other by the rabbinic? The discussion of these possibilities has persisted for over a century (see, e.g., Ephron, 1967; Kennard; Mantel; Rivkin; Tcherikover, 1964) and is likely to persist until the sources are subjected to a close historiographical analysis. And if after such analysis we are unable to determine which sources deserve preference, we may conclude that the problem is insoluble. (On the sanhedrin, see again below.)

If the study of ancient Jewish history is suffering from methodological insouciance, we may take comfort in the fact that classical history is similarly afflicted. Consider the following excerpts from the review by Keith Hopkins of Fergus Millar's *The Emperor in the Roman World*:

> One problem is that the ancient sources, the evidence, are elevated to the level of sacred texts. They are called upon to authenticate each event or practice. . . . It is convention that assertions about the Roman world are backed by references to ancient literature.

They are our authorities. Credit goes to the ancient historian who makes the best pattern out of the largest number of pieces and cites the most obscure sources relevantly. . . .

On the whole, Millar seems to assume that the sources by and large faithfully reported the world in which they lived. But it is conceivable that ancient sources, like modern newspapers, reported the abnormal more often than the normal; if so, then Millar's careful patchwork contains more than its fair share of oddities. The evidence is not whole; it is itself a social construct and so should not be taken at face value any more than one should take *The Times* or a contemporary academic political scientist as necessarily right. The historian should interpret his sources actively, by trying, for example, to understand what the ancient sources took for granted and so systematically underreported. Yet Millar consciously limits his perceptions of historical problems to the perceptions of the sources. This means that sometimes and at its worst, his history is not better than an annotated florilegium of sources in the style of a Byzantine excerptor, filing cards and glue. . . .

Even in the terms of his own conventions, Millar's detailed use of his sources leaves much to be desired. For example, Macrobius is used as evidence for what Augustus said at a dinner party . . . four hundred years earlier, without apparent consideration that such sources are quasi-fictional and that dramatic stories get attached with appropriate changes to stereotypes. . . . The citation of late or fictionalizing sources for Millar's type of chronological history is dangerous, especially if the point turns on specific words in the late source. . . . Of course, Millar recognizes that some stories do not report what actually happened and he seems understandably uncertain how to treat everyday detail in an otherwise unbelievable story—is that fiction too or contemporary detail from real life? . . . But he does not seem to have considered the problem that generalizations in synoptic historians may have been based on anecdotes now suppressed. The criterion for belief should not be the testimony itself.

Mutatis mutandis, these criticisms apply to contemporary work on ancient Jewish history. Historians of Jewish antiquity too often elevate their sources to the status of sacred texts and hail as a great historian the one who assembles the largest number of "facts" verified by references from these "sacred texts." Historians of Jewish antiquity too often rely on anecdotal sources written centuries after the events they purport to describe. Hopkins warns us that this is not as it should be. Historians must first investigate the character and assumptions of the ancient texts before those texts can become "sources." The value of historiographic work of this sort can be appreciated from some recent attempts to write a biography of a certain prominent figure of the first century of our era who is known to us primarily through four somewhat contradictory literary sources. Yet we are able to write a biography of this man because we can more or less determine the character, motives, and relative historicity of the sources. Without such historiographical work, we would be forced to create a *diatessaron* in an attempt to reconcile the four sources as best we could, but this procedure obviously would not yield an account that could withstand historical criticism. I am referring, of course, to the emperor Tiberius; see, for example, his biography by R. Seager.

THE GRECO-ROMAN CONTEXT

In many respects Josephus's work has served as the model for subsequent attempts to write the political history of the Jews in Greco-Roman antiquity. Beginning with the Maccabean period Josephus punctuates his narrative with digressions of various lengths on the history of the Seleucids, the Romans, and the Parthians. By this method Jewish and Greco-Roman history are juxtaposed rather than coordinated. Jewish history is treated as an autonomous series of events unfolding in its own world. When this world is penetrated by the events of the Greco-Roman world—as, for example, in the Maccabean period, when Seleucid history and Jewish history are closely intertwined, or in the Herodian period, for which a knowledge of Roman politics is essential in order to understand the actions of Herod the Great—Josephus provides the requisite data, but no more. He has no interest in Greco-Roman history per se and has no need to convince his audience that the Jews were part of the Greco-Roman world.

Most modern surveys follow Josephus's lead. Their focus is Jewish history and their aim is the elucidation of the inner dynamics of that history. The events of the Greco-Roman world are mentioned only when they impinge directly upon Jewish history. Some surveys devote a separate chapter or two to the ancient context, but most do not do even that. This practice is due not only to Josephus's enduring influence—for what, in the final analysis, are Schürer, the *WHJP*, Smallwood, et al., if not paraphrases of Josephus with footnotes?—but also to the fact that ancient Jewish history has been to a great extent the domain of theologians, not classicists. However, Josephus is not an adequate model. It is not as obvious to us as it was to Josephus and his contemporaries that the Jews, as constituent members of the Greco-Roman world, did what many other Greco-Roman nations did. Therefore, in addition to surveys and detailed studies that concentrate upon internal Jewish history, we require cross-cultural and thematic studies that will concentrate upon the Greco-Roman context of ancient Jewish history. Elias Bickerman, a classicist, pioneered this sort of research in the 1930s but has not had many followers. Fortunately, the postwar period has seen the publication by classicists of several handbooks that not only provide essential information for historians of Jewish antiquity but also help them gain a proper perspective. Jewish history is part of ancient history. For the Hellenistic period I may mention the work of H. Bengtson and E. Will; for the Roman period (until 200 c.e.) I may mention the work of A. Garzetti. I shall now discuss several topics that benefit from a cross-cultural approach.

The Maccabean Revolt

My first illustration is the Maccabean revolt and its background. As is well known, 1 and 2 Maccabees explain that the Maccabees rebelled in response to Antiochus's religious persecution and profanation of the Temple. This sequence leaves Antiochus's anti-Jewish actions unmotivated. During the period under survey several scholars have grappled with this difficulty. I shall treat briefly three reconstructions. The first is that of V. Tcherikover (1959), a member of the "Israeli school" (see above), who theorizes that the Jews, led by the Hasidim, revolted against the hellenizers and thus against the Seleucid state. Realizing the religious origins of the rebellion, Antiochus proscribed the religion that was responsible for the restiveness of his subjects. This simple and plausible reconstruction has the advantage of being paralleled by the events of the Bar Kokhba war. In their attempt to suppress a revolt which, at least to some extent, was inspired by religious ideas and led by religious leaders, the Romans prevented the Jews from performing many of their rites in order to undercut the religious roots of the rebellion (Lieberman). Tcherikover's reconstruction is supplemented by J. Goldstein, who suggests that Antiochus's program of "hellenization" was really "Romanization" since it was from the Romans that Antiochus had learned how to suppress cults that threatened the social order. Against Tcherikover, J. Bunge (469–79) maintains the sequence of 1 and 2 Maccabees (persecution followed by revolt) but accepts Tcherikover's idea that the persecution really had political, not religious, goals. What prompted the persecution, according to Bunge, was not a revolt but a refusal by the Jews to participate in a pagan ceremony whose purpose was to acknowledge Antiochus as god and king.

The fact that the evidence for all these theories is insufficient or ambiguous is not my concern here. These theories have in common a concern to portray Antiochus not as an irrational madman but as a Hellenistic monarch acting in good Greco-Roman fashion. They have in common also a lack of concern to portray the Maccabees as a Hellenistic phenomenon. The Maccabees remain uniquely Jewish, loyal to the law, and the enemies of (extreme) Hellenization. True, Tcherikover is aware that the Maccabees were motivated—at least in part—by social and economic considerations (see Kreissig [1962] for a Marxist discussion) and that they typify the renascent nationalism of the peoples of the East, but these factors are subordinated to those of a religious sort. A proper understanding of the Maccabees demands more than detailed exegesis of 1 Maccabees, 2 Maccabees,

Daniel, and Josephus; it demands a knowledge of the larger context. Beginning in the third century B.C.E. the native peoples of the East became restive under the Macedonian yoke. This restiveness first manifested itself in eschatological speculations, but by the second century B.C.E. revolts and riots were common not only in Judea but also in Egypt, Persia, and elsewhere. The slogan of these movements was hatred of the Greeks and Hellenism. Thus, both Jewish apocalyptic and the Maccabean movement have close analogies in the contemporary world of the Hellenistic Near East. Jewish apocalyptic has been studied from this comparative perspective by several scholars (see Collins, 1975; Hanson; Hengel, 1974; and, from the prewar period, H. Fuchs, whose work has been unjustly neglected). The Maccabees, however, have been studied from this perspective only by S. K. Eddy.

The Maccabees' role in Greco-Roman politics becomes more prominent after their initial victories. The coordination of Maccabean conquests with Seleucid decline has been charted many times, notably by E. Will, but we must realize further that the rise and fall of the Maccabean state fits well the political dynamics of its period. The established political order in Rome, Egypt, and the Seleucid empire began to collapse in the second half of the second century B.C.E., not to be restored until Augustus. The Maccabees were among those who caused and abetted the disintegration of the Seleucid empire until they themselves in the time of Jannaeus also fell victim to the forces of disintegration. The year 88 B.C.E. testifies to the general political disintegration of the eastern Mediterranean area. In this year Sulla marched on Rome, Ptolemy IX Soter II Lathyros retook Egypt and faced a large revolt in the Thebaid, Syria was torn by a set of claimants to the throne, Mithridates overran Asia Minor, and a six-year revolt against Jannaeus climaxed with a battle by the Hasmonean king against his subjects and their Seleucid ally. The history of the Maccabees is more than just a part of the history of the Seleucid empire, it is part of the history of the entire Hellenistic world.

The Great Revolt against Rome

The study of the revolutionary movements of the great war against Rome in 66–74 C.E. (the Sicarii, Zealots, Fourth Philosophy, etc.) might also benefit from a cross-cultural thematic study. The interrelationship of these groups to one another has been studied intensively in recent years, the consensus of American, British, and Israeli scholarship being that the groups were in fact distinct (S. Applebaum, 1971; D. Rhoads; M. Smith, 1971; M. Stern, against Hengel, 1961). But in addition to this internal study of Jewish revolutionaries we need a thematic study of ancient native revolts, which would place the Jewish groups in their proper context. S. Dyson has demonstrated (1971, 1975) that native revolts in the Roman

Empire follow certain patterns, and I may supplement Dyson's work (which ignores the Jewish wars) by indicating that the revolt of 66–74 c.e. and, to some extent, the revolt of Bar Kokhba as well, fit the pattern.

1. Landless peasants often figure prominently in native revolts. Motivated less by ideology than by economic distress, they formed bands of brigands which attacked not only Romans but even the local gentry (Dyson, 1975:148–50). S. Applebaum (1975, 1976, 1977) has shown that landless peasants were in the forefront of both Jewish revolts, and Kreissig (1970) has developed this theme from a Marxist perspective. The similarities between Josephus's *lēstai* and the revolutionary brigands of the Roman world have been well drawn by R. MacMullen (1966, 1974).

2. In spite of what has just been said, native revolts frequently were led by members of the local nobility who had grievances of their own against the Romans which obviously differed from those of the peasants (Dyson, 1975:153–60). Modern scholars have generally not sufficiently appreciated the role played by high priests and other aristocrats in fomenting and leading the great Jewish revolt. Men like Eleazar b. Ananias, who stopped the sacrifices for the emperor, and Ananus b. Ananus, who must have been prominent in the initial campaign, cannot be dismissed as "moderates" (Cohen: 187). The relationship of the revolutionary aristocrats to the peasants during the Jewish war, especially during its early stages, remains obscure.

3. Extortive Roman taxation frequently was to blame for native revolts. This is true of the Jewish revolt as well (*J.W.* 2.14.3 §293 and 2.16.5 §403).

4. In addition to social and economic difficulties, religious "messianic" speculations occasionally fueled native revolts. In 69 c.e. the Druids aided the revolt of Julius Civilis in Gaul by forecasting that Rome would be destroyed and that the rule of the empire would devolve upon the tribes of Transalpine Gaul (possessionem rerum humanarum Transalpinis gentibus portendi superstitione vana Druidae canebant [Tacitus *Histories* 4.54.2]). Their contemporaries in Jerusalem also believed that Rome was about to collapse and that the rule of the empire would devolve upon Judea (pluribus persuasio inerat antiquis sacerdotum litteris contineri, eo ipso tempore fore ut valesceret Oriens profectique Iudaea rerum potirentur [Tacitus *Histories* 5.13.2; cf. Josephus *J.W.* 6.5.4 §§312–13). Hengel (1961) has treated exhaustively the religious and eschatological motives of the revolutionaries of 66–74 c.e., but he omits any reference to the fact that other nations too were impelled to rebel against Rome for very similar reasons.

The Sanhedrin and the Patriarchate

My final example of a subject that should benefit from a comparative study is the sanhedrin (which was discussed briefly above). Both before and after 70 c.e., the Jews of Palestine enjoyed a substantial degree of autonomy. Before 70 the chief organ of this autonomy was the sanhedrin; after 70 it was the office of the patriarch. Regarding the sanhedrin, the following questions in particular have been treated in the postwar period: the meaning of the term *synedrion;* the contradiction between the rabbinic and the Greek sources concerning the composition and leadership of the sanhedrin (see the works cited above); and the competency of the sanhedrin to decide legal cases (practically all works on the trial of Jesus). One issue that has received surprisingly little attention is the place of the sanhedrin in the governance of Judea. Tcherikover (1964) has shown that this institution, as described by Josephus and the NT, was not the supreme council *(boulē)* of a Hellenistic city; Jerusalem was not a *polis.* What, then, was the sanhedrin? J. S. Kennard has suggested that it was a "provincial assembly" of the sort known to us from other areas of the Roman Empire, especially Asia Minor. A few years after the publication of Kennard's thesis, J. Deininger's study appeared. Usually called *koina* or *synedria,* these provincial assemblies were responsible for the provincial emperor cult and for the protection of the interests of the citizens of the province. The latter responsibility was exercised by honoring Roman governors who had performed well and by sending emissaries to Rome to accuse those who had not. These two responsibilities were vested in the central Jewish body as well (although we cannot be absolutely sure of this because of Josephus's terminological sloppiness). The high priests, the notables *(gnōrimoi),* the men of influence *(dynatoi),* and the notables of the Pharisees were apparently responsible for the sacrifices on behalf of the emperor, since it was they who tried to convince Eleazar b. Ananias to resume the offerings *(J.W.* 2.17.2-3 §§410-11) and who, after their failure, made sure to inform the governor that the cessation of the sacrifices was not their doing *(J.W.* 2.17.4 §418). The *archontes* and high priests might accuse a Roman governor of malfeasance *(J.W.* 2.16.1 §333, and 2.16.3 §342). The Jewish *synedrion,* like the *koinon* of Lycia, had administrative and judicial responsibilities in addition to the two just mentioned, although the details in each case are obscure. It is unfortunate that Deininger, a classicist, did not consider the Jewish *koinon* in his book; it is unfortunate that most historians of Judaism, except Kennard, have ignored the Roman realia of the first century. After 70 c.e. the Jews continued to have a central authority, the patriarchate. Some scholars, notably Alon (1953-55), Avi-Yonah (1976), and Mantel, have discussed the jurisdiction and powers of this rabbinic office, but they have not asked regarding the patriarch what Kennard asked regarding the sanhedrin: what was the patriarch in Roman terms? In a famous passage in *Ad Africanum,* Origen speaks of the patriarch of his own day as a "veritable king" who occasionally inflicted even capital punishment. May we conclude that the patriarch, who, by Origen's time at least, claimed Davidic pedigree, was regarded as a vassal king? If not, what was he? The place of the patriarch in the provincial administration of Palestine, and the relationship of the patriarchal courts to the provincial and municipal courts are subjects that remain obscure and might benefit from a comparative perspective.

My conclusion is that ancient Jewish history should no longer be, as it was in Schürer's day, exclusively in the hands of theologians and rabbis; it belongs as well in the hands of classicists and all students of antiquity.

SOCIAL HISTORY

In recent years numerous monographs have been devoted to the social history of antiquity. Modern study of the subject begins with the two magisterial works of M. Rostovtzeff, *The Social and Economic History of the Hellenistic World* and *The Social and Economic History of the Roman Empire*. Rostovtzeff adopted the broadest possible approach in these volumes, attempting to depict the developments in the structure of ancient society as a whole. Jewish material too had its place in this edifice. Most classicists who followed Rostovtzeff focused on Italy and senatorial elites, ignoring the Jews and other ethnic "sub-societies" in the Roman Empire. For example, the fine books by J. Gagé, *Les classes sociales dans l'empire romain*, and G. Alföldy, *Römische Sozialgeschichte*, contain nothing relevant to our theme. A notable exception is R. MacMullen's *Roman Social Relations*, a work mentioned above, which sheds Rostovtzeff's prejudice for the urban bourgeoisie but follows Rostovtzeff's concern for the entire society of antiquity, including the Jews.

A synthesis of the results of older scholarship on the social history of the Jews in antiquity is provided by S. Baron in the insufficiently appreciated first two volumes of his *Social and Religious History of the Jews*. The larger part of these volumes is devoted to religious developments, which do not concern us here, but no less significant are the chapters that describe the society of the Second Temple and rabbinic periods. Baron summarizes a wealth of data and well illustrates the fundamental aspects of the subject. Although a comparable study of the social history of early Christianity remains to be written, many publications devoted to this theme have appeared in recent years, notably by J. Gager, R. Grant, and G. Theissen. These works are valuable for the historian of Jewish society as well.

We turn now to those works which deal specifically with the social history of ancient Palestine. (I emphasize again that my discussion concerns primarily Palestine; the social history of Diaspora communities has a separate set of problems.) These works generally plot Jewish society along one of two grids, the first based on religious criteria and the second on economic criteria.

The religious grid looks something like this:

I. Jews
    A. The Religious Establishment
        1. High priests, priests, and levites
        2. The patriarch and his court
        3. Scribes, elders, rabbis, sages, members of the sanhedrin
    B. The Sects and "Unofficial" Authority Figures
        1. Hasidim, Pharisees, Sadducees, Boethusians, Essenes, Qumran sect, "Fourth Philosophy," Judeo-Christians, Samaritans (?), *Haberim* (?), rabbis (?)
        2. "Holy men," "magic men," charismatics, healers, exorcists, messiahs, etc.
    C. Other Jews
        1. The *'am hā'āreṣ* and other "nonsectarian" Jews
        2. "Hellenistic Jews"
        3. Proselytes
II. Non-Jews
    A. The Romans and the Roman army
    B. "Greeks," hellenized pagans, not-so-hellenized pagans
    C. Samaritans (?)

The economic grid looks something like this:

I. The Rich
    A. The city rich
    B. The country rich (owners of large estates)
II. The "Middle Class"
    A. Artisans, merchants, etc. (city)
    B. Owners of moderate estates (country)
III. The "Lower Class"
    A. The city poor
    B. The country poor
        1. Peasant farmers
        2. Landless peasants
IV. "Non-Persons"
    A. Women and children
    B. Slaves

These two grids differ fundamentally from each other. The first analyzes a uniquely Jewish situation. Many nations had temples and priests, and to some extent the privileges and prerogatives of the Jewish hierarchy were comparable to those of other hierarchies. Many societies had philosophical schools (sects). But all in all it is clear that the Jewish religious scene was unique; no other ancient society was so torn by religious strife. The second grid, however, could be used to analyze any specimen of Greco-Roman society.

Instead of treating modern contributions in detail, I would like to focus on one central problem: what is the relationship of these grids one to the other? Specifically, do the religious and social classifications coincide? Were, say, all Sadducees wealthy high priests, all Pharisees "middle-class," and all 'ammê hā'āreṣ peasants? Or, in the words of A. H. M. Jones, "Were the ancient heresies national or social movements in disguise?" Confusion and imprecision on these points begin with Josephus, who distinguishes between Pharisees and Sadducees in four ways: (1) the Pharisees and Sadducees were political parties (my terminology) intimately involved in the politics of the Maccabean court; (2) the Pharisees have the support of the masses, the Sadducees of the well-to-do; (3) the Pharisees and Sadducees disagree on fate, free will, and immortality of the soul; (4) the Pharisees and Sadducees disagree on the authority of the traditional laws not included in the Mosaic writings. In (1) and (2) Josephus applies a political-economic grid to Jewish society, in (3) and (4) a religious one. He does not correlate these four distinctions. Is there any necessary connection between the (alleged) fact that the Pharisees have the support of the masses and the fact that the Pharisees believe in the immortality of the soul? Is there any necessary connection between the fact that the Sadducees have the support of the well-to-do and the (alleged) fact that the Sadducees deny the validity of "the Oral Law"? Josephus does not answer these questions. (On the sects see chap. 2 below.)

Some modern scholars have no difficulty with this problem; they select one grid and ignore the other. For example, volume 2 of Schürer and volume 8 of the *WHJP* (entitled *Society and Religion in the Second Temple Period*) speak only about the religious divisions of ancient Jewish society, while Marxist historians like H. Kreissig (whose work has been analyzed at length by H. Kippenberg [1978]) deny the importance of religious divisions and utilize exclusively a Marxist version of the second grid. For the most part, however, scholars assume that the two grids are intimately related, even if the nature of the relationship is never fully worked out. Baron devotes one chapter to the first grid ("New Horizons") and one to the second ("Social Turmoil"). J. Jeremias, whose encyclopedic work *Jerusalem in the Time of Jesus* became available in English only in 1969, analyzes Jerusalemite society in accordance with "Economic Status" and "Social Status," the latter of which includes "The Clergy," "The Lay Nobility," "The Scribes," and "The Pharisees" but omits the other sects and the figures listed above in I.B.2 of the religious grid and shunts proselytes to another chapter. In a chapter of the *JPFC* entitled "Aspects of Jewish Society," M. Stern treats the clergy, the lay nobility, the sages, proselytes, and slaves, but omits everyone else. When analyzing Jewish society, scholars must determine precisely whether their primary frame of reference is a religious or an economic grid and should not pass indiscriminately from one to the other without justifying the transition.

The Status of the Rabbis

As a particular example of the difficulties in determining the relationship of these two grids, I suggest the status of the rabbis. Years ago Louis Finkelstein argued that the Pharisees and their descendants the rabbis were divided along economic lines, the Hillelites stemming from the urban lower class and the Shammaites from the rural upper class. Finkelstein's theory was based on an intuitive-fundamentalist reading of rabbinic texts —intuitive in that hypotheses were proposed or rejected solely on the basis of how satisfactorily they explained various rabbinic sources, and fundamentalist in that the rabbinic sources were always assumed to be reliable. By a similar intuitive-fundamentalist method, Y. Baer attempted to reconstruct the social ideals of the Second Temple period and E. E. Urbach (1968) spoke of "Class-Status and Leadership in the World of the Palestinian Sages." Baer assumes that extensive portions of our Mishna derive directly from the Maccabean or pre-Maccabean period, while Urbach (1968) accepts rabbinic anecdotes at face value as sources for rabbinic social history. But the social setting of rabbinic law must be determined not through mere conjecture or reliance upon anecdotes but through the analysis of legal texts. Intuition does not suffice to determine whether a given rabbinic text derives from the Second Temple period. The claim must be evaluated, not accepted on faith. Further, questions of *Tendenz* must also be considered. Does tannaitic legislation favor borrowers or creditors? Landowners or renters/sharecroppers? Merchants or farmers? Peasants or slaves? Slaves or slave owners? Etc. Answers to these questions are not easily determined, but at least the questions must be asked. Urbach (1964) has devoted another long and erudite article to the (rabbinic) laws regarding slavery as a source for social history, but he never considers the rabbis' own interests in their slave legislation or the interests of those classes and groups whose support the rabbis desired. Once again it is Jacob Neusner who has made the key methodological contributions to this discussion, but the analysis remains to be done.

Indeed, the social and economic status of the Tannaim is a puzzle. On the one hand, great tension existed between the rabbis and the local aristocracy of Galilee, especially of the city of Sepphoris, whose power base did not depend upon the rabbis and who resented the intrusion of the rabbis into their domain after the Bar Kokhba war. The patriarch attempted to reconcile the aristocrats by co-opting them into his judicial administration, but this development occurred over the strenuous objections of many rabbis. Matters did not come to a head until the third century, which is

beyond the purview of this article, but the roots of that crisis are in the
second century. The classic discussion of this is Büchler, upon which Alon
based his further researches. Thus, the rabbis were not on good terms with
at least some of the local aristocrats. On the other hand, we find that the
rabbis were on bad terms with the peasantry as well whom they regarded
as *'ammê hā'āreṣ*. These "people of the land" are rabbinically defined in
three ways. They are Jews who fail to observe the rabbinic laws either
(1) of tithing or (2) of purity or (3) of the Sabbath—prayer, study, and the
like. Most modern scholars agree that the third definition is later than the
first two; as the rabbis' own observance of purity and tithing declined, nonrabbinic Jews had to be defined in terms of other rabbinic norms whose
importance was maintained. The discovery of a seventh-century inscription from a synagogue near Beth Shean which quotes a section of the
Palestinian Talmud dealing with the laws of purity and tithing (Sussman)
suggests that this theory is no longer as obviously correct as it once appeared to be. In any event, as long as *'ammê hā'āreṣ* were defined by their
nonperformance of rabbinic agricultural laws, presumably the majority of
those designated by the title would have been peasants. As the definition
changed, the categories of the social status of those designated by the title
will have expanded. Even (especially?) the well-to-do might not observe
the laws of Torah study. Thus, it is not easy to transfer the *'am hā'āreṣ* from
the religious to the economic grid. The halakic aspects of this problem are
treated in some detail by A. Oppenheimer, but the social aspects are
ignored.

Who then were the rabbis, and what was their social status? At odds
with some elements, at least, of both the rich and the poor, both rural and
urban, the rabbis had no obvious power base. Who supported them and
why? Were the rabbis a religious elite exclusively, as Urbach (1968) argues,
or a guild, or a sect? Tannaitic texts speak of a *ḥăbûrâ*, an association of
pietists who specialize in the laws of tithing and/or purity, but its relationship to the Pharisees and to the rabbinic movement remains unclear (see,
e.g., Rabin). Some rabbis were appointed by the patriarch to judicial posts
while others apparently had no official function. All of these uncertainties
and ambiguities testify to our ignorance of the fundamental structure of
Jewish society in the rabbinic period. We can speak of rabbis versus nonrabbinic Jews and of the rich versus the poor, but we still cannot coordinate
the data.

Pagans

A final desideratum. Any account of Palestinian society would be
incomplete without taking into account the pagans of Palestine, but this is
rarely done. (Imagine, for example, a work on Alexandrian society which
omits the Jews.) The pagan population includes not only Roman soldiers,

bureaucrats, and businessmen (see *Ant.* 14.5.2 §83) but also local Semites, both rural and urban. Jewish-pagan tensions in the cities of Palestine and Syria contributed greatly, as is well known, to the outbreak of the war in 66 C.E. Many areas of Palestine had heavy concentrations of pagans. And yet, Jeremias's encyclopedic classic devotes not a word to these pagans. The *JPFC* has an article on paganism, not pagans. The Palestinian pagans of the rabbinic period have received attention from several Israeli Ph.D. theses (e.g., Yankelevitch), but these works derive their data almost exclusively from rabbinic sources and are interested almost exclusively in the relationship of the rabbis and rabbinic Jews to the pagans. A full study of Palestinian pagans and paganism, based on both literary and archaeological sources, remains to be written.

CONCLUSION

In this essay I have argued that scholarship on the political and social history of the Jews in Greco-Roman antiquity must become much more sensitive to methodological issues. What is the nature of our sources? What are their aims and methods? How can we assess their reliability? It is difficult to produce a methodologically sound history without answering these historiographical questions first, but these questions remain unanswered for many of our sources, notably, but not exclusively, rabbinic sources. I have argued too that scholars must pay much more attention to the Greco-Roman context of ancient Jewish history, that is, not only the events of the Greco-Roman world that impinged directly upon the Jews but also the Greco-Roman ideas, practices, and realia that make comprehensible many aspects of ancient Jewish history. I offer these criticisms not in order to detract from the considerable achievements of contemporary scholarship, but in order to encourage twentieth-century scholars to break out of the mold established by our nineteenth-century predecessors and to proceed to new questions.

BIBLIOGRAPHY

Abel, F. M.
    1952   *Histoire de la Palestine depuis la conquête d'Aléxandre jusqu'à l'invasion arabe.* Paris: Gabalda.

Aleksandrov, G. S.
    1973   "The Role of 'Aqiba in the Bar Kokhba Rebellion." Ed. J. Neusner. *REJ* 132: 65–77.

Alföldy, Geza
    1975   *Römische Sozialgeschichte.* Wiesbaden: F. Steiner.

Alon, Gedalyahu
1953–55   *History of the Jews in the Land of Israel during the Period of the Mishnah and the Talmud.* Israel: Hakibutz Hameuchad.
1977   *Jews, Judaism and the Classical World: Studies in Jewish History in the Times of the Second Temple.* Trans. I Abrahams. Jerusalem: Magnes Press.

Applebaum, Shimon
1971   "The Zealots: The Case for Revaluation." *JRS* 61: 156–70.
1975   "The Struggle for the Soil and the Revolt of 66–73 C.E." Pp. 125–28 in the *Nelson Glueck Memorial Volume.* Ed. B. Mazar. Eretz-Israel 12. Jerusalem: Israel Exploration Society.
1976   *Prolegomena to the Study of the Second Jewish Revolt.* Oxford: British Archaeological Reports.
1977   "Judaea as a Roman Province." Pp. 355–96 in *ANRW* 2.8. Ed. H. Temporini. Berlin: de Gruyter.

Avi-Yonah, Michael
1973   "Palaestina." PWSup 13: 321–454.
1975   *The World History of the Jewish People VII: The Herodian Period.* New Brunswick, NJ: Rutgers University Press.
1976   *The Jews of Palestine: A Political History from the Bar Kokhba War to the Arab Conquest.* Oxford: Blackwell; New York: Schocken Books.
1977   *The World History of the Jewish People VIII: Society and Religion in the Second Temple Period.* New Brunswick, NJ: Rutgers University Press.

Baer, Yitzhaq
1971   "Social Ideals of the Second Jewish Commonwealth." Pp. 69–91 in *Jewish Society through the Ages.* Ed. H. H. Ben-Sasson and S. Ettinger. New York: Schocken Books.

Baron, Salo Wittmayer
1952   *A Social and Religious History of the Jews.* I, *To the Beginning of the Christian Era;* II, *Christian Era — The First Five Centuries.* 2d ed. New York: Columbia University Press.

Bengston, Hermann
1969   *Griechische Geschichte von den Anfängen bis in die römische Kaiserzeit.* 4th ed. Munich: Beck.

Ben-Sasson, Haim Hillel
1976   *History of the Jewish People.* Cambridge, MA: Harvard University Press.

Bousset, Wilhelm
1903   *Die Religion des Judentums.* 1st ed. Tübingen: Mohr-Siebeck.

Bright, John
1972   *History of Israel.* 2d ed. Philadelphia: Westminster.

Büchler, Adolph
1909   *The Political and Social Leaders of the Jewish Community of Sepphoris.* London: Oxford University Press for Jews College.

Bunge, Jochen G.
1971   *Untersuchungen zum zweiten Makkabäerbuch.* Bonn: Rheinische Friedrich-Wilhelms-Universität.

Cohen, Shaye J. D.
1979 *Josephus in Galilee and Rome.* CSCT 8. Leiden: Brill.

Collins, John J.
1975 "Jewish Apocalyptic against its Hellenistic Near Eastern Environment." *BASOR* 220: 27–36.

Deininger, Jürgen
1965 *Die Provinziallandtage der römischen Kaiserzeit.* Munich: Beck.

Delehaye, Hippolyte
1962 *The Legends of the Saints.* Trans. D. Attwater. New York: Fordham University Press.

Derenbourg, Josephe
1867 *Essai sur l'histoire et la géographie de la Palestine.* Paris: L'imprimerie imperiale.

Dyson, Stephen L.
1971 "Native Revolts in the Roman Empire." *Historia* 20: 239–74.
1975 "Native Revolt Patterns in the Roman Empire." Pp. 138–75 in *ANRW* 2.3. Ed. H. Temporini. Berlin: de Gruyter.

Eddy, Samuel K.
1961 *The King is Dead.* Lincoln: University of Nebraska Press.

Ephron, Yehoshua
1962 "The Hasmonean Revolt in Modern Historiography." Pp. 117–43 in *Historians and Historical Schools.* Ed. S. Ettinger. Jerusalem: Historical Society of Israel.
1967 "The Sanhedrin as an Ideal and as Reality in the Period of the Second Temple." Pp. 167–204 in *Doron sive Commentationes . . . Benzioni Katz . . . dedicatae.* Tel Aviv: University of Tel Aviv Press.

Finkelstein, Louis
1966 *The Pharisees.* 3d ed. Philadelphia: Jewish Publication Society.

Fuchs, Harald
1938 *Der geistige Widerstand gegen Rom.* Berlin: de Gruyter.

Gagé, Jean
1966 *Les classes sociales dans l'empire romain.* Paris: Payot.

Gager, John
1975 *Kingdom and Community.* Englewood Cliffs, NJ: Prentice-Hall.

Garzetti, Albino
1974 *From Tiberius to the Antonines: A History of the Roman Empire A.D. 14–192.* Trans. J. R. Foster. London: Methuen.

Goldstein, Jonathan A.
1976 *I Maccabees.* AB 41. Garden City, NY: Doubleday.

Gowan, Donald E.
1976 *Bridge Between the Testaments.* Pittsburgh: Pickwick Press.

Grant, Robert M.
1977 *Early Christianity and Society.* San Francisco: Harper & Row.

Hanson, Paul D.
1975 *The Dawn of Apocalyptic.* Philadelphia: Fortress.

Hayes, John H., and J. Maxwell Miller
1977 *Israelite and Judean History.* Philadelphia: Westminster.

Hengel, Martin
1961   *Die Zeloten: Untersuchungen zur jüdischen Freiheitsbewegung in der Zeit von Herodes I. bis 70 n. Chr.* AGJU 1. Leiden: Brill.
1974   *Judaism and Hellenism: Studies in their Encounter in Palestine during the Early Hellenistic Period.* 2 vols. Trans. J. Bowden. Philadelphia: Fortress.

Hopkins, Keith
1978   "Rules of Evidence." *JRS* 68: 178–86.

Jeremias, Joachim
1969   *Jerusalem in the Time of Jesus.* Trans. F. H. Cave and C. H. Cave. Philadelphia: Fortress.

Jones, A. H. M.
1959   "Were the Ancient Heresies National or Social Movements in Disguise?" *JTS* 10: 280–98.

Kennard, J. Spencer
1962   "The Jewish Provincial Assembly." *ZNW* 53: 25–51.

Kippenberg, H. G.
1978   *Religion und Klassenbildung im antiken Judäa.* Göttingen: Vandenhoeck & Ruprecht.

Kreissig, Heinz
1962   "Der Makkabäeraufstand: Zur Frage seiner sozialökonomischen Zusammenhänge und Wirkungen." *Studii Classice* 4: 143–75.
1970   *Die Sozialen Zusammenhänge des judäischen Krieges.* Berlin: Akademie-Verlag.

Lieberman, S.
1974   "On Persecution of the Jewish Religion." Pp. 213–45 in *Salo W. Baron Jubilee Volume.* Hebrew section. Jerusalem: American Academy for Jewish Research.

MacMullen, Ramsay
1966   *Enemies of the Roman Order.* Cambridge: Harvard University Press.
1974   *Roman Social Relations 50* B.C. *to* A.D. *284.* New Haven: Yale University Press.

Mantel, Hugo
1965   *Studies in the History of the Sanhedrin.* Cambridge, MA: Harvard University Press.

Noth, Martin
1958   *The History of Israel.* New York: Harper & Bros.

Oppenheimer, Aharon
1977   *The 'Am Ha-aretz: A Study in the Social History of the Jewish People in the Hellenistic-Roman Period.* ALGHJ 8. Trans. I. H. Levine. Leiden: Brill.

Rabin, Chaim
1957   *Qumran Studies.* Oxford: Clarendon Press.

Reicke, Bo
1968   *The New Testament Era.* Trans. David Green. Philadelphia: Fortress.

Rhoads, David M.
1976   *Israel in Revolution 6–74 C.E.* Philadelphia: Fortress.

Rivkin, Ellis
1975   "Beth Din, Boulē, Sanhedrin." *HUCA* 46: 181–99.

Rostovtzeff, Michael
1941   *The Social and Economic History of the Hellenistic World.* Oxford:
          Clarendon Press.
1957   *The Social and Economic History of the Roman Empire.* Revised
          by P. M. Fraser. Oxford: Clarendon Press.

Russell, D. S.
1967   *The Jews from Alexander to Herod.* Oxford: Oxford University
          Press.

Safrai, Shmuel, and M. Stern, eds.
1974, 1976 *The Jewish People in the First Century: Historical Geography,
          Political History, Social, Cultural and Religious Life and Institu-
          tions.* 2 vols. CRINT, Section 1, vols. 1, 2. Philadelphia: Fortress.

Schalit, Abraham
1969   *König Herodes: Der Mann und sein Werk.* Berlin: de Gruyter.
1972   *The World History of the Jewish People VI: The Hellenistic Age.*
          New Brunswick, NJ: Rutgers University Press.

Schürer, Emil
1901–7   *Geschichte des jüdischen Volkes im Zeitalter Jesu Christi.* 3d/4th
          ed. Leipzig: J. C. Hinrichs. [Trans. J. MacPherson et al. from
          earlier German ed. *A History of the Jewish People in the Time of
          Jesus Christ.* 5 vols. Edinburgh: T. & T. Clark, 1897–98.]
1973–   *The History of the Jewish People in the Age of Jesus Christ (175
          B.C.–A.D.135),* 3 vols. New English version revised and edited by G.
          Vermes, F. Millar, and M. Black. Edinburgh: T. & T. Clark.

Seager, Robin
1972   *Tiberius.* Berkeley: University of California Press.

Smallwood, E. Mary
1976   *The Jews under Roman Rule from Pompey to Diocletian.* SJLA 20.
          Leiden: Brill.

Smith, Morton
1971   "Zealots and Sicarii, their Origins and Relations," *HTR* 64: 1–19.

Stern, Menahem
1977   "The Zealots." Pp. 263–301 in *The World History of the Jewish
          People VIII: Society and Religion in the Second Temple Period.* Ed.
          M. Avi-Yonah. New Brunswick, NJ: Rutgers University Press.

Sussman, Ya'aqov
1973–74   "A Halachic Inscription from the Valley of Beth Shean." *Tarbiz* 43:
          88–158.

Tcherikover, Victor
1957   *Corpus Papyrorum Judaicarum I.* Cambridge, MA: Harvard Uni-
          versity Press.
1959   *Hellenistic Civilization and the Jews.* Trans. S. Applebaum. Phila-
          delphia: Jewish Publication Society.
1964   "Was Jerusalem a 'Polis'?" *IEJ* 14: 61–78.

Theissen, Gerd
1977   *Sociology of Early Palestinian Christianity.* Trans. J. Bowden.
          Philadelphia: Fortress.

Turner, E. G.
    1968   *Greek Papyri: An Introduction.* Princeton, NJ: Princeton University Press.
Urbach, Ephraim E.
    1964   "The Laws regarding Slavery as a Source for Social History of the Period of the Second Temple, the Mishnah, and Talmud." *Papers of the Institute of Jewish Studies* (London). Ed. J. G. Weiss. 1: 1–94.
    1968   "Class-Status and Leadership in the World of the Palestinian Sages." *Proceedings of the Israel Academy of Sciences and Humanities* 2: 38–74.
Will, Edouard
    1966–67   *Histoire politique du monde hellénistique.* Nancy: Faculté des lettres . . . de l'université de Nancy.
Yankelevitch, Refael
    1975   "Jews and Gentiles in Palestine in the Period of the Mishna and Talmud." Ph.D. thesis, Bar Ilan University, Ramat-Gan, Israel.

2

DIVERSITY IN POSTBIBLICAL JUDAISM

Gary G. Porton

I

Hellenistic Judaism

In the past it was common to draw a sharp distinction between Judaism and Hellenism and to argue that much of the history of postbiblical Judaism was a record of the struggle between Jews loyal to Judaism and those who favored the new Hellenistic ideals. The implication was that one could not be truly Jewish and Hellenistic at the same time. Although W. R. Farmer (50–57), A. Guttmann, and A. Finkel (46) still favor this view, many others have now rejected it. Writing in general terms, M. Hadas states that "individual alien elements may be assimilated without consciousness of surrendering and indeed can themselves come to be regarded as part of the tradition which must be protected against encroachment by Hellenism" (9).

One argument in support of the new view emphasizes the long history of contact between the East and the West. Hadas argues that this contact originated in "pre-historic" times (8), which helps to explain the success of the hellenization of the East, for "certain basic outlooks and practices" surviving from a common heritage allowed for the meeting in historical times to be "in the nature of a recognition," rather than in the form of "a new experience" (7). M. Smith (1971a:57), Hadas (8), and M. Hengel (1974:32–55) discuss the early trading contacts between Greece and the East. E. Bickerman argues that the culture of Palestine during the fifth and fourth centuries B.C.E. "belonged to the belt of an eclectic Greco-Egyptian-Asiatic" type "which extended from the Nile Delta to Cilicia" (14–15).

Hengel (1974:5), V. Tcherikover, Hadas, Bickerman, and Smith (1971a) strengthen the new position by showing that the transition from the Persian period to the Hellenistic period was *not* marked by discontinuity. Smith notes that it was with the Persian conquest that Palestine first became part of an empire that included Greek territories (1971a:59). He concludes: "It is clear that the cultural history of Palestine from the beginning of the Persian period is one of constant subjection to Greek influences and that already in the Ptolemaic period every section of the country must have been shaped by that influence more or less."

According to this line of reasoning, Alexander's conquest of the East merely made the confrontation between the Jewish and the Hellenistic cultures more direct and intense (Hengel, 1974:3). Although Hadas (59–71) and Bickerman (54–71) draw a distinction between the Jewish scribe and the Greek gentleman, Hengel argues that the penetration of Greek education into Palestine "is confirmed" by the development of a Jewish literature in Greek "which was above all interested in the Jews' own history" (1974:104). He believes that the first climax of the "infiltration of Greek education" into Palestine occurred with Jason's construction of the gymnasium (1974:103); however, Hengel suggests that a Greek school existed in Jerusalem in preparation for Jason's new institution. Hengel writes, however, that "there need not have been conflict between a conscious preservation of the national traditions of the Jewish people and an affiirmative attitude toward Greek education" (1974:76).

The new scholarly consensus suggests that the issue during the early Hasmonean era was not Hellenism per se; rather, the issue must have been to determine exactly when one had become *too* hellenized. As Bickerman notes, it would have been impossible for the Jews to have rejected Hellenism totally: "For Judaism . . . , the question of its historical existence or disappearance depended upon its ability to accommodate itself to Western Culture" (105). "A man became a 'Hellene' without at the same time forsaking his gods and his people, but merely by adopting Hellenic culture" (103). From a slightly different perspective, Tcherikover (1958) interprets Aristeas to Philocrates as a plea for rapprochement between Jews and Greeks.

The fact that Palestinian Judaism continued to be affected by Hellenism throughout the late Hasmonean period is also brought in support of the new claims. Several aspects of the Hasmonean dynasty reflect Greek influences: Simon's drawing up a document as a constitution (Bickerman: 151; Hadas: 42), the appearance of Greek names among the later Hasmoneans and the priesthood (Hadas: 37; Bickerman: 153; Hengel, 1974:61–65), and the Hasmoneans' use of foreign mercenaries are only a few examples (Bickerman: 155–82; Hengel, 1974:60ff.). Hadas writes that "the object of the Hasmonean rulers was . . . to maintain a sovereignty which would be able to hold its head up. . . . Neither the rationalists nor even their opposition objected to Hellenism as such. . . . The controlling principle was something like 'accept the largest possible measure of Hellenization and retain the greatest measure of loyalty to the native traditions'" (43–44). Collins (1980) reads the epic poem of Theodotus as a manifestation of the persistence of Hellenistic culture under the Hasmoneans.

The influence of Hellenistic culture upon Palestinian Judaism did not end with the last Hasmonean. S. Lieberman suggests that many aspects of the ritual in the Jerusalem Temple as well as the design of the building itself and its implements "were common to all sanctuaries of the time" (1950:153–79). Bickerman notes that the idea of placing traditional usage alongside written law (as the Pharisees and probably other Jewish sects had done) and the Pharisaic (and rabbinic) emphasis on education were common in the Hellenistic world (162–63). J. Neusner states that "Palestinian Judaism overall and the Pharisaic sect in particular are to be seen as Jewish modes of a common, international cultural 'style' known as Hellenism" (1973:10; similarly Rivkin, 1978:242–43; W. D. Davies, 1967a:11; Simon: 13).

As many have pointed out, the influence of Hellenism can be found throughout rabbinic Judaism (Smith, 1956:68–71). Smith argues that the preserving of minority opinions is a result of Greek influences (1957–58:484 n. 3). He suggests that some of the concepts the rabbis "found" in the Bible were actually Hellenistic in origin (1957–58:473–74). H. A. Fischel has done considerable work on the *chria* and has shown that this Cynic literary form appears in rabbinic literature. Lieberman draws attention to the rabbis' use of material from the "vast stores of popular belief" in order to "attract the people to the world of the Torah." He argues that the rabbis were "familiar with the fashionable style of the civilized world" and that many were "highly educated" in Greek literature (1942:114, 67). He claims that Greek words are found in "every branch of Jewish life in Palestine insofar as it is recorded in Rabbinic literature of the first four centuries of the common era" (1942:39, 15, 6). In addition, Lieberman (1950:52–82) and D. Daube have demonstrated that the exegetical principles attributed to Hillel find parallels in Hellenistic culture.

The period under review is characterized by the transformation of the world view and concerns of the Hebrew Bible into the realities of rabbinic Judaism, most of which are firmly established at Usha at the end of the second and the beginning of the third century c.e. The major events at the end of the process are the disaster of the Bar Kokhba revolt, which changed the economic, social, and religious realities of Palestinian Judaism (Avi-Yonah) and the production of the Mishna, which took these new facts into account (Neusner, 1974). The replacement of the old leadership, the priesthood, by the Pharisee/rabbi is another major feature of this process (Neusner, 1971, 1973).

At the beginning of the period we find, according to Smith, the creation of Judaism, "that is, the religion of (most) Judeans" (1971a:145). During the period we see the replacement of the traditional high priestly family, the Zadokites/Oniads, by the Hasmoneans, the eventual destruction of the traditional modes of priestly succession to office, the growing centrality of Torah and conflicting claims of possessing the true word of God (Porton). In addition, the political, social, and economic changes experienced by the Palestinians were frequent and rapid. It is within this context of transformation, which was greatly affected by Judaism's encounter with Hellenism, that the varieties of Jews with which we are concerned arose. The continual *rapprochement* between Judaism and Hellenism was both a cause and an effect of this process.

II

Many scholars have argued that the scribes, the Hasidim, and the apocalyptic Jews formed recognizable groups; therefore, we shall begin by discussing these three varieties.

Scribes

Hadas (59–71) and Bickerman (54–71) note that the scribal class was a distinctive element of Eastern culture. It is common to describe the Jewish scribe as the copier, transmitter, and expounder of the Hebrew Bible. This picture is derived from the description of Ezra, the scribe who brought the Law from Babylonia to Jerusalem, the general tasks of the scribe in the larger Near Eastern setting, and the rabbinic claims that the scribes were the copiers of the biblical text and the transmitters and originators of certain laws (Bowker: 21–22; Finkel: 22–28; Black, 1972b; Bickerman: 67–70; Sandmel: 34–36; Guttmann: 8ff.; Meyer, 1965:42, 1974a:21–23). The scribe is also described as a member of the governmental, legal, and religious institutions of postbiblical Judaism (Bickerman: 69; Guttmann: 8; Rivkin, 1978:199–200). Furthermore, because the scribes supposedly had a close association with the biblical text and were expounders of that material, several scholars have connected the scribes with the Pharisees (Black, 1972b:247; Jeremias: 114, 151, 236; Hengel, 1974:78; Westerholm: 1; Rivkin, 1978:270; Marcus, 1952:155).

In drawing a relationship between the scribes and the Pharisees, M. Black, J. Jeremias, and S. Westerholm have relied heavily on the description of the scribes in the Christian Bible. M. J. Cook, however, has raised serious doubts concerning Mark's knowledge of the scribes and the other Jewish parties at the time of Jesus (1978a,b). Cook argues that, if the historical usefulness of Mark's descriptions is open to question, the same must be true of the derivative pictures drawn by Matthew and Luke.

Discussing the scribes of the Hellenistic era is a complex matter. First, the sources are few and far between, and they appear to deal with a variety of scribes. Therefore, many of the scholarly descriptions of the scribe are composites drawn from different sources written for different purposes over a long period of time. Second, attempts to discuss the scribes must be based on careful studies of a larger variety of documents. Cook has given us careful studies of Mark, but we have no similar studies of the scribe in rabbinic literature or Josephus. As far as I know, no one has even mentioned the fact that the scribe as such is not mentioned in the tannaitic stratum of the rabbinic texts or that our major descriptions of the scribe come from amoraic sources. In brief, at present we have few careful studies of the scribe that take into account the scope of the literary and historical problems; therefore, it is unclear whether or not we can even speak of the scribes as a single organized class of Jews.

Hasidim

Many scholars have suggested that the Hasidim are the forerunners of the Pharisees, the Essenes, or both (Sandmel: 37; Marcus, 1952:156; Hengel, 1974:176; Goldstein: 5–6; Plöger: 51; Simon: 19; Meyer, 1974a:14, 1965:18). Furthermore, the anti-Hellenistic nature of the Hasidim is widely accepted (Tcherikover: 197; Baron: 177–78; Guttmann: 17; Black, 1965:22–24). Some point to the Hasidim's strict adherence to the Law as an important characteristic of the group (Tcherikover: 197; Black, 1965: 20–23; Plöger: 7; Hengel, 1974:80; Meyer, 1974a:14; Tedesche and Zeitlin: 19). S. Tedesche and S. Zeitlin (19), J. A. Goldstein (64), and O. Plöger (8) emphasize the pacifist nature of the sect, whereas Guttmann (17), Tcherikover (197), and Black (1965:24) describe the sect as nonpacifist. There is also a debate concerning the priestly or lay origin of the group (Black, 1965:22; Sandmel: 37; Tcherikover: 197). Hengel (1974:179), following Plöger (23), stresses the apocalyptic nature of the Hasidim. Underlying these discussions is the assumption that the Hasidim were an organized and recognizable group during the Maccabean revolt.

P. Davies offers a detailed critique of the positions described above. He argues that there is no clear indication in 1 Macc 2:42, 1 Macc 7:12, or 2 Macc 14:6 that the Hasidim formed a group (133). He further claims that there is no evidence to connect the Hasidim mentioned in the Maccabean books with either the Essenes or the Pharisees (132). He also notes that, when the Hasidim mentioned in the Maccabean books are divorced from the appearance of the term in Daniel and from the Essenes, they lose their eschatological or apocalyptic nature (130–31; see also Collins, 1977: 195–210; Nickelsburg, 1983:647–48).

Apocalyptic Jews

The weight of scholarly opinion favors the view that Jewish apocalyptic is intimately connected with Hebrew prophecy (Hanson; Schmithals; Nickelsburg; Collins; Hengel, 1974). However, recent work has shown that it is more difficult to describe or to define "apocalyptic" than it is to show its connection to prophecy. Although many now reject the attempts of J. Lindblom, J. Schreiner, and D. S. Russell to construct lists of apocalyptic traits, contemporary scholars often select one element as essential to Jewish apocalyptic. Hengel points to the visionary and ecstatic experience (1974: 207), and W. Schmithals underscores the revelatory aspect of apocalyptic thought (14–17; cf. Nickelsburg, 1977a: 326; Hanson: 16; Rowland: 70). Schmithals also writes that "a basic characteristic of Apocalyptic is that history is presented as a continuity which can be viewed as a whole, is complete, and is moving toward a goal" (17); the concept of two ages "is [also] a basic principle" (20; similarly Collins: 110). This is close to P. Hanson's view that the "basic intent" of Jewish apocalyptic is to describe

to the "faithful the vision of Yahweh's future saving act on their behalf" (8).
Stone, on the other hand, stresses noneschatological aspects of apocalyptic
(1976).

Several writers have attempted to discuss the social, ideological, and
historical matrix in which Jewish apocalyptic arose (see Nickelsburg, 1983).
Hanson argues that this matrix is found "in an inter-community struggle
. . . between visionary and heirocratic elements" (29). B. W. Kovacs,
however, has argued against Hanson's position and has shown that it is
extremely difficult to apply contemporary sociological theory to the era in
which Jewish apocalyptic arose. Plöger argues that the development of
Jewish apocalyptic was inevitable, for the "transformation of the nation of
Israel into the community of Yahweh established the basis that eventually
led to the change of the prophetic eschatology into the apocalytic view"
(49–50); Schmithals, however, objects strongly to this view (138). A. J.
Saldarini (1975:356) and J. J. Collins (18) have found the essence of apocalyptic in its political posture, whereas Schmithals (45) argues that Jewish
apocalyptic was generally apolitical.

Hengel argues that the apocalyptic spirit arose as a result of the
struggle between the Jewish spirit and the Hellenistic spirit (1974:194). He
claims that the influence of "Hellenistic eschatology" was strongest in early
"hasidic-Essene apocalyptic" (1974:200). Independently of one another,
G. W. E. Nickelsburg (1977b:395–401) and R. Bartelmus (161–66) argue
for the influence of Greek myth on the apocalyptic narratives in *1 Enoch*
6– 11. Plöger (26) suggests that the "appropriation of foreign concepts" into
Jewish apocalyptic presupposes "a certain openness," and Schmithals (177)
believes that "to a large extent . . . specifically apocalyptic concepts" came
from Iran.

To date, no one has convincingly argued that apocalyptic Jews formed
a unique segment of the Jewish community. Apocalyptic thought was
widespread and probably affected a number of different Jewish groups (see
Saldarini, 1975:356–58). Davies has argued that apocalyptic thought was
much more compatible with Pharisaism than scholars traditionally argued
(1962). Given the failure of contemporary scholars to demonstrate more
than a *general* similarity among the various apocalyptic documents and
their failure to demonstrate a unified social, economic, political, or historical reality behind all the documents, we should probably *not* view
Jewish apocalyptic as a unitary phenomenon.

Contemporary scholarship on the scribes, the Hasidim, and the apocalyptic Jews has certain elements in common. In all three cases, scholars
have treated these phenomena as if they were unified entities; however, a
careful reading of the sources indicates that there were varieties of scribes,
Hasidim, and apocalyptic Jews. In all three cases scholars have failed to
take into account the variety of literature from which they must draw their

information, and several have failed to ask even the most basic literary questions of the texts.

III

Samaritans

It is generally agreed that the Samaritan redaction of the Pentateuch could not have been made before the second century B.C.E. (Purvis, 1968:16–87; Cross, 1964:281). J. D. Purvis suggests that the formation of the Samaritan community as a *distinct sect* may have occurred even later than the early Greek period (1968:213–18). Recent archaeological study has demonstrated large-scale activity at Shechem in the early Greek period, which follows a period of abandonment during the Persian period (Wright: 170–84). H. H. Rowley has shown that Josephus's story of Alexander's allowing Sanballat to build the Samaritan temple is possible. Against Josephus's account is the scholarly view that the Samaritans did not claim that their priesthood was derived from the Jerusalem priesthood (Coggins: 142–44; Kippenberg: 65–66) and that the action of the Samaritans in establishing their own sanctuary was an independent activity on their part and not a schism with Jerusalem (see Purvis, chap. 3, below). The period between the construction of the temple and the fall of Shechem in 107 B.C.E. was marked by a deterioration of relations between the Samaritans and the Jews (see Purvis, below). Some time after the building of their temple, the Samaritans produced their version of the Pentateuch, which emphasized the sanctity of Shechem/Gerizim as the divinely ordained center of Israel's cultic life. "It was this contention," writes Purvis, "which drove the permanent wedge between the Samaritans and the Jews" (Purvis, p. 89 below).

R. J. Coggins has shown that the religion and culture of the Samaritans should be understood within the broad context of Judaism (141–42, 162–65). Furthermore, although the Samaritans and the Jews understood Israel's traditions differently, both claimed to be the authentic representatives of that common tradition (Purvis, below). Although Purvis has demonstrated the complexity of the issue of the Samaritan's relationship to Judaism, we are safe to continue to speak of some sort of relationship. The ambiguity of the issue corresponds to the rabbinic view of the Samaritans (*b. Qidd.* 76a, *b. Ber.* 47b, *b. Giṭ.* 10a, *b. Ḥul.* 4a, *b. Ned.* 31a, *b. Soṭa* 33b, *b. Sanh.* 90b, *b. Ḥul.* 6a).

Qumran

The study of the documents from Qumran has developed into a multidiscipline, multifaceted venture unified by the texts with which it is concerned. The scope of Qumran scholarship is evidenced by the number of bibliographies and summary articles (LaSor, 1958; Burchard, 1957, 1965; Yizhar; Jongeling; Fitzmyer; J. A. Sanders; Vermes, 1975a, 1975b, 1976a, 1976b; Laperrousaz; et al.).

The texts from Qumran have illuminated several areas of interest for the scholar of Judaism. The biblical fragments and manuscripts have thrown much light on the history of the Hebrew Bible (Cross and Talmon). The scrolls have proved of interest and importance also to the scholars of earliest Christianity (Vermes, 1976b; Laperrousaz: 980–1014; Murphy-O'Connor, 1984; Fitzmyer: 119–30). In addition, the scrolls have evidenced the variety and diversity of postbiblical Judaism, for they contain many new points of view on a variety of topics.

Although the debate continues (Ory), the majority of scholars agree that the Essenes stand behind the Qumran texts. E. M. Laperrousaz offers a good summary of competing views and the major refutations of these theories (828–32). J. Murphy-O'Connor suggests that one can explain the disagreement between the external information about the Essenes in Philo, Josephus, and Pliny the Elder and the internal evidence in the texts from Qumran by realizing that the members of the Qumran community represented "the far right wing of a much larger Essene movement from which they broke off about the middle of the second century B.C." (1986: forthcoming). Whether or not we accept in full Murphy-O'Connor's reconstruction of the history of the community of Qumran (1974), his claim that they represent only a segment of the Essene movement is well argued.

The appearance of written documents at Qumran, many of which are halakic (legal) in nature, reopens the debate concerning the supposed Jewish practice of transmitting laws orally (Vermes, 1975b:8–9; Baumgarten, 1972). The finds at Qumran also raise the problem of the changing role of the temple and the sacrificial cult at the turn of the era. B. Gärtner (16ff.) argues that the people of Qumran saw themselves as the "new temple." He believes that the Qumran community did not break with the Temple and its cult completely; rather they "spiritualized" the complex so that the Temple and the community were now linked (18). This explains, according to Gärtner, why we find some texts in the Qumranean corpus that condemn the Temple, while we have others that contain many positive comments about the institution (19). This also explains the conflicting views found in the documents with regard to sacrifices (19ff., 25ff., 29–30). In general terms, J. Baumgarten's study of 1QpHab and CD reaches the same conclusions (1953). In his second essay on the issue, Baumgarten concluded again that the members of the community at Qumran did not offer sacrifices there and that they brought offerings to Jerusalem "when religious and political circumstances were favorable" (1977:74).

The Dead Sea Scrolls have increased our knowledge also concerning Jewish eschatology, apocalyptic, and messianism; furthermore, in addition to providing us with new documents that treat these issues, the finds at Qumran supplied copies also of some of the apocryphal and pseudepigraphic texts (Vermes, 1975b:6–8, 1976a:212; Laperrousaz: 818, 822–27). Some of the documents speak of a judgment of the world by God himself through a great flood (Laperrousaz: 977–78). The sect believed in the ultimate victory of justice and the eventual establishment of God's kingdom on earth and that this final age would be preceded by a period of war and tribulations (Vermes, 1976a:216; Cross, 1961:76–78). The doctrine found in the Qumran texts concerning the messiah or messiahs is rather complex, and it testifies to the great variety of messianic doctrines current in postbiblical Judaism (Laperrousaz: 974–77; Vermes, 1976a:216; Fitzmyer: 114–18). Related to these areas is the sect's belief that it was living in the end of time and that the eschatological words of some of the prophets spoke about the history of the sect. These ideas affected the sect's exegesis of biblical materials and stand behind the unique character of the Qumran *pesher* texts within Judaism (Porton: 125–27; Laperrousaz: 904–10; Fitzmyer: 110–11).

There are two areas into which research on the scrolls has not fully entered. As Murphy-O'Connor suggests (chap. 5, below), much more work needs to be done on the literary analyses of the scrolls. Until we know the constituent parts of the various documents and until we have some idea of the chronology of the documents and their elements, we shall fail to understand fully the material before us. In addition, more work on the scrolls as priestly documents needs to be done. The priestly origin of the Qumran sect is generally accepted (Gärtner, Porton); therefore, we have before us the largest corpus of documents affected by priestly values, concepts, and principles. Theoretically, we should be able to learn much about the Jewish priestly class from the Dead Sea documents.

Therapeutae

Contemporary scholarship draws a connection between the Essenes and the "Therapeutae." Several scholars of the last century suggested that the Therapeutae were a figment of Philo's imagination, but the weight of contemporary scholarship is on the side of those who accept the reality of the group (Daumas: 347–48). M. F. Daumas places the Therapeutae near Dikhela. There is general agreement that the Therapeutae have much in common with the Essenes, especially with Philo's description of the Essenes (Vermes, 1959–60:107; Geoltrain, 1959:49; Gärtner: 11). P. Geoltrain argues that both the Essenes and the Therapeutae studied scripture, composed hymns, and held special celebrations on Pentecost; however, he suggests that they had different "programs of contemplation" (1959:49–50). Gärtner stresses the important role of the temple priests and temple worship in both communities (13). In contrast to Geoltrain, G. Vermes sees a similarity between the contemplative lives of the Therapeutae and the Essenes (1959–60:110). In general, however, Geoltrain's view that the Therapeutae and the Essenes are related but not identical seems to be the most widely accepted opinion (1959:56–57). Vermes's opinion that the two groups are closely related and that the oldest title of the *De Vita Contemplativa* was *De Statu Essaeorum* (1975a:36) does not seem to have gained wide acceptance.

IV

The major Jewish groups of this period are the Sadducees and the Pharisees, and we now turn our attention to them.

Sadducees (and Boethusians)

Several scholars see a close relationship between the Sadducees and the priesthood (Goldstein: 57 n. 17; Sundberg: 160–61; Baumbach: 208; Jeremias: 230). This position rests on Josephus's references to the support of the Sadducees by the wealthy and the highest men (*Ant.* 18.1.4 §17), the few references to high priests who were Sadducees (*Ant.* 20.9.1 §199, *b. Sipra* 81b, *b. Yoma* 19b), perhaps the references in the Christian Bible that picture the Sadducees working in conjunction with the high priest (Acts 4:1–4, 15:17–18), and the name of the group, *ṣaddukim*, which many connect with Zadok, David's high priest. However, none of our sources equates the Sadducees with the priestly party; the most they claim is that certain priests were Sadducees. Some writers hold that the Sadducees were the Palestinian aristocracy (Mansoor, 1972b:621; Jeremias: 230; Le Moyne: 349; Baron: 35). This is a result of Josephus (*Ant.* 18.1.4 §17, 13.10.6 §297) and *'Abot R. Nat.* 5. The point of Josephus's two accounts however, is not the social status of the Sadducees. He refers to the social status of those who support the Sadducees *only* to bolster his claim that the Pharisees *alone* have the support of the masses (Smith, 1956:75–76). *'Abot R. Nat.* A 5 states that the Sadducees' ostentation was only a response to the "Pharisaic tradition to afflict themselves in this world, hoping to receive a reward in the world to come." The shorter version in *'Abot R. Nat.* B *does not* mention the Sadducees' ostentation. Several scholars have argued that the Sadducees were the upper class; therefore, they were the most hellenized. However, it is difficult to claim that one particular class of Jewish society was *more* hellenized than another. A. C. Sundberg's claim that the Sadducees were as hellenized as the Pharisees is probably closer to the truth (162). Others have argued that the Sadducees were the most nationalistic of the Jewish population (Meyer, 1974b:44; Zeitlin, 1961:125–26; Sundberg: 162). S. W. Baron believes, without seeing any contradiction between the two positions, that the Sadducees were at the same time the most hellenized and the most nationalistic of the Palestinian Jews (36). The nationalistic nature of the Sadducees is based on their supposed ties to the priesthood, which would have had the most to lose if the country lost its unique cultural, national, and religious roots.

Concerning matters of Sadducean doctrine there is virtual scholarly agreement that the Sadducees rejected the doctrine of resurrection and/or life after death. Josephus (J.W. 2.8.14 §165; Ant. 18.1.4 §§16–17, 13.5.9 §173), the Christian Bible (Matt 22:23–24; Mark 12:18–23; Luke 20:27; Acts 32:6–8), and two late rabbinic passages (b. Sanh. 90b, 'Abot R. Nat. A 5) support this claim. However, the concept does not play the same role in all of our sources. The importance of resurrection for the Christian writers is obvious. Josephus mentions the doctrine in only three of his four lists of Sadducean doctrines and beliefs, and we have only two late references to this doctrine in the entire corpus of the rabbinic texts.

Many scholars have argued that the essential element of Sadducean belief was their rejection of the oral law and their literalist interpretations of the Bible (Bowker: 18; Sandmel: 39; Guttmann: 127; Mansoor, 1972b: 621; Meyer, 1965:63; Le Moyne: 378–79). Josephus provides support for this position in only two texts (Ant. 13.10.6 §297, 18.1.4 §17). The rabbinic texts usually tell us that the Sadducees disagree with the Pharisees over particular issues, for example, purity. Sifre Num. 112 states that Num 15:31 ("for he despised the word of the Lord") refers to the Sadducees; however, the meaning of the comment is unclear. In b. Yoma 4a the Sadducees are excluded from the "students of the sages" and the "students of Moses"; the reason for their exclusion is their views on the rituals surrounding the high priest.

Just as we are unable to gain a clear picture of who the Sadducees were or what they believed, we are also unable to delineate clearly the history of the group. M. Mansoor argues that the sect originated about 200 B.C.E. (1972b:620), while Sundberg places its origin "not long before the reorganization of Judaism under Maccabean leadership" (160–61; see Baumbach: 204). J. Le Moyne merely states that in the first century B.C.E. "the Sadducees constituted a complete group inserted into Jewish life" (331). Generally, scholars tie the end of the Sadducees to the destruction of the temple in 70 C.E. (Jeremias: 243; Bowker: 10; W. D. Davies, 1967a:19; Meyer, 1974b:41; Sandmel: 58). This view rests on the assumed close relationship between the Sadducees and the priesthood and the success of the rabbinic heirs of the Pharisees after 70 C.E. Sundberg argues, however, that the end of the Sadducees did not come about simply with the destruction of the temple, for the Jews anticipated the rebuilding of the temple. "Probably," he writes, "the Sadducees, concentrated about Jerusalem and being implicated in the war, suffered heavily with the fall of the city" (161–62). V. Eppstein's theory that the end of the Sadducees is related to the Pharisaic doctrines concerning the waters of the Red Heifer is based on a naïve reading of the sources.

Several rabbinic stories mention the *Boethusians* in one version and the Sadducees in another (Le Moyne: 101–2). A. Oppenheimer argues that the two groups are synonymous (159). Sundberg states that Boethusians is a "popular derisive synonym for Sadducees, originating during Roman times" (160; see Rivkin, 1970a:210). Le Moyne argues that only with the redaction of Mishna and Tosefta in the beginning of the third century c.e. did the two terms become equated (334–35). Jeremias states that orginally Boethusians referred to only a section of the Sadducees; however, eventually all of the Sadducees became known as Boethusians (194). Guttmann believes that the Boethusians were "separate from but had affinities with the Sadducees" (32, 158–59). On the other hand, J. Bowker claims that Boethusians "does not necessarily refer to one single, identifiable group; it may have diverse references" (10).

Le Moyne has demonstrated that in all the texts concerning Pentecost, the Boethusians, not the Sadducees, appear (187). He concludes that a major issue separating the Boethusians from the Pharisees was the calendar (190–92). He also notes that it was the Boethusians who disagreed with the Pharisees concerning the *tefilin* and the beating of the willow on the last day of Sukkot, if that fell on the Sabbath (193–98). Because Le Moyne can isolate issues with which the Boethusians were concerned from those with which the Sadducees were concerned, his argument that they were originally two different groups seems correct. His explanation that by the middle of the third century c.e. the non-Sadducean compilers of Mishna and Tosefta had forgotten the differences between the Sadducees and the Boethusians is also plausible.

In conclusion, we have little information about the Sadducees, and what we do have comes from documents written by non-Sadducees. Furthermore, our sources do *not* present a consistent or coherent picture of the Sadducees, for each text deals with those issues that are related to its agendum. In fact, the only item that appears in each group of documents is the Sadducean rejection of resurrection. The social and political stance of the Sadducees is unclear, for all we learn is that some priests were Sadducees and that the Sadducees did not enjoy the support of the masses. Clearly, what is needed is a sober and careful study of the picture of the Sadducees in each of the corpora that contain information about them: Josephus, the Christian Bible, the tannaitic and the amoraic strata of rabbinic literature. The texts should be subjected to literary analyses, and the author's agenda should be analyzed and taken into account. After we have a clear picture of what each segment of the evidence has to tell us, the various images can be compared and contrasted.

Pharisees and Related Groups

It is generally assumed that the Pharisees were a large group which had the complete confidence and support of the masses and exercised a great deal of influence over them (Rivkin, 1978:276, 317; W. D. Davies, 1967a:17; Finkel: 68; Jeremias: 236, 266; Meyer, 1974a:31; Marcus, 1952:154). Smith, however, has carefully compared and analyzed Josephus's descriptions of the Pharisees in the *Jewish War* and the *Antiquities* and has concluded that Josephus's testimony in *Ant.* (e.g., 13.10.6 §297 and 13.15.5 §401) cannot be taken simply at face value (1956:75–76). His comments make it clear that we cannot gloss over the differences between Josephus's two works as many have done (e.g., Rivkin, 1978:34ff.).

Several have pointed to the Pharisaic conception of Torah as the group's principal characteristic. E. Rivkin states that the "Pharisees are in all texts the champions of the twofold law, the oral and the written" (1970a:234). He believes that the Pharisees were a "scholar-class dedicated to the supremacy of the twofold law" (1970a:247–48). Finkel claims that the Pharisaic teacher's main task was to "transmit to the people certain refutations handed down by former generations" (47). Black, basing his argument on the statements in the Christian Bible, focuses on the "fundamentally legalistic character" of the Pharisees and their respect for "the traditions of the elders" (1972a:776–77). Mansoor describes the Pharisees as following "an evolutionary and non-literal approach toward their legal decisions" and as believing that the oral law was "equally valid" with the written law (1972a:364; see Baron: 41; Bowker: 2; Guttmann: 98; Le Moyne: 247–48; Zeitlin, 1961:123–24). Scholars commonly claim that Josephus's description of the Pharisees supports the idea that they possessed oral traditions (Rivkin, 1978:46ff., 283, 297, 69; Finkel: 91–94; Zeitlin, 1961:105). Josephus does state that the Pharisees had their own traditions, but he does *not* claim that these were formulated or transmitted orally (*Ant.* 13.10.6 §297, 18.1.4 §17; *J. W.* 1.5.2 §110; see Mark 7:1–5). Neusner has demonstrated that the earliest claim for the oral transmission of rabbinic traditions postdates the Bar Kokhba war (1971, 3:143–79; see also 1:6).

Some have argued that the Pharisaic concern with purity was a central feature of the group (Meyer, 1965:43, 1974a:23; Le Moyne: 212). Neusner emphasizes the role of purity among the Pharisees, especially with reference to their "table fellowship." He notes that 67 percent of the rabbinic traditions about the Pharisees pertain to table fellowship. He has shown that many of the rulings of the House of Hillel and the House of Shammai are directly or indirectly concerned with food (1971, 3:294–97). Neusner argues, however, that the table fellowship did not demand a special occasion or a special ritual; rather, it applied to "ordinary daily life"

(1971, 3:297), and it was observed in private homes "in the same circumstances in which all *non-ritual* table-fellowship occurred. . . . This made the actual purity-rules and food restrictions all the more important, for only they set the Pharisees apart from the people among whom they constantly lived" (1971, 3:300).

Black expresses a fairly common view that the Pharisees' main concern was "separation from uncleanness and especially from the unclean people of the Land" (1972a:776). The relationship between the Pharisees and the 'ammê hā'āreṣ is obscure because the identification of the latter group is uncertain. Finkel argues that the 'ammê hā'āreṣ were country people who admired the Pharisees but were separated from them because the latter lived in the city. Furthermore, the former "could not abide by the strict code of conduct directed to their household or their produce" (57). Unfortunately, there is no evidence to support Finkel's sociological distinction. R. Meyer believes that the 'ammê hā'āreṣ were the "non-priestly majority" who "did not follow the priestly purity rules" (1974a:19, 1965:31). Again there is little evidence to support this formulation.

Oppenheimer's recent study on the 'am hā'āreṣ suffers from three major weaknesses. First, he virtually ignores modern non-Israeli scholarship. The major non-Israeli authors to whom he refers are the German-Jewish writers of the last century. Often one has the impression that many of the author's issues and problems are the result of the outdated scholarship upon which he relied. Second, Oppenheimer moves between a blind acceptance of the literal meaning of the text and some minor attempts at source and literary criticism. This vacillation produces arguments of unequal value. Third, he seems to ignore the possibility that the later rabbinic collections may not contain evidence of the same value as the earlier collections concerning the early period.

Despite these problems, Oppenheimer does offer some interesting observations. He suggests that the 'ammê hā'āreṣ "desired" to observe the commandments; however, they did not "devote" themselves "fully and completely to their observance" (67). In this Oppenheimer differs from Jeremias, who claimed that the 'ammê hā'āreṣ were uneducated Jews "from whom it was useless to expect exact observance of the Law" (105). Following amoraic sources, Oppenheimer distinguishes between the 'ammê hā'āreṣ concerning matters of law and the 'ammê hā'āreṣ concerning matters of study. It was the former group which most often stood in opposition to the Pharisees (118). He further argues that the majority of the 'ammê hā'āreṣ "probably" belonged to the masses; however, some of them could have been wealthy and members of the aristocratic classes (20). He finally suggests that the issues of purity and tithing were the major matters that separated the Pharisees from the 'ammê hā'āreṣ. This separation, however, was not absolute. Oppenheimer argues that a close relationship existed between the Pharisees and the ʿammê hāʾāreṣ "which continued unimpaired despite the caution of the Pharisees in refraining from contact with the ʿamme haʾarets in certain spheres" (159). This statement should be read in conjunction with Neusner's comment that "the separation of the Pharisees from the practices of common piety was almost certainly a long and gradual process . . . since new, precise laws in all details of religious life could not be invented at once" (1971, 3:235).

Related to the problems of the Pharisees and the ʿammê hāʾāreṣ is the issue of the ḥăbûrôt (conventicles, brotherhoods). It is generally argued that the fellows, ḥăbērîm, based their separation on purity and tithing (Westerholm: 15; Meyer, 1965:27–28; Neusner, 1960:125; Oppenheimer: 127, 17, 61, 132). Rivkin, on the other hand, argues that although the ḥăbērîm were "very close" to the Pharisees, they were not the same, for "the Pharisees constituted a spiritual social movement," while "the haverim belonged to closed associations" (119). Neusner argues that, although the ḥăbērîm were Pharisees, not all Pharisees were ḥăbērîm (1960:125 n. 1). Both Oppenheimer (140) and Neusner (1960:125) argue that the ḥăbērîm did not separate themselves completely from the rest of Palestinian society; however, Neusner favors a more formal separation than that favored by Oppenheimer.

The history of the Pharisees is obscure. Zeitlin placed their origin at the time of Ezra; the pĕrûšhîm were those who refused to follow the rule of the Zadokites in the postexilic community (1961). Mansoor argues that the name derives from the time that the pĕrûšhîm were expelled from the Sanhedrin under John Hyrcanus (1972a:364). Guttmann places their origin at the time of Jonathan; however, he does not offer any good reasons for this date (125). Meyer suggests that the Pharisees began "to organize themselves firmly" at the beginning of the first century c.e. (1965:23, 1974a:16), but that their beginnings reach back to the second century b.c.e. (1974a:13). M. Simon, unable to decide between the rabbinic version of the Pharisees' split with the Hasmoneans and the account preserved in Josephus, states that the Pharisees originated "either at Hyrcanus' or Jannaeus' time" (21). Rivkin claims that the Pharisees originated at the time of Simon the Hasmonean, for they legitimized Simon's rule. Rivkin's claim that the Pharisees could have been the only Jewish group to call the assembly that declared Simon ruler because the assembly had no biblical precedents is naïve.

Smith has given us some clues to how we should deal with Josephus, and Cook has presented some interesting arguments concerning the validity of the Gospels' testimony concerning the varieties of Judaism at the time of Jesus. Similarly, Neusner has drawn us to new paths in the study of rabbinic literature.

Instead of attempting to write a history of the Pharisees, Neusner set out to study the rabbinic traditions *about* the Pharisees before 70. Neusner attempts to move behind the content of the documents to the structure, context, and agenda of the documents and their discrete units (1971). He argues that before one can assess the historical validity of rabbinic literature, one must develop a theory of that literature (1971, 1973). Before one can accept a particular version of a given pericope, one must subject it to the analyses of literary criticism. To ignore the nature of the literature and the literary context of the evidence about the Pharisees is to ignore a basic datum of the evidence. Neusner has shown that many works on the Pharisees are flawed because their authors failed to realize that the texts themselves have a history and an agendum that stands behind them. As W. S. Green states, "we know . . . what the various authorities behind the documents want us to know, and we know it in the way they want us to know it" (80). Neusner has demonstrated over and over again that students of rabbinic Judaism must first deal with the literature that supplies the data before they can deal with the data themselves.

V

Zealots and Sicarii

The last two groups to occupy our attention are the Zealots and the Sicarii. Josephus is our only important source of information about these two parties, and as usual his evidence from the *War* and the *Antiquities* is less than consistent, coherent, or clear. J. Klausner identifies the Zealots with the Pharisees, the Hasidim, and the Fourth Philosophy throughout Palestine (4:201–2). Hengel and S. G. F. Brandon follow much the same line. Both argue that the sect was founded in 6 C.E., that the Zealots can be identified with the Sicarii, and that the party was behind all of the Jewish revolts in Palestine in the first and second centuries. Brandon argues further that the Zealots were also known as Galileans and that they were close to the Pharisees. C. Roth also identifies the Sicarii, the Zealots, and the Fourth Philosophy. In his insightful review article, Smith takes issue with these scholars and argues that the Zealots became "an organized and important group only late in the revolt" (1971b:11; see also Borg; Kingdon) and that there was no countrywide resistance movement before the war. Against H. P. Kingdon, M. Stern, and others, Smith argues that the Zealots were probably not a Jerusalem priestly party (1971b:15). Against Brandon, Klausner, Roth, and Hengel, Smith does not believe that the Zealots of the period of the war are related to the group founded by Judas of Galilee. Smith also disagrees with those who would connect the Sicarii and the Zealots, who were important in the final drama at Masada (1971b:19; against Roth, Hengel, Brandon). Stern takes an intermediate position. He argues that the Sicarii and the Zealots should not be equated, for they have at least three major differences: the Sicarii originated in the north, whereas the Zealots were directed by a group of priests in Jerusalem; the Sicarii accepted the dynasty of Judas the Galilean, whereas the Zealots were not committed to any particular dynasty; the Sicarii put their eschatological hopes in the person of their leaders, whereas the Zealots did not. However, Stern argues that there "was a certain connection and co-operation" between the Zealots and the Sicarii during Quirinius's census.

VI

Our review of the scholarly literature on postbiblical Judaism reveals one important trend that must be furthered. Smith, Cook, Murphy-O'Connor, and Neusner have demonstrated the importance of carefully reading the various sets of documents. Furthermore, each of these scholars has stressed the importance of applying the methods and canons of literary criticism to the documents with which we must deal. The documents themselves, and not just the data that they contain, must be analyzed. We must move behind the content of the texts and study the way in which the texts were created, the authors' agenda, and the history of the constituent units within each document. We should stop glossing over the differences among the various accounts. Instead, we should attempt to account for the variety and diversity of information before us. Related to this scholarly agendum is the belief that the documents of postbiblical Judaism must be treated in the same manner as any other ancient documents. They should be subjected to the same scholarly questions and techniques as the other written texts of late antiquity. Furthermore, consensus concerning Hellenistic Judaism suggests that Judaism is one example of a much larger cultural phenomenon and that it can be understood only in the light of the larger picture.

BIBLIOGRAPHY

Avi-Yonah, Michael
  1976   *The Jews of Palestine: A Political History from the Bar Kokhba War to the Arab Conquest.* Oxford: Blackwell; New York: Schocken Books.

Baron, Salo Wittmayer
  1952   *A Social and Religious History of the Jews.* I, *To the Beginning of the Christian Era;* II, *Christian Era — The First Five Centuries.* 2d ed. New York: Columbia University Press.

Bartelmus, Rüdiger
  1979   *Heroentum in Israel und seiner Umwelt.* ATANT 65. Zürich: Theologischer Verlag.

Baumbach, G.
  1973   "Der sadduzäische Konservativismus." Pp. 201–13 in *Literatur und Religion des Frühjudentums.* Ed. J. Maier and J. Schreiner. Würzburg: Echter-Verlag.

Baumgarten, J.
1953   "Sacrifice and Worship Among the Jewish Sectarians of the Dead
        Sea (Qumran) Scrolls." *HTR* 46: 141–59. Reprinted, pp. 39–56 in
        Studies in Qumran Law. SJLA 24. Leiden: Brill, 1977.
1972   "The Unwritten Law in the Pre-Rabbinic Period." *JSJ* 3: 7–19.
1977   *Studies in Qumran Law*. SJLA 24. Leiden: Brill.

Bickerman, Elias
1962   *From Ezra to the Last of the Maccabees: The Historical Founda-
        tions of Post-Biblical Judaism*. New York: Schocken Books.

Black, M.
1965   "The Tradition of Hasidaean Essene Asceticism: Its Origin and
        Influence." Pp. 19–32 in *Aspects du Judéo-Christianisme: Colloque
        de Strasbourg, April 23–25, 1964*. Paris: Presses universitaires de
        France.
1972a   "Pharisees." *IDB* 3: 774–81.
1972b   "Scribe." *IDB* 4: 246–48.

Borg, M.
1971   "The Currency of the Term 'Zealot,'" *JTS* 22: 504–12.

Bowker, J.
1973   *Jesus and the Pharisees*. Cambridge: University Press.

Brandon, S. G. F.
1968   *Jesus and the Zealots*. New York: Scribner.

Burchard, C.
1957   *Bibliographie zu den Handschriften vom Toten Meer*. BZAW 76.
        Berlin: Töpelmann.
1965   *Bibliographie zu den Handschriften vom Toten Meer II*. BZAW 89.
        Berlin: Töpelmann.

Coggins, R. J.
1975   *Samaritans and Jews: The Origins of Samaritanism Reconsidered*.
        Oxford: Blackwell; Atlanta: John Knox.

Collins, John J.
1974   *The Sibylline Oracles of Egyptian Judaism*. SBLDS 13. Missoula,
        MT: Scholars Press.
1977   *The Apocalyptic Vision in the Book of Daniel*. HSM 16. Missoula,
        MT: Scholars Press.
1980   "The Epic of Theodotus and the Hellenism of the Hasmoneans."
        HTR 73: 91–104.

Cook, M. J.
1976   "Judaism, Hellenistic." *IDBSup*, 505–9.
1978a   "Jesus and the Pharisees—The Problem as It Stands Today." *JES*
        15: 441–60.
1978b   *Mark's Treatment of the Jewish Leaders*. NovTSup 57. Leiden:
        Brill.

Cross, F. M.
1961   *The Ancient Library of Qumran and Modern Biblical Studies*. Rev.
        ed. Garden City, NY: Doubleday, Anchor Books.
1964   "The History of the Biblical Text in the Light of Discoveries in the
        Judaean Desert." *HTR* 57: 281–99.
1966   "Aspects of Samaritan and Jewish History in Late Persian and
        Hellenistic Times." *HTR* 59: 201–11.

Cross, F. M., and S. Talmon
1975   *Qumran and the History of the Biblical Text.* Cambridge, MA:
          Harvard University Press.

Dancy, J. C. J.
1954   *A Commentary on I Maccabees.* Oxford: Blackwell.

Daube, D.
1949   "Rabbinic Methods of Interpretation and Hellenistic Rhetoric."
          HUCA 22: 239–64.

Daumas, M. F.
1967   "La 'Solitude' des Therapeutes les antecedents egyptiens du mona-
          chisme Chretien." Pp. 347–58 in *Philon d' Alexandrie: Colloques
          Nationaux du Centre National de la Recherche Scientifique, Lyon:
          11–15 September, 1966.* Paris: Éditions du Centre National de la
          Recherche Scientifique.

Davies, P.
1977   "Hasidim in the Maccabean Period." *JJS* 28: 127–40.

Davies, W. D.
1962   *Christian Origins and Judaism.* Philadelphia: Westminster.
1966   *The Setting of the Sermon on the Mount.* Cambridge: University
          Press.
1967a   *Introduction to Pharisaism.* Philadelphia: Fortress. Introduction by
          J. Reumann.
1967b   *Paul and Rabbinic Judaism.* Rev. ed. New York: Harper Torch-
          books.

Eppstein, V.
1966   "When and How the Sadducees were Excommunicated." *JBL* 85:
          213–23.

Farmer, W. R.
1956   *Maccabees, Zealots, and Josephus: An Inquiry into Jewish Nation-
          alism in the Greco-Roman Period.* New York: Columbia University
          Press.

Finkel, A.
1974   *The Pharisees and the Teacher of Nazareth.* AGSU 4. Leiden: Brill.

Fischel, H. A.
1968   "Studies in Cynicism and the Ancient Near East: The Transforma-
          tion of a *chria.*" Pp. 372–411 in *Religions in Antiquity: Essays in
          Memory of Erwin Ramsdell Goodenough.* Ed. J. Neusner. Leiden:
          Brill.

Fitzmyer, J. A.
1975   *The Dead Sea Scrolls: Major Publications and Tools for Study.*
          Missoula, MT: Scholars Press.

Gärtner, B.
1965   *The Temple and the Community in Qumran and the New Testa-
          ment: A Comparative Study in the Temple Symbolism of the
          Qumran Texts and the New Testament.* Cambridge: University
          Press.

Geoltrain, P.
1959   "La Contemplation à Qoumran et chez les Therapeutes." *Sem* 9:
          49–57.

1960 "Le Traité de la Vie Contemplative de Philon d'Aléxandrie, Introduction, Traduction et Notes." *Sem* 10: 5–66.

Goldstein, Jonathan A.
1976 *I Maccabees*. AB 41. Garden City, NY: Doubleday.

Green, W. S.
1978 "What's in a Name? The Problematic of Rabbinic 'Biography.'" Pp. 77–96 in *Approaches to Ancient Judaism: Theory and Practice*. Ed. W. S. Green. Missoula, MT: Scholars Press.

Guttmann, A.
1970 *Rabbinic Judaism in the Making: A Chapter in the History of the Halakhah from Ezra to Judah I*. Detroit, MI: Wayne State University Press.

Hadas, M.
1972 *Hellenistic Culture: Fusion and Diffusion*. New York: W. W. Norton.

Hanson, Paul D.
1975 *The Dawn of Apocalyptic*. Philadelphia: Fortress.

Hengel, Martin
1961 *Die Zeloten: Untersuchungen zur jüdischen Freiheitsbewegung in der Zeit von Herodes I. bis 70 n. Chr*. AGJU 1. Leiden: Brill.
1974 *Judaism and Hellenism: Studies in their Encounter in Palestine during the Early Hellenistic Period*. 2 vols. Trans. J. Bowden. Philadelphia: Fortress.

Jeremias, Joachim
1969 *Jerusalem in the Time of Jesus*. Trans. F. H. Cave and C. H. Cave. Philadelphia: Fortress.

Jongeling, B.
1971 *A Classified Bibliography of the Finds in the Desert of Judah— 1958–1969*. STDJ 7. Leiden: Brill.

Kingdon, H. P.
1970 "Who Were the Zealots and their Leaders in A.D. 66?" *NTS* 17: 68–72.

Kippenberg, H. G.
1971 *Garizim und Synagogue: Traditionsgeschichtliche Untersuchungen zur samaritanischen Religion der aramäischen Periode*. Berlin: de Gruyter.

Klausner, J.
1950 *History of the Second Temple*. Jerusalem: Achiasaf Publishing House (Hebrew). Reprinted, 1968.

Kovacs, B. W.
1976 "Contributions of Sociology to the Study of the Development of Apocalypticism: A Theoretical Survey." Paper for the SBL Consultation on the Social World of Ancient Israel, St. Louis, MO, October 1976.

Laperrousaz, E. M., et al.
1978 "Qumran et Decouvertes au Desert de Juda." *Supplément au Dictionnaire de la Bible*. Ed. H. Cazelles, and A. Feuillet. Fas. 51, Sup. 9, *Qumran-Rabbinique (Littérature)*. Paris: Letouzey & Ané.

LaSor, W. S.
1958   *Bibliography of the Dead Sea Scrolls.* Fuller Library Bulletin 31.
        Pasadena: Fuller Theological Seminary Library.

Le Moyne, J.
1972   *Les Sadducéens.* Paris: Gabalda.

Lieberman, S.
1942   *Greek in Jewish Palestine: Studies in the Life and Manners of
        Jewish Palestine in the II–IV Centuries C.E.* New York: Jewish
        Theological Seminary.
1950   *Hellenism in Jewish Palestine: Studies in the Literary Transmission
        of Beliefs and Manners of Palestine in the I Century B.C.E. – IV
        Century C.E.* New York: Jewish Theological Seminary.

Lindblom, J.
1938   *Die Jesaija-apokalypse.* Lund: Gleerup.

Mansoor, M.
1972a   "Pharisees." *EncJud* 13: 363–66.
1972b   "Sadducees." *EncJud* 14: 620–22.
1972c   "Therapeutae." *EncJud* 15: 1111–12.

Marcus, Ralph
1952   "The Pharisees in the Light of Modern Scholarship." *JR* 32: 153–64.
1954   "Pharisees, Essenes, and Gnostics." *JBL* 73: 157–61.

Meyer, R.
1965   *Tradition und Neuschöpfung im antiken Judentum: Dargestellt an
        der Geschichte des Pharisäismus.* Sitzungsberichte der sächsischen
        Akademie der Wissenschaften zu Leipzig, philologisch-historische
        Klasse 110/2. Berlin: Akademie-Verlag.
1974a   "Pharisees." *TDNT* 9: 11–35.
1974b   "Sadducees." *TDNT* 7: 35–54.

Murphy-O'Connor, J.
1974   "The Essenes and their History." *RB* 81: 215–44.
1986   "Qumran and the New Testament." Forthcoming in *The New
        Testament and Its Modern Interpreters.* Ed. Eldon Jay Epp and
        George W. MacRae. Atlanta: Scholars Press. Philadelphia: Fortress.

Neusner, J.
1960   "The Fellowship (*hbwrh*) in the Second Jewish Commonwealth."
        HTR 53: 125–42.
1970   *Development of a Legend: Studies on the Traditions Concerning
        Yohanan b. Zakkai.* SPB 16. Leiden: Brill.
1971   *The Rabbinic Traditions About the Pharisees Before 70.* 3 vols.
        Leiden: Brill.
1973   *From Politics to Piety: The Emergence of Pharisaic Judaism.* Engle-
        wood Cliffs, NJ: Prentice-Hall.
1974–   *A History of the Mishnaic Law of Purities.* SJLA 6. Leiden: Brill.

Nickelsburg, G. W. E.
1977a   "The Apocalyptic Message of 1 Enoch 92–105." *CBQ* 39: 309–28.
1977b   "Apocalyptic and Myth in 1 Enoch 6–11." *JBL* 96: 383–405.
1983   "Social Aspects of Palestinian Jewish Apocalypticism." Pp. 641–46
        in *Apocalypticism in the Mediterranean World and the Near East.*
        Ed. D. Hellholm. Tübingen: Mohr-Siebeck.

Oppenheimer, Aharon
1977   *The Am Ha-aretz: A Study in the Social History of the Jewish People in the Hellenistic-Roman Period.* ALGHJ 8. Trans. I. H. Levine. Leiden: Brill.

Ory, G.
1975   *A la Recherche des Esseniens: Essai Critique.* Paris: Cercle Ernst-Renan.

Plöger, O.
1968   *Theocracy and Eschatology.* Trans. S. Rudman. Richmond, VA: John Knox.

Porton, G. G.
1979   "Midrash: Palestinian Jews and the Hebrew Bible in the Greco-Roman Period." Pp. 103–38 in *ANRW* 2.19.2. Ed. H. Temporini and W. Haase. Berlin: de Gruyter.

Purvis, James D.
1968   *The Samaritan Pentateuch and the Origin of the Samaritan Sect.* Cambridge, MA: Harvard University Press.
1981   "The Samaritan Problem: A Case Study in Jewish Sectarianism in the Roman Era." Pp. 323–50 in *Traditions in Transformation: Turning Points in Biblical Faith.* Ed. B. Halpern and J. D. Levenson. Winona Lake, IN: Eisenbrauns.

Rivkin, Ellis
1970a   "Defining the Pharisees: The Tannaitic Sources." *HUCA* 40: 205–49.
1970b   "Pharisaism and the Crisis of the Individual in the Greco-Roman World." *JQR* 61: 27–53.
1978   *A Hidden Revolution.* Nashville: Abingdon.

Roth, C.
1965   *The Dead Sea Scrolls: A New Historical Approach.* New York: Norton.

Rowland, C.
1983   *The Open Heaven: A Study of Apocalyptic in Judaism and Early Christianity.* New York: Crossroad.

Rowley, H. H.
1955   "Sanballat and the Samaritan Temple." *BJRL* 38: 166–98.

Russell, D. S.
1964   *The Method and Message of Jewish Apocalyptic.* Philadelphia: Westminster.

Saldarini, A. J.
1975   "Apocalyptic and Rabbinic Literature." *CBQ* 37: 348–58.
1977   "The Uses of Apocalyptic in the Mishna and Tosepta." *CBQ* 39: 396–409.

Sandmel, S.
1969   *The First Christian Century in Judaism and Christianity: Certainties and Uncertainties.* New York: Oxford University Press.

Sanders, E. P.
1977   *Paul and Palestinian Judaism.* Philadelphia: Fortress.

Sanders, J. A.
1973   "Palestinian Manuscripts 1947–1972." *JJS* 24: 74–83.

Schmithals, W.
1975   *The Apocalyptic Movement: Introduction and Interpretation.*
           Trans. J. E. Steely. Nashville: Abingdon.

Schönfeld, H. G.
1961   "Zum Begriff 'Therapeutae' bei Philo von Alexandrien." *RQ* 10:
           219–40.

Schreiner, J.
1969   *Alttestamentlich-jüdische Apokalyptik.* Munich: Kösel.

Simon, Marcel
1967   *Jewish Sects at the Time of Jesus.* Trans. J. H. Farley. Philadelphia:
           Fortress.

Smith, Morton
1956   "Palestinian Judaism in the First Century." Pp. 67–81 in *Israel: Its
           Role in Civilization.* Ed. M. Davis. New York: Israel Institute of the
           Jewish Theological Seminary.
1957–58   "The Image of God: Notes on the Hellenization of Judaism with
           Especial Reference to Goodenough's Work on Jewish Symbols."
           BJRL 40: 473–512.
1960–61   "The Dead Sea Sect in Relation to Ancient Judaism." *NTS* 7:
           347–60.
1971a   *Palestinian Parties and Politics that Shaped the Old Testament.*
           New York: Columbia University Press.
1971b   "Zealots and Sicarii, their Origins and Relations." *HTR* 64: 1–19.

Stern, Menahem
1973   "Zealots." *Encyclopedia Judaica Year Book.* Jerusalem: Keter.

Stone, M. E.
1976   "Lists of Revealed Things in the Apocalyptic Literature." Pp.
           414–52 in *Magnalia Dei: The Mighty Acts of God: Essays on the
           Bible and Archaeology in Memory of G. Ernest Wright.* Ed. F. M.
           Cross, W. E. Lemke, P. D. Miller. Garden City, NY: Doubleday.

Sundberg, A. C.
1962   "Sadducees." *IDB* 4: 160–63.

Tcherikover, Victor
1958   "The Ideology of the Letter of Aristeas." *HTR* 51: 59–85.
1959   *Hellenistic Civilization and the Jews.* Trans. S. Applebaum. Phila-
           delphia: Jewish Publication Society.

Tedesche, S., and S. Zeitlin
1950   *The First Book of Maccabees.* New York: Harper & Bros.

Thoma, C.
1973   "Der Pharisäismus." Pp. 254–72 in *Literatur und Religion des
           Frühjudentums.* Ed. J. Maier and J. Schreiner. Würzburg:
           Echter-Verlag.

Vermes, G.
1959–60   "Essenes-Therapeutae-Qumran." *Durham University Journal* 52
           (n.s. 21): 97–115.
1975a   *Post-Biblical Jewish Studies.* SJLA 8. Leiden: Brill.
1975b   "The Impact of the Dead Sea Scrolls on Jewish Studies During the
           Last Twenty-Five Years." *JJS* 26: 1–14.
1976a   "Dead Sea Scrolls." *IDBSup,* 210–19.

1976b   "The Impact of the Dead Sea Scrolls on the Study of the New Testament." *JJS* 27: 107–16.

Weiss, H. F.
1974   "The Pharisees in the New Testament." *TDNT* 9: 35–46.

Westerholm, S.
1978   *Jesus and Scribal Authority*. ConBNT 10. Lund: Gleerup.

Wright, G. E.
1965   *Shechem: Biography of a Biblical City*. New York: McGraw-Hill.

Yizhar, M.
1967   *Bibliography of Hebrew Publications on the Dead Sea Scrolls, 1948–1964*. HTS 23: Cambridge, MA: Harvard University Press.

Zeitlin, S.
1961   "The Pharisees: A Historical Study." *JQR* 52: 97–128.
1962   "Zealots and Sicarii." *JBL* 81: 395–98.
1969   "The Origin of the Pharisees Reconsidered." *JQR* 52: 97–128.

3

THE SAMARITANS AND JUDAISM

James D. Purvis

MAJOR CONTRIBUTIONS OF RECENT STUDIES

The Formative Stages of Samaritanism

Recent studies have contributed significantly to our understanding of Samaritans, especially with regard to the history of the community during the formative stages of its development. These have resulted from the assessment of previously unavailable data pertaining to Samaritan history and the institutions of early Samaritanism. Scholars have been concerned with the problem of Samaritan origins for some time but have been unable to attain unanimity, primarily because of the limited amount of (conflicting) data upon which their reconstructions have been based. Varieties of opinion still remain, but there is optimism that the problem is capable of resolution. Although a clear consensus has yet to emerge, it appears closer than at any previous time in the long history of Samaritan research (about four hundred years of scholarly activity; see the citations below, under "Recent Reconstructions of Early Samaritan History"). Most important, this means that with a clearer understanding of what the Samaritan community was in late antiquity—why it came into being and continued an autonomous life apart from its parent (or sister) faith—it is possible to make a clearer evaluation of Samaritanism in relation to Judaism (see the observations below, under "Samaritanism as a Variety of Judaism and Varieties of Samaritanism").

Samaritanism as a Complex Religious System

Of equal importance, a deeper appreciation of early Samaritanism as a complex religious system embracing a variety of theological positions has recently emerged. That the early Samaritan religion was not monolithic was well known, and the varieties of Samaritanism were generally understood after the model of a Samaritan orthodoxy and its heretical sects. The best known of the early Samaritan sects was the Dositheans, but it was not entirely clear (because of conflicting witnesses) exactly what this community represented in itself and how it may have related to other Samaritan groups or to Samaritanism as a whole. Recent studies have clarified the

81

identity of the Dositheans and their place within the Samaritan community (Bowman, 1958–59, 1964, 1975:37–56; Caldwell; Crown, 1967, 1967–68, 1972, 1972–73; Isser; Kippenberg: 128–71). It has also become apparent that at some point in the history of the Samaritans (some think as early as the fourth century [so Kippenberg]; others as late as the fourteenth [so Bowman]) an accommodation was made between Dosithean and non-Dosithean factions with the result that a standardization of Samaritan religion occurred, in which originally divergent theological traditions were syncretized. This understanding has resulted in a process of sorting out disparate traditions preserved in medieval and modern theological and liturgical texts to determine to which of the branches of early Samaritanism various traditions originally belonged. Consequently, a number of important studies have appeared in which attempts have been made to understand early Samaritan theology not simply against the background of Judaism but in terms of the social dynamics of the Samaritan community itself (see Bowman, 1958–59, 1964, 1975:37–56; Kippenberg: 175–349). This is an area in which the opinions of scholars have differed considerably and in which much work remains to be done.

Samaritan Culture

Finally, we would note the contribution to Samaritan research represented by the plethora of recent publications relating to Samaritan history, literature, liturgy, folklore, linguistics (Hebrew and Aramaic), and anthropology, as well as other dimensions of Samaritan life down to the present day. Most important, we note the publication (and reprinting) of texts and translations of Samaritan materials which have stimulated interpretive study and without which the second contribution noted above would not have been possible. A recent bibliographical study (by S. Noja, as cited in Pummer, 1976b:39) observed that of the numerous publications on Samaritan subjects since 1600, approximately 25 percent appeared between 1950 and 1970; the percentage would be even more impressive for the period 1950 to 1980. Not all of these publications can be mentioned here, but see especially the three "recent studies" articles by Reinhard Pummer (1976a, 1976b, 1977) and the bibliographies in Kippenberg (351–54), Macdonald (1964:457–63, 1969:226–27), and Purvis (1975:162–68). Special reference should be made to three publications by John Macdonald: *The Theology of the Samaritans* (1964), *Memar Marqah* (1963), and *The Samaritan Chronicle No. II* (1969). The first of these is a comprehensive view of Samaritan thought based on both early (fourth century C.E.) and later (medieval) texts. The last two are texts and translations of works that have stimulated further studies (see also the more recent publication by John Bowman, *Samaritan Documents* [1977]). The value of Macdonald's so-called Chronicle II is, however, problematic. (I have been informed by several members of the Samaritan community that the document was put together in the late nineteenth century. It is essentially a modern forgery of an alleged ancient document.)

THE PROBLEM OF SAMARITAN ORIGINS:
BACKGROUND OF PRESENT RESEARCH

To understand the present state of Samaritan studies, it is necessary to review briefly those questions which perplexed a previous generation of scholars. Not that these questions went without answers; the difficulty was that there were too many answers and they contradicted one another.

Who were the Samaritans?—What was the essential character of the Samaritan community when it attained a distinct and autonomous status?

How did the Samaritans come into being as a distinct religious community?—What were the specific issues that drove a permanent wedge between the Samaritans of Shechem and the Jews of Jerusalem?

When did the rupture between the Samaritans and the Jews occur?

What was the theological raison d'être of the Samaritan community?—What did the Samaritans affirm concerning Israel's sacred history which set them apart from the Jews, so that one may speak of Samaritanism as distinct from Judaism?

Closely related to these questions and considered by many to be *the* primary question was that of the Samaritan Pentateuch: What is it and what value does it have for OT historical and textual criticism? In contrast, the problem of the varieties of Samaritan belief in ancient times concerned only a few scholars.

Answers to these questions varied according to the inclination of scholars to follow one or another of the following approaches:

1. *Interpretations based upon the Samaritan view of their own history.* The Samaritans claim to be the descendants of the ancient Joseph tribes and the Levitical priests who have lived in Shechem and its environs since the days of the Israelite settlement in Canaan. Of the two surviving branches of the Israelite nation (i.e., the Samaritans themselves and the Jews), only the Samaritans have remained true to the historic Mosaic faith as set forth in the Torah and as established at Shechem under Joshua. Judaism is an Israelite heresy that was derived, ultimately, from the schismatic action of Eli when he established a rival sanctuary at Shiloh. The Judean error was perpetuated through the traditions that acknowledged Jerusalem as Israel's cultic center (i.e., the Prophets and the Writings of the Jewish scriptures) and through a falsified version of the Torah that obscured the importance of Shechem and Mount Gerizim (i.e., the Masoretic Text). The major villains of this reverse *Heilsgeschichte* were Eli (schism), Solomon (Jerusalem Temple), and Ezra (falsified scripture). (This view of Samaritanism vis-à-vis Judaism is found, for the most part, in the

Samaritan chronicles; see especially the *Sefer Hayyamin*, passim, Macdonald, 1969; *Chronicle Adler*, Bowman, 1977:89–103.) Although most scholars recognized the Samaritan position for what it is—a reconstructed sacred history to provide a raison d'être for the sect—a few were willing to accept it as essentially correct for understanding the origins of the sect (without at the same time accepting the theological position of the Samaritans). That is, Samaritanism was understood as the surviving, non-Judean branch of the ancient Israelite faith. Perhaps the most learned advocate of this position (learned in the sense of being knowledgeable about the Samaritan traditions) was Moses Gaster (1925). The position is still defended, essentially, by John Macdonald (1964: 11–23).

2. *Interpretations based upon an anti-Samaritan position known from Josephus and the rabbinic tradition.* According to this view, the Samaritans were understood as the descendants of the half-Yahwistic, half-pagan population of Samaria following the Assyrian colonization of northern Palestine in the late eighth century B.C.E. This opinion was based on the characterization of the Samaritan populace of that time in 2 Kgs 17:24–41. Indeed, this is the only passage in the Bible in which the gentilic *haššōměrōnîm* appears (17:29). But the view that the Samaritans of a later time had their origins in this corrupt and syncretistic community belongs specifically to the interpretation of 2 Kgs 17:14–41 by Josephus and the rabbis (*Ant.* 9.14.3 §§288–91; for the rabbinic traditions, see Montgomery: 165–203). This understanding was perpetuated in the Jewish community through the use of the designation *kûtîm* to refer to the Samaritans, from Cuthah (*kûtâ* of the Mesopotamian cities from which the race was said to have had its genesis. Josephus was aware of the Samaritans' claim to be descended from the Joseph tribes, but he declared emphatically that this was a fiction designed to obscure their foreign origins—and one they employed only when it was to their advantage. He also claimed that the Samaritan community of his day continued the same rites as those of its forefathers (*Ant.* 9.14.3 §§290–91). That Josephus overstated the case of his contemporary Samaritans is evident from rabbinic sources. The rabbis were much more ambivalent toward the Samaritans of their own time, seeing them as being somewhat like Gentiles and somewhat like Israelites, but mostly like Israelites. They also saw them as scrupulous in their observances. Thus, the idea that the Samaritan community originated in the pagan population of Samaria was never taken too seriously by scholars, except for the understanding that these pagans may have been among the ancestors of the Samaritans (see Rowley, 1962:222). Rather, an attempt was made to determine when the community emerged as an Israelite-type sect, with its own religious institutions and peculiar view of itself in relation to the Israelite *Heilsgeschichte*.

3. *Interpretations based upon the idea of a postexilic Samaritan schism, following Josephus.* Josephus claimed that the Cutheans (as he

called them) assumed a quasi-Israelite identity as the result of a schism in which disenfranchised Jerusalem priests went over to the Samaritans and established a rival sanctuary on Mount Gerizim. The occasion for this schism was the rejection by the Jewish leadership of a marriage between Manasseh, the brother of Jaddua, high priest in Jerusalem, and Nicaso, the daughter of Sanballat, the governor of Samaria. Josephus dated the event to the time of Alexander the Great, who allegedly granted Sanballat the privilege of erecting the Samaritan temple (*Ant.* 11.7.2–8.4 §§302–25). Thereafter, the Samaritan community continued to absorb disgruntled and renegade elements from Jerusalem (11.8.7 §§346–47). Inasmuch as this was the only literary source (excluding the Samaritan traditions) that actually offered an explanation for the origins of a Samaritan sect of Israelite identity, it was accepted by the majority of scholars. But Josephus's account was not without its difficulties: it represented Sanballat as a contemporary of Alexander, whereas the only Samaritan Sanballat known (until recently) was a contemporary of Nehemiah. Also, his story of the rejected intermarriage between the ruling houses of Jerusalem and Samaria was similar to (but not identical with) a story in Neh 13:28, although the Bible does not mention a Samaritan schism in connection with that (or any other) event. It seemed to many, then, that Josephus was actually bearing witness to a Samaritan schism that had occurred in the Persian rather than the Greek period. Still others, perhaps an equal number, accepted Josephus's account as indicating a schism in the time of Alexander (for a summary of both views, see Marcus; Rowley, 1955). Thus, Josephus was responsible for not just one theory of a Samaritan schism, but two. Those who followed either theory or a conflation of the two (schism in the Persian period; temple in the Greek period) were apparently not troubled by Josephus's strong anti-Samaritan bias, which would have led him to affirm that whatever Israelite character the Samaritans had was borrowed from Judaism, and all seemed to assume that the idea of a schism of the Samaritans *from* the Jews was axiomatic for the understanding of Samaritan origins.

RECENT RECONSTRUCTIONS OF
EARLY SAMARITAN HISTORY

It may be said that until recently the question of Samaritan origins was suspended upon the two horns of the dilemma posed by Josephus: *either* a schism in the Persian period *or* a schism in the time of Alexander. The question may well have remained there, unresolved, were it not for the coming to light of new data that moved the discussion in other directions. The new data were primarily archaeological, namely, (1) the discovery of the biblical fragments from the Essene library of Qumran, of inestimable value in the evaluation of the Samaritan Pentateuch; (2) the

excavations of Tel Balatah, the biblical Shechem, and Tel er-Ras on Mount
Gerizim, the site of a pagan Samaritan temple of the Roman period; and
(3) the discovery of the so-called Samaria papyri of the Wadi Daliyeh.
Much has been written about the importance of these materials for the
reconstruction of early Samaritan history; we summarize briefly what has
been learned from them.

It has become apparent that the promulgation of the Samaritans'
sectarian redaction of the Pentateuch was an activity that could not have
occurred before the second century (on the basis of paleography, orthography, and text; see Cross, 1964:281, 1966b:85; Skehan: 99; Purvis, 1968:
16–87, 1976a). This was an important datum in determining when the
final breach between the Samaritans and the Jews actually occurred, but
it meant entertaining possibilities other than those suggested by Josephus.
Most important, it meant that the constitution of the Samaritan community as a distinct sect may have occurred even later than the early Greek
period (Cross, 1966a:208–11; Purvis, 1968:213–18, 1976b; Kippenberg:
92–93; this was suggested as early as 1940 by W. F. Albright on the basis
of data then available [1957:346n]).

The excavations at Balatah indicated that the biblical city of Shechem
had experienced a renewal in the early Greek period, after a time of virtual
abandonment during the Persian period (Wright: 170–84; Campbell: bibliography cited), and the excavations of the er-Ras temple revealed bedrock
foundations of a Samaritan temple of the Hellenistic period (Bull; Campbell, bibliography cited). The Samaria papyri also provided evidence for
the existence of a Sanballat in addition to the biblical Sanballat the
Horonite, most likely the grandson of Nehemiah's contemporary. Although
this Sanballat (II) lived too early to have been a contemporary of Alexander
the Great, he could well have been the grandfather of the Sanballat (III)
of Alexander's account (Cross, 1971:47, 58–69; Klein). What was important for the problem of Samaritan origins was the evidence of the practice
of papponomy (naming the grandson after the grandfather) in the ruling
house of Samaria and the establishment of a time sequence of Samaritan
governors that would allow Josephus's report that the Gerizim temple had
been built by a Sanballat in the time of Alexander. That and the archaeological evidence from Balatah and er-Ras indicate that Josephus did not err
in placing the construction of the Samaritan temple in the early Hellenistic
period (cf., however, Reicke [28–29], who dates the building of the temple
to the time of the Sanballat (II) of the Samaria papyri, ca. 380; for a critique of Reicke's position see Coggins: 109–15). In addition, the excavations of the caves of the Wadi Daliyeh, in which the Samaria papyri were
found, provided additional information on the background of the
rebuilding and repopulation of Shechem. It is known that the ruling
families of Samaria were dispossessed of the leadership of that city by the

Macedonians as the result of an abortive revolt against foreign control. (The reconstruction of Samaria as a Greek *polis* had been known from classical sources; the caves gave testimony to the severity of the expulsion of the indigenous leadership.) The rebuilding of Shechem by the disenfranchised nobility of Samaria has provided the best explanation for the renascence of that site. The erection of a shrine on Gerizim would then be seen as a concomitant action in the development of a new base of operation by the former rulers of Samaria (Wright: 172–81; Cross, 1971:52–58).

It has now become possible to determine a sequence of events that led to the establishment of the Samaritan community as a clearly defined Israelite sectarian movement. What is revealed in this is an overview of Samaritan origins that differs from the previous reconstructions that were based primarily upon the testimony of Josephus (or, in the case of a minority opinion, on the testimony of the Samaritans).

1. At the beginning of the Greek period, the ruling family and associated nobility of Samaria were deprived of political leadership of the city and the region by the Macedonians. They resettled at the ancient site of Shechem, a city which had been abandoned but which they now rebuilt. The Samaritans who settled in Shechem had had, at that point, a long history of independent corporate life apart from the leadership Jerusalem had exercised over much of the Palestinian population. The relationship between the two had not been cordial. Mutual antipathies between the people of Samaria and Jerusalem had existed for at least two centuries (compare Ezra 4:1–5; 1 Esdr 5:66–73; Neh 4–6; 13:28). The people of Samaria were also held in contempt by some Judeans because of their mixed ethnic background and because of the long history of pagan worship and syncretistic Yahwism in the north. (It has long been evident that not all of the Judean nation felt the same contempt toward the northern Israelites as expressed by the Deuteronomic historians: see Gaster, 1925:12–14; Macdonald, 1964:22–24; Rowley, 1962; Coggins: 13–81.) The Samaritans who rebuilt Shechem were, however, worshipers of the Hebrew God, whether their forefathers had worshiped YHWH or Nergal (the deity of *kûtâ*, 2 Kgs 17:30) or any of the other deities brought to Samaria by the Assyrians (2 Kgs 17:29–32).

2. At the time of their settlement, the Samaritans of Shechem built a sanctuary to YHWH on the adjacent holy mountain, Gerizim. The Samaritans were thus making a conscious effort to relate themselves to the most ancient of Israel's traditions in order to maintain the support of the native Palestinian population of that region. (Compare the analogous action of Jeroboam I in establishing a cultic rallying point at Bethel with the establishment of the separate northern kingdom in 922 B.C.E., 1 Kgs 12:26–29.) The action of the Samaritans in reestablishing the Gerizim cultus relates well to what is otherwise known of political-religious establishments in the

eastern Mediterranean region. As Elias Bickerman has noted, "it often happened that when a Greek colony was formed, native villages under its control formed a union around an ancestral sanctuary" (43–44).

3. Aside from the highly prejudicial account of Josephus, there is no evidence that the priesthood of the Samaritan temple was derived from the Jerusalem cultus. The Samaritan high priestly genealogy represents their priestly chain as having been independent of Jerusalem, and this may well have been the case (Kippenberg: 60–68). Although some scholars continue to write of the Zadokite priesthood of Gerizim (e.g., Bowman, 1959, 1975:33–34, 1977:107), the Samaritans do not trace their priestly office to the Zadok of David's time. The name Zadok appears from time to time as the name of a high priest at Shechem, but this is unrelated to the Zadokite descent of Jerusalem's priesthood (see Kippenberg: 65–66; Coggins: 142–44). The Samaritan priest list could have been fabricated, but the same could be said of the Jerusalem priest list. What is most likely is that Sanballat and his associates would have had little difficulty in finding a Levitical or Aaronite order to function as the keepers of their shrine, and they, in turn, would have found little difficulty in producing credentials to legitimate their standing. Speculations on the origins of this non-Zadokite priestly line in ancient times remain just that, speculations (but see Kippenberg: 64–68). On the other hand, the Samaritans may have (as Josephus maintains) functioned originally with Zadokite priests—only to reject that priestly family at some subsequent point. But this seems less likely. (I myself was formerly of this opinion; Purvis, 1968:116–17.)

4. The action of the Samaritans in establishing their own sanctuary appears, then, to have been an independent activity on their part and not a schism from Jerusalem. But it (as well as the rebuilding of Shechem) was certainly undertaken with Jerusalem in mind, for it constituted, in the words of Coggins, "a kind of counterpoise to Jerusalem, an alternative center of loyalty" (110). It was clearly an event that was in time to shape the independent thought of the Samaritans as they came to understand more clearly their relationship to Jerusalem within the context of the Israelite tradition. But it does not appear, in and of itself, to have represented a claim that the Gerizim temple was the only legitimate sanctuary or that the Samaritans alone constituted the true Israel—the contention that was to divide Samaritans and Jews as two autonomous, hostile communities. Again, to quote R. J. Coggins:

> It would seem, therefore, that the temple on Mount Gerizim, though obviously important as a symbol of a different focus of loyalty to Yahweh from that represented by the Jerusalem temple, should not be seen as the decisive cause of cleavage between the two communities. It stands, rather, as one among different emphases which distinguished the Samaritans within the totality of Judaism" (113).

5. During their time at Shechem (the Samaritan temple was destroyed by John Hyrcanus in 128 B.C.E.; the city of Shechem in 107; Wright: 183–84; Bull; Campbell) relations between the Samaritans and the Jews badly deteriorated. This was due to several factors: (1) political tensions created by differing power alliances with the Ptolemies and the Seleucids (Purvis, 1965; compare Coggins: 84–85); (2) resentment by the Jews for the willingness of the Samaritans to accept Hellenization under Antiochus Epiphanes and for their failure to resist, as did the Maccabees (2 Macc 5:21–6:2; Josephus *Ant.* 12.5.5 §§257–64; see Kippenberg [74–85] for this and other traditions relating to Hellenism and the Samaritans; compare also Delcor; Schalit; Wacholder); (3) the development of hostilities between Jews and Samaritans in their respective Diaspora communities in Egypt under Ptolemy VI Philometor, 180–145 B.C.E. (Josephus *Ant.* 13.3.4 §§74–79); and (4) the expansionistic policies of the Hasmoneans, notably John Hyrcanus (Josephus *Ant.* 13.9.1 §§254–58; 13.10.2–3 §§275–81; *J. W.* 1.2.6–7 §§62–65; Purvis, 1968:113–17).

6. At some time subsequent to the building of their temple, the Samaritans produced an edition of the Pentateuch in which their theological legitimacy was decisively declared and through which the cultic traditions of Jerusalem were (in contrast) declared illegitimate. This was accomplished by deliberate textual manipulation to underscore the sanctity (and necessity) of Shechem/Gerizim as the divinely ordained center of Israel's cultic life (the texts are discussed in Purvis, 1976a). It was this contention, not simply the existence of a Samaritan temple, which drove the permanent wedge between the Samaritans and the Jews. For as long as the Samaritan community maintained this position (and they have continued to do so to this very day), there could be no basis of mutual respect or fraternal interchange between the two. Samaritanism and Judaism would exist side by side, not as two branches of a common tradition but as two rival faiths in which each made the same claim for itself—the claim of representing Israelite religion as it was meant to be. The Samaritan claim would, of course, have made little sense to the Jewish nation, viewing as it did Israel's sacred history from the perspective of the traditions that had developed in Jerusalem (now preserved in the second and third division of the Jewish scriptures). The Samaritans, in turn, were forced to affirm that these traditions represented not a sacred history but a perversion of it, a tragic error. And this was something that they and they alone perceived—that the sacred history did not belong to Jerusalem/Zion and its children but to Shechem/Gerizim and its heirs.

It had long been assumed that the Samaritans had produced their distinctive edition of the Pentateuch at the time of the construction of their temple. There was no evidence for this, but it seemed to make sense as long as the erection of the Samaritan temple was viewed as a schismatic action. But it is now clear, on the basis of palaeographical, orthographic and textual evidence, that this sectarian recensional activity took place closer in time to the destruction of that temple. Viewed in retrospect, this makes even more sense, for the despoiling of Gerizim and Shechem by John Hyrcanus was a decisive and offensive action by the Jewish community which demanded just the sort of response the Samaritan Pentateuch represented. The Samaritans had no intention of bending the knee to the Hasmoneans and of being brought within the religio-political orbit of Jerusalem. They had functioned apart from Jerusalem and would continue to do so, secure in the realization that they were fulfilling the manifesto of the Mosaic faith.

The reconstruction offered above is essentially that of Wright, Cross, and Purvis, as supported by others; Bull, Campbell, Klein, et al., in accordance with citations. It is followed in the main by Kippenberg in his exhaustive study [33–93], but with many additional insights and counter-suggestions; for example, that the loss of the Zadokite priesthood in Jerusalem in the early second century was a precipitating factor in the clarification of the Samaritans' self-understanding, that is, with respect to their sacerdotal traditions. A number of his suggestions will undoubtedly prove fruitful in future Samaritan studies, although I have not been able to incorporate all of these into this presentation. Similarly, this reconstruction appears to be generally accepted by Coggins, although somewhat cautiously and from the perspective of a devil's advocate. It should be noted, however, that Coggins does not see even the promulgation of the Samaritan Pentateuch (the late date of which he appears to accept) as the occasion for a decisive breach between the Samaritans and the Jews, but maintains that the breach was not reached until well into the Christian era (161–65). His judgment appears to be based on some conciliatory attitudes of the mishnaic teachers toward certain kinds of Samaritans. We shall see, however, that this issue is more pertinent to the problem of Jewish attitudes toward varieties of Samaritanism than toward Samaritanism as a whole (on which see especially Isser: 86–97).

SAMARITANISM AS A VARIETY OF JUDAISM
AND VARIETIES OF SAMARITANISM:
PROBLEMS AND PERSPECTIVES

Samaritanism is thus seen as the faith of a community which believed that it had correctly perceived the intent of the Mosaic legislation and had effectively executed that religion in its communal life. This claim is supported by the literature of the sect, beginning with the Samaritan Pentateuch, and is evident even in the reports of Samaritan practice in the literature of its detractors (once the polemical veneer is stripped away). It is particularly evident in the term the community has used of itself, haš-šamrîm, the Guardians or Observers (of the Torah). (The Samaritans have eschewed the geographical gentilic haššōměrōnîm, because of the pagan associations of 2 Kgs 17:29; *šamrîm* is most likely secondary, however, to *šōmĕrōnîm*—against Mikolásek and his interpretation.) The Samaritans were not, of course, the only party to make such a claim for themselves among the religious communities of Palestine during the late Second Commonwealth period, that is, among the sects and parties of Judaism. But Samaritanism differed from the other Jewish sects, or, one might say, from Judaism itself, in its rejection of the *Heilsgeschichte* tradition of Jerusalem. Many of the Jewish sects and parties entertained radically different views of the theological status of Jerusalem in their own time, but none so radical as the Samaritan position—that the entire history of Jerusalem as sacred center was in error.

Is it permissible, then, to speak of Samaritanism as a variety of Judaism? Not if one accepts the Samaritan view of their history as essentially correct historically, in which case it would be viewed as a variety of Israelite religion (so Macdonald, 1964:445–56). Nor could one speak of Samaritanism as a variety of Judaism if one restricted that term to its geographical field of reference (Judah). At one time it was fashionable to speak of the Samaritans as a Jewish sect (so Montgomery, in the title of his classic study *The Samaritans, the Earliest Jewish Sect*), but this was predicated upon the idea of a schism of the Samaritans from Judaism (following Josephus), and we have since come to view Samaritan origins from a different perspective.

Nonetheless, there are good reasons for viewing Samaritanism as a variety of Judaism, in spite of what might appear to be a semantic violation. First, Samaritanism must be understood not only in terms of the claim it made for itself, but also—perhaps even more important—against the background of the religious situation in Palestine during the last centuries before the common era, when the Samaritans emerged as a clearly defined sect. We are accustomed to speak of this religious context or milieu as Judaism, but as a Judaism broadly defined, not restricted by any particular standards or norms concerning what constituted a true or authentic Judaism. The term is used to cover a wide spectrum of theological opinion, including varieties of Hellenistic Judaism that would be rejected as Judaism by Pharisaic standards. That Samaritanism should be understood within the context of Judaism in the late Second Commonwealth period (differing views of cult, priesthood, halakah, calendar, etc.) has been convincingly argued by Coggins (141–42, 162–65). Moreover, there is a naiveté in the opposite approach of Macdonald, which has led him to affirm that Samaritanism was not influenced at all by Judaism (456; compare the similar view of Mikolásek). Second, both Jews and Samaritans understood themselves (first and foremost) as carriers of Israel's sacred traditions—not as representatives of Juda-*ism* or Samaritan-*ism* but as the latter-day representatives of Israel's religion. The two differed from each other in terms of the focus of the *Heilsgeschichte*, but both Jews and

Samaritans understood their faith (ideally) as Israelite. Moreover, although each judged the other in respect to its loyalties (Jerusalem/Zion versus Shechem/Gerizim), neither restricted its understanding of Israel to one tribe alone; compare the *Letter of Aristeas* (in which those who argued the value of Jewish philosophy were allegedly made up of representatives of all twelve of the original tribes of Israel) and 1QM (in which the Sons of Light were understood as Israel collectively, not just the Jewish nation) with certain Samaritan eschatological traditions that envisioned the eventual reconciliation of the Josephite and Judean branches of Israel (Bowman, 1955; Gaster, 1932:221–77).

Thus, it is not inappropriate to regard early Samaritanism as a variety of Judaism, if one views it contextually (i.e., within the context of a religious complex broadly defined as Judaism) and if one considers that the claim it made for itself was essentially what the Jewish sects and parties claimed for themselves—to represent the Israel of God. Its relationship to the spiritual traditions of Jerusalem would cause it to appear as an anomaly among the movements within Judaism, that is, as an anti-Jerusalem Jewish sect, but it was not absolutely unique in this regard. The Essenes also had a negative attitude toward the Jewish leaders in Jerusalem, although this was viewed as a temporary problem and did not constitute a rejection of the *Heilsgeschichte* tradition of the holy city. But a view of Jerusalem and its cultic traditions remarkably similar to that of the Samaritans is seen in the position of the so-called Hellenist branch of the early Jerusalem church (see especially Acts 7) and in the variety of Christian thought represented in the Fourth Gospel. Although these have been traditionally regarded as expressions of a developing animosity within the Christian movement toward its parent faith, they may very well have drawn upon an anti-Jerusalem (priesthood, temple, calendar) stream of thought within the Jewish tradition (broadly defined), of which Samaritanism was the major expression (compare Simon; Cullmann, 1957). (The Palestinian background of Johannine Christianity became evident after the discovery of the Dead Sea Scrolls: see Albright, 1956; Cullmann, 1957, 1975. More recently, Samaritan traditions have been utilized for the clarification of the Christian Hellenist and Johannine traditions; see especially Bowman, 1971, 1975:57–89; Buchanan; Freed, 1968, 1970; Meeks: 216–57, 286–319; Purvis, 1975; Scobie and the bibliography he cites; Spiro. Comparisons of the Samaritans with the Essenes may be found in Bowman, 1957, 1975:95–118; Ford.)

As useful as these comparisons may be in indicating that Samaritanism should be understood within the broad context of Judaism, they also indicate what has always been obvious—that Samaritanism was an aberrant position within this complex (a judgment that must stand considering that the majority of Jewish traditions related positively to Jerusalem). *But were there aspects of Samaritanism that would cause it to be seen as relating in positive ways to the mainstream of Judaism?* The difficulty in answering this question is that we are less sure than formerly of exactly what constituted that mainstream. Some would even deny that such existed before the emergence of Pharisaism as the dominant religious force. When it seemed that Judaism's mainstream was represented by a balance of power between the Pharisees and Sadducees, it was suggested that the Samaritan faith was a Sadducean-type religion and that some cordiality may have existed between the Sadducees (and Jerusalem's priesthood) and the Samaritan priests before or even after the final rupture between the two communities (Montgomery: 72-73, 86-88). (Most recently, this has been suggested by Coggins: 157-58.) This seemed to be a valid observation when one considers the power the Samaritan priests have always exercised within their community, even to the present day, and Josephus's claim (now moot) that the Samaritan priesthood was of Zadokite origin.

The difficulty with this perception of Samaritan religion is that the Samaritan community included both lay people and priests, and (as now appears evident) the priests were not the only articulate spokesmen of the Samaritan faith. Thus, any discussion of the character of Samaritan religion and its relations to the mainstream of Judaism must take into account the varieties of opinion within the Samaritan community. A major contribution of recent Samaritan studies has been the clarification of the respective roles of the Samaritan clergy and laity in the development of Samaritan religious thought. In this, that branch of Samaritanism known as the Dositheans has been viewed as an important (if not the major) expression of Samaritan lay opinion.

In the history of modern Samaritan research, it was John Bowman who first pointed out the significance of the Dositheans for the understanding of Samaritan lay movements and as providing the clue for the understanding of conflicting theological traditions preserved in the corpus of Samaritan literature (1958-59, 1964, 1975:37-56). In this he was most certainly correct, as has been demonstrated by the subsequent studies by his student A. D. Crown (1967, 1967-68, 1972, 1972-73), by H. G. Kippenberg (128-71) and by S. J. Isser (86-95, 109). Of these scholars, Bowman and Crown have been especially concerned with the problem of divergent theological traditions, notably in regard to eschatology (resurrection and eschatological agents). Both have argued that the Dositheans held more liberal views than the priests in regard to the resurrection of the dead and the day of judgment (roughly analogous to the liberal tendencies of the Pharisees vis-à-vis the Sadducees). Both have also maintained that the Dositheans believed in an eschatological figure patterned after Joshua, in contrast to the prophet like Moses supposedly expected by the priests (in addition to the works cited above see Bowman, 1971). Crown has also suggested that some Samaritan priests entertained the idea of a messiah like Joseph (1967:185-86). Not all who have worked with Samaritan traditions from the perspective of lay/priestly divergences have concurred in the Bowman-Crown theory of the Joshua messiah (see Isser: 124; Kippenberg: 321; Purvis, 1975:183–85), or Crown's theory of a Joseph messiah (see Kippenberg: 293; Purvis, 1975: 178–81).

Kippenberg has also maintained that early Samaritan theology was characterized by traditions that polarized around priestly and lay movements, but he has viewed that situation as having been more complex than a simple priestly/Dosithean dichotomy. Working with a tradition-historical methodology and positing two major groups in which distinct traditions would have developed (the Gerizim-based priests and the synagogue-based Dositheans), Kippenberg sought also to identify other lay groups to which distinct traditions could be credited—specifically, teachers of the Law, political leaders (*Stammesfürsten*), and judges, some of whom were at times at odds with the Dositheans. After having done this, he sought to lay out the major theological traditions of early Samaritanism and to trace the "history of tradition" of each [175–349]. This was an ambitious undertaking, but it must be added that Kippenberg's conjectures do not always rise to the level of certitude. Nonetheless, his work advanced the study of Samaritan traditions and their sociological backgrounds beyond the work of Bowman and Crown, and (from the standpoint of this writer) helped correct some of the misconceptions of those scholars (notably in regard to the Samaritan Joshua traditions, which Kippenberg has judged to be anti-Dosithean rather than Dosithean).

Isser's approach, in contrast to the work of Bowman, Crown, and Kippenberg, has been first to deal with the problem of the identity of the Dositheans and second to determine what they represented within Samaritanism that differed from the standpoint of the so-called priestly orthodoxy. The determination of the identity of the Dositheans had been a problem because of the conflicting testimony of Christian, Samaritan, and Arabic sources. The problem was one to which Bowman, Crown, and Kippenberg should have devoted more attention; but, now that Isser has dealt with it, it is possible to put the work of the other scholars in better perspective. Briefly, Isser sees the Dositheans as a sect that developed out of an early (pre-first century C.E.) lay movement within the Samaritan community which held views on halakah, calendar, and eschatology similar to those held by the Pharisees within the Jewish community. (This stage of Dositheanism is represented in sources that identify the group after an alleged heresiarch known as Dustan.) Later, many of this lay party accepted the Samaritan prophet Dositheus (Dusis) as the prophet like Moses. (Hence the Dustan/Dusis confusion; the so-called Dustan movement represents the earliest stage of the party that later took the name of Dositheus; there were not two major Dosithean sects, as some incorrectly supposed, but there were Samaritan sects that developed out of Dositheanism, many of which had Essene-like character: 80–81, 103–6.) Isser's identification of the

Dositheans and their background is convincing (see the writer's review in *JBL* 97 [1978] 290–91), and he has been able to bring many insights to bear in the critique of the earlier studies by other Samaritanologists.

In the review of these studies it is evident that early Samaritanism was a complex phenomenon. It was characterized generally by its loyalty to a Mosaic faith that rejected the Jerusalem-oriented *Heilsgeschichte* with which the mainstream of Judaism identified; it followed instead a *Heilsgeschichte* that centered on Gerizim/Shechem. And yet even within Samaritanism, there were differences of opinion about how that faith should be practiced (halakah, calendar) and there were different groups (priestly and lay) vying for leadership of the community. There were Samaritan sects, a situation not unlike that which existed in the Jewish communities.

It should be kept in mind, then, that comparisons between Judaism and Samaritanism which liken the Samaritans to the Jewish Sadducees are valid only in respect to the priestly tradition of the Samaritan community. A similar comparison could be made (and has been, Isser: 85–96) between a significant lay movement in early Samaritanism and Jewish Pharisees. Similarly, comparisons may be drawn between the Dositheans as a Samaritan sect (following an eschatological prophet) and the early Christians as a Jewish sect (following a messianic teacher). Moreover, similarities are evident between the subsects of the Dositheans and various Jewish sects (Essene, Baptist, Christian). The danger, of course, is in viewing Samaritanism only in terms of what was later to become (in the middle ages) a standard, normative Samaritanism.

BIBLIOGRAPHY

Albright, W. F.
    1956   "Recent Discoveries in Palestine and the Gospel of John." Pp. 153–71 in *The Background of the New Testament and Its Eschatology*. Ed. W. D. Davies and D. Daube. Cambridge: University Press.
    1957   *From the Stone Age to Christianity*. 2d ed. Garden City, NY: Doubleday.

Bickerman, Elias
    1962   *From Ezra to the Last of the Maccabees: The Historical Foundations of Post-Biblical Judaism*. New York: Schocken Books.

Bowman, John
    1955   "Early Samaritan Eschatology." *JJS* 6: 63–72.
    1957   "Contact between Samaritan Sects and Qumran?" *VT* 7: 184–89.
    1958–59 "The Importance of Samaritan Researches." *ALUOS* 1: 43–54.
    1959   "Is the Samaritan Calendar the Old Zadokite One?" *PEQ* 91: 23–37.

1964   "Pilgrimage to Mount Gerizim." Pp. 17–28 in *L. A. Mayer Memorial Volume (1895–1959)*. Ed. M. Avi-Yonah, et al. Eretz-Israel 7. Jerusalem: Israel Exploration Society.
1971   "The Identity and Date of the Unnamed Feast of John 5:1." Pp. 43–56 in *Near Eastern Studies in Honor of William Foxwell Albright*. Ed. H. Goedicke. Baltimore: Johns Hopkins University Press.
1975   *The Samaritan Problem: Studies in the Relationships of Samaritanism, Judaism, and Early Christianity*. Pittsburgh: Pickwick Press.
1977   *Samaritan Documents Relating to Their History, Religion and Life*. Pittsburgh: Pickwick Press.

Buchanan. G. W.
1968   "The Samaritan Origin of the Gospel of John." Pp. 149–75 in *Religions in Antiquity: Essays in Memory of Erwin Ramsdell Goodenough*. Ed. J. Neusner. Supplements to *Numen* 14. Leiden: Brill.

Bull, R. J.
1976   "Gerizim, Mount." *IDBSup*, 361.

Caldwell, T.
1962   "Dositheos Samaritanus." *Kairos* 4: 105–17.

Campbell, E. F.
1976   "Shechem." *IDBSup*, 821–22.

Coggins, R. J.
1975   *Samaritans and Jews: The Origins of Samaritanism Reconsidered*. Oxford: Blackwell; Atlanta: John Knox.

Cross, F. M.
1964   "The History of the Biblical Text in the Light of Discoveries in the Judaean Desert." *HTR* 57: 281–99.
1966a   "Aspects of Samaritan and Jewish History in Late Persian and Hellenistic Times." *HTR* 59: 201–11.
1966b   "The Contribution of the Qumran Discoveries to the Study of the Biblical Text." *IEJ* 16: 81–95.
1971   "Papyri of the Fourth Century B.C. from Daliyeh." Pp. 45–69 in *New Directions in Biblical Archaeology*. Ed. D. N. Freedman and J. Greenfield. Garden City, NY: Doubleday.

Crown, A. D.
1967   "Some Traces of Heterodox Theology in the Samaritan Book of Joshua." *BJRL* 50: 178–98.
1967–68   "Dositheans, Resurrection and a Messianic Joshua." *Antichton* 1: 70–85.
1972   "New Light on the Inter-Relationships of Samaritan Chronicles from Some Manuscripts in the John Rylands Library." *BJRL* 54: 282–313.
1972–73   "New Light on the Inter-Relationships of Samaritan Chronicles . . . , II." *BJRL* 55: 86–111.

Cullmann, Oscar
1957   "The Significance of the Qumran Texts for Research into the Beginnings of Christianity." Pp. 18–32 in *The Scrolls and the New Testament*. Ed. K. Stendahl. New York: Harper & Bros.
1975   *Der johanneische Kreis: Sein Platz im Spätjudentum, in der Jüngerschaft Jesu und im Urchristentum: Zum Ursprung des Johannesevangeliums*. Tübingen: Mohr-Siebeck.

Delcor, M.
1962   "Vom Sichem der hellenistischen Epoche zum Sychar des Neuen
            Testament." *ZDPV* 78: 34–48.

Ford, J. M.
1967–68   "Can We Exclude Samaritan Influence from Qumran?" *RevQ* 6:
            109–29.

Freed, E. D.
1968   "Samaritan Influences in the Gospel of John." *CBQ* 30: 580–97.
1970   "Did John Write His Gospel Partly to Win Samaritan Converts?"
            NovT 12: 241–56.

Gaster, Moses
1925   *The Samaritans: Their History, Doctrine, and Literature.* London:
            The British Academy.
1932   *Samaritan Oral Law and Ancient Traditions,* Vol. 1: *Samaritan
            Eschatology.* London: Search.

Isser, S. J.
1976   *The Dositheans: A Samaritan Sect in Late Antiquity.* SJLA 17.
            Leiden: Brill.

Kippenberg, H. G.
1971   *Garizim und Synagogue: Traditionsgeschichtliche Untersuchungen
            zur samaritanischen Religion der aramäischen Periode.* Berlin: de
            Gruyter.

Klein, R. W.
1976   "Samaria Papyri." *IDBSup,* 772.

Macdonald, John
1963   *Memar Marqah: The Teachings of Marqah.* 2 vols. BZAW 84.
            Berlin: A. Töpelmann.
1964   *The Theology of the Samaritans.* Philadelphia: Westminster.
1969   *The Samaritan Chronicle No. II (or Sepher Ha-Yamim).* Berlin: de
            Gruyter.

Marcus, Ralph
1951   "Josephus on the Samaritan Schism." Pp. 498–511 (Appendix B) in
            Josephus, Vol. 6. LCL. Cambridge, MA: Harvard University Press.

Meeks, Wayne
1967   *The Prophet-King: Moses Traditions and the Johannine Christol-
            ogy.* NovTSup 14. Leiden: Brill.

Mikolásek, A.
1969   "Les Samaritains Gardiens de la Loi Contre Les Prophetes." *Com-
            munio Viatorum* 12: 139–48.

Montgomery, James
1907   *The Samaritans, the Earliest Jewish Sect: Their History, Theology
            and Literature.* Philadelphia: J. C. Winston.

Pummer, Reinhard
1976a   "Aspects of Modern Samaritan Research." *Église et Théologie* 7:
            171–88.
1976b   "The Present State of Samaritan Studies: I." *JSS* 21: 39–60.
1977   "The Present State of Samaritan Studies: II." *JSS* 22: 27–47.

Purvis, James D.
1965   "Ben Sira and the Foolish People of Shechem." *JNES* 24: 88–94.

1968   *The Samaritan Pentateuch and the Origin of the Samaritan Sect.* Cambridge: Harvard University Press.

1975   "The Fourth Gospel and the Samaritans." *NovT* 17: 161–98.

1976a   "Samaritan Pentateuch." *IDBSup*, 772–75.

1976b   "Samaritans." *IDBSup*, 776–77.

Reicke, Bo

1968   *The New Testament Era.* Trans. David Green. Philadelphia: Fortress.

Rowley, H. H.

1955   "Sanballat and the Samaritan Temple." *BJRL* 38: 166–98.

1962   "The Samaritan Schism in Legend and History." Pp. 208–22 in *Israel's Prophetic Heritage: Essays in Honor of James Muilenburg.* Ed. B. W. Anderson and W. Harrelson. New York: Harper & Row.

Schalit, Abraham

1970–71   "Die Denkschrift der Samaritaner an König Antiochus Epiphanes zu Beginn der Grossen Verfolgung der Jüdischen Religion im Jahre 167 v. Chr." *ASTI* 8: 131–83.

Scobie, Charles H. H.

1972–73   "The Origins and Development of Samaritan Christianity." *NTS* 19: 390–414.

Simon, Marcel

1958   *St. Stephen and the Hellenists in the Primitive Church.* New York: Longmans, Green.

Skehan, P. W.

1965   "The Biblical Scrolls from Qumran and the Text of the Old Testament." *BA* 28: 87–100.

Spiro, Abram

1967   "Stephen's Samaritan Background." Pp. 285–300 (Appendix V) in *The Acts of the Apostles.* AB 31. Ed. J. Munck. Revised by W. F. Albright and C. S. Mann. Garden City, NY: Doubleday.

Wacholder, Ben Zion

1963   "Pseudo-Eupolemus' Two Greek Fragments on the Life of Abraham." *HUCA* 34: 83–113.

Wright, G. E.

1965   *Shechem: Biography of a Biblical City.* New York: McGraw-Hill.

4
JUDAISM AS SEEN BY OUTSIDERS

John G. Gager

Few fields in the area of biblical studies have been immune to the impact of World War II and its aftermath. No area has been more traumatized than the study of pagan and Christian views of Jews and Judaism. As never before, the result has been an urgent examination of the role of Christian thought and institutions in the history of Western anti-Semitism. Studies have concentrated in two separate areas: (1) the presence of anti-Semitism or anti-Judaism in the writings of the NT and in succeeding centuries; and (2) pagan views of Judaism and their impact on Christian attitudes.

At one level, it may be appropriate to evaluate these studies in purely historiographic terms, that is, as efforts to reexamine important fields in the history of Western thought and institutions. But for many others, these historiographic undertakings have prompted nothing less than a profound theological crisis (Davies, 1969; Eckardt). The configuration of this crisis has varied according to circumstances, but the underlying issues have remained the same: Is Christianity the primary source of anti-Semitism in the West? How deep are the Christian roots of anti-Semitism? Is anti-Semitism an accidental by-product of Christian history or can it be said to inhere in the very structure and essence of historical Christianity itself? Can it be argued that key figures in the early years of Christian history, for example, Jesus and Paul, are themselves devoid of an anti-Jewish bias and consequently that their use by later writers is based on a misunderstanding?

At its deepest point, the theological crisis takes the form of Rosemary Ruether's question whether "anti-Judaism is too deeply embedded in the foundations of Christianity to be rooted out entirely without destroying the whole structure" (1974:228). Given this analysis of the relationship between Christianity and anti-Semitism, it is not surprising to discover that efforts to dissolve the dilemma have moved in two separate directions. The first of these, which may be called historical, offers exegetical reexaminations of NT writings with a view to arguing that interpretations which presuppose anti-Semitic elements in Paul or the Synoptic Gospels are profoundly mistaken (Gaston; Hare; Harrington; Koenig; Sloyan). The second direction, which might be dubbed theological, concedes that anti-Semitism is to be found throughout the NT and seeks to construct an entirely new model for Christian views of Jews and Judaism, a model based not only on new interpretations of the literature and history of early Christianity but also on the experience of Jews and Christians in the modern world.

ANTI-SEMITISM AND ANTI-JUDAISM IN EARLY CHRISTIANITY: THE DEBATE SINCE WORLD WAR II

The early years following World War II saw the appearance of several independent studies dealing with early Christian attitudes toward Jews and Judaism (Wilde; Goppelt; Simon; Isaac). For the English-speaking world, the most influential among these have been the works of Jules Isaac. Following the decimation of his own family, Isaac, who had already acquired enormous prestige as a modern historian and as Inspector General of the French educational system, turned his attention to the question of Christianity and anti-Semitism. His *Jesus and Israel*, written between 1943 and 1946 and published in 1948, followed later by *Genèse de l'antisémitisme* (1956) and *The Teaching of Contempt* (1967), unleashed a series of shock waves whose reverberations are still felt today. In a series of terse propositions, with accompanying exposition and documentation, Isaac argued (1) that Jesus and his earliest followers were thoroughly immersed in Judaism and that they had neither advocated nor presupposed any break with Judaism; (2) that beginning with the Gospels, Christians began to paint a hostile portrait of Judaism and that this portrait has served throughout subsequent Christian history as the basis and justification for Christian anti-Semitism; and (3) that anti-Semitism has not been a constant companion of Judaism and that pre-Christian pagan anti-Semitism in particular is of little consequence when compared with its Christian counterpart.

The responses to Isaac's prophetic declaration have tended to follow two basic courses. The first simply denies Isaac's basic claim: it holds that the NT cannot properly be described as anti-Semitic, that pagan anti-Semitism was widespread in the Roman world and exercised considerable influence within Christianity, and that modern anti-Semitism has little to do with Christian anti-Semitism in late antiquity and the Middle Ages (Arendt). The second response takes the form of conceding, to varying degrees, the heart of Isaac's case. Like Isaac, those who have expressed agreement with him also argue that true Christianity is not anti-Semitic and could never give voice to or tolerate anti-Semitism. Thus, it has been in efforts to reach a historical definition of true Christianity—Paul? Jesus? one or more of the Synoptic Gospels?—that the degrees of assent to Isaac's indictment have found expression. Alan T. Davies has summarized this position as follows:

Other Christian scholars (mostly Protestants), however, are more willing to acknowledge the presence of distinct anti-Jewish sentiments in the NT, but insist that these must be interpreted in their proper historical setting, as polemical reflections of the mutual animosity between the church and the synogogue towards the end of the first century. Once this fact is understood, it only remains to separate the essential gospel from its accidental human expression during an unfortunate time of troubles in order to show that Christianity is not really anti-Semitic. (1969:61)

The strongest advocate of Isaac's position, and still very much at the center of the debate, is Rosemary Ruether. Her *Faith and Fratricide. The Theological Roots of Anti-Semitism* (1974) represents not only the most forceful reformulation of Isaac's views but also the most serious response to those critics who have rejected or even moderated his position. In essence, her argument is twofold: first, that Christian anti-Judaism arose not toward the end of the first century or in the middle of the second, but at the very beginning; and, second, that this anti-Judaism arose not as the accidental by-product of conflict between local churches and synagogues, of the increasing number of Gentile Christians, or of the Bar Kokhba revolt, but rather as the left hand of Christology, that is, a systematic effort to depreciate Judaism as part of Christianity's effort to demonstrate that it, and it alone, represented the true Israel (1974:64). "For Christianity, anti-Judaism was not merely a defense against attack but an intrinsic need of Christian self-affirmation" (1974:181). This systematic anti-Judaism involved the replacement of Judaism by Christianity as the recipient of the divine promise of salvation, the abrogation of the Mosaic Law, and the denigration of Judaism itself. Only at the very beginning, "within the teachings of Jesus himself" (1979:235) was there a complete absence of such sentiments.

The work of the Catholic scholar Gregory Baum may be taken as a measure of Ruether's impact on the field. In his earlier writings (1961) Baum adamantly rejected Isaac's views. But in his introduction (1974) to Ruether's *Faith and Fratricide,* he confessed to a change of heart: "Writing this introduction gives me the opportunity to declare that the book I wrote in the late fifties and published in 1961 no longer represents my position on the relationships between Church and Synagogue" (1974:3f.).

Although it would be difficult to overestimate the impact of the Isaac-Ruether line of interpretation, the overall picture of the field still requires modification at several points. The first concerns the work of the French scholar Marcel Simon, whose *Verus Israel* (1948), published independently of Isaac's work, traces relations between Christians and Jews from 135 to 425 C.E., and thus provides a comprehensive view of the context within which early Christian views of Judaism took shape. Of major significance for the understanding of Christian authors like Cyril of Alexandria and

John Chrysostom are Simon's observations regarding the continued strength and appeal of Judaism among pagans in the Roman Empire and the persistence of Judaizing Christians, that is, Christians who frequented synagogues and observed Jewish holy days, in an unbroken sequence from the first century onward. In the republication of *Verus Israel* in 1964, Simon appended a lengthy survey ("Post-Scriptum") of critical reaction to his work as well as his own reactions to the writings of Isaac. Among its many virtues, this survey documents the extent of Simon's own influence on the historical debate in this area.

The second modification in the picture drawn thus far concerns work produced before World War II. While it would be difficult to overestimate the amount and significance of work produced since the 1940s, it would be equally erroneous to leave the impression that this work was without precedent among earlier scholars. A list of such pioneers would include Jean Juster, T. Reinach, I. Heinemann, G. F. Moore and James Parkes.

A third modification is made manifest in a volume of essays (Davies, 1979) produced in response to Ruether's *Faith and Fratricide*. Three essays in particular deserve mention. D. R. A. Hare's contribution on the rejection of the Jews in the Synoptic Gospels and Acts challenges Ruether on a number of important issues. As part of his argument he proposes a refined typology for the varieties of anti-Judaism in early Christian literature: (a) *prophetic anti-Judaism*, found in Jesus' sayings, which involves no rupture of any kind with Israel and has clear precedents in earlier Israelite literature; (b) *Jewish-Christian anti-Judaism*, which claimed that Israel's history culminated in the life, death, and resurrection of Jesus and was accompanied by energetic missionary efforts among fellow Jews; and (c) *gentilizing anti-Judaism*, which adds the final claim that Israel's rejection of the Messiah has led God to reject the Jews in favor of a new people, that is, Christians.

Equally important in this collection of essays is D. P. Efroymson's treatment of early patristic literature. In particular, he has demonstrated that the violent reaction to Marcion by such figures as Justin Martyr, Irenaeus, Tertullian, and Origen led to a marked intensification of anti-Jewish sentiment in the mainstream of Christianity. Finally, and most radically, Lloyd Gaston's essay on Paul and the Torah (1979) advances the position that all interpretations of Paul, ancient as well as modern, have misread Paul as a result of failing to observe two fundamental features of his letters: first, that the letters deal exclusively with Gentile Christians and their problems, including the question of their standing in relation to Torah as covenant and observance; and, second, that Paul's opponents in his letters are never Jews or Judaism as such but rather Jewish or Judaizing Christians. Thus, Gaston is able to conclude that "for Paul, Jesus was neither a new Moses, nor the messiah, nor the climax of the history of God's dealing with Israel, but the fulfillment of God's promises concerning the gentiles. . . ." (1979:66). In this and other essays, Gaston has joined a growing number of those who are inclined to reverse the genetic-causal relationship between Paul and the history of Christian anti-Judaism (Stendahl; Howard). Instead of taking Paul's statements on Israel and the Torah as substantiating later Christian anti-Judaism, they assert that Paul can be read in this manner only by bringing anti-Jewish presuppositions to the interpretation of Pauline texts.

The significant new results in the treatment of early Christian attitudes toward Jews and Judaism may be classified as follows:

Terminology. Much discussion has been given to the terms anti-Semitism and anti-Judaism (Simon; Sevenster; Ruether; Lovsky; Hare). Although it has become customary to use anti-Judaism when speaking of early Christianity and anti-Semitism when referring to pagan antiquity or the modern world, the terms continue to be used interchangeably. More often than not, anti-Judaism and anti-Semitism refer to the same set of phenomena, that is, beliefs, feelings, and actions that manifest hostility toward Jews, even when an effort is made to establish distinctions on the basis of differing motivations (Hare).

Causes. More than anyone else, Rosemary Ruether is responsible for having intensified the debate on the causes and sources of Christian anti-Semitism. She has argued that its basic cause is christological reflection, that is, the claim that the divine promises to Israel have been fulfilled in Jesus and not in Judaism. Thus, Christian anti-Semitism, absent from the message of Jesus and his earliest followers, is present in the first Christian reflections about Jesus. Largely in response to Ruether's position, other causes have been proposed: conflicts between local churches and synagogues (Richardson; Townsend; Hare); the growth of Gentile Christianity (Hare; Gaston); the impact of the Bar Kokhba revolt (Simon; Richardson); the need to formulate a theological critique of Marcion (Efroymson); the presence of Judaizing Christians in many Christian communities (Simon, Meeks and Wilken); the continued vigor of Judaism throughout late antiquity (Simon; Blumenkranz); and the influence of pagan anti-Semitism (Lovsky; Simon). Some have denied the link between Christology and anti-Semitism (Hare), and others have denied the presence of anti-Semitism altogether in certain early Christian writers, for example, Paul (Gaston).

Finally, a number of psychologists and sociologists have examined the causes of anti-Semitism within the framework of the social sciences (Loewenstein; Glock and Stark).

Studies of individual Christian texts and authors. Perhaps the greatest benefit to have emerged from recent discussion has been the increased attention given to individual Christian texts and authors as well as to their social and cultural context. In general it may be said that the movement has been from broad assertions (e.g., Isaac; Ruether), through a closer examination of individual texts, themes, and authors (e.g., Richardson; Stendahl; Neusner), to an analysis of the context and development of Christian anti-Judaism in the early centuries (e.g., Wilken; Meeks and Wilken; Efroymson; Simon).

Images of ancient Judaism in modern Christian scholarship. One of the least recognized victims of Western anti-Semitism has been Christian scholarship on early Judaism. The work of Isaac, Moore, Simon, and more recently of Charlotte Klein and E. P. Sanders has drawn attention to the fact that the negative image of Judaism which pervades early Christian literature has had a profound impact on modern scholarship as well. Klein in particular has shown the extent to which much of the standard academic literature on early Judaism illustrates Moore's claim that "Christian interest in Jewish literature has always been apologetic or polemic rather than historical" (197).

Periods, stages and areas. One important area of discussion involves the determination of periods and stages in the development of early Christian attitudes toward Judaism. In one area it is possible to speak of general consensus: the decisive turning point in relation between Jews and Christians coincides approximately with the suppression of the Bar Kokhba revolt in 135 (Simon), in the sense that from that time forward Christians began to use the term "true Israel" to describe themselves (Richardson). What distinguishes the period after the mid-second century is the increasing internal consolidation of Christianity as well as the widespread belief that Israel's "rejection" of the Christian message had resulted in its permanent and irreversible replacement by Christianity as the chosen people of God.

But the significance of agreement on this issue must not be exaggerated. For at the same time there is a growing awareness that the "official" Christian stance toward Israel and Judaism often had little effect on the attitudes and behavior of many believers. As the anti-Jewish sermons and the anathemas of various councils in the fourth century make abundantly clear, the phenomenon of Judaizing among Gentile Christians was widespread and deeply entrenched (Meeks and Wilken). It is now apparent that Judaism remained a lively competitor with Christianity into the fourth century and beyond, attracting not simply pagans but many Christians as well (Simon, Blumenkranz). In some cases this attraction led to conversion, but for most it took the form of Judaizing in one way or another. This general picture is confirmed by a number of recent studies which deal with relations of Christians and Jews in specific geographic areas: Alexandria (Wilken), Antioch (Meeks and Wilken), Caesarea (Levine), Cyrene (Applebaum, 1979), Sardis (Kraabel, 1971, 1978) and Syria (Murray; Neusner; Vööbus).

JEWS AND JUDAISM IN PAGAN PERSPECTIVE

Although the earliest pagan response to Judaism antedates the rise of Christianity by some three hundred years, the study of pagan attitudes has been shaped in large part by the problem of anti-Semitism in early Christianity. In particular, there has been a persistent trend toward minimizing Christianity's contribution to anti-Semitism in the later Roman Empire and in the early Middle Ages by stressing the importance of the hostile attitudes which converts to Christianity would have brought along (Lovsky; Sevenster) from their Greco-Roman environment. In order for this argument to work, however, it is necessary to assume that the environment was generally unsympathetic to Jews and Judaism. Much of the research since World War II has sought to examine and challenge the validity of this assumption. The single greatest contribution in this field is undoubtedly the work of Menahem Stern (1974, 1980). His two-volume work, which includes texts, translations, introductions, and commentaries for all of classical antiquity, replaces the earlier work of Theodore Reinach.

The Hellenistic Era (to 60 B.C.E.)

The earliest and most abiding response to Judaism by the Greco-Roman world took the form of describing the Jews as a nation of philosophers. Writers like Theophrastus (ca. 300 B.C.E.), Megasthenes (ca. 300 B.C.E.), Clearchus of Soli (ca. 300 B.C.E.), Hermippus of Smyrna (ca. 200 B.C.E.), and Ocellus Lucanus (second century B.C.E.) all associate Judaism with the sources of ancient wisdom. A similar image appears among Hellenistic ethnographers. Hecataeus of Abdera (ca. 300 B.C.E.) and others indicate a strong and positive interest in Jewish history and culture throughout the Hellenistic period. In short, there is considerable evidence to substantiate M. Hengel's observation that "down to Posidonius (ca. 50 B.C.E.) . . . the earliest Greek witnesses, for all their variety, present a relatively uniform picture: they portray the Jews as a people of 'philosophers'" (255).

Beyond these figures, mention must be made of numerous Hellenistic writers on Jewish history and culture many of whom are known only by name—for example, Hieronymus of Cardia, Eratosthenes, Polybius, Timachares and Agatharchides of Cnidus. Undoubtedly the most significant of these was Alexander Polyhistor whose work *On the Jews*, preserved in Eusebius's *Praeparatio Evangelica*, included an anthology of Jewish Hellenistic writings.

Palestine

During the period of Seleucid control in Palestine, under Antiochus IV Epiphanes and following the successful Jewish revolt under the Maccabees, the tradition of good relations was interrupted. The traditional view, according to which Antiochus's invasion of Jerusalem was prompted by his own anti-Semitic sentiments, has been called into question by various scholars (Bickerman; Hengel). At the same time, there is evidence to suggest that these conflicts marked the beginnings of pagan anti-Semitism in a double sense: (1) A passage from Diodorus of Sicily portrays certain advisers of Antiochus VII Sidetes as urging the king to punish the Jews for their misanthropic and impious customs (Stern, 1974:181–85). Although Antiochus rejected this advice, the speech of his advisers reads like a script for much of the subsequent anti-Semitism in Greek and Latin authors. (2) The material accusations in the speech of Antiochus's advisers are not unrelated to the accounts of the earlier Hellenistic ethnographers. Hecataeus in particular, following the conventions of ancient historiography and ethnography, had noted certain distinctive and peculiar elements of Jewish culture, including what he described as "a way of life which was somewhat unsocial and hostile to foreigners" (Stern, 1974:26–35). But when enmity later arose between Jews and various political and military opponents, these originally disinterested observations served as the starting point for unmistakably anti-Semitic statements. No single item illustrates this transformation better than the stories about the Jews' departure from Egypt under Moses. Versions which in Hecataeus and later writers like Strabo are reported in a straightforward and noncondemnatory fashion are appropriated by others—Apion, Lysimachus, the adviser of Antiochus VII and Tacitus—to vilify the Jews by depicting their ignominious origins as polluted Egyptian exiles.

Apart from this period of Jewish-Seleucid conflict in the mid-second century B.C.E., there is little information on pagan views of Judaism in Palestine before the Roman occupation. The sole exceptions are Mnaseas of Patara (ca. 200 B.C.E.) and Posidonius (ca. 50 B.C.E.). Mnaseas, who is the first to record the story that the Jews worshiped the head of an ass, reports this libel in the context of a military struggle between the Jews and the Idumeans—in other words, a typical situation for the invention or transmission of slanderous tales about one's enemy. Much has been written on Posidonius. Some are inclined to give credence to Josephus's words about "the authors who supplied him [Apion] with his materials, I mean Posidonius and Molon" (Ag.Ap. 2.7 §79) and to conclude that Posidonius's sentiments regarding Judaism were unfriendly (Tcherikover; Sevenster). Others have argued that the impreciseness of Josephus's references, as well as the more general difficulty of ascertaining Posidonius's views on any matter, means that "we must pronounce a *non liquet* on the question of Posidonius' real views on the Jews and their religion" (Stern, 1974:143).

Rome

The Maccabean struggle marks the beginning of official dealings between Rome and Judea, as the Jewish leaders sought and found support for their cause in Rome. From this point onward, the history of Roman attitudes toward Judaism would follow three separate courses: (1) the official policy of the Roman government, (2) the issues of Roman *literati*, and (3) popular attitudes in Rome and other cities and towns of the empire.

1. Recent studies have indicated that official Roman policy toward Judaism was laid down as early as the mid-second century B.C.E. and continued in effect, with occasional exceptions, until the early fifth century C.E. (Cohen). The basic element of this policy was the right to live according to their ancestral laws, and it included the privilege of annual donations to the Temple in Jerusalem, of settling most disputes within the community, and of freedom from civic obligations on the Sabbath. It did not, as a matter of course, include citizenship. In return, the community was expected to maintain its own internal order and not to engage in proselytism among non-Jews. Virtually all legal measures against the Jews can be traced to these two restrictions.

2. It has been customary to assert that Roman literary circles were uniformly hostile toward Jews and Judaism. In part this is due to the figure of Cicero. Taken together, Cicero's unfriendly remarks and the incorrect assumption that they remained normative, have created a misleading point of departure for surveying later Roman views of Judaism. The case of Varro is instructive. In his work on ancient religious customs, he sought to identify the god of the Jews as Jupiter and praised the Jewish cult for its prohibition of images. In his effort to blend the Jewish diety into the pagan pantheon, he is but one among many—pagans and Jews—to make use of the technique of *theokrasia*.

3. There is sparse evidence for popular attitudes toward Judaism. What little there is suggests that among some there was an attraction to Judaism and a willingness to embrace certain Jewish practices. This pattern of Judaizing emerged strongly during the empire and would play an important role in Christianity as well.

Egypt

In many respects, Ptolemaic Egypt is strikingly similar to Hellenistic Palestine and Syria with regard to the reception of Judaism. Jewish settlers and mercenaries figured prominently in the affairs of the early Ptolemies (Fuks and Tcherikover), particularly during the reign of Ptolemy Philometor (181–145 C.E.). From that time on, the dangers of this involvement became increasingly apparent in the internal dynastic struggles of the Ptolemies and later still with the intervention of Rome, for by making friends with one side, the Jewish mercenaries automatically made enemies with the other. In particular, the Greek population seems to have resented the role played by Jewish military advisers. This resentment exploded into action when the Jews of Alexandria later placed their full weight behind the Romans.

There is, however, general agreement regarding Egypt that, as Tcherikover puts it, "during the whole Hellenistic period, anti-Semitism does not pass beyond the limits of the purely literary" (Fuks and Tcherikover, 1957:25). Put more directly, anti-Semitism is a minor theme. Nonetheless, the sudden turn of events in the 30s of the first century c.e. was not entirely without antecedent causes. The much-debated texts attributed by Josephus to Manetho, a Greco-Egyptian priest of high standing in early Ptolemaic Egypt (ca. 300 b.c.e.), are relevant here. Whether they are authentic (so Tcherikover; Sevenster; Stern with reservations) or later fabrications (so Heinemann; Gager), their hostile versions of the Jewish exodus from Egypt under Moses demonstrate the potential for an anti-Semitism whose form and roots are religious as well as political. Ironically, a second important factor in the rise of anti-Semitism during the 30s and 40s of the first century was the privileged position of the Jews in Ptolemaic Egypt. E. Mary Smallwood proposes that the favor which the Jews enjoyed under the Ptolemies may have accounted for or contributed to the rise of later anti-Semitism. In short, the violent anti-Semitism that flares up in early Roman Egypt may be seen in large part as the Greek and Egyptian response to the Jew's firm alliance with the Roman oppressor.

The Roman Empire (30 B.C.E.–135 C.E.)

Egypt under Roman Rule

The case for interpreting Alexandrian anti-Semitism in the light of Egyptian anti-Romanism emerges most clearly in the *Acts of the Pagan Martyrs,* a series of fictitious hearings in which the civic leaders of Alexandria make insulting speeches before various Roman emperors (Fuks and Tcherikover, 1960:25–107). One recurrent theme in these speeches is that the emperors are avid supporters of the Jews. Although these documents date from the third and fourth centuries c.e., they reveal a set of tensions whose beginnings go back to the first appearance of Roman power in Egypt. These tensions came to a head in the anti-Jewish riots of 38 c.e., during Flaccus's reign as prefect of Egypt. The long-standing causes of the riots were the fervent anti-Roman feelings of certain Alexandrian patriots and the efforts by some Jews to obtain full Alexandrian citizenship, efforts prompted no doubt by Augustus's imposition of a poll tax, the *laographia,* on all noncitizens in Egypt. More immediately, it was the ability of certain

Alexandrian patriots to draft Flaccus's support for their cause by offering to intervene on his behalf before the new emperor, Caligula.

With the removal of the restraint provided by Rome's protection of the Jewish *politeuma*, anti-Semitic feelings quickly gave way to actions. These actions, which Claudius later characterized as a war, had as their pretext, and in the minds of the instigators as their chief goal, to clarify the civic status of the Jews. In fact, their aim was to restrict Jewish privileges to the maximum. Their chosen means were a series of riots, burnings, and murders which lasted two or three months. After several delegations appeared before Caligula and later Claudius, the issue was resolved provisionally by Claudius's famous *Letter to the Alexandrians* of 41 C.E.

During this period, anti-Semitism reached its climax in the ancient world. Lysimachus, Chaeremon, and Apion produced the first extensive anti-Semitic tracts. *The Acts of the Pagan Martyrs* must have originated at the same time. In all cases, their purpose was to awaken and reinforce the anti-Semitic beliefs and feelings which constantly threatened to erupt into action. Indeed, Claudius's letter and its ominous warning that the Jews not invite others from Egypt and Syria, failed to settle the issue permanently. From the time of Caligula on, new voices began to speak for Judaism. Philo took up the pen to fight for the Jewish cause; others began to take up the sword. Caligula's death was greeted by a momentary Jewish uprising against their Alexandrian antagonists. In 66 C.E., there was renewed fighting. And from 115 to 117, there was serious strife in Alexandria and the Egyptian countryside, as the Jewish uprising in Cyrene spilled into Cyprus and Egypt. Mutual hatred was widespread, as scattered papyrus fragments and the continued popularity of the *Acts of the Pagan Martyrs* attest. After 117, we hear little from or about Jews in Egypt for some time. And the voices of figures like Philo and the armed Jewish insurgents will not be heard from again. But the presence of Jewish motifs in magical and alchemical recipes of the third, fourth, and fifth centuries suggests that an assimilated, popular Judaism—perhaps present all along—continued to play a significant role in the popular culture of Egypt to the very end of late antiquity.

Rome

The story of Roman attitudes toward Judaism involves three recurrent motifs: (1) the continuing policy regarding the protection of Jewish rights and attempts to restrict proselytism; (2) the persistent appeal of Judaism for many Romans, reaching as far as the imperial family; and (3) a small coterie of conservative Roman authors who saw in Judaism the antithesis of Roman values and who thus reacted with particular violence to the adoption of Jewish practices by non-Jews.

Commonly, and mistakenly, undue emphasis has been given to this third motif. Although it is true that various Roman writers—including

Seneca, Persius, Petronius, Martial, Horace, and Juvenal—poke fun at circumcision, abstinence from pork, and Sabbath observance, their jokes must be seen as part of their literary calling, which required them to resist the invasion of foreign cults and customs. In any case, the tone of their comments is scarcely anti-Semitic. Juvenal and Seneca are perhaps exceptions. Their greater stridency is no doubt related to the fact that they were deeply troubled by the appeal of this *barbara superstitio* among their contemporaries. The evidence for this appeal, and thereby for some kind of proselytism—no doubt more active than has been traditionally allowed—is overwhelming. The conversions of prominent figures like Flavius Clemens and his wife, Flavia Domitilla, show just how strong this appeal could be, especially toward the end of the first century c.e.

In light of the evidence just surveyed, it is perhaps not surprising that the great Jewish War of 66–73 c.e. has left so little trace in Roman literature. Apart from brief references in military epics from the period, almost nothing is extant. There is, of course, Tacitus, who produced his infamous excursus on Jewish history and customs as a preface to his account of the Jews in Book 5 of the *Histories*. Together with Juvenal, and behind them Quintilian, Tacitus clearly represents the views of a conservative, literary, and political elite. His excursus functioned as a semiofficial justification for the anti-Semitic views of this elite. The war itself is not singled out for special attention because, in Tacitus's eyes, it merely illustrates the fundamentally anti-Roman character of Jewish culture. And, like Juvenal, he was both dismayed and angered that such a culture might appeal to fellow Romans. Finally, it should be noted that of these authors only Tacitus singled out Jews for special consideration and that in general these authors' dislike of Judaism was part of a much broader reaction against the growing presence of foreign groups in Rome.

Opposition to Judaism stemmed primarily from this limited and interconnected circle of conservative *literati*, whose opinions were often at odds with the populace, with certain aristocratic circles, and with a wide variety of other Roman authors. Among historians and ethnographers, Judaism appears prominently in the works of Livy, Pompeius Trogus, Strabo, Nicolaus of Damascus, and Diodorus of Sicily. These figures make it possible to speak of something like an official attitude of sympathy with and respect for Judaism, at least among Greek writers of Augustus's time. If we add to these the sympathetic treatment of Judaism by Longinus and Plutarch, as well as the several references to the Essenes as an ideal community of wise men, it becomes apparent that the earlier Hellenistic tendency toward interpreting Judaism as a school of philosophy persisted throughout the early Roman Empire. In this sense the philosophical dialogue between Jews and pagans (Galen, Celsus, Numenius, Porphyry, Julian, Syrianus, and Proclus) must be seen as representing an important and continuous aspect of the encounter between the Greco-Roman world and Judaism.

Recent scholarship has emphasized that the first century in particular must be reevaluated in these terms. As M. Stern has put it, "the first century C.E. was not only the age of Apion, Chaeremon and Seneca, but was also a century marked by the unprecedented diffusion of Jewish ideas and customs among various classes of society" (1974:362). This new view may be summarized as follows:

1. The cumulative evidence makes it necessary to dismiss any claim that the ancient world in general, or the early Roman Empire in particular, disliked Jews and Judaism. This traditional view must now be stood upside down. The example of Rome in the first century indicates that Roman public opinion was deeply divided on the matter of Judaism. The critics, who seem to have been a minority, were motivated less by a distaste for Judaism itself than by a concern about its inroads in Roman circles. In a way that is strongly reminiscent of Christian anti-Jewish polemic in John Chrysostom and others, it seems likely that it was precisely the unprecedented diffusion of Jewish ideas and customs of various classes of society that prompted the occasional words and acts of protest.

2. The tendency of earlier scholarship to explain sympathetic references to Judaism by calling them later interpolations or by referring to the authors themselves as Jews in some sense is no longer either acceptable or necessary. Speaking of Longinus, Stern remarks that, given what we now know of Judaism's appeal in the first century, "it would be the lack of any literary expression that would call for an explanation" (1974:362).

3. The literary sources, including those known only by title and author, have shown that Judaism was a recurrent topic of conversation throughout the Hellenistic and Roman worlds, perhaps most prominently from the late first century B.C.E. on. The specific items in these commentaries included the identity and nature of the Jewish god, the question of Jewish origins, the peculiarity of Jewish customs, the figure of Moses, and the phenomenon of Judaizing in pagan circles.

4. Many ancient observers, pagan as well as Jewish, portray Judaism as a philosophy. It has been customary to dismiss such characterizations either as apologetic efforts by Jews to enhance the appeal of Judaism to non-Jews or as idealizing tendencies inherent in ancient historiography and ethnography. Morton Smith (78–81) has argued that such dismissals are unwarranted in that the term *philosophia* is best translated as "cult of wisdom" and that it most closely corresponds to what we call religion.

5. Josephus surely exaggerates in his claim that "the masses have long since shown a desire to adopt our religious observances; and there is not one city, Greek or barbarian, nor a single nation, to which our custom of abstinence from work on the seventh day does not spread and where the fasts and lighting of lamps and of our prohibitions in the matter of food are not observed" (*Ag.Ap.* 2.39 §282). Nonetheless, Josephus turns out to be a more reliable witness than has commonly been assumed. This is not to say

that his words apply to official Alexandria, although the evidence of the magical and alchemical papyri suggest that there was a greater openness to Jewish ideas and practices in popular circles and perhaps in the country-side. Nor do they imply large numbers of full converts. More exactly, Josephus's words indicate what the other evidence corroborates, namely, that many pagans were drawn to specific ideas and practices of Judaism. No less a figure than the emperor Augustus prided himself as a scrupulous observer of the Sabbath, though according to Suetonius, who records the boast, he took the Sabbath to be a day of fasting (Goldenberg). In short, not every Judaizer—here the term must cover a wide range of types— could be said to possess an intimate knowledge of Jewish history and culture.

6. Two aspects of ancient Judaism are frequently alleged to have placed limits on its attractiveness to outsiders—nationalism and separat-ism. There can be no doubt that radical expressions of Jewish nationalism were incompatible with the political ambitions of the Hellenistic and Roman Empires. As the various revolts and rebellions make clear, the strains of nationalism ran deep in the Judaism of the Roman period and were not limited to Palestine. By the same token, however, militant Jewish nationalism was for many pagans and Jews quite distinguishable from what we have called Judaism as a philosophy or religion. This is confirmed by two important observations; first, that Judaism remained an attractive option for numerous pagans despite the war of 66–73 c.e.; and, second, that Roman policies and attitudes reverted rapidly to the status quo in the aftermath of the Bar Kokhba revolt of 135–138 c.e. In brief, Jewish nationalism was a sporadic, if powerful, force in generating antipathy in official circles. But when it was absent, as seems generally to have been the case, it played no role at all.

The matter of Jewish *separatism* is equally problematic. Along with nationalism, it has served as the most frequent explanation of ancient anti-Semitism. Whereas the equation of Judaism with nationalism fails to account for the non-nationalistic perception of Judaism that was dominant in the Greco-Roman world, and thereby overstates the issue of anti-Semitism, the emphasis on separatism presupposes what must be demon-strated—a classic *petitio principii*—namely, that the observance of Jewish customs, whether by pagans or Jews, necessarily separated them from the mainstream of the Greco-Roman culture. The tradition of Judaizing of Gentiles would appear to indicate otherwise. Here again we need to remind ourselves that those authors who ridiculed the peculiarity of Jewish prac-tices were equally offended by other non-Roman religions—and philos-ophies—and even so represented only one element of public opinion. Jewish separatism became an issue only in conjunction with other factors, for example, the anti-Romanism of Greek and Egyptian elements in Alex-andria or efforts by individual Jews to attain full citizenship in the local town or city. In the second instance, allegations of Jewish separateness are at least as much a pretext as a cause of the antagonism, inasmuch as those Jews who would be enticed by the prospect of citizenship were certainly those who were the least separate. Once again it has become apparent that the diversity of attitudes toward Judaism in Gentile society reflects a deep division within that society. Wherever the reality or the dream of a closed community survived, antagonism toward Judaism might be sparked by Jewish proselytism or militant nationalism. But in the Hellenistic and Roman worlds, such a reality was a rare commodity and even the dream belonged to only a few.

BIBLIOGRAPHY

Applebaum, Shimon
  1974   "Domitian's Assassination: The Jewish Aspect." *Scripta Classica Israelica* 1: 116–23.
  1979   *Jews and Greeks in Ancient Cyrene.* SJLA 28. Leiden: Brill.
Arendt, Hannah
  1973   *The Origins of Totalitarianism.* New York: Harcourt Brace Jovanovich. First published, 1951.
Baum, Gregory
  1961   *The Jews and the Gospel.* London: Bloomsbury.
  1974   Introduction to Ruether, *Faith and Fratricide* (see below).
Bickerman, E.
  1962   *From Ezra to the Last of the Maccabees: The Historical Foundations of Post-Biblical Judaism.* New York: Schocken Books.
Blumenkranz, B.
  1961   *Juifs et Chrétiens dans le monde occidental (430–1096).* Paris and The Hague: Mouton.
Cohen, Jeremy
  1976   "Roman Imperial Legislation Toward the Jews from Constantine Until the End of the Palestinian Patriarchate (ca. 429)." *Byzantine Studies* 3: 1–29.
Davies, Alan T.
  1969   *Anti-Semitism and the Christian Mind: The Crisis of Conscience after Auschwitz.* New York: Herder & Herder.
Davies, Alan T., ed.
  1979   *Anti-Semitism and the Foundations of Christianity.* New York: Paulist Press.
Eckardt, A. Roy
  1973   *Elder and Younger Brothers: The Encounter of Jews and Christians.* New York: Schocken Books.
Efroymson, David P.
  1979   "The Patristic Connection." Pp. 98–117 in Davies, ed.
Fuks, A., and V. Tcherikover
  1957,1960, *Corpus Papyrorum Judaicarum.* 3 vols. Cambridge, MA: Harvard
  1964   University Press.

Gager, John
1972   *Moses in Greco-Roman Paganism.* SBLMS 16. Nashville: Abingdon.
1983   *The Origins of Anti-Semitism: Attitudes toward Judaism in Pagan and Christian Antiquity.* New York: Oxford University Press.

Gaston, Lloyd
1979   "Paul and the Torah." Pp. 48–71 in Davies, ed.
1980   "Abraham and the Righteousness of God." *Horizons in Biblical Theology* 2: 39–68.
1982   "Israel's Enemies in Pauline Theology." *NTS* 28: 400–423.

Glock, C. Y., and R. Stark
1966   *Christian Beliefs and Anti-Semitism.* New York: Harper & Row.

Goldenberg, Robert
1979   "The Jewish Sabbath in the Roman World up to the Time of Constantine the Great." Pp. 414–47 in *ANRW* 2.19.1. Ed. H. Temporini. Berlin: de Gruyter.

Goppelt, L.
1954   *Christentum und Judentum im ersten und zweiten Jahrhundert.* Gütersloh: Bertelsmann.
1964   *Jesus, Paul and Judaism.* New York: Nelson. A translation of the first half of Goppelt (1954).

Hare, D. R. A.
1979   "The Rejection of the Jews in the Synoptic Gospels and Acts." Pp. 27–47 in Davies, ed.

Harrington, D. J.
1980   *God's People in Christ: New Testament Perspectives on the Church and Judaism.* Philadelphia: Fortress.

Heinemann, I.
1931   "Antisemitismus." PWSup 5: 3–43.
1940   "The Attitude of the Ancient World Toward Judaism." *RR* 4: 385–400.

Hengel, Martin
1974   *Judaism and Hellenism: Studies in their Encounter in Palestine during the Early Hellenistic Period.* 2 vols. Trans. J. Bowden. Philadelphia: Fortress.

Howard, George
1969   "Christ and the End of the Law: The Meaning of Romans 10:4ff." *JBL* 88: 331–37.
1970   "Romans 3:21–31 and the Inclusion of the Gentiles." *HTR* 63: 223–33.

Issac, Jules
1956   *Genèse de l'anti-sémitisme.* Paris: Calmann-Levy.
1965   *The Teaching of Contempt: Christian Roots of Anti-Semitism.* New York: McGraw-Hill. First French ed., 1962.
1971   *Jesus and Israel.* New York: Holt, Rinehart and Winston. First French ed., 1948.

Juster, Jean
1914   *Les juifs dans l'empire romain: Leur condition juridique, économique et sociale.* 2 vols. Paris: Geuthner.

Klein, Charlotte
1978   *Anti-Judaism in Christian Theology.* Trans. Edward Quinn. Philadelphia: Fortress.

Koenig, John
1979   *Jews and Christians in Dialogue: New Testament Foundations.* Philadelphia: Westminster.

Kraabel, A. T.
1971   "Melito the Bishop and the Synagogue at Sardis: Text and Context." Pp. 77–85 in *Studies Presented to George M. A. Hanfmann.* Ed. D. G. Mitten, J. G. Pedley, and J. A. Scott. Mainz: Philipp von Zabern.
1978   "Paganism and Judaism: The Sardis Evidence." Pp. 13–33 in *Paganisme, Judaisme et Christianisme: Mélanges offerts à Marcel Simon.* Ed. A. Benoit, M. Philonenko, and C. Vogel. Paris: Boccard.

Levine, Lee
1975   *Caesarea under Roman Rule.* SJLA 7. Leiden: Brill.

Loewenstein, R. L.
1951   *Christians and Jews: A Psycho-Analytic Study.* New York: International Universities Press.

Lovsky, F.
1955   *Antisémitisme et mystère d'Israël.* Paris: Albin Michel.

Meeks, Wayne A.
1972   "The Man from Heaven in Johannine Sectarianism." *JBL* 91: 44–72.
1975   "'Am I a Jew?' Johannine Christianity and Judaism." Pp. 163–86 in *Christianity, Judaism and Other Greco-Roman Cults: Studies for Morton Smith at Sixty.* SJLA 12. Ed. J. Neusner. Leiden: Brill.

Meeks, Wayne A., and Robert L. Wilken
1978   *Jews and Christians in Antioch in the First Four Centuries of the Common Era.* Missoula, MT: Scholars Press.

Moore, G. F.
1921   "Christian Writers on Judaism." *HTR* 14: 197–254.

Murray, Robert
1975   *Symbols of Church and Kingdom: A Study in Early Syriac Tradition.* Cambridge: University Press.

Neusner, J.
1971   *Aprahat and Judaism: The Christian-Jewish Argument in Fourth-Century Iran.* SPB 19. Leiden: Brill.

Parkes, James
1961   *The Conflict of the Church and Synagogue: A Study in the Origins of Anti-Semitism.* Cleveland and New York: Meridian. First published, 1934.

Reinach, T.
1895   *Textes d'auteurs grecs et romains relatifs au judaisme.* Paris: Leroux. Reprinted, 1963.

Richardson, Peter
1969   *Israel in the Apostolic Church.* Cambridge: University Press.

Ruether, Rosemary
1974   *Faith and Fratricide: The Theological Roots of Anti-Semitism.* New York: Seabury.

1979   "The *Faith and Fratricide* Discussion: Old Problems and New Dimensions." Pp. 230–56 in Davies, ed.

Sanders, E. P.
1977   *Paul and Palestinian Judaism*. Philadelphia: Fortress.

Sevenster, J. N.
1975   *The Roots of Pagan Anti-Semitism in the Ancient World*. NovTSup 41. Leiden: Brill.

Simon, Marcel
1948   *Verus Israel: Étude sur les relations entre chrétiens et juifs dans l'empire romain (135–425)*. Paris: Boccard.
1964   "Post-Scriptum" to *Verus Israel*. Paris: Boccard.

Sloyan, Gerard S.
1978   *Is Christ the End of the Law?* Philadelphia: Westminster.

Smallwood, E. Mary
2976   *The Jews under Roman Rule from Pompey to Diocletian*. SJLA 20. Leiden: Brill.

Smith, Morton
1956   "Palestinian Judaism in the First Century." Pp. 67–81 in *Israel: Its Role in Civilization*. Ed. M. Davis. New York: Harper.

Stendahl, Krister
1976   *Paul among Jews and Gentiles*. Philadelphia: Fortress.

Stern, Menahem
1964   "Sympathy for Judaism in Roman Senatorial Circles in the Period of the Early Empire." *Zion* 29: 155–67.
1974   *Greek and Latin Authors on Jews and Judaism*. Vol. 1, *From Herodotus to Plutarch*. Jerusalem: Israel Academy of Sciences and Humanities.
1980   *Greek and Latin Authors on Jews and Judaism*. Vol. 2, *From Tacitus to Simplicius*. Jerusalem: Israel Academy of Sciences and Humanities.
1984   *Greek and Latin Authors on Jews and Judaism*. Vol. 3, *Appendices and Indexes*. Leiden: Brill.

Tcherikover, Victor [see also Fuks]
1961   *Hellenistic Civilization and the Jews*. Trans. S. Applebaum. Philadelphia: Jewish Publication Society.

Townsend, John
1979   "The Gospel of John and the Jews: The Story of a Religious Divorce." Pp. 72–97 in Davies, ed.

Vööbus, A.
1958   *History of Asceticism in the Syrian Orient: A Contribution to the History of Culture in the Near-East*, I: *The Origin of Asceticism: Early Monasticism in Persia*. Louvain: Durbecq.

Wilde, R.
1949   *The Treatment of the Jews in the Greek Christian Writers of the First Three Centuries*. Washington, DC: Catholic University of America Press.

Wilken, Robert L.
1971   *Judaism and the Early Christian Mind: A Study of Cyril of Alexandria's Exegesis and Theology*. New Haven, CT: Yale University Press.

Part Two

Recent Discoveries

5
THE JUDEAN DESERT

Jerome Murphy-O'Connor, O.P.

Even though only about 60 percent of the documents have been published, a check of the bibliographies (Burchard; La Sor; Jongeling), completed by the periodic listings in *RevQ*, reveals some seven thousand contributions to Qumran studies. This is a clear indication not only of the difficulties presented by the Dead Sea Scrolls but of the interest they inspire. The scrolls shed welcome light on the text and interpretation of the OT, on key sectors of the intertestamental period, on the development of Hebrew and Aramaic, on three critical centuries of the history of Palestine, and on the religious background of the NT.

The vast body of secondary literature has been briefly surveyed by G. Vermes (1977) and in much greater detail in the article "Qumran et découvertes au désert de Juda" in *DBSup* (1978). These demonstrate that it has become impossible to consider all contributions, and extremely difficult to deal adequately with all aspects. Hence, in this short survey I intend to concentrate on the most fundamental elements, namely, the documents themselves and their historical context, paying particular attention to the evolution of Qumran research.

THE DISCOVERIES

The saga of the original scrolls has been told by the scholars directly involved, J. C. Trever and E. L. Sukenik, and with particular reference to the site from which they came by G. L. Harding. From that moment it became a race between the archaeologists and the Ta'amireh Bedouin, which has been summarized with admirable objectivity by R. de Vaux (1973:49–53), who provides the original references omitted by E.-M. Laperrousaz (1978). A detailed listing of all the manuscripts found in the Qumran area has been provided by J. A. Fitzmyer (1975:11–39).

Manuscripts of a type different from those found in the Qumran region began to be offered for sale in Jerusalem in late November 1951. Adroit diplomacy, gleefully recounted by de Vaux (1960:3–7), induced the Ta'amireh to reveal that the scrolls had come from the Wadi Murabba'at, whose caves were immediately excavated (de Vaux, 1960:7–49). Among the most significant elements thus brought to light (see the complete list in

Fitzmyer, 1975:41–45) were a papyrus palimpsest of the eighth pre-Christian century and a letter of Shimon ben Kosba (Milik, 1960a:93–100, 161–63) similar to that bought from Kando, the Bethlehem shoemaker to whom the Taʿamireh sold the first scrolls (de Vaux, 1960:7; Milik, 1960a:159–61). A Hebrew scroll containing the Minor Prophets was discovered in a nearby cave two years later (de Vaux, 1960:50).

Tighter controls in the Qumran-Murabbaʿat area forced the Taʿamireh further afield, and new manuscripts appeared on the market in Jerusalem in July 1952, the most important of which was a manuscript of the Minor Prophets in Greek (Barthélemy, 1953, 1963). At this point the Israelis had already heard of Bedouin activity in Naḥal Ḥever, and Y. Aharoni found traces of their passage in what was later to become known as the "Cave of the Letters" (Yadin, 1963:1). This then was assumed to be the "unknown source" until, at the end of 1959, a new rumor suggesting that the documents had come from Naḥal Ṣeʾelim produced a frantic burst of Israeli activity in the wadis between En Gedi and Masada (Yadin, 1963:3–6). Fragments found in a cave on the south side of Naḥal Ḥever proved it to have been the source of the Greek Minor Prophets manuscript (Lifshitz; see Barthélemy, 1963:168 n. 9). Other manuscript finds were made in Naḥal Ṣeʾelim (Aharoni, 1961:22–24; 1962:197) and Naḥal Mishmar (Bar-Adon, 1961:27; 1962:216), but these paled into insignificance beside the "Cave of Letters" on the north side of Naḥal Ḥever, whose treasures are listed in Fitzmyer (1975:46–49); virtually all these manuscripts are from the second century of the Christian era.

In 1963 excavations at Masada brought to light a series of manuscripts of which the most important were portions of the Hebrew of Sirach, fragments of *Jubilees* and of an Essene text "The Songs of the Sabbath Sacrifice" (Yadin, 1965:103–14), copies of which had also been found at Qumran (Strugnell, 1960).

Finally, mention must be made of the discovery of Christian-Palestinian Aramaic, Greek, and Arab documents at Khirbet Mird (Wright), first by the Taʿamireh and subsequently by a Belgian expedition directed by Robert De Langhe (Milik, 1953:526); the Aramaic manuscripts are dated to the sixth/seventh Christian centuries (Milik, 1953:537; Perrot: 550).

None of the other discoveries provoked anything like the interest stimulated by the Qumran manuscripts, partly because they came later and no one was any longer surprised to find that manuscripts could be preserved for two thousand years, partly because they were of a nature to interest only specialists, who quickly came to agreement regarding their origin and interpretation.

THE EDITORIAL COMMITTEE

Once it became clear that there was an enormous quantity of material coming out of the Qumran region, an international and interconfessional editorial committee was organized under the direction of Roland de Vaux. The original members of this group, appointed in 1952, were D. Barthélemy, M. Baillet, and J. T. Milik. In 1953, F. M. Cross, Jr., and J. M. Allegro were added, to be joined in 1954 by J. Starcky, P. W. Skehan, J. Strugnell, and C.-H. Hunzinger (who later withdrew). Supported by a Rockefeller grant, this group was able to work full-time on the scrolls until 1960. After that year, only Baillet, Milik, and Starcky, all supported by the French National Center for Scholarly Research (CNRS), were free to devote all their energies to the scrolls; the others had to make time from onerous teaching and administrative responsibilities.

A preliminary report was provided in *RB* 63 (1956) 49–67, and four volumes of Discoveries in the Judaean Desert had appeared before the 1967 war complicated the situation. At that stage DJD 5 was already in press, and it appeared in 1968. The long delay before the appearance of DJD 6 in 1977 is explained in the preface to that volume by P. Benoit, who assumed the direction of the committee after the death of R. de Vaux in 1971. M. Baillet (1978) has provided a detailed presentation of the contents of DJD 7, which eventually appeared in 1982. In *RB* 86 (1979) 277, P. Benoit gave news of what can be expected in the future. According to the wishes of P. W. Skehan (d. 1979), responsibility for his material has passed to E. Ulrich.

Different arrangements were made for the Cave 11 material. Responsibility for its publication was assumed by the American Schools of Oriental Research and the Koninklijke nederlandse Akademie van Wetenschappen. The former nominated J. A. Sanders, who produced DJD 4, and D. N. Freedman, and the latter appointed J. P. M. van der Ploeg and A. S. van der Woude, who have issued the *editio princeps* of 11QtgJob.

THE ANTIQUITY OF THE SCROLLS

H. H. Rowley was the first to use the phrase "the battle of the scrolls" (1952:31), and it would be difficult to find a more accurate description of the first decade or so of research into the Qumran material. Skepticism was the natural reaction when the first scrolls were touted around Jerusalem (Trever: 108), because forgeries were far from unknown (Allegro, 1979). The trustworthiness of the intermediaries could not be assumed, and their credibility was further compromised by contradictory testimony (Trever: 25, 75). The authority of W. F. Albright (1948) ensured that the find would be taken seriously, even though many preferred to reserve judgment. Few scholars, however, immediately took a definite position.

Though devoid of any scientific basis or support, the position of S. Zeitlin is part of the history of Qumran research and remains a lesson of the dangers of haste and obstinacy in scholarship. According to Zeitlin, the scrolls could not be authentic because "during the Second Commonwealth the Jews did not write commentaries [the reference is to 1QpHab] on biblical books" (1949a:180). They must be dated in the Middle Ages, since 1QpHab, with which Zeitlin associated 1QIsa and 1QS, exhibited affinities with CD (1949b:236–37), which was nothing more than a tendentious attempt by Karaites to establish their antiquity (1952:5–23, 29). The scrolls came from the Cairo Geniza (1950a:50) via the Hebron synagogue (1956:151) and were planted in the cave shortly before being presented for sale (1950b:271)!

Independently of Zeitlin, P. R. Weis dated 1QpHab around 1096 of the Christian era because of allusions to the Seljuks and Crusaders (147). A medieval date was proposed also by E. R. Lacheman because the scribes had ruled the parchment (34). This feature was also noted by G. R. Driver, who pointed out that the earliest known ruled Hebrew manuscript was of the ninth Christian century (1949a:129), but the orthography, the errors in the use of Hebrew, and the possible influence of Arabic all led him (at this time) to date the scrolls between 650 and 800 of the Christian era (1949b:370–372). An examination of 1QIsa convinced J. Reider that it and the associated scrolls were from the third or fourth Christian century.

Such conclusions now appear inconceivable, but at this stage paleography was not as well based as it now is, and the archaeological data were not complete. More important, errors were induced by a failure to distinguish between the date of composition of the *Damascus Document* and the date of the medieval copy found in the Cairo Geniza. Naturally, such conclusions did not go unquestioned, and during the 1950s the pages of *BA*, *BASOR*, *JQR*, *RB*, and *TLZ* were filled with argument and counterargument. Here I can mention only the key points in the demonstration that has become the basis of the current consensus that all the Qumran manuscripts antedate the year 68 of the Christian era.

That the manuscripts were actually found in the caves and not planted there by the Ta'amireh was confirmed by the archaeologists' independent discovery of fragments in every cave (1, 2, 4, 6, 11) from which the Bedouin had taken manuscripts; in certain instances, notably for Cave 4, the fragments belonged to the same manuscripts sold by the Bedouin (de Vaux, 1959:89–90). The archaeologists themselves discovered Caves 3, 5, 7–10, which contained manuscript fragments of the same type (ibid.).

With the exception of Cave 5, all the caves contained pottery, none of which is later than the first century of the Christian era (de Vaux, 1973:101–2). According to Muhammed edh-Dhib, he found two of the scrolls wrapped in cloth in a jar (Trever: 104); during the excavation of Cave 1 "one scroll, or part of a scroll, was found still in its linen wrapper, stuck together to the neck of a jar" (Harding: 7). This link between the scrolls and the pottery can be taken a step further because "the paste, form and decoration [of the latter] were sufficiently homogeneous to suggest a common place of manufacture" (Cross, 1961:20). The very reasonable assumption is made that this was the potter's workshop at Khirbet Qumran (de Vaux, 1973:16–17) because of the obvious similarities between the cave pottery and that found in the ruins (de Vaux, 1973:54). It is extremely improbable, therefore, that the manuscripts were placed in the caves after the year 68 when the community was dispersed (de Vaux, 1973:107).

The weave of the cloth in which the Cave 1 manuscripts were wrapped provided no clue to its date, but a carbon 14 test dated it to 33 of the Christian era, plus or minus two hundred years, that is, between 168 pre and 233 post (Sellers: 25). Much greater precision was attained in a test applied to uninscribed manuscript fragments from Qumran and Murabba'at; the fragment from Qumran was found to be older than that from Murabba'at (Burton et al.), and the latest date for the latter was the second Christian century. When taken together, these tests positively excluded any date subsequent to the early Roman period.

While this external framework was being developed, other approaches were also being perfected. Paleography was at the center of the controversy over the dating of the scrolls, and the doubts and criticisms of certain scholars provided the stimulus to advance a science that had made little progress since Albright's programmatic analysis of the Nash papyrus in 1937. Close attention was paid to possible sources of new data, and the mass of documents from the Judean Desert greatly extended the material available for typological analysis. A consensus quickly emerged: the manuscripts found in the Qumran caves range from the mid-third century before the Christian era to the third quarter of the first Christian century (Avigad; Birnbaum; Cross, 1965; Milik, 1959a:133–36).

Finally, by 1956, fragments of 173 manuscripts containing all the books of the Hebrew canon (save Esther) had been found (Skehan, 1978a:806). They revealed a very fluid textual situation. The Pentateuchal material embodied three distinct textual traditions, whereas the historical books exhibited a text much closer to the LXX than to the MT (Cross, 1956:56–57). One copy of Exodus reflected the Samaritan recension (Skehan, 1956:58), and another attested the *Vorlage* of the LXX (Cross, 1956:57). The Hebrew and Greek versions of Job did not contain precisely the same text (Milik, 1956:60). One manuscript of Jeremiah contained the long recension known from the MT, whereas another manifested the short recension preserved in the LXX (Skehan, 1978a:813). These few examples, of the many that could be adduced, unambiguously indicate that the biblical manuscripts from Qumran must be dated prior to the establishment of a uniform authoritative text, which is estimated to have taken place around 100 of the Christian era (Cross, 1961:170). This conclusion is confirmed by Milik's assessment that "the biblical fragments 1 and 88 [from Murabba'at] are the oldest witnesses to the received text of the Hebrew bible, separated by only a few decades from the archetype conscientiously established by the School of Jamnia" (1960a:69).

THE PEOPLE OF THE SCROLLS

As the arguments just outlined were seen to converge and strengthen each other, a number of hypotheses that had been proposed to identify the group responsible for the Qumran scrolls simply faded into the outer darkness visited only by authors of survey articles. In addition to all the theories based on a post-first Christian century date for the manuscripts, such was the fate of views that considered this group to be Ebionites (Teicher; cf. Fitzmyer, 1955), Sadducees (North), Pharisees (Rabin, 1957:53-70), or Zealots (Roth, 1958, 1965; Driver, 1965; cf. de Vaux, 1966).

Very early W. H. Brownlee (1950) and A. Dupont-Sommer (1950: chap. 8) independently identified the people of the scrolls with the Essenes, a hypothesis that now commands unanimous assent. Although the relationship between Khirbet Qumran and the caves had not been established at this point, the known existence of the ruins was sufficient to permit the use of Pliny the Elder's location of an Essene settlement on the west bank of the Dead Sea; the site was some distance from the shore and was defined by the phrase "infra hos Engada oppidum fuit" (*Natural History* 5.17.4). For reasons that will become apparent, this became the cornerstone of the argument. However, in order to fit Pliny's text to the topography, "infra" had to be translated "farther south" or "downstream," whereas hitherto it had been understood to mean that the Essenes lived on the heights above En Gedi. Inevitably, the novel translation—though Dupont-Sommer was not as original as he claimed (1959:49 n. 1; cf. Bardtke, 1958:39 n. 2)—was challenged (Audet; Driver, 1965:400), but the overdue critical examination of Pliny's text that this produced (Laperrousaz, 1962; Burchard, 1962) showed that the meaning "downstream" was perfectly compatible with Pliny's usage.

Around this time it became clear that above En Gedi there were no ruins of the period when the Essenes were known to have existed (Mazar). It was assumed, evidently on the basis of the silence of previous explorers, that there was no other settlement between Khirbet Qumran and En Gedi, and so the former must necessarily be the settlement mentioned by Pliny. Hence, shock waves began to radiate out when it was announced that other ruins had been discovered south of Qumran (Bar-Adon, 1970; Blake; Stutchbury and Nicholl). One did in fact reveal strong affinities with Khirbet Qumran (Bar-Adon, 1977) and may have been an outstation of the same type as En Feshkha (de Vaux, 1973:135 n. 3); it could not have accommodated the numbers implied in Pliny's description, even if we discount an element of hyperbole.

Other ancient texts that refer to the Essenes have been conveniently collected by A. Adam, and the more important translated in Dupont-Sommer (1959:chap. 1). Comparison of these texts with the contents of the scrolls (Grinz; Schürer-Vermes-Millar: 555–85) highlights so many striking similarities in social organization, doctrines, rites, and customs that the identification of the people of the scrolls with the Essenes is virtually certain. However, there are notable differences. These have been exaggerated by opponents of the identification (Gottstein; Roth, 1959a, 1959b; Ory: 74–75), but the force of the geographical argument has led proponents of the identification to explain away such differences (e.g., Schürer-Vermes-Millar: 584) rather than justify them convincingly. A serious literary analysis of all the ancient texts referring to the Essenes—such as has been attempted for Josephus and Hippolytus (Smith)—is a prerequisite for any valid comparative study. Sources and supplements need to be determined and not merely speculated about. Contradictory information, at present merely juxtaposed (e.g., Schürer-Vermes-Millar: 567, 570), requires adequate explanation. Such research will, it is hoped, throw some light on the critical question of the homogeneity of the Essene movement.

THE SECTARIAN DOCUMENTS

Since the biblical texts from Qumran (Skehan, 1978a:805–22) are to be dealt with elsewhere in terms of their contribution to the text of the OT (see E. Tov below, chap. 9), I limit myself in this section to the nonbiblical documents that are agreed to have originated within the sect, giving priority to those which have been considered most important for the determination of the history of the sect. (For a full list see Fitzmyer, 1975.)

After the novelty of the discovery had worn off and the first translations had been disseminated, differences between the documents became apparent. The solution was to place them in a relative order. On the basis of his understanding of the historical allusions H. H. Rowley considered 1QM and 1QpHab to be the oldest, followed by 1QS, and CD to be the most recent (1952:76). A year later, however, I. Rabinowitz, using the attitude toward eschatological consummation as the criterion, proposed the following descending order: 1QS, the Admonition of CD, 1QM, 1QpHab, and finally the Laws of CD. Both authors agreed in placing 1QS before CD, and by 1963 this could be considered to represent the consensus (Cothenet: 140).

It did not go unchallenged. Having selected the theme of conflict as his criterion, H. A. Butler discerned three groups of documents, the earliest being 1QpHab, CD, and 1QH, followed by 1QM and 1QSa, and the most recent being 1QS. A.-M. Denis (1964), on the other hand, using a variety of criteria, found the order to be: CD (minus the Laws), 1QpHab, 1QS, and finally 1QM. Considering only the documents that he attributed to the Teacher of Righteousness, J. Carmignac (1963:86) concluded that 1QM was composed after 1QS and 1QSa, but before parts of 1QH.

When one looks back at this period of Qumran research, it is striking to note the confidence with which highly ambiguous criteria were employed. Even more striking, however, is the assumption that each document could be treated as a homogeneous literary unit. How those who were trained in the literary dissection of both OT and NT could operate with such a presupposition, particularly since so many of the pseudepigrapha were known to be composite, is one of the mysteries of Qumran studies. There were, of course, discordant voices, but it took some time for them to make themselves heard. Once this happened they were to dominate the future course of research on the sectarian documents.

The Damascus Document
(Bardtke, 1974; Delcor, 1978b:834–51)

Israel Levi's disregarded intuition that CD was of Essene origin (10) was confirmed by the discovery of eight copies of this work in Caves 4, 5, and 6, which rendered obsolete many other hypotheses (Iwry: 82 n. 8). The relationship of the published and unpublished Qumran material to the medieval copies from Cairo has been conveniently summarized by Fitzmyer (1970:18–19, supplemented by Murphy-O'Connor, 1971:299). The Cave 4 fragments are by far the most important because, in addition to supplying missing portions of the document, they provide a *terminus ante quem* in that the oldest manuscript is dated 75–50 before the Christian era (Milik, 1959a:58; Cross, 1961:82).

CD falls naturally into two parts, the Admonition and the Laws, an association that Rabin (1954:x) considers to be entirely accidental, a medieval scribe having copied two different documents into the same codex. Unsupported by any arguments, this judgment has won no adherents; a hortatory introduction to legal material is not unusual.

It has become axiomatic to explain the differences between the Laws and 1QS by claiming that "the Community Rule legislates for a kind of monastic society, whilst the statutes of the Damascus Rule are concerned with town communities leading a lay existence" (Schürer-Vermes-Millar: 575). In reality this view is nothing more than a facile harmonization of Josephus's description of the Essenes with the situation at Qumran and cannot be considered an adequate solution of the problem. L. Ginzberg's thorough and comprehensive investigation of the Laws remains superior to that of L. Schiffman. His reconstruction of the history of the sect must now be abandoned, but his observations of detail retain all their value. He concluded that the Laws could only have been designed for "the peculiar social and economic situation of a Jewish colony in a pagan country" (281). Apparently independently, M. H. Segal insisted that we have to do with "legislation for a community living in a gentile environment" (141). Precisely the same point has been strongly underlined by S. Iwry (85). This aspect, though questioned by M. Knibb (1983:104), has obvious importance for any reconstruction of the history of the Essene movement, but as yet it has failed to receive the attention it deserves.

Shortly after the discovery of CD, the composite character of the Admonition was recognized. Metrical considerations led R. H. Charles to bracket a series of interpolations. Basically the same approach was adopted by I. Rabinowitz (1954:14) and R. A. Soloff, but the value of such a criterion is nil. A consistent meter cannot be established for the Admonition; it is written in a solemn rhythmic prose (Cothenet: 134). Following K. G. Kuhn (1960:651–51), J. Becker (1963:57) employed an equally unsatisfactory criterion; he considered all midrashic elements to be secondary. The assumption that a single author could not combine the literary forms of "homily" and "midrash" is untenable; midrashic exegesis is often used to sustain a homiletic point.

A much more sophisticated attitude toward the literary criticism of the Admonition became evident toward the end of the 1960s. Reliance on a single criterion was abandoned, and the hypotheses became much more complex. In 1967 A.-M. Denis distinguished three sources. Two (1:1–4:6 and 4:6–6:11) are coherent documents. The first, whose vocabulary resembles Daniel, is the older and witnesses to a movement, whereas the second shows the movement to have evolved into an organized community. The third source (7:4–8:21 = 19–20) has three literary levels. Two of these (7:13–8:13 and 20:22–34) can be related to the other two sources, but the third supposes long experience of community life. When viewed together the three sources reflect the developing self-understanding of the Qumran community. Despite many valuable points of exegesis, Denis' analysis ultimately fails to carry conviction.

For Stegemann (1971:183–84), the Admonition is one document whose concern was to rebut the false teaching of a group that had once formed part of the New Covenant. The original tenor of this text was disturbed by a series of interpolations (1:13–18; 4:19–5:17; 8:12–13; 20:13–15) designed to identify the Man of Lies as the source of such teaching. Our understanding of the Admonition is greatly advanced by Stegemann's acute observation and controlled historical imagination, but his concentration on the opponents of the sect has unconsciously led him to overlook aspects of the text that need to be accounted for as well.

In a series of articles written between 1970 and 1972 J. Murphy-O'Connor pursued the field of research opened up by Denis and Stegemann, but came to very different conclusions (1972a:562–63). Murphy-O'Connor distinguished four source documents which had existed independently prior to the settlement of some Essenes at Qumran: the Missionary Document (2:14–6:1), the Memorandum (6:11–8:3), the Critique of the Princes of Judah (8:3–18), and the Appeal for Fidelity (19:33–20:1b, 8b–13, 17b–13). The purpose of the compilation made at Qumran was to bolster the morale of the community by showing the advantages of membership and the consequences of failure to observe "the exact interpretation of the Law." In addition to supplying a conclusion (20:22–34), the compiler reinforced the hortatory purpose of the collection by minor insertions and by identifying the source of outside opposition (4:19–8:13).

The only critical evaluation of Murphy-O'Connor's hypothesis comes from P. Davies (1983a). Although Davies disagrees on the delineation of sources, he concurs with the most novel element of the hypothesis, namely, the presence of pre-Qumran material in the Admonition. In his view, the original work comprised 1:1–7:9 plus 20:27–34. It was later supplemented by the addition of the warnings in 7:10–8:21. The final section (19:33–20:26) was added at Qumran and at the same time a number of minor interpolations were inserted throughout the supplemented source document.

Given the amount of unpublished material from Cave 4, all the above solutions can only be considered provisional, and the variety of hypotheses indicates the need for a closer examination of the methodologies employed. It is, however, an appreciable advance to be certain that the Admonition is not a literary unity, and the pre-Qumran material throws new light on the most obscure period of the history of the sect.

The Rule of the Community
(Bardtke, 1973; Delcor, 1978b:851–57)

1QS is the oldest copy of the *Rule* (Cross, 1965:258 n. 116) and is dated 100–75 before the Christian era. The Qumran community, therefore, was solidly established at this period. The fragments of the ten manuscripts of the *Rule* from Cave 4 have not yet been published, but Milik (1960b:411–16) has provided a list of the variants (all minor), noting in particular that three manuscripts offer a shorter and more intelligible version of col. 5 and that 8:16–9:11 is missing in one manuscript.

From among the vast literature on 1QS, H. Bardtke (1973:263) was certainly correct in singling out the studies devoted to literary criticism as the most important, since they must influence all other conclusions. In the same year in which 1QS was published H. E. del Medico claimed to find five distinct sources broken up into thirty fragments and arbitrarily reassembled by the copyist of 1QS (1951:27–30). The audacity of the dissection was exceeded only by the confidence with which del Medico restored the original order of the sources. Inevitably such excess provoked a reaction, and for the next decade authors contented themselves with vague remarks regarding the composite character of 1QS without ever descending to the specific (Dupont-Sommer, 1953:90; Kuhn, 1960:652; Maier, 1960:I, 21). During this period P. Guilbert was the only one to raise his voice in support of the literary unity of 1QS; it met with no echo.

The shift that took place in the 1960s is highlighted by a comparison of the commentaries of P. Wernberg-Møller (1957) and A. R. C. Leaney (1966). Apart from one vague reference to multiple sources, the former ignored the literary problems completely (56 n. 49), whereas the latter was concerned with defining and dating the various literary units. Leaney considered 8:1–9:26 to be the oldest element and dated it ca. 130 before the Christian era, prior to the advent of the Teacher of Righteousness, to whom he attributed 10:1–11:11, which he dated ca. 110 before the Christian era. A number of Leaney's observations had been anticipated by J. Becker, who, unfortunately, dealt only very summarily with the key section 5:1–10:9 (1963:39–42). A.-M. Denis (1964:40–44), on the contrary, paid particular attention to cols. 8–9, in which he discerned a number of interpolations (8:10b–12 and 8:16–9:2 [1965:40–44]). These studies conclusively demonstrated that 1QS is not a literary unity, but none advanced a general theory to explain the composition of the document.

The 1960s also saw the appearance of a number of very valuable analyses of portions of 1QS. M. Weise's investigation of the cultural calendar in col. 10 remains fundamental. P. von der Osten-Sacken's theory of three literary levels (17–27) made a significant contribution to our understanding of the Instruction on the Two Spirits (3:13–4:26); his analysis was subsequently refined by J. Duhaime (1977b). G. Klinzing subjected 8:1–9:11 to a minute examination that brought to light elements that had been overlooked (50–66), but his source criticism is not convincing (Murphy-O'Connor, 1972b:436–38).

The first attempt to construct a comprehensive hypothesis to explain the composition of 1QS was made by Murphy-O'Connor (1969). He saw it as a three-stage development from the Manifesto (8:1–16; 9:3–10:8), in which the Teacher of Righteousness proposed the move to Qumran. Penal legislation for a small community (8:16–9:2) was later added. Subsequently, the community redefined itself (5:1–13) and enacted more elaborate legislation (5:15–7:25). Finally, material from various sources was combined to form an exhortation to authentic observance (1:1–4:26; 10:9–11:22). Murphy-O'Connor's hypothesis was subjected to a severe book-length evaluation by J. Pouilly. He found it to be substantially correct with regard to the four-stage evolution, but convincingly argued that certain details needed modification. In consequence, he assigned 8:10–12 to stage two, and 5:13–6:8 to stage four. Since Pouilly also considered all other contributions to the literary analysis of 1QS it would appear that his conclusions should be accorded a very high degree of probability.

The Hodayot
(Bardtke, 1975; Delcor, 1978b:861–904)

Of all the scrolls from Cave 1, the *Hymns* had suffered the most physical damage. E. L. Sukenik reconstructed eighteen columns, but was unable to locate sixty-six fragments. J. Carmignac (1961:129) proposed a different order for the columns and placed a significant number of fragments. I and others have had the opportunity to see an unpublished manuscript by H. Stegemann in which he established the original order of the columns and placed all sixty-six fragments (H. W. Kuhn: 16). It is unfortunate that this extremely important work has not been given to the scientific world, but obviously the author is waiting for the publication of the six manuscripts found in Cave 4 (Strugnell, 1956:64).

Since other aspects of the hymns are studied by J. Charlesworth in chapter 16 of this volume, I shall concentrate on the question of authorship, which highlights the literary problem of 1QH. At a time when only parts of 1QH had been published, both Sukenik (39) and Dupont-Sommer (1950:86) claimed that the author of the hymns could only have been the Teacher of Righteousness. For ten years this remained the dominant view (references in Jeremias: 168 n. 6), even though adequate evidence was never adduced. Convenience and the magisterial affirmations of "authorities" commanded more attention than the protestations of those who could not see a single historical figure behind the "I" of the hymns and who were not convinced of the uniformity of the hymns (Bardtke, 1956; Burrows, 1958:328; Molin).

The attack on the homogeneity of the hymns was led by S. Holm-Nielsen (312–23) and G. Morawe (107). Working independently and using different criteria both agreed in classifying 2:3–7:25 and 8:4–9:36 as individual thanksgiving psalms; the remainder they categorized as "hymns." These conclusions were later modified on only one point: H. W. Kuhn (22) showed that 3:19–36 was not a "psalm" but a "hymn." Such unanimity deserves to be noted as an unusual feature of Qumran literary criticism! It probably inspired the renewed attack on the relationship of 1QH to the Teacher of Righteousness that took place in the brilliant group inspired by K. G. Kuhn at the University of Heidelberg (Delcor, 1978a:17–21).

Three scholars were involved in this quest between 1963 and 1966, and the high degree of agreement in their conclusions is made evident in the table of the hymns they attribute to the Teacher of Righteousness (see page 131). It will be noticed that all these hymns belong to Holm-Nielsen's and Morawe's category of "individual thanksgiving psalms." Jeremias's criterion appears to have been exclusively lexicographical, whereas Becker first notes four hymns (5:5–19; 6:1–36; 7:6–25; 8:4–40) in which the "I" is formally distinguished from the community and then includes four others because of internal links. His arguments for the inclusion of 2:20–30 (also

Jeremias (171)	Becker (1963:53)	H. W. Kuhn (23)
2:1–19		2:1–19
	2:20–30	
2:31–39		
3:1–18	3:1–18	
	3:37–4:4	
4:5–5:4	4:5–29	4:5–29
5:5–19	5:5–19	5:5–19
5:20–7:5	6:1–7:5	5:20–6:36
7:6–25	7:6–25	7:6–25
8:4–40	8:4–40	8:4–40

attributed to the Teacher by Stegemann, 1971:188) and 3:37–4:4 are weak, but his characterization of 4:29–5:4 as a secondary addition has been confirmed by H. W. Kuhn (23 n. 3). This latter obtained his restricted list by insisting that hymns attributed to the Teacher of Righteousness must include the motifs of "bearer of revelation" and "individual plaint" (22).

The cumulative force of the arguments of a series of scholars whose central concerns all differ is impressive, and the conclusion that the hymns of Kuhn's list (on which all agree) have a single author is inescapable (Schulz). Given what we now know of the history of the sect, a refusal to identify this figure with the Teacher of Righteousness smacks of pedantic prudence.

In contrast to the highly individualized "I" of the Hymns of the Teacher, the "I" in the rest of the hymns could be appropriated by any member of the community. These Hymns of the Community have been studied by Becker (1963:126–28) and in particular by H. W. Kuhn. Earlier hypotheses regarding the purpose of the hymns, notably the view that they constituted a set of spiritual exercises to aid meditation (Bardtke, 1958:138; Carmignac, 1961:133), were rendered obsolete by the proof that 1QH was not a literary unity. Once the Hymns of the Teacher were removed it became evident that a cultic context must be postulated for the Hymns of the Community. Becker thought in terms of the daily prayers and liturgies of the sect (1963:167), but this was too vague for H. W. Kuhn (31–33). The key formal elements of the Hymns of the Community are "a soteriological confession" and "a misery meditation," which suggests that these hymns were designed either for the ceremony of entrance into the community or for the annual ceremony of the renewal of the covenant. Kuhn opts for the latter, while admitting that from this ceremony the Hymns of the Community probably passed into more general use. Perhaps the most important aspect of Kuhn's study is his demonstration that these hymns display a realized eschatology which had hitherto been considered distinctive of the preaching of Jesus.

The dates of the Hymns of the Teacher can be fixed within the lifespan attributed to this personage. The dates of the Hymns of the Community have not so far been established, nor has the question of their provenance been seriously investigated. Were they exclusive to Qumran or did they belong to the liturgical heritage of the wider Essene movement? This question is made all the more urgent by the clear parallels between the Hymns of the Community and some of the liturgical material preserved in the NT (Deichgräber).

The War Scroll
(Bardtke, 1972; Delcor, 1978b:919–31)

Most of the Cave 4 material relating to 1QM is still unpublished. 4QMᵃ has been partially published, and C.-H. Hunzinger claimed that it represented an older recension. This was questioned by Carmignac (1958:270–72) on the grounds that the variants were not significant, and by P. Davies (1977a:17), who speculated that it might be a question of a recension not of M itself, but of one or two hymns later incorporated into M. However, this is not very likely because, in his detailed report on the seven unpublished manuscripts from Cave 4, M. Baillet revealed that 4QMᵃ also offers a very different version of col. 15 (1972b:220). Baillet, although conceding that 4QMᵃ has much to contribute to our understanding of M, tends to diminish the importance of its readings by pointing out that it is a very small manuscript, a sort of pocket book and thus necessarily a very secondary edition (1972b:221).

The text of 1QM is often obscure and sometimes contradictory. In consequence, its interpretation has been much disputed. The only hope for real clarification lies in source analysis, and it is in this direction that research has moved. In the first major commentary, Y. Yadin (1962:14–17) made vague references to sources but in practice assumed the literary unity of M, a position that is still maintained by Carmignac (1961:85), who obstinately has refused to take seriously all evidence to the contrary. This might be understandable had he to deal only with the magisterial statement of Dupont-Sommer (1955:29) that cols. 15–19 were a supplementary rule that was added to the principal war rule in cols. 2–14, col. 1 being a general introduction to the whole. But van der Ploeg (1959:11–22) had produced a series of cogent objections to the unity of authorship. On the positive side, van der Ploeg (1963) discerned a primitive document (cols. 1, 10–12, 15–19) which was later expanded by the addition of cols. 2–9. He allowed that cols. 10–12 may have undergone some revision and thought that cols. 13–14 may have been represented in the primitive document.

J. Becker (1963:43–50) also found two levels in M. One recension was composed of cols. 1; 7:9–8:10; 15–19, and the other was made up of cols. 2; 3–7:7; 10–14. He does not locate col. 9, nor does he determine the relative ages of the two recensions within which, moreover, he discerned a number of originally independent smaller units.

The precision of P. von der Osten-Sacken's analysis of 1QS 3:13–4:26 is unfortunately absent in his treatment of 1QM (42–115), principally because he permitted his theory of the development of dualism at Qumran to interfere with his literary investigation. Basically, his position is that the war rule in cols. 15–19 was constructed on the framework provided by the more ancient col. 1. An originally independent war rule appears in 7:9–9:9. It may have been associated with other elements of M, but he provides no clear picture either of the origin of these elements or of when and why they were inserted. For von der Osten-Sacken, the two war rules are based on Maccabean practices, and so he would apparently date them in the second century before the Christian era.

The most comprehensive literary study of 1QM is that of P. Davies (1977a), who critically refines the observations of his predecessors. He distinguishes three sources and two fragments. Originally independent, these were regarded as belonging together and were eventually integrated into a coherent war rule prefaced by col. 1 sometime in the first half of the first Christian century. On the level of sources, cols. 2–9 are a compilation made in the Hasmonean period of traditions going back to the Maccabean wars. Cols. 15–19 are the end product of a long development from an original Maccabean war rule represented by 14:2–12; these columns underwent their final redaction in the second half of the first century before the Christian era. Cols. 10–12, on the other hand, were originally a collection of hymns and prayers many of which reflect a Maccabean setting. The two fragments were cols. 13 (also analyzed by J. Duhaime, 1977a) and 14. Carmignac's (1978) flat rejection of Davies's hypothesis is more a manifestation of his own hostility to literary criticism and ignorance of its methods than a serious critique. In particular, his objection that Davies's view of 1QM cannot be correct because 4QM[a] is dated to the first half of the first century before the Christian era (602; Baillet, 1972b:226) gratuitously supposes that these fragments belonged to a complete text of M, even though Baillet (1972b:222) states that they do not have an exact parallel in 1QM! P. Skehan's (1978b) assessment is much more positive, but he is certainly correct in pointing out that the paleography of 1QM excludes the very late date that Davies has postulated for the final redaction.

Obviously, nothing resembling a consensus has been attained in the literary analysis of 1QM. It is perhaps the most difficult document to deal with from a literary point of view, but it would be unfortunate if the effort to determine its composition were abandoned. It has much to contribute to our understanding of an obscure aspect (the holy war) of a difficult period in Jewish history.

The Pesharim
(Delcor, 1978b:904-10)

Even before the discovery of copies at Qumran, CD had been drawn into the initial discussions on the scrolls because it contained a series of allusions to historical personages—the Teacher of Righteousness, the Man and Men of Mockery, the Man of Lies, "Saw," the Removers of Bounds, Ephraim, Judah, etc. When 1QpHab was published in 1950, it was immediately noted that it also contained references to the Teacher of Righteousness and the Man of Lies; it also introduced a number of new puzzles: the Wicked Priest, the House of Absalom, and above all the Kittim. These latter appeared to provide the best bridge between Essene and world history, and thus a key indication of the temporal framework in which the other figures were to be sought. However, some saw the Kittim as the Seleucids, but others as the Romans, and so a lively but rather inconclusive debate developed (Burrows, 1955:123-42; Rowley, 1956; Delcor, 1978b:927-29).

In 1954 J. M. Allegro began to publish the *pesharim* from Cave 4 (references in Fitzmyer, 1969) and as new information became available all the hypotheses were reshuffled. In 1954 and 1956 Allegro presented such a bizzare publication of portions of 4QpPs37 (later known as 4QpPs[a]) that they had to be reedited by H. Stegemann (1963); the quality of the edition did little to facilitate the identification of His Elect, Ephraim, Manasseh, the Priest, the Teacher of Righteousness, and the Wicked Priest. In 1956 the Kittim again appeared in 4QpIsa[a] and in 4QpNah but the latter, in addition to the first historical names ("Demetrius king of Yavan" and "Antiochus"), also furnished new enigmas: the Seekers of Smooth Things and the Furious Young Lion. Two years later the Seekers of Smooth Things and the Scoffers appeared in 4QpIsa[b-c]. Published in 1959, 4QpHos[a] mentioned the Last Priest and, once again, Ephraim. The final portion of 4QpNah was revealed in 1962 and added the Mediator of Knowledge and the House of Peleg to the list of cryptic names.

New fragments were added to most of these documents when Allegro published his *editio princeps* (DJD 5) in 1968. Very few were surprised when this edition proved to be extremely inadequate, but the scholarly world was very fortunate to have necessary joins made and the errors in transcription and the faults of translation remedied in most exemplary fashion by J. Strugnell (1970).

At the beginning of Qumran research 1QpHab was drawn into the web of speculation that had grown up around CD, but once archaeology and paleography had established the *terminus ante quem* of the scrolls, the references in the *pesharim* became the key to the history of the sect. It is in this context that we shall consider the identifications that have been proposed. Here it must suffice to underline the obvious; studies written prior to 1970 are unreliable because they did not have access to all the material now available.

Developing van der Ploeg's (1957) observations on the use of tenses in the *pesharim*, Carmignac (1963:50) has concluded that 1QpHab, 4QpNah, and 4QpPs[a] were all composed during the lifetime of the Wicked Priest. The majority of scholars ignore this criterion because it attributes too great a precision to Hebrew tenses, but no alternative explanation for the consistency of the usage has been proposed. At present the general assumption is that each *pesher* is the work of a single author, but this has not been tested by serious literary analysis. Texts such as 1QpHab 2:1-10 and the variations in the introductory formulas (see M. Horgan below, chap. 10) suggest that this line of research might prove fruitful. Unfortunately, it has not been touched on in the most recent full commentary on 1QpHab (Brownlee, 1979).

Other Documents

Given the space allotted to this article there can be no question of dealing with all the other sectarian manuscripts. However, considerations extrinsic to the documents themselves demand that mention be made of three:

The Copper Scroll (Bardtke, 1968:185–204)

K. G. Kuhn's brilliant deduction that the Copper Scroll contained a list of buried treasures greatly intensified interest in its publication (1954a:204). Commissioned to provide an immediate transcription lest the copper rolls disintegrate as they were being cut open in 1956, J. M. Allegro exploited his position by organizing a treasure hunt in 1959–60 (de Vaux, 1961:147). This pillage expedition, which proved completely fruitless, is not mentioned in his pirated edition of the document (1960). The preliminary edition by the official editor, J. T. Milik (1959b), indicated his belief that it dealt with imaginary treasures, a conviction confirmed by the quantity of gold and silver and the discovery of literary parallels (Milik, 1959c:567–75). Though dated paleographically in the period 25–75 of the Christian era (Cross, 1962:217), the content suggests a date around the end of that century (Milik, 1962:283; Lehmann). Milik denies that it is of Essene origin (1962:276–78), a view that has been questioned by L. Moraldi (714) and Delcor (1978b:955), but is accepted by E.-M. Laperrousaz, who, however, believes that the treasures are real and constituted the war-chest of Bar Kokhba (1976:131–47). The document makes important contributions to the study of the topography of Palestine and of the development of the Hebrew language.

The Greek Fragments from Cave 7

In 1972 a series of articles by J. O'Callaghan astounded the scientific world. He claimed to have identified parts of Mark, Acts, Romans, 1 Timothy, James, and 2 Peter in the Greek fragments from Cave 7 (7Q1–18). If he were correct, the implications (revision of the dating of most NT books) and the dangers (sensationalized fundamentalism; see Estrada and White) were obvious, and an intense discussion followed (Fitzmyer, 1975:120–23). The most fundamental objections came from P. Benoit (1972, 1973) and M. Baillet (1972a, 1973) who showed that a number of readings critical to O'Callaghan's restorations were either extremely dubious or without foundation. Others with greater likelihood attempted to identify the fragments with the LXX. Although there appears to be some unanimity regarding 7Q4 (Fee: 110; Urban, 1973:248–50; 1974), there is none concerning 7Q5 (Roberts; Garnet; Parker). O'Callaghan's reaction to his critics failed to make any new converts (1974). The fragments are simply too small for secure identification, even by a computer (Aland: 374–76).

The Temple Scroll

Parts of the large scroll liberated by the Israelis in 1967—an imprudence that made sellers so nervous that no new material has since appeared—were published in order to clarify particular points in 4QpNah (Yadin, 1971) and CD (Yadin, 1972). The *editio princeps* appeared (in modern Hebrew) in 1977 (see van der Ploeg, 1978). The English edition by Yadin appeared in 1984 (Israel Exploration Society) after the completion of this article, and good translations are available also in French (Caquot) and German (Maier, 1978). J. Milgrom's objective presentation of the scroll (1978a) has been followed by a series of studies (1978b, 1980) in which he takes issue with Yadin on points of detail, as does A. Qimron.

Thus far the most stimulating reaction has come from B. A. Levine, who raises the fundamental question of whether the scroll is sectarian in precisely the same way 1QS is. Yadin claims that it is, on the grounds that the Qumran calendar is presupposed, but Levine (11) finds the scroll's prescriptions for the "set-times" to be too ambiguous to compel the conclusion that the author was using this calendar. Even if Yadin were correct, Levine argues, it would not prove his point because no one claims *Jubilees* as sectarian even though it uses this calendar. Yadin's legal comparisons show that the *Temple Scroll* has a particular affinity with CD. Rather than use such contacts to prove Essene origin, Levine speculates that we should rather presume that CD and the *Temple Scroll* were not authored by the same group that produced 1QS, 1QH, etc. (12). In fact, the three contacts discussed by Levine all come from levels of CD which in the view of Murphy-O'Connor (1974:223–27) antedate the establishment of the

Essenes at Qumran. Insofar as Levine's question assumed the literary unity of 11QTemple it will have to be reformulated in view of the work of Wilson and Wills. Using a variety of criteria, they have shown that 11QTemple is composite. The basic document consisted of regulations concerning the construction of the temple (2:1–13:8 plus 30:3–47:18), followed by legal material adapted from Deuteronomy 12–22 (51:11–56:21 plus 60:1–66:17). A redactor added the festival calender (13:9–30:2) and the purity laws (48:1–51:10). Both of these and the Torah of the King (57–59), which may have been incorporated into the basic document earlier, all originally circulated as independent documents.

The direction of future research is clearly indicated by the questions that Wilson and Wills do not attempt. What are the dates and life situations of the component documents? How are they related to *Jubilees* and to the pre-Qumran material in CD? Did the final redaction take place at Qumran? If so, what were the redactor's concerns?

PSEUDEPIGRAPHA

Since a survey of all the fragments that might be grouped under this rubic (see Charlesworth, 1976:41–44) is impossible here, I propose to limit myself to the three major works, *1 Enoch, Jubilees,* and *Testaments of the Twelve Patriarchs* (Skehan, 1978a:822–28).

Jubilees

The importance of *Jubilees* at Qumran is attested by the presence of twelve manuscripts, the oldest dated ca. 100 before the Christian era (Baillet, 1962:77–79; Milik, 1966:104; van der Woude, 1971). The value of these fragments was to prove that *Jubilees* had been written in Hebrew and to provide a criterion for judging the reliability of the Ethiopic version (the only complete text), which was based on a Greek translation. J. C. VanderKam (1977:94) has shown that the Ethiopic reproduces the Hebrew literally and precisely in almost all instances. To A. Jaubert belongs the credit for the systematic development of D. Barthélemy's (1952:200–202) insight that the calendar supposed by *Jubilees* was also that of Qumran, a hypothesis that gave rise to an intense discussion (Fitzmyer, 1975:131–32) that has been recently evaluated by VanderKam (1979), whose own hypothesis (1981) has been criticized by Davies (1983b).

1 Enoch (Nickelsburg, 1981)

In 1976 J. T. Milik (with M. Black) published the *editio princeps* of fragments of eleven copies of *1 Enoch* dating from the last part of the third pre-Christian century to the early years of the first Christian century. Milik's elaborate theory to explain the growth and development of the

Enoch literature has been conveniently summarized by Fitzmyer (1977: 337–41). Milik's most controversial assertion (91–96) has proved to be the thesis that the Book of Parables (*1 Enoch* 37–71), of which no trace appears at Qumran, was composed in Greek by a Christian around the year 270 and was substituted for the Book of the Giants in the fifth century. This conclusion was accepted by R. Leivestad (246) and originally by M. Black (6), who, however, later changed his mind (Charlesworth, 1979:321). Although he disagrees radically with Milik's date of composition for the Parables, C. L. Mearns apparently accepted the Christian origin of the Book of Parables. Fitzmyer (1977:342) found Milik's arguments concerning both date and provenance generally unconvincing, as did G. W. E. Nickelsburg (1978:417–18). More sustained criticism came from J. Greenfield and M. E. Stone, and in particular from M. A. Knibb (1979a). All of these authors date the Book of Parables in the first Christian century, which would now constitute the majority opinion (Suter). In order to explain the absence of the Book of Parables at Qumran, J. Coppens's suggestion of a progressive lack of interest within the Qumran community is less probable than D. Flusser's observation (reported by Greenfield and Stone: 56) that this work would have been unacceptable at Qumran because chap. 41 puts the moon on the same level as the sun. Of course, if the current consensus is correct regarding the date of composition, then the Book of Parables would have come into being only after the Qumran community had been dispersed.

The Aramaic fragments also furnished an opportunity to evaluate the quality of the Ethiopic version. Milik's extremely negative judgment, "one should never trust any detail of this version" (1976:88), has been justly criticized for exaggeration by Nickelsburg (1978:415; 1981:210–11) and others. Progress on this issue and in the debate whether the Ethiopic was translated from the Aramaic original or from a Greek version will certainly be fostered by the publication of Ethiopic manuscripts superior to those that were available to Milik (Charlesworth, 1979:316).

Testaments of the Twelve Patriarchs

Perhaps because of M. de Jonge's defense of its literary unity against previous critical opinion (Murphy-O'Connor, 1968), research on *T. 12 Patr.* was strongly influenced by the pan-Qumranism of the 1950s. Though conceding to de Jonge that it was a Christian work, Milik considered its Essene character incontestable (1955b:298). Others went much further. According to K. G. Kuhn (1954b:173), A. van der Woude (1957:215), and M. Philonenko, it originated in the Qumran community. Such views, however, were much more impressions than well-argued positions. Those who undertook detailed comparisons found the evidence for Qumran origin inadequate (Otzen) or considered it to prove the opposite (Braun).

However, it is now becoming clear that Qumran is likely to provide the most significant clues to the enigmatic origin of *T. 12 Patr.*

J. T. Milik, who had previously published part of *T. Levi* in Aramaic from Cave 4 (1955a), recently provided a rather detailed overview of the unpublished material relating to *T. 12 Patr.* (1978:95–102). There are five fragmentary copies of *T. Levi*, one dated ca. 100 before the Christian era, two incomplete columns of *T. Naph.*, two fragments of *T. Judah*, dated 100–50 before the Christian era, and two fragments of *T. Jos.*, also dated 100–50 before the Christian era. All are in Aramaic with the exception of *T. Naph.*, but its Hebrew can be shown to be a translation. The place names in *T. Levi* and *T. Judah* demonstrate that they originated in Samaria. At this point Milik becomes rather vague. There was a Judean version that was translated into Greek and then abbreviated by the author of *T. 12 Patr.* (Milik, 1978:96, 98, 99), a Judeo-Christian (100) writing in the second century (96). Full publication of the evidence underlying this hypothesis will be awaited with impatience, and the discussions of the SNTS Seminar on this topic (Charlesworth, 1977) will have been complicated even more so, not only by Milik but also by J. Becker's (1970) literary analysis of *T. 12 Patr.*

THE HISTORY OF THE SECT

Within the framework provided by paleography (the events mentioned in the scrolls must have taken place before ca. 50 before the Christian era), there have been two principal centers of concern—the identification of the Wicked Priest and of the Teacher of Righteousness—and two minor ones—the pre-Qumran history of the sect and the identification of the Man of Lies.

The Wicked Priest

At this point in Qumran research many candidatures have lapsed or been withdrawn, but a short list made up of two candidates from the first pre-Christian century and two from the second is still being canvassed.

J. Starcky (1978) still supports the candidacy of Hyrcanus II, even though his claim has been shown to be without textual foundation (Jeremias: 49–57), and J. Carmignac (1980) keeps the name of Alexander Jannaeus in circulation. For Carmignac, however, this identification of the Wicked Priest is a consequence of his identification of the Teacher of Righteousness as Judah the Essene (see below).

Simon Maccabeus has found a recent advocate in G. Nickelsburg (1976), whereas M. A. Knibb (1979b:297–98) champions the cause of Simon's brother Jonathan, who is certainly the current favorite (Charlesworth, 1980:218–22). The objectivity, thoroughness, and methodology of the analyses of Jeremias (36–78) and Stegemann (1971:202–7) have not been surpassed; the profile they have established fits only Jonathan.

Recently, the validity of this profile has been questioned. In an article published just after his death, Brownlee (1982) maintained that the various references to the demise of the Wicked Priest cannot be made to fit a single known individual. Independently, van der Woude (1982) had come to the same conclusion, but whereas Brownlee limited the allusions to John Hyrcanus and his two sons, Aristobulus I and Alexander Jannaeus, van der Woude insists that the references in 1QpHab successively evoke all the high priests from Judas Maccabeus to Alexander Jannaeus. Both authors interpret the ambiguous statements of the *pesharim* too literally, and in the light of recent studies their confidence in the details supplied by Josephus appears somewhat exaggerated (Cohen; Broshi).

The Teacher of Righteousness

Periodic efforts to see "teacher of righteousness" as indicating a function carried out by different individuals (Rabinowitz, 1958; Buchanan; Starcky) have met with little success; it is generally understood as the title of a particular personage. The majority of scholars go no further than the position that he must be a contemporary of Jonathan, but a few are much more precise.

Though proposed with much erudition, the identification of the Teacher with John the Baptist (Thiering: 213–14), which would imply that Jesus was the Wicked Priest, is ruled out by paleography. For Carmignac (1980), he is Judah the Essene mentioned by Josephus (*J.W.* 1.3.2–5 §§73–80; *Ant.* 13.11.1–2 §§304–13), but the arguments fail to carry conviction (Burgmann, 1977) because they exaggerate the relation of this figure to the Temple and fail to distinguish the two branches of the Essene movement.

H. Stegemann (1971:102, 210–20) made an extremely important contribution by showing that the Teacher must have been a high priest, an insight that has been ignored by Carmignac (1973) and Vermes (1977), accepted by Knibb (1979b:298), and unconvincingly refused by Charlesworth (1980:222). This might seem to lend credibility to the identification of the Teacher with Onias III (Rowley, 1966:220), but in this case the Wicked Priest would have to be his brother Jason or the latter's successor Menelaus, neither of which fits the profile established by the scrolls. Hence, Stegemann (1971:220) has argued that the Teacher was high priest during the intersacerdotium of 159–152. In order to explain more satisfactorily the silence of Josephus (*Ant.* 20.10.3 §237), Murphy-O'Connor (1974:230) modified Stegemann's position by suggesting that the Teacher was merely the senior Zadokite, who *de facto* functioned as high priest and who is mentioned in 1 Macc 10:38 (Murphy-O'Connor, 1976). Forced from office by Jonathan, this individual took refuge with the Essenes. For them he was the true high priest and perhaps the one who would teach righteousness at the end of days according to CD 6:11a (Davies, 1983a:124, 203), but even without this traditional claim on their loyalty the powerful spiritual personality revealed by his hymns would have imposed itself. Jeremias (264–66) has correctly argued against Carmignac (1960) that the hymns cannot be used to provide biographical data uncorroborated by CD and the *pesharim*.

The Man of Lies

The role of this figure, also known as the Babbler, "Saw," and the Man of Mockery, is ignored in what is likely to prove the most influential outline of Essene history (Schürer-Vermes-Millar: 585–90), an inexplicable denial of the importance the scrolls accord him, particularly since the view—once widely held (references in Jeremias: 76)—that he is to be identified with the Wicked Priest has been proved wrong (Jeremias: 79–126; Stegemann, 1971:41–53).

Both Jeremias (126) and Stegemann (1971:225–26) agree that he was a leader in the Essene movement who broke away from the group that accepted the authority of the Teacher because of the latter's insistence on a break with the Temple. Murphy-O'Connor believes this break to have taken place earlier and attributes the split to the Teacher's proposal to move to Qumran (1974:237). This is of less importance, however, than the clear evidence of hostile groups within the Essene movement. Since hostility implies serious differences, the texts of Pliny, Philo, Josephus, etc., that refer to the Essenes must be used with great caution. It cannot be assumed that what is said of the Essenes in general applies to the Qumran branch or vice versa.

Burgmann (1978) identifies the Man of Lies with Simon Maccabeus, and Murphy-O'Connor (1981) suggests Judah the Essene. Burgmann's claim that the community of the Man of Lies is to be identified with the Pharisees rejoins Stegemann's position (1971:230). At present the evidence for this view is not satisfactory (Murphy-O'Connor, 1974:240–41), and J. Neusner has shown that Josephus's information on the early stages of the Pharisaic movement must be read with extreme critical control, a quality that is unfortunately lacking in E. Rivkin's study.

The Pre-Qumran History of the Sect

From CD 1:9–11 it is clear that the movement existed for "twenty years" before the advent of the Teacher of Righteousness. There is a firm consensus that the movement was a Palestinian phenomenon. It originated as a reaction to the religious persecution of the Seleucids (Carmignac, 1963:52; Schürer-Vermes-Millar: 586) or more concretely to the murder of Onias III (Stegemann, 1971:247) or to the introduction of a new cultic

calender in 167 (VanderKam, 1979:411; 1981). This latter hypothesis is
disputed by Davies (1983b). Others (Milik, 1959a:80; Cross, 1961:141;
Hengel: 1. 224; Vermes, 1977:148; Brownlee, 1982) are more specific and
identify the pre-Teacher movement with the Hasidim mentioned in 1 Maccabees. The weakness of this convenient assumption—it has never been
developed into anything more serious—has been convincingly demonstrated
by L. Rabinowitz, P. Davies (1977b) and Nickelsburg (1983:647–48).

An alternative to the Hasidim hypothesis was first proposed by
Albright, who claimed that the Essenes originated in Babylon (1957:376,
1969:19). It was taken up by Murphy-O'Connor (1974:215–19) and integrated with the observations of a number of other scholars. The Laws of
CD (Ginzberg; Segal; Iwry) and 4Q159 (Weinert) are legislation for a
Jewish community living in a Gentile environment. Babylonian names in
1QIsa^c are correctly vocalized (Albright, 1955) and the proto-Masoretic
tradition may have developed independently in Babylon before being re-
introduced into Palestine in the Hellenistic period (Cross, 1961:192). Many
of the "alien influences" (Albright, 1957:376) that Hengel (1. 228–41) has
so much difficulty in explaining are of Babylonian origin (K. G. Kuhn,
1952; pace Knibb, 1983:103). Finally, there is the connection between
certain Essene and Babylonian Karaite halakot (Paul: 30).

The hypothesis that the Essenes originated in Babylon has met with
a somewhat mixed reception. It has been dismissed without discussion by
Charlesworth (1980:220) and refused on the basis of a caricature of the
argument by Vermes (1981:28). On the other hand, it has been accepted
as possible by Brownlee (1982:17), as plausible and illuminating by Fitzmyer (1981:358), and as the most adequate background against which to
understand 4Q159 by Weinert. A detailed response has come from Knibb,
who, despite an initial negative bias (1979b:299), is forced to conclude,
"Nothing that has been said here makes Murphy-O'Connor's thesis completely unacceptable and it may still be right" (1983:113–14). Substantial
support for the Babylonian hypothesis is furnished by P. Davies's new
literary analysis of CD. He finds that the component documents consistently place the origins of the community during the exile and that contextually, "Damascus" can only mean Babylon. In consequence, he correctly
emphasizes the methodological point that "recognition of this perspective
undermines the conventional view that the community originated in the
Maccabean period, and it requires to be shown that the exilic perspective
of this document cannot be historically accurate before the possibility can
be dismissed" (1983a:123).

Those who place the origins of the Essene movement in Babylon
postulate a return to Palestine in the Maccabean period and at this point
rejoin the partisans of the Hasidim theory in recognizing that the group
which eventually settled at Qumran was once part of a wider movement.

This obscure period is perhaps the most important segment of Essene history. It is hoped that it will be illuminated by a more profound analysis not only of the pre-Qumran material in CD and 11QTemple but also of *Jubilees* and of texts such as the Epistle of Enoch (*1 Enoch* 92–105), which according to Nickelsburg (1982) is addressed to outsiders and was probably composed in circles ancestral to the Essenes of Qumran. The parallel between the intention of this document and one of the sources of CD is noteworthy (Murphy-O'Connor, 1970; Davies, 1983a:56–104).

CONCLUSION

The central thrust of this survey both explains and justifies what many consider an inadmissible lacuna in such a study, namely, the complete absence of any mention of Essene doctrines, particularly in the important areas of messianism, eschatology, and anthropology. With the exception of the dissertations related directly or indirectly to the Heidelberg Qumran seminar of K. G. Kuhn, all the studies in these areas rest on a pre-critical reading of the texts which fails to take into account the differences between documents and developments within the sect. It is now recognized that the history of the sect is considerably more complicated than was once thought and the possibility of such wide-ranging syntheses can no longer be taken for granted. In the case of anthropology it has already been shown to be impossible (Lichtenberger).

The most significant feature of recent research has been the appearance of new literary analyses and the renewed critical discussion of old proposals. It is too early to speak of anything like a consensus, but a certain convergence of views is beginning to be perceptible. Those who claim that the Qumran community conserved and adapted for its own use documents that antedated its foundation and continued to function in the wider Essene community are no longer negligible voices. Their differences are rooted in a coherent basic harmony whose message is clear. The most fruitful research will focus on the period prior to the establishment of Qumran. It is in this period that Qumran studies intersects with the illuminating work that is being done on other documents of the intertestamental period. In the past, many problems seemed insoluble because the assumption was that the documents were literary unities. Now as the constituent elements (the sources) of these documents are compared and contrasted new correlations should become apparent, which will permit more precise descriptions of genres and a better appreciation of the social contexts that gave them birth. Questions of influence and dependence, which control the dating of documents, are going to become ever more critical, but the answers will be useless unless derived from a sound methodology of comparison, which is probably the prime desideratum in this field.

BIBLIOGRAPHY

Adam, Alfred
1961   *Antike Berichte über die Essener*. Kleine Texte, 182. Berlin: de Gruyter.

Aharoni, Yohanan
1961   "The Expedition to the Judean Desert 1960." *IEJ* 11: 11–24.
1962   "The Expedition to the Judean Desert 1961." *IEJ* 12: 186–99.

Aland, Kurt
1974   "Neue Neutestamentliche Papyri III." *NTS* 20: 357–81.

Albright, William Foxwell
1937   "A Biblical Fragment from the Maccabaean Age: The Nash Papyrus." *JBL* 56: 145–76.
1948   "Notes from the President's Desk." *BASOR* 110: 2–3.
1955   "New Light on Early Recensions of the Hebrew Bible." *BASOR* 140: 27–33.
1957   *From the Stone Age to Christianity*. 2d ed. Garden City, NY: Doubleday.
1969   "Qumran and the Essenes: Geography, Chronology and Identification of the Sect." Pp. 11–25 in *The Scrolls and Christianity*. Ed. M. Black. London: SPCK.

Allegro, John M.
1960   *The Treasure of the Copper Scroll*. London: Routledge and Kegan Paul.
1968   *Qumran Cave 4, I (4Q158–4Q186)*. DJD 5. Oxford: Clarendon Press.
1979   "The Shapira Affair." *BAR* 5: 12–27.

Audet, Jean-Paul
1961   "Qumrân et la notice de Pline sur les Esséniens." *RB* 68: 346–87.

Avigad, Nahman
1958   "The Palaeography of the Dead Sea Scrolls and Related Documents." Pp. 56–87 in *Aspects of the Dead Sea Scrolls*. Ed. C. Rabin and Y. Yadin. Scripta Hierosolymitana 4. Jerusalem: Magnes Press.

Baillet, Maurice
1962   Pp. 45–166 in *Les 'petites grottes' de Qumrân*. DJD 3. Oxford: Clarendon Press.
1972a   "Les manuscrits de la Grotte 7 de Qumrân et le Nouveau Testament." *Bib* 53: 508–16.
1972b   "Les manuscrits de la Règle de la Guerre de la Grotte 4 de Qumrân." *RB* 79: 217–26.
1973   "Les manuscrits de la Grotte 7 de Qumrân et le Nouveau Testament." *Bib* 54: 340–50.
1978   "Le volume VII de 'Discoveries in the Judaean Desert': Presentation." Pp. 75–89 in *Qumrân: Sa piété, sa théologie et son milieu*. Ed. M. Delcor. BETL 46. Paris and Gembloux: Duculot; Leuven: University Press.

Bar-Adon, Pessah
1961   "The Expedition to the Judean Desert 1960." *IEJ* 11: 25–35.
1962   "The Expedition to the Judean Desert 1961." *IEJ* 12: 215–26.

1970	"Rivage de la Mer Morte: Un établissement essénien." *RB* 77: 398–400.
1977	"Another Settlement of the Judean Desert Sect at 'En el-Ghuweir on the Shores of the Dead Sea." *BASOR* 227: 1–26.

Bardtke, Hans
1956	"Das 'Ich' des Meisters in den Hodajoth von Qumran." *Wissenschaftliche Zeitschrift der Karl-Marx-Universität Leipzig* 6: 93–104.
1958	*Die Handschriftenfunde am Toten Meer: Die Sekte von Qumran.* Berlin: Evangelische Haupt-Bibelgesellschaft.
1968	"Qumran und seine Probleme." *TRu* 33: 97–119, 185–226.
1972	"Literaturbericht über Qumran. VI. Teil: Die Kriegsrolle." *TRu* 37: 97–120.
1973	"Literaturbericht über Qumran. VII. Teil: Die Sektenrolle 1QS." *TRu* 38: 257–91.
1974	"Literaturbericht über Qumran. VIII. Teil: Die Damaskusschrift CD." *TRu* 39: 189–221.
1975	"Literaturbericht über Qumran. IX. Teil: Die Loblieder (Hodajoth) von Qumran." *TRu* 40: 210–226.

Barthélemy, Dominique
1952	"Notes en marge de publications récentes sur les manuscrits de Qumran." *RB* 59: 187–218.
1953	"Redécouverte d'un chainon manquant de l'histoire de la Septante." *RB* 60: 18–29.
1963	*Les devanciers d'Aquila: Première publication intégrale du texte des fragments du Dodécaprophéton.* VTSup 10. Leiden: Brill.

Becker, Jürgen
1963	*Das Heil Gottes: Heils- und Sündenbegriffe in den Qumrantexten und im Neuen Testament.* SUNT 3. Göttingen: Vandenhoeck & Ruprecht.
1970	*Untersuchungen zur Entstehungsgeschichte der Testamente der zwölf Patriarchen.* AGJU 8. Leiden: Brill.

Benoit, Pierre
1972	"Note sur les fragments grecs de la grotte 7 de Qumrân." *RB* 79: 321–24.
1973	"Nouvelle note sur les fragments grecs de la grotte 7 de Qumrân." *RB* 80: 5–12.

Birnbaum, S. A.
1952	*The Qumran (Dead Sea) Scrolls and Palaeography* (BASOR Supp. Studies 13–14). New Haven: ASOR.

Black, Matthew
1976	"The 'Parables' of Enoch (1 En. 35–71) and the 'Son of Man.'" *ExpTim* 88: 5–9.

Blake, Ian
1966	"Rivage occidental de la Mer Morte." *RB* 73: 564–66.

Braun, François M.
1960	"Les Testaments des XII Patriarches et le problème de leur origine." *RB* 67: 516–49.

Broshi, Magen
1982	"The Credibility of Josephus." *JJS* 33: 379–84.

Brownlee, William H.
1950   "A Comparison of the Covenanters of the Dead Sea Scrolls with pre-Christian Jewish Sects." *BA* 13: 50–72.
1979   *The Midrash Pesher of Habakkuk.* SBLMS 24. Missoula, MT: Scholars Press.
1982   "The Wicked Priest, the Man of Lies, and the Righteous Teacher — The Problem of Identity." *JQR* 73: 1–37.

Buchanan, George W.
1969   "The Priestly Teacher of Righteousness." *RevQ* 6: 553–58.

Burchard, Christoph
1957   *Bibliographie zu den Handschriften vom Toten Meer.* BZAW 76. Berlin: A. Töpelmann.
1962   "Pline et les Esséniens: A propos d'un article récent." *RB* 69: 533–69.
1965   *Bibliographie zu den Handschriften vom Toten Meer,* II. BZAW 89. Berlin: A. Töpelmann.

Burgmann, Hans
1977   "Gerichtsheer und Generalankläger: Jonathan und Simon." *RevQ* 9: 3–72.
1978   "Der Gründer der Pharisäergenossenschaft: Der Makkabäer Simon." *JSJ* 9: 153–91.

Burrows, Millar
1955   *The Dead Sea Scrolls.* New York: Viking.
1958   *More Light on the Dead Sea Scrolls.* New York: Viking.

Burton, D., J. B. Poole, and R. Reed
1959   "A New Approach to the Dating of the Dead Sea Scrolls." *Nature* 184: 533–34.

Butler, Harry A.
1960   "The Chronological Sequence of the Scrolls of Qumran Cave One." *RevQ* 2: 534–36.

Caquot, André
1978   Le rouleau du Temple de Qoumran." *ETR* 53: 443–500.

Carmignac, Jean
1958   *La Règle de la Guerre.* Paris: Letouzey & Ané.
1960   "Les éléments historiques des Hymnes de Qumrân." *RevQ* 2: 205–22.
1961   "La Règle de la Guerre." "Les Hymnes." Pp. 81–282 in *Les textes de Qumran, I.* Ed. J. Carmignac and P. Guilbert. Paris: Letouzey & Ané.
1963   "Interprétation de Prophètes et des Psaumes." Pp. 45–130 in *Les textes de Qumran, II.* Ed. J. Carmignac, E. Cothenet, and H. Lignée. Paris: Letouzey & Ané.
1973   Review of H. Stegemann, *Die Entstehung der Qumrangemeinde. RevQ* 8: 277–81.
1978   Review of P. R. Davies, *1QM, the War Scroll from Qumran: Its Structure and History. RevQ* 9: 599–603.
1980   "Qui était le Docteur de Justice?" *RevQ* 10: 235–46.

Charles, R. H.
1913   "Fragments of a Zadokite Work." *APOT* 2: 785–834.

Charlesworth, James H.
1976   *The Pseudepigrapha and Modern Research.* SBLSCS 7. Missoula, MT: Scholars Press.
1977   "Reflections on the SNTS Pseudepigrapha Seminar at Duke on the Testaments of the Twelve Patriarchs." *NTS* 23: 296–304.
1979   "The SNTS Pseudepigrapha Seminars at Tübingen and Paris on the Books of Enoch." *NTS* 25: 315–23.
1980   "The Origin and Subsequent History of the Authors of the Dead Sea Scrolls: Four Transitional Phases among the Qumran Essenes." *RevQ* 10: 213–33.

Cohen, Shaye J. D.
1979   *Josephus in Galilee and Rome, His Vita and Development as a Historian.* Leiden: Brill.

Coppens, Joseph
1975   "Le Fils d'Homme dans le Judaisme de l'époque néotestamentaire." *OLP* 6–7: 65–68.

Cothenet, E.
1963   "Le Document de Damas." In *Les textes de Qumran, II.* Ed. J. Carmignac, E. Cothenet, and H. Lignée. Paris: Letouzey & Ané.

Cross, Frank Moore
1956   "Le travail d'édition des fragments manuscrits de Qumrân." *RB* 63: 56–58.
1961   *The Ancient Library of Qumran and Modern Biblical Studies.* Rev. ed. Garden City, NY: Doubleday, Anchor Books.
1962   "Excursus on the Palaeographical Dating of the Copper Document." Pp. 217–21 in *Les 'petites grottes' de Qumrân.* DJD 3. Oxford: Clarendon Press.
1965   "The Development of the Jewish Scripts." Pp. 170–264 in *The Bible and the Ancient Near East: Essays in Honor of William Foxwell Albright.* Ed. G. E. Wright. Garden City, NY: Doubleday.

Davies, Philip R.
1977a   *1QM, the War Scroll from Qumran: Its Structure and History.* BibOr 32. Rome: Biblical Institute Press.
1977b   "Hasidim in the Maccabean Period." *JJS* 28: 127–40.
1983a   *The Damascus Covenant: An Interpretation of the "Damascus Document."* JSOT Supp. 25. Sheffield: JSOT Press.
1983b   "Calendrical Change and Qumran Origins: An Assessment of VanderKam's Theory." *CBQ* 45: 80–89.

Deichgräber, Reinhard
1967   *Gotteshymnus und Christushymnus in der frühen Christenheit: Untersuchungen zu Form, Sprache und Stil der frühchristlichen Hymnen.* SUNT 5. Göttingen: Vandenhoeck & Ruprecht.

De Jonge, M.
1953   *The Testaments of the Twelve Patriarchs: A Study of their Text, Composition and Origin.* Van Gorcum's Theologische Bibliotheek 25. Assen: Van Gorcum.

Delcor, Mathias
1978a   "Où en sont les études Qumrâniennes?" Pp. 11–46 in *Qumran: Sa piété, sa théologie et son milieu.* Ed. M. Delcor. BETL 46. Paris and Gembloux: Duculot; Leuven: University Press.
1978b   "Littérature essénienne." *DBSup* 9: 828–960.

Del Medico, H. E.
1951 *Deux manuscrits hébreux de la Mer Morte.* Paris: Geuthner.

Denis, Albert-Marie
1964 "Evolution de structures dans le secte de Qumrân." Pp. 23–49 in *Aux origines de l'Eglise.* RechBib 7. Bruges: Desclée.
1967 *Les thèmes de connaissance dans le Document de Damas.* StudHell 15. Louvain: Publications Universitaires.

Driver, Godfrey Rolles
1949a "New Hebrew Manuscripts." *JQR* 40: 127–34.
1949b "New Hebrew Manuscripts." *JQR* 40: 359–72.
1965 *The Judean Scrolls: The Problem and a Solution.* Oxford: Blackwell.

Duhaime, Jean
1977a "La rédaction de 1QM xii et l'évolution du dualism à Qumrân." *RB* 84: 210–38.
1977b "L'instruction sur les deux esprits et les interpolations dualistes à Qumrân." *RB* 84: 566–94.

Dupont-Sommer, André
1950 *Aperçus préliminaires sur les manuscrits de la mer Morte.* Paris: Maisonneuve.
1953 *Nouveaux aperçus sur les manuscrits de la mer Morte.* Paris: Maisonneuve.
1955 "Réglement de la Guerre des Fils de Lumière." *RHR* 148: 25–43, 141–80.
1959 *Les écrits esséniens découverts près de la mer Morte.* Paris: Payot.

Estrada, David, and William White
1978 *The First New Testament.* Nashville and New York: Nelson.

Fee, Gordon D.
1973 "Some Dissenting Notes on 7Q5 = Mark 6:52–53." *JBL* 92: 109–12.

Fitzmyer, Joseph A.
1955 "The Qumran Scrolls, the Ebionites and Their Literature." *TS* 16: 335–72.
1969 "A Bibliographical Aid to the Study of the Qumran Cave IV Texts 158–186." *CBQ* 31: 59–71.
1970 Prolegomenon to S. Schechter, *Documents of Jewish Sectaries.* New York: Ktav.
1975 *The Dead Sea Scrolls: Major Publications and Tools for Study.* SBLSBS 8. Missoula, MT: Scholars Press.
1977 "Implications of the New Enoch Literature from Qumran." *TS* 38: 332–45.
1981 "The Dead Sea Scrolls and the New Testament after Thirty Years." *TD* 29: 351–67.

Garnet, Paul
1973 "O'Callaghan's Fragments: Our Earliest New Testament Texts?" *EvQ* 45: 8–9.

Ginzberg, Louis
1976 *An Unknown Jewish Sect.* Moreshet Series 1. New York: Jewish Theological Seminary.

Gottstein, M. H.
1954 "Anti-Essene Traits in the Dead Sea Scrolls." *VT* 4: 141–47.

Greenfield, Jonas C., and Michael E. Stone
1977 "The Enochic Pentateuch and the Date of the Similitudes." *HTR* 70: 51–65.

Grinz, Y. M.
1973 "Die Männer des Yachad-Essener: Zusammenfassungen, Erlauterungen und Bemerkungen zu den Rollen vom Toten Meer." Pp. 294–336 in *Zur Josephus-Forschung*. Ed. A. Schalit. Wege der Forschung 84. Darmstadt: Wissenschaftliche Buchgesellschaft.

Guilbert, P.
1959 "Le Plan de la Règle de la Communauté." *RevQ* 3: 323–44.

Harding, G. Lankester
1955 Pp. 3–7 in *Qumran Cave 1*. DJD 1. Oxford: Clarendon Press.

Hengel, Martin
1974 *Judaism and Hellenism: Studies in their Encounter in Palestine during the Early Hellenistic Period*. 2 vols. Trans. J. Bowden. Philadelphia: Fortress.

Holm-Nielsen, Svend
1960 *Hodayot: Psalms from Qumran*. ATDan 2. Aarhus: Universitetsforlaget.

Hunzinger, Claus-Hunno
1957 "Fragmente einer älteren Fassung des Buches Milḥamā aus Höhle 4 von Qumran." *ZAW* 69: 131–51.

Iwry, Samuel
1969 "Was there a Migration to Damascus? The Problem of *šby yśr'l*." Pp. 80–88 in *W. F. Albright Volume*. Ed. A. Malamat. Eretz-Israel 9. Jerusalem: Israel Exploration Society.

Jaubert, Annie
1953 "La calendrier des Jubilés et de la secte de Qumrân: ses origines bibliques." *VT* 3: 250–64.

Jeremias, Gert
1963 *Der Lehrer der Gerechtigkeit*. SUNT 2. Göttingen: Vandenhoeck & Ruprecht.

Jongeling, Bastiaan
1971 *A Classified Bibliography of the Finds in the Desert of Judah 1958–1969*. STDJ 7. Leiden: Brill.

Klinzing, Georg
1971 *Die Umdeutung des Kultus in der Qumran Gemeinde und im Neuen Testament*. SUNT 7. Göttingen: Vandenhoeck & Ruprecht.

Knibb, Michael A.
1979a "The Date of the Parables of Enoch: A Critical Review." *NTS* 25: 345–59.
1979b "The Dead Sea Scrolls: Some Recent Publications." *ExpTim* 90: 294–300.
1983 "Exile in the Damascus Document." *JSOT* 25: 99–117.

Kuhn, Heinz-Wolfgang
1966 *Enderwartung und gegenwärtiges Heil: Untersuchungen zu den Gemeindeliedern von Qumran*. SUNT 4. Göttingen: Vandenhoeck & Ruprecht.

Kuhn, Karl Georg
1952   "Die Sektenschrift und die iranische Religion." *ZTK* 49: 296–316.
1954a   "Les rouleaux de cuivre de Qumrän." *RB* 61: 193–205.
1954b   "Die beiden Messias Aarons und Israels." *NTS* 1: 167–79.
1960   "Der gegenwärtige Stand der Erforschung der in Palästina neu gefundenen hebräischen Handschriften." *TLZ* 85: 649–58.

Lacheman, Ernest R.
1949–50 "A Matter of Method in Hebrew Palaeography." *JQR* 40: 15–36.

Laperrousaz, E.-M.
1962   "'Infra hos Engadda.' Notes à propos d'un article récent." *RB* 69: 368–80.
1976   *Qoumrân: L'établissment essénien des bords de la mer Morte: Histoire et archéologie du site.* Paris: Picard.
1978   "Qumran: Topographie des lieux et historique des recherches." *DBSup* 9: 738–44.

La Sor, William S.
1958   *Bibliography of the Dead Sea Scrolls.* Fuller Theological Seminary Bibliography Series 2. Pasadena: Fuller Theological Seminary.

Leaney, A. R. C.
1966   *The Rule of Qumran and Its Meaning.* London: SCM.

Lehmann, M. R.
1964   "Identification of the Copper Scroll based on its Technical Terms." *RevQ* 5: 97–105.

Leivestad, Ragnar
1971   "Exit the Apocalyptic Son of Man." *NTS* 18: 243–67.

Levi, Israel
1912   "Un écrit sadducéen antérieur à la destruction du Temple." *REJ* 63: 1–19.

Levine, Baruch A.
1978   "The Temple Scroll: Aspects of its Historical Provenance and Literary Character." *BASOR* 232: 5–23.

Lichtenberger, Hans
1980   *Studien zum Menschenbild in Texten der Qumrangemeinde.* SUNT 15. Göttingen: Vandenhoeck & Ruprecht.

Lifshitz, B.
1962   "The Greek Documents from the Cave of Horror." *IEJ* 12: 201–7.

Maier, Johann
1960   *Die Texte vom Toten Meer, I–II.* Munich and Basel: Reinhardt.
1978   *Die Tempelrolle vom Toten Meer.* Munich and Basel: Reinhardt.

Mazar, Benjamin
1967   "En-Gedi." Pp. 223–30 of *Archaeology and Old Testament Study.* Ed. D. Winton Thomas. Oxford: Clarendon Press.

Mearns, Christopher L.
1979   "Dating the Similitudes of Enoch." *NTS* 25: 360–69.

Milgrom, Jacob
1978a   "The Temple Scroll." *BA* 41: 105–20.
1978b   "Studies in the Temple Scroll." *JBL* 97: 501–23.
1980   "Further Studies in the Temple Scroll." *JQR* 71: 1–17.

Milik, Josef T.
1953   "Une inscription et une lettre en araméen christo-palestinien." *RB* 60: 526–39.
1955a   "Le Testament de Levi en araméen: Fragment de la grotte 4 de Qumrân." *RB* 62: 398–406.
1955b   Review of M. de Jonge, *The Testaments of the Twelve Patriarchs.* *RB* 62: 297–98.
1956   "Le travail d'édition des fragments manuscrits de Qumrân." *RB* 63: 60–62.
1959a   *Ten Years of Discovery in the Wilderness of Judaea.* Trans. J. Strugnell. SBT 26. London: SCM.
1959b   "Le rouleau de cuivre de Qumrân (3Q15). Traduction et commentaire topographique." *RB* 66: 321–57.
1959c   "Notes d'epigraphie et de topographie palestiniennes." *RB* 66: 550–75.
1960a   Pp. 67–208 in *Les grottes de Murabba'at.* DJD 2. Oxford: Clarendon Press.
1960b   Review of P. Wernberg-Moller, *The Manual of Discipline. RB* 67: 410–16.
1962   Pp. 211–302 in *Les 'petites grottes' de Qumrân.* DJD 3. Oxford: Clarendon Press.
1966   "Fragment d'une source du psautier (4Q Ps 89) et fragments des Jubilés, du Document de Damas, d'une phylactère dans la grotte 4 de Qumrân." *RB* 73: 94–106.
1978   "Ecrits préesséniens de Qumrân: d'Henoch à Amram." Pp. 91–106 in *Qumran: Sa piété, sa théologie et son milieu.* Ed. M. Delcor. BETL 46. Paris and Gembloux: Duculot; Leuven: University Press.

Milik, Josef T., with M. Black
1976   *The Books of Enoch: Aramaic Fragments of Qumrân Cave 4.* Oxford: Clarendon Press.

Molin, G.
1957   *Lob Gottes aus der Wüste: Lieder und Gebete aus den Handschriften vom Toten Meer.* Freiburg and Munich: Alber.

Moraldi, Luigi
1971   *I manoscritte di Qumran.* Turin: Unione tipografico — Editrice Torinese.

Morawe, G.
1961   *Aufbau und Abgrenzung der Loblieder von Qumran: Studien zur gattungsgeschichtlichen Einordnung der Hodajoth.* Theologische Arbeiten 16. Berlin: Evangelische Verlagsanstalt.

Murphy-O'Connor, Jerome
1968   "Testamente der zwölf Patriarchen." Cols. 1733–35 in *Bibel-Lexikon.* Ed. H. Haag. Einsiedeln: Benziger.
1969   "La genèse littéraire de la Règle de la Communauté." *RB* 76: 528–49.
1970   "An Essene Missionary Document? CD 2:14–6:1." *RB* 77: 201–29.
1971   Review of S. Schechter, *Documents of Jewish Sectaries. RB* 78: 298–99.
1972a   "A Literary Analysis of Damascus Document xix, 33–xx, 34." *RB* 79: 544–64.

1972b   Review of G. Klinzing, *Die Umdeutung des Kultus in der Qumran Gemeinde und im Neuen Testament. RB* 79: 435–40.
1974   "The Essenes and their History." *RB* 81: 215–44.
1976   "Demetrius I and the Teacher of Righteousness." *RB* 83: 400–420.
1981   "Judah the Essene and the Teacher of Righteousness." *RevQ* 10: 579–86.

Neusner, Jacob
1972   "Josephus's Pharisees." Pp. 224–44 in *Ex Orbe Religionum: Studia Geo Widengren oblata,* Vol. 1. Studies in the History of Religions 21. Leiden: Brill.

Nickelsburg, George W. E.
1976   "Simon — A Priest with a Reputation for Faithfulness." *BASOR* 223: 67–68.
1978   Review of J. T. Milik, *The Books of Enoch: Aramaic Fragments of Qumrân Cave 4. CBQ* 40: 411–19.
1981   "The Books of Enoch in Recent Research." *RelSRev* 7: 210–17.
1982   "The Epistle of Enoch and the Qumran Literature." *JJS* 33: 333–48.
1983   "Social Aspects of Palestinian Jewish Apocalypticism." In *Apocalypticism in the Mediterranean World and the Near East: Proceedings of the International Colloquium on Apocalypticism, Uppsala, August 12–17, 1979.* Ed. David Hellholm. Tübingen: Mohr-Siebeck.

North, Robert
1955   "The Qumran 'Sadducees.'" *CBQ* 17: 44–68.

O'Callaghan, José
1972a   "¿Papiros neotestamentarios en la cueva 7 de Qumran?" *Bib* 53: 91–104.
1972b   "¿1 Tim 3, 16; 4, 1.3 en 7Q4?" *Bib* 53: 362–67.
1972c   "Tres probables papiros neotestamentarios en la cueva 7 de Qumran." *SPap* 11: 83–89.
1972d   "Notas sobre 7Q tomadas en el 'Rockefeller Museum' de Jerusalén." *Bib* 53: 517–33.
1974   *Los papiros griegos de la cueva 7 de Qumran.* BAC 353. Madrid: Editorial catolica.

Ory, G.
1975   *A la recherche des Esséniens: Essai critique.* Paris: Cercle Ernest-Renan.

Osten-Sacken, Peter von der
1969   *Gott und Belial: Traditionsgeschichtliche Untersuchungen zum Dualismus in den Texten aus Qumran.* SUNT 6. Göttingen: Vandenhoeck & Ruprecht.

Otzen, B.
1954   "Die neugefundenen hebräischen Sektenschriften und die Testamente der XII Patriarchen." *ST* 7: 125–57.

Parker, Pierson
1972   "Enthält das Papyrusfragment 5 aus der Höhle 7 von Qumran einen Markustext?" *Erbe und Auftrag* 48: 467–69.

Paul, André
1969   *Écrits de Qumran et sectes juives aux premiers siècles de l'Islam: Recherches sur l'origine du Qaraïsme.* Paris: Letouzey & Ané.

Perrot, Charles
1963 "Un fragment christo-palestinien découvert à Khirbet Mird (Actes des Apôtres x, 28–29, 32–41)." *RB* 70: 506–55.

Philonenko, Marc
1960 *Les interpolations chrétiennes des Testaments des XII Patriarches et les manuscrits de Qoumran.* Cahiers de la *RHPR* 35. Paris: Presses universitaires de France.

Ploeg, J. P. M. van der
1957 "L'usage du parfait et de l'imparfait comme moyen de datation dans le Commentaire d'Habacuc." Pp. 25–35 in *Les manuscrits de la Mer Morte: Colloque de Strasbourg, 25–27 Mai 1955.* Paris: Presses universitaires de France.
1959 *Le rouleau de la guerre.* STDJ 2. Leiden: Brill.
1963 "Zur literarischen Komposition der Kriegsrolle." Pp. 293–98 in *Qumran-Probleme: Vorträge des Leipziger Symposions über Qumran-Probleme.* Ed. H. Bardtke. Berlin: Akademie-Verlag.
1978 "Une *halakha* inédite de Qumran." Pp. 107–13 in *Qumrân: Sa piété, sa théologie et son milieu.* Ed. M. Delcor. BETL 46. Paris and Gembloux: Duculot; Leuven: University Press.

Pouilly, Jean
1976 *La Règle de la Communauté de Qumran: Son évolution littéraire.* Cahiers de la *RB* 17. Paris: Gabalda.

Qimron, A.
1978 "New Readings in the Temple Scroll." *IEJ* 28: 161–72.

Rabin, Chaim
1954 *The Zadokite Documents.* Oxford: Clarendon Press.
1957 *Qumran Studies.* Scripta Judaica 2. Oxford: University Press.

Rabinowitz, I.
1953 "Sequence and Dates of the Extra-Biblical Dead Sea Scrolls Texts and 'Damascus' Fragments." *VT* 3: 175–85.
1954 "A Reconsideration of 'Damascus' and '390 Years' in the 'Damascus' ('Zadokite') Fragments." *JBL* 73: 11–35.
1958 "The Guides of Righteousness." *VT* 8: 391–404.

Rabinowitz, L.
1959 "The First Essenes." *JSS* 4: 358–61.

Reider, Joseph
1950 "The Dead Sea Scrolls." *JQR* 41: 59–70.

Rivkin, Ellis
1979 *A Hidden Revolution: The Pharisees' Search for the Kingdom Within.* Nashville: Abingdon; London: SPCK.

Roberts, C. H.
1972 "On Some Presumed Papyrus Fragments of the New Testament from Qumran." *JTS* 23: 446–47.

Roth, Cecil
1958 *The Historical Background of the Dead Sea Scrolls.* Oxford: Blackwell.
1959a "Why the Qumran Sect cannot have been Essenes." *RevQ* 1:417–22.
1959b "Were the Qumran Sectaries Essenes?" *JTS* 10: 87–93.
1965 *The Dead Sea Scrolls: A New Historical Approach.* New York: Norton.

Rowley, Harold H.
1952   *The Zadokite Fragments and the Dead Sea Scrolls.* Oxford: Blackwell.
1956   "The Kittim and the Dead Sea Scrolls." *PEQ* 88: 92–109.
1966   "The History of the Qumran Sect." *BJRL* 49: 203–32.

Schiffman, Lawrence H.
1975   *The Halakhah at Qumran.* SJLA 16. Leiden: Brill.

Schulz, Paul
1974   *Der Autoritätsanspruch des Lehrers der Gerechtigkeit in Qumran.* Meisenheim am Glan: Hain.

Schürer, Emil
1979   *The History of the Jewish People in the Age of Jesus Christ (175 B.C.–A.D. 135),* Vol. 2. New English version revised and edited by G. Vermes, F. Millar, and M. Black. Edinburgh: T. & T. Clark.

Segal, M. H.
1951   "The Habakkuk 'Commentary' and the Damascus Fragments. A Historical Study." *JBL* 70: 131–47.

Sellers, Ovid R.
1951   "Radiocarbon Dating of Cloth from the 'Ain Feshkha Cave." *BASOR* 123: 24–26.

Skehan, Patrick W.
1956   "Le travail d'édition des fragments manuscrits de Qumrân." *RB* 63: 58–60.
1978a   "Littérature de Qumran. A: Textes bibliques; B: Apocryphes de L'Ancien Testament." *DBSup* 9: 805–28.
1978b   Review of P. R. Davies, *1QM, the War Scroll from Qumran: Its Structure and History. CBQ* 40: 602–3.

Smith, Morton
1958   "The Description of the Essenes in Josephus and the Philosophumena." *HUCA* 29: 273–313.

Soloff, R. A.
1958   "Towards Uncovering Original Texts in the Zadokite Documents." *NTS* 5: 62–67.

Starcky, Jean
1978   "Les Maîtres de Justice et la chronologie de Qumrân." Pp. 249–56 in *Qumrân: Sa piété, sa théologie et son milieu.* Ed. M. Delcor. BETL 46. Paris and Gembloux: Duculot; Leuven: University Press.

Stegemann, Hartmut
1963   "Der Pesher Psalm 37 aus Höhle 4 von Qumran (4QpPs37)." *RevQ* 4: 235–70.
1971   *Die Entstehung der Qumrangemeinde.* Bonn: privately published.

Strugnell, John
1956   "Le travail d'édition des fragments manuscrits de Qumrân." *RB* 63: 64–66.
1960   "The Angelic Liturgy at Qumran—4Q Serek Sîrôt 'Ôlat Haššabbat." Pp. 318–45 in *Congress Volume: Oxford, 1959.* VTSup 7. Leiden: Brill.
1970   "Notes en marge du volume V des 'Discoveries in the Judaean Desert of Jordan.'" *RevQ* 7: 163–276.

Stutchbury, H. E., and G. R. Nicholl
1962   "Khirbet Mazin." *Annual of the Department of Antiquities of Jordan* 6–7: 96–103.

Sukenik, E. L.
1955   *The Dead Sea Scrolls of the Hebrew University.* Ed. N. Avigad and Y. Yadin. Jerusalem: Magnes Press.

Suter, David W.
1981   "Weighed in the Balance: The Similitudes of Enoch in Recent Discussion." *RelSRev* 7: 217–21.

Teicher, J. L.
1951   "The Dead Sea Scrolls — Documents of the Jewish-Christian Sect of Ebionites." *JJS* 2: 67–99.

Thiering, Barbara E.
1979   *Redating the Teacher of Righteousness.* Australian and New Zealand Studies in Theology and Religion 1. Sydney: Theological Explorations.

Trever, John C.
1965   *The Untold Story of Qumran.* London: Pickering & Inglis.

Urban, A. C.
1973   "Observaciones sobre ciertos papiros de la cueva 7 de Qumran." *RevQ* 8:233–51.
1974   La identificacion 7Q4 con Num 14, 23–24 y la restauracion de textos antiguos." *EstBib* 34: 219–44.

VanderKam, James C.
1977   *Textual and Historical Studies in the Book of Jubilees.* HSM 14. Missoula, MT: Scholars Press.
1979   "The Origin, Character, and Early History of the 364-Day Calendar: A Reassessment of Jaubert's Hypotheses." *CBQ* 41: 390–411.
1981   "2 Macc 6:7a and Calendrical Change in Jerusalem." *JSJ* 12: 1–23.

Vaux, Roland de
1959   "Les manuscrits de Qumrân et l'archéologie." *RB* 66:87–110.
1960   Pp. 3–50 in *Les grottes de Murabba'at.* DJD 2. Oxford: Clarendon Press.
1961   Review of J. M. Allegro, *The Treasure of the Copper Scroll. RB* 68: 146–47.
1966   "Esséniens ou Zélotes: A propos d'un livre récent." *RB* 73: 212–35.
1973   *Archaeology and the Dead Sea Scrolls.* Schweich Lectures 1959. Rev. ed. in an Eng. trans. by D. Bourke. London: Oxford University Press.

Vermes, Geza
1981   "The Essenes and History." *JJS* 32: 18–31.

Vermes, Geza, with Pamela Vermes
1977   *The Dead Sea Scrolls: Qumran in Perspective.* London: Collins.

Weinert, Frank D.
1977   "A Note on 4Q159 and a New Theory of Essene Origins." *RevQ* 9: 223–30.

Weis, P. R.
1950–51   "The Date of the Habakkuk Scroll." *JQR* 41: 125–53.

Weise, M.
1961   *Kultzeiten und kultischer Bundesschluss in der Ordensregel vom Toten Meer.* SPB 3. Leiden: Brill.

Wernberg-Møller, P.
1957   *The Manual of Discipline.* STDJ 1. Leiden: Brill.

Wilson, Andrew M., and Lawrence Wills
1982   "Literary Sources of the *Temple Scroll.*" *HTR* 75: 275–88.

Woude, A. S. van der
1957   *Die messianische Vorstellungen der Gemeinde von Qumran.* Studia semitica neerlandica 3. Assen: Van Gorcum.
1971   "Fragmente des Buches Jubiläen aus Qumran Höhle XI (11QJub)." In *Tradition und Glaube: Das frühe Christentum in seiner Umwelt: Festgabe für Karl Georg Kuhn.* Ed. G. Jeremias, H.-W. Kuhn, and H. Stegemann. Göttingen: Vandenhoeck & Ruprecht.
1982   "Wicked Priest or Wicked Priests? Reflections on the Identification of the Wicked Priest in the Habakkuk Commentary." *JJS* 33: 349–59.

Wright, G. R. H.
1961   "The Archaeological Remains at el-Mird in the Wilderness of Judaea." *Bib* 42: 1–21.

Yadin, Yigael
1962   *The Scroll of the War of the Sons of Light against the Sons of Darkness.* Oxford: University Press.
1963   *The Finds from the Bar Kokhba Period in the Cave of Letters.* JDS. Jerusalem: Israel Exploration Society.
1965   "The Excavation of Masada 1963/64. Preliminary Report." *IEJ* 15: 1–120.
1967   "The Temple Scroll." *BA* 30: 135–39.
1971   "Pesher Nahum (4QpNahum) Reconsidered." *IEJ* 21: 1–12.
1972   "L'attitude essénienne envers la polygamie et le divorce." *RB* 79: 98–99.
1977   *The Temple Scroll* (Hebrew). 3 vols. and a supplement. Jerusalem: Israel Exploration Society.
1983   *The Temple Scroll* (Engl. trans.). 3 vols. and a supplement. Jerusalem: Israel Exploration Society.

Zeitlin, Solomon
1949a   "The Hoax of the 'Slavonic Josephus.'" *JQR* 39: 171–80.
1949b   "'A Commentary on the Book of Habakkuk': Important Discovery or Hoax?" *JQR* 39: 235–47.
1950a   "The Hebrew Scrolls: Once More and Finally." *JQR* 41: 1–58.
1950b   "The Hebrew Scrolls: A Challenge to Scholarship." *JQR* 41: 251–75.
1952   *The Zadokite Fragments: Facsimile of the Manuscripts in the Cairo Genizah Collection in the Possession of the University Library, Cambridge, England.* JQRMS 1. Philadelphia: Dropsie College.
1956   *The Dead Sea Scrolls and Modern Scholarship.* JQRMS 3. Philadelphia: Dropsie College.

6

OTHER MANUSCRIPT DISCOVERIES

Sebastian P. Brock

In this chapter the aim will be to draw attention to some of the important discoveries of manuscripts and inscriptions made since 1945, to the extent that these have not been covered in chapters 5 and 7. At the outset certain problems of demarcation should be kept in mind. Manuscripts written in this period may contain texts composed at a very much earlier date (this, of course, applies above all to biblical manuscripts). At the other end of the scale it should be noted that, although our concern will be focused mainly on those manuscripts and inscriptions written within the half millennium that constitutes the Hellenistic and early Roman period (approximately 300 B.C.E. to 200 C.E.), some mention will be made of discoveries of much later manuscripts (up to the sixteenth century) which are nevertheless of great significance for the study of literary works first written down in the period under review. Furthermore we have, in some instances, the added problem of not knowing for certain whether a particular manuscript is of Jewish or of Christian provenance, or whether the origins of a particular work can be traced back to the period we are studying or not. With these provisos this survey will cover the following types of literature: biblical, apocryphal and pseudepigraphal, liturgical, subliterary, nonliterary (including inscriptions), and finally a brief glance at some non-Jewish manuscript discoveries of significance for the study of Judaism in this period. The languages involved are Hebrew, Aramaic, and Greek. As will become apparent, "discoveries" do not necessarily involve new manuscripts; in some instances they consist of identifications of manuscripts that have long been lying unexploited in Western libraries.

JEWISH BIBLICAL TEXTS

The last three and a half decades have witnessed major finds of Jewish biblical manuscripts in three different languages—Hebrew, Aramaic, and Greek—as a result of which it has become possible to gain totally new insights into the way in which the texts of the Hebrew Bible and of its daughter versions in Greek and Aramaic have been transmitted to us. In the present section we shall attempt to draw attention to some of the more important finds.

The new textual materials, which date from the third century B.C.E.

to the sixteenth century C.E., derive from five main sources: (1) the Judean Desert (Qumran, Masada, Murabbaʿat, Naḥal Ḥever), (2) Egyptian sands, (3) Cairo Geniza, (4) Western libraries, and (5) inscriptions. Before these finds are examined by language groupings (and the inscriptions separately) a few words should be said about the first three of these sources. The rich biblical materials from the Judean Desert (including fragments from about two hundred biblical manuscripts ranging in date from the third century B.C.E. to the second century C.E.) have received a great deal of attention (though some important materials still await publication), and a convenient inventory can be found in Fitzmyer (see also the bibliography of the preceding chapter). Whereas the finds from the Judean Desert do not antedate the *terminus a quo* for this volume (1945), discoveries of fragmentary biblical manuscripts (mostly Christian, but some Jewish), usually on papyrus and from Egypt, go back to the end of the nineteenth century, and invaluable inventories of this Greek material up to ca. 1975 have now been made by K. Aland, who covers biblical manuscripts, including Jewish — despite the title — and J. van Haelst, who treats biblical and literary papyri (for the relationship between the two works, see Skeat, 1978). The Geniza biblical material, the discovery of which again goes back well before 1945, has been less intensively studied. Attention has been focused primarily on the vocalization systems these manuscripts contain, and, although P. Kahle made considerable use of Geniza manuscripts in the apparatus to *Biblia Hebraica* (3d ed., 1937), there is room for much work in this area. For example, no complete inventory either for Hebrew or for Aramaic biblical manuscripts yet exists. Much information on this scattered and fragmentary material can be found in Chiesa; Davis; Díez Macho, 1971; Díez Merino; and Revell.

Hebrew

Before 1945 the only known early Jewish biblical manuscript in Hebrew was the Nash papyrus. Otherwise, the earliest fragments (from the Cairo Geniza) dated only from the last centuries of the first millennium C.E., and the earliest complete manuscripts were from the tenth century. The discoveries in the Judean Desert have now completely revolutionized the picture. For the first time we are in possession of quite extensive materials predating the fixing of the consonantal text sometime around 100 C.E. This has allowed scholars to sketch out, at least in tentative form, the history of the biblical text in its fluid state during the centuries immediately preceding the stabilization and fossilization of the consonantal text in the form with which we are familiar, which has been transmitted to us by the entire medieval manuscript tradition.

It is the very variety of the textual traditions represented at Qumran that is most instructive. Particularly important are the very fragmentary texts of Samuel and Jeremiah from Cave 4, as yet not fully published (see Janzen, Ulrich), which exhibit a Hebrew text with affinities to that presupposed by the LXX. This lends renewed respectability to the careful use of the LXX for the textual criticism of the Hebrew Bible—a much-needed corrective, since biblical scholarship of the 1930s and 1940s had overreacted against the use (admittedly sometimes uncritical) made of the LXX by scholars of the late nineteenth and early twentieth century. In a few instances we can actually observe how changes in the textual alignment of biblical manuscripts came to be made: thus the first hand of 5QDeut copied a text almost identical to the traditional consonantal text, but a second hand inserted here and there supralineal readings which bring the text into line with the slightly variant textual tradition that underlies the LXX.

Although the importance of the Qumran biblical manuscripts lies primarily in the light they shed on the transmission of the Hebrew Bible, a few are also of considerable significance for the history of the Hebrew language and its orthography (notably 1QIsa^a, studied by E. Y. Kutscher) or for the literary prehistory of certain biblical texts or collections (e.g., 11QPss, 4QPs89, and 4QPrNab, which so neatly confirms the conjecture, first made in 1902, that behind the Nebuchadnezzar of Daniel 4 there must lie traditions originally connected with Nabonidus).

It is only natural that the finds of biblical manuscripts from the Judean Desert (including Masada, Murabbaʿat, Naḥal Ḥever, as well as Qumran) should have stolen the limelight. If it were not for these finds, relatively more attention would have been paid to the fact that fragments of biblical scrolls in Hebrew, written on leather, have also been found in Egypt at Antinoopolis. According to their editor, W. D. McHardy, these date from sometime between the third and the sixth century C.E.

Greek Manuscripts of Jewish Scripture (LXX, Old Greek)

The obvious fact that the LXX originated as a Jewish version of the Bible is often unconsciously forgotten. Before 1945 only one fragment of a pre-Christian (and hence definitely Jewish) manuscript of the Greek Jewish scriptures was known (*P. Rylands Gr.* 248, second century B.C.E.). Since then, however, several new Jewish manuscripts have turned up. By far the most important, because of the implications for the early textual history of the Greek Bible suggested by the revision of the Old Greek which it contains, are the fragments from Naḥal Ḥever of the Twelve Prophets (Rahlfs MS 943), which received preliminary publication and brilliant interpretation by D. Barthélemy (the final publication, with full photographs, is still awaited; further fragments were published by B. Lifshitz, 1962). The manuscript probably dates from between ca. 50 B.C.E. and 50 C.E.; a good outline and critique of Barthélemy's revolutionary hypothesis can be found in Kraft.

From Egypt, fragments of three further Jewish manuscripts dating to the turn of the Christian era are now available (*P. Fuad Inv.* 266), containing parts of Genesis (Rahlfs MS 942) and especially Deuteronomy (Rahlfs MSS 847 and 848); the readings of these fragments (published by F. Dunand and Z. Aly) are now incorporated into the recent editions of Genesis and Deuteronomy in the Göttingen LXX. Yet other fragments of Jewish Greek biblical manuscripts have been found at Qumran, which contain portions of Exodus (7QLXXExod = Rahlfs MS 805), Leviticus (4QLXXLev[a,b] = Rahlfs MSS 801, 802), Numbers (4QLXXNum = Rahlfs MS 803), and the Letter of Jeremiah (7QLXXEpJer = Rahlfs MS 804). Manuscripts 801, 803, and 805 contain texts that point to activity on the part of scribes who "corrected" their LXX text on the basis of the Hebrew original, an activity that was to culminate in the early second century C.E. in the *ekdosis* of Aquila, whose work, it now appears, was a radical revision of the available Old Greek materials rather than a completely new translation.

With manuscripts of the Jewish Greek scriptures from the early Christian period it is often difficult to discern which are Jewish and which Christian. The use of contracted forms for *nomina sacra* and of the codex format are considered to be fairly certain indications of Christian provenance (see Roberts: 74–78). On the whole it seems likely that we now possess at least a few Jewish manuscripts of the Old Greek Bible that postdate the commencement of the Christian era.

Aquila, Theodotion, and Symmachus

According to Barthélemy, the author of the revision of the Old Greek contained in the Naḥal Ḥever Twelve Prophets fragments is none other than Theodotion, whose traditional dating to the second century C.E. should accordingly be corrected. However, there still remains a good deal of uncertainty surrounding the interrelationship of the various texts and readings attributed to Theodotion. The Naḥal Ḥever manuscript represents the only find for Aquila, Theodotion, or Symmachus in a manuscript earlier than our strict limit of ca. 200 C.E. Since, however, important material in much later manuscripts has come to hand, at least passing mention should be made of this as well. Although discovered at the end of the nineteenth century, it was only in 1958 that the famous Milan fragments of the Hexapla Psalter were published in a magnificent edition by G. Mercati. Other "finds" of new material containing excerpted readings of Aquila, Theodotion, and Symmachus are all derived from catenae or marginalia in other medieval manuscripts. The most extensive collection of such readings is that made by A. Schenker for the Psalter. A few further readings of Aquila, from Geniza manuscripts, have been published by H.-P. Rüger and N. de Lange.

Another important collection of new readings of "the Three" is to be found in a rather late manuscript of the Syrohexapla Pentateuch, found in southeast Turkey and variously dated to the twelfth or to the fifteenth century, which has been published in a photographic edition by A. Vööbus. This new material has not yet been fully excerpted and analyzed, although J. Wevers was able to draw upon it for his editions of Genesis, Numbers, and Deuteronomy in the Göttingen LXX.

Aramaic

Prior to the Qumran finds the only extant manuscripts of the Aramaic targums belonged to the Middle Ages (the oldest Geniza fragments going back perhaps to the eighth century). Today we have quite extensive parts of a targum of Job (11QtgJob) in a manuscript dating from the turn of the Christian era and a very small piece of another manuscript of the same book (4QtgJob). It is possible that this targum may be the one referred to with disapproval by R. Gamaliel the Elder (early first century c.e.); it is totally unrelated to the printed targum of Job which is based on late medieval manuscripts. Another possible targum fragment is 4Q156, which contains some verses from Leviticus, but it is too brief to permit certainty and it might just as well belong to a liturgical work for the Day of Atonement.

Finds of other targum materials all involve medieval manuscripts. Best known is the discovery, announced in 1956, that ms 1 of the Neophyti library in Rome contained not *Targum Onqelos*, as had previously been assumed, but a Palestinian targum (*Targum Yerushalmi*) of the entire Pentateuch. Although claims that this manuscript (dated 1504) represents a targum of the first or second century in a dialect that would have been used by Jesus must be discounted, the discovery is nevertheless of great significance and has led to a new impetus in targum studies. The text, with its important marginalia, which represent a slightly different recension of the Palestinian targum tradition, has now been fully published in a sumptuous edition by A. Díez Macho (with Spanish, French, and English translations).

Several other, much less dramatic, finds of new Palestinian targum materials have been made in Western libraries, and a collection of this material has been promised by M. L. Klein, who has already provided an important republication of the *Fragmentary Targum* manuscripts. An identification that has interesting implications for the prehistory of certain poetic passages incorporated into Palestinian targum manuscripts was recently made by J. Yahalom, who pointed out that the *piyyut* "Go, Moses . . ." in the *Fragmentary Targum* (Exodus 14) was to be found in an Aramaic papyrus fragment from Egypt, dating from the fourth/fifth century c.e.

Finally, mention should be made of the new edition of the *Samaritan*

Targum, based on the oldest manuscripts available (early medieval). Volume 1, containing Genesis and Exodus, appeared in 1980, and volume 2, Leviticus to Deuteronomy, appeared in 1981, both edited by A. Tal.

Other Finds of Biblical Texts

Biblical texts are not only to be found in manuscripts written on papyrus, leather, or parchment; a third-century ostracon, possibly of Jewish origin, in fact happens to be the earliest extant witness to the text of Judith (Rahlfs MS 999). Already before 1945 a number of Samaritan inscriptions containing the text of the Decalogue in Hebrew were known, and since then several further examples have come to light. Of much greater interest, however, is another Samaritan inscription of the fourth century C.E. found in Saloniki (Greece), which contains the text of Num 6:22–27 in Greek together with two benedictions in Hebrew (Lifshitz and Schiby). As E. Tov has subsequently pointed out, the Greek text represents a "revised" LXX text.

Another unexpected epigraphic find is that of a mosaic inscription, consisting of Greek quotations from Judges, from a fifth-century building, which may be either a synagogue or a church, at Mipsis (ancient Mopsuestia in Cilicia). This has been discussed in particular by R. Stichel.

APOCRYPHA AND PSEUDEPIGRAPHA

The title is unsatisfactory but convenient, and here again we are faced with problems of demarcation. The vast majority of new finds of manuscripts dating from 300 B.C.E. to 200 C.E. are fragments in Hebrew and Aramaic from Qumran, of works previously known and unknown. Very little new material in Greek has become available in papyri, and some of this in fact stems from identifications of texts that had been published long before. Both these categories are considered briefly below. A great deal of energy in postwar years has been devoted to the reediting of known apocrypha and pseudepigrapha (in several cases it is difficult to determine whether a particular work is originally of Jewish or of Christian provenance) on the basis of much wider manuscript and versional attestation. A good survey of this material is Denis; a new edition, with much fuller coverage of the oriental and Slavic materials, is in preparation. For reasons of space no further reference to this important sphere of activity will be made here.

Discoveries of New Manuscripts

Here virtually all the new material comes from Qumran, from which we have numerous, but mostly very fragmentary, manuscripts. These contain either books previously known primarily from Greek or other translations, such as Tobit, *Jubilees,* and *Enoch,* or entirely new works, such as the comparatively well-preserved *Genesis Apocryphon.* In the former category particular importance attaches to the fragments of Ben Sira, from both Qumran and from Masada, since it now becomes clear that the Geniza fragments of this book (and of the *Damascus Document* and the *Testament of Levi*) must have been copied from manuscripts descended from those found in the Qumran area around 800 c.e. (see Di Lella). One of the more astonishing discoveries, made by J. T. Milik (1971a), was that among the fragments of the Enoch cycle found at Qumran were parts of the Book of the Giants (a "book" absent from the *Ethiopic Enoch*), which had hitherto been known only from some Manichean fragments found in central Asia earlier this century and written in a Middle Iranian dialect.

Identifications of Published Texts

Here a few identifications deserve mention: (1) fragments of the otherwise lost *Book of Jannes and Jambres* (Maraval; additional fragments of this work that have recently come to light are to be published by A. Pietersma); (2) fragments of a text related to *Jubilees* and preserved in Syriac (Brock); and (3) fragments of *Enoch* (Milik, 1971b).

Geniza Texts

Although none of the Geniza manuscripts dates from earlier than the end of the first millennium c.e., three publications in particular contain new texts that are of interest for the study of early postbiblical Judaism, even though the texts themselves were probably only committed to writing in the Talmudic period. *Sepher ha-Razim,* or *Book of Secrets,* published by M. Margalioth, is a book of magic lore that purports to have been transmitted to Noah by the angel Raziel. S. Hopkins's *Miscellany of Literary Pieces from the Cambridge Genizah Collections* includes a variety of pseudepigraphical fragments such as the *Apocalypse of Zerubbabel,* the *Scroll of Antiochus,* and the *Alphabet of Ben Sira,* as well as some leaves of Tobit in Hebrew. Further texts of some of these, as well as other similar works, are to be found in S. A. Wertheimer's *Batei Midrashot.*

LITURGICAL AND SUBLITERARY TEXTS

Liturgical

Before 1945 the only Jewish liturgical texts preserved in manuscripts of the Roman period were some very fragmentary Hebrew and Aramaic papyri and the Hebrew *P. Dura* 11. It is possible that the Nash papyrus should be classified as liturgical rather than biblical. The texts from Egypt are listed by M. Beit Arye (10 n. 3; for the identification of one of these see the section above entitled "Aramaic"). The only new Hebrew papyri from

Egypt (as opposed to leather, for which see the section above entitled "Hebrew") are some very fragmentary texts of uncertain character, published by F. Díaz Esteban. Numerous fragments from Qumran have now vastly increased the material available in these two languages (see chap. 5). In Greek the only addition consists of some fragments of a prayer against evil spirits, published by P. Benoit. (For some Greek texts claimed as Jewish but probably Christian, see Roberts: 74–78.)

Onomastica

Although it is likely that Philo already had access to onomastica explaining the meaning of Hebrew proper names, the earliest extant onomasticon had previously been a papyrus fragment in Heidelberg of the third or fourth century. To this has now been added a slightly more extensive fragment, *P. Oxyrhynchus* 2745, of approximately the same date (published by D. Rokeah).

Magic Bowls

Magic bowls of uncertain date (perhaps late Sassanian), inscribed in Mandean, Jewish Aramaic, and Syriac, have long been known. The number of bowls of Jewish provenance has now been increased by several new items (published by Franco, Kaufman, Smelik, and McCullough), and a corpus of seventy-two texts (the majority discovered before 1945) has been assembled by C. D. Isbell in a volume that needs to be used with caution. Their interest lies not only in the light they shed on popular beliefs but also in the links they have with the Enochic literature (see Greenfield).

NONLITERARY TEXTS

On Papyrus, Leather, Ostracon, etc.

Here it will be most convenient to list the main finds according to location.

Wadi ed-Daliyeh

Although they date from the fourth century B.C.E., the "Samaria papyri," discovered by Bedouin in a cave in Wadi ed-Daliyeh, north of Jericho, in 1962 should be mentioned. According to the preliminary report by F. M. Cross, these are administrative documents mentioning, among others, a Sanballat who is to be identified as the grandson of the Sanballat mentioned in Nehemiah. Despite their very fragmentary character, these texts are of prime importance for the little-known history of this period. The language is Aramaic, but the script, fourth-century cursive. They still await publication.

Masada

Excavations carried out in 1963–65 uncovered a number of texts left by the Zealot garrison from the time of the first Jewish revolt. Of the biblical manuscripts, the quite extensive fragments of Ben Sira have already been mentioned. Besides a few nonbiblical literary texts (including a fragment of the *Angelic Liturgy* known from Qumran Cave 4), there are more than two hundred ostraca inscribed in Hebrew and Aramaic. These have yet to be published (for a preliminary report, see Yadin, 1965).

Murabbaʿat

Caves in Wadi Murrabaʿat, some eleven miles south of Qumran, excavated in 1952, produced texts ranging in date from seventh/eighth century B.C.E. to the eleventh century C.E. To the period here under consideration belong the following materials, published by Benoit, Milik, and R. de Vaux: a few biblical texts (early second century C.E.); two nonbiblical literary fragments, one Hebrew (a hymn?), the other Aramaic (a narrative text on an ostracon); legal texts in Hebrew, Aramaic, and Greek (republished with commentary by Koffmahn); and various Hebrew letters belonging to the time of the second revolt. Of these the legal documents and the letters are by far the most important because of the scarcity and the usually hostile nature of the sources for the second revolt. Now for the first time we have documentation from the participants themselves, and two of the letters are from none other than the leader of the revolt, Bar Kokhba (whose real name is now shown to have been Simeon bar Kosiba). The legal texts (several of which are precisely dated) likewise fill in a gap in our knowledge of Jewish legal history in the first and second centuries of the Christian era.

Naḥal Ḥever

Exploration of the caves in the wadis southwest of En Gedi, in 1960–61, brought to light a number of fragmentary texts written on papyrus, parchment, leather, wood, and ostraca, dating mostly from the first to second century C.E. Among these, two groups of texts found in the "Cave of Letters" in Naḥal Ḥever are of particular importance: some further letters and documents (in Hebrew, Greek, and Aramaic) concerning Bar Kokhba; and a documentary archive (in Aramaic, Greek, and Nabatean) concerning Babatha, daughter of Simeon. The Bar Kokhba archive not only adds very significantly to our knowledge of the course of the second revolt, but it also sheds interesting light on the use of different languages at this time. The Hebrew letters are of especial value for the study of the history of the Hebrew language in a transitional period and for a better understanding of the emergence of Mishnaic Hebrew. The rather well-preserved Babatha archive consists of thirty-five legal documents concerning this woman's family affairs over the years 93/4–132 c.e. Twenty-six of these are in Greek, six in Nabatean, and three in Aramaic. Thus far only a preliminary report concerning these dramatic finds has been given (Yadin, 1961, 1962). Like many other important, but fragmentary, texts discovered in the Judean Desert, these too clamor for publication.

Inscriptions

As far as Jewish inscriptions (in Hebrew, Aramaic, Greek, and [rarely] Latin) are concerned, the period under discussion has seen the publication of a number of important collections of materials, notably the Beth She'arim necropolis (Schwabe and Lifshitz; Avigad, 1976:230–58), ossuary and other inscriptions from Mount Olivet (Bagatti and Milik), graffiti and ostraca from the Herodion (Testa), and some Jewish pilgrim inscriptions from Wadi Haggag (Negev). Many other ossuary inscriptions dating from the turn of the Christian era have been published since 1945. Of particular interest is a collection from a family tomb in the Jewish necropolis of Jericho (see Hachlili, where references to other publications can be found).

Among the most interesting epigraphic finds outside Palestine is an inscription of the early third century b.c.e. from Oropos (Greece) concerning the manumission of "Moschos the Jew, son of Moschion," which constitutes the earliest evidence for Jews in Greece (see Lewis). The Samaritan synagogue inscription from Saloniki has already been mentioned. Further new evidence for Samaritans in Greece has recently come from a Samaritan amulet found at Corinth (Kaplan).

Useful collections (mostly of earlier finds) have appeared since 1945. The second volume of J.-B. Frey's *Corpus inscriptionum judaicarum* (Vatican City: Institute of Christian Archaeology) (covering Asia and Egypt) was published in 1952, and in 1975 the first volume (covering Europe) was reprinted with addenda and corrigenda by B. Lifshitz. Vol. 2 now requires considerable supplementation (in addition to the Egyptian materials covered by an appendix in Tcherikover and Fuks, vol. 3), especially for Palestine, from which a large variety of new inscriptions has subsequently turned up. Important Greek materials are to be found in Lifshitz, 1967, 1974, and newly published texts are noticed in due course in the *Supplementum Epigraphicum Graecum*. For Aramaic, J. A. Fitzmyer and D. J. Harrington provide a convenient collection, and synagogue inscriptions in Hebrew and Aramaic (but not those in Greek) are collected by J. Naveh (many of these, of course, belong to the later Roman period). For coin inscriptions the most important new publications are mentioned in Schürer-Vermes-Millar, Vol. 1, Appendix 4 (see further below, chap. 8).

Among the rather rare Jewish inscriptions of the Hellenistic period, the inscribed bulla of a high priest Jonathan (probably Alexander Jonathan Jannaeus), published by Avigad, could be singled out, since it is the first known seal impression of any of the Hasmoneans. Although it falls outside the time limit of this discussion, passing reference should be made to an extraordinary find (made in the Beth Shean valley, 1974) of a long seventh-century mosaic inscription in Hebrew. Its contents are entirely halakic, and almost all are paralleled in the Palestinian Talmud. Here we have a unique correlation between an inscription and a literary text (see Naveh: 79–85; Sussman).

SOME RELEVANT NON-JEWISH TEXTS

Finally, we should have a cursory glance at non-Jewish texts that have a bearing on Judaism of the Hellenistic and early Roman period. Of importance for chronological matters is the Babylonian king list of the Hellenistic period published by Sachs and Wiseman, and the publication of some prophetic texts, also in Akkadian, provides a significant background for Jewish apocalyptic (Grayson).

An astonishing discovery, which is likely to have wide repercussions, concerns *P. Amherst* 63 of the late fourth century B.C.E. This papyrus contains a fairly extensive collection of pagan Aramaic texts written in Demotic script, and among these S. P. Vleeming and J. W. Wesselius have identified a hymn that has close parallels with Psalm 20. The full publication of the manuscript, promised for 1984, is clearly going to be of great significance.

Papyri that mention Jews are now conveniently collected by V. Tcherikover and A. Fuks in their *Corpus Papyrorum Judaicarum*. Most of the texts included were first published before 1945, but among the few subsequent texts of relevance are some further Zenon papyri concerning Tobias (Skeat, 1974) and *P. Oxyrhynchus* 3021, another fragment of the pagan *Acta Alexandrina* (first century C.E.) that mentions Jews.

New evidence for the popularity of the *Wisdom of Ahiqar* in the Hellenistic period has come to light with a fragment of a Demotic text of Ahikar (who is mentioned in Tobit), which has recently been published by K.-T. Zauzich.

Something of the appeal that Judaism had among pagan intellectuals in the second century C.E. is indicated by the funerary inscription of the sophist Amphikles, recently studied by L. Robert (245–52).

The dramatic finds of Manichaica (mostly not published until after 1945) and Gnostica (from Nag Hammadi) have only indirect bearing on Judaism. We have already noted that the Manicheans read one of the *Enoch* texts (Book of the Giants), which turned out to be attested in Aramaic also at Qumran. What is termed the Apocalypse of Enoch is also quoted in the recently found Greek *Life of Mani*. Several of the new

Gnostic texts show the influence of Judaism—notably the *Apocalypse of Adam* (V), the *Paraphrase of Shem* (VII), the *Second Treatise of Seth* (VII), the *Three Stelai of Seth* (VII) and *Melkizedek* (IX)—but none directly originates from a Jewish milieu. Whether or not they can be used as evidence for a Jewish gnosticism remains hypothetical.

CONCLUSION

New finds rarely solve problems; rather they have a habit of showing that things were more diverse and complex than scholars had previously imagined. Just as the discovery of the literature of the Qumran community has opened up to our eyes an entirely new facet of Judaism, so too the finds of biblical manuscripts from the Judean Desert have revealed an unsuspected multiplicity of text forms current in Palestine around the turn of the era during the time immediately preceding the standardization of the consonantal text at the end of the first century c.e. Next in importance probably come the Bar Kokhba documents, which provide such direct sidelights on the obscure period of the second revolt. The remaining, less dramatic, textual finds of the last three and a half decades generally confirm the picture that is now emerging of the very rich variety of Jewish culture during the Hellenistic and early Roman period, when Semitic and Greek civilizations met and interacted in such diverse manners.

BIBLIOGRAPHY

Aland, Kurt
    1976   *Repertorium der griechischen christlichen Papyri. I, Biblische Papyri*. Patristische Texte und Studien 18. Berlin and New York: de Gruyter.

Aly, Zaki
    1980   *Three Rolls of the Early Septuagint, Genesis and Deuteronomy: A Photographic Edition*. Papyrologische Texte und Abhandlungen 27. Bonn: Habelt.

Avigad, Nahman
    1975   "A Bulla of Jonathan the High Priest." *IEJ* 25: 8–12.
    1976   *Beth She'arim: Report on the Excavations during 1953–58*. Vol. 3, *Catacombs 12–13*. New Brunswick, NJ: Rutgers University Press.

Bagatti, B., and J. T. Milik
    1958   *Gli scavi del "Dominus Flevit."* Parte 1, *La necropoli de periodo Romano*. Publicazioni dello Studium Biblicum Franciscanum 13. Jerusalem: Franciscan Printing Press.

Barthélemy, Dominique
    1963   *Les devanciers d'Aquila: Première publication intégrale du texte des fragments du Dodécaprophéton*. VTSup 10. Leiden: Brill.

Beit Arye, M.
1976   *Hebrew Codicology*. Paris: Centre National de la Recherche Scientifique.

Benoit, Pierre
1951   "Fragment d'une prière contre les esprits impurs?" *RB* 59: 549–65.

Benoit, Pierre, J. T. Milik, and Roland de Vaux
1960   *Les grottes de Murabba'at*. DJD 2. Oxford: Clarendon Press.

Brock, Sebastian P.
1978   "Abraham and the Ravens: A Syriac Counterpart to Jubilees 11–12 and Its Implications." *JSJ* 9: 135–52.

Chiesa, Bruno
1978   *L'Antico Testamento Ebraico secondo la tradizione palestinese*. Turin: Bottega d'Erasmo.

Cross, Frank M.
1963   "The Discovery of the Samaria Papyri." *BA* 26: 110–21.

Davis, M. C.
1978–80   *Hebrew Bible Manuscripts in the Cambridge Genizah Collection*. Vol. 1, *Taylor-Schechter Old Series*. Vol. 2, *New Series*. Cambridge: Cambridge University Library.

Denis, Albert-Marie
1970   *Introduction aux pseudépigraphes grecs d'Ancien Testament*. SVTP 1. Leiden: Brill.

Díaz Esteban, F.
1968   "Cuatro nuevos papiros hebreos postcristianos." *SPap* 7: 111–28.

Díez Macho, A.
1968–79   *Neophyti 1. Targum Palestinense ms. de la Biblioteca Vaticana*. 6 vols. Madrid: Consejo Superior de Investigaciones Científicas.
1971   *Manuscritos hebreos y arameos de la Biblia*. Studia Ephemeridis "Augustinianum" 5. Rome: Institutum Patristicum "Augustinianum."

Díez Merino, Luis
1975   *La Biblia Babilonica*. Madrid: the author.

Di Lella, Alexander
1966   *The Hebrew Text of Sirach*. The Hague: Mouton.

Dunand, Françoise
1971   "Papyrus grecs bibliques (Papyrus Fuad Inv. 266): Volumina de la Genèse et du Deutéronome." *Études de Papyrologie* 9: 81–150.

Fitzmyer, Joseph A.
1975   *The Dead Sea Scrolls: Major Publications and Tools for Study*. SBLSBS 8. Missoula, MT: Scholars Press.

Fitzmyer, Joseph A., and Daniel J. Harrington
1978   *A Manual of Palestinian Aramaic Texts*. BibOr 34. Rome: Biblical Institute Press.

Franco, F.
1978–79   "Five Aramaic Incantation Bowls from Tell Baruda." *Mesopotamia* 13/14: 233–49.

Grayson, A. K.
1975   *Babylonian Historical-Literary Texts*. Toronto and Buffalo: University of Toronto Press.

Greenfield, Jonas C.
1973 "Notes on Some Aramaic and Mandaic Magic Bowls." *JANESCU* 5: 149–56.

Hachlili, R.
1979 "The Goliath Family in Jericho: Funerary Inscriptions from a First Century A.D. Jewish Monumental Tomb." *BASOR* 235: 31–65.

Haelst, Joseph van
1976 *Catalogue des Papyrus littéraires juifs et chrétiens.* Paris: Publications de la Sorbonne.

Hopkins, Simon
1978 *A Miscellany of Literary Pieces from the Cambridge Genizah Collections.* Cambridge: Cambridge University Library.

Isbell, Charles D.
1975 *Corpus of the Aramaic Incantation Bowls.* SBLDS 17. Missoula, MT: Scholars Press.

Janzen, J. Gerald
1973 *Studies in the Text of Jeremiah.* HSM 6. Cambridge, MA: Harvard University Press.

Kaplan, J.
1980 "A Samaritan Amulet from Corinth." *IEJ* 30: 196–98.

Kaufman, Stephen A.
1973 "A Unique Magic Bowl from Nippur." *JNES* 32: 170–74.

Klein, Michael L.
1980 *The Fragment-Targums of the Pentateuch according to Their Extant Sources.* AnBib76. Rome: Biblical Institute Press.

Koffmahn, Elisabeth
1968 *Die Doppelurkunden aus der Wüste Juda.* STDJ 5. Leiden: Brill.

Kraft, Robert A.
1965 Review of Barthélemy (1963) in *Gnomon* 37: 474–83.

Kutscher, E. Y.
1974 *The Language and Linguistic Background of the Isaiah Scroll.* STDJ 6. Leiden: Brill.

Lange, Nicholas R. M. de
1980 "Some New Fragments of Aquila on Malachai and Job?" *VT* 30: 291–94.

Lewis, David M.
1957 "The First Greek Jew." *JSS* 2: 264–66.

Lifshitz, Baruch
1962 "The Greek Documents from the Cave of Horror." *IEJ* 12: 201–7.
1967 *Donateurs et fondateurs dans les synagogues juives.* Cahiers de la RB 7. Paris: Gabalda.
1974 "Varia Epigraphica." *Euphrosyne* 6: 23–48 = *Epigraphica* 36: 78–100.
1975 "Prolegomenon." Pp. 21–104 in J.-B. Frey, *Corpus Inscriptionum Iudaicarum*, Vol. 1. 2d ed. New York: Ktav.

Lifshitz, Baruch, and J. Schiby
1968 "Une synagogue samaritaine à Thessalonique." *RB* 75: 368–78.

McCullough, W. S.
1967   *Jewish and Mandaean Incantation Bowls in the Royal Ontario Museum.* Toronto: University of Toronto Press.

McHardy, W. D.
1950   Appendix in *Antinoopolis Papyri*, Vol. 1. Ed. C. H. Roberts. London: Egypt Exploration Society.

Maraval, P.
1977   "Fragments grecs du Livre de Jannès et Jambré." *Zeitschrift für Papyrologie und Epigraphik* 25: 199–207.

Margalioth, M.
1966   *Sepher ha-Razim: A Newly Discovered Book of Magic from the Talmudic Period.* Jerusalem: Yediot Acharonot Print (Hebrew).

Mercati, Giovanni
1958   *Psalterii Hexapla Reliquiae.* Vol. 1. *Codex rescriptus Bybliothecae Ambrosianae 0.39 supp. phototypice expressus et transcriptus.* Rome: Bybliotheca Vaticana.

Milik, J. T.
1971a   "Turfan et Qumran: Livre de Géants juif et manichéen." Pp. 117–27 in *Tradition und Glaube: Festgabe für K. G. Kuhn.* Göttingen: Vandenhoeck & Ruprecht.
1971b   "Fragments grecs du livre d'Henoch (P.Oxy.XVII.2069)." *Chronique d'Egypte* 46: 321–43.

Naveh, Joseph
1978   *On Stone and Mosaic: the Aramaic and Hebrew Inscriptions from Ancient Synagogues.* Jerusalem: Carta (Hebrew).

Negev, Abraham
1977   *The Inscriptions of Wadi Haggag, Sinai.* Qedem 6. Jerusalem: Institute of Archaeology.

Rahlfs, A.
1914   *Verzeichnis der griechischen Handschriften des Alten Testaments, für das Septuaginta-Unternehmen.* Berlin: Weidmann.

Revell, E. J.
1977   *Biblical Texts with Palestinian Pointing and Their Accents.* SBLMasS 4. Missoula, MT: Scholars Press.

Robert, Louis
1978   "Malédictions funéraires grecques." *CRAIBL:* 241–89.

Roberts, Colin H.
1979   *Manuscript, Society and Belief in Early Christian Egypt.* The Schweich Lectures 1977. London: British Academy.

Rokeah, David
1968   "A New Onomasticon Fragment from Oxyrhynchos and Philo's Etymologies." *JTS* n.s. 19: 70–82.

Rüger, Hans-Peter
1959   "Vier Aquila-Glossen in einem hebräischen Proverbien-Fragment aus der Kairo-Geniza." *ZNW* 50: 275–77.

Sachs, A. J., and Donald J. Wiseman
1954   "A Babylonian King-List of the Hellenistic Period." *Iraq* 16: 202–12.

Schenker, Adrian
1975　　　*Hexaplarische Psalmenbruchstücke: Die Handschriften Vaticanus graecus 752 und Canonicianus graecus 62.* OBO 8. Freiburg: Universitätsverlag; Göttingen: Vandenhoeck & Ruprecht.

Schürer, Emil
1973　　　*The History of the Jewish People in the Age of Jesus Christ.* Vol. 1. New English version revised and edited by G. Vermes and F. Millar. Edinburgh: T. & T. Clark.

Schwabe, Moshe, and Baruch Lifshitz
1967　　　*Beth She'arim.* Vol. 2. *The Greek Inscriptions.* Jerusalem: Israel Exploration Society (Hebrew).

Skeat, Theodore C.
1974　　　*Greek Papyri in the British Museum.* Vol. 7, *The Zenon Archive.* London: British Library Board.
1978　　　Review of Aland (1976) and van Haelst (1976) in *JTS* n.s. 29: 175–86.

Smelik, K. A. D.
1978　　　"An Aramaic Incantation Bowl in the Allard Pearson Museum." *BO* 35: 174–77.

Stichel, Rainer
1978　　　"Die Inschriften des Samson-Mosaiks in Mopsuestia und ihre Beziehung zum biblischen Text." *Byzantinische Zeitschrift* 71: 50–61.

Sussman, Y.
1974　　　"A Halakhic Inscription from the Beth Shean Valley." *Tarbiz* 43: 88–158, V–VII (Hebrew).

Tal, Abraham
1980–81　*The Samaritan Targum of the Pentateuch: A Critical Edition.* Vol. 1, *Genesis, Exodus.* Vol. 2, *Leviticus-Deuteronomy.* Tel Aviv: Tel-Aviv University Press.

Tcherikover, Victor A., and Alexander Fuks
1957–64　*Corpus Papyrorum Judaicarum.* 3 vols. Cambridge, MA: Harvard University Press.

Testa, E.
1972　　　*Herodion, IV, I graffiti e gli ostraca.* Jerusalem: Franciscan Printing Press.

Tov, Emanuel
1974　　　"Une inscription grecque d'origine samaritaine." *RB* 81: 394–99.

Ulrich, Eugene Charles
1978　　　*The Qumran Text of Samuel and Josephus.* HSM 19. Missoula, MT: Scholars Press.

Vleeming, S. P., and J. W. Wesselius
1982　　　"An Aramaic Hymn from the Fourth Century B.C." *BO* 39: 501–9.

Vööbus, Arthur
1975　　　*The Pentateuch in the Version of the Syro-Hexapla.* CSCO 369, Subsidia 45. Louvain: Sécrétariat du CSCO.

Wertheimer, S. A.
1980　　　*Batei Midrashot.* 2d ed. Jerusalem: Ktab waSepher.

Yadin, Yigael
    1961   "Expedition D." *IEJ* 11: 36–52.
    1962   "Expedition D: The Cave of Letters." *IEJ* 12: 227–57.
    1965   "The Excavations of Masada: The Documents and Inscriptions."
                IEJ 15: 103–14.
Yahalom, Joseph
    1978   "'Ezel Moshe'—according to the Berlin Papyrus." *Tarbiz* 47:
                173–84, III (Hebrew with English summary).
Zauzich, K.-T.
    1976   "Demotische Fragmente zum Ahikar Roman." Pp. 180–85 in *Folia
                Rara W. Voigt dedicata*. Ed. H. Franke, W. Heissig, W. Treue.
                Wiesbaden: Steiner.

7

ARCHAEOLOGY, ICONOGRAPHY, AND NONLITERARY WRITTEN REMAINS

Eric M. Meyers and A. Thomas Kraabel

The American quest to recover the material culture of ancient Palestine dates back to the pioneering explorations of Edward Robinson in 1838. But Robinson, like so many who followed him, was primarily interested in "biblical" or OT sites. The orientation and bias of American scholarship toward OT and ancient Near Eastern archaeology relating to Hebrew scripture, therefore, has existed from the beginning. It is only in recent times that this has been balanced by a more direct interest in and excavation of sites relating to the so-called postbiblical world of early Judaism and early Christianity.

With systematic survey of Palestine well under way by the 1880s, led by the British (Conder and Kitchener), French (Guerin), and Germans (Dever), it was but a matter of time before the significant relics of the Greco-Roman period began to receive the attention they deserved. The founding of the Palestine Exploration Society, and later the Israel Exploration Society, after the establishment of the State of Israel, enabled the emerging discipline of the archaeology of early Judaism to go forward at a pace commensurate with that in other disciplines. While W. F. Albright and his followers set about to refine an appropriate scientific method of excavation of Palestinian mounds, which led ultimately to the development of ceramic typology as a subdiscipline of archaeology, scholars like M. Avi-Yonah (Cassuto-Salzmann), B. Mazar (1973, 1975), and E. L. Sukenik (1932, 1934) sought to recover the remains of the major Jewish synagogue sites and burial centers and to refine our topographic understanding of Eretz Israel in Roman Palestine. Studies on Jewish art in relation to oriental art, the development of synagogue architecture and furnishings, and Jewish burial customs all contributed to a growing awareness of the newly revealed data from excavation and chance finds. The study of Jewish numismatics also received new and concentrated efforts during this formative period (see chap. 8).

On occasion, the general phrase "talmudic archaeology" is used to refer to the study of the artifactual heritage of Greco-Roman Palestine, but the Talmud as a literary document of the amoraic sages did not come into existence until around 400 C.E. in its Palestinian form and around 500 C.E. in its Babylonian form; the time from 200 B.C.E. to 400 C.E. can hardly be referred to as a period of "talmudic Judaism." Thus, we prefer a term coined by G. Ernest Wright, "the archaeology of early Judaism," within which we may also include the Diaspora.

175

The development of the Palestinian arm of this field was in the main uninfluenced by American scholarship until after the 1967 Six-Day War when the American Schools of Oriental Research decided to field the joint expedition to Khirbet Shema' (Meyers, Kraabel, and Strange), subsequently known as the Meiron Excavation Project, and the joint excavation of Caesarea Maritima. Outside Palestine, excavations at Dura Europos, Jerash, Sardis, Stobi, and Ostia greatly illuminated the material culture of Judaism in those diverse lands; all of these efforts have been American except for the Italian work at Ostia. Recent Israeli excavations in the Golan Heights (Syria), especially at Qisrin and Gamala, have been extremely productive, but full publication of this material is still in the distant future (Urman, 1976, Levine, 1981a). This work has unfortunately not been widely disseminated in American circles, though several recent dissertations will help to rectify this situation (Urman, 1979).

With such a record of field work and with so great an accumulation of new material, one might assume that a different kind of scholarship has emerged today which takes into account both nonliterary remains and epigraphic discoveries as well as literary evidences. However, it is fair to say that a wide gap still separates archaeologists from students of the written evidence; little cross-fertilization characterizes the field. Though E. R. Goodenough elevated the questions of the relevance of the data from material culture to a place of singular importance (Goodenough, 1953–68), he did not turn the state of affairs around as he had hoped he would. Perhaps because of his strong theories of interpretation, perhaps because of the sheer weight of the evidence with which he worked, the distance between these two kinds of historical inquiry is still great today.

To say, therefore, that a methodological consensus exists today among those who would like to bring texts and monuments into closer dialogue is to be overly optimistic. But it can be argued that the recent quest for the recovery of the "social history" of ancient Judaism is available only within such a framework. No one today would discuss the Dead Sea community without recourse to the archaeology of Qumran. Yet some social historians of early Judaism or of early Christianity continue to view Jerusalem of the first century as if it were in an archaeological vacuum, or as if it were as abstruse as the "heavenly" Jerusalem. Nothing could be farther from reality. This brief résumé of material remains from Palestine and the Diaspora is presented with the methodological assumption that the historians' task requires an evaluation of *all* the evidence available to them, even if some of it does not fall within the often confining and narrow limits of their primary disciplines.

ARCHAEOLOGICAL SITES

Palestine

In assaying a field as all-embracing as the archaeology of Greco-Roman Palestine, one is faced with the dilemma of choosing that material which is best suited to illustrate the integrative historical-archaeological approach suggested above. All the data cannot be presented, and thus the highlights offered here are intended merely to indicate the wide array of new materials available to the historian of early Judaism and to suggest a meaning and context for understanding them.

The following paragraphs reveal a strong emphasis on *regional* archaeology. This is due to the conviction, shared with nearly all field archaeologists, that future work must take into account the distinctive features of material culture region by region. Although there are obvious ties between the culture of one area and that of another, between Palestine and the Diaspora, each individual area or region can be said to be identifiable through the unique social, cultural, and economic influences that are operative in it. One region may be culturally dominated by several or more Hellenistic cities; another may be more attuned to the culture of surrounding villages. Here geography and political history may well provide the clues to understanding the particular cultural setting of a given area whose material culture, although part of the larger Greco-Roman cultural world, still reflects individual features of the local setting.

ASOR Upper Galilee Project

The authors undertook in 1970 the beginning of a long-term project to excavate ancient synagogues and their settlements in the context of a single geographical region, the Upper Galilee. To date, four sites have been excavated, three of which had been previously surveyed by the German team of H. Kohl and K. Watzinger. These four sites are Khirbet Shema‘ (Teqo‘a of Galilee), Meiron, Gush Halav (Giscala), and Nabratein (Niborayya).

Prior to this work most scholars believed that the development of the Palestinian synagogue proceeded along typological lines that were easily categorized and which fit neatly into a developmental chronological pattern (Meyers and Strange). Thus, the basilical synagogue was thought to be early (second-third century c.e.), the apsidal synagogue late (fifth century c.e.), and the broadhouse transitional (fourth century c.e.). The excavation and publication of Khirbet Shema‘ (Meyers, Kraabel, and

Strange) demonstrated the inadequacy of such a theory to accommodate
the variety of new evidence which contradicted that scheme. For example,
Khirbet Shema' turned out to be an "early" broadhouse, and Capernaum
a "late" basilica. Gush Halav was found to be a most unusual basilica
which survived late into the Byzantine era (mid-sixth century) (Meyers,
Strange, and Meyers, 1979). A different form of broadhouse synagogue
without interior columns was discovered simultaneously at Susiya, south of
Hebron, which was in continual use from the fourth to the ninth century
(Gutmann, Yeivin, and Netzer; Levine, 1981a).

The Upper Galilee Project also sought to recover the historical setting
of these sanctuaries. Several significant conclusions resulted. First, it took
about a century for Jews to relocate and adjust successfully in Galilee after
the two wars with Rome. Evidence is very sparse prior to the first century
C.E., when there was systematic renovation and rebuilding in the Middle
Roman period. Second, by the third century synagogues were being built
in most communities, and they were continuously repaired and rebuilt into
the late Byzantine era. Third, at Meiron and Nabratein, at least, there is
significant evidence that there was a systematic abandonment around the
time of the so-called revolt under Casesar Gallus (351–52 C.E.) until the
great earthquake of 363 C.E. Although the effects of this rebellion have thus
far not been documented for the entire region, the 350s must now be
reevaluated in view of these excavations (Meyers, Strange, Meyers, 1981).
Fourth, the Byzantine period is a surprisingly flourishing time for Upper
Galilee. The Gush Halav and Nabratein synagogues and settlements apparently prospered until the late sixth and the seventh century C.E. respectively. Fifth, the data from private houses indicate a highly developed
society that enjoyed the luxuries of fine imported ceramic household wares
and excellently made local glass. Finally, there is evidence both to corro-
borate traditional Jewish religious practice (e.g., ritual baths, study
houses) and to call it into question (e.g., pig bones, placement of tombs)
(Strange, 1979).

Franciscan Excavations

Capernaum. Surely one of the most controversial excavations of recent years has been that of Capernaum, an important Jewish and Christian
site on the northwestern shore of the Sea of Galilee. The major issues
surrounding this excavation are two: the proposed late dating for the
synagogue in the fourth-fifth centuries C.E. (Avi-Yonah, 1973; Loffreda,
1973), and the pluralistic nature of the community there (Strange, 1976b,
1977). The latter point relates to the placement of the synagogue literally
across the street from the octagonal Church of St. Peter, built over the
earlier remains of the house-church (Meyers and Strange: 128–30, 142–44).

Although the late dating of the synagogue has withstood strong criticism, it remains a central issue in the discussion of synagogal remains. In the main, the Israelis have maintained its earlier dating, relying mainly on art-historical considerations. The recent discovery of an earlier (first century) structure, however, may change the nature of the debate. The late chronology raises important issues that are still unresolved concerning the nature of relations between Jews and Christians (or Jewish Christians).

Magdala. The Franciscan excavations at Tarichaeae (Magdala) have also aroused great interest (Corbo). Originally, building D, a rectangular structure 8.16 m. by 7.25 m., was identified as a small synagogue and dated to the first century C.E. Located at the intersection of two well-paved Roman streets, equipped with five stone benches on the north wall, it forms a small basilica with nave and two aisles the length of the building. It has an aisle across its back, southern side as well (Strange, 1976a). Of special interest are the several heart-shaped corner columns, which are tradition-ally associated with synagogue structures. Many scholars have accepted the identification of the synagogue, but others suggest that it is rather an elaborate bath. Recently there has been a disposition even among the excavators to question the designations anew.

The Golan Synagogues

Since the Six-Day War in 1967 more than twenty-five synagogues have been positively identified in the Golan Heights. Two (Gamala and Qisrin) have been extensively excavated by the Israelis (Urman, 1976; Maoz, 1981b). Both survey (Kochavi; Meyers, Strange, and Groh, 1978) and excavation have demonstrated how integral the Golan Jewish community was to the community flourishing in Palestine in the Roman and Byzantine periods. Indeed, the types of synagogue found and the great variety of decorated architectural elements discovered underscore the vitality of com-munal life there. In general, these buildings and their decoration conform more with those uncovered in Upper Galilee. Similarly, the epigraphy associated with these remains is almost exclusively Hebrew and Aramaic.

One of the most significant aspects of the Jewish finds is their location alongside but separate from important Christian and pagan ruins. The juxtaposition of these several settlement patterns reinforces a picture of religious pluralism within distinct and apparently rigid geographical parameters (Urman, 1979). Recent investigations into the pagan and Christian epigraphy should shed light on this issue (Ovadiah, 1976).

The excavations at Gamala have presented convincing data to sub-stantiate Josephus's narrative of the Jewish struggle there against Rome in 70 C.E. (Shanks; Levine, 1981a; Gutmann, 1981a). They have also pro-duced an undisputed first-century synagogue. Its rectangular hall on the exterior measures 17 m. by 20.5 m. and is oriented NE by SW. Internally, it measures 15.1 m. by 9.6 m. Heart-shaped corner columns are to be found at each of the four corners. Two individual columns are proposed for both the north and the south between the heart-shaped columns, with four between them on the east and west. Four rows of benches surround the assembly hall except on the south, where they give way to a solitary entrance.

The importance of the Golan material cannot be overstressed. Unfortunately, there is still little published in English.

Other Synagogue Sites

Because of the paucity of published scientific reports it is best to summarize the state of synagogue study and make reference to the new standard handbook on Palestinian synagogue sites, the Tübingen Atlas (Hüttenmeister and Reeg), and to another recent catalogue of synagogue art and architecture organized by regions (Chiat, 1982). These two publications provide basic comparative data and full bibliography for most Jewish sites in Palestine. The Israel Exploration Society's most recent collection of essays on newly excavated synagogues rounds out the recent literature on this subject (Levine, 1981a). The new surveys make it unavoidable that any further study of Jewish sites must be informed by a consideration of regional differences which influenced both the architecture and decoration of synagogues, homes, etc., as well as the language associated with them (Meyers, 1976a). The colorful mosaics which characterize Hammath Tiberias (Dothan, 1983), Beth Shean, Naaran near Jericho, or Susiya near Hebron, are simply absent in the Upper Galilee or Golan, where the architecture, although it adheres closely to Roman and Byzantine patterns, is strongly influenced by the Syrian oriental style. Building plans do not conform to rigid patterns, but local planning which takes into account topography and town plan exerts a very strong influence.

The real question is to what extent the diversity attested in synagogue art and architecture might represent religious diversity in the Judaism of late antique Palestine. The new data do suggest that the variety of religious expression which characterizes pre–70 c.e. Judaism can be said to continue into the rabbinic period. Sensitivity to such regional differences will doubtless contribute substantially to the quest for an understanding of the religious pluralism of all of Palestine as well.

Beth She'arim

Of all the necropolises in ancient Palestine, none is more important than Beth She'arim in western Galilee, the traditional burial site both of sages and of common folk from all over the Diaspora until ca. 350 c.e. The published remains constitute the single most important resource for understanding the material culture of the rabbinic period (Mazar, 1973; Avigad, 1976). We are presented with a stunning array of sarcophagi decorated in the manner of the day, objects of everyday life, including wood and bone implements, glass, pottery, and metal objects of every kind. The inscriptions from these catacombs, nearly 80 percent of which are in Greek, provide entrée into the world of the rabbis as no other corpus of material does in all Palestine (Schwabe and Lifshitz).

The remains of Beth She'arim underscore the following aspects of Jewish life at the dawn of the Byzantine era: (1) the ascendancy of Greek language; (2) the subtle refinement of Jewish beliefs in afterlife to accommodate Greek ideas; (3) the continuing importance of Palestine in the mind of Diaspora Jews who are reburied here; (4) the adoption of oriental and pagan motifs in decoration as evidence of the provincial character of this center; and thus (5) the absorption by the rabbis and their people of the dominant Hellenistic-oriental culture of the day (Meyers and Strange).

Jericho

The recent excavations in the necropolis of Hellenistic-Roman Jericho provide extensive new evidence from tombs antedating the destruction in 70 C.E. (Hachlili, 1978, 1979). Not only do they make available an important new corpus of Jewish onomastics of the period, but they also throw light on the circumstances and time of the introduction of the wooden coffin into Palestine. The total reconstruction of one inlaid wood example, together with other specimens of wooden burial containers, finally corroborates the presence and influence of wooden prototypes in Jewish ossuaries and sarcophagi. Moreover, the Jericho tombs provide us with primary burials and secondary burials in a single context and thus clarify the Jewish custom of reburial (Meyers, 1971).

Excavations in Jericho proper conducted by E. Netzer (1974, 1977, 1978) show how data from the broader setting of the city itself can provide new insight into matters of everyday concern, which include irrigation, landscaping, bathing, industry, and general recreation. With the revelation of the winter palaces of the latter Hasmoneans and Herod the Great, no other site except Jerusalem or Masada provides the visitor and scholar with such an opportunity for grasping the realia of Palestinian culture at this time. The uncovering of so many *miqvaot* (ritual baths) of the latter Hasmoneans indicates a degree of ritual observance perhaps surprising. On another level, the proximity of the site to Jerusalem via the Wadi Kelt (ca. 13 mi.), accentuates the influence of topography and climate as factors in Judean history. This tropical watering spot set high in the Judean hills, so close to Jerusalem, not only enabled the Jewish leadership and elite to escape to the Jordan Valley for rest and recuperation but also offered a delightful haven for many others who sought to leave Jerusalem's urban setting and wintry weather.

The high level of sophistication revealed at Jericho, often reminiscent of other Herodian sites such as Masada or Herodium, provides a picture of a Jewish life that was more and more part of the cultural mainstream of the day. When the site of the winter palaces is viewed together with its nearby necropolis, however, it becomes apparent that strong elements of conservatism still linger on. Moreover, the proximity to Khirbet Qumran, home of the Dead Sea sectarians, affords a special opportunity to compare two disparate elements in society in a common physical setting. The contrast is revealing: the communal center of Qumran in its simple, quiet elegance; Jericho in its pure and unabashed opulence.

For other Herodian sites of significance, see the *Encyclopedia of Excavations in the Holy Land* (Avi-Yonah, 1975–78).

Jerusalem

The recent excavations in the city of Jerusalem now permit close observations of the setting of first-century Judaism at its very heart. The Jerusalem excavations, which began in 1967 and continue to this day in any number of forms, provide the basic new corpus of evidence for consideration (Yadin). Most remarkable, perhaps, is the image of the strikingly splendid area adjacent to the Temple enclosure, south and southwest of the Temple Mount (Mazar, 1975). Such a picture is also confirmed by the Jewish Quarter excavations of Avigad (1983) and those in the Armenian Quarter conducted by M. Broshi. Both confirm Pliny the Elder's description of the holy city as "by far the most famous city of the East, and not of Judaea only" (*Natural History* 5.15.70). As for the Temple itself, the words of the Gospel are most apt: "And some spoke of the temple, how it was adorned with noble stones and offerings" (Luke 21:5). The findings here indicate that the Herodian planners and builders made decisive changes in the topography of the Temple area, which enabled the elaborate structures in this area to be executed. They also make it probable that some of the work begun by Herod was still continuing at the eve of the first Jewish war with Rome.

It is the impression of the splendid and urban quality of Jerusalem, more than anything else, which has been a surprise to those who have followed these extensive excavations. The texts present Jerusalem as a center of national religious life, but if we were to rely upon the literary notices alone we would surely miss the urban and cosmopolitan character of this great city. It is, in fact, this feature which enables us now to comprehend the contrast with many of the rural areas that dotted the landscape not only of Judea but of Samaria and Galilee as well.

Conclusion

In attempting to highlight some of the new evidence uncovered in recent years and to identify new trends in the archaeology of Palestinian Judaism, we have perforce omitted a great deal. The bibliographical aids referred to will enable serious students to pursue further their special interests.

Several general conclusions may be observed. It may be noted that the introduction of the Hellenistic *polis* left a permanent mark on Palestinian society (Freyne: 101–54). In many ways the Greco-Roman period may be viewed as a dialogue between city and village, between the urban and rural. At first the cities were the sponsors of the new culture, as Jerusalem continued to be until it was made a pagan city in 135 C.E. But after a while other areas, such as the Rift Valley, surrounded by many cities, became closely identified with Hellenistic language, art, decorative style, and many other elements of Gentile civilization.

Perhaps the closer one lived to a Hellenistic *polis*, the more hellenized one was. Perhaps the relative isolation of the northern Upper Galilean hinterland and the Golan Heights is an adequate justification of its cultural simplicity. Still, trade and other east–west and north–south traffic made most of Palestine subject to the dominant cultural trends and modes of the day. It is important, therefore, to keep in mind the nature of the particular environment in which a particular site or artifact is located. The Jews of Ancient Syria-Palestine, like their Diaspora brethren were some city people and some village folk, and often the voices with which they speak suggest corresponding tensions and feelings.

The Diaspora

In contrast to the sites just described, the newer Jewish evidence from the western Diaspora (the rest of the Mediterranean world under Roman control, Palestine apart) comes, in the main, from substantial excavation projects concerned with extensive ancient environments. Earlier descriptions of "Diaspora Judaism" were often wonderfully sweeping and vague; that is no longer possible. The publications on each site described below will run into many volumes, only a fraction concerned with the Jewish population; these masses of evidence permit us to see the context of *particular* Diaspora communities with a clarity and detail never possible before. No less than in Palestine, there is a kind of regionalism here too, much of it depending on social historical factors beyond the scope of this survey (Kraabel, 1981). The discussion below presupposes for each location the overview and bibliography available from *The Princeton Encyclopedia of Classical Sites* (Stillwell); for additional bibliography and information on each synagogue, see Kraabel, 1979a.

Dura Europos

Dura Europos on the Syrian Euphrates was first excavated by Franz Cumont in 1922–23, and then as a joint undertaking of Yale University and the French Academy of Inscriptions and Letters from 1928 to 1937. The synagogue was discovered in 1932, its pictures provoking a number of interpretations, along with a many-sided discussion of the nature and origins of "Jewish art." It also stimulated E. R. Goodenough to move to the study of Jewish art and symbolism, which became his life's chief work. Dura's principal excavator has given a fascinating account of its discovery (Hopkins); Kraeling produced the official report on the synagogue; and Goodenough (1964) issued two volumes of text and a third of illustrations in his massive reinterpretation. The discussion continues: see Gutmann (1966, 1973, 1975) and, on Goodenough, Smith (1967) and Neusner (1975; Part III).

The Dura Jews are best known for their paintings, but the splendor of this folk art and its utility for larger questions of the history of art and of religion must not hide the evidence that the excavations provide for the *entire* life of a Diaspora Jewish community from the late Hellenistic period on. In addition to the pictures and the small building itself, in its two stages, there is some information about its furnishings, as well as twenty-two Aramaic, nineteen Greek, and sixteen Middle Iranian inscriptions.

Sardis

The new Jewish evidence from Sardis in western Asia Minor comes from the largest synagogue ever excavated, and perhaps the most substantial known from any ancient source. Its implications for iconography are discussed below under that heading.

The present expedition was begun in 1958 by G. M. A. Hanfmann. An overall account of the excavations is available in Hanfmann (1983), and a sector-by-sector summary in Hanfmann and Waldbaum. These two publications are presently the best sources of plans, photographs, and reconstruction drawings for the synagogue, discovered in 1962. A. R. Seager is chief author of the final publication, forthcoming in the series *Archaeological Exploration of Sardis*. For the relationship of the building to Diaspora Judaism, Christianity, and pagan piety, see Goodenough, 1965: 191–97; Kraabel, 1969, 1971, 1978; and Wilken.

The synagogue was previously a public secular basilica, a part of the municipal bath-gymnasium complex in the center of the Roman city (Seager, 1973). It came under the control of the large Jewish community in the late second century. The final interior plan dates from the fourth century. The distance from apse to front steps is nearly 100 m., the width nearly 10 m. The two major spaces are the main hall, 60 m. in length, and the atrium-like forecourt, over 20 m. long. (Furnishings are reviewed in the section below on iconography.) Over eighty inscriptions were recovered from the building; six—very fragmentary—are Hebrew, the rest Greek (Robert, 1964; see also Lifshitz, 1967).

In the context of the later Roman Empire, the Dura synagogue and its paintings appear exotic, even bizarre, whereas Sardis is much closer to the norm. The city itself is an old one, antedating the Trojan War, and during its long history was usually a political, economic, and intellectual center in the Gentile world. It also contained a strong, early Christian community, established about the middle of the first century. The Jewish community dates from the end of the third century B.C.E. It was wealthy and apparently powerful, and the present synagogue is the most recent of at least three it controlled. Even in its later history the Jewish community had much more to do with pagan Sardis than with local Christians (Kraabel, 1981).

There is no reason to suspect the Gentiles of Sardis of being particularly philo-Semitic; rather, this synagogue and its community may be seen as one typical kind of Jewish enclave in a Diaspora city under Rome. There are other models, Rome for example, where the Jews apparently enjoyed less wealth and prestige. The reasons for the differences between Jews in Sardis and in a city like Rome are socioeconomic and have to do also with the period in which the Jews arrive, as well as their status at that time: perhaps prisoners of war, sometimes prosperous merchants, or something in between. One's place of origin probably is a factor as well, though it is more difficult to determine. Thus, the earliest Jews in the Rome community appear to have come perhaps as prisoners from Palestine, but the first at Sardis were brought from exile communities in Babylonia and Mesopotamia, because the Seleucid ruler saw them as responsible and established people and a pacifying influence on this part of his empire.

Delos

The evidence for Jews on the Aegean island of Delos has recently been fully reviewed by P. Bruneau. If the first-century B.C.E. building on which he reports is actually a synagogue, it is the earliest excavated anywhere. But the identification is disputed because the iconography and other evidence are ambiguous, as might be expected from a synagogue so early. A. Plassart, the original excavator, considered it a synagogue. He was followed by E. L. Sukenik at first (1934) and by J.-B. Frey (CII, 726–31). Sukenik later reversed his position (1949) but did not convince Goodenough (1953), Lifshitz (1967), or Avi-Yonah (1971).

The Delos building is a complex of rooms in a residential area. The main room is 16.9 m. north–south, 14.4 m. east–west, but in a later stage it was divided with an east–west wall. Marble benches along the west wall are interrupted by a fine white marble throne, similar to the one provided for the priest of Dionysus in an ancient Greek theater. It is often identified as a "seat of Moses" (Matt 23:2). A series of small rooms was discovered south of the main room; a roofed portico runs north–south on the east.

The inscriptions are also ambiguous. The term *theos hypsistos* ("highest god") occurs in four ex-votos found in the building. This is a common designation for God in the LXX, but is not always to be taken as such, since it may refer to one or another pagan deity. In later times the term is avoided in Diaspora Jewish inscriptions lest it be misunderstood, but the individuals in Delos who set up these texts might well be using the terms as LXX language, oblivious to the danger of "syncretism"—indeed it could be argued that that danger is perceived only later, after the destruction of the Jerusalem Temple, as Judaism becomes even more decentralized and Diaspora Jews more sensitive to the religious language of their Gentile neighbors (Kraabel, 1969). Certainty is impossible at this point, but the identification of the Delos building as a synagogue is the most likely one. (New epigraphic evidence attests to the presence of a Samaritan community on Delos contemporary with the Delos synagogue; see Kraabel, 1984.)

Athens

A small piece of Pentelic marble revetment from Athens is the first architectural evidence that might come from a synagogue here. It bears an incised menorah, and, to the right, a palm branch or *lulav*. The fragment was discovered in the Agora excavations, which suggests that a synagogue may have stood in the very heart of this center of classical antiquity; it was found in the late fourth- to early fifth-century C.E. fill (Kraabel, 1979a).

Stobi

Systematic excavation of the synagogues of Stobi in southern Yugoslavia began in 1970 as a part of a joint Yugoslavian-American project headed by James R. Wiseman and Djordje Mano-Zissi (Wiseman). Important information had been available for four decades before that: in *CII* (694), a late third-century inscription in which the wealthy donor Klaudios Tiberios Polycharmos describes extensive construction work done at his expense on the synagogue and related structures; the "holy place," a *triklinion*, a *tetrastoon*, and "upper chambers" are all mentioned as parts of this complex (Hengel, 1966; Poehlmann).

The present excavators distinguish three buildings, one above another: a fifth-century basilica (a church, formerly misidentified as a synagogue), which by design supplants a fourth-century synagogue, below which is a still earlier synagogue. The middle building, the later synagogue, had a mosaic floor of geometric design and walls decorated with frescoes. The main room is approximately 7.9 m. by 13.3 m. A rectangular brick and concrete foundation, perhaps the base of a Torah shrine, stands against the east wall. A bench may have run along the south wall (Moe). The plan and mosaic immediately suggest the synagogue on the island of Aegina, near Athens, whose dimensions are nearly identical to that of Stobi (Kraabel, 1979a n. 9).

The earlier synagogue beneath had frescoed walls, but other features and dimensions are still unclear; references to Polycharmos in the fresco inscriptions make it probable that this building and the one described in *CII* 694 are the same.

After centuries of occupying the same site, the Jews of Stobi were dispossessed by local Christians in the fifth century. The archaeological data are evidence for Christian power in Stobi in late antiquity but also for a Jewish presence of some duration and wealth for most of the Roman period previous.

Ostia

Ostia, the port of ancient Rome, has been under systematic investigation for over a century. The synagogue was discovered and excavated in 1961–62 (Floriani Squarciapino, 1963). The building as restored dates to the fourth century; like the buildings at Dura, Delos, and Stobi, it is a complex of rooms, with the overall dimensions 36.6 m. by 23.5 m. The synagogue proper is 24.9 m. by 12.5 m. and includes an entrance area, a four-columned gateway, and the main hall; immediately south are a kitchen and dining hall.

Two phases are attested for the synagogue proper. In the earlier there were three doors into the main hall, the center one framed by two pairs of columns, set in a square pattern. A permanent *bēma* occupied the wall opposite this entrance. The *bēma*-wall is curved, which suggests that the room was built as a synagogue, not (as at Sardis) converted from some other use. The later stage of this building is attested by the massive Torah shrine which now dominates the reconstructed building. It is a kind of off-center apse, built of regular courses of brick and tufa-block, which completely blocks the southernmost of the three entrances to the main hall; that is, it is at the *back* of the main hall, on the east wall, opposite the *bēma*. It immediately recalls the two shrines added to the *back* of the Sardis synagogue. Beneath this fourth-century building the excavator has identified an earlier structure of similar plan, which she believes is an earlier synagogue, of the first century.

Discussion of the Ostia evidence has all but ceased in the past decade, but increased clarity will likely come from a more comprehensive study of the Jewish communities of ancient Italy, similar to that done for western Asia Minor (Kraabel, forthcoming). Such a project may be beginning with Venosa (see below). The extensive archaeological evidence for Rome is summarized in Leon, 1960; see also the relevant sections of Goodenough

and more recently Kraabel, 1979b. Lifshitz (1975) provides further information and new data on the Jewish inscriptions of Rome and the rest of
Italy.

Venosa

Renewed interest in the Jewish catacombs of Venosa, the site of
Horace's Venusia, date to the visit in 1951 of H. J. Leon, a classicist whose
main interest had been the Jewish catacombs in Rome. His work at Venosa
(Leon, 1953–54) consisted mainly of checking the fifty inscriptions published by Frey in *CII* and offering new suggestions on readings of both the
dipinti and *graffiti*. The Venosa texts, although overwhelmingly Greek,
attest to an increased usage of both Latin and Hebrew by Jews of the later
periods. The inscriptions are chiefly from the fourth through the seventh
centuries C.E. Similarly, the Venosa sepulchral formulas demonstrate important differences from those in Rome and these find some parallels in
ancient Palestine, Beth She'arim, and elsewhere in the eastern Mediterranean world.

More recent explorations, inspired by natural collapses and vandalism
have led to some new inscriptional evidence (Colafemmina, 1975) as well
as new data on the plan of the catacombs (Colafemmina, 1974, 1978; Dell
'Aquila). The excitement surrounding Colafemmina's discovery of a frescoed
arcosolium tomb (1975b), featuring a large candelabrum, *lulav*, *ethrog*,
and incense shovel, has generated much new interest in these catacombs.
Colafemmina and E. M. Meyers conducted a new survey in October 1980.
A plan to excavate new catacombs under joint American (World Jewish
Congress: Heritage Committee) and Italian (University of Bari: Institute
of Christian Archaeology) auspices has been initiated and approved, and
the first campaign was conducted in May 1981 (Colafemmina, 1981;
Meyers, 1983).

The 1980 survey produced one important new piece of evidence: an
architectural cornerstone with a feline in bas relief, accompanied by a long
Hebrew inscription. Found in the town of Venosa, it provides the first
documentary evidence of Jewish life there; previous data had come exclusively from the catacombs beyond the town limits. It remains to be seen
whether this piece is from a synagogue or public building of some kind.
Cursory study of the script suggests a late fourth- or fifth-century date. The
fact that the cemetery includes Jewish and Christian catacombs in close
proximity suggests a peaceful coexistence at least until the early medieval
period, ca. the seventh century.

Cyrenaica

The archaeological evidence for the Jews of ancient Cyrenaica in
North Africa is of a wholly different sort, relating to the Jewish uprising

there in 115–117. It is collected and subjected to a kind of proto-Zionist interpretation by S. Applebaum (1979). The data are the evidences of the destruction of Gentile sites, particularly in the city of Cyrene, dated to this period. The preoccupation of the emperor Trajan with military campaigns in Dacia, Parthia, and Mesopotamia had the effect of encouraging the revolt of hostile forces elsewhere, for example, in northern Britain; and in his last years the Jews in Cyrenaica, Cyprus, and the often-volatile Egypt attacked their Gentile neighbors, with the result that thousands died on both sides, particularly after Roman armies entered the battle. It is this story that Applebaum tells, concentrating on Cyrenaica and the archaeological evidence for the demolition of pagan temples and other Gentile property there. These Jews, landless and dispossessed, differ greatly from those of Dura or Sardis; Diaspora Judaism was never monolithic. Applebaum pulls the archaeological and literary evidence together and tells their story well, but his emphasis on the movement as messianic and apocalyptic gives insufficient weight to its nonreligious causes.

Priene

At the end of the nineteenth century, German excavators working on Priene, a Hellenistic and Roman city on the west coast of Asia Minor, identified a certain small structure as a Christian "house-church," although they noted that the tiny apse was so small as to provide room for "only one priest" (Wiegand and Schrader). Two incised menorahs which they found in the room make it clear that the "apse" is in fact a Torah niche and the "church" a synagogue. In all probability a great deal of unknown archaeological evidence for Diaspora Judaism has already been excavated, but through misidentification some of it has been lost forever. The rest remains to be discovered again in the records and reports of other "Prienes." Some present "Jewish" evidence will doubtless be lost too, like the building in Stobi once called the "synagogue of Polycharmos" but now seen to be a fifth-century Christian basilica. In the next decades, the increasingly cooperative efforts of classicists, archaeologists, and historians of religion may be expected to produce a substantially more comprehensive and coherent picture of the Diaspora communities whose present evidence is sampled here.

ICONOGRAPHY

In the examination of ancient Judaism and ancient Christianity from the standpoint of religious studies, previous discussion of iconography has been dominated by authoritative statements from the Bible, the rabbis, and the church fathers. The archaeological evidence is slowly forcing a change. For Judaism at least, it is becoming obvious that what the rabbinic leadership might say about, for example, the art of the ancient synagogue need not be more than the view of a small group, one lacking an influential role in synagogue life (Neusner, 1968, 1975). American students of rabbinic literature are already sorting out the implications of these data for their texts. The purpose of this section is to review the nontextual evidence presently available.

Dura

The pivotal "artifact" is the synagogue of Dura, a small fortified city on the Euphrates, destroyed in 256 c.e. The biblical paintings preserved on the synagogue walls reveal Jewish iconography of late antiquity in the most vivid and direct fashion. They are from the later synagogue, in existence for a decade in the middle of the third century.

The earlier synagogue, from the late second century, was more modestly decorated. The motifs of its ornamentation are largely architectural rather than pictorial and recall the Greco-Roman artistic tradition. The designs were similar to those found in Dura's private houses. No animal or human figures were represented—in all, a proper building, quite in conformity with a conservative Jewish tradition.

The meeting room was completely rebuilt about 244. Initially, the decorative scheme of the new synagogue was also comparatively simple, recalling the earlier building. But then a second, more ambitious plan was developed and executed whose pictures are under consideration here. They had been completed and had become so well known as to attract visitors from the East, from Mesopotamia, before all of Dura was destroyed in 256. In the final design, the four walls of the main room were covered with paintings; at the top and bottom the decoration is conventional, but the main part of the wall on all four sides was covered with vivid scenes, perhaps one hundred in all, arranged in three horizontal bands, each well over a meter high. Over half of the pictures are still preserved. Some are instantly recognizable biblical stories (the exodus, Elijah reviving the widow's child, Samuel anointing David); others display puzzling symbolism (the open temple/the closed temple)—all with a bewildering mixture of costume (Persian caftan and trousers, Greek chiton and himation, Jewish prayer shawl with zizith or ritual fringes), imagery (biblical, mythological, astrological, apotropaic), and languages (legends and graffiti in Aramaic, Greek, Middle Persian, and Parthian).

The importance of these paintings can scarcely be overestimated. Located in an important frontier town, they are an extraordinary iconographic document from an otherwise unknown Jewish community. There have been many attempts at explanation (Gutmann, 1966, 1973, 1975), most of which were flawed by their use of an antiquated understanding of "rabbinic Judaism," assumed to be dominant among all Jews of this period. An adequate interpretation will take into account the following: (1) The style suggests a blend of artistic trends from the hellenized East, rather than from the Greco-Roman world to the west. (2) The community that owned the building was likely the only synagogue community in Dura. For Dura this *is* "normative" Judaism, and there is no indication that it was controlled by Jewish authorities from elsewhere. (3) The final form of the paintings, created in a few years, is greatly different from the decoration in the first synagogue and that originally planned for the second. Was some new element injected into the Judaism of Dura to bring this change about? (4) The religious creativity of these paintings is not an isolated phenomenon. They date from a period of extraordinary religious productivity by Jews and by Gentiles of several religious traditions in early Sassanid Iran (Neusner, 1975:207–8).

Sardis

The Sardis synagogue was no less startling a discovery than Dura (the two buildings are compared in Seager, 1973). It is not as rich in iconography, but in several respects the picture is clearer, and Sardis may reveal more about Diaspora communities generally than Dura does. The major images at Sardis are the eagles of the Eagle Table, the pairs of lions which flanked that table, and the crater, vines, and peacocks of the apse mosaic. (The extensive mosaics in the main hall and forecourt are sufficiently well preserved to show that they contained only ornamental geometric designs.) The eagles and the lions are particularly striking, in the emphasis placed upon them by their location and in view of the fact that they were obviously Gentile, pagan objects boldly reused by the Sardis Jews. The eagles were cut from a Roman monument of the late Hellenistic or early imperial period, where they had been symbols of Roman power. The lions just as quickly recall pagan Lydia and Sardis. ("The Lydians suffered from a regular *leontomania*," writes senior excavator Hanfmann.) The great Anatolian goddess Cybele had lions as her attributes in this region since well into the second millennium B.C.E. The two pairs in the synagogue date from about 400 B.C.E. In the small lot of Lydian and Persian sculpture recovered by the current expedition, there are twenty-one lions. Lions and eagles are biblical images, of course, and were found on other synagogues and in Jewish tombs; but to any Gentile at Sardis, and to the Jews as well, the Gentile and pagan associations of the figures from this synagogue would have been unavoidable.

A clue to understanding Sardis iconography may come from a series of coins minted in the mid-third century at Apameia in Phrygia, not far east of Sardis. They clearly show a double scene from the biblical story of Noah's ark, the ark itself being clearly labelled *Noe* = Noah (Kindler). Perhaps in combination with local flood stories, the biblical account had apparently become part of the town's mythological history, without losing its Jewish identity (Kraabel, 1978).

At Sardis the bold appropriation of Gentile imagery by Jews is even more obvious, since eagles and lions are prominent *in the synagogue itself.* It suggests a strong, self-confident Judaism at home in a Gentile world. It also points the way to an understanding of the Gentile motifs evident in the Dura paintings. There is considerable boldness in the paintings themselves; and, further, the disaster that ended the life of the synagogue was no pogrom—the whole town suffered the same fate. Self-confident appropriation of Gentile images seems to have characterized both synagogue communities. But Sardis goes one step further. Not only are these images taken over from the Gentiles; so are the table, other furnishings, and indeed the building itself. The table serves as a lectern, installed or reinstalled in the first half of the fourth century in its present position, on the central axis of the building, and before the apse. Its size and decorations surely enhanced the impressiveness of the reading of the Torah. But this is the *only* such table known from any excavated synagogue. No matter how useful or impressive, such a furnishing was not employed in any other known synagogue, probably because it recalled an altar—pagan or even Christian.

In the same way the true Roman basilica had strong secular and pagan association. Until the Jews took it over, the apse of the Sardis building was provided with niches for statues of rulers or deities. Thus, the same connotations must have been alive here in the public building and would not have instantly vanished when it was given over to religious use. No other excavated synagogue building takes over a Gentile architectural form and makes it Jewish in this fashion. In the main hall two massive *aediculae,* both on the east wall, the one closest to Jerusalem, flank the central door. Hellenistic structures in reuse, they were added in the last major remodeling. At least one was surely a Torah shrine, its impressive architecture enhancing the sanctity of the scriptures it held (Kraabel, 1974). (A similar addition, a single Torah shrine awkwardly placed, was discovered simultaneously in the Ostia synagogue.)

Neither in Dura nor in Sardis can there be any support for a claim that a heavily hellenized, syncretized, or "fringe" Judaism is responsible. These are the buildings of the Jewish *communities,* which were made up of most or all of the Jews resident in these locations. Their Jewish identity and their attachment to their traditions are undeniable.

Synagogue Iconography in Palestine

The explosion of new evidence from the synagogues of this area since World War II has been reviewed above. Questions of iconography arise at many points. We have selected two: the "zodiac pavements" of at least four buildings and the David-Orpheus mosaic of the synagogue at Gaza.

The first zodiac floor was exposed by World War I shellfire during a battle at Naaran, near Jericho. This example and the magnificent folk-art

Beth Alfa zodiac discovered a decade later occasioned lively speculation about "pagan" influence and about "secret groups" of "unorthodox Jews" using this motif in late antiquity. The four clear examples are at Hammath Tiberias (fourth century), Hussifa (fifth century), Beth Alfa, and Naaran (both sixth century). In each case the zodiac is made up of two concentric circles in a square. The central circle shows the sun-god in his chariot; the other circle is divided in twelve segments for the signs of the zodiac, each identified in Hebrew. The corners of the square each display a symbol of one of the four seasons.

The reader should not substitute our bald summary for a taste of the debate on "the zodiac in the ancient synagogue," which has been carried on in print over the past half-century (Hüttenmeister and Reeg; Hachlili, 1977). But these points should be kept in mind: (1) Astrology was a conceptual *lingua franca* throughout the Roman world. Sharing in its presuppositions and vocabulary did not oblige one to a particular creed, nor make one a "member" of a particular religious group. (2) Astral and solar symbolism and the rhythm of the year and its seasons are almost inevitable elements of a geocentric world view with agrarian roots. Such "language" occurs in Israelite religion and in postbiblical Judaism. (3) The existence of a rich Jewish mysticism in late antiquity has been established beyond question, chiefly by G. Scholem, on the evidence of both talmudic and extra-talmudic literature. But (4) these pavements occur in synagogues used by an entire Jewish town (Tiberias is the exception, since it is not the only synagogue in this larger and more cosmopolitan city). Their symbols should make sense somehow to the common people of the community, even if the mosaics were laid by artisans, not all of them Jewish, who worked also on Gentile buildings. (5) There is a certain informality with regard to detail. Only at Tiberias are the signs of the seasons coordinated with the zodiac signs that should go with them. At Beth Alfa and Tiberias the zodiac signs progress *counterclockwise*; at Hussifa and Naaran, *clockwise*. But the four seasons at Naaran are in a *counterclockwise* sequence! This suggests that the overall effect is paramount, rather than the details of the design.

This design—and any other religious symbol—may have meaning on several levels, but we would argue that its primary function was related to the calendar, as a permanent reminder of that cycle of annual rites which helped to create a reality structure for any synagogue community in late antiquity. Given the importance of the annual ritual acts performed by the priests while the Temple still stood, the liturgical calendar was probably implied as well. Synagogue life, like Temple life, followed a repeatable annual pattern, the zodiac being the preeminent symbol available in late antiquity to make this point vividly in graphic form.

The Gaza synagogue "Orpheus" is dated to 508/509 c.e. by a dedicatory text in the mosaic. He wears royal garments and a crown and plays a lyre-like instrument; he is attended by a lioness and other animals (the mosaic is too damaged to permit precision). It is clear that the origin of this image is Greek mythology, in the singer and poet Orpheus, whose sweet music charmed even the wild beasts. It is equally clear that for the Jews of this community this figure represented King David, for it is labeled "David" unmistakably, in Hebrew. The Gentile Orpheus is not represented as a king until the high Middle Ages. Although there was an extensive use of Orphic themes in Hellenistic Jewish literature, for apologetic purposes, the only other certain iconographic example from ancient Judaism appears in Dura, where a lyre-playing seated musician, dressed in royal garments and attended by a large bird and a lioness, is shown in the painting over the synagogue's Torah shrine. Like the zodiacs, the Gaza "Orpheus-David" poses questions for historians both of art and of religions. Exploration of the context of this motif and the forces that produced it has only begun (Finney).

The Palestinian synagogues raise other issues, of course, but these two are particularly striking. Note finally that in late antiquity all five sites discussed in this section are on major highways, open presumably to Gentile influence from traders, governing officials, and the military, an ostensibly likely explanation for the "Gentile" mosaics. But all inscriptions in the mosaics are in Hebrew. Perhaps this was seen as a way of capturing alien iconography and making it one's own.

Funerary Art

In the Greco-Roman world, burials are the most consistent source of Jewish imagery. The evidence comes from all the Mediterranean lands, from Spain clockwise around to North Africa (Goodenough, 1965:22–39). The major site outside Palestine is, of course, Rome, whose six Jewish catacombs have been extensively studied (Leon, 1960); the last was discovered in 1919, however, though stray finds continue to appear (Kraabel, 1979b). In the period for which we are responsible, the major source of funerary art has been the State of Israel, and the preeminent site the necropolis of Beth She'arim, excavated by B. Mazar in 1935–40 and 1969 and by N. Avigad in 1953–58.

The images of Beth She'arim are astonishing. Along with the clearly Jewish symbols—a number of menorahs, Torah shrines, and ritual objects—are warrior figures (one with a great menorah projecting from his head) and themes from pagan myth. The juxtapositions are striking: centered over one tomb door is a woman's face (Medusa?) in high relief, flanked by the name "Sokrates" on the right and a menorah on the left (catacomb 19). In the largest tomb, catacomb 20, nearly all inscriptions are in Hebrew (though Greek is the rule elsewhere in the necropolis). Six rabbis are mentioned by name, and the implication is that this catacomb was reserved for rabbis and their families. Along with some 125 stone sarcophagi, excavators found broken fragments of perhaps twenty additional marble coffins. Among the images in this rabbis' catacomb are the face of a deity (Zeus? Helios?), *Nikai, Erotes*, Aphrodite, a bull's head, and an Amazonomachy. Families of symbols suggest themselves. The triple entrance to catacomb 20 recalls synagogue facades with their three doors, but in the iconography these are perhaps linked to the columned front of the Torah shrine, a synagogue furnishing which itself became a religious symbol in mosaics, on lamps, and in the Beth She'arim catacombs—and in Jewish art also recalls the ark of the covenant!

The town of Beth She'arim could not be more central to rabbinic Judaism. Located in Lower Galilee, it grew rapidly in importance as Jews moved north after the Bar Kokhba revolt, and it became the seat of the Sanhedrin, and home and then burial place of Rabbi Judah I, the head of the Sanhedrin and editor of Mishna (d. ca. 220). Its catacombs were constructed in the two centuries between the revolt of Bar Kokhba and that of Gallus (ca. 352). Avigad has attempted to cope with the implications of such an iconography in such a location (1976:275–87). The evidence has been fully published (Mazar, 1973; Schwabe and Lifshitz; Avigad, 1976), but the debate has little more than begun.

Temple, Synagogue, and Torah Shrine

One final puzzle is not restricted to a single type of excavated site, nor to one area of the ancient world. (Specific examples are mentioned in several parts of this chapter.) It may in fact be several puzzles, but if so they are closely related. The Torah shrine, and in some sense the synagogue itself and the scripture which is central to them, carries some of the symbolic value of the Jerusalem Temple. After a great deal of work on the problem in the first half of the century, S. Krauss declared that the ancient synagogue was a substitute, an *Ersatz* for the Temple.

There are changes, of course, analogous to the shift in leadership from priest or cultic official to lay scholar or rabbi. The Torah shrine is a "shrine," an "ark" for the Torah, itself a powerful symbol in later Judaism. The Dura synagogue uses substantial Temple imagery, including the puzzling closed temple. Over time the sanctity of the synagogue itself increased, as the language of the inscriptions shows. Centuries after the destruction of Jerusalem, the image and meaning of the Temple and its cult are never something wholly of the past, as the persistent debates of rabbinic literature make clear. There are archaeological data in quantity to this point and masses of literary evidence, but a satisfactory analysis of the relationship of all the elements and a convincing explication of the meaning of these powerful, interlocked images still eludes us. Only a fully interdisciplinary approach will provide the answer.

Conclusion

A number of other themes might well have been explored more extensively in this section: the function of the second commandment, the effect of the destruction of the Temple in 70 C.E., rabbinic attitudes toward popular symbols, Judaism in relation to a dying paganism and a blossoming Christian art, elitist "mystic" or heterodox Judaism as the creator of the Jewish forms of originally pagan symbols. These are vital issues in their place, but this essay begins from the artifacts themselves and the often-ordinary people who commissioned the designs and to whom presumably they made sense.

If the "answers" which have been given in earlier generations have not been persuasive, it may be because researchers have brought the questions to the data rather than permit them to arise out of the discoveries themselves. This will all change, we predict, as more archaeologists and historians of religion become involved. We suggest that more satisfactory solutions will appear as the result of working inductively, asking simple questions: What was the repertoire of images available? Which ones were in fact used most frequently by Jews, and which do not appear? The corpus of symbols used is diverse, but remarkably small (Neusner, 1981); why are menorahs, Torah shrines, incense shovels, eagles, the Akedah (the sacrifice of Isaac) found again and again in communities across the very large Mediterranean world? Why do other symbols, well known in ancient literature, not occur in the synagogues? And why are clearly Gentile symbols so rare when the examples of the zodiac and the Gaza Orpheus prove that they are not excluded altogether?

There were criteria that were followed in antiquity and theological statements made iconographically, but the map that plots their location and displays the entirety of this terrain is yet to be drawn. The deductive approach, which imports criteria—literary, theological, psychological—from outside, has proved to yield unsatisfying and incomplete results. Any new solution will have to begin with the realia themselves, in their context. This is the task to be carried out by archaeologists, art historians, and historians of religion in the rest of this century.

Appendix:
Symbolism of the Jewish-Christians
(Testa, Mancini, Manns)

Evidence for the iconography of "Jewish-Christians" has been assembled over the past two decades from scraps of archaeological data (e.g., graffiti and fragmentary figures which are usually open to several quite different explanations), brief references in church fathers and later customs within (or nearly within) traditional Christianity (Saunders). In circular fashion this reconstruction has also been used to identify and define communities of "Jewish-Christians" in Roman Palestine, a process that appears highly arbitrary on the archaeological side and as yet nearly untested from the literary side. This Palestinian "Jewish-Christianity" is thus a wobbly edifice erected on a shaky foundation. It will remain precarious until more powerful literary, historical, and archaeological tools are used on the data (Strange, 1979:674 n. 135).

THE NONLITERARY WRITTEN EVIDENCE

Since 1888 publications of inscriptions in the classical languages have been reviewed in *Année Epigraphique* (abbreviated *AE*) and in the "Bulletin Epigraphique" (abbreviated "Bull. epigr." or "Bull." or BE) of the *Revue des Etudes Grecques*. For many years the latter has been produced by Louis Robert, who has demonstrated frequently in his own publications an informed sensitivity to Jewish texts in Greek. Inscriptions in Semitic languages published since 1964 are reviewed in "Bulletin d'epigraphie semitique" (abbreviated BES) by J. Teixidor, in the periodical *Syria* 44– (1967–). For each of the three, individual entries are cited in the literature by the abbreviation, the year of publication of the review, and the number of the entry, for example, Bull. epigr. 1979, no. 671.

Palestine Epigraphy

There has been a virtual eruption of new epigraphic data from Palestine since 1948. The Jewish material, mainly from tombs and synagogues, is best understood in the light of all the comparative linguistic evidence that has been retrieved from pagan, Christian, Samaritan, and other contexts. The languages of Judaism in the Greco-Roman period are Aramaic, Hebrew, and Greek, and it is possible to trace the spread of Greek culture through the gradual displacement of Semitic language by Greek (Meyers and Strange, 1981:62–91; Safrai and Stern: 1976: 1007–64). Many scholars would perceive in the gradual ascendancy of Greek the logical outcome of a very long accommodation to external forces which came to dominate not only Palestine but the whole of the eastern Mediterranean world (Freyne).

Just as Aramaic was the *lingua franca* of the Near East in the postexilic period, so was Greek from about the third century b.c.e. on. Aramaic continued both as a literary language and as a vernacular, household language throughout the Roman period (for a convenient collection of Palestinian Aramaic texts, see Fitzmyer and Harrington). It was Pompey's invasion in 63 b.c.e., however, that established Greek as a popular language in Palestine. After that time multilingualism was to characterize the Jewish people (Hengel, 1974; Fitzmyer; Barr).

Epigraphy from Funerary Contexts

In the main, Jewish epigraphy from the end of the Second Temple period has come from ossuary and sarcophagi inscriptions. Much of the older material is readily available in Frey (1952) or in Klein. Although no systematic new corpus has been prepared, access to the material is provided in a number of excellent survey articles. Both N. Avigad (1958) and F. M. Cross (1961) have studied the paleography. R. Hachlili has compiled an impressive array of comparative data on the onomastica (1979). B. Bagatti and J. T. Milik have provided a most important corpus of material from Jerusalem (1958). Two recent Ph.D. dissertations attempt to catalogue all the ossuary material in relation to decorative and funerary art (Figueras, 1975, cf. 1983; Rahmani). See also the discussion of funerary texts in Fischer.

This material, which is both Semitic and Greek, is essential to a full understanding of Jewish burial practices and beliefs in afterlife at a critical juncture in religious history. Moreover, the texts provide us with an important unedited corpus of names which may shed light on literary and political development of the day. A clear desideratum is the publication of a full catalogue of all this new material with philological notes.

Beth She'arim

This necropolis provides the most important and coherent corpus of Palestinian Jewish Greek epigraphy (Schwabe and Lifshitz). The corpus cannot be studied, however, without access to the excavation reports of Mazar (1973) and Avigad (1976). It is noteworthy that the Greek used in these epitaphs is colloquial, for that underscores the fact that Greek was used as a normal everyday language. We have already noted how this material has illuminated Jewish accommodations to Hellenization. It also demonstrates how Jewish epigraphy may be used to study beliefs in afterlife and contemporary attitudes toward family and the Holy Land. The availability of this material in English will mean that a much better and more informed history of Palestinian Judaism can now be written.

Unfortunately there is no systematic collection of other Jewish Greek material. Whereas B. Lifshitz (1975) has attempted a systematic updating of Vol. 1 of Frey's *CII* (Europe), no such work on Vol. 2 has appeared. In order to find the Jewish Greek material available from Palestinian tombs or synagogues, one must consult Hüttenmeister and Reeg, or Chiat (1982), the annual surveys of Robert, the essays of G. Mussies (in Safrai and Stern) and A. Ovadiah (1978), *and* the notes in Schürer-Vermes-Millar.

Synagogue Inscriptions in Hebrew and Aramaic

The publication of J. Naveh's catalogue (1978) has filled a gap in the literature on Jewish epigraphy of ancient Palestine. A model of clarity and brevity, it presents in handy form all the data up to around 1977. A number of excellent tables provide ready access to personal and place names. (See also Levine, 1981a, for a brief discussion of this subject.)

Several of its inscriptions deserve special attention. The most important single item in the catalogue is the long inscripton from Rehov in the Beth Shean valley. It is the most extensive Hebrew inscription ever found in Palestine, some twenty-nine lines, 4.3 m. by 2.75 m. on mosaic. It is assigned to the early Byzantine period, though there is still some discussion about its precise date. It contains valuable information concerning the status of certain rabbinic texts at that time and provides an invaluable listing of place names and foods which pertain to Jewish life at the end of the rabbinic period. It also sheds light on the observance of Jewish laws pertaining to sabbatic release, relations with non-Jews and the borders of Palestine. No other single discovery can rank with Rehov in importance.

In his commentary, Naveh displays his skill as a paleographer and a philologist and offers new insight into recent discoveries. Important inscriptions from En Gedi, Khirbet Susiya, and many others receive fresh and illuminating treatment.

For non-synagogue material no comprehensive source exists. The authors must refer the student and the scholar to the scholarly literature and standard aids; a new systematic corpus of these data is needed badly.

Linguistic Regionalism

In view of all the new material uncovered or published since 1948 it is possible to make several generalizations. It would appear that a lively bilingualism (Greek and Semitic) characterized most of Jewish life until the wars with Rome (multilingualism characterized it afterward). Hebrew seems to achieve more and more the status of a holy language. With the huge population shift to Galilee that came in the second century C.E., the several areas of the country developed different language preferences. Western Galilee, the coastal plain, the Rift Valley, the areas situated near Roman municipalities, the areas along trade routes, all became dominated by the Greek language. Hebrew was retained as the language of liturgy and synagogue, and the vernacular Aramaic was displaced. But the Galilean highlands, Upper Galilee in particular, and the Golan Heights became centers of Aramaic and Hebrew. The villagers in these areas continued to understand and converse in Greek, but they seem to have consciously preferred Semitic, as the paucity of Greek inscriptions in these areas attests.

It remains for the present generation to make better sense of this rather complex set of data. The richness and diversity of such linguistic competency testifies to a lively Jewish life in late antiquity, a vitality that is expressed in the variety of Jewish communities as well.

Diaspora Epigraphy

The basic source for Jewish inscriptions in Greek and Latin is *CII* (ed. J.-B. Frey). Europe is covered in the first volume (1936), the eastern Mediterranean from Asia Minor to Egypt in the second (1952); the numeration is continuous. Criticism of the corpus has been severe; see Robert, 1946, and his "Bull. epigr." 1954, no. 24. Frey died in 1939, and Gerhard Kittel joined the project in 1943. But the second volume remained lacunulose, and a third, though planned, was never published. But there has been considerable revision and updating by others, who preserved the *CII* numeration. Leon provides transcriptions and translations of the texts from Rome, and D. M. Lewis does the same for Egypt in *CPJ* 3. Recently the first volume of *CII* was reissued with a long and often useful prolegomenon by Lifshitz (1975), adding new inscriptions and bibliography.

In the Roman Diaspora, Greek was the first language of Jews (Treu) and of most other groups that came out of the East. Even in Rome itself Jewish epitaphs are 76 percent Greek and 23 percent Latin; only 1 percent are in Semitic languages, a striking figure in view of the usual conservatism of funerary texts (Leon, 1960). Outside the capital, and especially farther east, the predominance of Greek is even greater. Before the Sardis discoveries only one Anatolian Jewish inscription in Hebrew had been published, MAMA VI 334 from Acomonia in Phrygia, a Hebrew-Greek bilingual, possibly a biblical quotation.

Final publications of Diaspora sites usually include the Jewish inscriptions, for example, Kraeling for Dura, Bruneau for Delos. In the forthcoming final publication of the Sardis synagogue, J. H. Kroll is responsible for the Greek inscriptions, I. Rabinowitz for the Hebrew. Robert has already published a number of the most significant Sardis Greek texts with excellent commentary (1964). Applebaum makes extensive use of the Berenike and Teuchira inscriptions in his study of North African Judaism. Goodenough in *Jewish Symbols* frequently used the inscriptions available to him (1968 index). For decades the extensive *Polycharmos* inscription (*CII* 694) was the only evidence for the synagogue of Stobi in Yugoslavia (Hengel, 1966), but current excavations there make it imperative to attempt to mesh this text with new epigraphic and archaeological data (Poehlmann).

Lifshitz, whose contribution to this field is second only to Robert's, brought together many of the dedication inscriptions from Diaspora synagogues in a collection now widely used (1967). Unfortunately, he left out the inscription most fascinating to historians of religion, the dedication of the Ostia Torah shrine, a Greek text but beginning with the well-known Latin formula in behalf of the emperor's well-being, *pro salute Aug(usti)* (Floriani Squarciapino, 1965).

In the past, Diaspora Jewish inscriptions along with others alleged to be Jewish have been used out of context to draw irresponsible conclusions. Kittel may be the most egregious example, but the practice was widespread, prompted in part by a genuine desire to say *something* on an ancient topic even when the evidence was really too skimpy to permit it. For examples, with correctives, see Kraabel, 1969; and Lane. For a more responsible use of the data, see Delling, drawing on Bickerman, in regard to an altar from Pergamon in western Asia Minor. Apparently it had been dedicated to the God of the LXX.

Often the epigraphic evidence remains tantalizingly obscure, and its precise relevance to Diaspora Judaism all but unfathomable. A final set of examples: IG III2 13209, 13210 = SIG 1239 (from Athens) and SIG 1240 (from Chalcis in Euboea) employ curses resembling those in Deut 28:22, 28 to protect the graves of well-to-do sophists of the second century c.e. (for a recent study of possible connections with Judaism, see Robert, 1978).

The early medieval revival of Hebrew in the Jewish inscriptions of the classical world lies outside the scope of this review.

GENERAL CONCLUSIONS

As a result of this very brief survey of recent archaeological evidences, a number of general conclusions may be made. First, it should be quite clear that everywhere in the classical world the main vehicle for the transmission of ancient Judaism was the synagogue. Even in the day when the Temple in Jerusalem still stood, Jews were seeking out means to live and worship far away from the holy city. The material evidence for ancient synagogues and their context thus constitutes one of the major sources for the study of ancient Judaism.

Second, additional sorts of archaeological evidence, from tombs and other contexts, provide data that must also be taken into account. It is the blending of data both from the public and the private spheres of life which allows archaeological interpretation to be somewhat objective in its reconstruction of ancient life. For example, the existence of many Diaspora inscriptions and much art provides a rich opportunity to supplement the literary record and the evidence from synagogues. Similarly, in Palestine the nonsynagogal finds (e.g., Meiron, Beth Shean) may often be of more significance for the understanding of Jewish communal life and practice than are the monumental remains.

Third, it is clear that in private and in public Jews in Palestine and in the Diaspora often adopted Gentile culture with enthusiasm. Such an accommodation not only resulted in the gradual erosion of the Hebrew language but also in the emergence of new ways of religious expression in language and in art. Consideration of regional factors in both Palestine and in the Diaspora allows for a much more nuanced understanding of Jewish culture. Through such considerations it is possible to understand more fully the complex social and historical factors that underlie distinctive regional patterns and trends. Moreover, it is quite clear that such an approach enables one to understand the Judaism of the town and the Judaism of the city in an entirely new perspective.

Fourth, although there is clear continuity between the Jewish communities of Palestine and the Diaspora, a great discontinuity may be seen as well. It is now possible, for example, to speak of the Jews of Italy or of Asia Minor or of North Africa, or of an eastern Diaspora, and of the Jews of Palestine. For all that links these communities one to another, archaeological evidence unmistakably points to many areas of change and modification. Hence the terms "rabbinic Judaism" or "talmudic Judaism" are not particularly helpful. In fact, they are often misleading as general descriptions of the Jews of late antiquity.

Perhaps it is the language of Jewish art, the symbols that accompany Jews in their wanderings, which provides the strongest archaeological evidences for continuity (see Neusner, 1981). It is the Torah shrine and Temple symbols which recur in the frescoed catacombs of Rome or Venosa or on the wall paintings of Dura. But it is also the documentation of Jewish loyalty to tradition conveyed in inscriptions which points to the tenacity of a community that survives despite the ascendancy of Christianity as the dominant and restrictive religious tradition of the West.

Finally, the material culture of postbiblical Judaism provides a challenge to the modern interpreter. By its random nature it has no axe to grind. By its variety it has no dominant form to proclaim. Through study of it questions yet unasked will come forward. Surely the time has come for synthesis. Archaeological data will doubtless come to play a more and more critical role in achieving this goal in the years and decades ahead. This essay, it is hoped, will help pave that way by creating an opportunity for dialogue not only between texts and monuments but also among the scholars represented in this volume.

BIBLIOGRAPHY

Applebaum, S.
    1974   "The Legal Status of the Jewish Communities in the Diaspora." Pp.
                420–53 in Safrai and Stern, eds., section 1, vol. 1
    1979   *Jews and Greeks in Ancient Cyrene.* SJLA 28. Leiden: Brill.

Aquila, F. Dell'
    1979   "Struttura e planimetria della catacombe ebraica di Venosa."
                Lucania Archeologica 1: 10–16.

Avigad, N.
    1958   "The Paleography of the Dead Sea Scrolls and Related Documents."
                Pp. 56–87 in *Aspects of the Dead Sea Scrolls.* Ed. C. Rabin and Y.
                Yadin. Scripta Hierosolymitana 4. Jerusalem: Magnes Press.

1976 *Beth She'arim: Report on the Excavations during 1953–1958.* Vol. 3, *Catacombs 12–23.* New Brunswick, NJ: Rutgers University Press.
1983 *Discovering Jerusalem.* Nashville: Nelson.

Avi-Yonah, Michael
1971 "Synagogue: Architecture." *EncJud* 15: 595–600.
1973 "Ancient Synagogues." *Ariel* 32: 29–43. Reprinted in Gutmann, ed., 1975.

Avi-Yonah, Michael, ed.
1975–78 *Encyclopedia of Archaeological Excavations in the Holy Land.* 4 vols. Jerusalem: Israel Exploration Society.

Bagatti, B., and J. T. Milik
1958 *Gli scavi del "Dominus Flevit."* Parte 1, *La necropoli de periodo Romano.* Publicazioni dello Studium Biblicum Franciscanum 13. Jerusalem: Franciscan Printing Press.

Barr, James
1970 "Which Language Did Jesus Speak? Some Remarks of a Semitist." *BJRL* 53: 9–29.

Bickerman, Elias
1958 "The Altars of Gentiles: A Note on the Jewish 'ius sacrum.'" *Revue internationale des Droits de l'Antiquite* 5: 137–64.

Bruneau, Philippe
1970 *Recherches sur les cultes de Délos à l'époque hellénistique et à l'époque impériale.* Bibliothèque des Écoles françaises d'Athènes et de Rome 217. Paris: Boccard.

Cassuto-Salzmann, Milka
1974 "Bibliography of M. Avi-Yonah." *IEJ* 24: 287–315.

Chiat, M. J. S.
1981 "First-Century Synagogue Architecture: Methodological Problems." Pp. 49–60 in Gutmann, ed., 1981.
1982 *Handbook of Synagogue Architecture.* Brown Judaic Studies 29. Ed. J. Neusner. Chico, CA: Scholars Press.

Colafemmina, C.
1974 "Nova e vetera nella catacomba ebraica di Venosa." Pp. 87–95 in *Studi Storici dedicati a M. Miglietta.* Ed. C. Colafemmina. Molfetta: Mezzina.
1975 "Nuove iscrizioni ebraiche a Venosa." Pp. 41–46 in *Studi in Memoria Di P. Adiuto Putignani.* Molfetta: Societia Di Storia Patia per La Puglia, sezione de Taranto, 1975.
1978 "Nuove scoperte nella catacombe ebraica di Venosa." *Vetera Christianorum* 15: 369–81.
1981 "Saggi di scavo in località 'collina della Maddalena' a Venosa. Relazione preliminare." *Vetera Christianorum* 18: 443–51.

Conder, Claude R., and H. H. Kitchener
1881–84 *The Survey of Western Palestine: Memoirs of the Topography, Orography, Hydrography, and Archaeology.* Ed. E. H. Palmer and W. Besant. London: The Committee of the Palestine Exploration Fund.

Corbo, V.
1976 "La città romana di Magdala: Rapporto preliminare dopo la quarta campagna di scavo." Pp. 355–78 in *Studia Hierosolymitana.* Jerusalem: Fransican Printing Press.

Cross, Frank M., Jr.
1961 "The Development of the Jewish Scripts." Pp. 133–202 in *The Bible and the Ancient Near East: Essays in Honor of William Foxwell Albright.* Ed. G. E. Wright. Garden City, NY: Doubleday.

Delling, G.
1964 "Die Altarinschrift eines Gottesfuerchtigen in Pergamon." *NovT* 7: 73–80.

Dever, W. G.
1974 *Archaeology and Biblical Studies: Retrospects and Prospects.* Evanston, IL: Seabury-Western.

Dothan, Moshe
1983 *Hammath Tiberias: Early Synagogues and the Hellenistic and Roman Remains.* Jerusalem: Israel Exploration Society.

Figueras, P.
1975 "Jewish Ossuaries and Their Decoration." Diss., Hebrew University.
1983 *Decorated Jewish Ossuaries.* Leiden: Brill.

Finney, Paul C.
1978 "Orpheus-David: A Connection in Iconography between Greco-Roman Judaism and Early Antiquity." *Journal of Jewish Art* 5: 6–15.

Fischer, Ulrich
1978 *Eschatologie und Jenseitserwartung im hellenistischen Diaspora-judentum.* BZNW 44. Berlin: de Gruyter.

Fitzmyer, Joseph A.
1970 "The Languages of Palestine in the First Century A.D." *CBQ* 32: 501–31.

Fitzmyer, Joseph A., and Daniel J. Harrington
1978 *A Manual of Palestinian Aramaic Texts.* BibOr 34. Rome: Biblical Institute Press.

Floriani Squarciapino, M.
1963 "The Synagogue at Ostia." *Archaeology* 16: 194–203.
1965 "La sinagoga di Ostia: Seconda Campagna di Scavo." Pp. 299–315 in *Atti del VI Congresso intern. di arch. crist. 1962.* Rome: Institute of Christian Archaeology.

Foerster, G.
1981 "A Survey of Ancient Diaspora Synagogues." Pp. 164–72 in Levine, ed., 1981a.

Frey, Jean-Baptiste, ed.
1936, 1952 *Corpus Inscriptionum Iudaicarum.* Sussidi allo Studio delle Antichità Cristiane 1, 3. Rome: Institute of Christian Archaeology. Reprint (vol. 1 only) New York: Ktav, 1975.

Freyne, S.
1980 *Galilee from Alexander the Great to Hadrian: 325 B.C.E. to 135 C.E.* Wilmington, DE: Michael Glazier. Notre Dame, IN: University of Notre Dame Press.

Goodenough, Erwin R.
1953-68   *Jewish Symbols in the Greco-Roman Period.* New York: Pantheon
           Books, 1953 (vols. 1–3), 1954 (vol. 4), 1956 (vols. 5–6), 1958 (vols.
           7–8), 1964 (vols. 9–11), 1965 (vol. 12), 1968 (vol. 13).

Goodenough, Erwin R., and Michael Avi-Yonah
1971   "Dura-Europas." *EncJud* 6: 275–298.

Guérin, Victor
1868-80   *Description Géographique, Historique et Archéologique de la
           Palestine.* Paris: Imprimé par autorisation de l'empereur à l'Impr.
           impériale.

Gutmann, Joseph
1966   "Dura-Europos. C. Die Synagogue." *Reallexikon zur byzanti-
           nischen Kunst.* Stuttgart: Hiersemann. 1: 1230–1240.
1981a   "The Synagogue at Gamla." Pp. 30–34 in Levine, ed., 1981a.
1981b   "Synagogue Origins: Theories and Facts." Pp. 1–6 in Gutmann, ed.,
           1981.

Gutmann, Joseph, ed.
1973   *The Dura-Europos Synagogue: A Re-evaluation (1932–1972).*
           RelArts 1. Missoula, MT: American Academy of Religion and
           Society of Biblical Literature.
1975   *The Synagogue: Studies in Origins, Archaeology, and Architecture.*
           New York: Ktav.
1981   *Ancient Synagogues: The State of Research.* Chico, CA: Scholars
           Press.

Gutmann, J., S. Yeivin, and E. Netzer
1978   "Susiya." In Avi-Yonah, ed., 1975–78, vol. 4.

Hachlili, R.
1977   "The Zodiac in Ancient Jewish Art: Representation and Signifi-
           cance." *BASOR* 228: 61–77.
1978   "A Jerusalem Family in Jericho." *BASOR* 230: 45–56.
1979   "The Goliath Family in Jericho: Funerary Inscriptions from a First
           Century A.D. Jewish Monumental Tomb." *BASOR* 235: 31–66.

Hanfmann, G. M. A.
1972   *Letters from Sardis.* Cambridge, MA: Harvard University Press.
1983   *Sardis from Prehistoric to Roman Times: Results of the Archaeo-
           logical Exploration of Sardis 1958–1975.* Cambridge, MA: Harvard
           University Press.

Hanfmann, G. M. A., and J. C. Waldbaum
1975   *A Survey of Sardis and the Major Monuments outside the City
           Walls.* Archaeological Exploration of Sardis, Report 1. Cambridge,
           MA: Harvard University Press.

Hengel, Martin
1966   "Die Synagogeninschrift von Stobi." *ZNW* 57: 145–83. Reprinted in
           Gutmann, ed., 1975.
1974   *Judaism and Hellenism: Studies in their Encounter in Palestine
           during the Early Hellenistic Period.* 2 vols. Trans. John Bowden.
           Philadelphia: Fortress.

Hoffman, Lawrence A.
1981   "Censoring In and Censoring Out: A Function of Liturgical Lan-
           guage." Pp. 19–37 in Gutmann, ed., 1981.

Hopkins, C.
1979   *The Discovery of Dura-Europos.* New Haven, CT, and London: Yale University Press.

Hüttenmeister, F., and G. Reeg
1977   *Die antiken Synagogen in Israel.* Beihefte zum Tübinger Atlas des vorderen Orients 12/1, Teil 1: Die jüdischen Synagogen, Lehrhäuser und Gerichtshöfe. Wiesbaden: Reichert.

Kindler, A.
1971   "A Coin-Type from Apameia in Phrygia (Asia Minor) Depicting the Narrative of Noah." *Museum Haaretz Bulletin* 13: 24–32.

Kittel, Gerhard
1944   "Das Kleinasiatische Judentum in der hellenistische-römischen Zeit." *TLZ* 69: 9–20.

Klein, S.
1920   *Jüdisch-Palästinisches Corpus Inscriptionen.* Pressburg: R. Loewit.

Kloner, A.
1981   "Ancient Synagogues in Israel: An Archaeological Survey." Pp. 11–18 in Levine, ed., 1981a.

Kochavi, Moshe, ed.
1972   *Judaea, Samaria and the Golan: Archaeological Survey 1967–1968.* Jerusalem: Archaeological Survey of Israel (Hebrew).

Kohl, H., and C. Watzinger
1916   *Antike Synagogen in Galiläa.* Wissenschaftliche Veröffentlichung der Deutschen Orient-Gesellschaft 29. Leipzig. Reprint, Jerusalem: Kedem, 1973.

Kraabel, A. T.
1969   "*Hypsistos* and the Synagogue at Sardis." *GRBS* 10: 81–93.
1971   "Melito the Bishop and the Synagogue at Sardis: Text and Context." Pp. 77–85 in *Studies Presented to George M. A. Hanfmann.* Ed. D. G. Mitten, et al. Cambridge, MA: Harvard University Press.
1974   "Synagogues, Ancient." Pp. 436–39 in *NCE, Supplement 1967–1974.*
1978   "Paganism and Judaism: The Sardis Evidence." Pp. 13–33 in *Paganisme, Judaisme, Christianisme: Mélanges offerts à Marcel Simon.* Ed. A. Benoit, M. Philonenko, and C. Vogel. Paris: Boccard.
1979a   "The Diaspora Synagogue: Archaeological and Epigraphic Evidence since Sukenik." Pp. 475–510 in *ANRW* 2.19.1. Ed. W. Haase. Berlin and New York: de Gruyter.
1979b   "Jews in Imperial Rome: More Archaeological Evidence from an Oxford Collection." *JJS* 30: 41–58.
1981   "Social Systems of Six Diaspora Synagogues." Pp. 79–91 in Gutmann, ed., 1981.
1984   "New Evidence of the Samaritan Diaspora Has Been Found on Delos," *BA* 47: 44–46.
Forthcoming *The Jews of Western Asia Minor under the Roman Empire.*

Kraeling, C. H.
1956   *The Synagogue: The Excavations at Dura-Europos. Final Report,* VIII.1. New Haven, CT: Yale University Press.

Krauss, S.
1922   *Synagogale Altertümer.* Berlin-Vienna: Harz.

Lane, E.
1979   "Sabazius and the Jews in Valerius Maximus: A Re-examination."
            JRS 69: 35–38.

Leon, Harry J.
1953–54   "The Jews of Venusia." *JQR* 44: 267–84.
1960   *The Jews of Ancient Rome.* Philadelphia: Jewish Publication
            Society.

Levine, L. I., ed.
1981a   *Ancient Synagogues Revealed.* Jerusalem: Israel Exploration
            Society.
1981b   "Ancient Synagogues: A Historical Introduction." Pp. 1–10 in
            Levine, ed., 1981a.

Lifshitz, B.
1967   *Donateurs et fondateurs dans les synagogues juives.* Cahiers de la
            RB 7. Paris: Gabalda.
1975   "Prolegomenon." Pp. 21–104 in J.-B. Frey, *Corpus Inscriptionum
            Iudaicarum*, Vol. 1. 2d ed. New York: Ktav.

Loffreda, Stanislao
1973   *A Visit to Capharnaum.* 2d. ed. The Holy Places of Palestine. Jeru-
            salem: Franciscan Printing Press.
1974   *Cafarnao II: La Ceramica.* Pubblicazioni dello Studium Biblicum
            Franciscanum 19. Jerusalem: Franciscan Printing Press.

Mancini, Ignazio
1970   *Archaeological Discoveries Relative to the Judaeo-Christians: His-
            torical Survey.* Trans. G. Bushell. Publications of the Studium
            Biblicum Franciscanum, Collectio minor 10. Jerusalem: Franciscan
            Printing Press.

Manns, Frederic
1979   *Bibliographie du Judeo-Christianisme.* Studium Biblicum Fran-
            ciscanum, Analecta 13. Jerusalem: Franciscan Printing Press.

Maoz, T.
1979   *The Jewish Settlement and Ancient Jewish Synagogues in the
            Golan.* Qatsrein: Field School of the Golan and Ministry of Educa-
            tion and Culture (Hebrew).
1981a   "The Synagogue at Gamla and the Typology of Second-Temple
            Synagogues." Pp. 35–41 in Levine, ed., 1981a.
1981b   "The Art and Architecture of the Synagogues of the Golan." Pp.
            98–115 in Levine, ed., 1981a.

Mazar, Benjamin
1973   *Beth She'arim.* Vol. 1, *Catacombs 1–4.* Jerusalem: Israel
            Exploration Society; New Brunswick, NJ: Rutgers University Press.
1975   *The Mountain of the Lord.* Garden City, NY: Doubleday.

Meyers, Eric M.
1971   *Jewish Ossuaries: Reburial and Rebirth.* BibOr 24. Rome: Biblical
            Institute Press.
1976a   "Galilean Regionalism as a Factor in Historical Reconstruction."
            BASOR 221: 93–101.
1976b   "Synagogue, Architecture." *IDBSup*, 842–44.
1980   "Ancient Synagogues in Galilee: Their Religious and Cultural
            Setting." *BA* 43: 97–108.

1981   "Ancient Gush Halav (Giscala): Palestinian Synagogues and the
            Eastern Diaspora." Pp. 61–77 in Gutmann, ed., 1981.
1983   "Report on the Excavations of the Venosa Catacombs, 1981."
            Vetera Christianorum 20: 455–59.

Meyers, E. M., A. T. Kraabel, and J. F. Strange
1976   *Ancient Synagogue Excavations at Khirbet Shema‘, Upper Galilee,
            Israel, 1970–1972.* Durham, NC: Duke University Press.

Meyers, E. M., and J. F. Strange
1981   *Archaeology, the Rabbis and Early Christianity: The Social and
            Historical Setting of Palestinian Judaism and Christianity.* Nash-
            ville: Abingdon.

Meyers, E. M., J. F. Strange, and D. Groh
1978   "Survey of Galilee and Golan." *BASOR* 230: 1–24.

Meyers, E. M., J. F. Strange, and Carol Meyers
1979   "Preliminary Report on the 1977 and 1978 Seasons at Gush Halav
            (el-Jish)." *BASOR* 233: 35–58.
1981   *Excavations at Ancient Meiron, Upper Galilee, Israel.* American
            Schools of Oriental Research and Meiron Excavation Project Publi-
            cation no. 3. Cambridge, MA: ASOR.

Moe, D.
1977   "The Cross and the Menorah." *Archaeology* 30: 148–57.

Mussies, G.
1976   "Greek in Palestine and in the Diaspora." Pp. 1040–64 in Safrai and
            Stern, eds., section 1, vol. 2.

Naveh, J.
1978   *On Stone and Mosaic: The Aramaic and Hebrew Inscriptions from
            Ancient Synagogues.* Jerusalem: Carta (Hebrew).

Netzer, E.
1974   "The Hasmonean and Herodian Winter Palaces at Jericho." *Qad-
            moniot* 23/26: 28–36 (Hebrew)
1977   "The Winter Palaces of the Judean Kings at Jericho at the End of
            the Second Temple Period." *BASOR* 228: 1–13.
1978   "Miqvaot (Ritual Baths) of the Second Temple Period." *Qadmoniot*
            42: 54–59. (Hebrew).

Neusner, Jacob
1975   *Early Rabbinic Judaism: Historical Studies in Religion, Literature,
            and Art.* Leiden: Brill.
1968   "Rabbis and Community in Third-Century Babylonia." Pp. 438–59
            in *Religions in Antiquity: Essays in Memory of Erwin Ramsdell
            Goodenough.* Ed. J. Neusner. Supplements to *Numen* 14. Leiden:
            Brill.
1981   "The Symbolism of Ancient Judaism: The Evidence of the Syna-
            gogues." Pp. 7–17 in Gutmann, ed., 1981.

Ovadiah, A.
1976   "Greek Inscriptions from the Northern Bashan." *Liber Annuus* 26:
            170–212.
1978   "Early Christian Inscribed Tombstones in the D. Pinkus Collection,
            Israel." *Liber Annuus* 28: 127–41.

Poehlmann, W.
1981   "The Polycharmos Inscription and Synagogue I at Stobi." Pp. 235–48 in *Studies in the Antiquities of Stobi*, vol. 3. Eds. Blaga Aleksova and James Wiseman. Titov Veles: Macedonian Review Editions.

Rabin, Chaim
1976   "Hebrew and Aramaic in the First Century." Pp. 1007–39 in Safrai and Stern, eds., section 1, vol. 2.

Rahmani, L. Y.
1978   "A Catalogue of Jewish Ossuaries." Diss., Hebrew University (Hebrew).

Robert, L.
1946   "Un corpus des inscriptions juive." *Hellenica* 3: 90–108.
1964   *Nouvelles inscriptions de Sardes I.* Paris: Maisonneuve.
1978   "Malédictions funéraires grecques." *CRAIBL:* 241–89.

Safrai, S., and M. Stern, eds.
1974, 1976 *The Jewish People in the First Century: Historical Geography, Political History, Social, Cultural and Religious Life and Institutions.* 2 vols. CRINT, section 1, vols. 1, 2. Philadelphia: Fortress.

Saunders, E.
1977   "Christian Synagogues and Jewish-Christianity in Galilee." *Explor* 3: 70–77.

Schürer, Emil
1973, 1979 *The History of the Jewish People in the Age of Jesus Christ (175 B.C.–A.D. 135).* 2 vols. Ed. G. Vermes, and F. Millar. Edinburgh: T. & T. Clark.

Schwabe, Moshe, and Baruch Lifshitz
1974   *Beth She'arim.* Vol. 2, *The Greek Inscriptions.* Jerusalem: Israel Exploration Society; New Brunswick, NJ: Rutgers University Press.

Seager, A. R.
1973   "The Architecture of the Dura and Sardis Synagogues." Pp. 79–116 in Gutmann, ed., 1973. Reprinted in Gutmann, ed., 1975.
1981a   "Ancient Synagogue Architecture: An Overview." Pp. 39–47 in Gutmann, ed., 1981.
1981b   "The Synagogue at Sardis." Pp. 178–84 in Levine, ed., 1981a.

Shanks, H.
1979   "Gamla: The Masada of the North." *BARev* 5: 12–59.

Smith, Morton
1967   "Goodenough's 'Jewish Symbols' in Retrospect." *JBL* 86: 53–68. Reprinted in Gutmann, ed., 1975.

Stillwell, R., ed.
1976   *The Princeton Encyclopedia of Classical Sites.* Princeton, NJ: Princeton University Press.

Strange, James F.
1976a   "Magdala." *IDBSup,* 561.
1976b   "Capernaum." *IDBSup,* 140–41.
1977   "Review Article: The Capernaum and Herodian Publications." *BASOR* 226: 65–73.
1979   "Archaeology and the Religion of Judaism in Israel." Pp. 646–85 in *ANRW* 2.19.1. Ed. W. Haase. Berlin and New York: de Gruyter.

Sukenik, Eliezer L.
1932   *The Ancient Synagogue of Beth Alpha.* London and Jerusalem:
        Oxford University Press. Reprint, Hildesheim, 1975.
1934   *Ancient Synagogues in Palestine and Greece.* The Schweich Lec-
        tures on Biblical Archaeology, 1930. London: Humphrey Milford.
1949   "The Present State of Ancient Synagogue Studies." Pp. 1–23 in
        *Louis M. Rabinowitz Fund for the Exploration of Ancient
        Synagogues,* Bulletin 1. Jerusalem: Museum of Jewish Antiquities,
        The Hebrew University.

Testa, E.
1962   *Il Simbolismo dei Giudeo-Cristiani.* Publications of the Studium
        Biblicum Franciscanum 14. Jerusalem: Franciscan Printing Press.

Treu, K.
1973   "Die Bedeutung des Griechischen für die Juden im römischen
        Reich." *Kairos: Zeitschrift für Religionswissenschaft und Theologie*
        15: 123–44.

UNESCO
1960   *Israel: Ancient Mosaics.* Preface by M. Shapiro. Introduction by M.
        Avi-Yonah. UNESCO World Art Series 14. Greenwich, CT: New
        York Graphic Society.

Urman, D.
1976   "Golan." Pp. 453–67 in Avi-Yonah, ed., 1975–78, vol. 2.
1979   "The Golan during the Roman and Byzantine Periods: Topo-
        Settlements, Economy." Ph.D. diss., New York University.

Vogel, E. K.
1971   "Bibliography of Holy Land Sites." *HUCA* 42: 1–96.

Wiegand, T., and H. Schrader
1904   *Priene: Ergebnisse der Ausgrabungen und Untersuchungen in den
        Jahren 1895–1898.* Berlin: Reimer.

Wilken, R. L.
1976   "Melito, the Jewish Community at Sardis, and the Sacrifice of
        Isaac." *TS* 37: 53–69.

Wiseman, J.
1973   *Stobi: A Guide to the Excavations.* Austin: University of Texas
        Press; Beograd: National Museum of Titov Veles.

Yadin, Yigael, ed.
1975   *Jerusalem Revealed: Archaeology in the Holy City 1968–1974.* Jeru-
        salem: Israel Exploration Society.

INDEX OF SITES DISCUSSED

Athens, Greece, 186, 201; Beth Alfa, 193; Beth Shean, 180; Beth She'arim, 180-81, 194-95,
198; Capernaum, 178-79; Chalcis, Euboea, 201; Cyrenaica, North Africa, 188-89; Delos
(Aegean island), 185-86, 187, 200; Dura Europos, Syria, 184, 190-91, 195, 200; Gamala,
179-80; Gaza, 193-94; Gush Halav, 177, 178; Hammath Tiberias, 180, 193; Hussifa, 193;
Jericho, 181-82; Jerusalem, 182; Khirbet Shema', 177, 178; Magdala, 179; Meiron, 177, 178;
Naaran, 180, 193; Nabratein, 177, 178; Ostia, Italy, 187, 200; Priene, Ionia, 189; Qisrin,
179-80; Rehov, 199; Rome, Italy, 187-88, 194, 200; Sardis, Lydia, 184-85, 191-92, 200; Stobi,
Macedonia, 186-87; Susiya, 178, 180; Venosa, Italy, 188.

8
JEWISH NUMISMATICS

Yaakov Meshorer

Jewish coins have been studied quite intensively during the past three centuries. Individual investigations have contributed not only new material but also more comprehensive attributions and identifications. Nevertheless, it seems that the biggest advance in the understanding of ancient Jewish coins has taken place during the last forty years. New discoveries in archaeology and numismatics coupled with a better understanding of Jewish history have enabled the scholars of the recent generation to solve many enigmas and to propose solid evidence derived from ancient Jewish coins. This paper attempts to describe the various stages of progress for each relevant historical period, from the fourth century B.C.E. up to the Bar Kokhba war (132–135 C.E.).

UNDER THE PERSIAN REGIME
FOURTH CENTURY B.C.E.

In 1934, E. L. Sukenik identified for the first time coins of the Persian Jewish province of Judea, "Yehud," and since then they have been called "Yehud" coins. At first two types were clearly identified as such, but recently L. Mildenberg (1979) and Y. Meshorer have published what seem to be more or less complete collections of Yehud coins struck in Jerusalem during the end of the Persian period. This group of coins has been shown to contain thirteen different types. The designs are mainly imitations of contemporary Greek or Cilician coins, but they also have some Jewish flavor, such as the lily flower, a popular design in the Temple in Jerusalem. The inscriptions include either the name of the province Yehud (YHD) in ancient Jewish script or the name of the Jewish governor and his title (YHZQYH HPHH = Yehezkiah the governor).

The quantity of known Yehud coins was very limited until fifteen years ago, but since then hundreds of these tiny coins have been found. Among the new types not known before, coins struck even after the conquest of Alexander have been discovered (Mildenberg, 1979; Meshorer).

SAMARITAN COINS?

Other recent discoveries include some small silver coins depicting the name of Jeroboam and others, bearing the name ŠMRYN (Samaria). These coins apparently represent an issue parallel to the Jerusalemite Yehud coins, Yehud being the name of the city of Jerusalem as well as that of the province while Yehezkiah was governor. At the same time Shomron (Samaria) was the name of the province under Jeroboam's governorship (Meshorer: 1: 32; Spaer: 218).

UNDER THE PTOLEMIES

Jewish coins struck in Jerusalem under the Ptolemies are sensational new discoveries. They were struck mainly in small denominations of silver half-obols, of which hundreds have been found, but two half-drachm coins are also known (Meshorer: 1: 184). These coins imitate the prototype of the Ptolemaic currency, depicting the king's head on the obverse and the eagle on the reverse. The inscriptions are in paleo-Hebrew and show the name of the province as either YHD, YHWD, or YHWDH (Judea).

It seems that these coins were struck under Ptolemy II Philadelphus, during which time relations between the Ptolemaic ruler and the Jewish government in Jerusalem were flourishing. According to the *Letter of Aristeas* 68, the king ordered the translation of the Jewish scriptures into Greek for his library at Alexandria. He sent many precious gifts to the Temple in Jerusalem and freed from their masters in Egypt the Jewish slaves captured by his father, Ptolemy I.

UNDER THE HASMONEANS

The dispute over the chronology of the Hasmonean coins is still the major issue in the field of Jewish numismatics. The question of who struck the first Hasmonean coins remains unresolved. Many scholars maintain that John Hyrcanus I (135–104 B.C.E.) was the first to mint Hasmonean coins (Kindler, 1958:17; Rappaport; Barag and Qedar), whereas others suggest that Alexander Jannaeus (103–76 B.C.E.) was the first (Meshorer: 1: 35–98), arguing that all the Hasmonean coins with the name Yehohanan were struck under John Hyrcanus II (63–40 B.C.E.), and that those with the name Yehudah were struck under Aristobulus II (67–63 B.C.E.) rather than Aristobulus I (104 B.C.E.). Until recently, publications on Hasmonean coins had described only the major types, but in 1982 over six hundred different Hasmonean coins were systematically published and classified into twenty-six groups and subgroups. This publication included enlarged photographs of the coins as well as a survey of their paleography (Meshorer: 1). This study constitutes a basis from which further numismatic and paleographic study can proceed.

The investigation into the possible meanings of the symbols and emblems on these coins is also progressing. B. Kanael, to cite one example out of many, demonstrated that the eight-spoked star on Jannaeus coins is actually surrounded by a diadem rather than by a "wheel"; this makes it quite clear that the star symbolizes Jannaeus and the diadem his royal title.

THE HERODIANS

Herod the Great's coins have always been intriguing with respect to their symbolism, the meanings of which have been a source of scholarly dispute. Some have seen in them Jewish symbols and, therefore, a plant resembling a poppy was interpreted as a pomegranate and some pagan cult vessels were related to the cult objects in the Temple in Jerusalem. Others, who considered Herod to be more pagan-oriented because of his Edomite origins or his devotion to Roman masters, have explained some of the designs on his coins as depicting pagan ceremonial vessels such as "a tripod and lebes-symbols of the worship of Apollo." This interpretation is well represented by E. R. Goodenough (1953, 1: 274).

> The coins of Herod I can only doubtfully be considered to belong to the history of Jewish art. He used a number of pagan symbols, such as the Dionysiac tripod with pot (lebes), a ceremonial ordinary helmet, the winged caduceus, a little square cross, a war galley, and the eagle along with the anchor, wreath, palm branch, and the crossed cornucopiae, which had been used before in Jewish coinage.

A total change in the chronology of Herod's coinage can help to solve this problem. If all the dated coins of Herod (bearing a monogram and the year "3") are assigned to 40 B.C.E. rather than 37 or later, it can be argued that all these coins were struck at Samaria and not at Jerusalem where Mattathias Antigonus ruled. This enables us to connect the symbols on these dated coins to either Samaria itself or to the historical circumstances of that year, and indeed it seems that these symbols are inspired by contemporary Roman coins or from the repertoire of local Samarian cults (Meshorer: 2: 9–12, 18–30). Recent publications have brought the total number of published coin types of Herod to twenty-three.

In the coinage of Herod's sons, many interesting new types have been published during the last few decades. One type, the Antipas coins of "Year 24," which corresponds to 19/20 C.E., suggests that this year witnessed the foundation of Tiberias by Antipas (Spijkerman: 302, no. 10). Another discovery among these coins is the earliest portrait on Jewish coins, found on the coins of Philip, struck at Paneas in 1/2 C.E. (Kindler, 1971: 161–63) and later in 30 and 33 C.E. (Meshorer: 2: 45–47). These portraits from Paneas explain the appearance of portrait coins struck under Agrippa I at Paneas a short time later in 38 C.E., when he took over Philip's territory.

Studies of the coins of Agrippa I conclude that this king struck his coins at four different mints, according to the different territories he ruled while king. First he struck his coins at Paneas; then after receiving Antipas's territory, he moved to Tiberias (41 C.E.). In his sixth year (42 C.E.), Agrippa I struck his famous "three ears of barley" coins in Jerusalem, and finally, in his seventh and eighth (last) year, coins were minted at Caesarea.

Among the coins of Agrippa II are some which bear double dates reflecting two different dating systems. It now seems that the problems connected with these double-dated coins have been solved. It is widely accepted that Agrippa II's Flavian coins (which total over 95 percent of his coinage) are all dated according to the year 61 c.e., which makes his last dated coin "Year 35" (= 95/96 c.e.), the last year of Trajan's rule (Barag). The coins bearing "Year 19," which also depict the maritime symbols of galleys and anchors, refer to the voyage of Agrippa's sister Berenice to Rome in 79 c.e. to try to realize Titus's promise of marriage (Meshorer: 2: 78, 79).

The coins of the first revolt against Rome received very careful study as soon as their identification was certain. In a monograph specially devoted to these coins (Kadman) and in other studies (Kanael), the famous silver shekels and the much-discussed coins of "Year 4" along with the bronze prutot of "Year 2" and "Year 3" were finally attributed with confidence to the first revolt. The excavations at Masada, the last stronghold of this war, and at Jerusalem, where thousands of these coins were found in destruction layers, make this attribution certain.

The development of the types of inscriptions found on the coins of the period of the first revolt is quite clear now. The slogans of war such as "Freedom of Zion," found on the coins of Years 2 and 3 (67–68 c.e.), show that these coins were struck at a time when there was still hope for victory over the Romans in battle. These inscriptions give way to slogans like "For the Redemption of Zion," found on coins of Year 4 after most of the country had been captured by the Romans and only Jerusalem was left to defend itself from the legions of Titus. The expression "redemption" on these coins indicated the hope of the defenders for help from heaven, a hope that is mentioned by Josephus.

Except for some new varieties added recently to the repertoire of coins struck during this period (Meshorer: 2: nos. 1, 9, 14), the only new type not known previously is represented by a crude bronze coin found at the excavations at Gamla on the Golan Heights (four specimens). This coin bears a crude chalice resembling the vessels on the shekels of the first year. The inscription (in paleo-Hebrew) reads: "For the Redemption of Holy Jerusalem" (Meshorer: 2: 129–31). This type was struck at Gamla, probably during the siege of the Romans at the beginning of the revolt. Such coins were not found at the excavations of Jerusalem or Masada; consequently, it can be concluded that this coin type was Galilean.

The only change in identification concerns the so-called "half-prutot" of the third year described by G. F. Hill (275, nos. 55–57), A. Reifenberg (nos. 149–50), and L. Kadman (nos. 46–59). These coins are practically small minimas of Caesarea imitating Jewish coins and are not part of the minting of the first revolt coins. This is demonstrated by the many hybrid coins where vine leaves or amphora imitating first revolt types are found on one side, whereas on the other side depictions of the Roman emperor or a head of Tyche appear. These representations stem from dies of other types of minimas struck at Caesarea which themselves imitate coins of Alexandria, Sidon, or Tyre (Meshorer: 2: suppl. 6, 1–12, pp. 188–89).

Regarding the series of provincial "Judea Capta" coins struck at Caesarea, the greatest progress has been made in identifying the coins of the emperor Domitian and arranging them in their proper types, such as "the coins of the Roman administration of Judea" (Kindler, 1968). Several new coin types have been identified among these and the "Judea Capta" coins during the past few years (Meshorer: 2: suppl. 7, no. 4; suppl. 8, nos. 1, 2, 4).

THE COINS OF THE BAR KOKHBA REVOLT (132–135 C.E.)

Until twenty-five years ago, the coins of Bar Kokhba were practically the only archaeological evidence from this war. The discoveries of the Judean Desert excavations of the caves to which some refugees of the war escaped, including letters and other written documents of the time as well as objects from daily life, have complemented our picture of the period.

The coins are all overstruck on contemporary Roman coins which had been struck in Rome or the provinces. Overstriking these Roman coins, which bore the portraits of the Roman emperors, with new designs not only saved the stage of preparing flans but also enabled Bar Kokhba to demolish the pagan symbols and designs of the foreign rulers and to replace them with his own symbols and slogans. The silver and bronze coins bear designs related to the Temple in Jerusalem, the one destroyed by Titus in 70 C.E., which Bar Kokhba planned to rebuild after his victory. The designs include the façade of the temple and a selection of ceremonial vessels. A detailed study of the Bar Kokhba coins appeared recently (Mildenberg, 1984).

One of the difficulties that has not yet been satisfactorily explained and has become even more complicated is the undated coins. The coins of the first year are dated, "Year 1 of the redemption of Israel." The coins of the second year are dated "Year 2 of the freedom of Israel." All the later coins, struck during the third and fourth years, are undated and are inscribed "For the freedom of Jerusalem." The fact that the written documents of Bar Kokhba found in the Judean Desert caves do bear the dates "Year 3" and "Year 4" indicate that the counting of the years did not cease and its absence from the coins remains a mystery.

THE COINS OF THE ROMAN PROCURATORS

The Romans sent various categories of administrators to their provinces, some of whom even struck provincial coins such as those struck at Antioch by the local Roman legates. However, the coins struck in Judea (probably in Jerusalem) by the Roman procurators/prefects sent there after 6 C.E. were different from all other Roman provincial issues, in that they do not have any Roman characters, but rather Hebrew. It seems that they were struck in this manner in order to avoid offending the Jews, possibly after consultation with the Jewish authorities. Only the coins of Pontius Pilate depict pagan designs such as the *lituus* and the *simpulum*, but this appears to have been done out of ignorance of Jewish culture rather than deliberately to irritate the Jews (Meshorer: 2: 177–80)

The minting of coins by the procurators/prefects was interrupted during the reign of Agrippa I (37-44 C.E.), and it stopped in 59 C.E. The complete repertoire of procuratorial coins was established long ago and practically no new types have been discovered. The only innovations are hybrid coins bearing new combinations not previously known among the coins of Valerius Gratus, Pontius Pilatus, and Antonius Felix (Meshorer: 2: nos. 7, 9, 11, 26–28, 34). There is little doubt that Festus, not Felix, minted the last and largest issue, struck in the fifth year of Nero, 59 C.E. (Meshorer: 2: 183).

LIST OF PRINCIPAL COINS

1. *YHD* coin, silver obol, ca. 340 B.C.E.
2. Silver obol of "Yehezkiah the governor," ca. 340 B.C.E.
3. Silver hemiobol of Judea under Ptolemy II, ca. 275 B.C.E.
4. Bronze prutah of Judas Aristobulus, 67–63 B.C.E.
5. Bronze prutah of Alexander Jannaeus, 103–76 B.C.E.
6. Bronze prutah of John Hyrcanus II, 63–40 B.C.E.
7. Bronze double prutah of Herod, struck at Samaria, 40 B.C.E.
8. Bronze double prutah of Herod, struck at Jerusalem, 37–4 B.C.E.
9. Bronze coin of Herod Antipas, struck at Tiberias, 19/20 C.E.
10. Bronze coin of Philip bearing his portrait and that of Augustus, struck at Paneas, 1 C.E.
11. Bronze coin of Agrippa I bearing his portrait, struck at Paneas, 38 C.E.
12. Bronze coin of Agrippa I depicting Caligula and Germanicus, struck at Tiberias, 41 C.E.
13. Bronze prutah of Agrippa I, struck at Jerusalem, 42 C.E.
14. Bronze coin of Agrippa I bearing his portrait, struck at Caesarea, 43 C.E.
15. Bronze coin of Agrippa II, struck at Paneas, 61 C.E.
16. Bronze coin of Agrippa II, struck at Paneas, 79 C.E., to commemorate the voyage of Berenice to Rome
17. Silver shekel of the Jewish war, struck at Jerusalem, 67 C.E.
18. Bronze prutah of the Jewish war, struck at Jerusalem, 67 C.E., with the inscription "The freedom of Zion"
19. Bronze coin of the Jewish war, struck at Jerusalem, 69 C.E., with the inscription "For the redemption of Zion"
20. Bronze "barbaric" coin of the Jewish war, struck at Gamla, 67 C.E.
21. Silver denarius of Bar Kokba, undated (134/5 C.E.).
22. Bronze prutah, struck at Jerusalem under Festus, 59 C.E.

1

2

3

4

5

6

7

8

9

10

11

12

13

14

15

16

17

18

19

20

21

22

BIBLIOGRAPHY

Barag, D.
1978   "The Palestinian 'Judea Capta' Coins of Vespasian and Titus and
          the Era of the Coins of Agrippa II Minted under the Flavians." NC
          7th ser.: 14–23.

Barag, D., and S. H. Qedar
1980   "The Beginning of Hasmonean Coinage." INJ 4: 8–21.

Goodenough, E. R.
1953–76   Jewish Symbols in the Greco-Roman Period. 13 vols. New York:
          Pantheon Books.

Hill, G. F.
1914   Catalogue of the Greek Coins of Palestine. London: British
          Museum. Reprint, Bologna: Arnaldo Forni, 1965.

Kadman, L.
1960   The Coins of the Jewish War of 66–73 C.E. Corpus nummorum
          Palaestinensium, series 2, vol. 3. Jerusalem: Schocken.

Kanael, B.
1963   "Ancient Jewish Coins and Their Historical Importance." BA 26:
          38–62.

Kindler, A.
1958   "The Coinage of the Hasmonaean Dynasty." Pp. 10–28 in The
          Dating and Meaning of Ancient Jewish Coins and Symbols.
          Numismatic Studies and Researches. Jerusalem: Israel Exploration
          Society.
1968   "The Coin Issues of the Roman Administration in the Provincia
          Ivdaea During the Reign of Domitian." Bulletin of the Museum
          Haaretz 10: 6–16.
1971   "A Coin of Herod Philip — the Earliest Portrait of a Herodian
          Ruler." IEJ 21: 161–63.

Meshorer, Y.
1982   Ancient Jewish Coinage. 2 vols. Dix Hills, NY: Amphora Books.

Mildenberg, L.
1979   "Yehud: A Preliminary Study of the Provincial Coinage of Judaea."
          Pp. 183–96 in Greek Numismatics and Archaeology: Essays in
          Honor of Margaret Thompson. Ed. Otto Morkholm and Nancy M.
          Waggoner. Wetteren: n.p.
1984   The Coinage of the Bar Kokhba War. Ed. and trans. Patricia
          Erhart Mottahedeh. Typos: Monographien zur antiken Numis-
          matik 6. Aaran, Switzerland and Frankfurt am Main and Salzburg:
          Sauerländer.

Rappaport, U.
1976   "The Emergence of Hasmonean Coinage." AJSReview 1: 171–86.
          Reprinted in Studies in the History of the Jewish People and the
          Land of Israel. Tel Aviv: University of Haifa, 1978. 4: 77–85
          (Hebrew).

Reifenberg, A.
1947   Ancient Jewish Coins. 2d ed. Jerusalem: Rubin Mass.

Spaer, A.
   1979   "A Coin of Jeroboam?" *IEJ* 29: 218.
Spijkerman, A.
   1962–63   "Some Rare Jewish Coins." *SBFLA* 13: 302, no. 10.
Sukenik, E. L.
   1934   "The Oldest Coins of Judaea." *JPOS* 14: 178–84.

Part Three

The Literature

9

JEWISH GREEK SCRIPTURES

Emanuel Tov

The study of ancient Greek translations of Jewish scriptures has changed in the past four decades, if only because of new discoveries: Greek scrolls (see chap. 6 in this volume) made possible a better understanding of the LXX and its revisions, and Hebrew scrolls from Qumran (see below) improved understanding of the use of the LXX for textual criticism of the Hebrew Bible. These new finds stimulated a number of valuable studies which, together with new editions, have served to open new horizons. Enthusiasm has also been generated by the founding, largely through the energy of the late S. Jellicoe, of the International Organization for Septuagint and Cognate Studies (IOSCS), which sponsors conferences and publishes an annual *Bulletin* (since 1968) containing information about research accomplished and in progress. Other publications of general significance include an extensive classified bibliography (Brock, Fritsch, and Jellicoe) and new introductions (Jellicoe, 1968, intended to update H. B. Swete's still valuable work; Fernández Marcos, 1979). Research in the period covered by this chapter is reviewed in Seeligmann, 1940; Orlinsky, 1947; Katz; Wevers, 1954, 1968; Howard; Jellicoe, 1974:XIII-LXI; and Fernández Marcos, 1976.

THE LXX PROPER

Editions and Tools

The most significant events in the period under review were the discontinuation of the Cambridge LXX (1906–1940) and the publication of several eclectic editions in the Göttingen Septuagint series, prepared by the Septuaginta-Unternehmen: Isaiah (1939, ²1967), Ezekiel (1952, ²1977), Jeremiah (1957, ²1976), Minor Prophets (1943, ²1967), Daniel (1954), Wisdom of Solomon (1962), Jesus Sirach (1965) and Job (1983), all by J. Ziegler. The very first volume was Psalms by A. Rahlfs (1931, ²1967). W. Kappler edited 1 Maccabees (1936, ²1967), and R. Hanhart has prepared 2 and 3 Maccabees (1959, 1960), Esther (1966), 1 Esdras (1974), Judith (1979) and Tobit (1984). J. W. Wevers has edited Genesis (1974), Deuteronomy (1977), and Numbers (1981) and is presently preparing Leviticus and Exodus. W. Baars is editing 4 Maccabees. Each edition includes an extensive introduction, which describes the textual witnesses and analyzes matters of orthography and grammar, and is accompanied by a volume of textual studies (see Hanhart and Wevers). Recent Göttingen editions provide more information on the nature of the "Editionstechnik" and on textual problems than did earlier volumes. However, the user still lacks guidance concerning why in any given instance the editor preferred one reading as archetypal and relegated the others to the apparatus. Admittedly, the otherwise desirable inclusion of such remarks in an appended commentary would have delayed the publication of the editions for many years.

The missing parts of M. L. Margolis's valuable edition of Joshua (1931 [-1938]) have now been rediscovered by E. Tov at Dropsie University, Philadelphia (see *Bulletin of the IOSCS* 14 [1981] 17–21).

For editions of recently discovered papyri and scrolls, see Pietersma, 1977, 1978; additional papyri of the LXX have been listed in Aland and in van Haelst.

Of the other versions made from the LXX, the Syro-Palestinian translation was reedited by M. Goshen-Gottstein (1975). Several new Syro-Hexapla texts have been published by Baars, and that of the entire Pentateuch has appeared in a facsimile edition of a manuscript recently found in Tur-Abdin (Vööbus). To date, the Vetus Latina Institute in Beuron has published only Genesis (Fischer) and Wisdom of Solomon (Thiele); at present, work is concentrated on the Apocrypha and the NT rather than on the Hebrew Bible. M. Peters has published a major study on the Bohairic Coptic translation of Deuteronomy.

A useful reverse index to the concordance of Hatch-Redpath has been prepared by E. C. dos Santos, and X. Jacques has published another index to that concordance which arranges the Greek words by roots.

A computer tape of Rahlfs's edition of the LXX has been prepared by the Thesaurus Linguae Graecae (TLG) project at the University of California at Irvine, and similar work is under way in Edinburgh. Computerized concordances, prepared from these tapes, have been made available for private use. The tape of the TLG project provides the data base for the LXX material prepared by the multilingual concordance project in Maredsous (Belgium), directed by F. Poswick, and also for the Computer Assisted Tools for LXX Studies (CATSS) project directed by R. A. Kraft and E. Tov (Kraft and Tov; Kraft, 1979). The first publication of a computer-assisted concordance is the one of Baruch by R. A. Martin (1977).

LXX Origins and the Nature of the Canon of the LXX

New data have become available that are relevant to understanding the origins of the LXX and the nature of its canon, but they have been interpreted in different ways. The analysis by D. Barthélemy (1963) of the

Dodekapropheton scroll from Naḥal Ḥever (8HevXII gr) has demonstrated once again that the collection of Greek scriptures grew through continuous revision of previous translations. At the same time, the analyses by P. W. Skehan of the unrevised 4QLXXLev[a] and by Wevers (1977) of *P. Rylands Gk.* 458 (Deut) showed that the text of the great uncials, which in most books has always been considered a good representative of the original translation, had in fact often been revised toward a more literal representation of the MT. The same trend had been pointed out earlier by D. W. Gooding (1955) on the basis of an analysis of the uncial manuscripts themselves.

The old controversy between the followers of P. de Lagarde's theory (an "Urtext" subsequently diffusing into different text forms) and those following P. Kahle (multiple translations converging into one central text) has not been settled because each group has claimed that the recent finds support its own views. For instance, Kahle and A. Sperber failed to recognize the revisional nature of some of the newly found scrolls and, hence, exaggerated the amount of difference between the various Greek traditions and cited evidence that is not relevant to the issue of the Urtext. At the same time scholars have read too much into the views of de Lagarde and Kahle and have tended to present them as two diametrically opposed views. The different views on the relevance of the *Letter of Aristeas* to these issues have been summarized by Gooding (1963).

On the basis of the work of E. Bickerman (1950), a synthetic view has been suggested by Tov (1981:42), which may be characterized as a theory of multiple textual traditions. According to this view, one Greek translation must be presupposed as the base of the manuscripts of most, if not all, books of the LXX. The original wording of this translation was soon corrupted. As the original translation was copied and transmitted in different scrolls, it split into several secondary textual traditions, since various types of corrections (mainly toward the Hebrew) were inserted into the various individual scrolls.

As a result of recent finds and studies of early recensions, the heterogeneity of the canon of the LXX has become increasingly evident. It has been recognized that "the LXX" contains translations of different types, early and late, relatively original and significantly revised, official and private, literal and free (see especially Kraft, ed.). In view of this situation it must be assumed that those responsible for selecting the translations included in the collection of Jewish-Greek scriptures apparently did not attempt or were unable to insure uniformity of the translations included.

The Greek of the LXX

In the past, the supposedly unusual character of LXX Greek has been described in various ways: as a development within the Greek of Hellenistic

Egypt, as a Jewish-Greek dialect, or as translation Greek. Less realistic descriptions referred to the language of the LXX and the NT as "the language of the Holy Spirit," whereas others described it as an exponent of classical Greek. The various positions until the 1940s have been depicted by J. Vergote and J. Ros (with the unavoidable mixture of terminology referring to both LXX and NT as "biblical" Greek).

In the last decades, research on the background of LXX Greek has not progressed in any particular direction. Even the more remote theory referring to a living Jewish-Greek dialect has found adherents among prominent scholars such as H. S. Gehman and N. Turner. In a detailed study J. A. L. Lee centers on the contemporary background of LXX (Pentateuch) words—Hellenistic Egypt as reflected in the papyri. In Hellenistic Egypt there undoubtedly existed a limited vocabulary of Jewish technical terms, especially relating to religion, which formed the basis for the vocabulary of the original LXX (Pentateuch). Furthermore, the LXX contains several local Egyptian terms. In my view, however, the idiosyncrasies of the vocabulary and syntax of the LXX have been caused mainly by the special nature of the translation. The translators' adherence to stereotyped renderings of words, roots, and syntactical constructions, which also generated etymologizing renderings and the coining of new words, created a special type of language (unusual words and meanings, lack of variation in vocabulary, and lack of distinction between poetic and prosaic words). For recent studies of the translational (Semitic) elements in the LXX, see Rapallo; Martin, 1974; Tov, 1976a,b; and Daniel.

Lexicography

The need for lexicographical studies on the LXX was felt by all those interested in the Hellenistic background of the LXX, its translation technique, the text-critical value of the LXX for biblical research, the history of the Greek language, and the background of the NT. However, the number of full lexicographical studies has remained small, since LXX words (often called "concepts") have often been analyzed for limited purposes only and with preconceived ideas. The search for theological ideas behind common translation equivalents, advocated by R. Kittel's *Theologisches Wörterbuch* (especially through the many articles by G. Bertram), has become more widely known in the last decade through its English translation. The issues have been clarified by J. Barr (1961), whose approach stressed the linguistic background of the translators' equivalents, in contrast to Kittel's theological approach.

In more recent years, the approach to lexicography has become more comprehensive, as the translation aspect of Septuagintal words has been taken into greater consideration. In the period under review, see especially word studies by E. Repo, M. Paeslack, S. Daniel, Barr (1962), L. Monsengwo Pasinya, and D. Hill, as well as methodological studies by G. B. Caird, Lee (1970, 1980) and Tov (1976b). The history of the planning of the proposed LXX lexicon can be followed in Kraft, 1979, ed., 1972; Tov, 1976a; Kraft and Tov; and Silva.

Translation Technique and Exegesis

The study of the translation technique and exegesis reflected in the LXX is interesting in its own right, but it is also of much interest for an understanding of the LXX as a document of Hellenistic Judaism and as a prerequisite for an analysis of the language of the LXX. At the same time, translation technique and exegesis are analyzed often as a necessary preparatory step for the textual analysis of the individual books. Since the LXX is a translation of a Hebrew text often different from the MT, analysis of the LXX is in need of criteria that help to distinguish between exegetical elements in that translation and elements that are based on a Hebrew text different from the MT.

Individual books in the LXX differ much with regard to their patterns of exegesis and translation technique. Therefore, few studies have been written on all or some aspects of the exegesis of the LXX as a whole. Most studies have been confined to individual books; see, e.g., Ziegler, 1934; Seeligmann, 1948; Allen; Orlinsky, 1975. For further references, see Brock et al., sections 10-14, 16.

The scientific study of the translation technique of the LXX as a separate line of investigation is in the process of being developed. However, the definition of what falls under the heading of translation technique needs to be defined more precisely, since this is not at all clear, for example, from the relevant sections in either Brock et al. or Jellicoe, 1974. The most promising exponents of a modern approach to translation technique have been offered by I. Soisalon-Soininen in a major study (1965) and several smaller studies both by him and by his students (e.g., R. Sollamo). For this purpose, Soisalon-Soininen has classified in a card-index system the major grammatical and syntactical categories of the Hebrew text that have been translated into Greek (e.g., infinitives, construct forms, relative clauses, prepositions) and of the Greek text (e.g., *echō*, verbs with neuter plural subjects). These data are analyzed in detailed studies, and in due course they will form the basis for a full description of the translation technique and syntax of the Pentateuch.

The study by Barr (1979) on literalism (with examples mainly from the LXX) greatly advanced our understanding of translation technique. Studies by C. Rabin and Brock (1979) clarified the background of the LXX translation within its setting in the ancient world.

The LXX and Qumran

Discovery of Hebrew scrolls at Qumran relates directly to the use of the LXX as a text-critical tool in biblical scholarship (see Brock et al.; Cross, 1953, 1961, 1964, 1975; Cross and Talmon; Fitzmyer; Tov, 1972a, 1981). The use of the LXX as a text-critical tool can now for the first time be supported by an independent source such as the Qumran scrolls. In the past, scholars have often oscillated between recognition of exegetical elements or Hebrew variants deviating from the MT. This issue can never be settled completely, but there is now at least more evidence in favor of the second possibility. Hundreds of examples can be adduced from the Qumran scrolls to show that the LXX, when analyzed correctly, reflects Hebrew variants also found in these scrolls. There is thus no longer any need to justify the use of a non-Hebrew source such as the LXX in the text-critical analysis of the Hebrew Bible. However, caution should be used in evaluating agreements between the LXX and a particular scroll, since many of them do not bear on the text-critical analysis. This is especially true in regard to agreements in grammatical categories such as the addition or omission of the article and pronouns as well as various harmonizations, differences in verbal forms, etc. In all these instances the agreement may have derived from independent exegesis by a Hebrew scribe and a Greek translator, as suggested by Goshen-Gottstein (1963). In such passages the text-critical value of the agreements cannot be determined (against Ziegler, 1959, with regard to 1QIsa[a]).

Beyond the general relevance of the Qumran scrolls to the overall evaluation of the LXX, some scrolls are directly related to the text of some Greek translations. The relationship between the LXX and the Hebrew scrolls found at Qumran differs from scroll to scroll, and therefore generalizations should be avoided. Moreover, much material still awaits publication, so that no final judgment is possible, even concerning fragments that have already been published, such as the fragments of the Samuel scrolls. Several scrolls often coincide with details in the LXX, either with the central or with a specific group of its manuscripts. Although these details are often significant, no published scroll—with the exception of 4QJer[b]—agrees with the LXX in *most* of its details.

The relationship between the LXX and the Qumran scrolls has been discussed in analyses of the individual scrolls (see Cross, 1953–1975; Skehan; Cross and Talmon; Ulrich, 1978, 1980). Many scrolls agree with the LXX in several significant details: 4QExod[a], 11QpaleoLev, 4QDeut[q], 1QIsa[a], and 11QPs[a]. However, none of these is, as a whole, very close to the LXX, for although they agree in several details, both the scrolls and the LXX contain various independent readings. A different situation obtains with regard to 4QJer[b] and 4QSam[a,b,c], which have many readings in common with the LXX. The close relation between 4QJer[b] and the LXX has been described in Janzen and in Tov, 1982:264. The number of agreements between the LXX and 4QSam[a,b,c] is impressive (Cross, 1953–1975; Ulrich, 1978, 1980). However, both the scrolls and the LXX also contain many independent readings. The significance of the agreements should therefore not be overstated, especially since many of them refer to readings that are more original than the parallel readings in the MT. Moreover, the readings common to the LXX and the scrolls of Samuel are not typologically similar, as in the case of Jeremiah (see further the articles in Tov, ed.; on the proto-Lucianic problem in Samuel, see below).

The Text-critical Use of the LXX in Biblical Research

Together with the Qumran scrolls, the LXX forms the most significant source for variant readings. Hence, details in this translation are often analyzed for perusal in the textual criticism of the Hebrew Bible. It is noteworthy that most surveys like the present one include some statement on the uncritical use of the LXX by OT scholars (see, e.g., Orlinsky, 1947; and especially Katz: 198: "Never was the LXX more used and less studied"). Despite the sound methodological rules formulated by M. Margolis in an earlier period (*JAOS* 30 [1910] 301–12; *JQR* 1 [1910] 5–41) and by Goshen-Gottstein (1963), Barr (1967, 1968) and Tov (1981) in the period under review, scholars too often approach the LXX atomistically. On the one hand, there has been much progress in the understanding of the text-critical use of the LXX (see the aforementioned studies and further Allen; Barr, 1968, 1979; Barthélemy, 1978; Gooding, 1979; Goshen-Gottstein, 1975; Orlinsky, 1969; Seeligmann, 1948; Wevers, 1978). On the other hand, the widening gap between specialists in textual criticism and non-specialists leaves much to be desired in biblical commentaries. Some of these commentaries show great textual understanding, but others do not reflect the progress of scholarship in this discipline. *BHS*, for example, does improve the third (seventh) edition of *BH* in its more cautious approach to the ancient versions, but its choice of data included in the apparatus is less judicious. On the whole, this widely used edition does not reflect the advanced critical understanding of modern times. The edition by Goshen-Gottstein (1975) reflects a more cautious approach to the LXX and the other versions, and its apparatus reflects a good choice of the available data, but to date little has been published of that edition.

REVISIONS OF THE LXX

Terminology

A given textual tradition can be considered a revision of the LXX if the following two conditions are met: (1) The LXX and the revision share a common textual basis, established by the existence of distinctive agreements.

(2) The supposed revision was revised in a certain direction, generally toward a more precise reflection of its Hebrew source. However, the purpose of some revisions was the clarification and stylistic improvement of the Greek wording without any connection to the Hebrew *Vorlage*. Scholars have not always paid attention to these two conditions, and, consequently, the revisional nature of some textual traditions has not been established. In the period under review, older terms (as well as the views behind them) have become extinct, and new terms have been introduced into the scholarly discussion:

Old Greek. With the unraveling of a series of subsequent revisions of the original Greek translations, it has become customary, especially among American scholars, to refer to the oldest recoverable translation as the Old Greek (OG), to distinguish it, on the one hand, from the term "LXX" proper (Pentateuch) and, on the other, from later editorial activity (e.g., Lucian).

Kaige-Theodotion. In the provisional publication of 8HevXIIgr by Barthélemy (1963), it was suggested that this text, together with several sections of the so-called LXX (2 Sam 11:1 [10:1]–1 Kgs 2:11; 1 Kings 21–2 Kings; Ruth; Lamentations; and possibly other sections; see Barthélemy, 1963:47) reflects an early revision of the Old Greek. This revision has been named by Barthélemy *kaige*, because one of its easily recognizable characteristics is the frequent rendering of *gam* by *kaige*—a rendering that Barthélemy linked with the rabbinic "rule of inclusion and exclusion." Barthélemy also showed that the readings (sections) that in antiquity have been ascribed to Theodotion (the sixth column of the Hexapla) also belong to the *kaige* revision. Accordingly, this revision has usually been named the *kaige*-Theodotionic revision.

Ur-Theodotion. The term Ur-Theodotion had been invented to describe the quotations reflecting a Theodotionic text in the period preceding the historical Theodotion (second century C.E.), for example, in the NT. However, if the existence of the *kaige*-Theodotionic revision is assured, the very assumption of "Ur-Theodotion" becomes superfluous.

"LXX." Because it has been realized that the canon of the LXX contains an amalgam of revised and unrevised translations, and because the term "Septuagint" traditionally refers to the first translation (of the Pentateuch, later expanded to the whole of the Greek scriptures), some scholars place the term "LXX" in quotation marks to indicate the special nature of the collection of Greek scriptures.

Lucian. Even though Barthélemy (1963) argued against the assumption of a historical Lucian, the term Lucian has continued in scholarly use, albeit in a different sense. In recent years it has become customary to refer to two *strata* of text extant in the Lucianic tradition. According to most scholars, the second and last stratum of that tradition was superimposed upon an earlier text by the historical Lucian. The nature of the first stratum is disputed. According to Barthélemy (1963) and Tov (1972b), it reflects the Old Greek translation (for Barthélemy the term OG designates the whole body of the Lucianic tradition, since he rejected the existence of the historical Lucian). For Cross (1964–1975), this stratum reflects a proto-Lucianic revision (see below).

Proto-Lucian. In the period prior to Barthélemy (1963), the term proto-Lucian (or Ur-Lucian) was often used to denote elements in the Lucianic tradition that were attested in the period preceding the historical Lucian (d. 312), for example, in Josephus or in the Old Latin translation. (The nature of this first stratum of the Lucianic tradition has not yet been clarified.) The simplest solution would seem to be to use the term "proto-Lucian" in a neutral way to denote the textual tradition upon which Lucian superimposed his revision. However, in contemporary research this layer is described in different ways. As a result, the neutral application of the term is used less frequently. According to Barthélemy (1963) and Tov (1972b), this layer reflects the Old Greek in the historical books; thus, for them a term like proto-Lucian would be superfluous in those books. A different course, however, is taken by Cross (1964–1975), who finds in this layer a proto-Lucianic *revision* of the Old Greek toward a Hebrew text similar to the Samuel scrolls from Qumran Cave 4. Hence, especially in American research, one notes frequent reference to the proto-Lucianic revision, even though the very existence of the revisional element has not yet been demonstrated (see Tov, 1972a). The latest statement by Cross on this issue (1975) is less insistent than earlier ones, but there is no basic change in his position.

New Directions

Modern research in the wake of Barthélemy's study has been amply summarized by Tov (1972a), Kraft (1976) and K. O'Connell, so that only the major issues are reviewed here. Many recent studies support the suggestion of Barthélemy (1963) that there existed a *kaige*-Theodotionic revision that incorporated the sections mentioned above (O'Connell; Tov, 1972a; Venetz; Ulrich, 1978; for bibliographic references, see Tov, 1972a, and below). There has been no inner-Greek study of the proto-Lucianic layer beyond that of Brock (1966). There is much need of such studies as well as of a concordance of that text, especially in the historical books. J. Abercrombie and the CATSS project are preparing such a concordance (computer-assisted) for Samuel–Kings.

The question of the precise relationship between the proto-Lucianic stratum and the Samuel scrolls from Qumran needs to be investigated in full after the publication of these Hebrew texts. Ulrich (1978) presents much valuable material; it appears that in the *kaige* sections of Samuel the proto-Lucian stratum agrees more with the Qumran scrolls than in the non-*kaige* sections, where agreements are closer to the Old Greek (thus already Cross, 1964). The material of the "Three" is now more accessible through the concordances of Reider and Turner, Busto Saiz, and A. Schenker.

BIBLIOGRAPHY

For further bibliography see Tov, 1972a, and especially Brock et al., which covers from 1860 to 1969 inclusive.

Aland, Kurt
  1971   *Repertorium der griechischen christlichen Papyri. I, Biblische Papyri.* Patristische Texte und Studien 18. Berlin and New York: de Gruyter.

Allen, Leslie C.
  1974   *The Greek Chronicles: The Relation of the Septuagint of I and II Chronicles to the Massoretic Text.* Vol. 1, *The Translator's Craft.* Vol. 2, *Textual Criticism.* VTSup 25, 27. Leiden: Brill.

Baars, W.
  1968   *New Syro-Hexaplaric Texts.* Leiden: Brill.

Barr, James
  1961   *The Semantics of Biblical Language.* Oxford: Oxford University Press.
  1962   *Biblical Words for Time.* SBT 33. London: SCM.
  1967   "Vocalization and the Analysis of Hebrew among the Ancient Translators." Pp. 1–11 in *Hebräische Wortforschung: Festschrift zum 80. Geburtstag von Walter Baumgartner.* VTSup 16. Leiden: Brill.
  1968   *Comparative Philology and the Text of the Old Testament.* Oxford: Oxford University Press.
  1979   *The Typology of Literalism in Ancient Biblical Translations.* MSU 15. Nachrichten der Akademie der Wissenschaften in Göttingen. I. Phil.-Hist. Kl. Göttingen: Vandenhoeck & Ruprecht.

Barthélemy, Dominique
  1963   *Les devanciers d'Aquila: Première publication intégrale du texte des fragments du Dodécaprophéton.* VTSup 10. Leiden: Brill.
  1974   "Qui est Symmaque?" *CBQ* 36: 451–65.
  1978   *Études d'histoire du texte de l'ancien Testament.* OBO 21. Freiburg: Universitätsverlag; Göttingen: Vandenhoeck & Ruprecht.

Bickerman, Elias J.
  1950   "Some Notes on the Transmission of the Septuagint." Pp. 149–78 in *A. Marx Jubilee Volume.* New York: Jewish Theological Seminary.
  1959   "The Septuagint as a Translation." *PAAJR* 28: 1–39.

Bodine, Walter R.
  1980   *The Greek Text of Judges: Recensional Developments.* HSM 23. Chico, CA: Scholars Press.

Brock, Sebastian
1966 "The Recensions of the Septuagint Version of I Samuel." Diss., Oxford University.
1972 "The Phenomenon of the Septuagint." *OTS* 7: 11–36.
1979 "Aspects of Translation Technique in Antiquity." *GRBS* 20: 67–87.

Brock, Sebastian, Charles T. Fritsch, and Sidney Jellicoe
1973 *A Classified Bibliography of the Septuagint.* Leiden: Brill.

Busto Saiz, José Ramon
1978 *La Traduccion de Simaco en el libro de los Salmos.* Textos y estudios "Cardenal Cisneros" 22. Madrid: Consejo Superior de Investigaciones Cientificas.

Caird, George B.
1968, 1969 "Towards a Lexicon of the Septuagint." *JTS* n.s. 19: 453–75; 20: 21–40. Reprinted in Kraft, ed.

Charlesworth, James H.
1976 *The Pseudepigrapha and Modern Research.* SBLSCS 7. Missoula, MT: Scholars Press.
1978 "New Developments in the Study of the *Ecrits Intertestamentaires.*" *Bulletin of the IOSCS* 11: 14–15.

Cross, Frank M., Jr.
1953 "A New Qumran Fragment Related to the Original Hebrew Underlying the Septuagint." *BASOR* 132: 15–26.
1961 *The Ancient Library of Qumran and Modern Biblical Studies.* Rev. ed. Garden City, NY: Doubleday, Anchor Books.
1964 "The History of the Biblical Text in the Light of Discoveries in the Judaean Desert." *HTR* 57: 281–299.
1975 "The Evolution of a Theory of Local Texts." Pp. 306–20 in Cross and Talmon.

Cross, F. M., Jr., and Shemaryahu Talmon, eds.
1975 *Qumran and the History of the Biblical Text.* Cambridge, MA: Harvard University Press.

Daniel, Suzanne
1966 *Recherches sur le vocabulaire du culte dans la Septante.* Études et Commentaires 61. Paris: Klincksieck.

Fernández Marcos, Natalio
1976 "Los estudios de 'Septuaginta.' Visión retrospectiva y problemática más reciente." *Cuadernos de filología clásica* 11: 413–68.
1979 *Introduccion a las versiones griegas de la Biblia.* Textos y estudios "Cardenal Cisneros" 23. Madrid: Consejo Superior de Investigaciones Cientificas.

Fischer, Bonifatius
1951 *Vetus Latina: Die Reste der altlateinischen Bibel.* 2, *Genesis.* Freiburg: Herder.

Fitzmyer, Joseph A.
1975 *The Dead Sea Scrolls: Major Publications and Tools for Study.* SBLSBS 8. Missoula, MT: Scholars Press.

Gehman, Henry S.
1951 "The Hebraic Character of Septuagint Greek." *VT* 1: 81–90.

Gooding, David W.
1955 *Recensions of the Septuagint Pentateuch.* London: Tyndale.

1963   "Aristeas and Septuagint Origins." *VT* 12: 357–79.
1976a   *Relics of Ancient Exegesis: A Study of the Miscellanies in 3 Reigns 2.* SOTSMS 4. Cambridge: University Press.
1976b   "An Appeal for a Stricter Terminology in the Textual Criticism of the OT." *JSS* 21: 15–25.
1979   *Current Problems and Methods in the Textual Criticism of the OT.* Inaugural Lecture, The Queens University of Belfast, 10 May 1978. Belfast.

Goshen-Gottstein, Moshe H.
1963   "Theory and Practice of Textual Criticism—The Text-Critical Use of the Septuagint." *Textus* 3: 130–58.
1973   *The Bible in the Syro-Palestinian Version.* Jerusalem: Magnes Press.
1975   *The Hebrew University Bible: The Book of Isaiah, Part 1-2.* Jerusalem: Magnes Press.

Haelst, J. van
1976   *Catalogue des papyrus littéraires juifs et chrétiens.* Paris: Publications de la Sorbonne.

Hanhart, Robert, and John W. Wevers
1977   *Das Göttinger Septuaginta-Unternehmen.* Göttingen: Vandenhoeck & Ruprecht.

Hill, David
1967   *Greek Words and Hebrew Meanings.* SNTSMS 5. Cambridge: University Press.

Howard, George E.
1970   "The Septuagint: A Review of Recent Studies." *Restoration Quarterly* 13: 154–64.

Hyvärinen, Kyösti
1977   *Die Übersetzung von Aquila.* ConBOT 10. Lund: Gleerup.

Jacques, Xavier
1972   *List of Septuagint Words Sharing Common Elements.* Subsidia Biblica 1. Rome: Biblical Institute Press.

Janzen, J. Gerald
1973   *Studies in the Text of Jeremiah.* HSM 6. Cambridge, MA: Harvard University Press.

Jellicoe, Sidney
1968   *The Septuagint and Modern Study.* Oxford: Oxford University Press.

Jellicoe, Sidney, ed.
1974   *Studies in the Septuagint: Origins, Recensions, Interpretations.* New York: Ktav.

Kahle, Paul E.
1959   *The Cairo Geniza.* 2d ed. Oxford: Blackwell.

Katz, Peter
1956   "Septuagintal Studies in the Mid-Century." Pp. 176–208 in *The Background of the New Testament and Its Eschatology.* Ed. W. D. Davies and D. Daube. Cambridge: University Press. See also Walters.

Kittel, Gerhard, ed.
1968–1976 *Theological Dictionary of the New Testament.* Trans. G. W. Bromiley. Grand Rapids, MI: Eerdmans.

Klein, Ralph W.
1974   *Textual Criticism of the Old Testament: From the Septuagint to Qumran*. Guides to Biblical Scholarship. Philadelphia: Fortress.

Kraft, Robert A.
1976   "Septuagint. B, Earliest Greek Versions." *IDBSup*, 811–15.
1979   "Lexicon Project: Progress Report," *Bulletin of the IOSCS* 12: 14–16.

Kraft, Robert A., and Emanuel Tov
1981   "Computer Assisted Tools for Septuagint Studies," *Bulletin of the IOSCS* 14: 22–40.

Kraft, Robert A., ed.
1972   *Septuagintal Lexicography*. SBLSCS 1. Missoula, MT: Scholars Press.

Lee, John A. L.
1970   "A Lexical Study of the Septuagint Version of the Pentateuch." Diss., Cambridge University.
1980   "Equivocal and Stereotyped Renderings in the LXX." *RB* 87: 104–17.

Martin, Raymond A.
1974   *Syntactical Evidence of Semitic Sources in Greek Documents*. SBLSCS 3. Missoula, MT: Scholars Press.
1977   *Syntactical and Critical Concordance to the Greek Text of Baruch and the Epistle of Jeremiah*. The Computer Bible 12. Wooster, OH: Biblical Research Associates.

Monsengwo Pasinya, Laurent
1973   *La notion de "nomos" dans le Pentateuque grec*. AnBib 52. Rome: Biblical Institute Press.

O'Connell, Kevin
1976   "Greek Versions (Minor)." *IDBSup*, 377–81.

Orlinsky, Harry M.
1947   "Current Progress and Problems in Septuagint Research." Pp. 144–61 in *The Study of the Bible Today and Tomorrow*. Ed. H. R. Willoughby. Chicago: University of Chicago Press.
1969   "The Hebrew *Vorlage* of the Septuagint of the Book of Joshua." Pp. 187–95 in *Congress Volume: Rome, 1968*. VTSup 17. Leiden: Brill.
1975   "The Septuagint as Holy Writ and the Philosophy of the Translators." *HUCA* 46: 89–114.

Paeslack, Meinhard
1953–54   "Zur Bedeutungsgeschichte der Wörter φιλεῖν 'lieben'; φιλία 'Liebe', 'Freundschaft'; φίλος, 'Freund' in der Septuaginta und im NT." *Theologia Viatorum* 5: 51–142.

Peters, Melvin K. H.
1982   *An Analysis of the Textual Character of the Bohairic of Deuteronomy*. SBLSCS 9. Missoula, MT: Scholars Press.

Pietersma, Albert
1977   *Chester Beatty Biblical Papyri IV and V*. American Studies in Papyrology 16. Toronto and Sarasota: Samuel Stevens Hakkert.
1978   *Two Manuscripts of the Greek Psalter in the Chester Beatty Library Dublin*. AnBib 71. Rome: Biblical Institute Press.

Rabin, Chaim
1968   "The Translation Process and the Character of the Septuagint."
        Textus 6: 1–26.

Rapallo, Umberto
1971   *Calchi ebraici nelle antiche versioni del "Levitico."* Studi Semitici
        39. Rome: Istituto di Studi del Vicino Oriente.

Reider, Joseph, and Nigel Turner
1966   *An Index to Aquila.* VTSup 12. Brill: Leiden.

Repo, Eero
1951   *Der Begriff 'Rhēma' im Biblisch-griechischen. I, "Rhēma" in der
        Septuaginta.* AASF B. 75, 2. Helsinki: Suomalainen Tiedeakatemia.

Ros, Jan
1940   *De studie van het bijbelgrieksch van Hugo Grotius to Adolf Deiss-
        mann.* Nijmegen: Dekker en van de Vegt.

Santos, Elmaro Camilo dos
1973   *An Expanded Hebrew Index for the Hatch-Redpath Concordance
        to the Septuagint.* Jerusalem: Dugith.

Schenker, Adrian
1975   *Hexaplarische Psalmenbruchstücke: Die Handschriften Vaticanus
        graecus 752 und Canonicianus graecus 62.* OBO 8. Freiburg: Uni-
        versitätsverlag; Göttingen: Vandenhoeck & Ruprecht.

Seeligmann, Isaac L.
1940   "Problemen en perspectieven in het moderne Septuaginta-
        onderzoek." *Jaarbericht Ex Oriente Lux* 7: 359–90.
1948   *The Septuagint of Isaiah.* Leiden: Brill.

Silva, Moises
1978   "Describing Meaning in the LXX Lexicon." *Bulletin of the IOSCS*
        11: 19–26.

Skehan, Patrick W.
1957   "The Qumran Manuscripts and Textual Criticism." Pp. 148–60 in
        Volume du Congrès: Strasbourg, 1956. VTSup 4. Leiden: Brill.

Soisalon-Soininen, Ilmari
1965   *Die Infinitive in der Septuaginta.* AASF B 132, 1. Helsinki: Suoma-
        lainen Tiedeakatemia.

Sollamo, Raija
1979   *The Renderings of the Hebrew Semiprepositions in the Septuagint.*
        AASF Diss. Hum. Litt. 19. Helsinki: Suomalainen Tiedeakatemia.

Sperber, Alexander
1940   "NT and Septuagint." *JBL* 59: 193–293.

Talmon, Shemaryahu
        See Cross and Talmon.

Thiele, Walter
1977   *Vetus Latina: Die Reste der altlateinischen Bibel.* 11, *Sapientia
        Salomonis.* Freiburg: Herder.

Tov, Emanuel
1972a   "The Methodology of Textual Criticism in Jewish Greek Scriptures,
        with Special Attention to the Problems in Samuel– Kings—The
        State of the Question: Problems and Proposed Solutions." Pp. 3–15
        in Kraft, ed.

1972b   "Lucian and proto-Lucian—Toward a New Solution of the Problem." *RB* 79: 101–13.
1976a   "Some Thoughts on a Lexicon of the LXX." *Bulletin of the IOSCS* 9: 14–46.
1976b   "Three Dimensions of LXX Words." *RB* 83: 529–44.
1981   *The Text-Critical Use of the Septuagint in Biblical Research.* Jerusalem: Simor.

Tov, Emanuel, ed.
1980   *The Hebrew and Greek Texts of Samuel: 1980 Proceedings IOSCS, Vienna.* Jerusalem: Academon.

Turner, Nigel
1974   "Jewish and Christian Influence on New Testament Vocabulary." *NT* 16: 149–60.

Ulrich, Eugene C.
1978   *The Qumran Text of Samuel and Josephus.* HSM 19. Missoula, MT: Scholars Press.
1980   "4QSamᶜ: A Fragmentary Manuscript of 2 Samuel 14–15 from the Scribe of the *Serek Hay-yahad* (1QS)," *BASOR* 235: 1–25.

Venetz, Hermann-Josef
1974   *Die Quinta des Psalteriums: Ein Beitrag zur Septuaginta- und Hexaplaforschung.* Hildesheim: Dr. H. A. Gerstenberg.

Vergote, J.
1938   "Grec Biblique." *DBSup* 3: 1320–69.

Vööbus, Arthur
1975   *The Pentateuch in the Version of the Syro-Hexapla: A Facsimile Edition of a Midyat MS. Discovered 1964.* CSCO 369. Louvain: Secrétariat du CSCO.

Walters, Peter
1973   *The Text of the Septuagint, Its Corruptions and Their Emendation.* Cambridge: University Press. See also Katz.

Wevers, John W.
1954   "Septuaginta Forschungen." *TRu* n.s. 22: 85–137, 171–90.
1968   "Septuaginta Forschungen seit 1954." *TRu* n.s. 33: 18–76.
1977   "The Earliest Witness to the LXX Deuteronomy." *CBQ* 39: 240–44.
1978   "Text History and Textual Criticism in the Septuagint." Pp. 392–402 in *Congress Volume: Göttingen, 1977.* VTSup 29. Leiden: Brill.

Ziegler, Joseph
1934   *Untersuchungen zur Septuaginta des Buches Isaias.* ATA 12, 3. Münster: Aschendorff.
1959   "Die Vorlage der Isaias-Septuaginta (LXX) und die erste Isaias-Rolle von Qumran (1QIsᵃ)." *JBL* 78: 34–59.
1971   *Sylloge.* MSU 10. Göttingen: Vandenhoeck & Ruprecht.

10
PALESTINIAN ADAPTATIONS OF
BIBLICAL NARRATIVES AND PROPHECIES

I. The Bible Rewritten (Narratives)

Daniel J. Harrington, S.J.

In his exciting and provocative book entitled *Scripture and Tradition in Judaism* (1961), G. Vermes used the term "rewritten Bible" to describe works from various periods in Jewish history that try to make the biblical story more attractive, edifying, and intelligible. The nature of the rewritten Bible is explained in these words: "In order to anticipate questions and to solve problems in advance, the midrashist inserts haggadic development into the biblical narrative—an exegetical process which is probably as ancient as scriptural interpretation itself" (95). The terms "midrashist" and "haggadic" may not be entirely appropriate in dealing with books from the so-called intertestamental period, and so in this essay the expression "rewritten Bible" is used simply to refer to those products of Palestinian Judaism at the turn of the era that take as their literary framework the flow of the biblical text itself and apparently have as their major purpose the clarification and actualization of the biblical story. The most important adaptations of biblical narratives treated here are *Jubilees*, *Assumption* (or, *Testament*) *of Moses*, the Qumran *Temple Scroll* (11QTemple), *Genesis Apocryphon* (1QapGen), Pseudo-Philo's *Biblical Antiquities*, and Josephus's *Jewish Antiquities*. By way of a postscript, mention will also be made of *Paralipomena of Jeremiah*, *Life of Adam and Eve/Apocalypse of Moses*, and *Ascension of Isaiah*—all based on biblical narratives to some degree and all probably of Palestinian origin.

The restriction to Palestinian writings taking the flow of the biblical narrative as their structural principle is admittedly artificial, since there is a good deal of possible biblical interpretation in *1 Enoch*, the other Qumran writings, 4 Ezra, 2 Baruch, etc. Some of the writings of Philo of Alexandria could conceivably be included, though his literary form of exposition and his allegorical method set him apart from the books that we are discussing. Even with these restrictions, very diverse pieces of literature are considered in this part of the article. What holds all of them together is the effort to actualize a religious tradition and make it meaningful within

239

new situations. The material in this part is somewhat difficult to categorize from a literary and historical standpoint and illustrates the diversity within Judaism at the turn of the era.

The narratives that are the focus of attention here are based on specific Jewish scriptural texts. *Jubilees*, which is probably the oldest of the works under consideration, retells material from Gen 1:1 through Exod 12:50. *Assumption of Moses* is the farewell speech of Moses (based on Deuteronomy 31–34) in which he presents an overview of Israel's "future" history and ends with an apocalypse. The Qumran *Temple Scroll* begins with a description of the temple building and moves outward, pausing at key installations to cite related biblical laws. But from col. 51 to the end it follows Deuteronomy 12–26. The legible portions of the Qumran *Genesis Apocryphon* are free reworkings of Gen 6:8–9; 9:2–4, 20; 10(?); 12:8–15:4. In recounting Israel's history from Adam to David, Pseudo-Philo's *Biblical Antiquities* interweaves biblical incidents and legendary expansions of accounts in the Pentateuch, Joshua-Judges, and 1–2 Samuel. Josephus's *Jewish Antiquities* tells ancient Israel's story in its first ten books and naturally relies on the Bible as the primary source. All but the last of these books are of Palestinian origin, and even Josephus reflects the strong influence of Palestinian tradition.

The areas in which the most significant scholarship on these works has been carried out are the following: (A) *Jubilees, Genesis Apocryphon, Biblical Antiquities, Jewish Antiquities,* and perhaps *Assumption of Moses* presuppose the use of Hebrew biblical texts that, according to the categories developed by F. M. Cross (1964, 1966), can be traced back to Palestine. (B) If we understand the term "targum" to describe a more or less paraphrastic translation of the Bible and if we understand the term "midrash" to mean a body of literature that takes the biblical text itself as the focus of attention, then these books are not correctly called targum or midrash in the narrow or traditional senses of those terms. Using the framework of scripture, these documents include elements from the biblical narrative but freely omit words and whole incidents and add material without any foundation in the text. (C) The mechanical and simplistic application of labels like "Pharisaic" or "Sadducean" to these books has been halted by our increased knowledge of the complexity of Palestinian Judaism.

Biblical Texts

The discovery of the biblical manuscripts at Qumran and environs led Cross (1964, 1966) to elaborate a theory of local texts corresponding to the three great centers of the Jewish population: the Septuagint (Egypt); the Masoretic tradition and the "*kaige*" Greek recension (Babylon); and Chronicles, some Qumran manuscripts, the Samaritan Pentateuch, and the Hebrew underlying the proto-Lucianic recension of the Septuagint (Palestine). This theory of local texts has found striking support in several studies of extrabiblical books undertaken by Cross's students. Where there is sufficient evidence to allow us to determine the kind of biblical text used, several of these books (*Jubilees, Genesis Apocryphon, Biblical Antiquities, Jewish Antiquities,* and perhaps *Assumption of Moses*) seem to reveal a stage in the development of the Palestinian type of the biblical text. Since this type of text appears to have been suppressed by 100 c.e., its presence in these works provides some indication of their latest possible date of composition and of their place of composition. Even if Cross's formulation of the theory of local texts were to be refuted, one would still have to explain why these works of Palestinian origin or, in the case of Josephus, with Palestinian roots, from around the turn of the era have the kind of biblical texts that they do.

J. C. VanderKam's detailed examination of texts from Genesis and Exodus in the Ethiopic *Jubilees* (1977) indicates little or no evidence of alteration due to the direct influence of the Septuagint, the Ethiopic Bible, or the Masoretic Text. Rather, the many affinities with the Septuagint and the striking number of agreements with the Syriac and the Samaritan texts point to the use of a Palestinian biblical text, probably quite an early one. VanderKam (1978) has also listed the instances in which the biblical text of *Genesis Apocryphon* agrees with the Samaritan Pentateuch and the Septuagint versus the Masoretic Text (six), SP versus LXX and MT (three), MT and SP versus LXX (eleven), and LXX versus MT and SP (nineteen). The combined data of these lists indicate that *Genesis Apocryphon*, along with the Samaritan Pentateuch, 1 Chronicles 1–9, *Jubilees,* and some Qumran fragments, is a witness to the Palestinian (as opposed to the Babylonian and Egyptian) textual family in the book of Genesis.

D. J. Harrington has argued that the Latin text of Pseudo-Philo's *Biblical Antiquities* allows us a glimpse of the Hebrew biblical text used in the original composition. The texts in the Joshua–Judges–1 Samuel sections are related to the Hebrew texts on which the Lucianic or proto-Lucianic revisions of the Septuagint (a Palestinian text-type) were based. Even in the Pentateuch there are many agreements with the Septuagint, Lucian, and the Samaritan Pentateuch and few instances of uniquely Masoretic readings. E. C. Ulrich's study of the text of the major Samuel scroll from Qumran (4QSam[a]) has shed light on at least part of the biblical text in Josephus's *Antiquities.* Josephus used a slightly revised form of the Old Greek based on the tradition represented by 4QSam[a]—a Bible fitting the description of the proto-Lucianic Greek text and reflecting the Hebrew text used in Palestine. Finally, Klein has at least established the possibility that a non-Masoretic text was employed in *Assumption of Moses.*

Literary Character

Too frequently in the past (and unfortunately even in the present) these books have been treated according to the categories of later Jewish literature (Bloch; Patte; Porton; Haas; Wright). Because they paraphrase the biblical text, they have been called targumic. Because these books interpret biblical texts, they have been seen as midrashic. But careful literary analysis has demonstrated that they are neither targums nor midrashim.

The problem of the literary character of these books has been clarified to some extent by J. A. Fitzmyer's discussion of the *Genesis Apocryphon* (1971). Though it depends on the biblical text of Genesis and displays traits of targumic and midrashic composition, it is neither a targum (because the reworking is too free) nor a midrash (because the focus is not the explication of the biblical text). Fitzmyer (1971:11) sees the book as representing a third type of literature: "an example of late Jewish narrative writing, strongly inspired by the canonical stories of the patriarchs, but abundantly enhanced with imaginative details (accounts of dreams, reports of plagues, descriptions of beauty, accounts of journeys, explanations of geographical terms, and modifications of the text to eliminate difficulties or apparent contradictions)."

C. Perrot's discussion of Pseudo-Philo's *Biblical Antiquities* proceeds along lines similar to those used in Fitzmyer's treatment of *Genesis Apocryphon* but employs different terminology. If targum is taken to mean a more or less paraphrastic translation of the biblical text, then *Biblical Antiquities* is not a targum. But when Perrot comes to the question of whether or not it is a midrash, he introduces a distinction between *texte expliqué* and *texte continué*. In the case of *texte expliqué* the written biblical text is the focus of attention, and what is sought is a better understanding of the text itself. The term *texte expliqué* is parallel to Fitzmyer's restricted definition of midrash. In the case of *texte continué* the point of reference is the sacred history revealed in the Bible. Using the framework of scripture, Pseudo-Philo included elements from the biblical narrative but felt free to omit words and passages that did not fit his plan and to add material entirely without foundation in the text. He did not cite the Bible as Matthew did ("for so it was written") but produced a new entity by combining material from the Bible and from other traditions. Within the larger genre of *texte continué*, Pseudo-Philo used smaller literary forms: for example, genealogies, speeches, hymns, and prayers. So like *Genesis Apocryphon* and all the other works considered in this section, *Biblical Antiquities* is a free rewriting of parts of Israel's sacred history, not a targum or midrash.

In some respects this discussion is really a quarrel over words. But what Fitzmyer and Perrot want to insist upon is quite important and valid. The use of the terms "targum" and "midrash" in connection with these books brings more confusion than illumination. Nevertheless, establishing that these books are not appropriately described as targums or midrashim is not the same as proving that they all represent a distinctive literary genre called the "rewritten Bible." In fact, it seems better to view rewriting the Bible as a kind of activity or process than to see it as a distinctive literary genre of Palestinian Judaism. On the one hand, the rewriting of the Bible can be traced backward to the books of Chronicles and forward to the use of the scriptures in American Negro spirituals. Such a widespread and hallowed activity can scarcely be confined to Palestine around the turn of the era. On the other hand, while taking most of their content from the Bible, *Jubilees* and *Assumption of Moses* are formally revelations or apocalypses. *Assumption of Moses* illustrates the point nicely, since the book uses as its primary source Deuteronomy 31–34 but reaches its climax in an apocalypse. Furthermore, Josephus proposes to write a precise version of the Bible, "neither adding nor omitting anything" (*Ant.* 1.1.3 §17), though he is not entirely faithful to his promise. In conclusion, it is tempting to place all these books, as well as others, under the broad literary genre of "rewritten Bible," but unfortunately the diversity and complexity of the materials will not allow it.

Theological Tendencies and Setting in Life

What did these writers think that they were doing when they composed their books? It is not possible to give a general answer to this question. Rather, each piece of literature has to be approached on its own terms. The discovery of the Dead Sea Scrolls has both clarified and complicated our understanding of Judaism at the turn of the era. Having access to the library of one Essene group has enabled us to make judgments about the truth or falsity of the ancient testimonies about the Essenes. However, it has become increasingly difficult to assign documents to the Pharisees, Sadducees, or Essenes with the confidence displayed by R. H. Charles and those of his generation.

Paleographic data from the Qumran fragments of *Jubilees* has established 100 B.C.E. as the book's latest possible date of composition, and its several Maccabean references require that it be dated no earlier than the time of Judah the Maccabee. G. W. E. Nickelsburg (1981:78–79) suggests a date of composition in 168 B.C.E. on the basis of the apocalypse in chap. 23 and the negative attitudes toward Gentile practices. VanderKam (1977) maintains that it was written betweeen 161 and 152, that is, in the *intersacerdotium* before Jonathan was appointed high priest in Jerusalem. Though he admits that there are many theological affinities between *Jubilees* and the writings of the Qumran sect, VanderKam cautions against supposing that the author and his party had gone into a Qumran-like exile. In fact, *Jubilees* 49:21, which demands that the Passover be celebrated "before the tabernacle of the Lord or before His house where His name has dwelt," presupposes that the author was still a member of the community that worshiped in Jerusalem. In other words, *Jubilees* came from the time before the Qumran schism of the Essenes. G. L. Davenport envisions a more complex process of composition in three stages: a basic document consisting of 1:1–4a, 29a; 2:1–50:4 (minus 4:26; 23:14–31; 31:14) composed around 200 B.C.E., an updating around 160 B.C.E. with references to Antiochus's persecution; and a Qumran revision between 140 and 104 B.C.E.

Since the time of Charles, scholars have generally assumed that *Assumption of Moses* was composed between 7 and 30 C.E., that is, after the death of Herod the Great and the removal of Herod Archelaus from power in Judea in 6 C.E. This position is based on clear historical references in chaps. 6–7. But J. Licht and Nickelsburg (1972:28–31, 43–45) have argued for an original composition in the persecution of Antiochus IV Epiphanes and have seen the addition of chaps. 6–7 as part of a revision undertaken after 6 C.E. If this hypothesis is correct (and it makes excellent sense from a literary-critical standpoint), then we are dealing with a book first composed in the same situation as the book of Daniel—during the persecution by Antiochus. Chapter 9 suggests that the group behind the document may have been the "pious ones" who, according to 1 Macc 2:29–38, went out to the wilderness rather than transgress the Lord's commandments. The connecting of this with the apocalyptic material in chap. 10 makes it clear that, for the author, the martyrs' deaths would trigger God's eschatological vengeance. Viewed in this perspective, the original version of *Assumption of Moses* can be called a Hasidic or proto-Essene document.

J. Milgrom's description of the Qumran *Temple Scroll* suggests that the last fifteen columns (cols. 51–66 [67]) follow Deuteronomy 12–26, but neither in sequence nor in entirety. The most striking literary feature of the text is the change of scriptural quotations to the first person, which thus makes the entire scroll the "revealed word of God." Scriptural texts are clarified by emendations and glosses (e.g., Deut 17:14–20; 21:10–14; 21:22), and innovations and polemics on a wide variety of issues are included. The *Temple Scroll* was probably composed during the reign of John Hyrcanus I (135–104 B.C.E.) or slightly earlier. Yadin believed that this scroll corroborates the identification of the Qumran sect with the Essenes.

On the basis of a philological analysis of *Genesis Apocryphon*, E. Y. Kutscher concluded that the language of the scroll dates either from the first century B.C.E. or from the first century C.E. Since the manuscript itself can be dated to some time between 50 B.C.E. and 70 C.E., we probably have a very early copy of the text, perhaps even the autograph. The relation of this scroll to other texts used by the Essenes, the discovery of it in an Essene cave at Qumran, and the date of both the composition and the copy could suggest an Essene origin. But in fact there is nothing in the text that clearly links it to any of the known beliefs or customs of the Essene sect. Fitzmyer (1971:13) concludes: "As far as we can see, there is nothing in the *Genesis Apocryphon* which forces us to affirm the Essene authorship of the text. Nor does anything exclude it." He observes also that "it is hardly likely that this text was used in the synagogue as a targum, but it was most likely composed for a pious and edifying purpose (11)."

Several factors point to Palestine as the place in which Pseudo-Philo's *Biblical Antiquities* originated. It was composed in Hebrew. The biblical text used by the author was of the Palestinian type. There are many literary affinities with 4 Ezra and 2 *Baruch*, both apparently of Palestinian origin. The author's theological interests (the temple, rules of sacrifice, covenant and law, eschatology, angelology, geography) point to Palestine before 70 C.E., though Nickelsburg (1980) suggests that the portrayals of good and bad leaders allude to the events surrounding the first Jewish revolt. But efforts to connect the work with specific groups or sects in Palestine (Pharisees, Essenes, Samaritans, anti-Samaritans, Hellenists, Gnostics, etc.) have never won general acceptance. Perrot describes it as a corpus of haggadic traditions prepared for the use of homilists and targumists active in the synagogues of Palestine (perhaps dominated by the Pharisees). The many references to the synagogue found in the work seem to indicate this as the setting for the work's composition.

In what ranks as the most extensive examination of the theological tendency of any of these books, H. A. Attridge has called attention to Josephus's apologetic theology, which reworks Jewish traditions in categories derived from and comprehensible to a Greco-Roman public. Many details of the scriptural paraphrases derive from oral traditions of biblical exegesis, either those which Josephus knew from his youth in Palestine, or those which developed in the synagogal homiletics of the Diaspora. Josephus used this material to illustrate and inculcate a religiously-based morality and to demonstrate the significance of Jewish tradition. Two themes emerge as central: (1) History is a series of examples substantiating the belief that God exercises providential concern that justice be done. (2) Morals are important because of their religious foundation and function, that is, participation in the divine. Attridge observes that many of the interpretative elements in *Jewish Antiquities* are not inconsistent with rabbinic Judaism and thus perhaps with Pharisaism. These agreements, however, are not so specific that we are compelled to call Josephus a Pharisee because of them.

T. W. Franxman has focused on Josephus's retelling of the book of Genesis in *Ant.* 1.1.1–2.9.1 §§1.27–2.200 and distinguished between the episodes in which Josephus noticeably expanded the biblical account, shortened it, and struck an even balance. His analysis justifies to some extent Josephus's claim that he followed Genesis quite closely and indicates that his alterations may represent exegetical traditions much better thought out than had previously been supposed (Feldman). However, the reliance on the Masoretic Text and the fluid literary milieu (targums, pseudepigrapha, rabbinic writings) supposed for Josephus led Franxman to a slighting of the Hellenistic elements established by Attridge and others. F. G. Downing's examination of Josephus's redactional techniques as seen in the use of biblical material in *Antiquities* yields the following list: omissions (discrepancies, duplicates, interruptions, miracle and magic, inappropriate theology, apologetic awkwardness); additions (harmony and continuity, providence and prophecy, piety and moral uplift, apologetics, interest and clarity); rearrangement (harmony and continuity); assembly (thematic coherence and verbal coincidence); and conflation (harmony and continuity).

By way of a postscript, note can be made of some research on three short narratives that might qualify as examples of rewritten Bible: *Paralipomena of Jeremiah, Life of Adam and Eve/Apocalypse of Moses,* and *Ascension of Isaiah.* Though these documents are less obviously keyed to the structure and flow of the biblical narrative than the other works treated here, they are in considerable debt to it. From an examination of the language of *Paralipomena of Jeremiah,* G. Delling argued that the document up to 9:11 is clearly Jewish, that its thought world is close to that of later Pharisaic Judaism, and that behind the Greek text there is an original written in the Palestinian vernacular. Nickelsburg (1973) suggested that both *Paralipomena of Jeremiah* and *2 Baruch* depend on a common source that retold the story of the last days of Jerusalem in 587 B.C.E., perhaps under Jeremiah's name. In dealing with the figure of Adam in *Life of Adam and Eve/Apocalypse of Moses,* J. L. Sharpe called attention to the twofold portrayal of Adam as sinner and exalted one and compared this with Paul's notion of the first and second Adam. A. Caquot has tried to isolate the Jewish material in *Ascension of Isaiah* (1:6–7 [apart from the trinitarian formula], 8–11; 2:1, 4–6, 12 [minus the transitional phrase]; 3:6–12; 5:1b–6, 8–10) and to connect the story with the tragic fate of the Teacher of Righteousness or of the visionaries persecuted by the religious and secular authorities of Jerusalem.

Conclusion

The discovery of the Dead Sea Scrolls has revivified or begun research on these adaptations of biblical narratives to a considerable extent. By exposing the inadequacies of older notions about the history of the biblical text, about the literary forms available to writers in early Judaism, and about the sociological makeup of Palestinian Judaism at the turn of the era, the discovery of the Qumran scrolls has allowed scholars to study these works in new and more effective ways. The Hebrew biblical texts used in these works conform neither to the Masoretic tradition nor to the Septuagint nor to any known translation. Rather, these books seem to provide precious information about the type of biblical texts current in Palestine at the turn of the era. Furthermore, the application of terms like "targum" and "midrash" to these books appears to be more of a hindrance than a help. In fact, there is doubt whether the "rewritten Bible" represents a literary genre at all or whether one can speak about the single genre of these writings. Finally, these books illustrate in microcosm some of the problems involved in talking about the shape of Palestinian Judaism prior to the destruction of the Second Temple.

II. The Bible Explained (Prophecies)

Maurya P. Horgan

Among the documents from the Qumran caves that have been published thus far are eighteen texts distinguished by the fact that each is a continuous commentary on or an interpretation of a single biblical book. These texts have been called *pesharim* because each section of interpretation following a biblical citation is introduced by one of several formulas using the word *pesher*, meaning "interpretation" (plural: *pesharim*). Thus far the following texts have been identified as pesharim: 1QpHab (formerly designated DSH), 1QpMic (1Q14), 1QpZeph (1Q15), 1QpPs (1Q16), 3QpIsa (3Q4), 4QpIsa[a-e] (4Q161–165), 4QpHos[a,b] (4Q166–167), 4QpMic (4Q168), 4QpNah (4Q169), 4QpZeph (4Q170), 4QpPs[a,b] (4Q171, 173), and 4QpUnid (4Q172, unidentified fragments presumed to be of pesharim).

Because of the special problems connected with the initial publication of previously unknown texts, most of the secondary literature on the pesharim has focused either on the transcription, translation, or restoration of the texts themselves (Fitzmyer, 1977), or on the historical allusions found in these texts and the light that they shed on the history of the Qumran community (Bardtke). These elements are not treated here. Rather, this report will be concerned with work that has contributed, first, to illuminating the nature of these texts as a literary genre and to understanding the use of the biblical texts in these documents, and, second, to placing the pesharim in the history of interpretative writings. The subjects surveyed here are treated in greater detail in Horgan (1979), in which the Hebrew texts are presented with translations, notes, and a description of the literary genre of the documents.

Among the documents of the Dead Sea Scrolls the texts listed above are neither the only texts in which the key word pesher occurs, nor are they the only texts that reflect aspects of biblical interpretation and study among the members of the Qumran community. But these are the texts in which this special kind of interpretation assumes its most systematic form. J. Carmignac (360–61) distinguished between "continuous pesher" (*pesher continu*), in which a single biblical book is methodically interpreted section by section, and "thematic pesher" (*pesher thematique*), in which certain citations to be interpreted are grouped artificially around a central idea, for example, 11QMelchizedek (11QMelch) and 4QFlorilegium (4QFlor). This section treats the continuous pesharim of Qumran.

Description of the Texts

From the initial study of these documents has emerged a picture of them that is a composite of observations on the word *pesher*, the structure of the texts, the use of formulas, the modes of interpretation, and the content of the interpretations.

The starting point for understanding these texts and their use of scripture is the word *pesher*, by which the texts are identified and described. The root *pšr*, from which the Hebrew *pēšer* is derived, is a common Semitic root attested in Akkadian, Aramaic, Hebrew, and Arabic, meaning "loosen," "dissolve." The root appears with this basic meaning throughout the Hebrew and Aramaic of the biblical and postbiblical periods. The extended meaning "interpret" appears already in Akkadian, where it refers especially to the interpretation of dreams by magic. The translation "interpretation" is not ideal, since it does at times connote scholarly exegetical analysis of the modern type, especially in a biblical context. But the English word "interpretation" does not have to imply this and can serve as an adequate translation of the word *pesher* if it is understood to refer to the "loosing" or "unravelling" of mysteries.

The mystery to which the pesher corresponds is designated by the word *rāz*, a Persian loanword that does not occur in biblical Hebrew but is found in biblical Aramaic in Dan 2:18, 19, 27, 28, 29, 30, 47 (twice); 4:6 (English 4:9). The concept of mystery expressed by the term *rāz* developed out of the idea of the ancient prophets' being introduced in their visions into the heavenly assembly and there learning the secret divine plans for cosmic history (Brown, 1958a,b). In the pesharim the word refers to the mystery concerning the things that are going to come, which were hidden in the prophetic writings (1QpHab 7:4–5), not made known fully to the prophets. This mystery could not be unravelled or solved by human wisdom; the pesher or interpretation was made known by God.

The continuous pesharim regularly follow this pattern: citation, section by section, of a single biblical book, each lemma being followed by an interpretation. The documents usually exhibit the same divisions as the Masoretic Text, and the citations vary in length from one-fourth of a verse to five verses, but most of the lemmas are from one-half to two verses long. The length of the interpretation-sections varies from as little as one-half line to as much as nine and one-half lines, but most of the interpretations are about two to three lines long. The commentaries are not divided into sections or chapters, though some of the documents show fairly regular patterns of spacing or identation.

To introduce an interpretation of a lemma, the documents always use a formula containing the word *pšr* ("interpretation"). The most frequent construction is *pšrw 'l*+substantive+ *'šr*+verb ("the interpretation of it concerns x, which/who . . ."). Also regularly used are *pšr hdbr 'l*+substantive + *'šr*+verb ("the interpretation of the passage concerns x, which/who . . ."), *pšr hdbr*+*'šr*+verb ("the interpretation of the passage [is] that . . ."), and *pšrw 'šr* ("the interpretation of it [is] that . . ."). In some instances a portion of the lemma is repeated, and it might be introduced by the phrase *ky' hw' 'šr 'mr* ("for this is what it [scripture] says"), or *w'šr 'mr* ("and as for what it [scripture] says" or "and when it says").

An examination of the ways in which the Qumran commentators drew out the prophetic meaning of the biblical texts reveals four main categories of interpretation: (1) The pesher may follow the action, ideas, and words of the lemma closely, developing a similar description in a different context. (2) The pesher may grow out of one or more key words, roots, or ideas, developing the interpretation from these isolated elements apart from the action or description of the lemma. (3) The pesher may consist of metaphorical identifications of figures or things named in the lemma, with or without a description or elaboration of action. (4) There are instances in which the pesher seems to be only loosely related to the lemma. Within these general forms, the pesher is often drawn out or developed by means of one or more of the following techniques: use of synonyms for words in the lemma; use of the same roots as in the lemma, appearing in the same or different grammatical forms; play on words in the lemma; changing the order of letters or words in the lemma; use of a different biblical textual tradition; and referring back to an earlier lemma or anticipating a following lemma.

The Qumran interpretations of the prophetic texts deal with history— the past history of the community and the events of the last days, in which the Qumran authors believed that their congregation was living. The Qumran authors believed that the meaning of the emergence of the community and all Yahweh's plans for the judgment of the wicked and the deliverance of the righteous were hidden in the mysteries of the prophetic words.

This description, which is a collation of observations by modern commentators who have studied the texts, can be summarized thus: The pesharim are a group of sectarian writings that present, section by section, continuous commentaries on biblical books, namely, prophets and Psalms. The interpretations and sometimes the citations are introduced by formulas, several of which use the word *pēšer*. The interpretations refer the biblical citation to the history of the sect—past, present, or future—and use modes of interpretation such as metaphor, plays on words, and developments of key words or key ideas in the text.

Complementing this description is the picture outlined by the texts themselves. If the author of the Habakkuk pesher can be taken as representative, the Qumran commentators believed (1) that the words of the biblical books contained mysteries revealed by God ("and God told Habakkuk to write down the things that are going to come upon the last generation, but the fulfillment of the end-time he did not make known to him" [1QpHab 7:1–2]; "all the mysteries of the words of his servants the prophets" [1QpHab 7:4]); (2) that the mysteries hidden in the biblical books referred to history, specifically, the history of their community ("the words of his servants the prophets by whose hand God enumerated all that is going to come upon his people and upon his congregation" [1QpHab 2:9–10]; "God told Habakkuk to write down the things that are going to come upon the last generation" [1QpHab 7:1]); and (3) that the interpretation of these mysteries was revealed to the Teacher of Righteousness and to selected interpreters who followed him ("the interpretation of it concerns the Teacher of Righteousness, to whom God made known all the mysteries of his servants the prophets" [1QpHab 7:4–5]; "when they hear all that is going to come upon the last generation from the mouth of the priest into whose heart God put understanding to interpret all the words of his servants the prophets" [1QpHab 2:7–10]). Thus, the picture of the pesharim drawn by the Qumran author is that the pesher is an interpretation revealed by God of a mystery (*rāz*) revealed by God concerning history.

Pesharim and Other Interpretative Writings

In the attempts to identify the literary genre of the pesharim, these texts have been compared to other writings in the collection of Qumran literature (e.g., *Damascus Document*), to rabbinic midrashic and targumic writings, to Jewish apocalyptic works (especially Daniel), and to writings outside the Jewish tradition (e.g., the Egyptian *Demotic Chronicle*).

Concentrating mainly on the concept of searching into the Torah as it emerges from a study of the *Manual of Discipline* and the *Damascus Document*, O. Betz has examined the attitude toward and the use of scripture in the pesharim. He brought out that the sect believed that a new time of revelation had begun with the work of the Teacher of Righteousness. Neither did the Teacher bring a new Torah, nor did he reproduce the Torah of Moses as Ezra had (4 Ezra 12:38–50); but he exacted guiding principles or regulations from the interpretation of the Torah. For Betz, the pesher interpretation of the prophetic message is a corresponding concept referring to the correct understanding of history rather than the precise meaning of regulations. In discussing the technique of pesher interpretation, Betz compares the dream interpretation in Daniel and suggests that pesher and apocalyptic are closely related, since both speak of the signs of the times that make the end known. The pesher, however, is more rigorous in its use of scripture than the apocalypse, whose visions and mysterious images sometimes spin off from isolated dates and names in scripture. More will be said of apocalyptic below.

While studying the Habakkuk commentary, W. H. Brownlee compared the pesharim to rabbinic midrash and characterized them as a new type of midrash, the midrash pesher, related to, but different from, the midrash halakah and midrash haggadah. G. Brooke prefers the designation "Qumran midrash." Brownlee (1951) made a detailed examination of the interpretation of the Habakkuk pesher for the purpose of showing that the Qumran exposition of scripture is "essentially midrashic." He set out thirteen techniques, which he referred to as "hermeneutical principles or presuppositions," that he believed could be found in the document. Following Brownlee's lead, many authors began to view these texts in terms of rabbinic midrashic techniques, but this approach was criticized by G. Vermes (1955), who suggested that the pesharim were closer to the targumic writings, and by K. Elliger, who concluded that the pesharim were closer to the type of interpretation found in the book of Daniel.

There has been considerable debate about the origin, nature, development, and extent of midrash, and it cannot be assumed that there is a commonly accepted definition of the term. However, the word usually calls to mind the written works resulting from the rabbinic process of oral and written biblical interpretation. These midrashic works in their present form date from the second century c.e. and onward. To attempt to illuminate the pesharim—all of which were written before 70 c.e.—by pointing to apparently similar elements in rabbinic midrashic writings can be anachronistic and misleading. Moreover, the comparisons have focused on possible similarities in techniques of biblical interpretation. That means that the comparisons are based on characteristics of the pesharim that are observed by modern commentators, which neglects the essential consideration of what the texts say about themselves—that they are revealed interpretations of revealed mysteries concerning history. The first question that should be asked is this: Do the midrashic writings purport to be revealed interpretations of revealed mysteries? No rabbinic texts have been cited to show that the midrashim make this claim. From this perspective the term "midrash" is neither a useful nor an informative term by which to characterize the pesharim.

A more fruitful area of comparison was opened up by the observation of the verbal similarities between the pesharim and the book of Daniel. It was pointed out from the start that the root pšr and the word rāz were used both in the pesharim (in Hebrew) and in Daniel (in Aramaic) in similar contexts. In his exhaustive study of the Habakkuk commentary, Elliger (164) called attention to this similarity, and, as was noted above, concluded that in its method of interpretation the work is closer to the book of Daniel than it is to rabbinic literature. But do the interpretations in the book of Daniel purport to be revealed interpretations of revealed mysteries? Indeed, in Daniel it is stated that the dream, the hidden mystery or *rāz*, was sent by God and that its interpretation was revealed by God to a chosen interpreter ("Then the mystery [*rāzâ*] was revealed by God to Daniel in a vision of the night " [2:19]; "No wise men, enchanters, magicians, or astrologers can show to the king the mystery . . . but there is a God in heaven who reveals mysteries" [2:27–28]).

The interpretations in the book of Daniel provide other points of comparison. There is one place where a formulaic introductory phrase appears that is reminiscent of the formulas in the pesharim. When Daniel interprets the writings on the wall at Belshazzar's feast, he says *děnâ pěšar millětā'* ("this is the interpretation of the matter" [5:26]). Some of the same modes of interpretation that are observed in the pesharim can be found in Daniel, and just as the content of the interpretation sections in the pesharim refers to the clarification of past history, present and future circumstances of the community and the world, or eschatological events, so too the interpretations in Daniel refer to history. The relationship between the Qumran Habakkuk commentary and Daniel has been the subject of an investigation by A. Mertens (114–41). His examination of word usage in Daniel and in the Qumran writings, along with angelology, methods of interpretation, and eschatological beliefs, led him to suggest that there was a connection between the Maccabean redactor of Daniel and the community of the Dead Sea Scrolls.

The existence of such significant similarities between the type of interpretation found in the book of Daniel and that observed in the pesharim has led to a widening of the field of comparison to illuminate further the character and background of this type of interpretation. Daniel is an eschatologically oriented work—specifically, an apocalyptic work—and, beginning with this fact, some studies have compared the pesharim to other Jewish apocalyptic writings (Collins). In the context of a larger study on the background of early Christian prophecy, G. Dautzenberg investigated the terminology of interpretation and the understanding of revelation in Daniel, the Qumran writings, *1 Enoch*, *4 Ezra*, *2 Baruch*, and Josephus. But apocalypticism is not restricted to the Jewish writings. It can be found throughout the ancient Near East, and some instructive parallels to the pesher type of interpretation have been noted. F. Daumas discussed the similarity between the pesharim and the Egyptian *Demotic Chronicle*, which is a fragmentary papyrus document that can be dated on paleographic grounds to the early Ptolemaic period. It is supposed to have contained an obscure text of prophetic value, an oracle dealing with Egyptian history and kingship. The oracle is cited in short sections, each of which is interpreted. The interpretations are sometimes introduced by a formulaic expression that can be translated "this is," and the interpretations refer to national history, sometimes by means of metaphorical or figurative equation. The field of comparison can be extended further to include Assyrian traditions. In a study of dream interpretations in the ancient Near East, A. L. Oppenheim explored the meaning of the Akkadian verb *pašāru*, which is derived from the same common Semitic root as is the Hebrew *pēšer*.

Collecting these points of comparison within a history-of-religions framework, J. J. Collins has included the pesharim in the category of Jewish apocalyptic as examples of interpretative writing within the broader Near Eastern context. With the demise of native monarchies that resulted from the conquests of Alexander the Great, national resistance to Hellenistic rule flared, producing a renewed interest in native traditions and myths and eschatological prophecy. Collins calls this "prophecy by interpretation," and he regards the pesharim, Daniel, and the *Demotic Chronicle* as examples of this type of prophecy.

Conclusion

Research on the Qumran pesharim, focusing on the nature of the texts and their relationships to other interpretative literature, has laid the groundwork for future investigations, which might include (1) a detailed examination of the biblical texts that are preserved in the pesharim in the light of Cross's theory of local texts, (2) an attempt to pinpoint the setting of these commentaries within the life and history of the Qumran community, and (3) continuing efforts to understand the pesharim not only within the framework of Jewish interpretative tradition but also within the broad outline of perceptions of revelation in ancient civilizations. Thus far the pesharim emerge as interpretations revealed by God of mysteries revealed by God concerning history. They appear to be more closely related to apocalyptic writings like Daniel than they are to various forms of rabbinic midrashic literature.

III. Future Research

Daniel J. Harrington, S.J.

The scope of our presentation has been confined to reviewing research related to several Palestinian adaptations of biblical narratives and to a relatively small corpus of commentaries on biblical prophecies. Little or nothing has been said about the book of Wisdom, Philo, the New Testament, and the rabbinic midrashim—all works containing substantial amounts of biblical interpretation and adaptation. Even the range of issues raised in the course of discussing scholarship on these few documents has been limited. Can we now pass from some of the particulars involved in the presentation of research on a few documents to some general comments on studying the rereading of the Bible in the so-called intertestamental period? How would one go about a comprehensive investigation of biblical interpretation in intertestamental Judaism and early Christianity?

The emphasis on the historical and theological individuality of the documents treated in this paper is of paramount importance. Every Jewish or Christian religious movement has to come to grips with the Jewish scriptures and adapt traditions to its own purposes. That challenge was taken up in antiquity in a variety of ways, and it is still carried on by churches and synagogues today. It is an inescapable and indispensable task facing any person or any group claiming to stand within the Judeo-Christian tradition. The various responses to this challenge will inevitably have some features in common. Yet what is more significant from a history-of-religions perspective is the peculiar shape that the response takes in a particular writing or in a particular group. The central question is this: Why does this author or this community interpret the biblical passage in this way? Much of our impatience with scholars who use terms like midrash and targum or rely heavily on the rabbinic rules of interpretation stems from a fear that the distinctive characteristics of each interpretation will be passed over and assimilated to the literary categories and hermeneutical procedures of rabbinic Judaism.

The starting point must be the particular historical setting and theological tendencies of individual documents, not generalizations derived from the much later rabbinic materials. Of course, the specific documents transmit exegetical traditions. Nevertheless, the ways in which such traditions have been modified and reshaped by a particular writer or community ought to take precedence over attempts at generalization applying to large quantities of literary material. Therefore, the necessary first step in a comprehensive investigation of biblical interpretation and adaptation in Judaism and early Christianity is a thorough inventory of specific documents or corpora taken on their own historical and theological terms. Such a description would include the material covered in this essay as well as other Jewish and early Christian works that try to actualize Israel's religious heritage. The basic concern in such an investigation should be the distinctive place that adapting the biblical tradition holds in the overall construction of the particular writing or corpus.

The outline of a methodology for carrying out this kind of investigation is latent in the first two sections of this article. The first and most obvious area of concern is the biblical text used in the document. That determination is easy enough where a Hebrew document is being studied, but it is still possible even when the Hebrew text has been translated into Aramaic, Greek, Latin, Ethiopic, etc. The second area of concern involves the logic of the interpretation. Particular attention should be given to the techniques customarily used by homilists; for example, direct transference, allegorization, spiritualization, parallelism of situations, demythologizing, retelling the story, universalization, identification. In addition, an effort should be made to uncover the hermeneutical principles used to draw meaning out of the biblical texts. At this point, relying on the elementary processes of logic will probably be more fruitful and less prejudicial than going too quickly to the *middôt* of Hillel or Rabbi Ishmael. Here one should also look for the presence (or the absence) of a basic hermeneutical key like the community's history at Qumran or the person of Jesus in the early church that opened up the biblical tradition to thoroughgoing reevaluation. The third and final area of concern has to do with the character of the document under consideration: its historical and social setting, the literary genre in which the interpretative material is presented, the theological tendencies, and the attitude shown toward the biblical text. Future research on adaptations of biblical narratives and prophecies will demand even greater attention to particular cases than in the past.

BIBLIOGRAPHY

Attridge, Harold W.
1976   *The Interpretation of Biblical History in the* Antiquitates Judaicae *of Flavius Josephus*. HDR 7. Missoula, MT: Scholars Press.

Bardtke, Hans
1976   "Literaturbericht über Qumran. X. Teil: Der Lehrer der Gerechtigkeit und die Geschichte der Qumrängemeinde." *TRu* 41: 97–140.

Betz, Otto
1960   *Offenbarung und Schriftforschung in der Qumransekte*. Tübingen: Mohr-Siebeck.

Bloch, Renée
1955   "Midrash." *DBSup* 5: 1263–81.

Brooke, Gerald
1981   "Qumran Pesher: Towards the Redefinition of a Genre," *RevQ* 10: 483–503.

Brown, Raymond E.
1958a   "The Pre-Christian Semitic Concept of 'Mystery.'" *CBQ* 20: 417–43.
1958b   "The Semitic Background of the New Testament *Mysterion*." *Bib* 39: 426–48.

Brownlee, William H.
1951   "Biblical Interpretation among the Sectaries of the Dead Sea Scrolls." *BA* 14: 54–76.
1979   *The Midrash Pesher of Habakkuk*. SBLMS 24. Missoula, MT: Scholars Press.

Caquot, André
1973   "Bref commentaire du 'Martyre d'Isaïe.'" *Semitica* 23: 65–93.

Carmignac, Jean
1969-71   "Le document de Qumrân sur Melchisédeq." *RevQ* 7: 343-78.

Charles, Robert H.
1897   *The Assumption of Moses Translated from the Latin Sixth Century MS.* London: Black.

Collins, John J.
1975   "Jewish Apocalyptic against its Hellenistic Near Eastern Environment." *BASOR* 220: 27-36.

Cross, Frank M.
1964   "The History of the Biblical Text in the Light of Discoveries in the Judaean Desert." *HTR* 57: 281-99.
1966   "The Contribution of the Qumran Discoveries to the Study of the Biblical Text." *IEJ* 16: 81-95.

Daumas, François
1961   "Littérature prophétique et éxégetique égyptienne et commentaires esséniens." Pp. 203-21 in *À la rencontre de Dieu: Mémorial Albert Gelin*. Bibliotheque de la faculté catholique de théologie de Lyon 8. Le Puy: Editions Xavier Mappus.

Dautzenberg, Gerhard
1975   *Urchristliche Prophetie: Ihre Erforschung, ihre Voraussetzungen im Judentum und Struktur im ersten Korintherbrief.* Stuttgart: Kohlhammer.

Davenport, Gene L.
1971   *The Eschatology of the Book of Jubilees.* Leiden: Brill.

Delling, Gerhard
1967   *Jüdische Lehre und Frömmigkeit in den Paralipomena Jeremiae.* BZAW 100. Berlin: Töpelmann.

Downing, F. Gerald
1980   "Redaction Criticism: Josephus' *Antiquities* and the Synoptic Gospels (I)." *JSNT* 8: 46-65.

Elliger, Karl
1953   *Studien zum Habakkuk-Kommentar vom Toten Meer.* BHT 15. Tübingen: Mohr-Siebeck.

Feldman, Louis H.
1981   "Josephus' Commentary on Genesis." *JQR* 72: 121-31.

Fitzmyer, Joseph A.
1971   *The Genesis Apocryphon of Qumran Cave I: A Commentary.* 2d ed. BibOr 18a. Rome: Biblical Institute Press.
1977   *The Dead Sea Scrolls: Major Publications and Tools for Study.* Rev. ed. SBLSBS 8. Missoula, MT: Scholars Press.

Franxman, Thomas W.
1979   *Genesis and the "Jewish Antiquities" of Flavius Josephus.* BibOr 35. Rome: Biblical Institute Press.

Haas, Lee
1981   "Bibliography on Midrash." Pp. 93-103 in *The Study of Ancient Judaism I: Mishnah, Midrash, Siddur.* Ed. J. Neusner. New York, Ktav.

Harrington, Daniel J.
    1971   "The Biblical Text of Pseudo-Philo's *Liber Antiquitatum Biblicarum.*" *CBQ* 33: 1–17.

Horgan, Maurya P.
    1979   *Pesharim: Qumran Interpretations of Biblical Books.* CBQMS 8. Washington, DC: Catholic Biblical Association.

Klein, Ralph W.
    1973   "The Text of Deuteronomy Employed in the Testament of Moses." P. 78 in *Studies on the Testament of Moses.* Ed. G. W. E. Nickelsburg. SBLSCS 4. Missoula, MT: Scholars Press.

Kutscher, Eduard Y.
    1965   "The Language of the 'Genesis Apocryphon': A Preliminary Study." Pp. 1–35 in *Aspects of the Dead Sea Scrolls.* Ed. C. Rabin and Y. Yadin. Scripta Hierosolymitana 4. Jerusalem: Magnes Press.

Licht, Jacob
    1961   "Taxo, or the Apocalyptic Doctrine of Vengeance." *JJS* 12: 95-103.

Mertens, Alfred
    1971   *Das Buch Daniel im Lichte der Texte vom Toten Meer.* Stuttgart: Katholisches Bibelwerk; Würzburg: Echter-Verlag.

Milgrom, Jacob
    1978   "The Temple Scroll." *BA* 41: 105-20.

Nickelsburg, George W. E.
    1972   *Resurrection, Immortality and Eternal Life in Intertestamental Judaism.* HTS 26. Cambridge, MA: Harvard University Press.
    1973   "Narrative Traditions in the Paralipomena of Jeremiah and 2 Baruch." *CBQ* 35: 60-68.
    1980   "Good and Bad Leaders in Pseudo-Philo's *Liber Antiquitatum Biblicarum.*" Pp 49-65 in *Ideal Figures in Ancient Judaism: Profiles and Paradigms.* Ed. G. W. E. Nickelsburg and J. J. Collins. SBLSCS 12. Chico, CA: Scholars Press.
    1981   *Jewish Literature Between the Bible and the Mishnah.* Philadelphia: Fortress.

Oppenheim, A. Leo
    1956   *The Interpretation of Dreams in the Ancient Near East: With a Translation of an Assyrian Dream-Book.* Philadelphia: American Philosophical Society.

Patte, Daniel
    1975   *Early Jewish Hermeneutic in Palestine.* SBLDS 22. Missoula, MT: Scholars Press.

Perrot, Charles
    1976   *Pseudo-Philon: Les Antiquités Bibliques. Tome II.* SC 230. Paris: Cerf.

Porton, Gary G.
    1981   "Defining Midrash." Pp. 55-92 in *The Study of Ancient Judaism I.* Ed. J. Neusner. New York: Ktav.

Sharpe, John L.
    1973   "The Second Adam in the Apocalypse of Moses." *CBQ* 35: 35-46.

Ulrich, Eugene C.
    1978   *The Qumran Text of Samuel and Josephus.* HSM 19. Missoula, MT: Scholars Press.

VanderKam, James C.
   1977   *Textual and Historical Studies in the Book of Jubilees.* HSM 14.
               Missoula, MT: Scholars Press.
   1978   "The Textual Affinities of the Biblical Citations in the Genesis
               Apocryphon." *JBL* 97: 45-55.
Vermes, Geza
   1955   "A propos des Commentaires bibliques découverts à Qumrân."
               RHPR 35: 96-102.
   1961   *Scripture and Tradition in Judaism: Haggadic Studies.* Leiden:
               Brill.
Wright, Addison G.
   1967   *The Literary Genre Midrash.* Staten Island, NY: Alba House.
Yadin, Yigael
   1984   *The Temple Scroll.* 3 vols. Jerusalem: Israel Exploration Society.

11
TESTAMENTS

I. The Literary Genre "Testament"

Anitra Bingham Kolenkow

The testament was a commonly used genre in the Second Temple period. The last words of a parent facing death were viewed as of primary importance. Death was believed to be a time when God granted prophetic knowledge and visions of the other world to the righteous. Testaments were viewed as authoritative because no person would be expected to tell an untruth at the hour of death/judgment, nor would the dying person fail to give children both goods and truth (or warning). Thus, testaments may include information received from the other world (usually forecasts of the future and scenes of judgment) as well as ethical teaching and distribution of inheritance.

In the period covered by this essay, the discussion of testaments has profited from a number of works ranging from general encylopedia articles (Stauffer, Behm, Schnackenburg) to the recent books by E. Cortès and E. von Nordheim, as well as works on particular testaments and studies that confront issues important to the discussion of the genre. The major interests of these works relate to the following topics: (1) the formal characteristics of the genre, (2) ethics and apocalytic in contents and genre, (3) pseudepigraphy and midrash, and (4) relationships to other genres (common forms, rationales, and divergent purposes).

FORMAL CHARACTERISTICS
RELATING TO SETTING

Recent scholarship has come to recognize that ancient writers sometimes used formal settings characteristic of testaments (death bed, bequeathal, etc.) to construct their works and give their works new meaning. The study of the *Testaments of the Twelve Patriarchs*, the *Testament of Abraham* (together with those of Isaac and Jacob), and NT works with testamentary characteristics has provided particular insight in this respect.

The *T. 12 Patr.* has received particular attention because it contains the word "testament" in its title and provides twelve examples of testament format. The slight differences in form among the individual parts have encouraged analysis of the form of the testament and also fostered the study of the redaction of *T. 12 Patr.* itself. To some scholars the structure of *T. 12 Patr.* seemed basic and ordinary. M. de Jonge (1953) and K. Baltzer suggested that there was a uniform schema of testamental characteristics in *T. 12 Patr.* J. Becker (1970) analyzed the major formal constituents of the settings in *T. 12 Patr.* and was able to establish a variety of types from the differences in expression of the constituents. However, like de Jonge and Baltzer, he also argued for a uniform schema for the whole. A. B. Kolenkow was able to build on Becker's work, noting that the differences in the formulas corresponded to the differences in types noted by Becker. Kolenkow therefore argued for various levels of redaction based on differences in formulas (1975a). The importance of formal characteristics is highlighted by attempts in this literature to build upon the external framework of a story and to rely on formal characteristics normally associated with deathbed scenes to establish a point that may not be generally accepted. For example, some testaments also contain (1) the request for a particular burial place (the burial place being a subject of dispute; see Jeremias on *T. 12 Patr.* and various Greek tragedies that end with a request that the person be buried in a place other than what is expected, e.g., Oedipus and Theseus at Athens); (2) the citation of and thus support for certain, perhaps controversial, books (such as Enoch books cited in *T. 12 Patr.*); (3) the forecasts that descendants will not heed the command to be obedient after the father's death (see *T. 12 Patr.*, where disobedience to certain brothers is predicted; this is also paraenetic, but associated with the idea of distribution of goods and power to one other than the elder brother; see also *T. Job* on the giving of girdles to daughters).

The *Testament of Abraham* has been another focus for study of testamentary literature. Although its title proclaims it to be a testament, the work does not contain a formal testament. Scholars have thus been forced to define the genre testament in relationship to *T. Abr.*, and then to try to explain why a work so labeled does not include a testament. The general scholarly solution has been to point out that the work does have a deathbed location and does give revelation. F. Schmidt (19, 41), for example, uses a definition of testament that includes knowledge of heaven and end-time judgment, thus focusing on the question of content rather than form.

It is possible that *T. Abr.* may have gained its title from its association with the *Testaments* of Isaac and Jacob. In the Hebrew scriptures, Abraham is not said to have left a testament. In its present position, the story of *T. Abr.* becomes a context for *Testament of Isaac*'s heavenly vision of Abraham, the intercessor for those who have made no testament (see *T. 12 Patr.*'s emphasis on certain brothers as important, with attention focused on those brothers' special revelations). Abraham's value as an intercessor and model is that he is like those (the monks??) who give no testaments. Abraham's pleas for those without testaments are witnessed in heaven by Isaac, and the pleas are the contents of the special revelation that is told to Jacob (*T. Isaac* 6.1–23). Isaac's name and festival are remedial for those who do not have testaments (see Kolenkow, 1974:183).

Some articles in encyclopedias and elsewhere have made the NT a focus of their studies of testaments (Stauffer, Behm, Schnackenburg). Precisely because the NT texts were not generally labeled as testaments, critics found it essential to establish formal characteristics of testaments and identify as many other examples as possible outside the NT. Stauffer's excellent article both gives a number of examples of testaments and lists contextual characteristics. J. Munck, without having read Stauffer (Munck: 156), studied the Miletus speech in Acts as a testament. Munck comments on the use of the testament form in the ancient Near East (especially Jewish scriptures) and in the Greco-Roman world. He stresses two features of such accounts beyond the biographical summary and the location of death: the transmission of power by a person about to depart and the prediction of the future (159). He also identifies other texts, such as John 13–17, as testaments.

Following Stauffer and Munck, H. J. Michel also studied Paul's Miletus speech as a testament. To define it as a testament, he compared it with testaments from the Jewish biblical period on. He noted that the form of (or emphasis on) testament was provided by the redactional introductory verses (35; cf. also Genesis 49). He also discussed how other testaments functioned as parts of books; he suggested that one is alerted to them by statements referring to one's age, the calling together of children, etc. However, he claimed that the relationships between testaments, such as *T. 12 Patr.*, are not limited to similarities of testamentary beginning and ending characteristics. Note, for example, the relationship between the eschatological parts of *T. 12 Patr.* and what is found in Deuteronomy 33 (see below).

Michel cites not only early Jewish literature in his parallels to Paul's Miletus speech in Acts but also parallels in the NT (as did Munck, but in more detail, especially with materials such as John 13–17). He identifies a testament as a work given by those who are dying or rising to heaven. E. Käsemann had already defined chap. 17 of John as a testament like those of the *T. 12 Patr.* and compared it to the apocalyptic discourse of Mark (which had been recognized as a testament by A. Farrer and others). Käsemann moved to a definition of testament as not merely "last will and testament" but the final declaration of will by one whose proper place is in heaven (not simply one who is going to heaven).

Two caveats need to be mentioned at this point: (1) Agreements in form between several of the individual testaments in *T. 12 Patr.* show what one or two authors' models for testament were, not what a general model for testament may have been. (2) Those who lived at the time *T. Abr.* was written knew that Abraham had not left a testament and were able to make up testaments for him (cf. *Jubilees* 21–22, which shows that they knew the form) or could make Abraham's failure to leave one a purposeful tool. It is indeed in places like *Jubilees* or NT passages that one sees most clearly what the form was and the range of options in emphasis that it provided (for example, *Jubilees* 21–22 has both "commands" and "blessings").

ETHICS AND APOCALYPTIC: CONTENT AND STRUCTURE

The two most recent books on testaments (Cortès and von Nordheim) show the two major viewpoints on the contents of testaments. Cortès, who follows Munck, emphasizes how apocalyptically oriented the genre is. Von Nordheim, a student of G. von Rad and Baltzer, says that if there is no "Verhaltensanweisung" ("ethical instruction"), there is no testament (1980: 233); ethics is primary. These two authors express the essential poles of the continuing question in testamental research: What is the relative importance of ethics and apocalyptic in testaments?

Recognition that these approaches represent two different schools of thought is important. The school of Munck attempted to study the genre testament in a descriptive history-of-religions manner (without conscious reference to modern theological concerns). The Baltzer group, following R. Bultmann's approach, worried about supernatural authority as a basis for teaching "in a world come of age." This concern engendered an attempt to separate from certain genres (like testament, which was associated with wisdom) any contamination by supernatural authority—or to try to explain (with careful analysis of genre) the development of apocalyptic in the testamental genre.

The internal form of the ethical testament and its contents were emphasized especially by Baltzer in his analysis of *Jubilees* and *T. 12 Patr.* In this examination, he shows how the various constituents of testaments may correspond to the features of biblical "covenant formulas." He sees these points as history, parenesis, blessing and curse, and quite rightly recognizes that example (life) may replace covenant history in the formulation (146; in fact this happens in Jewish scriptures as well when an account of evil deeds sometimes replaces or supplements the formulaic references to the mighty acts of God; Baltzer: 133, 146). Baltzer sees the use of apocalyptic as a "reasonable development" of the blessing and curse section (and not as a part of parenesis; 155). He thus can combine ethics and apocalyptic without viewing them as essentially related. Baltzer recognizes that where in the Hebrew Bible, "the present is the focus of history," in the literature of the Second Temple period, the present "stands at the beginning of history to come." As a result, Baltzer argues that the presence of apocalyptic in postbiblical early Jewish literature is a legitimate development of the older covenant formulations.

Michel, influenced by Munck, criticizes Baltzer's work for citing motifs but not really showing how a testament is organized. He notes that *Jubilees* does not fit Baltzer's structures. Michel also follows J. Thomas and others in their criticism of Baltzer's analysis of *T. 12 Patr.* J. Becker, for example, criticized Baltzer on the ground that the analysis did not fit *T. Levi* (1974:153). Michel himself hypothesizes the following structural outline: the situation of the speaker, the calling together of hearers, and the ending. This becomes a framework for "Mahnung und Prophezeiungen," admonition and prophecy. Although Michel criticizes Baltzer's presentation as putting too narrow a frame (that of covenant formulary) on testaments, Michel admits that one can hardly find a better locus than change of generation (57). Michel also emphasizes the presence of apocalyptic in the prophetic part of testament. He rightly sees this as a genre of difficult times and emphasizes not only how one gains authority from the past in a genre, but how this genre allows the present generation to relate itself both to present difficulty and to the relevance of God to that present.

Several of J. Strugnell's Harvard students have worked separately on the issue of forecasts of the future in testaments. R. Spittler followed Munck in identifying forecasts as characteristic of testaments (although Spittler saw *T. Job* as moving away from this emphasis). Kolenkow became aware of the use of testament as a particular vehicle for revelation of the future in the apocalyptic historiography of *2 Apoc. Bar.* To put the issue in a locus outside *2 Apoc. Bar.* she widened her research to apply her analysis of structure to the examples of Hellenistic-type trips to the other world to reinforce the authority of testaments in giving revelation of the future.

Becker criticized Baltzer's analysis for not being appropriate to the material of *T. Levi* (1974:153), and Kolenkow (1975a) agreed with Becker that there seemed to be a problem with Baltzer's structured analysis of *T. Levi* and in this connection studied a number of related Jewish works. She suggested that these works show a "blessing-revelation" structure (named after *1 Enoch* and Deuteronomy 33). In reaction to Baltzer, she questioned the adequacy of any definition of testament limited solely to an ethical model and argued for two variant types: the ethical testament and the blessing testament. The blessing type includes authority for revelation history (often a trip to or vision of heaven), the revelation itself, and an urging to righteousness (blessing and curse). Although the juxtaposition of the two types of testaments in *T. Levi* may be evidence for their separate existences, it does not mean that they reflect different testament forms. If a life history represents the "basis of authority in heavenly relationship" and parenesis is seen as an alternative to apocalyptic (since both are authoritative teaching), then the same form is represented by both types, with variation concerning authority and teaching according to the need of the subject. Apocalyptic teaching needs heavenly authority (vision or trip to heaven); ethical teaching needs the authority of experience; and both assume reward and punishment.

The relationships may be schematized as follows:

(descriptive content)	Baltzer	Kolenkow
life history	history/life	heavenly trip/vision
material learned from above by the testamentor	parenesis	forecast/revelation
authoritative urging as last gift from the testamentor	blessing/curse	urging

In her study of the ethical aspect of testaments, Kolenkow hypothesized that behind such testaments there often must have been (as part of the life section) a *nekyia*, or trip to the world of the dead, in which the visitor sees examples of other judgments and is warned to reform (1975a:69 #18; 1975b:45 #15; cf. in *T. Abr.* the sin of "wanting to destroy," which is recognized on a trip to heaven; 1976:142). She also recognized in *T. 12 Patr.* the use of a particular type of testamentary introduction in the same redactional layer as the contrasting pictures of Joseph and his brethren *and* the forecast of sin against Levi (1975b:40ff.).

Another of Strugnell's students, J. Collins, studied *T. Job* according to Baltzer's structural outline and in relation to other parallels, and found prediction in *T. Moses* where *T. 12 Patr.* contains historical recollection (and not at the end of the work, as Baltzer argued for *T. 12 Patr.*). In *T. Job*, Collins notes, there is more emphasis on narrative and less on exhortation than in *T. 12 Patr.*, but "the narrative is expected to carry a word." Thus, in *T. Job* (as well as in *T. Abr.*, which Collins also mentions) narrative becomes message-exhortation. Story has become message (see midrash below), and Job is the proper "type of example" (1974:39). In the same seminar volume, H. C. Kee emphasizes that eschatology occurs throughout *T. Job* (1974:64), including the beginning of the work (1974:61). Collins, for his part, found no "eschatological section in TJ" (1974:39), but Kee's emphasis suggests that eschatology may be part of the exhortation-story of *T. Job*.

PSEUDEPIGRAPHY AND MIDRASH:
BEYOND ETHICS

As Cortès had related apocalyptic to testament, he also related pseudepigraphy to testaments (64ff.) and to midrash. Both apocalyptic and pseudepigraphy were problems for a "world come of age." Bultmann, P. Ricoeur, and others had sought to get beyond the question of "authoritative" genre (apocalyptic, pseudepigraphy, etc.) by emphasizing the role of ethics, prophecy, and law as valuable for the present. Using the issue of pseudepigraphy, Morton Smith (1972) struck at the biblical basis of such an emphasis by stressing that both law (in Deuteronomy) and prophecy (in Deutero-Isaiah) were supported by pseudepigraphy in the Jewish scriptures.

The "midrash" answer had been given long before for testaments by K. Kohler (1897) and by E. Fascher (1921), who described such works as a combination of Märchen and Lehrstücke (legends and instructions). The relation between story and teaching was also a major focus of M. Hengel's article and reply to Smith. Hengel rightly answers the moral issue raised by Smith by saying that Jewish haggada shows a picture of how the past (and this includes speeches) was continuously renewed and fitted to new situations (253; Fritz: 221). Hengel's argument moves beyond the common observation that the Pythagorean or Mosaic traditions tended to attribute new thoughts to the founders of their schools. When Hengel cites the midrashic play on the words and lives of famous people, one realizes that one is working with a tradition that was accustomed to producing stories about a figure that both suited the biblical (and later midrashic) options for the figure and also served as a vehicle for the author's viewpoint. In the midrashim and in the literature of the Second Temple period about Solomon or Abraham, one also may transfer motifs from one biblical figure to another (e.g., Abraham and Moses). This activity is similar to the traditions of NT apophthegms or rabbinic sayings that may find new settings or new speakers for a given quotation. The Jews indeed felt free to dramatize lives as did Ezekiel the Tragedian. The *Letter of Aristeas* tells the story of the tragic poet Theodectes who was afflicted with cataracts in both eyes because he was about to adapt incidents in the existing material for one of his plays (3:14).

This midrash or apophthegm approach (although it may seem too much of a scholarly cliché) opens two paths: a study of haggadic options available and a study of the writers as authors using their literary freedom to combine sources and genres, to change and to speak new words to produce their story for the present. Their midrash must be self-justifying and must speak to an audience like a parable.

The study of options available (and how one may place the author in a particular haggadic tradition or use of tradition) illumines the importance of the various articles in which members of the SBL Pseudepigrapha Group discussed the presentation of a particular testamental spokesman (Abraham, Joseph, etc.) in relation to other presentations of the same spokesman as found in contemporary writers such as Philo, Josephus, or the rabbis. Although some have complained that a few of these articles produce nothing new, it is nevertheless important to know where authors or communities have lines of representation in common. When common motifs have been identified, one may establish possible contexts and focus on other points in a work—now made evident when they are seen as options (e.g., Schmidt; Sanders et al., on Abraham's virtue of hospitality; or Kolenkow on sin in "seeking to destroy," 1976:143–47). One may further note how the figure chosen relates to the point of the teaching: Job, who suffered afflictions, gives girdles of healing; Joseph and the patriarchs tell which of the patriarchal descendants should be obeyed; Solomon can speak about demons because he once controlled them. The question of suitability may also help explain the transfer of a story from one figure to another (Moses to Abraham, Abraham to Job, or vice versa). Sometimes each figure is equally appropriate and the transfer may be suitable for other reasons (ancient apologetics, etc.).

The author of a testament has to become a convincing historical novelist, putting likely options into the events of his protagonist's life so that the audience will say, "Oh, yes," and be able to make the leap of imagination that is required. Further, the story may become part of the revelation as in *T. Abr.* or *T. Job.* The revelation must also be believable. One must be able to validate the argument of the new revelation from scripture or from the logic of the story. For example, when *T. Abr.* has divine revelation, it has God speak using the theology of the prophet Ezekiel (Kolenkow, 1976). Likewise, when one produces apocalyptic presentations of history and the future, the reader must be moved both by the use of the commonplaces of apocalyptic history and by the new internal logic of history through which the author argues the case (Kolenkow, 1971).

RELATIONSHIP TO OTHER GENRES

Since many works (both labeled and not labeled "testament") have testamental characteristics, one scholarly quandary was whether to classify as "testament" all those works that contain either a testamantary label or testamentary characteristics. (See the discussion of *T. Mos* and *T. Abr.* in the SBL Pseudepigrapha Seminars, and reviews of their work.) Are other genres joined to testamental form to acquire testamental authority? The question of analysis of genres and analysis of authors' purposes becomes important. Scholars have taken apart works to arrive at their "original" sources. Now one must ask why an author used a source at a particular point or tied together separate genres.

Since testaments contain ethical parenesis and apocalyptic forecasts, one may expect that testaments may contain the language of ethical paraenesis and apocalyptic forecast in predictable locations. On a larger scale, trips to the other world are a common part of apocalyptic. They therefore may be used in testaments that reveal the future. This both gives authority to revelation and is an apologetic motif that (along with pseudepigraphic nomenclature) would speak to the Greco-Roman world, which was accustomed to such trips from its own literature (Kolenkow, 1975a:66–67).

Martyr acts are also important as an authoritative contextual setting. Collins (1974) ties the "surface" genre testament with the general genre of martyr acts (see also Fischer). Noting the combination in *T. Job* of the gift of healing by the hero, one should consider whether the gift of healing becomes a functional proof of the authority of the martyr (power beyond death)—as Jesus gives to his disciples in the NT; note also the *Martyrdom of Felicitas and Perpetua*, where the martyr is able to heal in heaven.

In discussion of the interplay of genres (as well as working with the problems of insertion), it becomes important to understand the structural purposes of the author—especially in those works like *T. 12 Patr.* where previously it had been common to argue for maladroit insertion of material (on structural purposes see *T. Levi;* on apocalyptic, Thomas: 87; Kolenkow, 1975a, 1982:664; *T. Jos.;* on ethics, Kolenkow, 1975b:37–40). Collins makes a good argument for a similar case for *T. Job* (1974:44–48); see also Michel (43, 45, 50, 56) on the takeover of material from wisdom and apocalyptic in the account of Kenaz in *Liber Antiquitatum Biblicarum.* In the case of several redactors beyond the first author, Michel is correct that it may be necessary to move beyond the question of sources to the question of the final redactor's understanding of the materials.

CONCLUSION

In surveying the study of the testament genre during the past thirty years, what is most astonishing is the real movement toward unity of scholarly outlook in spite of differences of opinion. Apocalyptic and ethics indeed both occur in testaments. One can even argue that accounts of sins (see *T. Abr., T. Levi*) serve as validators of revelation. Further elaboration of older stories (including visits to heaven) is common. Authors feel free to change divine revelation and patriarchal story for their own purposes (e.g., the two versions of *T. Abr.*). Historicization of contemporary problems and sins provides the audience with perspective. The scholar observes the authors' careful attempts to convince an audience by logic and by biblical commonplaces put in new perspectives. What scholarship in a "world come of age" may find valuable is to study those areas which seem most alien to it—the uniting of ethics and apocalyptic or forecast and the use of stories (whether of trips to heaven or ills in life) to give a perspective on present reality. The ancient world had the ability to set problems outside its own world and thus gain new insight into its present. The writer is heard because the writings tell "how it could have been" to an audience for whom story was a vehicle of argument, and "gnostics" as well as sober Jews tried to explain the process of evil in the world through revelation and story.

II. The Testamentary Literature
in Recent Scholarship

John J. Collins

Most of the scholarly literature on testaments in the postwar period has been devoted to the *Testaments of the Twelve Patriarchs*. In addition to this there have been a few studies of the *T. Job*; the *Assumption of Moses* has been recognized as a testament and relabeled accordingly; and the *Testament of Abraham* has been recognized as a misnomer since it does not involve a formal testament at all.

THE TESTAMENTS OF THE TWELVE PATRIARCHS

Two factors especially stimulated the lively debates on the *Testaments of the Twelve* in the postwar period: the discovery of the Qumran scrolls and the publication in 1953 of the dissertation of M. de Jonge, which challenged the scholarly consensus of the previous half century. The ensuing debates, primarily devoted to the provenance of the *Testaments*, have been chronicled at length in a number of recent publications (Becker, 1970:129–58; de Jonge, 1975:183–92; Slingerland, 1977a). Our purpose here is not to document every contribution but to outline the main issues and assess the current state of the discussion.

Provenance

Three main theories on the provenance of the *Testaments* may be distinguished. The position which is most widely defended, in variant forms, is that formulated by J. E. Grabe in 1698: "Testamenta XII Patriarcharum a Judaeo olim scripta, a Christiano autem postea interpolata esse" (The Testaments of the XII Patriarchs were originally written by a Jew, but later were interpolated by a Christian). This position became dominant after the work of F. Schnapp (1884) and was adopted in the authoritative collections of the pseudepigrapha by E. Kautzsch and R. H. Charles. The influence of Charles, in particular, has remained pervasive down to the present. In recent years this position has been most elaborately defended by J. Becker, but also in different forms by several scholars including most recently H. C. Kee and A. Hultgård. The main rival to this position is the view that the *Testaments* are a Christian composition. This position had in fact been the dominant one prior to the work of Schnapp (Singerland, 1977a:5–18). In recent years it has been associated mainly with M. de Jonge. A minority view regards the *Testaments* as an Essene document or as a product of the Qumran community. This theory, proposed by A. Dupont-Sommer and M. Philonenko, differs from the usual theory of Jewish origins in seeking to explain many of the apparent Christian allusions as Essene.

The Qumran Hypothesis

Since the Qumran theory has found fewest recent advocates it may be treated first and most briefly. Similarities between the *Testaments* and the Scrolls were noted already in 1952 (Slingerland, 1977a:45–47) and more thoroughly by B. Otzen in 1953. It was Dupont-Sommer, however, followed by his student Philonenko, who developed the extreme view that the *Testaments* were products of Qumran and that the Christian element was negligible. The arguments of Philonenko that the apparently christological passages should be applied to the Teacher of Righteousness have been widely rejected (Slingerland, 1977a:60–65). The most striking similarity between the *Testaments* and the scrolls is undoubtedly their common expectation of two messiahs, although they refer to them in different terms. This point has led a number of scholars (Kuhn; Liver; van der Woude) to posit an Essene origin for the *Testaments*. A few other points of similarity are generally admitted, such as the references to Belial and the elements of moral dualism. Yet these affinities must be weighed against numerous points of difference (Becker, 1970:149–51). The *Testaments* lack any clear reference to the history of the Qumran community and indeed do not reflect a sectarian ideology at all. The determinism of the scrolls is lacking in the *Testaments*, and mythological dualism is much less prominent. The fact that much of the *Testaments* seems to have been composed in Greek and cannot be easily retroverted into a Semitic language also weighs against a Qumran origin. Further, it must be said that the actual discoveries at Qumran have lent little support to the theory of Qumran provenance. Semitic parallels to *T. Naph.* and *T. Levi* had been known since the turn of the century (Charles, 1908). The Hebrew text of *T. Naph.*, published by M. Gaster (1893–94) has been evaluated in various ways: de Jonge saw it as a late and inferior form of an original Hebrew text (1953:52–60). Becker regards it as a late product only loosely related to the Greek *Testament* (1970:105–13). Now a further parallel to *T. Naph.* 1:6–12 has been discovered in a Qumran fragment (Cave 4), written in Hebrew, which contains the genealogy of Bilhah. This work is yet unpublished, but again is only loosely related to the Greek *Testament* (Milik, 1959:34). In the case of *T. Levi*, Charles printed in the third appendix to his edition (1908) two Aramaic fragments of the same manuscript from the Cairo Geniza, which had been discovered at Oxford and Cambridge. These fragments provide a partial parallel to *T. Levi* 8–13 and a remote parallel to *T. Levi* 6. Charles also published in the same appendix a Greek fragment that was inserted at *T. Levi* 18:2 in a manuscript from Mount Athos (denoted *e*). This fragment provides a close parallel to the Aramaic. The Mount Athos manuscript has another important addition at *T. Levi* 2:3. Further fragmentary Aramaic parallels have now been found at Qumran. Milik has published fragments from Cave 1 and "some more important pieces" from

Cave 4 which parallel the texts from the Geniza and the two inserted passages in the Mount Athos manuscript (Milik, 1959:34; 1966; DJD 1: 88–89). The relationship between these Qumran fragments and the Greek *T. Levi* is disputed. De Jonge (1953:39) argued that *T. Levi* and the fragments go back to a common source. Becker (1970:69–105) argues for a more remote relationship. Fragments of other testaments that have been identified are extremely scanty. Milik refers to two Aramaic fragments of *T. Judah* (4QA Ju 1 a–b) and even more fragmentary remains of *T. Jos.* (Milik, 1978:97–102). Baillet (78) claims to have identified Hebrew fragments of *T. Judah* (4Q484, 3Q7) but again they are extremely fragmentary. Finally, J. Starcky's unpublished fragments from Cave 4 reportedly include an Aramaic fragment of *T. Benjamin* (Fitzmyer: 405). The identification of these smaller fragments is less than certain, and they can bear little weight in reconstructions of the history of the *Testaments*.

The fragments from Qumran and from the Cairo Geniza can be understood as reflecting sources on which the Greek *Testaments* drew or as independent, related materials. Parallel narrations of the exploits of Judah in *T. Judah* 3–7 are known in *Jub* 34:1–9 and in *Midr. Wayissa'u* (which is printed in Charles's edition of the *Testaments*, Appendix 1). Such parallel materials are not necessarily direct sources for the Greek *Testaments*. It is apparent, then, that the Qumran discoveries have not significantly changed our knowledge of the history of the *Testaments*. They do not prove that there was a Jewish corpus of twelve testaments, nor do they exclude the possibility that such a corpus may have been composed in Greek at an early date. The editor of the Aramaic fragments, J. T. Milik, emphatically denied that the Qumran materials lent any support to the theory of Qumran provenance, and he himself espoused the position of de Jonge that the *Testaments* are a Christian composition that drew on Jewish sources (Milik, 1955:405–6).

M. de Jonge

De Jonge's dissertation has had a far more enduring impact on the discussion than have the discoveries at Qumran. This impact has been evident in two areas: the textual criticism of the *Testaments* and the question of distinguishing Jewish and Christian elements.

Text Criticism

Prior to the work of de Jonge, textual criticism of the *Testaments* had been dominated by the edition of Charles (1908). Charles had used nine Greek manuscripts, twelve Armenian, and a Slavonic translation. He distinguished two families in the Greek manuscripts, designated alpha and beta, and regarded both as independent translations from Hebrew. The MS *c* of the family alpha was regarded as the best manuscript of the *Testaments*.

The Armenian text (A) is somewhat shorter than the Greek. Since some of the passages lacking in A are Christian, Charles sought to use this shorter text to remove the Christian influence on the *Testaments*, at least in part.

Charles's position has been rendered obsolete by further discoveries of manuscripts (H. J. de Jonge in M. de Jonge, 1975:45–62). More significant, his critical decisions have been challenged. The hypothesis of Hebrew originals for families alpha and beta is now widely rejected. De Jonge, in his dissertation (in part following J. W. Hunkin) argued that the alpha text is a late inferior recension of the beta text and that *b* is the best manuscript of the beta family. Accordingly, de Jonge used the *b* manuscript in his *editio minor* (1964, 1970). More recently, in the preparation of the new *editio major* (1978), he has accepted the conclusions of his student H. J. de Jonge that Charles's classification of alpha and beta must be completely discarded. Instead, the textual tradition is divided into two branches or families: family I, consisting of the witnesses *b* and *k*; and family II, comprising all other witnesses. That is, the split is located within Charles's family beta, and alpha is only a late recension within family II (de Jonge, 1975:174–79; H. J. de Jonge in de Jonge, 1975:45–62).

De Jonge also argued against Charles that the Armenian version "has been greatly overrated" and that "its omissions disfigure the text in many places" (1953:30–31). It is of little value for the removal of Christian interpolations. The Slavonic version is also of little value in reconstructing the Greek text, but is most closely related to the gamma subgroup of Charles's group beta (1953:22–23).

Subsequent studies have generally supported de Jonge against Charles. Major studies of the Armenian version by C. Burchard and M. E. Stone supported the view that "many variants noted in Charles' edition are inner-Armenian variants and do not represent differences between the prototype of the Armenian version and the Greek. The Greek text from which A derives will not have been so very different from the Greek manuscripts in our possession" (de Jonge, 1975:124). Hultgård (1971) also supported a close relationship to the Greek (MSS *b, d, g, k, l*, especially *d* and *g*), although he still felt that the Armenian could be used to correct the Greek in many passages (see the critique by de Jonge, 1975:130–35). E. Turdeanu's study of the Slavonic version argued that it was derived from a Greek text similar to de Jonge's gamma subgroup.

The re-appraisal of the textual tradition by de Jonge and his students has not gone unchallenged. Becker (1974:18–21) sees alpha and beta as variant traditions with a long parallel history and rates the Armenian more highly than does de Jonge. He avoids the selection of the best witness to the text and follows an eclectic procedure by which the text of each passage is determined separately. Hultgård also professed an eclectic method in his dissertation (1971). These scholars have in turn been sharply criticized for arbitrariness by de Jonge and his collaborators (de Jonge, 1975:80–86,

130–35). Nevertheless, even de Jonge's critics now reject Charles's views on the text. It seems safe to say that the attempt to remove Christian interpolations by means of textual criticism has been thoroughly undermined.

Both the importance of textual criticism for the question of composition and its limitations must be appreciated. On the one hand, "textual criticism cannot provide information about the time prior to the archetype (or archetypes) from which all extant witnesses are descended" (de Jonge, 1975:153). This archetype, according to H. J. de Jonge (in de Jonge, 1975:79) is "earlier than the ninth century" but otherwise cannot be dated precisely. There is no doubt that the *Testaments* had been Christianized by then. Strictly, text criticism can neither prove nor disprove the existence of a Jewish composition before the Christian era. On the other hand, it is crucial to know "where to work back from" (de Jonge, 1975:153). De Jonge has repeatedly criticized his opponents for the textual readings on which they base their source- and redaction-critical theories. At the very least he has established the need to scrutinize the textual evidence on which reconstructions of the history of the *Testaments* are based.

The Composition of the Testaments

De Jonge (1953) also argued that it was incorrect to speak of interpolations—rather, a Christian compilation or composition that used much Jewish material. He dated this composition to approximately 190–225 C.E., but in 1957 moved the date back to the middle or second half of the second century C.E. (de Jonge, 1975:184). He has subsequently admitted that he reached his conclusion on Christian composition "a little rashly" (1975:184) and that it is "probably as much an oversimplification as the interpolation theory" (1975:311). The main emphases in his recent work have been on the need to explain the final stage of the *Testaments* as a whole, and on the complexity that confronts any attempt to reconstruct an earlier Jewish stage. Thus, he insists on the primacy of the Christian completion of the *Testaments*, and although he no longer rules out the possibility of a Jewish stage, he does not seem to regard it as a fruitful subject of investigation.

De Jonge's insistence on the importance of the final stage is salutary and highlights a dimension of the pseudepigrapha that is often neglected. In this respect J. Jervell's study of the Christian redaction of the *Testaments* is noteworthy, all the more so since Jervell himself assumed a Jewish original. Yet, as de Jonge himself has recognized, it is not sufficient to speak of the *Testaments* simply as a Christian document: "it remains important to show how various traditions in the Testaments were used, especially in what form and with what contents and within which groups, *in Jewish and Christian circles*" (de Jonge, 1975:189–90, emphasis added). Any approach to the *Testaments* as *both* Jewish *and* Christian (Slingerland, 1977a:107) is inevitably thrown back on source criticism and the need to find some criterion of dissimilarity by which the Jewish stage can be recognized. Although it is clearly legitimate to treat the final text as Christian, the Jewish stage remains problematic. The main issue here is whether the framework of twelve testaments was first introduced by a Christian or was already found in a Jewish document (de Jonge, 1975:189).

Although de Jonge has seen and posed this question, he has made little headway toward answering it. In his earlier work he tended to regard everything compatible with Christianity as Christian, and he still objects to the attempts to reduce the Christian elements to the obvious minimum (1975:189). On his own admission he has made relatively little use of form and redaction criticism, although his recognition of the sin–exile–return and the Levi–Judah passages has been rightly hailed as a major contribution (Becker, 1970:143). Substantial formal and generic studies have been contributed (Aschermann; Baltzer; Becker; von Nordheim; see the essay of A. B. Kolenkow in this volume), but de Jonge has not dealt adequately with the potential of using formal and generic criteria to distinguish an earlier stage. He merely insists on their hypothetical character and the primacy of the final text (e.g., 1975:310). Yet if the use of the *Testaments* (or their sources) in Jewish circles is admitted as important, some criteria must be found for moving behind the extant text form(s).

J. Becker

By far the most thorough formal and redactional analysis of the *Testaments* was contributed by J. Becker in 1970. Becker distinguishes (1) separate distinct narratives within a testament, such as *T. Reub.* 1:5–10 and 3:9–4:5, or *T. Jos.* 1:3–10:4 and 10:5–18:4; (2) independent self-contained lists of vices and virtues, e.g., *T. Reub.* 4:6–6:4; *T. Dan* 2:2–4:7; *T. Gad* 4:1–5:2; 1:3–6:6; (3) similarly independent complexes of apocalyptic material at the end of *T. Levi* or *T. Judah* (Becker, 1974:24). These blocks of material are held together by the introductory and concluding formulas, which characterize the works as testaments. According to Becker's analysis the testament form belongs to the earliest stage of the corpus. The individual testaments were then expanded by the incorporation of traditional, usually hortatory, material. Finally, a Christian editor made minor adaptations in the text. So, for example, in *T. Reub.*, Becker would distinguish an original frame in 1:1–10 and 6:9–7:2. Within this original testament the treatise on the seven spirits in 2:1–3:8 and the long paraenetic section in 3:9–6:8 are self-contained units that were inserted later (not necessarily at the same time). Finally, Christian adaptations were made in 6:8, in the phrase *archiereōs christou* and in 6:12 in the statement "he will die for you in wars seen and unseen and will be among you an eternal king." Even in these passages Jewish authorship is not entirely impossible, although less probable. In *T. Jos.* the first story, in chaps. 3–9, is not regarded as part of the original testament. It constitutes a self-contained story, which should follow *T. Jos.* 10–19 chronologically rather than precede it, and it shows far more points of contact with Hellenistic literature than the second story. It can therefore be most readily understood as an independent unit inserted in the testament in the second stage. Christian elements are found in *T. Jos.* 19:8 and 11, which refer to the birth of a lamb from a virgin (8) and to the "lamb of God" (11).

There is no doubt that Becker has made a great contribution to understanding the formal structure of the *Testaments.* His reconstruction of their history, however, is very hypothetical and rests on two assumptions: that only those elements which are distinctively Christian need be regarded as such and that formally distinct units must be ascribed to different stages. The first of these assumptions has been repeatedly challenged by de Jonge. In fact both the distinctively Jewish (e.g., the two messiahs) and the distinctively Christian elements are quite limited, and much of the *Testaments* is compatible with either (see, e.g., Amstutz's study of *Aplotes* in Jewish and Christian literature). However, it has rightly been said that the distinctively Christian element in the *Testaments* is less than what we find in such Christian works as Hermas, with which it is often compared (Becker, 1970:145). When the Christian elements are removed it is possible to read the *Testaments* as a coherent Jewish composition. Given the certainty that Jewish material is used and the limitation of the distinctively Christian, it is not unreasonable for Becker to attribute the ambiguous material to the Jewish stage, especially since the overall structure of the *Testaments* can be explained in this way. Becker certainly risks minimizing the Christian element, but some such risk is inevitable if we are to reconstruct a Jewish stage at all. At the same time the hypothetical nature of the undertaking must be underlined. Becker's reconstruction provided an ingenious and plausible impression of what the Jewish *Testaments might* have looked like, but it can scarcely count as independent evidence for Judaism.

Becker's correlation of formal units and historical strata leads him to distinguish two Jewish editions. Although this is possible, the argument is by no means a necessary one, and no weight can be placed on the results.

Provenance and Date

Most recent scholars who reconstruct a Jewish stage of the Testaments emphasize contacts with Egyptian Judaism (Becker; Thomas; Rengstorf; Thomas differs from the others in suggesting that the original composition was produced in Palestine but addressed to the Diaspora). There is now a virtual consensus that the *Testaments* were written in Greek, contrary to the view of Charles, although R. Martin has recently argued that *T. Jos.* is in part translation Greek. The ethics of the *Testaments*, with their emphasis on specific virtues, finds its closest Jewish parallels in the Diaspora. The prominence of Joseph, not only in *T. Jos.* but also in the testaments of Reuben, Simeon, Dan, Gad, and Benjamin, may reflect on Egyptian provenance, since Joseph was obviously associated with Egypt. A Diaspora origin would also help to explain the absence of the *Testaments* from Qumran. None of these arguments is conclusive. The parallels between the *Testaments* and Qumran clearly show that they drew on some material that was current in Palestine. Greek language and Hellenistic ethics are not incompatible with a Palestinian origin. The references to Joseph and parallels with Hellenistic literature are more common in Becker's second stratum than in the framework. On the whole it seems probable that the *Testaments* underwent an edition in the Diaspora, but here again the conclusion is very tentative and no great weight can be placed upon it.

There is general agreement that the Christian redaction of the *Testaments* must be dated to the second century C.E. There is no consensus on the Jewish stages. Since the article of E. J. Bickerman in 1950, a number of scholars have argued that the original *Testaments* were written before the Maccabean revolt (Becker; Thomas; Harrelson). In *T. Levi* 17:11 the sinful priests of the seventh week who immediately precede the "new priest" of the eschatological age have been identified with the Hellenizers prior to the Maccabean revolt. *T. Naph.* 5:8 states that "Assyrians, Medes, Persians, Chaldeans, Syrians shall possess in captivity the twelve tribes of Israel." Since no reference is made to the Romans, this passage must be dated before Pompey, and probably before the expulsion of the Syrians in 141 B.C.E. It cannot be earlier than 200 B.C.E., since it presupposes Syrian, not Ptolemaic, rule. The lack of reference to the Maccabean revolt may narrow the range to 200–170, but this is not conclusive, since the silence may be due to lack of sympathy. It is also possible that *T. Naph.* 5:8 is an isolated fragment and not representative of the composition as a whole. Here again the hypothesis of pre-Maccabean *Testaments* must be regarded as extremely tentative.

A similar redactional theory, different in its specific details, has been proposed by A. Hultgård. He locates the original *Testaments* in Galilee in the early part of the first century B.C.E. The distinction of two messiahs was developed in opposition to the Hasmonean priest-kings. He then allows for one or more Jewish redactions, reflected in the translation into Greek and development of the priestly savior figure, which is dated about the turn of the era on the basis of parallels with Augustus (1977:370). Finally, there was a Christian redaction in the second century. Hultgård's study is erudite and rich in cross references to Hellenistic literature, but the evidence on which he bases his reconstruction also admits of other explanations.

H. C. Kee has argued for a date about 100 B.C.E. on the basis of parallels with middle Stoicism. Kee's parallels are interesting for the ethics of the *Testaments*, but the ideas in question cannot be confined to such a narrow time period and are of little help for dating. Kolenkow (1975) suggests another approach to the composition of the *Testaments* which focuses on the contrasts between Joseph and some of his brothers. Her suggestions await fuller elaboration.

Not all study of the *Testaments* has focused on the question of origins. The ethics and piety of the *Testaments* have also been studied repeatedly (Eppel; Hollander). Like much of the Diaspora literature, the *Testaments* emphasize ethical issues that could be appreciated even by Gentiles, rather than distinctive Jewish customs (Collins, 1983:154–62). Nickelsburg (1981) takes an agnostic position on the question of provenance but emphasizes that most of the *Testaments* share a common structure (see also Baltzer). Küchler locates them more broadly in the tradition of Jewish wisdom teaching.

Summary

The only point that has been definitively clarified by recent research is that the Christian elements in the *Testaments* cannot be removed by textual criticism. The discussion of provenance remains divided between two main options (since the Qumran hypothesis has apparently receded). On the one hand, de Jonge quite rightly insists on the need to study the final Christian stage and on the extremely hypothetical character of any pre-Christian construct. On the other hand, Becker, Hultgård, and others have ventured hypotheses and produced a history that is highly suggestive but must remain very tentative. The abiding conviction, admitted even by de Jonge, that the *Testaments* are not simply a Christian composition, demands that hypotheses such as Becker's be ventured and refined but in the end the *Testaments* can be used much more confidently in the study of second-century Christianity than of pre-Christian Judaism.

THE TESTAMENT OF JOB

Relative to the *Testaments of the Twelve Patriarchs*, the discussion of the other testaments has been uncomplicated. The view that *T. Job* is Christian (James; Schürer) has not been defended in any recent study. There is a consensus that the work originated in the Egyptian Diaspora (Job is king of Egypt) about the turn of the era (Philonenko, 1958, 1969; Delcor, 1968; Kee, 1974; Schaller leaves the place of origin open). In fact, there is little precise evidence for the date. *T. Job* can scarcely be earlier than the first century B.C.E., since it depends on the LXX of Job, but a *terminus ante quem* is hard to find. The consensus dating to the turn of the era rests primarily on parallels with other Jewish writings. The attempt to attribute *T. Job* to the Therapeutae (Philonenko; Spittler) has been sharply and rightly criticized by B. Schaller. The mystical tendencies of the work have been repeatedly noted in recent studies (Collins, 1974; Kee, 1974;

Schaller). A convenient text and translation of *T. Job* can be found in Kraft, 1974, and an edition of the Greek of MS P in Brock.

THE TESTAMENT OF MOSES

R. H. Charles (1913:407) had already recognized that the so-called *Assumption of Moses* was really a testament, and this insight has been confirmed by recent studies (Laperrousaz; Kolenkow, 1973). The main point at issue in recent study has been the date of the document. Charles had dated it about the turn of the era, after the attack on the Jews by Varus in 4 B.C.E. J. Licht challenged this view and argued that the work was composed during the persecution by Antiochus IV Epiphanes and only updated after 4 B.C.E. This view was developed by Nickelsburg (1972:43–45). Collins (1973a) and Rhoads argued for the coherence of the document in a setting after the death of Herod, but Collins (1973b) ultimately accepted Nickelsburg's argument (1973) that the specificity of the parallels in chap. 8 to the Antiochan persecution is more easily explained if the post-Maccabean material in chaps. 6 and 7 is a later insertion, so that in the original document the historical persecution is the prelude to the eschatological climax. This two-stage understanding of *T. Moses* was supported by A. Yarbro Collins's redaction-critical study of *T. Moses* 10. A number of scholars (Brandenburger; Priest) still reject the Antiochan stage.

THE TESTAMENT OF ABRAHAM

In contrast to the *Testament/Assumption of Moses, T. Abr.* is not a testament and is in fact characterized by Abraham's refusal to make a testament (Kolenkow, 1974, 1976). There is wide agreement that it is a Jewish work (contra James and Schürer; see Janssen: 199). The date is usually put in the first Christian century, on the basis of parallels with other Jewish writings (Delcor, 1973:51), but hard evidence is lacking. Scholarly debate has involved the issues of the original language, the place of composition, the relation of the two recensions, and the coherence of the work. A convenient text and translation of both recensions can be found in Stone, 1972.

Most scholars now agree that the original language was Greek. N. Turner initially argued for a Hebrew original of recension B (1953) but later modified this view to allow the possibility of "Jewish Greek" (1955). Martin (1976:95–101) suggests that "the producer of Recension A (and possibly also the producer of Recension B) is editing a Greek text which was earlier translated from a semitic language," but Martin allows that some "additions" may not go back to a Semitic original.

The most plausible location of the work is in Egypt, in view of several parallels to Egyptian mythology and to Egyptian Jewish literature (Delcor, 1973:67–68). Janssen (199–201) objects that Egyptian influence was possible in Palestine, but he fails to adduce positive evidence for a Palestinian origin. F. Schmidt argues that Egyptian influence is only evident in recension A, whereas both recensions A and B show Iranian influence. He concludes that B was composed in Palestine, but there is no reason why Iranian influence should be more likely in Palestine than in Egypt (Nickelsburg, ed., 1976:15–16).

There is no consensus about whether the longer (A) or shorter (B) recension is earlier. Many scholars reject the idea that one recension depends directly on the other and suppose that both can ultimately be traced to a common original (Delcor, 1973:13–14; Janssen: 195). Schmidt defends the priority of B, but Nickelsburg (1976:92) has shown persuasively that "numerous elements, *which are simply present* in Rec B, *with no clearly delineated function, are of the essence* of the structure and plot of Rec A," and that therefore the longer Rec A better preserves the outline of the story.

Delcor (1973:57) suggested that recension A, chaps. 10–15 (the ride in the chariot) may be a *corps étranger*. Against this Nickelsburg (1976:85) has shown that recension A is "neatly divided into two parallel and symmetrical parts," 1–15 and 16–20. In the first part Michael comes to take Abraham; in the second part, Death comes. In both cases Abraham refuses to go and asks for a revelation, the chariot ride and the revelation of Death. In the end he is taken by deceit. Nickelsburg argued that the point of the book was the inevitability of death, but he also noted that it is a veritable parody on the biblical Abraham. Kolenkow (1976:142) saw the point of the story as the recognition of a "new sin"—Abraham's excessive zeal in destroying sinners, which becomes manifest during the chariot ride. These insights may be seen as complementary. The problem raised by the book is Abraham's reluctance to die. The reader can identify with Abraham in this. Yet the terror of death is mitigated by the revelations that God does not share the severity of righteous humans such as Abraham. The revelation of Abraham's "new sin" and of the various kinds of death serves to put the problem of death in perspective (Collins, 1983:226–28).

CONCLUSION

There is little doubt that the testamentary literature occupied a significant place in Judaism in the period covered by this volume. Appreciation of that place is hindered by the lack of consensus on basic questions of date and provenance, especially in the case of the *Testaments of the Twelve Patriarchs*. Unless significant (and unexpected!) progress is made in clarifying these questions, only tentative use can be made of the testaments in the broader studies of the religious and social history of Judaism.

BIBLIOGRAPHY

Amstutz, J.
1968   ΑΠΛΟΤΗΣ: *Eine begriffsgeschichtliche Studie zum jüdisch-christlichen Griechisch.* Bonn: Hanstein.

Aschermann, P. H.
1955   "Die paränetischen Formen der 'Testamente der zwölf Patriarchen' und ihr Nachwirken in der frühchristlichen Mahnung." Diss., Humboldt-Universität, Berlin.

Baillet, M.
1978   "Le volume VII de 'Discoveries in the Judaean Desert.' Presentation." Pp. 75–89 in *Qumran: Sa piété, sa théologie et son milieu.* Ed. M. Delcor. BETL 46. Paris and Gembloux: Duculot; Leuven: University Press.

Baltzer, K.
1971   *The Covenant Formulary.* Philadelphia: Fortress.

Becker, J.
1970   *Untersuchungen zur Entstehungsgeschichte der Testamente der zwölf Patriarchen.* AGJU 8. Leiden: Brill.
1974   *Die Testamente der zwölf Patriarchen.* JSHRZ 3.1. Gütersloh: Mohn.

Behm, J.
1964   "διαθήκη." *TDNT* 2: 102–34.

Bickerman, E. J.
1950   "The Date of the Testaments of the Twelve Patriarchs." *JBL* 69: 245–60.

Brandenburger, E.
1976   *Himmelfahrt Moses.* JSHRZ 5.2. Gütersloh: Mohn.

Brock, S. P.
1967   *Testamentum Iobi.* PVTG 2. Leiden: Brill.

Burchard, C.
1969   "Zur armenischen Überlieferung der Testamente der zwölf Patriarchen." Pp. 1–29 in Eltester.

Charles, R. H.
1908   *The Greek Versions of the Testaments of the Twelve Patriarchs, Edited from Nine MSS. together with the Variants of the Armenian and Slavonic Versions and Some Hebrew Fragments.* Oxford: Clarendon.
1913   *APOT.*

Charlesworth, J. H., ed.
1983   *The Old Testament Pseudepigrapha.* Vol. 1, *Apocalyptic Literature and Testaments.* Garden City, NY: Doubleday.

Collins, J. J.
1973a   "The Date and Provenance of the Testament of Moses." Pp. 15–32 in Nickelsburg, ed., 1973.
1973b   "Some Remaining Traditio-Historical Problems in the Testament of Moses." Pp. 38–43 in Nickelsburg, ed., 1973.
1974   "Structure and Meaning in the Testament of Job." Pp. 35–52 in *Society of Biblical Literature 1974 Seminar Papers,* Vol. 1. Ed. G. W. MacRae. Missoula, MT: Scholars Press.

1983 *Between Athens and Jerusalem: Jewish Identity in the Hellenistic Diaspora.* New York: Crossroad.
1984 "Testaments." In *Jewish Literature of the Second Temple Period.* Ed. M. E. Stone. Philadelphia: Fortress.

Cortès, E.
1976 *Los discursos de Adiós de Gn 49 a Jn 13–17: Pistas para la historia de un género literario en la antigua literatura judía.* Colectánea San Paciano 23. Barcelona: Herder.

Delcor, M.
1968 "Le Testament de Job, la prière de Nabonide et les traditions targoumiques." Pp. 57–74 in *Bibel und Qumran.* Ed. S. Wagner. Berlin: Evangelische Haupt-Bibelgesellschaft.
1973 *Le Testament d'Abraham.* SVTP 2. Leiden: Brill.

Dupont-Sommer, A.
1953 *Nouveaux aperçus sur les manuscrits de la mer Morte.* Paris: Maisonneuve.

Eltester, W., ed.
1969 *Studien zu den Testamenten der zwölf Patriarchen.* BZNW 36. Berlin: Töpelmann.

Eppel, R.
1930 *Le Piétisme Juif dans les Testaments des Douze Patriarches.* Paris: Alcan.

Farrer, A.
1951 *A Study in St. Mark.* London: Oxford University Press.

Fascher, E.
1921 *Prophètes.* Giessen: Töpelmann.

Fischel, H.
1946-47 "Martyr and Prophet." *JQR* 37: 265–80, 303–89.

Fitzmyer, J. A.
1974 "The Contribution of Qumran Aramaic to the Study of the New Testament." *NTS* 20: 382–407.

Flusser, D.
1971 "The Testaments of the Twelve Patriarchs." *EncJud* 13: 184–86.

Fritz, K. von, ed.
1972 *Pseudepigrapha I: Pseudopythagorica, Lettres de Platon, Littérature pseudépigraphe juive.* Entretiens sur l'antiquité classique 18.

Gaster, M.
1893-94 "The Hebrew Text of One of the Testaments of the Twelve Patriarchs." Pp. 33–49, 109–17 in *Proceedings of the Society of Biblical Archaeology.*

Grabe, J. E.
1698 *Spicilegium SS. Patrum ut et Haereticorum seculi post Christum natum. I. II & III.* 2 vols. Oxford: Oxford University Press.

Greenfield, J. C., and M. E. Stone
1979 "Remarks on the Aramaic Testament of Levi from the Cairo Geniza (Planches XIII-XIV)." *RB* 86: 214–30.

Harrelson, W.
1975 "Patient Love in the Testament of Joseph." Pp. 29–35 in Nickelsburg, ed., 1975.

Hengel, M.
1972 "Anonymität, Pseudepigraphie und 'literarische Fälschung' in der jüdisch-hellenistischen Literatur." Pp. 231–308 in Fritz, ed.

Hollander, H. W.
1981 *Joseph as an Ethical Model in the Testaments of the Twelve Patriarchs.* SVTP 6. Leiden: Brill.

Hollander, H. W., and M. de Jonge
1985 *The Testament of the Twelve Patriarchs: A Commentary.* SVTP 8. Leiden: Brill.

Hultgård, A.
1971 "Croyances messianiques des Test. XII Patr.: Critique textuelle et commentaire des passages messianiques." Diss., Uppsala.
1977 *L'eschatologie des Testaments des Douze Patriarches.* Vol. 1, *Interprétation des textes.* Acta Universitatis Upsaliensis, Historia Religionum 6. Stockholm: Almqvist & Wiksell.
1982 *L'Eschatologie des Testaments des Douze Patriarches.* Vol. 2, *Composition de l'ouvrage; textes et traductions.* Acta Universitatis Upsaliensis, Historia Religionum 7. Stockholm: Almqvist & Wiksell.

Hunkin, J. W.
1914 "The Testaments of the Twelve Patriarchs." *JTS* 16: 80–97.

James, M. R.
1892 *The Testament of Abraham.* Texts and Studies 2.2; Cambridge: University Press.
1897 "The Testament of Job." In *Apocrypha Anecdota.* 2nd Series. Texts and Studies 5. Cambridge: University Press.

Janssen, E.
1975 "Testament Abrahams." In JSHRZ 3.2. Gütersloh: Mohn.

Jaubert, A.
1963 *La notion d'alliance dans le judaïsme aux abords de l'ère chrétienne.* Patristica Sorbonensia 6. Paris: Seuil.

Jeremias, J.
1958 *Heiligen Gräben in Jesu Umwelt.* Göttingen: Vandenhoeck & Ruprecht.

Jervell, J.
1969 "Ein Interpolator Interpretiert: Zu den christlichen Bearbeitung der Testamente der zwölf Patriarchen." Pp. 30–61 in Eltester.

Jonge, M. de
1953 *The Testaments of the Twelve Patriarchs: A Study of Their Text, Composition and Origin.* Assen: van Gorcum.
1964,1970 *Testamenta XII Patriarcharum Edited according to Cambridge University Library MS Ff 1.24 fol. 203a–261b with short notes.* PVTG 1. Leiden: Brill.
1978 *The Testaments of the Twelve Patriarchs: A Critical Edition of the Greek Text.* In cooperation with H. W. Hollander, H. J. de Jonge, and T. Korteweg. PVTG 1, 2. Leiden: Brill.

Jonge, M. de, ed.
1975 *Studies on the Testaments of the Twelve Patriarchs. Text and Interpretation.* SVTP 3. Leiden: Brill.

Käsemann, E.
1968 *The Testament of Jesus.* Philadelphia: Fortress.

Kautzsch, E.
1900   *Die Apokryphen und Pseudepigraphen des Alten Testaments*. 2
            vols. Tübingen: Mohr.

Kee, H. C.
1974   "Satan, Magic and Salvation in the Testament of Job." Pp. 53–76 in
            Society of Biblical Literature 1974 Seminar Papers, vol. 1. Ed.
            G. W. MacRae. Missoula, MT: Scholars Press.
1978   "The Ethical Dimensions of the Testaments of the XII as a Clue to
            Provenance." *NTS* 24: 259–70.
1983   "Testaments of the Twelve Patriarchs." Pp. 775–828 in Charles-
            worth, ed.

Kohler, K.
1897   "The Testament of Job as Essenic Midrasch." Pp. 264–338 in *Semitic
            Studies in Memory of Dr. Alexander Kohut*. Berlin: Calvary.

Kolenkow, A. B.
1971   "An Introduction to II Bar. 53, 56–74: Structure and Substance."
            Diss., Harvard University.
1973   "The Assumption of Moses as a Testament." Pp. 71–77 in Nickels-
            burg, ed., 1973.
1974   "What is the Role of Testament in the Testament of Abraham?"
            HTR 67: 182–84.
1975a   "The Genre Testament and Forecasts of the Future in the Helle-
            nistic Jewish Milieu." *JSJ* 6: 57–71.
1975b   "The Narratives of the TJ and the Organization of the Testaments
            of the XII Patriarchs." Pp. 37–46 in Nickelsburg, ed., 1975.
1976   "The Genre Testament and the Testament of Abraham." Pp.
            139–52 in Nickelsburg, ed., 1976.
1982   Review of von Nordheim. *JAOS* 102: 663–64.

Korteweg, T.
1975   "The Meaning of Naphtali's Visions." Pp. 261–90 in de Jonge, ed.

Küchler, M.
1979   Pp. 415–545 in *Frühjüdische Weisheitstraditionen*. Göttingen:
            Vandenhoeck & Ruprecht.

Kraft, R. A., et al.
1974   *The Testament of Job*. SBLTT 5; Pseudepigrapha Series 4. Mis-
            soula, MT: Scholars Press.

Kuhn, K. G.
1954   "Die beiden Messias Aarons und Israels." *NTS* 1: 167–79.

Laperrousaz, E.-M.
1970   *Le Testament de Moïse*. Semitica 19.

Licht, J.
1961   "Taxo, or the Apocalyptic Doctrine of Vengeance." *JJS* 12: 95–103.

Liver, J.
1959   "The Doctrine of the Two Messiahs in Sectarian Literature in the
            Time of the Second Commonwealth." *HTR* 52: 149–85.

Lohmeyer, E.
1913   *Diatheke*. Leipzig: Hinrichs.

Martin, R. A.
1975   "Syntactical Evidence for a Semitic *Vorlage* of the Testament of
            Joseph." Pp. 105–27 in Nickelsburg, ed., 1975.

1976 "Syntax Criticism of the Testament of Abraham." Pp. 95–120 in Nickelsburg, ed., 1976.

Michel, H. J.
1973 *Die Abschiedsrede des Paulus an die Kirche Apg 20 17–38.* SANT 35. Munich: Kösel.

Milik, J. T.
1955 "Le Testament de Lévi en araméen: fragment de la grotte 4 de Qumrân." *RB* 62: 398–406.
1959 *Ten Years of Discovery in the Wilderness of Judaea.* Trans. J. Strugnell. SBT 26. London: SCM.
1966 "Fragment d'une source du psautier (4Q Ps 89) et fragments des Jubilés, du Document de Damas, d'une phylactère dans la grotte 4 de Qumrân." *RB* 73: 94–106.
1978 "Ecrits prééesséniens de Qumrân: d'Henoch à Amram." In *Qumran: Sa piété, sa théologie et son milieu.* Ed. M. Delcor. BETL 46. Paris and Gembloux: Duculot. Leuven: University Press.

Milik, J. T., with M. Black
1976 *The Books of Enoch.* Oxford: Clarendon.

Munck, J.
1950 "Discours d'adieu dans le Nouveau Testament et dans la littérature biblique." Pp. 155–70 in *Aux sources de la tradition chrétienne: Festschrift Maurice Goguel.* Neuchâtel and Paris: Delachaux & Niestlé.

Nickelsburg, G. W. E.
1972 *Resurrection, Immortality and Eternal Life in Intertestamental Judaism.* HTS 26. Cambridge, MA: Harvard University Press.
1973 "An Antiochan Date for the Testament of Moses." Pp. 33–37 in Nickelsburg, ed., 1973.
1981 *Jewish Literature Between the Bible and the Mishnah.* Philadelphia: Fortress.

Nickelsburg, G. W. E., ed.
1973 *Studies on the Testament of Moses.* SBLSCS 4. Missoula, MT: Scholars Press.
1975 *Studies on the Testament of Joseph.* SBLSCS 5. Missoula, MT: Scholars Press.
1976 *Studies on the Testament of Abraham.* SBLSCS 6. Missoula, MT: Scholars Press.

Nordheim, E. von
1980 *Die Lehre der Alten.* Vol. 1, *Das Testament als Literaturgattung im Judentum der Hellenistisch-Römischen Zeit.* Leiden: Brill.

Otzen, B.
1953 "Die neugefundenen hebräischen Sektenschriften und die Testamente der zwölf Patriarchen." *ST* 7: 125–57.

Philonenko, M.
1958 "Le Testament de Job et les Therapeutes." *Sem* 8: 41–53.
1960 *Les interpolations chrétiennes des Testaments des XII Patriarches et les manuscrits de Qoumrân.* Cahiers de la RHPR. Paris: Presses universitaires de France.
1969 "Le Testament de Job." *Sem* 18: 9–24.

Priest, J.
1977   "Some Reflections on the Assumption of Moses." *Perspectives in Religious Studies* 4: 92–111.
1983   "Testament of Moses." Pp. 919–34 in Charlesworth, ed.

Rengstorf, K. H.
1974   "Herkunft und Sinn der Patriarchen Reden in den Testamenten der zwölf Patriarchen." Pp. 28–47 in *La littérature juive entre Tenach et Mischna: Quelques problèmes.* Ed. W. C. van Unnik. RechBib 9. Leiden: Brill.

Rhoads, D. M.
1973   "The Assumption of Moses and Jewish History: 4 B.C.–A.D. 48." Pp. 53–58 in Nickelsburg, ed., 1973.

Robinson, S. E.
1982   *The Testament of Adam: An Examination of the Syriac and Greek Traditions.* SBLDS 52. Chico, CA: Scholars Press.

Sanders, E. P.
1983   "The Testament of Abraham." Pp. 869–918 in Charlesworth, ed.

Schaller, B.
1979   *Das Testament Hiobs.* JSHRZ 3.3. Gütersloh: Mohn.

Schnapp, F.
1884   *Die Testamente der zwölf Patriarchen untersucht.* Halle: Niemeyer.

Schmidt, F.
1971   "Le Testament d'Abraham: Introduction, édition de la recension courte, traduction et notes." Diss., Strasbourg.

Schnackenburg, R.
1957   "Abschiedensreden Jesu." *LTK* 1: 68–69.

Schürer, E.
1909   *Geschichte des jüdischen Volkes im Zeitalter Jesu Christi.* 4th ed. Vol. 3. Leipzig: Hinrichs.

Slingerland, H. D.
1977a   *The Testaments of the Twelve Patriarchs: A Critical History of Research.* SBLMS 21. Missoula, MT: Scholars Press.
1977b   "The Testament of Joseph: A Redaction-Critical Study." *JBL* 96: 507–16.

Spittler, R.
1971   "The Testament of Job: Introduction, Translation and Notes." Diss., Harvard University.
1983   "The Testament of Job." Pp. 919–26 in Charlesworth, ed.

Smith, Morton
1972   "Pseudepigraphy in the Israelite Literary Tradition." Pp. 191–215 in Fritz, ed.

Stauffer, E.
1950   "Abschiedsreden." *RAC* 1: 29–35.

Stone, M. E.
1969   *The Testament of Levi: A First Study of the Armenian MSS of the Testaments of the Twelve Patriarchs in the Convent of St. James, Jerusalem.* Jerusalem: St. James Press.

1972 *The Testament of Abraham: The Greek Recensions.* SBLTT 2;
Pseudepigrapha Series 2. Missoula, MT: Scholars Press.

1975 *The Armenian Version of the Testament of Joseph: Introduction,
Critical Edition and Translation.* SBLTT 6; Pseudepigrapha Series
5. Missoula, MT: Scholars Press.

1977 "New Evidence for the Armenian Version of the Testaments of the
Twelve Patriarchs." *RB* 84: 94–107.

Thomas, J.
1969 "Aktuelles in Zeugnis der Zwölf Vater." Pp. 62–150 in Eltester, ed.

Turdeanu, E.
1970 "Les Testaments des douze Patriarches en slave." *JSJ* 1: 148–84.

Turner, N.
1953 "The Testament of Abraham: A Study of the Original Language,
Place of Origin, Authorship and Relevance." Diss., London.

1955 "The 'Testament of Abraham': Problems in Biblical Greek." *NTS* 1:
219–23.

Woude, A. S. van der
1957 *Die messianischen Vorstellungen der Gemeinde von Qumrân.*
Studia semitica neerlandica 3. Assen: Van Gorcum.

Yarbro Collins, A.
1976 "Composition and Redaction of the Testament of Moses 10." *HTR*
69: 179–86.

12
NARRATIVE LITERATURE

Robert Doran

INTRODUCTION

In the wide diversity of the literature examined, this chapter reflects the richness of narrative writing in the Second Temple period. The works considered here are only the remnant of what must have been produced, but this sample evidences the creative adaptation of traditional tale types to reflect a Jewish world view. This variety defies precise classification; one must simply put the stories side by side and enjoy their differences.

However, the narratives are linked in some way to biblical traditions, either to a biblical character or a historical event. Since the dating of each work presents difficulties, I have decided to order them according to the biblical reference fictionally presupposed in these works, but even this order is not without chronological problems. For example, Tobit is a young man at the secession of the northern tribes (931), and his son sees the downfall of Nineveh (612); Judith is set in the days of Nebuchadnezzar but presupposes the return from captivity. I have placed first stories about patriarchs (Abraham and Joseph), then stories about prophets (Isaiah and Jeremiah), about exilic heroes (Tobit and Daniel), and finally the story of a postexilic heroine, Judith.

THE TESTAMENT OF ABRAHAM

The *Testament of Abraham* narrates how the righteous Abraham came to die, although not without the protest of Abraham and the necessity of trickery on Death's part.

Text

The *Testament of Abraham* exists in a long and a short recension. R. A. Kraft enumerated the various possibilities for relationship between the two recensions ranging from direct dependence of one on the other to dependence on various individual traditions. Because of the basic similarity of plot line between the two recensions, scholars have generally agreed that they derive from a common original (Delcor, 1973:13–14; Janssen: 195; Sanders: 872). Scholars disagree, however, about which of the two recensions better reflects the original form of the work. F. Schmidt (1971,

1976) defends the priority of B, whereas G. W. E. Nickelsburg argues on the grounds of story line that A preserves the better narrative structure (1976:92). E. P. Sanders (872–73) concludes that the original contained approximately the structure of A, but he concurs with N. Turner that B may frequently represent more closely the original wording.

Recent scholarship agrees that *T. Abr.* is a Jewish work, but opinion is split on its original language. Turner (1953) first argued for a Hebrew original for B if not for A, but he has since stated in a letter to Sanders (873) that he "cannot believe either recension to be a translation." Schmidt (1971, 1:120) and R. A. Martin (95–101) posit a Semitic original for B, but for the most part scholars argue for a Semitizing Greek (Delcor, 1973:34; Janssen: 198–99; Sanders: 873–74).

Genre

The *Testament of Abraham* is not in the form of a testament: it does not employ a deathbed scene as a setting for ethical and eschatological teaching, and, in fact, Abraham dies without making any disposition (Kolenkow, 1974, 1976a; Nickelsburg, 1981:251).

Nickelsburg has shown that the book "is divided into two parallel and symmetrical sections" (1976:86–87; 1981:249–51). First Michael comes to take Abraham, then Death. In both sections Abraham refuses to go and stalls by asking for a revelation. Nickelsburg notes the humor throughout the narrative and suggests that Abraham's disobedient refusal to die creates "a veritable parody on the biblical and traditional Abraham" (1981:250–51). That the excessive zeal of the righteous Abraham to punish sinners is itself a sin heightens the parody, Collins suggests (542). Nickelsburg does not seem to use the term "parody" in a genre sense, however. Collins classifies the chariot ride, but not the work as a whole, as an apocalypse (541).

More needs to be done to determine the genre. If *Testament of Abraham* is a parody, examples of the literary form parodied need to be provided. Does not much of the humor come from watching Abraham bicker over dying, and does not this simply continue the portrayal of Abraham in Genesis 18 and 23 as a consummate haggler? Are heavenly tours being parodied?

Message

Schmidt, using a structuralist approach, argues that the book shows that death is but a passage to real life (1971 as summarized by Nickelsburg, 1976:32–34). Nickelsburg (1976:16) questions Schmidt's interpretation, and he sees death as the central theme: "the moment of death, and its inevitable consummation, are in the hands of the sovereign God, and there is none who can resist" (1976:87). Kolenkow notes that the *Testament of Abraham* highlights a sin not generally recognized—the desire of the righteous to destroy sinners (1976a:142). Nickelsburg accepts this (1976: 294–95; 1981:252), as does Collins, who holds that the book's ethical message is that "mercy rather than severity is pleasing to God" (542–43). Sanders takes a different tack and emphasizes the "lowest-common-denominator universalism of its soteriology" (876–87). The *Testament of Abraham* makes no distinction between Jew and Gentile and mentions sins such as theft and immorality condemned by Jews and Gentiles. Everyone is judged by the same standard, and the only means of atonement, available to all, are repentance and premature death. Sanders contrasts this universalism with the spirit of works, which insists on strict adherence to dietary laws and to the Mosaic covenant. Is such a contrast valid? The author, as Sanders suggests (873–74), imitates classical biblical prose style. Is he also reflecting the distinction in Genesis 18 between righteous and sinners rather than post-Mosaic attitudes?

Provenance

Janssen proposes a Palestinian origin for the work (198–99), and Schmidt places the origin of the short recension in Palestine and that of the long recension in Egypt (1971:119–21). The papers in Nickelsburg's collection suggest an early presence of the short recension in Egypt. This presence, coupled with the parallels to Egyptian mythology and other Egyptian Jewish literature brought forward by M. Delcor (1973:59–68), argues in favor of an Egyptian origin. Nickelsburg (1976:16–19) criticizes Schmidt's suggestion of an Essene provenance, but is less firm in rejecting Delcor's suggestion that the *Testament of Abraham* had its origin among the Therapeutae (Delcor, 1973:69–72; Nickelsburg, 1976:298).

Arguments for the date are based largely on a comparison with other works. C. W. Fishburne attempts to show that in 1 Corinthians Paul was writing against the background of the *Testament of Abraham*. His three parallels, however, do not demand dependence of one on the other, but reference to a common judgment tradition. S. E. Loewenstamm argues that the traditions about Moses' refusal of death are more ancient and are presupposed by the *Testament of Abraham* (219–25), and he is followed in this by Sanders (879), though this comparison does not provide a certain *terminus a quo*. Kolenkow shows how the angelology is common to 2 *Enoch*, the *Life of Adam and Eve* and the *Assumption of Moses* (1976b:153–62). Sanders (874–75) argues that, if Egyptian, it must predate 117 C.E., and that its dependence on the Moses traditions and its similarities to 2 *Enoch* and 3 *Baruch* suggest a date around 100 C.E.

The judgment scene in the *Testament of Abraham* clearly needs to be compared with the eschatology of early Christianity. This has been started by Fishburne, but much more needs to be done for a comparison of thought world.

JOSEPH AND ASENETH

In 1952/53, G. D. Kilpatrick and J. Jeremias argued that *Joseph and Aseneth* was produced at the beginning of the Common Era. The consensus of recent scholarship is that it was written in Greek (Burchard, 1965:91–99), probably in Egypt (Burchard, 1965:140–43; Philonenko, 1968:27–32). As for its date, Burchard (1965:143–51) and Nickelsburg (1981:263) prefer the more general dating at the turn of the era, whereas Philonenko (1968:99–109) suggests a time just prior to the Jewish revolt in Egypt in 116 C.E., a clear *terminus ad quem* if the work was written in Egypt. S. West points out how tentative such conclusions are and suggests a date earlier than the increasingly anti-Semitic atmosphere under Roman rule (79–80). Her dating depends on a close parallelism between social conditions in the story and those prevailing at the time the story was written, a parallelism that needs to be explored.

Three major problem areas of the work remain: the text, its genre, and its religious background.

The Textual Problem

Burchard (1965) thoroughly analyzed the manuscript evidence and concluded that there were four textual families—a, b, c, and d. Family d is a short text, only two-thirds the length of a, b, and c. The edition of P. Battifol was based on the text family a. Philonenko saw this text as late and edited a text based on d, which he saw as the earliest witness (1968), independent of the long tradition which for him ran from b as earliest through c to a as the latest (1974:74–75). Philonenko even suggested that one should abandon any attempt to reconstruct an "original" text but simply be content with two different versions (1974:74). Burchard now sees the development as more complex (1974:81–84). He rejects d as witness to a short earlier version but sees it simply as an abbreviated text. He holds that a, c, and d are certainly three text families, but he is not sure that the manuscripts assigned to b really constitute a family (1974:83). Burchard has published a provisional Greek text (1979b) that is the basis for his translation in J. H. Charlesworth's *Old Testament Pseudepigrapha*, and he continues to work on the manuscript tradition (1977–78, 1979a). Until his edition appears, one should consult his provisional text and Philonenko's edition.

The Genre

Philonenko and Burchard are fundamentally in agreement about the genre of the work: it should be classed among the Greek and Latin romances. Philonenko argues that the author drew on motifs familiar from the Greek romance (1968:32–48); Burchard stresses parallels with the tale of Cupid and Psyche in Apuleius (*Metamorphoses* 4.28–6.24), the transformation of Lucius in *Metamorphoses* 11, and the marriage of Habrocomes and Anthia in Xenophon of Ephesos (1970:59–86; 1974:84–96). West approves of such a classification. While recognizing the presence of such motifs, R. Pervo rejects the notion that *Joseph and Aseneth* is a Jewish equivalent of the Greek romances. He would place *Joseph and Aseneth* within the tradition of the Jewish sapiential novel, a tradition that would include Ahikar, Tobit, and Daniel 1–6 (174–75). His two criteria for this classification seem to be length—it is much shorter than the extant Greek romances—and the heavy-handed insertion of wisdom material, that is, the symbolic and allegorical character of the narrative of Aseneth's conversion. Although the first criterion is not convincing, the second does raise an important issue. Nickelsburg, for example, mentions only in passing that the author uses "a popular erotic literary genre" (1981:263; 1984:59) and concentrates rather on the symbolic character of the work, describing *Joseph and Aseneth* as "functionally a religious myth that explains the origins of proselytism" (1981:262; 1984:57). Here the old question arises: Is the genre just a popular veneer to get the author's religious message across?

What urgently needs to be done is an analysis of the literary structure of the work. It is not enough to point to motifs held in common between works. It is how the motifs are arranged and structured that is primary to understanding a work. The arrangement of motifs in the extant Greek romances and *Joseph and Aseneth* is markedly different.

The literary structure of *Joseph and Aseneth* has nothing in common with the court contests of Ahikar and Daniel 1–6, and religious myth is too vague a term for a literary definition. Nickelsburg has begun a literary analysis by showing how the pattern of events in chaps. 3–8 is repeated in chaps. 18–20, but with significant changes (1981:258–59). One should also start to examine the narrative at the level of a common denominator and to look for comparable tales: tales of the winning of a princess by a suitor might be compared and contrasted, as well as the foiled plot of the jealous rival (the latter suggestion being that of Pervo: 178). Once the pattern is taken seriously, one can appreciate better how the author has adapted it for his purpose. The combination of two such traditional tale patterns—the winning of the princess and the defeat of the rival—may not be as jejune as Pervo claims nor simply an example of how God protects those who convert to him (Nickelsburg, 1981:263). These patterns are used to describe how Joseph, low in status compared with Pharaoh's son, actually succeeds to the throne.

The Religious Background

In this area much progress has been made. Scholars have by and large rejected the thesis of major Christian interpolations, although T. Holtz still argues for this. Much discussion centers on the description of the initiation meal of Aseneth. Should it be connected with the meal of the Essenes or the Therapeutae (Kuhn; Delcor, 1962)? Both Burchard and Philonenko reject this, but D. Sänger has made the fullest rebuttal (1980:48–58). Philonenko (1968) and E. W. Smith, Jr., have collected wide-ranging parallels in Hellenistic literature and religion. Sänger (1980:29–48, 58–83) has made a trenchant critique of those who wish to interpret the narrative in the light of a Gnostic redemption drama or as modeled on a liturgy of initiation into a Jewish mystery religion (Philonenko, 1965, 1975). Sänger follows in the line of Jeremias and Burchard (1968:191–233), who saw in Aseneth's honey-meal not a reflexion of a cultic meal but *theologoumena* about Jewish dietary practices in contrast to non-Jewish. Through an analysis of initiation into the mysteries of Eleusis and Isis as in Apuleius *Met.* 11, Sänger also argues that one could find in *Joseph and Aseneth* a modified formula for the reception of proselytes into the community (1980:174–87). Sänger could have paid more careful attention to the elements of the form of the symbolic vision which are clearly present in the appearance of Michael. He has perhaps been too emphatic in his rejection of influences from the mystery religions, but he has done an important service in emphasizing the Jewishness of the narrative. On this point he is in complete agreement with Nickelsburg (1981:261–62), who underscores the symbolism of Joseph and Aseneth as prototypes for the community and connects the description of Joseph to the language of Wisdom 2 and 5 (1981:271 n. 63). Sänger notes resonances in Philo and, in particular, connects Aseneth's meal with the symbolical interpretation of the manna of the exodus (1980: 191–208; 1981:232–40). For Sänger, the purpose of *Joseph and Aseneth* is to instill a sense of self-worth and identity in a group of Jews and proselytes, and therefore only in a secondary sense is it directed to Gentiles (1980:213–14). Nickelsburg allows for religious syncretism and so sees it as directed at Gentiles in order to convert them to Judaism (1981:262). The larger context of the history of proselytism in Judaism in this period has so far not been explored in the discussion.

Here the question of the social background of the work comes into play. Thus far it has been a neglected factor in the literature on *Joseph and Aseneth*, which has mainly concentrated on the interplay between Michael and Aseneth within the first narrative of the work. At what strata of society would this work be aimed? In this connection the second narrative of the work may be more important. Here one finds a distinction made between the sons of Rachel and Leah and those of her maid-servants. Sänger sees the latter as representing indifferent Jews, but the distinction is based on social standing (1980:213). What does this say about the makeup of the audience addressed?

THE MARTYRDOM OF ISAIAH

The *Martyrdom of Isaiah* exists now only as part of a larger Christian work, the *Ascension of Isaiah*. Most scholars (Hammershaimb: 19; Caquot; Nickelsburg, 1984:34) agree with Charles (*APOT* 2:156–57) that the work probably included the following verses: *Ascension of Isaiah* 1:1–2a; 1:7–3:12; 5:1–14. The biblical basis for the narrative is 2 Kgs 20:16–21:18 and 2 Chr 32:32–33:20, but the author has created his own story.

Date

Hammershaimb concludes that this Jewish work was first written in Hebrew (19). However, he does not decide much beyond this concerning its date. He maintains that *Ascension of Isaiah* was written in the last third of the first century C.E. and that the *Martyrdom of Isaiah* legend is much earlier, but he states that no further precision can be gained (19). The grounds for his dating of the *Ascension of Isaiah*—it is not likely that a Christian writer of the second century C.E. would have used a Jewish legend and that 4:3 refers to Peter's martyrdom by Nerva—are not convincing, and so his *terminus ad quem* for the *Martyrdom of Isaiah* is also questionable. Attempts at a more precise dating have come particularly from O. Eissfeldt and D. Flusser. Eissfeldt connects Isaiah's and his friends' retreat to the wilderness with the stories about Mattathias and Judas Maccabeus and the martyrdom legends of 2 Maccabees 6–7. Nickelsburg, writing against such a view, states that "the archvillain ought not to be an Israelite king—or false prophet—but a foreign oppressor" (1981:144)

Provenance

Flusser interpreted the work as a product of the Qumran community, and in this he was followed enthusiastically by Philonenko (1967) and moderately by Nickelsburg (1981:144–45). Especially important is the polarity in the narrative between Satan, who dwells in Manasseh and supports Bechir-ra, and the Holy Spirit, who supports Isaiah. Notable here are the names used of Satan: Beliar and Sammael. Isaiah's condemnation of Jerusalem as Sodom and the princes as the people of Gommorah would parallel Qumranite criticism of Jerusalem. Isaiah's retreat into the wilderness to escape the wickedness of Jerusalem compares with the retreat of the Qumran community. The charge leveled against Isaiah could reflect the claims by the Teacher of Righteousness to have special revelations into the interpretation of the scriptures. Stone labels this a typological interpretation (1971a:9.72), and one must ask if one is forced to see the *Martyrdom of Isaiah* as a *roman à clef*. Are the incidents in the story so peculiar that they can only be explained by this allegorical approach? Nickelsburg mentions only that Isaiah's withdrawal to the wilderness and the presence of a group of prophets in his company are not required for the dramatic action of the story (1981:143). However, Josephus mentions several prophets who went into the wilderness with their followers—surely this is an exodus motif. The typological approach also does not explain the emphasis on Bechir-ra as a Samaritan, nor does it do justice to the parallels already adduced by Charles to Persian traditional literature. The confrontation between Isaiah and Manasseh/Bechir-ra has been raised to the mythical level of the battle between God and Satan, but is this universality only to be found at Qumran? With Nickelsburg (1981:145) it is probably safer to say that the work emanates from a group with ideas similar to those found in the Qumran literature.

Because of this, both date and provenance are difficult to determine. Flusser (45–47) compared the prophets' departure for Tyre and Sidon with the withdrawal to Damascus (CD 7:140) and suggested that the *Martyrdom* was written in Damascus to justify the exile. Hammershaimb suggested that Elijah's stay in this region (1 Kgs 17:9) could have inspired this reference (32), and Nickelsburg noted that this incident is too brief and parenthetical to be *the* point of the story (1984:40).

Message

The *Martyrdom of Isaiah* makes an early connection between prophecy and persecution. O. H. Steck (245–47) sees this as a confusion of two types, but H. Fischel perhaps offers the best context for seeing this reinterpretation of the role of the prophet, as does S. Niditch.

THE REST OF THE WORDS OF JEREMIAH

This intriguing narrative has not yet received proper attention. Scholars who have treated it have followed the agenda set out by J. R. Harris (1889) in his introduction and critical edition of the Greek text. Is the work originally Jewish or Christian, and when is it to be dated? More recently, Kraft and A.-E. Purintun published a provisional edition containing a wider range of textual materials; but M. E. Stone rightly laments the lack of a thorough study of the textual tradition (1971b:276).

Jewish or Christian

In its present form, the work is clearly Christian. Harris suggested that it was written as a peace offering in which Christians encouraged Jews to be baptized and to return to their home city after the second Jewish revolt (1889:13–17). P. M. Bogaert alone takes up this idea, suggesting that it was written to Jewish Christians by a Jewish Christian or that it is a Jewish work edited by a Christian (216–21). Most scholars maintain a Jewish origin (Delling: 68–74; Stone, 1971b:276; Nickelsburg, 1981:316). G. Delling (72–73) even posits a Hebrew or Aramaic original. The approval of sacrifice and temple cult, as well as the prohibition against mixed marriages and the hatred of Samaritans, strongly points to Jewish origin. Delling's study highlights the presence of Jewish religious ideas and terminology, particularly in the predicates of God in the prayers.

Date

Nickelsburg writes: "The apocalypses of 4 Ezra and 2 Baruch testify to the fact that Nebuchadnezzar's destruction of Jerusalem was viewed as a prototype of the destruction of 70 C.E. A similar typology seems to be operative here" (1984:64). The work would thus have been written some time after the destruction of the Second Temple. Delling (2–3) dates it to the first third of the second century C.E. Bogaert (220–21) follows Harris (1889:1–25), dating it to 136 C.E. By adding the sixty-six years of Abimelech's sleep to the date of the Temple's destruction, 70 C.E., one arrives at the precise date of 136 C.E. This date is also a year after Hadrian had crushed the Bar Kokhba revolt and issued an edict forbidding Jews to enter Jerusalem. Nickelsburg sees this date as possible, but allows for an earlier date (1984:65).

Bogaert argues that the work depends on *2 Baruch* (177–221), but Nickelsburg provides evidence that the author used a source common to himself and *2 Baruch* (1973). This source would have been written in the name of Jeremiah and would have explained the events that led up to the destruction of Jerusalem in 587 B.C.E. In this connection Nickelsburg points to the traditions found in 2 Macc 2:1–8 and posits that a pseudo-Jeremianic account of the fall of Jerusalem originated during the time of Antiochus IV Epiphanes and formed the basis for the narratives in *2 Baruch* and in the *Rest of the Words of Jeremiah* (1981:316).

Here one must be aware of the assumptions behind the interpretation. At play is a typological argument (or is it allegorical; see above on *Martyrdom of Isaiah*): Nebuchadnezzar stands for Hadrian or Antiochus IV, the destruction of the first Temple stands for the destruction of the second Temple, the exile to Babylon for the exile from Jerusalem under Hadrian. All of this may be true, but one wishes there were some evidence for this approach in the structure of the text itself. What one finds is the use of the Rip Van Winkle story to fulfill Jeremiah's prediction in Jer 39:15–18 that Ebed-melech would be saved, and the motif of the talking eagle messenger for the communication of letters between Baruch and Jeremiah. The suspended animation of Ebed-melech lasts sixty-six years, after which Jeremiah and some exiles return home. Does this not fulfill Jeremiah's prediction that the exile would last seventy years (Jer 25:11; 29:10)? One knows from Dan 9:2 that this prediction of Jeremiah was a problem; the *Rest of the*

Words of Jeremiah gives a different answer from that found in Dan 9:2.

The elements that stand out are the anti-Samaritan polemic, the emphasis on resurrection, and the prohibition of mixed marriage. This combination may point to the same period as previous scholars have suggested, but it does not allow for more precision. One major problem still exists: Where does the Jewish original of the *Rest of the Words of Jeremiah* end? Did it end with Jeremiah's offering sacrifice in Jerusalem at 9:6, or did it have a narrative of Jeremiah's execution by stoning? This may be important for dating as well as for the overall view of the work as optimistic or pessimistic.

THE BOOK OF TOBIT

Concerning Tobit, new finds have not settled old questions. This story about life among the Israelite exiles in Assyria still puzzles scholars with regard to its text, literary analysis, message, and provenance.

Text

There are two major recensions in Greek of the book of Tobit—the longer, represented mainly by Codex Sinaiticus (Rs), and the shorter, found primarily in Codex Vaticanus and Codex Alexandrinus (Rv). Older scholars debated which was the more original: Was Rv a reduction of a longer text or Rs an expansion that added little (Zimmermann, 1958a:127–38; Wikgren: 659). The five manuscripts of Tobit found among the Qumran scrolls, four in Aramaic and one in Hebrew (Milik: 522 n. 3), which appeared to be closest to Rs, seemed to settle the question. Through word-count analysis, J. D. Thomas attempted to show conclusively that Rv abbreviated Rs and that, since Rs is more Semitic, it was based on a Semitic original. Thomas argued (471) that this original was Aramaic primarily on the basis of mistranslations, which could be explained by the multivalent character of the Aramaic particle *di*. A strong objection has been raised against Thomas's method, however, by P. Deselaers (19), who objects to word statistics that do not take account of a thorough analysis of the work from many angles. Deselaers argues for the priority of Rv. On the basis of his source-critical conclusions, he concludes that originally Tobit was written in Greek (342–43), then expanded once in Greek (448–50), and then a second time (449–500). Although he does not explicitly address the question, Deselaers would presumably argue that the Qumran fragments are a translation from Greek into Aramaic and Hebrew.

Source Analysis

Wikgren states that, although a very small minority might see in Tobit some elaboration and additions, there "is no conclusive evidence against the general integrity of the composition" (661). Among that minority is Zimmermann (1958a:24–26), who argued that chaps. 13 and 14 are late additions. However, the presence of part of all fourteen chapters at Qumran discredits some of Zimmermann's argument. Deselaers now claims on the basis of source analysis to have uncovered three main levels of composition in Tobit (48–49). The original narrative would have been 1:1–2, 3*, 9, 13–14; 2:1*, 2–5, 6*, 7, 9–10a; 3:1–5, 6*, 7, 17; 4:1–3a, 20*, 21a; 5:3–14a, 15–17; 7:1–6, 7*, 11–12, 14–15a, 16a, 18b–19; 7:1–10a, 12–14; 8:1–5, 7–15, 17*, 18–19; 10:8–11, 14a; 11:1–6, 10–16a, 17–18; 12:1–2, 3*, 4–6a, 15–18, 21, 22*; 14:2*, 3*, 9a, 11b–14. A first expansion (Deselaers: 52) would mainly encompass the warnings of 4:3b–19 and 12:6b–14 and the hymn in 13:1–9a. A second minor expansion (Deselaers: 53) would have included the Aḥikar material, and a third expansion (Deselaers: 53–54) would have brought in eschatological and apocalyptic motifs, particularly in 13:10b–18. Deselaers's source-critical methodology must be questioned—how dependent is it on an assumption of absolute consistency in a narrative—but is this not a problem for most source-critical explanations?

Literary Analysis

Scholars have long recognized that Tobit reflects folktale tradition. For many the folktale represented was "The Fable of the Grateful Dead" (Wikgren: 661). Zimmermann (1958a:5–12) made several references to motifs listed in Stith Thompson's analysis of folktales. T. F. Glasson tried to sort out the parallels and argued that the narrative in Tobit was not primarily concerned with the burial of the dead but with the marriage of Tobias and Sara and the overpowering of the demon (275–77). Glasson preferred the narrative of Admetus as the main source of Tobit, but he has not been widely followed. Deselaers (281–92), relying on the work of S. Liljeblad, prefers the tale-type "The Demon's Bride" (Stith Thompson's "Monster in the Bridal Chamber" Type 507B) and presents a detailed comparison between the folktale structure and that of Tobit. Deselaers concludes that a Jewish author took this widely known traditional tale and created out of it the book of Tobit (306–8).

Herein lies an emphasis found in recent research. Whereas Zimmermann was content to list references to biblical writers (1958a:12–13), L. Ruppert suggested that the author reformed and modeled his narrative mainly on the Joseph story. Deselaers prefers as a model Genesis 24, where Isaac takes a bride (292–308). There is great promise in this kind of analysis, which takes seriously both the traditional type of the narrative and yet seeks to show how the author of Tobit has creatively used this narrative structure. Nickelsburg also makes significant steps in showing how the plot of the Tobit story is paralleled in the subplot of Sarah (1984:16–17).

Tobit's piety	(2:1-7)	Sarah's innocence	(presumed, e.g., 3:14)
Blindness	(2:9-10)	The demon	(3:8a)
Reproach	(2:11-14)	Reproach	(3:7, 8b-9)
Prayer	(3:1-6)	Prayer	(3:10-15)

The author thus skillfully weaves his story together, incorporating motifs and themes from many sources including those most frequently found in apocalyptic literature (Nickelsburg, 1984:22).

Message

Zimmermann drew out specific ethical and theological statements contained in Tobit (1958:27-32), but recent studies attempt to tie more closely the message of the book to its overall structure. Nickelsburg, who accepts the integrity of the work, sees the story as moving from piety to blessing: "The figure of Tobit is paradigmatic in his movement from despair (or rather a vacillation between despair and faith) to doxology" (1984:19). Stressing the doxological character of the work, Nickelsburg states that the primary purpose of the work is to assure its readers that God is with them even in dispersion and that he will bring them back together. The readers, therefore, should constantly praise the God in whose hands they are. A second purpose, according to Nickelsburg (1984:20), is paraenetic—to teach that which constitutes the pious life.

Deselaers concentrates on the story of Tobit that he has reconstructed through source analysis, but his conclusions are quite similar to those of Nickelsburg. Deselaers concentrates on the terms *hodos, eleēmosynai* and *eulogein.* Of particular interest is his insistence that the term "mercy," "almsgiving," has sociological implications and thus is bound up with uniting the family, kin, and people together (348-58). Since this term is also used frequently to describe God's dealings, Deselaers sees the author as stressing God's close relationship to his people and that no wall exists between humanity and God (373). By his sociological analysis, Deselaers has tied together neatly the two purposes that Nickelsburg kept separate.

Deselaers proposes that the first expansion of the Tobit narrative emphasizes Tobit's wisdom and his role as a medium of revelation (374-423); the second, primarily through the use of Aḥikar, stresses again the need for deeds to build up the community (424-25); the third portrays Tobit in colors of apocalyptic eschatology as part of the propaganda of the Jerusalem priestly circles to the worldwide Diaspora against the hellenizing tendencies of the Seleucid kings (451-500). Here might be noted the thesis of Milik which places the original Tobit as a Samaritan work aimed at giving luster to the politically influential Tobiad family by emphasizing the piety of their ancestor. Milik claims that this original was then reworked by a more orthodox party. He alludes to the teasing problem that Tobit is a northerner and the obvious similarity to the Tobiads, but he does not provide a satisfactory analysis of the whole work.

Date and Provenance

The discovery of the Tobit fragments at Qumran has given a *terminus ad quem*. Zimmerman had pointed to the "historical inaccuracies and hazy geography" in the book to show that it could not have been written early and suggested the time of Antiochus IV (1958:23–24), certainly after 200 B.C.E., given the quotation of the prophetic books. Wikgren (660) felt that Tobit did not reflect a situation of crisis and dated it with most scholars to 200–170 B.C.E. Nickelsburg (1984:21) dates it before Antiochus IV and, citing J. Lebram, even holds that a date before 200 B.C.E. is permissible. Deselaers (342) dates the original Tobit to the middle or second half of the third century B.C.E.; the first expansion to the end of the third century B.C.E. around 220 B.C.E. (423); the second expansion around 195 B.C.E. (450); and the third between the reigns of Antiochus III and IV, that is, ca. 185 B.C.E. With regard to the final form of Tobit, then, Deselaers does not differ greatly from his predecessors.

The mainstream of scholars holds that the book was written in the eastern Diaspora (Lebram: 331; Grintz, 1971c:1185; Nickelsburg, 1984:21 n. 62). Zimmermann concludes that behind the Assyrian capital Nineveh should be seen the Seleucid capital Antioch (1958a:19–21). Milik suggests Samaria and Galilee as its origin, but his thesis has not received much support. R. H. Pfeiffer (273–75) insists on Jerusalem, but most scholars have felt that much in the book suggests a Diaspora setting, particularly the neighbors' lack of sympathy with Tobit's pious concerns and the insistence on endogamy (Nickelsburg, 1984:21). Deselaers rounds out the list: originally Tobit was written in Alexandria (333–43), then expanded in Jerusalem (423), then again in Alexandria (450), and finally in Jerusalem (500).

This survey of scholarship on Tobit shows a general lack of consensus among scholars, although the attempts to treat the work as a whole are producing interesting results.

THE ADDITIONS TO DANIEL

There are in the Greek versions of Daniel three additions to the canonical text: The Prayer of Azariah and the Hymn of the Three Young Men, Susanna, and Bel and the Dragon. Although the prayer and the hymn may once have existed independently (Moore: 40–49), it is not an independent narrative and so will not be discussed here.

Susanna

Some manuscript traditions place the story either before chap. 1 or after chap. 12. However, Moore (90) shows that it originally preceded Daniel 2 and explained why Daniel was held in high repute.

Text

The differences between the Old Greek and Theodotion of Daniel are considerable, particularly when Daniel comes on the scene (Moore: 78–80, 114–16), although the plot remains essentially the same. J. Schüpphaus regards Theodotion as a reediting of the Old Greek, whereas A. Schmitt (100–112) argues that it is a separate translation of a Semitic text. Moore (80) cautiously states that the Old Greek and Theodotion are separate translations of two similar Semitic texts and that Theodotion had the Old Greek before him. The debate continues, not least in regard to the original language. The wordplay in vv. 54–55 and 59–60 may indicate composition in Greek as O. Plöger (67) and Nickelsburg (1981:26) maintain. Moore (81–84) argues that the puns could have been made by the Greek translator guided by puns in the Semitic text and that the overwhelming evidence favors a Semitic original. Moore (25–26), however, also refers to an unpublished paper by R. A. Martin which concludes from an analysis of syntactical features that, although vv. 50–59 were originally in Greek, a Semitic text probably lay behind most of Susanna.

Relation to the Canonical Text

If the Greek Susanna is based on a Semitic original, one wonders why the story was not included with the text of Daniel in the Hebrew scriptures. R. A. F. MacKenzie (214) points to a conflict with mishnaic halakah. Moore (80–81) suggests that a story unfavorable to elders would have been rejected by them.

Literary Analysis

Earlier in this century G. Huet (1912, 1917) and W. Baumgartner (1926, 1929) recognized the folktale character of Susanna, and this identification was accepted by Pfeiffer (453–54). Two motifs were singled out: the innocent woman falsely accused (Stith Thompson motif K 2112) and the clever young judge (Stith Thompson motif J 1140–1150). Moore (89) is less enthusiastic about this view. His skepticism seems to stem from the misconception that traditional folktale structure necessarily means that a Jewish author has transformed a specific "secular folk-tale with no value apart from entertainment" (Moore: 89; Pfeiffer: 454) into a religious story. Such a diachronic judgment is, of course, unwarranted. Traditional typology is a tool for uncovering the structure of the story, not for tracing the history of a particular tale. Attention to narrative structure shows that the plot functions primarily to highlight the success of the young man, in this case Daniel. On structural grounds one cannot say, as Moore does (91), that Susanna, not Daniel, is the hero of the story. The false conviction of Susanna is precisely the problem that the wise man has to solve.

Here one comes to the fascinating question of why the story is concerned with a false accusation of adultery against an innocent woman. Pfeiffer (451–52; Moore: 87–88) was right to criticize the theory of N. Brull that the story is a Pharisaic polemic against Sadducean court procedure. Both he and Moore (84–86) point out the weaknesses in an allegorical reading that finds Susanna to be a cryptogram for historical figures. MacKenzie and Nickelsburg (1981:25–26) both suggest that the story is one of persecution and vindication as are Daniel 3 and 6. MacKenzie (217) also emphasizes that the Susanna story rounds out the tales about Daniel: Daniel 3 is against worshiping idols; Daniel 1 is against eating unclean food; and Susanna is against committing adultery. Busto Saiz follows MacKenzie, but he places more emphasis on the judicial role of Daniel and on the contrast between Susanna and the lecherous judges called descendants of Canaan. Busto Saiz interprets Susanna as a midrash inspired by Hos 4:12–15. Such a generalization, however, does little to elucidate the actual narrative line.

The story cannot be situated geographically. As for its date of composition, the *terminus ad quem* is the Greek translation of the Old Greek of Daniel, which Moore (92) dates to around 100 B.C.E.

Bel and the Dragon

The two Greek versions agree with one another more in Bel and the Dragon than in Susanna (Schmitt: 101; Schüpphaus: 50; Moore: 129).

Source Analysis

The narrative itself divides easily into two stories. Moore argues for the independence of the two narratives on the basis of stylistic differences between the versions (147–48). Whereas Theodotion tells the story of Bel more effectively, the Old Greek tells the story of the Dragon more convincingly. Nickelsburg, however, emphasizes well that the two episodes in their present form are "inextricably interwoven into a single plot (the conversion of Cyrus) which is resolved only at the end of the second episode" (1981:26–27). A. K. Fenz has provided form-critical arguments for the common view that the Habbakuk incident is an insertion. Recent scholars (Zimmermann, 1958; Plöger: 767; Moore: 119–20) argue for a Semitic original, though whether it is Hebrew or Aramaic remains uncertain; Nickelsburg is undecided (1983:13).

Relation to the Canonical Text

Whereas Moore (121) stressed the similarities to the cycle of confrontation stories in Daniel 1–6, Nickelsburg has argued strongly that Bel and the Dragon is typologically later (1981:27; 1984:11–12). The plot is more

complex; the court setting is missing; Daniel's enemies are not rival sages
but pagan priests; the king's conversion is explicit; and the miraculous
character is heightened in comparison with the version of the lions' den in
Daniel 6.

Genre

The primary thrust of the narrative is an explicit polemic against
idolatry, although Grintz (1971a) questions this. As such, it stands in a long
tradition of idol mockery, so that W. Roth speaks of a genre called "idol
parody." Pfeiffer hears echoes of the myth about the combat of Marduk
and Tiamat and the dragon-slayer myth (455–56), and Moore (122–23)
maintains that the tales are haggadic in nature and based on Jer 51:34–35.
Nickelsburg points more convincingly to Isaiah 45 and 46 (1981:27). It may
prove fruitful to compare and contrast this account to other conversion
accounts such as that of Heliodorus in 2 Maccabees 3. Moore suggests that
Bel and the Dragon was added to the visions of Daniel to complete an "ABA
pattern *in terms of literary genre*" so that the prologue and epilogue would
be stories of similar type and the middle section would consist of visions.
Nickelsburg proposes that Bel and the Dragon may have presupposed the
collection of Daniel 1–6 and "was composed to supply a story about the last
of the kings under whom Daniel served according to Dan 6:28" (1984:13)

Date and Provenance

The date and place of composition remain unknown. The *terminus ad
quem* is the date of the Greek translation of Daniel, that is, late second or
early first century B.C.E. Roth (42–43) argues for an Egyptian provenance
(its purpose being to ridicule zoolatry). Moore (128) is more tempted by a
Palestinian provenance on the basis of the Qumran Danielic stories. Grintz
(1971) suggests that they were popular works "composed in Babylon when
Bel was no longer worshipped," that is, between the destruction of the
temple of Babylon by Artaxerxes (485–465 B.C.E.) and its rebuilding by
Alexander the Great (332 B.C.E.).

JUDITH

Of all the narratives discussed in this chapter, Judith has received the
most thorough attention as a work of literature. Basic questions still remain, however.

Text

Most scholars posit a Hebrew original, no longer extant, from which
the Greek versions derive (Dancy: 71; Enslin: 40; Grintz, 1971:459; Skehan,
1966:348; Zenger, 1981:430–31). A. M. Dubarle holds a minority view,
namely, that the Hebrew textual tradition is independent of the Greek text

and the Vulgate (1966, 1969, 1975). T. Craven has called into question the general consensus: "It seems equally plausible that the Greek text could have been written from the outset in elegant hebraicized Greek" (1983:5).

Literary Genre

Because Judith abounds in anachronisms and historical inaccuracies (Pfeiffer: 292–95), scholars have classified it as didactic literature (Zeitlin: 1) or as a short historical novel (Dancy: 67). E. Zenger likens its style to the Greek, oriental, and Jewish-Hellenistic novel (1981:437). P. Skehan is impressed by the way Judith is modeled on the exodus story and sees it as "a conscious and systematic meditation on the providence of God for Israel, prepared as a *haggadah* for Passover" (1963:108; 1966:349). Delcor calls it midrash (1967:179).

E. Haag (1962:291–98; 1963:61–117) and, following him, Zenger (1974; 1981:438–39) stress the way in which Nebuchadnezzar takes on a suprahistorical character. To use Haag's term, Judith is a "parabolic presentation of history." This suprahistorical characterization is evident in Zenger's literary division of the narrative (1981:432–33): (1) Nebuchadnezzar as God, 1–3:10; (2) Who is God—Nebuchadnezzar or Yahweh? 4:1–7:32; (3) Yahweh proves himself God, 8:1–16:25. Such a theomachy is certainly present. Craven's (1983) detailed alternative division of the narrative, however, exploits parallels and chiastic structures to show how the narrative is divided into two—chaps. 1–7 and chaps. 8–16. She builds consciously on the suggestions of Alonso-Schökel regarding the composition, irony, denouement, and character portrayal in Judith, although she focuses more strictly on the compositional arrangement of the work.

Throughout her "text-oriented" study, Craven considers Judith a story, but she offers no further clarification of the genre of the story. Although she uses many of the collected responses to Alonso-Schökel's paper, she does not deal with M. P. Coote's (21–26) analysis of the story as belonging to Stith Thompson Type 888 (The Faithful Wife), in which the female assumes the hero's role and saves the male. Although one might quarrel with Coote's classification, she forces one to consider the traditional narrative qualities of the tale. Nickelsburg notes the wisdom quality of Judith, and Judith uses precisely the wisdom of the traditional narrative heroine (1981:107). Further exploration of this traditional narrative quality would be of great help and may illuminate the connections between Judith and Miriam (Exodus 15), Deborah and Jael (Judges 4–5) and other wise and warlike heroines of the Bible.

Date and Provenance

Scholars have stressed the influences of both the Persian period and the Maccabean revolt. Holofernes and Bagoas have the same names as one of the generals of Artaxerxes III and his eunuch, and the story offers some parallels to Artaxerxes' campaign against Phoenicia, Syria, and Egypt in 353 B.C.E. and in the Satraps' Revolt in the reign of Artaxerxes II (Pfeiffer: 294; Dubarle, 1966:131–32). Grintz argues that many items in Judith reflect the Persian period and that there was a Jewish-Simeonite settlement in Samaria at the time of the exile (1971b:452).

On the other hand, Delcor finds in the Greek text terms that point to a Seleucid setting for the narrative (1967). H. Y. Priebatsch argues that the setting was the result of the author's use of Hellenistic materials—the Jewish historian Eupolemus, as well as the historians of Alexander the Great—to create his historical novel.

Scholars have mainly dated Judith to the time of Judas Maccabeus. Especially noteworthy are the connections between Judith and Judas's defeat of Nicanor (Zeitlin: 28–30; Nunes Carreira). Both Nunes Carreira and Delcor (1967:174–79) connect Judith and Daniel, although the links here are less persuasive.

Here one must caution against reading Judith in too allegorical a manner—that is, to suggest that Judith refers to Judas Maccabeus, Nebuchadnezzar to Antiochus IV, Holofernes to Nicanor. Zenger (1981:435) states that Bethulia is a theological cryptogram for Jerusalem, and he finds in the date of the eighteenth year of Nebuchadnezzar's reign a critical stance vis-à-vis the capitulation theology of Jeremiah (Jer 32:1; 52:29). Nickelsburg (1981:109) hints at *pesher* modes of interpretation behind the characters in the story, but I believe he gives the proper solution when he suggests that a "tale which originated in the Persian period has been rewritten in Hasmonean times." The author would then not be primarily motivated to write an allegory, but would be writing a story in larger-than-life terms that would be equally applicable to any case of oppression against Israel.

CONCLUSION

Scholars have not resolved exactly when or where these narratives were produced, but marked progress has been made in recognizing that these are not the first questions to ask of a narrative. Attempts to locate these texts on a Pharisee/Sadducee grid have been abandoned, and one is much more sensitive to the complexity of the parties and politics of early postbiblical Judaism. Each narrative must be listened to for its own voice, whether it be the praise of the righteous, as in Tobit, or the parody, as in the *Testament of Abraham*. Scholarship is also moving from an interpretation of these texts whereby characters and events in the narrative are ciphers for historical persons and events. The assumption that events in the narrative closely parallel the social conditions of the real author needs more careful consideration. It is an assumption we are only too glad to make when we know nothing about the real author.

Thus, we come to the major development in the study of these narratives—examination of them as works of literature. The narratives have been treated as wholes, and attempts have been made to understand their present structure. A deviation from this is Deselaers's work on Tobit, but, as noted above, one has questions about the literary assumptions behind his source analysis. Such an approach to the narratives as wholes has already borne fruit. However, with these narratives, as with narratives in both the Hebrew and Christian scriptures, scholars are still groping. Which method of literary analysis should one adopt? Within the corpus studied in this chapter, several have surfaced. Craven pays close attention to the way rhetorical devices shape the narrative of Judith, and Nickelsburg is always careful to note how parts of a narrative parallel others in the same narrative. Reference has been made to folktale types, the branch of folklore exemplified by Stith Thompson's work. These approaches underscore that various types of structures can operate at the same time in one work. Finally, no scholar so far has attempted to apply to these texts other methodologies such as reader response or narrative criticism. The literary analysis of the narratives has just begun.

BIBLIOGRAPHY

Alonso-Schökel, Luis
    1975   "Narrative Structures in the Book of Judith" Pp. 1–20 in *The Center for Hermeneutical Studies in Hellenistic and Modern Culture, Colloquy 11*. Berkeley, CA: Center for Hermeneutical Studies in Hellenistic and Modern Culture.

Battifol, Pierre
    1889/90 *Le livre de la prière d'Aséneth.* Pp. 1–115 in *Studia Patristica 1.2.* Paris: Leroux.

Baumgartner, Walter L.
    1926   "Susanna—Die Geschichte einer Legende." *ARW* 24: 259–90.
    1929   "Der Weise Knabe und die des Ehebruches Beschuldigte Frau." *ARW* 27: 187–88.

Bogaert, Pierre-Maurice
    1969   *Apocalypse de Baruch.* SC 144, 145. Paris: Cerf.

Brull, Nehemiah
    1877   "Das apokrphische Susanna Buch." *Jahrbücher für Jüdische Geschichte und Literatur* 3: 1–69.

Burchard, Christoph
    1965   *Untersuchungen zu Joseph und Aseneth.* WUNT 8. Tübingen: Mohr-Siebeck.
    1970   *Der dreizehnte Zeuge: Traditions- und kompositionsgeschichtliche Untersuchungen zu Lukas' Darstellung der Frühzeit des Paulus.* FRLANT 103. Göttingen: Vandenhoeck & Ruprecht.

1974   "Joseph et Aséneth, Questions actuelles." Pp. 77–100 in *La littéra-
           ture juive entre Tenach et Mischna: Quelques problèmes.* RechBib
           9. Ed. W. C. van Unnik. Leiden: Brill.
1977–78   "Joseph und Aseneth neugriechisch." *NTS* 24: 68-84.
1979a   "Joseph und Aseneth armenisch." *JSJ* 10: 1–10.
1979b   "Ein vorläufiger Text von Joseph und Aseneth." *Dielheimer Blätter
           zum Alten Testament* 14: 2–53.

Busto Saiz, José Ramon
1982   "La interpretación del relato de Susana." *Estudios Eclesiásticos* 57:
           421–28.

Caquot, André
1973   "Bref commentaire du Martyre d'Isaïe." *Sem* 23: 65-93.

Collins, John J.
1983   "The Genre Apocalypse in Hellenistic Judaism." Pp. 531–48 in
           Apocalypticism in the Mediterranean World and the Near East. Ed.
           D. Hellholm. Tübingen: Mohr-Siebeck.

Coote, Margaret P.
1975   "Response." Pp. 21–26 in *The Center for Hermeneutical Studies in
           Hellenistic and Modern Culture, Colloquy 11.* Berkeley, CA: Center
           for Hermeneutical Studies in Hellenistic and Modern Culture.

Craghan, John F.
1982a   "Esther, Judith and Ruth: Paradigms for Human Liberation." *BTB*
           12: 11–19.
1982b   "Judith Revisited." *BTB* 12: 50–53.

Craven, Toni
1977   "Artistry and Faith in the Book of Judith." *Semeia* 8: 75–101.
1983   *Artistry and Faith in the Book of Judith.* SBLDS 70. Chico, CA:
           Scholars Press.

Dancy, John C.
1972   "Judith." Pp. 67–131 in *The Shorter Books of the Apocrypha.* The
           Cambridge Bible Commentary on the New English Bible. Cam-
           bridge: University Press.

Delcor, M.
1962   "Un roman d'amour d'origine thérapeute: Le Livre de Joseph et
           Aséneth." *BLE* 63: 3–27.
1967   "Le Livre de Judith et l'époque grecque." *Klio* 49: 151–79.
1973   *Le Testament d'Abraham.* SVTP 2. Leiden: Brill.

Delling, Gerhard
1967   *Jüdische Lehre und Frömmigkeit in den Paralipomena Jeremiae.*
           BZAW 100. Berlin: Töpelmann.

Deselaers, Paul
1982   *Das Buch Tobit: Studien zu seiner Entstehung, Komposition und
           Theologie.* Göttingen: Vandenhoeck & Ruprecht.

Dubarle, Andre M.
1966   *Judith: Formes et sens des diverses traditions.* 2 vols. AnBib 24.
           Rome: Biblical Institute Press.
1969   "L'authenticité des textes hébreux de Judith." *Bib* 50: 187–211.
1975   "Les textes hébreux de Judith: Un nouveau signe d'originalité." *Bib*
           56: 503–11.

Eissfeldt, Otto
1965   *The Old Testament: An Introduction.* Trans. P. R. Ackroyd. New
            York: Harper & Row.

Enslin, Morton S., and Solomon Zeitlin
1972   *The Book of Judith.* Leiden: Brill.

Fenz, Augustinus K.
1970   "Ein Drache in Babel: Exegetische Skizze über Daniel 14:23– 42."
            SEÅ 35: 5–16.

Fischel, Henry
1946/47   "Martyr and Prophet." *JQR* 37: 265–80; 363–86.

Fishburne, Charles W.
1970   "1 Corinthians 11.10–15 and the Testament of Abraham." *NTS* 17:
            110–15.

Flusser, David
1953   "The Apocryphal Book of Ascensio Isaiae and the Dead Sea Sect."
            IEJ 3: 30–47.

Glasson, T. F.
1959   "The Main Source of Tobit." *ZAW* 71: 275–77.

Grintz, Yehoshua M.
1957   *Sefer Yehudith.* Jerusalem: Bialik Institute.
1971a   "Bel and the Dragon." *EncJud* 4:412.
1971b   "Judith, Book of." *EncJud* 10: 451–59.
1971c   "Tobit." *EncJud* 15: 1183–86.

Haag, Ernst
1962   "Die besondere literarische Art des Buches Judith und seine theo-
            logische Bedeutung." *TTZ* 71: 288–301.
1963   *Studien zum Buch Judith.* Trierer Theologische Studien 16. Trier:
            Paulinus-Verlag.

Hammershaimb, Erling
1973   "Das Martyrium Jesajas." Pp. 15–34 in *Unterweisung in erzählender
            Form.* JSHRZ 2.1. Gütersloh: Mohn.

Harris, J. Rendel
1889   *The Rest of the Words of Baruch: A Christian Apocalypse of the Year
            136 A.D.* London: Clay.

Holtz, T.
1967   "Christliche Interpolationen in 'Joseph und Aseneth.'" *NTS* 14.
            482–97.

Huet, Gedeon
1912   "Daniel et Susanne: Note de littérature comparée." *RHR* 65: 277–84.

Janssen, Enno
1975   *Testament Abrahams.* JSHRZ 3.2. Gütersloh: Mohn.

Jeremias, Joachim
1952/3   "The Last Supper." *ExpTim* 64: 91–92.

Kilpatrick, G. D.
1952/3   "The Last Supper." *ExpTim* 64: 4–8.

Kolenkow, Anitra B.
1974   "What is the Role of Testament in the Testament of Abraham?"
            HTR 67: 182–84.

1976a   "The Genre Testament and the Testament of Abraham." Pp.
         139–52 in Nickelsburg, ed., 1976.
1976b   "The Angelology of the Testament of Abraham." Pp. 153–62 in
         Nickelsburg, ed., 1976

Kraft, Robert A.
1976   "Reassessing the 'Recensional Problem' in Testament of Abraham."
         Pp. 121–37 in Nickelsburg, ed., 1976.

Kraft, Robert A., and Ann-Elizabeth Purintun
1972   *Paraleipomena Jeremiou*. SBLTT 1. Missoula, MT: Scholars Press.

Kuhn, Karl G.
1957   "The Lord's Supper and the Communal Meal at Qumran." Pp.
         259–65 in *The Scrolls and the New Testament*. Ed. K. Stendahl.
         New York: Harper & Bros.

Lebram, J.
1964   "Die Weltreiche in der jüdischen Apokalyptik: Bemerkungen zu
         Tobit 14, 4–7." *ZAW* 76: 328–31.

Liljeblad, Sven
1927   *Die Tobiasgeschichte und andere Märchen mit toten Helfern*.
         Lund: P. Lindsted.

Loewenstamm, Samuel E.
1976   "The Testament of Abraham and the Texts Concerning the Death
         of Moses." Pp. 219–25 in Nickelsburg. ed., 1976.

MacKenzie, Roderick A. F.
1957   "The Meaning of the Susanna Story." *CJT* 3: 211–18.

Martin, Raymond A.
1976   "Syntax Criticism of the Testament of Abraham." Pp. 95–120 in
         Nickelsburg, ed., 1976.

Milik, Jozef T.
1966   "La Patrie de Tobie." *RB* 73: 522–30.

Moore, Carey A.
1977   *Daniel, Esther and Jeremiah: The Additions: A New Translation
         with Introduction and Commentary*. AB 44. Garden City, NY:
         Doubleday.

Nickelsburg, George W. E.
1981   *Jewish Literature Between the Bible and the Mishnah*. Philadel-
         phia: Fortress.
1984   "Stories of Biblical and Early Post-Biblical Times." Pp. 33–87 in
         *Jewish Writings of the Second Temple Period: Apocrypha, Pseud-
         epigrapha, Qumran, Sectarian Writings, Philo, Josephus*. Ed.
         M. E. Stone. CRINT 2.2. Philadelphia: Fortress.

Nickelsburg, George W. E., ed.
1976   *Studies on the Testament of Abraham*. SBLSCS 6. Missoula, MT:
         Scholars Press.

Niditch, Susan
1982   "Merits, Martyrs, and 'Your Life as Booty': An Exegesis of *Melkilta*,
         Pisha 1." *JSJ* 13: 170–71.

Nuñes Carreira, J.
1973   "O gênero literário de 'Judite' eo Macabeus." *Didaskalia* 3: 215–30.

Pervo, Richard I.
1976   "Joseph and Aseneth and the Greek Novel." Pp. 171–81 in *Society of Biblical Literature 1976 Seminar Papers*. Ed. G. W. MacRae. Missoula, MT: Scholars Press.

Pfeiffer, Robert H.
1949   *History of New Testament Times with an Introduction to the Apocrypha*. New York: Harper.

Philonenko, Marc
1965   "Initiation et mystère dans Joseph et Aséneth." Pp. 147–53 in *Initiation*. Ed. C. J. Bleeker. Leiden: Brill.
1967   "Le Martyre d'Esaie et l'historie de la secte de Qoumrân." Cahiers de la *RHPR* 41: 1–10.
1968   *Joseph et Aséneth: Introduction, texte critique, traduction et notes*. SPB 13. Leiden: Brill.
1974   "Joseph et Aséneth: Questions actuelles." Pp. 73–76 in *La littérature juive entre Tenach et Mischna: Quelques problèmes*. RechBib 9. Leiden: Brill.
1975   "Un mystère juif?" Pp. 65–70 in *Mystères et syncretismes*. Ed. F. Dunand et al. Etudes d'histoire des religions 2; Paris: Geuthner.

Plöger, Otto
1973   "Die Zusätze zur Daniel." Pp. 63–87 in *Historische und legendarische Erzählungen*. JSHRZ 1.1. Gütersloh: Mohn.

Priebatsch, H. Y.
1974   "Das Buch Judith und seine hellenistischen Quellen." *ZDPV* 90: 50–60.

Roth, Wolfgang M. W.
1975   "For Life, He Appeals to Death (Wis 13:18): A Study of Old Testament Idol Parodies." *CBQ* 37: 21–47.

Ruppert, Lothar
1972   "Das Buch Tobias—Ein Modellfall nachgestaltender Erzählung." Pp. 109–19 in *Wort, Lied und Gottesspruch: Beiträge zur Septuaginta I: Festschrift Joseph Ziegler*. Ed. J. Schreiner. Würzburg: Echter-Verlag.

Sanders, E. P.
1983   "The Testament of Abraham." Pp. 871–902 in *The Old Testament Pseudepigrapha*. Vol. 1, *Apocalyptic Literature and Testaments*. Ed. J. H. Charlesworth. Garden City, NY: Doubleday.

Sänger, Dieter
1980   *Antikes Judentum und die Mysterien: Religionsgeschichtliche Untersuchungen zu Joseph und Aseneth*. WUNT 5. Tübingen: Mohr-Siebeck.
1981   "Jüdisch-hellenistische Missionsliteratur und die Weisheit." *Kairos* 23: 231–43.

Schmidt, Francis
1971   "Le Testament d'Abraham: Introduction, édition de la recension courte, traduction et notes." 2 vols. Diss., Strasbourg.
1976   "The Two Recensions of the Testament of Abraham: In Which Way did the Transformation Take Place?" Pp. 85–93 in Nickelsburg, ed., 1976.

Schmitt, Armin
1966 *Stammt der sogenannte "O"-Text bei Daniel wirklich von Theodotion?* Göttingen: Vandenhoeck & Ruprecht.
Schüpphaus, Joakim
1971 "Der Verhältnis von LXX- und Theodotion-Text in den apokryphen Zusätzen zum Danielbuch." *ZAW* 83: 49–72.
Skehan, Patrick
1963 "The Hand of Judith." *CBQ* 25: 94–109.
1966 Review of A. M. Dubarles, *Judith: Formes et sens des diverses traditions. CBQ* 28: 347–49.
Smith, Edgar W., Jr.
1974 "Joseph and Aseneth and Early Christian Literature: A Contribution to the Corpus Hellenisticum Novi Testamenti." Diss., Claremont Graduate School.
Steck, Odil H.
1967 *Israel und das gewaltsame Geschick der Propheten.* WMANT 23. Neukirchen-Vluyn: Neukirchener Verlag.
Stone, Michael E.
1971a "Isaiah, Martyrdom of." *EncJud* 9: 71–72.
1971b "Baruch, Rest of the Words of." *EncJud* 4: 276–77.
1972 *The Testament of Abraham: The Greek Recensions.* SBLTT 2; Pseudepigrapha Series 2. Missoula, MT: Scholars Press.
Thomas, J. D.
1972 "The Greek Text of Tobit." *JBL* 91: 463–71.
Thompson, Stith
1955–58 *Motif-Index of Folk-Literature.* 6 vols. Rev. ed. Bloomington, IN: Indiana University Press.
Turner, Nigel
1953 "The Testament of Abraham: A Study of the Original Language, Place of Origin, Authorship, and Relevance." Diss., London.
1955 "The 'Testament of Abraham': Problems in Biblical Greek." *NTS* 1: 219–23.
West, S.
1974 "Joseph and Aseneth: A Neglected Greek Romance." *CQ* 24: 70–81.
Wikgren, Allen
1962 "Tobit, Book of." *IDB,* 4: 658–62.
Zeitlin, Solomon (see also Enslin)
1950 "Jewish Apocryphal Literature." *JQR* 40: 236.
Zenger, Erich
1974 "Der Juditroman als Traditionsmodell des Jahweglaubens." *TTZ* 83: 65–80.
1981 "Das Buch Judit." Pp. 428–534 in *Historische und legendarische Erzählungen.* JSHRZ 1.6. Gütersloh: Mohn.
Ziegler, Joseph
1954 *Susanna, Daniel, Bel et Draco. VT Graecum* 16.2. Göttingen: Vandenhoeck & Ruprecht.
Zimmermann, Frank
1957/58 "The Story of Susanna and its Original Language." *JQR* 48: 236–41.
1958a *The Book of Tobit.* New York: Harper and Brothers.
1958b "Bel and the Dragon." *VT* 18: 438–40.

13
JEWISH HISTORIOGRAPHY
Harold W. Attridge

Within the large corpus of narrative literature produced by Jews during the Hellenistic and early imperial periods, certain texts may be distinguished as attempts to relate significant events of the Jewish people within a chronological framework. These historical texts do not represent a single simple genre, nor are they to be considered "objective" historiography in a modern sense. They all approach their task with various partisan or apologetic tendencies and many share characteristics of other genres, such as exegetical literature (Demetrius) or popular romance (Artapanus). Some texts were originally composed in Hebrew (1 Maccabees) and operate within the canons of traditional biblical historiography; others (2 Maccabees, Eupolemus, Josephus) follow one or another model of Greek historiography. Hence, although it is useful to treat these works as a separate category, the development of Jewish historiography cannot be isolated from the more general cultural and literary developments of the period.

The Jewish historical works reviewed here have been subjected to intensive study since World War II. The fragments of Greco-Jewish historians offer a tantalizing glimpse of the process of hellenization within Judaism and special attention has been devoted to exploring that process. The major historical works about the events of the second century B.C.E. have received several important new commentaries. Progress has been made in elucidating their historical value and their literary affinities. Philo's apologetic works with historical dimensions have been explored in depth, with special attention paid to their value as historical sources. Perhaps the greatest progress has been made in the study of the chief historian of the period, Josephus, and the literature devoted to his work has grown tremendously.

FRAGMENTARY GRECO-JEWISH HISTORIANS

During the third and second centuries B.C.E., numerous Jewish authors composed historical works in Greek. Most of their work has perished, but a few fragments survive, largely because of the efforts of a scholar of the first century B.C.E., Alexander Polyhistor, who provided, for the educated Roman public, information on the Eastern nations with which the Republic had been put in contact by the military activity of Pompey. Alexander's compilation of earlier Greco-Jewish literature served as the primary source for Eusebius and other church fathers who used Jewish material for their own apologetic purposes. Among the authors excerpted by Alexander were several historians: Demetrius, a third-century chronographer; an anonymous author, probably a Samaritan, of the same period (Pseudo-Eupolemus); Eupolemus, a historian of Jerusalem from the mid-second century; and Artapanus, a novelistic historian of the second century, probably from Alexandria. These four figures have left the more substantial remains. Brief fragments survive from three other historians, Aristeas, Theophilus, and Cleodemus Malchus, and we have a simple reference to another figure, Philo "the elder." In addition to these authors, known through Alexander Polyhistor, there are several fragments attributed to Hecataeus of Abdera, an ethnographer of the late fourth century B.C.E., which may have been composed by Jews. The relationship of these fragments to one another and to the genuine Hecataeus has been a long-standing problem.

The classic study of the fragments preserved by Alexander Polyhistor was that of J. Freudenthal over a century ago. In recent years, significant new interest in these figures has developed, evidenced first by the study of P. Dalbert, who analyzed their work as part of the "missionary literature" of Hellenistic Judaism. That categorization raises a fundamental issue in the study of these texts. It suggests that all these works were designed in one way or another to convert Gentiles to Judaism. It is certainly clear that all the works in question were apologetic, but it is far from certain that apologetics is to be understood simply as literature with a missionary aim. An important article by V. Tcherikover (1956) raises this question in a forceful way. He suggests that Jewish apologetic literature, including apologetic historiography, with its encomiastic fervor for Judaism was as much directed to Jews as to Gentiles. It reinforced a sense of identity and worth in communities confronted with the challenge of Hellenic culture. In many cases this literature also attempts to build bridges to the surrounding culture and to provide a basis for Jewish self-understanding within that culture. Tcherikover's perspective on the literature in question informs much of the more recent scholarly discussion (e.g., Walter, 1976:117, 125).

In addition to Dalbert's theological study of Jewish apologetic historiography, followed in many respects by the work of D. Georgi in his attempt to reconstruct the theology of Paul's opponents in 2 Corinthians, there have been important philological studies that have placed the investigation of the fragmentary historians on sounder footing. The Greek text of all the fragments has been made available in F. Jacoby's collection of the fragments of Greek historians and by A.-M. Denis (1970a:175–202), who also produced a major bibliographical tool (1970b:241–69), summarizing the results of scholarship since Freudenthal. Further bibliography may be found in Charlesworth, and Delling (1969). An introduction to the literature has also been done in modern Hebrew by Y. Gutman. These publications have been followed by a German translation of the fragments with a brief but valuable commentary by N. Walter (1976), which incorporates the results of several earlier studies (Walter, 1965, 1966). A convenient translation of all the fragments into English is offered in the new collection of pseudepigrapha under the editorship of James H. Charlesworth (1985).

The recent contributions to the study of the fragmentary historians by Walter and B. Z. Wacholder have brought clarity on a number of detailed points. Walter (1966), for example, has provided a new analysis of the transmission of some of the fragments, suggesting that Josephus did not know Alexander Polyhistor's work on the Jews but had direct access to some of the authors such as Artapanus, whose influence is felt in the retelling of the Moses saga in *Ant.* 2.9.1–2.16.6 §§201–349. Walter (1976:116–39) also deals with the hypothesis that several of the fragments were the work of Samaritan historians. Freudenthal (260), for example, followed by Dalbert (11) and Denis (1970b:260), had made this claim for Cleodemus, but a North African provenance is much more likely. The only author with likely Samaritan affinities remains Pseudo-Eupolemus.

Wacholder's important study of Eupolemus (1974), which summarizes and incorporates the results of two earlier studies (Wacholder, 1963, 1968), provides a detailed commentary on the fragments of this historian, but also attempts to place him within the tradition of Hellenistic historiography and to illuminate the phenomenon of Greco-Jewish literature generally. Wacholder accepts the identification of the historian with the Maccabean ambassador to Rome mentioned in 1 Macc 8:17 and 2 Macc 4:11. The embassy to Rome took place in 161 B.C.E., and a date for the historical work of Eupolemus in the same period is provided by the chronological reference to 150/57 B.C.E. in fragment 5 (Clement of Alexandria *Strom.* 1.141.4). This dating and identification enable Wacholder (1974:7–21) to sketch the biographical background of Eupolemus, a member of the priestly house of Haqqos (cf. 1 Chr 24:10; Ezra 2:61; 1 Macc 8:17), the son of another diplomat, John, who secured from Antiochus III privileges for the Jerusalem Temple and its aristocratic priesthood. Thus, Eupolemus was probably a Jewish aristocrat of the faction that initially supported Seleucid hegemony over Judea, and yet he himself was an intimate advisor of Judas. His familiarity with a wide variety of Greek historical works, plus his diplomatic ability, indicates the degree of hellenization among all factions of the Jerusalem aristocracy in the Maccabean period. At the same time, Eupolemus's concern with and intimate knowledge of the history of his people suggest that his education was traditional, although tradition did not prevent him from reworking biblical material in the same tendentious way evidenced by other Palestinians who rewrote their sacred traditions in *Jubilees*, the *Genesis Apocryphon*, or the *Biblical Antiquities* of Pseudo-Philo (Wacholder, 1974:13).

Wacholder's detailed analysis of the fragments of Eupolemus shows clearly the affinities of the Jewish historian with Hellenistic ethnographic literature and in particular with the work of Hecataeus on Egypt, which combined a rationalist or euhemerist view of religion with a sympathetic view of Egyptian civilization as the source of all culture. The exaltation of Moses by Eupolemus as the true source of ancient culture must be seen, according to Wacholder, as a response to such ethnography, which often served as a basis for cultural polemics in the Hellenistic period (Wacholder, 1974:71–96).

Wacholder's analysis of Eupolemus against this Greek literary background also suggests important insights into the work of other early hellenized Jews. The works of Artapanus and Pseudo-Eupolemus make similar claims about the revered figures of Jewish antiquity, but with an even higher degree of syncretism than is evident in Eupolemus. Thus, in the Moses romance of Artapanus, the Jewish legislator is credited with the establishment of all the significant features of Egyptian civilization, including its religious practices (Wacholder, 1974:87).

Wacholder (1968; 1974:97–128) also devotes a significant share of his analysis of Eupolemus to the chronological elements in his fragments and shows how in his work, as in the work of the third-century chronographer Demetrius, the attempt to effect a synchronization of Jewish and world history served the apologetic aim of demonstrating the antiquity, and hence superiority, of Jewish culture. The nature and significance of the work of Demetrius have been explored also by E. Bickerman (1975).

Some of the insights into the process of hellenization that the fragments of the Greco-Jewish authors reveal may also be found in the important study by M. Hengel, who treats briefly (1974:88–100) the Samaritan Pseudo-Eupolemus, Eupolemus, and Jason of Cyrene, the historian whose work was epitomized by the author of 2 Maccabees. Hengel emphasizes the rationalism and universalism of the pre-Maccabean anonymous Samaritan and the patriotic bias and freedom in handling the biblical text that are characteristic of Eupolemus.

Wacholder (1974:254–306) goes beyond Hengel in his analysis of Greco-Palestinian literary tradition, in which he would include, in addition to Eupolemus and Pseudo-Eupolemus, the fragments of two works attributed to Hecataeus; Demetrius the chronographer; the verse compositions of the epic poet Philo; the Samaritan Theodotus; the tragic poet Ezekiel; some of the *Sibylline Oracles*; some of the translators of the Septuagint, including the grandson of Ben Sira; a novella on Alexander the Great in Palestine (in Josephus, *Ant.* 11.8.1 §§304–5; 11.8.3–7 §§313–47); the Tobiad novella (in Josephus, *Ant.* 12.4.1–12.4.11 §§154–236); the memoires of Herod (in Josephus, *Ant.* 15.6.1–3 §§164–74); the universal history of Nicolaus of Damascus (discussed in detail in Wacholder, 1962); and the later works of Josephus and Justus of Tiberias. The assignment of all this literature to Palestine, especially the work of Demetrius and the poets, is speculative, but suggestive. In any case, it is clear that there remain important bits of evidence for the impact of Hellenistic culture on Judaism which require further analysis.

To the list of Wacholder might be added some works attributed to pagan authors, but which may, in fact, be Jewish. One example is the account of Moses and his people in Strabo *Geographica* 16.2.35–40, now conveniently published with an introduction, translation, and commentary in the new collection of Greco-Roman authors on Judaism by M. Stern (1974:294–311). This piece is often considered to be a fragment of the important Stoic philosopher of the first century B.C.E., Posidonius, but several scholars such as A. D. Nock and J. Gager (1972:44–47) have suggested that it, in fact, is a piece of Jewish propaganda. Arguments to this effect have most recently been developed by J. C. H. Lebram (1974:241–44), who sees an anti-Hasmonean *Tendenz* in the cosmopolitan, phil-hellenic tendency of the account of Moses and his ideal polity.

The first items on Wacholder's list of Greco-Palestinian literature are especially problematic. As noted in connection with the work of Eupolemus, the historiography of Hecataeus of Abdera of the late fourth century exercised significant influence on Hellenistic Jewish historiography. A major reason for this was an excursus in his work on Egypt which provided a rather favorable account of Moses and the polity that he established. This fragment is preserved through a fragment of the first-century B.C.E. historian Diodorus Siculus, and a convenient edition is available in Stern (1974: 20–35). The fragment is almost universally recognized to be authentic. Only Lebram (1974:247–50) has argued that this fragment, like the fragment in Strabo, is a piece of Jewish polemic.

Apart from the probably authentic fragment of Hecataeus, there are four fragments that derive from works attributed to Hecataeus, as well as several other texts that provide attestation for these works. The relationship of these fragments and testimonia and the possible authenticity of some of the fragments has been a matter of much debate. Both Walter (1964:187–200; 1976:144–60) and Wacholder (1974:262–73) have provided new, independent, and divergent analyses of this material. Both agree that one pseudepigraphon is to be found in Josephus, *Ag. Ap.* 1.22 §§183–205, 1.23 §§213b–214a. The judgment that this text is pseudepigraphical is, however, frequently disputed, and among recent scholars its authenticity is defended by Gutman (38), Gager (1969) and, with some hesitation, by Stern (1974: 22–24). Agreeing with Walter and Wacholder that the piece is pseudonymous are B. Schaller and Hengel (1974). Walter includes in this first pseudonymous work the fragment of Hecataeus in Josephus *Ag. Ap.* 2.4 §43; he sees a testimonium to the work in the critical remarks of Philo of Byblos from the second century C.E. (preserved in Origen *Contra Celsum* 1.15); and he dates the pseudepigraphon to the end of the second century B.C.E. Wacholder, on the other hand, sees Josephus, *Ag. Ap.* 2.4 §§43–47 as part of a second pseudepigraphon, dating from the time between the *Letter of Aristeas* and Josephus. The fragment in *Ag. Ap.* 1.22 §§183–214 he dates around 300 B.C.E.,, and he argues that the work influenced the *Letter of Aristeas* 83–120. The second pseudepigraphon, from Josephus *Ag. Ap.* 2 is, according to Wacholder, reflected in Josephus *Ant.* 12.1.1 §§3–8 and in the *Letter of Aristeas* 12–27, 31. Yet another pseudepigraphon is found by both scholars in the allusion to a work by Hecataeus on Abraham in Josephus *Ant.* 1.7.2 §159, which, according to Walter, provided the nonbiblical material on the patriarch in *Ant.* 1.7.1–3 §§154–68. The same work, it is generally agreed, is mentioned in Clement of Alexandria *Strom.* 5.113.1–2, where a spurious fragment of Sophocles is recorded. Wacholder dates this work before Aristobulus, the Jewish exegete of the second century B.C.E. Walter, more properly, dates the piece between the first century B.C.E. and Josephus.

The material relevant to Pseudo-Hecataeus is obviously complex and deserves further study. Wacholder is probably correct in distinguishing the work mentioned in *Ag. Ap.* 2 from that in *Ag. Ap.* 1, but Walter's dating of the pieces seems to rest on better grounds. Yet neither of the two treatments is entirely satisfactory.

THE MACCABEAN HISTORIES

The political and religious crises in Judaism during the fourth decade of the second century substantially shaped the course of subsequent Jewish history. The story of that crisis is recorded in the two books of Maccabees, which view the events of the revolt against Seleucid domination from two different perspectives and recount those events in two quite distinct ways.

There is now available for both books a critical Greek text, produced by W. Kappler (1936) and R. Hanhart (1959). These editions, along with the analysis of the text of 2 Maccabees by Hanhart (1961), provide a good basis for study of the text, although they have been criticized in several respects by P. Katz (1960, 1961), B. Metzger, G. D. Kilpatrick, and C. Habicht (1976a:191–94; 1976b:8, 11).

During the period under consideration in this review, several noteworthy commentaries have been published. Both histories are treated in Schötz; Abel, 1949; Penna, 1953; Abel and Starcky; and Bartlett. Separate commentaries on 1 Maccabees have been published by Zeitlin and Tedesche, 1950; Dancy; Goldstein, 1976; and Schunck, 1980. Commentaries on 2 Maccabees include Zeitlin and Tedesche, 1954; Habicht, 1976a; and Goldstein, 1983. Among these commentaries the most important are the works of Abel, 1949; Goldstein, 1976, 1983; and Habicht, 1976. In addition to these works there have been numerous specialized monographs and studies during the period, the most important of which will be mentioned below.

On most of the issues connected with 1 Maccabees there is a large measure of scholarly consensus, the outlines of which can easily be found in Bellet, 1963; Hanhart, 1964b; Lefèvre; Brownlee; McEleney; Nickelsburg, 1971; and Schunck, 1960; 1980:289–93). The work was originally composed in Hebrew toward the end of, or slightly after, the reign of John Hyrcanus (135–104 B.C.E.), as is indicated by a reference to an official chronicle of that ruler (1 Macc 16:23–24). Goldstein (1976:63) dates 1 Maccabees slightly later, in the reign of Alexander Jannaeus, but before 90 B.C.E.

Earlier challenges to the unity of the book, made on the grounds that Josephus did not use the account of 1 Maccabees for the period after the reign of Simon (*Ant.* 13.214), have been almost uniformly rejected (Schunck, 1954:7–15; Abel and Starcky: 9, 16; Arenhoevel, 1967:94–96). Only Zeitlin (1950:27–33) argues, on wholly inadequate grounds, for the lack of integrity of the work and for a late date for the final composition, suggesting that chaps. 1–13 were composed under Hyrcanus, then reworked and joined with chaps. 14–16 after the destruction of the Temple in 70 C.E.

The sources of 1 Maccabees have been carefully analyzed by Schunck (1954:32–82), who suggests that 1 Maccabees depends on (1) documents in the historical archives mentioned in 1 Macc 14:49 (cf. 2 Macc 2:13); (2) an official Seleucid chronicle; (3) an account of Mattathias, the father of the Maccabean family; (4) a life of Judas, possibly composed by the historian and diplomat Eupolemus; (5) other Jewish accounts of the reigns of Jonathan and Simon. The work is also punctuated by numerous poetic pieces, which may be the compositions of the author himself. These pieces have recently been the subject of a monograph by G. O. Neuhaus (1974), who, on the basis of his study, has called into question the general outlines of Schunck's analysis and dramatically reduced the material in the work that may be attributed to written sources (Neuhaus, 1973–74).

Wacholder (1974:27–38) also devotes attention to the question of the role of Eupolemus in the formation of 1 Maccabees. He rightly rejects the possibility advanced earlier by A. Schlatter and G. Favoloro that Eupolemus was the author of 1 Maccabees and casts doubt on the suggestion that he was the author of the life of Judas. Wacholder suggests, however, that Eupolemus may have been a source of that biographical work.

Goldstein's treatment of the source question departs in several interesting ways from that of Schunck. He suggests (1976:102) that 1 Maccabees used oral traditions and documents from the Hasmonean family and a Gentile history. He also suggests (1976:39–54) that 1 Maccabees knew several apocalyptic works that the author used in various ways. These include the *Testament of Moses*, written in 166 or early 165, *1 Enoch* 85–90, and Daniel 7–12, which the author of 1 Maccabees wished to discredit. Furthermore, Goldstein hypothesizes (1976:92–103) that there were two further non-extant works that heavily influenced both books of Maccabees:

a Semitic work sympathetic to Judas, written in 159 B.C.E., "On the Death of Persecutors"; and a work by Onias IV, the legitimate heir to the high priesthood displaced during the Maccabean struggles (1975:85–123; 1976:55–61). This source-critical analysis is modified in Goldstein's commentary on 2 Maccabees (1983:28–53). He continues to posit a Seleucid chronicle, oral and documentary Hasmonean traditions, and the memoirs of Onias IV. He abandons the highly speculative description for the other common Jewish source for the two Maccabean histories. The analysis of precise contributions of the various sources also differs in many details (1976:102–3; 1983:50–53).

The tendency and biases of 1 Maccabees are generally recognized. The author wrote to glorify the Hasmonean family and probably to defend the legitimacy of the dynasty against its pietist opponents. The theological dimensions of this pro-Hasmonean tendency have been explored in several of its details by Adinolfi; Renaud; Penna, 1965; and more thoroughly in Arenhoevel, 1963, 1967. Arenhoevel notes that the legitimacy of the dynasty is made to depend on its status as God's representatives, who are presented in wholly traditional patterns as priests and judges over Israel (1967:40). Arenhoevel further argues that the reign of the dynasty is portrayed as one that fulfills the traditional expectations of Israel and thus inaugurates a period of eschatological bliss (1967:58–69). Goldstein attempts to be even more specific in his analysis of the *Tendenz* of the work. He argues that 1 Maccabees was designed to refute several of the hypothetical documents that he postulates as sources in an attempt to defend specifically the legitimacy of Alexander Jannaeus (1976:62–89). Goldstein imaginatively suggests the sorts of objections to that legitimacy that could have been leveled by opponents of the dynasty and tries to show how details of the history in 1 Maccabees are designed to refute those objections. Much in this reconstruction of party propaganda of the early first century B.C.E. is highly speculative, but Goldstein's reconstruction is certainly suggestive and it does shed some light on the possible environment in which 1 Maccabees was composed. Although Arenhoevel and Goldstein approach the issue independently and from quite different perspectives, their analyses usefully complement and correct each other. 1 Maccabees was no doubt more concerned with the specifics of partisan propaganda than Arenhoevel's analysis suggests, yet its defense of the Hasmoneans is made within a theological perspective that is not apparent from Goldstein's analysis.

One central historical problem affecting the interpretation of both 1 and 2 Maccabees and the assessment of them as sources of historical information is the issue of chronology. The numerous dates in 1 Maccabees in many cases present inconsistencies, and they contradict some of the few dates in 2 Maccabees. The most glaring contradiction appears in the dating of the death of Antiochus IV Epiphanes, which 1 Macc 6:16 places in year 149 of the Seleucid era and after the rededication of the Temple in

Jerusalem. 2 Maccabees 9, on the other hand, places the death of Antiochus before the dedication of the Temple.

Most of the chronological problems in the two works can be resolved once it is recognized that there are two calendrical systems at work in the sources of 1 Maccabees. This fundamental discovery was made by Bickerman (1930:781–84; 1937:154–57), who argued that the dates for royal Seleucid history in 1 Maccabees are given according to one calendar that fixed the beginning of the Seleucid era in the fall of 312, the Macedonian Seleucid era, whereas dates of local Jewish history are reckoned according to a calendar that fixed the beginning of the Seleucid era in the spring of 311, the Babylonian Seleucid era. Most recent discussions of the chronology of the two works have operated with and have attempted to refine this basic proposal by Bickerman. The major dissenting voices have been Zeitlin (1950:48–50, 252–65), who dates the inception of the Seleucid era to the spring of 313 B.C.E. and attempts to interpret the chronological data of 1 and 2 Maccabees on that basis; Abel (1949:li), who argues that all dates in 1 Maccabees are reckoned on a Seleucid calendar beginning in the spring of 311 B.C.E.; and Schunck (1954:16–31), who accepts Bickerman's basic hypothesis, but attempts to show that the Jewish Seleucid era was reckoned from the spring of 312 B.C.E., not 311. These chronological schemes are inadequate. Zeitlin's chronology is internally inconsistent, and it ignores external evidence for Seleucid chronology, as M. B. Dagut clearly showed. The major piece of evidence for Schunck's scheme, 1 Macc 6:20, is probably simply an error (cf. 2 Macc 13:1). Abel's scheme does not explain satisfactorily all the internal chronological data and is modified toward Bickerman's scheme in the work of Abel and Starcky (35–38).

An important new piece of external evidence for Seleucid chronology has clarified several problems of Maccabean chronology. This discovery is a cuneiform king list from Babylon, originally published by A. J. Sachs and D. J. Wiseman. This list indicates that Antiochus IV died in 148 S.E. (Babylonian) and that news of his death reached Babylon in the ninth month of that year, that is, November–December 164 B.C.E. This means that he died shortly before that time, just after the beginning of 149 S.E. (Macedonian), in October 164 B.C.E. This datum thus can explain the divergent chronologies of 1 and 2 Maccabees on this crucial point. 1 Maccabees dates the event according to the official Seleucid calendar; 2 Maccabees according to the Babylonian-Jewish calendar.

The implications of the discovery of the Babylonian king list for Maccabean chronology have been explored in detail by several scholars (Lebram, 1970; Zambelli; and esp. Schaumberger; and Hanhart, 1964a), who come to somewhat different conclusions. J. B. Schaumberger, for instance, argues that the relative chronology of the death of Antiochus IV found in 2 Maccabees is correct and that the king died before the rededication of the Temple (428, 434). This inference has been widely accepted in subsequent discussions (e.g., Abel and Starcky: 37–38; McEleney: 464; Hengel, 1974, 1:96, 2:66), but it has been criticized by Hanhart (1964a:80–84). Although agreeing with Hanhart on this point, Goldstein (1976:21–26) has criticized Hanhart's detailed chronology and suggests his own chronological system (1976:161–74, 540–44), which further improves the basic model of Bickerman. Goldstein takes full account of the chronological data in 1 and 2 Maccabees as well as the data of Daniel and the Jewish list of days when fasting is forbidden, the *Megillat Ta'anit*. In addition, he introduced a further hypothesis which enables him to explain several detailed discrepancies in the accounts. He maintains that the Jewish calendar used to date several inner-Jewish events of 1 Maccabees was defective because it was not properly intercalated following the persecution of 167 B.C.E. Thus, what had been a fixed point in earlier chronological discussions, the rededication of the Temple of 25 Kislev, must, according to Goldstein, be dated not in December of 164 B.C.E., but in October of that year.

Research into the chronology of 1 and 2 Maccabees illustrates the complexity of a detailed reconstruction of the events of the revolt against Seleucid domination. 1 Maccabees remains the most reliable framework for that reconstruction, although some of its accounts are still open to question, and 2 Maccabees does preserve some valid historical data. For surveys of the whole history of the period, see Abel, 1946a, 1946c; Aymard, 1952, 1953; Bunge, 1975; Giovannini and Muller; Kiechle; Kreissig; Liebermann-Frankfort; Mejía, 1958, 1959; Mölleken; Mørkholm; North; Plöger; Schalit, 1972; Stein; Stern, 1960; and Wibbing.

If there has been some measure of consensus on the major problems of 1 Maccabees, there has been continuing dispute about 2 Maccabees during the period under review. This work covers a much briefer period of history than 1 Maccabees, beginning with the events leading up to the revolt and ending just before the death of Judas. It is a much more deliberately theological work with a much more complex literary history. That complexity has given rise to the continuing disputes.

The work purports (2 Macc 2:23) to be an epitome by an unnamed author of an earlier five-volume history written by Jason of Cyrene. The epitome is prefaced by two letters (2 Macc 1:1–9 and 1:10–2:18), containing a fragment of the third (1:7–9), the relationship of which to the work of the epitomator is unclear. Thus, the literary history of 2 Maccabees may have involved either two or three stages: two, if both the letters were prefixed by the epitomator himself; three, if one or both of the letters are the work of a later editor, who may also be responsible for additions and rearrangements in the body of the work. The theory of two stages of composition has been defended by A. Momigliano (1930:78; 1975:83), and J.-G. Bunge (1971:102, 158–63, 195). A three-stage theory of composition seems to have gained more support among recent scholars; see Schunck, 1954:99; Brownlee: 208; Arenhoevel, 1967; Hanhart, 1964a:74; Habicht,

1976a:175; Goldstein, 1976:36, 545–57; 1983:25–27; and Doran, 1977a:16.

The dating of 2 Maccabees is obviously closely connected with the assessment of its literary history. If, as argued by Abel and Starcky (34), Momigliano (83), Bunge (1971:195), and Habicht (1976a:174), the epitomator prefixed the first letter to his abridgment of Jason's work, he may well have composed his epitome in or shortly after 124 B.C.E., which, since Bickerman (1933), has been recognized as the date of the first festal letter. If the epitomator is also responsible for the second letter (2 Macc 1:10–2:18), the whole work would date from the same period. Although this position has been defended by Momigliano and Bunge, the discrepancies between the account of the death of Antiochus IV in that second letter and the report in the body of the work (2 Macc 9:1–18) suggest that at least the second letter is the work of a subsequent redactor. As Habicht notes, he may have worked at any time between 124 B.C.E. and 70 C.E., the date of the destruction of the Temple, the existence of which is presupposed in all the strata of 2 Maccabees (1976a:76). Various dates have been proposed, without convincing evidence. Thus Schunck places the final redaction at the turn of the Christian era (1954:127); I. Levy (33) places it under Claudius. Goldstein, holding that the final redactor is responsible for prefixing both letters to the epitome, places his activity shortly after 78/77 B.C.E. (1976:551–57). The significance of this date derives from the supposition that it was at this point that the book of Esther was brought to Egypt and that this work provided the model for a festal scroll into which the epitome was transformed by the addition of the prefixed letters.

Dates for the literary activity of Jason, on whom the epitomator relied, also vary considerably. It has even been proposed by W. Richnow (41–42) that Jason is a fiction of the epitomator, but this view has little to recommend it. Jason's knowledge of many details of Seleucid officialdom and administrative practices, as noted by Hengel (1974, 1:98), and the possible reference to Eupolemus as a contemporary in 2 Macc 4:11, noted by Habicht (1976a: 175), suggest that Jason was a contemporary of the events that he describes, a position also supported by Abel (1949:xiii) and Abel and Starcky (1961:34). Goldstein again maintains a significantly different position. He argues that Jason's work was written after 1 Maccabees, in an attempt to refute the pro-Hasmonean claims of that work and to defend the prophecies of Daniel (1976:62–89; 1983:71–83). Here Goldstein's hypothetical reconstructions of party propaganda, frequently based on arguments from silence, become much less convincing than his analysis of the *Tendenz* of 1 Maccabees, and they have been properly criticized on that account (Saldarini: 289; see also S. Cohen: 44 n. 77).

The general question of the aims of 2 Maccabees is obviously affected by the assessment of the literary history of the work. The two prefixed letters are deeply concerned with the Jerusalem Temple and its sanctity. This fact further suggests that the work was polemically directed against the claims of the rival temple at Leontopolis in Egypt, which had been constructed by the descendants of the legitimate high-priestly line displaced during the persecution of Antiochus IV (Bunge, 1971:530–31, 600–601; Habicht, 1976a:186; Goldstein, 1976: 545–50). The only major question, then, is whether the epitomator of Jason's history designed his work as an appendix to the letters, as, for instance, a festal scroll. This thesis is defended by those scholars such as Abel and Starcky (25–26), Momigliano (1975:83), and Bunge (1971:184–90), who hold that the epitomator is responsible for prefixing at least the first epistle. The thesis is, however, rejected by many other recent scholars, such as Arenhoevel (1967:118–63), on the basis of his detailed analysis of the theology of 2 Maccabees, and Doran (1977a:184–88), primarily on literary grounds.

The theology of 2 Maccabees is certainly an amalgam of several beliefs that were at home among the pietists of the second century and among their Essene and Pharisaic followers (Schunck, 1954:125; Abel and Starcky: 18–26; Momigliano, 1975:85; Habicht, 1976:185–91), although given the uncertainty about the history of Jewish sects in the second century, many commentators have properly advised caution in identifying any stage in the composition of 2 Maccabees as "Pharisaic" (Habicht, 1976a:189, with further references).

One important element in the theology of 2 Maccabees is the doctrine of resurrection, especially pronounced in the famous seventh chapter, which describes the martyrdoms of a pious mother and her seven sons; see 2 Macc 7:9, 14, 33. To place this belief in the history of ideas has been the object of several studies: Schubert: 206; Nickelsburg, 1972:93–109; and Kellermann.

2 Maccabees is obviously a work with an elaborate theological program, however the components of that program are to be ascribed to the various stages through which the work passed. At the same time it is, as is often noted (e.g., Habicht, 1976a:189), a work that is heavily indebted to Greek historiography. During the period under review, there have been several attempts to illuminate the degree and nature of that debt, in particular the brief works by L. Gil and P. M. Bellet (1953), and, in more depth, the studies by Richnow and Doran. The latter's work constitutes a careful analysis of the style, sources, and literary structure of 2 Maccabees. His most significant conclusion is to challenge (1977a:143–91; 1977b) the commonly accepted notion that the work is an example of the genre of "pathetic" or "tragic" history, the existence of which he properly calls into question. From his work there emerges a picture of the epitome as a unified literary composition, composed in a style that in many details approaches that of classical literature. Even its theology, which emphasizes the epiphanic defense by God of his people and his Temple, draws on motifs of Greek historiography.

Despite the fact that 2 Maccabees is written with a pronounced theological program, the work is also important as a source of the history of the revolt against Antiochus IV. In particular, it provides significant data, lacking in 1 Maccabees, on the tensions within the Jewish community prior to the revolt. These details, especially in 2 Maccabees 3–4, provided Tcherikover the basis for his persuasive reconstruction of the events leading up to the revolt (1966:117–203). 2 Maccabees also provides several primary documents from the time of the revolt (2 Macc 9:19–27; 11:16–38), which are not to be found in 1 Maccabees. The assessment of these documents has been advanced significantly in this period, especially by the investigations of Habicht. The authenticity of several of these documents has frequently been questioned. Habicht (1976b:5–7), following Levy (27–32) and Zambelli (234–43), shows that only the first (2 Macc 9:19–27) is spurious. He also argues persuasively that the order of the four authentic letters in chap. 11 has been misunderstood. It must now be recognized that the first of these is a letter of Antiochus IV (2 Macc 11:27–33), the second a letter of the general Lysias to Judas (2 Macc 11:16–21), the third a letter of two Roman emissaries (2 Macc 11:34–38), and the last a letter of Antiochus V (2 Macc 11:22–26). This arrangement casts significant light on the course of events at the end of the revolt.

It is clear from this brief review of work on 2 Maccabees that numerous problems in assessing that important work remain unresolved. Given the nature of the material, this problematic text will, no doubt, continue to generate scholarly dispute.

PHILO

Two works in the Philonic corpus need to be considered in this survey—*In Flaccum* and *Legatio ad Gaium*—which are valuable sources for the history of the Alexandrian Jewish community in the fourth decade of the first century C.E. The first recounts the activities of Avillius Flaccus, the prefect of Egypt during the last years of Tiberius and the beginning of the reign of Gaius. The second covers the same events and adds information about the embassy of Alexandrian Jews, which included Philo himself, sent to Rome to plead the community's case. This was also the period when Gaius tried to have a statue of himself erected in the Temple of Jerusalem, and Philo provides information on this incident as well. Both works proclaim the reality of God's providential care for Israel and offer an apology for Judaism.

Several new editions of these important texts have been published during the period under review. That of the Loeb Classical Library, by F. H. Colson (1941, 1962), is perhaps the most readily available. The translations, as in the whole Loeb edition of Philo, are excellent and are accompanied by brief notes and introductions. Similar editions in the French translations of the Philonic corpus have been produced by A.

Pelletier (1967, 1972). In addition, the *Legatio* has been published with an extensive commentary by E. M. Smallwood (1961). In addition to these major studies, brief treatments of some of the major historical problems that are raised by the text have been published in Delling, 1972; Sherwin-White; and Solomon.

JOSEPHUS

Our major source for much of Jewish history in the Hellenistic and early Roman eras is the corpus of the historian Josephus, and in recent years there has been a steadily growing interest in his works. His corpus consists of (1) *The Jewish War*, an account in seven books of the revolt against Rome in 66–73 C.E., with a brief survey of the history that preceded it from the time of the Maccabean revolt, written in Rome between 75 and 82 C.E.; (2) *The Jewish Antiquities*, a history in twenty books of the Jewish people from Adam to the beginnings of the revolt, composed in Rome in 93–94 C.E. (see *Ant.* 20.267); (3) the *Life*, an autobiographical appendix to the *Antiquities* that focuses on the activity of the historian while he was in command of the Jewish forces in Galilee in the early stages of the revolt; and (4) the tract *Against Apion*, a frankly apologetic work that details and refutes various slanders against Jews.

A major stimulus to the current interest in Josephus has been the production of several new annotated translations of his works into various modern languages. In Germany, the Institutum Delitzchianum, under the leadership of O. Michel and K. H. Rengstorf, has completed an edition of the *War* (Michel and Bauernfeind, 1959–69). The *Antiquities* has been translated into Hebrew by A. Schalit (1967). The English translation of the entire corpus in the Loeb Classical Library, which was begun by the late H. St. John Thackeray (1926), has been completed. Before his death Thackeray had translated the *Vita, Against Apion*, the *War*, and the *Antiquities* through Book 8. The work was continued by R. Marcus, whose archaeological notes on *Antiquities* 12–14 are valuable, although in need of updating on the basis of more recent discoveries. The last volume in the Loeb series, by L. H. Feldman (1959), has the most extensive notes and bibliographical aids of any in the series and provides a model of a brief but detailed commentary. For other translations of the works of Josephus, published during the period under review, see Endrös; Larraya; Ricciotti; and Williamson, 1959.

A second stimulus to further study of Josephus are the bibliographical reference tools produced by Feldman (1962a) and Schreckenberg (1968, 1979). The first of these is more useful for the limited period that it covers (1937–62), since the entries are annotated and topically arranged. The second is more comprehensive, attempting to cover the entire history of scholarship on Josephus. The entries are arranged chronologically, although the works are indexed according to the subjects treated. This brief survey will not attempt to duplicate the detailed bibliographical information in those studies. Our interest will focus on works that deal directly with Josephus and his literary productions and not on those that explore the historical or archaeological problems raised by his accounts.

A third important research tool for study of Josephus has been produced under the auspices of the Institutum Delitzchianum under the leadership of K. H. Rengstorf. This is a complete concordance to the works of Josephus, which supplants the incomplete lexicon compiled by Thackeray and Marcus. The work is of high quality, although the editors have occasionally left words undefined and have missed the proper sense of others (Feldman, 1975, 1977, 1981, 1985).

Finally, in the category of basic research tools, two important studies of the history of the transmission of Josephus have been produced by Schreckenberg (1972, 1977). These studies incorporate the results of several treatments of the direct and indirect witnesses to the text of Josephus (Bardy; Black; Blatt; Bulhart; Burchard, 1974, 1977; Dubarle, 1973; Flusser, 1953, 1974; Höcherl; Meshcherskii; Mras; Pascal; Philonenko; Reiner; Rubinstein; Scheidweiler; Schreckenberg, 1970, 1973; and Smith, 1958), which have laid the groundwork for a new and much-needed critical edition of the Greek text of Josephus's works.

During the period under review there have been no new comprehensive studies of Josephus. Thackeray's set of general lectures has been reprinted (1967), with an introduction by S. Sandmel, and this remains the best short introduction to Josephus in English. The survey by F. J. Foakes Jackson has also been reprinted (1977), although this is a rather superficial treatment. There is also a useful survey in the new edition of Schürer (1973:43–63), a rather popular work by G. A. Williamson (1964), and a treatment of Josephus in the context of Jewish historiography by Zeitlin (1969, 1978).

There has been considerable interest in reassessing the personality of the historian in an attempt to break free from traditional condemnations of Josephus as a totally reprehensible renegade or traitor. Several brief studies (Brandon; Daube; Mayer and Möller; and Schwark) tend to be more sympathetic and try to elucidate the historian's own self-understanding. Nonetheless, it is important to recognize Josephus's pro-Flavian tendencies, and these have been further illuminated by Z. Yavetz.

There has been, in this period, some attention to the complicated problems of the sources of Josephus's works. The sources of Flavian history in the *War* have been explored by A. Briessmann and M. Durry. H. Lindner (95–141) reviews work on the sources of the last books of the *War*, and this analysis then provides support for an analysis of the historian's theological viewpoint. Rajak has studied the *War* in the context of Josephus's life and career (1983). The sources of the biblical history in the first part

of the *Antiquities* have also been extensively explored. Schalit assembles the
evidence for the use of Greek, Hebrew, and Aramaic sources, although the
evidence in the last category is weak (1965; 1967:xxxii–xxxv). E. C. Ulrich
has shown clearly that Josephus uses a proto-Lucianic form of the LXX for
his Samuel–Kings material. Various scholars have noted the use of or parallels to extrabiblical material (Feldman, 1971; Haacker and Schäfer). The
documentary sources in the *Antiquities*—which have often been taken to
be authentic, for example, by Bickerman (1953) and Schalit (1960)—have
been subjected to a critical examination by H. R. Moehring (1975). The
possible Roman sources for *Antiquities* Book 19 have been explored by
Feldman (1962b) and D. Timpe. A major source of Josephus, Nicolaus of
Damascus, has been carefully studied by Wacholder (1962). For a general
survey of earlier work, see Schürer, 1973:48–52.

Some of the most significant studies of Josephus in recent years have
attempted to analyze, more closely than has been the case in the past, the
literary techniques employed by Josephus in composing his several works.
The well-known thesis of Thackeray about the literary activity of Josephus—that he employed, in the composition of different parts of the
Antiquities, various assistants who had predilections for different classical
historians—has been criticized by various scholars (see Ek; Petersen; and
Shutt), who show that allusions to a wide range of classical authors occur
throughout the work of Josephus. Further studies of the way that sources
have been used by the historian, in particular the careful examination by
Pelletier (1962) of redaction of the *Letter of Aristeas*, show how Josephus
was concerned with producing literature acceptable to the atticizing tastes
of his own day.

Moreover, it is clear that Josephus was concerned with more than
style. His paraphrase of scriptural material has been intensively studied in
Bruce; N. Cohen; Feldman, 1968a, 1968b, 1970, 1978; Jervell; Melamed;
van Unnik, 1974a, 1974b; Tiede: 207–40; Attridge; Holladay: 47–102;
Hata; Franxman; and Downing. Most of these authors note the way in
which Jewish traditions have been hellenized, often with a dramatic or
romantic tendency. Similar novelistic characteristics have been found in
other sections of the historian's work (Justus; Moehring, 1957).

Josephus was also concerned with rhetorical effects and, like classical
historians generally, freely composed speeches for his leading characters
through which his own interpretation of events is presented. Studies by
Michel and Bauernfeind (1967) and by Lindner (21–48) have emphasized
the importance of such rhetorical pieces in the *War*.

Josephus's dependence on classical historians is not confined to matters
of language and style. Several rather general studies have attempted to
show how the broad approach to historiography adopted by Josephus
reflects Greek practice (Collomp; Sobel; Sowers; Stern, 1962; and van
Unnik, 1978). Closer examination shows that Josephus follows two distinct

historiographical patterns in his two major works. The *War* conforms more to the tradition of "pragmatic" military and political history represented in the Hellenistic period by Polybius. The *Antiquities* conforms more to the patterns of rhetorical historiography exemplified by the primary model for this work, the *Roman Antiquities* of Dionysius of Halicarnassus (Attridge: 29–70).

Attention has also been focused in this period on various aspects of the theological or religious tendencies of Josephus. The classical problem here has been to assess the self-description of Josephus as a Pharisee made in the *Life* 12. The validity of this claim has most recently been challenged by M. Smith (1956) and J. Neusner, who indicate that Josephus's "Pharisaism" is much more pronounced in his later works. It is thus clear that Josephus's self-description does not provide a simple key to the understanding of his theological program. That must rather be understood through a careful analysis of the literary techniques and dominant motifs and concerns that are found in his works.

Many of the details of these interpretative motifs have been studied in recent years. For example, concern with prophecy is important in both the *War* and the *Antiquities* (Blenkinsopp; Delling, 1974; Lindner: 49–68; Michel, 1954; and Reiling). Josephus is also concerned with the miraculous element in Jewish history as a vehicle for the manifestation of God's concern for his people (Betz; Delling, 1958; MacRae; Attridge: 92–104).

It is also clear that Josephus uses special terminology for fate and providence, drawn from the Greek historiographical tradition, to express his belief in the divine governance of history, although this terminology varies between his two major works. Some studies of this important terminology (such as Stählin) do not adequately note that variation. In fact, the *War* relies heavily on the terms τύχη and εἱμαρμένη to suggest a scheme of world history, possibly related to apocalyptic literature, in which God's favor is now being shown to the Romans. Josephus thereby criticizes the revolutionary theologies that fostered or were used to support the war against Rome (Lindner: 42–48, 89–94). For further studies of the apocalyptic elements in the *War*, see Böcher; Hahn; de Jonge; Michel, 1963, 1969; and Thoma. The tendentious polemic against the Zealots which characterizes the work as a whole is investigated by Hengel (1961) and by W. R. Farmer's study of Zealot theology, which Farmer sees as a continuation of Maccabean ideology. He does not, however, note the important differences between the two revolutionary movements.

In the *Antiquities*, Josephus instead relies heavily on πρόνοια terminology as a substitute for the biblical theology of the covenant, which is lacking in his treatment of biblical history (Jaubert), in order to express a belief in God's universal moral sovereignty. This sovereignty treated the Jews in a favored way not on any idiosyncratic grounds but because they exhibited in an exemplary way the virtue that is proper to God himself (Attridge:

71–144). Through these analyses the apologetic theology that runs throughout the works of Josephus has emerged with greater clarity.

Particularly problematic texts in Josephus continue to excite a good
deal of scholarly interest. The authenticity of all or part of the *Testimonium
Flavianum* (*Ant.* 18.63–64) remains a hotly contested issue. The earlier
discussion on the subject is summarized conveniently by Feldman (1962a:
42–43) and Schürer (1973:428–41). In recent discussion, usefully summarized by Dubarle (1977), various scholars have defended the authenticity
of at least part of the text (Koester; Pines; Pötscher; Winter). Some have
suggested that the point of the text is, in fact, to ridicule or satirize Jesus
(Bammel; Bell) because of its context in Book 18 of the *Antiquities*, where
it is followed by the story of the seduction of the Roman matron Paulina,
although the connection of that episode to the *Testimonium* is weak. In
Dubarle's own reconstruction of the original *Testimonium* (1973; 1977:50),
which relies heavily on the "indirect tradition" in patristic sources, Josephus appears more favorably disposed to Jesus than most other scholars
would allow.

The *Life* of Josephus presents many difficulties because of its discrepancies with the parallel accounts in the *War*. The work was apparently
issued as an epilogue to the *Antiquities*. Dating is problematic. The work
was clearly written after the death of Agrippa II (*Life* 354–60), which,
according to Photius, took place in 100 c.e. This would mean that the work
was appended to a second edition of the *Antiquities*, if the date of Agrippa's
death is reliable (Pelletier, 1959:xii; Feldman, 1962:45). Numismatic evidence for Agrippa's reign ends, however, in 94 and it has been suggested
that the date in Photius is incorrect and that the *Life* is to be dated shortly
after the *Antiquities* (Frankfort; Schürer, 1973:54, 481–82; Barish).

The *Life* was written as a direct response to criticism of Josephus
leveled by a rival historian, Justus of Tiberias, the subject of a recent study
by T. Rajak (for earlier work, see Schürer, 1973:34–37). The thesis of R.
Laqueur that the *Life* represents the reworking of an official report of
Josephus composed during his stay in Galilee has been generally rejected
(Pelletier, 1959:xvi–xviii; Schürer, 1973:53). The historical value of the
account of Josephus's activity in the *Life* has been defended by M. Gelzer,
although that defense is unconvincing. The whole account has been recently subjected to a careful analysis by S. Cohen, who revives, in modified
form, the theory of Laqueur and explores both the biographical and historiographical implications of the text. S. Freyne, in his recent study of
Galilee, also makes useful comments on Josephus's military career and its
social setting (71–78, 241–45).

CONCLUSIONS

As this selective survey indicates, work on Jewish historiographical
literature from the "intertestamental" period has progressed on several

fronts. The most significant progress has been made in detailed analysis of particular issues, although there have also been important developments in appreciating the apologetic and theological programs evidenced by the works in question. These texts will continue to be a major source not only for the political and social history of the period but also for the intellectual and religious life of the Jewish people in this pivotal period in Jewish and Christian history.

BIBLIOGRAPHY

Abel, Felix-Marie
> 1946a   "Hellénisme et orientalisme en Palestine au déclin de la période seleucide." *RB* 53: 385–402.
> 1946b   "Les lettres préliminaires du second livre des Maccabées." *RB* 53: 513–33.
> 1946c   "La Fête de la Hanoucca." *RB* 53: 538–46.
> 1949   *Les Livres des Maccabées.* 2d ed. Paris: Gabalda, 1954.
> 1952   *Histoire de la Palestine depuis la conquête d'Aléxandre jusqu'à l'invasion arabe.* Paris: Gabalda.

Abel, Felix-Marie, and Jean Starcky
> 1961   *Les Livres des Maccabées.* La sainte Bible III. Paris: Cerf.

Adinolfi, M.
> 1964/65 "Il testamento di Mattatia e i suoi esempi etici (I Mac 2, 46–69)." *SBFLA* 15:74–97.

Arenhoevel, Diego
> 1963   "Die Eschatologie der Makkabäerbücher." *TTZ* 72: 257–69.
> 1967   *Die Theokratie nach dem 1. und 2. Makkabäerbuch.* Walberger Studien 3. Mainz: Grünewald.

Attridge, Harold W.
> 1975   *The Interpretation of Biblical History in the Antiquitates Judaicae of Flavius Josephus.* HDR 7. Missoula, MT: Scholars Press.

Aymard, A.
> 1952   "Tutelle et usurpation dans les monarchies hellénistique." *Aegyptus* 32: 85–96.
> 1953   "Autour de l'avènement d'Antiochus IV." *Historia* 2: 49–73.

Bammel, Ernst
> 1974   "Zum Testimonium Flavianum." Pp. 9–22 in Betz et al., eds.

Bardy, G.
> 1948   "Le souvenir de Josèphe chez les Pères." *RHE* 43: 179–91.

Barish, David A.
> 1978   "The *Autobiography* of Josephus and the Hypothesis of a Second Edition of his *Antiquities.*" *HTR* 71: 61–75.

Bartlett, John R.
> 1973   *The First and Second Books of the Maccabees.* Cambridge: University Press.

Bell, A. A., Jr.
> 1976   "Josephus the Satirist? A Clue to the Original Form of the Testimonium Flavianum." *JQR* 68: 16–22.

Bellet, Paulinus M.
1953   "El gènere literari del II Libre dels Macabeus." Pp. 303–21 in
        Miscellenea Biblica B. Ubach. Ed. R. M. Diaz. Scripta et Docu-
        menta 1. Montisserrati: Cusa Provincial de Caridad.
1963   "Libros de los Macabeos." *Enciclopedia de la Biblia*. Barcelona:
        Garriga. 4: 1137–42.

Betz, Otto
1974   "Das Problem des Wunders bei Flavius Josephus im Vergleich zum
        Wunderproblem bei den Rabbinen und im Johannesevangelium."
        Pp. 23–44 in Betz et al., eds.

Betz, Otto, et al., eds.
1974   *Josephus-Studien: Untersuchungen zu Josephus, dem antiken
        Judentum und dem Neuen Testament: Otto Michel zum 70.
        Geburtstag gewidmet*. Göttingen: Vandenhoeck & Ruprecht.

Bickerman, Elias
1930   "Makkabäerbücher." *PW* 14: 781–84.
1933   "Ein jüdischer Festbrief vom Jahre 124 v. Chr." *ZNW* 32: 233–54.
        Reprinted in *Studies in Jewish and Christian History*, 136–58.
        AGJU 9.2. Leiden: Brill, 1980.
1937   *Der Gott der Makkabäer*. Berlin: Schocken. Translated by H. R.
        Moehring. SJLA 32. Leiden: Brill, 1979.
1947   *The Maccabees: An Account of their History from the Beginnings
        to the Fall of the Hasmonean House*. New York: Schocken Books.
1949   "The Historical Foundations of Post-Biblical Judaism." Pp. 70–114
        in *The Jews: Their History, Culture and Religion*. Ed. L. Finkel-
        stein. New York: Harper.
1953   "Une question d'authenticité: Les privilèges juifs (parmi les Séleu-
        cids)." Pp. 11–34 in *Mélanges Isidore Levy, Annuaire de l'Institute
        de Philologie et d'Histoire orientales et slaves* 13.
1962   *From Ezra to the Last of the Maccabees: The Historical Founda-
        tions of Post-Biblical Judaism*. New York: Schocken Books.
1975   "The Jewish Historian Demetrius." Pp. 72–84 in *Christianity,
        Judaism and Other Greco-Roman Cults: Studies for Morton Smith
        at Sixty*, vol. 3. Ed. J. Neusner. SJLA 12. Leiden: Brill. Reprinted
        in *Studies in Jewish and Christian History*, 347–58. AGJU 9.1.
        Leiden: Brill, 1980.

Black, Matthew
1956   "The Account of the Essenes in Hippolytus and Josephus." Pp.
        172–75 in *The Background of the New Testament and Its Escha-
        tology: Studies in Honor of C. H. Dodd*. Cambridge: University
        Press.

Blatt, Franz
1958   *The Latin Josephus*. I, *Introduction and Text. The Antiquities,
        Books I–IV*. Acta Jutlandica 30.1. Hum. Ser. 44. Aarhus and
        Copenhagen: Munksgaard.

Blenkinsopp, J.
1974   "Prophecy and Priesthood in Josephus." *JJS* 25: 239–62.

Böcher, Otto
1974   "Die heilige Stadt im Völkerkrieg: Wandlungen eines apokalypti-
        schen Schemas." Pp. 55–76 in Betz et al., eds.

Brandon, S. G. F.
1958   "Josephus, Renegade or Patriot." *History Today* 8: 830–36.

Breissman, Adalbert
1955   *Tacitus und die flavische Geschichtsbild.* Hermes Einzelschrift 10. Wiesbaden: Steiner.

Brownlee, William H.
1962   "Maccabees, Books of." *IDB* 3: 201–15.

Bruce, F. F.
1965   "Josephus and Daniel." *ASTI* 4: 148–62.

Bulhart, V.
1953   "Textkritische Studien zum lateinischen Flavius Josephus." *Mnemosyne* 6: 140–57.

Bunge, Jochen-Gabriel
1971   *Untersuchungen zum zweiten Makkabäerbuch.* Bonn: Rheinische Friedrich-Wilhelms-Universität.
1975   "Zur Geschichte und Chronologie des Untergangs der Oniaden und des Aufstiegs der Hasmonäer." *JSJ* 6: 1–46.

Burchard, Christian
1974   "Zur Nebenüberlieferung von Josephus' Bericht über die Essener: Bell. 2, 119–161 bei Hippolyt, Porphyrius, Josippus, Niketas Choniates und anderen." Pp. 77–96 in Betz et al., eds.
1977   "Die Essener bei Hippolyt, Ref. ix, 18, 2–28, 2 und Josephus, Bell. 2, 119–161." *JSJ* 8: 1–41.

Charlesworth, James H.
1976   *The Pseudepigrapha and Modern Research.* SBLSCS 7. Missoula, MT: Scholars Press.
1983   *The Old Testament Pseudepigrapha.* Vol. 1, *Apocalyptic Literature and Testaments.* Garden City, NY: Doubleday.
1985   *The Old Testament Pseudepigrapha.* Vol. 2, *Expansions of the "Old Testament" and Legends, Wisdom and Philosophical Literature, Prayers, Psalms, and Odes, Fragments of Lost Judeo-Hellenistic Works.* Garden City, NY: Doubleday.

Cohen, Naomi G.
1963–64   "Josephus and Scripture: Is Josephus' Treatment of the Scriptural Narrative Similar Throughout the Antiquities I–XI?" *JQR* 54: 311–32.

Cohen, Shaye J. D.
1979   *Josephus in Galilee and Rome: His Vita and Development as a Historian.* Studies in the Classical Tradition 8. Leiden: Brill.

Collomp, P.
1947   "La place de Josèphe dans la technique de l'historiographie hellénistique." Pp. 81–92 in *Études historiques de la Faculté des lettres de Strasbourg.* Publ. de la Fac. de lettr. de l'Univ. de Strasbourg 106. Mélanges 1945, III: Études historiques. Paris: Belles lettres.

Colson, F. H., ed.
1941   *Philo. Quod omnis probus liber sit, De vita contemplativa, De aeternitate mundi, In Flaccum.* LCL 9. Cambridge, MA: Harvard University Press. London: Heinemann.
1962   *Philo. The Embassy to Gaius.* LCL 10. Cambridge, MA: Harvard University Press. London: Heinemann.

Dagut, M. B.
1953 "II Maccabees and the Death of Antiochus IV Epiphanes." *JBL* 72: 149–57.

Dalbert, Peter
1954 *Die Theologie der hellenistisch-jüdischen Missionsliteratur unter Ausschluss von Philo und Josephus.* Theologische Forschung 4. Hamburg-Volksdorf: Reich.

Dancy, John C.
1954 *A Commentary on I Maccabees.* Oxford: Blackwell.

Daube, David
1976 "'I believe' in *Jewish Antiquities* xi. 237." *JJS* 27: 142–46.
1980 "Typology in Josephus." *JJS* 31: 18–36.

Delling, Gerhard
1958 "Josephus und das Wunderbare." *NovT* 2: 291–309.
1965 "Josephus und die heidnischen Religionen." *Klio* 43: 263–69. Reprinted in *Studien zum N.T. und zum hellenistischen Judentum: Gesammelte Aufsätze 1950–68,* 34–42. Göttingen: Vandenhoeck & Ruprecht, 1970.
1969 *Bibliographie zur jüdisch-hellenistischen und intertestamentarischen Literatur.* TU 106. Berlin: Akademie-Verlag. 2d ed., 1975.
1972 "Philons Enkomion auf Augustus." *Klio* 54: 171–92.
1974 "Die biblische Prophetie bei Josephus." Pp. 109–21 in Betz et al., eds.

Denis, Albert-Marie
1970a *Fragmenta Pseudepigraphorum quae supersunt Graeca.* PVTG 3. Leiden: Brill.
1970b *Introduction aux pseudépigraphes grecs d'Ancien Testament.* SVTP 1. Leiden: Brill.

Doran, Robert
1977a "Studies in the Style and Literary Character of 2 Maccabees." Diss., Harvard.
1977b "2 Maccabees and 'Tragic History.'" *HUCA* 48: 107–14.
1981 *Temple Propaganda: The Purpose and Character of 2 Maccabees.* CBQMS 12. Washington, DC: Catholic Biblical Association.

Downing, F. G.
1980 "Redaction Criticism: Josephus' *Antiquities* and the Synoptic Gospels (I)." *JSNT* 8: 46–65.

Dubarle, A. M.
1973 "Le témoignage de Josèphe sur Jésus d'après la tradition indirecte." *RB* 80: 481–513.
1977 "Le témoignage de Josèphe sur Jésus d'après des publications récentes." *RB* 94:38–58.

Durry, M.
1956 "Les empereurs comme historiens d'Auguste à Hadrien." Pp. 213–45 in *Fondation Hardt pour l'étude de l'antiquité classique. Entretiens 4: Histoire et historiens dans l'antiquité.* Geneva: Fondation Hardt.

Ek, S.
1945–46 "Herodotismen in der Jüdischen Archaeologie des Josephos und ihre textkritische Bedeutung." *Skrifter utgivna av Kungl. Humanistiska Vetenskapssamfundet i Lund. Acta Regia Societatis Humaniorum Litterarum Lundensis* 2: 27–62.

Endrös, Hermann
1965–66 *Flavius Josephus: Der Jüdische Krieg.* 2 vols. Munich: Goldmann.

Farmer, William R.
1956 *Maccabees, Zealots and Josephus: An Inquiry into Jewish National-ism in the Greco-Roman Period.* New York: Columbia University Press. Reprinted Westport, CT: Greenwood Press, 1973.

Feldman, Louis H.
1959 *Josephus.* LCL 9. Cambridge, MA: Harvard University Press. London: Heinemann.

1962a *Scholarship on Philo and Josephus (1937–1962).* Studies in Judaica. New York: Yeshiva.

1962b "The Sources of Josephus' Antiquites, Book 19." *Latomus* 21: 320–33.

1968a "Abraham the Greek Philosopher in Josephus." *Transactions and Proceedings of the American Philological Association* 99: 143–56.

1968b "Hellenizations in Josephus' Portrayal of Man's Decline." Pp. 336–53 in *Religions in Antiquity: Essays in Memory of Erwin Ramsdell Goodenough.* Ed. J. Neusner. Supplements to *Numen* 14. Leiden: Brill.

1970 "Hellenizations in Josephus' Version of Esther (Ant. Jud. 11.185–295)." *Transactions and Proceedings of the American Philological Association* 101: 143–70.

1971 *The Biblical Antiquities of Pseudo-Philo.* Trans. M. R. James. Prolegomenon by L. H. Feldman. New York: Ktav.

1975 Review of K. H. Rengstorf et al., *A Complete Concordance to Flavius Josephus,* Vol. I. *JBL* 94: 628–31.

1977 Review of K. H. Rengstorf et al., *A Complete Concordance to Flavius Josephus,* Vol. II. *JBL* 96: 132–33.

1978 "Josephus as an Apologist to the Greco-Roman World: His Portrait of Solomon." Pp. 68–98 in *Aspects of Religious Propaganda in Judaism and Early Christianity.* Ed. E. S. Fiorenza. Notre Dame, IN: University of Notre Dame Press.

1981 Review of K. H. Rengstorf et al., *A Complete Concordance to Flavius Josephus,* Vol. III. *JBL* 100: 151–54.

1985 Review of K. H. Rengstorf et al., *A Complete Concordance to Flavius Josephus,* Vol. IV. JBL 104: 739–742.

Flusser, David
1953 "The Author of the Book of Josippon: His Personality and His Age" (Hebrew). *Zion* 18: 109–26.

1974 "Der lateinische Josephus und der hebräische Josippon." Pp. 122–32 in Betz et al., eds.

1978– *The Josippon: Josephus Gorionides.* Jerusalem: Bialik Institute (Hebrew).

Foakes Jackson, Frederick J.
1977 *Josephus and the Jews.* New York: Smith. Reprint from the 1930 ed.

Frankfort, T.
1961 "La date de l'Autobiographie de Flavius Josèphe et des oeuvres de Justus de Tiberiade." *Revue Belge de Philologie et d'Histoire* 39: 52–58.

Franxman, T. W., S. J.
1979　　　*Genesis and the "Jewish Antiquities" of Flavius Josephus.* BibOr 35. Rome: Biblical Institute Press.

Freudenthal, Jacob
1874–75　*Hellenistische Studien.* Breslau: Grass.

Freyne, Sean
1980　　　*Galilee from Alexander the Great to Hadrian: 323 B.C.E. to 135 C.E.* Wilmington, DE: Michael Glazier; Notre Dame, IN: University of Notre Dame Press.

Gager, John
1969　　　"Pseudo-Hecataeus Again." *ZNW* 60: 130–39.
1972　　　*Moses in Greco-Roman Paganism.* SBLMS 16. Nashville: Abingdon.

Gelzer, M.
1952　　　"Die Vita des Josephus." *Hermes* 80: 67–90.

Georgi, Dieter
1964　　　*Die Gegner des Paulus im 2. Korintherbrief.* WMANT 11. Neukirchen-Vluyn: Neukirchener Verlag.

Gibbert, J.
1963　　　"Eupolème et l'historiographie du Judaïsme hellénistique." *ETL* 39: 539–54.

Gil, Luis
1958　　　"Sobre el estilo del Libro Segundo de los Macabeos." *Emerita: Revista de Linguistica y Filologia Clasica* 26: 11–32.

Giovannini, Adalberto, and Helmut Muller
1971　　　"Die Beziehungen zwischen Rom und den Juden im 2. Jahrhundert v. Chr." *Museum Helveticum* 28: 155–71.

Goldstein, Jonathan A.
1975　　　"Tales of the Tobiads." Pp. 85–123 in *Christianity, Judaism and Other Greco-Roman Cults: Studies for Morton Smith at Sixty,* vol. 3. Ed. J. Neusner. SJLA 12. Leiden: Brill.
1976　　　*I Maccabees.* AB 41. Garden City, NY: Doubleday.
1983　　　*II Maccabees.* AB 41A. Garden City, NY: Doubleday.

Gutman, Yehoshua
1958, 1963　*The Beginnings of Jewish Hellenistic Literature.* 2 vols. Jerusalem: Bialik Institute (Hebrew).

Haacker, Klaus, and Peter Schäfer
1974　　　"Nachbiblische Traditionen vom Tod Moses." Pp. 147–74 in Betz et al., eds.

Habicht, Christian
1976a　　*2. Makkabäerbuch.* JSHRZ 1.3. Gütersloh: Mohn.
1976b　　"Royal Documents in Maccabees II." *Harvard Studies in Classical Philology* 80: 1–18.

Hahn, I.
1963　　　Josephus und die Eschatologie von Qumran." Pp. 167–91 in *Qumran Probleme.* Ed. H. Bardtke. Berlin: Akademie-Verlag.

Hanhart, Robert
1959　　　*Maccabaeorum liber II.* Septuaginta, Vetus Testamentum Graece, Auctoritate Societatis Göttingensis editum 9.2. Göttingen: Vandenhoeck & Ruprecht.

1961   "Zum Text des 2. und 3. Makkabäerbuches: Probleme der Über-
        lieferung, der Auslegung und der Ausgabe." Pp. 427–86 in
        Nachrichten der Akademie der Wissenschaften in Göttingen, I.
        Phil.-hist. Kl. Göttingen: Vandenhoeck & Ruprecht.
1964a   "Zur Zeitrechnung des I und II Makkabäerbuches." Pp. 55–96 in
        Untersuchungen zur israelitisch-jüdischen Chronologie. Ed. A.
        Jepsen und R. Hanhart. BZAW 88. Berlin: Töpelmann.
1964b   "Makkabäerbücher." Pp. 1126–30 in *Biblisch-Historisches Wörter-
        buch.* Göttingen: Vandenhoeck & Ruprecht.

Hata, Gohei
1975   "Is the Greek Version of Josephus' *Jewish War* a Translation or a
        Rewriting of the First Version?" *JQR* 66: 89–108.

Hengel, Martin
1961   *Die Zeloten: Untersuchungen zur jüdischen Freiheitsbewegung in
        der Zeit von Herodes I. bis 70n. Chr.* AGJU 1. Leiden: Brill.
1974   *Judaism and Hellenism: Studies in their Encounter in Palestine
        during the Early Hellenistic Period.* 2 vols. Trans. J. Bowden.
        Philadelphia: Fortress.

Höcherl, Alfons
1970   *Zur Übersetzungstechnik des altrussischen Jüdischen Krieges des
        Josephus Flavius.* Slavistische Beiträge 46. Munich: Sagner.

Holladay, Carl
1977   *Theios Aner in Hellenistic Judaism: A Critique of this Category in
        New Testament Christology.* SBLDS 40. Missoula, MT: Scholars
        Press.

Jacoby, Felix
1958   *Die Fragmente der griechischen Historiker.* 3 c, ##722–34. Leiden:
        Brill.

Jaubert, Annie
1963   *La notion d'alliance dans le judaïsme aux abords de l'ère chrétienne.*
        Patristica Sorbonensia 6. Paris: Seuil.

Jervell, Jacob
1974   "Imagines und Imago Dei: Aus der Genesis-Exegese des Josephus."
        Pp. 197–204 in Betz et al., eds.

Jonge, Marinus de
1974   "Josephus und die Zukunftserwartungen seines Volkes." Pp. 205–19
        in Betz et al., eds.

Justus, Bernard
1973   "Zur Erzählkunst des Flavius Josephus." *Theokratia* 2: 107–36.

Kappler, Werner
1967   *Maccabaeorum liber I.* Septuaginta, Vetus Testamentum Graece,
        Auctoritate Societatis Litterarum Göttingensis editum 9.1. 2d ed.
        Göttingen: Vandenhoeck & Ruprecht.

Katz, Peter
1960   "The Text of 2 Maccabees Reconsidered." *ZNW* 51: 10–30.
1961   "Eleazar's Martyrdom: The Latin Evidence for a Point of the
        Story." Pp. 118–24 in *Studia Patristica.* Ed. F. L. Cross. TU 78.
        Berlin: Akademie-Verlag.

Kellermann, Ulrich
1979   *Auferstanden in den Himmel: 2 Makkabäer 7 und die Auferstehung der Märtyrer.* SBS 95. Stuttgart: Katholisches Bibelwerk.

Kiechle, Franz
1963   "Antiochus IV und der letzte Versuch einer Konsolidierung des Seleukidenreiches." *Geschichte in Wissenschaft und Unterricht* 14: 159–70.

Kilpatrick, George D.
1963   Review of Kappler, and Hanhart (1959, 1961), *Göttingische Gelehrte Anzeigen*, 10–22.

Koester, Helmut
1971   "The Historical Jesus: Some Comments and Thoughts on Norman Perrin's *Rediscovering the Teaching of Jesus.*" Pp. 123–36 in *Christology and a Modern Pilgrimage: A Discussion with Norman Perrin.* Ed. H. D. Betz. Claremont, CA: New Testament Colloquium.

Kreissig, H.
1962   "Der Makkabäeraufstand: Zur Frage seiner sozialökonomischen Zusammenhänge und Wirkungen." *Studii Clasice* 4: 143–75.

Laqueur, R.
1920   *Der jüdische Historiker Flavius Josephus: Ein biographischer Versuch auf neuer quellenkritischer Grundlage.* Giessen: Münchow. Chaps. 6 and 8 reprinted in *Zur Josephus Forschung*, 70–113, ed. A. Schalit. Wege der Forschung 84. Darmstadt: Wissenschaftliche Buchgesellschaft.

Larraya, J. A. G.
1952   *Las guerras de los Judios.* Barcelona: José Janés.

Lebram, J. C. H.
1970   "Zur Chronologie in den Makkabäerbüchern." Pp. 63–70 in *Das Institutum Judaicum der Universität Tübingen 1968–70.* Tübingen: Institutum Judaicum.
1974   "Der Idealstaat der Juden." Pp. 233–53 in Betz et al., eds.

Lefèvre, A.
1957   "Maccabés (livres I et II)." *DBSup* 5: 597–612.

Lévy, Isidore
1955   "Les deux livres des Maccabées et le livre hébraique des Hasmonéens." *Sem* 5: 15–36.

Liebermann-Frankfort, Thérese
1969   "Rome et le conflict judéo-syrien (164–61 avant notre ère)." *L'Antiquité classique* 39: 101–20.

Lindner, Helgo
1972   *Die Geschichtsauffassung des Flavius Josephus im Bellum Judaicum.* AGJU 12. Leiden: Brill.

McEleney, Neil J.
1968   "1-2 Maccabees." *JBC* 1: 461–86.

MacRae, George W.
1965   "Miracle in the *Antiquities* of Josephus." Pp. 129–47 in *Miracles: Cambridge Studies in their Philosophy and History.* Ed. C. F. D. Moule. London: Mowbray.

Marcus, Ralph
1937–43   *Josephus*. LCL 6–8. Cambridge, MA: Harvard University Press; London: Heinemann.

Mayer, Reinhold, and Christa Möller
1974   "Josephus—Politiker und Prophet." Pp. 271–84 in Betz et al., eds.

Mejía, J.
1958   "Possibles contactos entre los manuscritos de Qumrân y los Libros de los Macabéos." *RevQ* 1: 51–72.
1959   "Contribución de Qumrân a la exegesis de los libros de los Macabéos." Pp. 20–27 in *Sacra Pagina: Miscellanea biblica congressus internationalis catholici de re biblica*. Ed. J. Coppens et al. BETL 13. Paris: Gabalda.

Melamed, E. Z.
1951   "Josephus and Maccabees I: A Comparison." Eretz-Israel 1: 122–30. Jerusalem: Israel Exploration Society.

Meshcherskii, N. A.
1958   *Istoriga iudeskoig voiny Josifa Flaviga*. Moscow and Leningrad: n.p.

Metzger, Bruce
1962   "Lucian and the Lucianic Recension of the Greek Bible." *NTS* 8: 189–203.

Michel, Otto
1954   "Spätjüdisches Prophetentum." Pp. 60–66 in *Neutestamentliche Studien für R. Bultmann*. BZNW 21. Berlin: Töpelmann.
1968   "Ich komme (Jos. Bell. III. 400)." *TZ* 24: 123–24.
1969   "Studien zur Josephus, Apokalyptische Heilsansagen im Bericht des Josephus (BJ 6, 290 f., 293–295); Ihre Umdeutung bei Josephus." Pp. 240–44 in *Neotestamentica et Semitica: Festschrift M. Black*. Edinburgh: T. & T. Clark.
1971   "Zur Arbeit an den Textzeugnis des Josephus." ZAW 83: 101–2.

Michel, Otto, and Otto Bauernfeind
1959–69   *Flavius Josephus: De bello Judaico. Der jüdische Krieg*. 3 vols. Darmstadt: Wissenschaftliche Buchgesellschaft.
1967   "Die beide Eleazarreden in Jos. Bell. 7, 323–336; 7,341–388." ZNW 58: 267–72.

Moehring, Horst R.
1957   "Novelistic Elements in the Writings of Josephus." Diss., University of Chicago.
1975   "The *Acta pro Judaeis* in the Antiquities of Flavius Josephus." Pp. 124–58 in *Christianity, Judaism and Other Greco-Roman Cults: Studies for Morton Smith at Sixty*, vol. 3. Ed. J. Neusner. SJLA 12. Leiden: Brill.

Mölleken, Wolfgang
1953   "Geschichtsklitterung im I. Makkabäerbuch (Wann wurde Alkimos Hohepriester?)." ZAW 65: 205–28.

Momigliano, Arnoldo
1930   *Prime linee di storia della tradizione Maccabaica*. Rome: Foro Italiano.
1975   "The Second Book of Maccabees." *Classical Philology* 70: 81–88.

Mørkholm, Otto
1966   *Antiochus IV of Syria.* Historisk-filosofiske meddelelser udgivet af det kongelige Danske Videnskabernes Selskab 40.3. Copenhagen: Munksgaard.

Mras, Karl
1958   "Die Hegesippus-Frage." *Anzeigen der Oesterreichen Akademie der Wissenschaften.* Phil.-hist. Kl. 95: 143–53.

Neuhaus, Gunter O.
1973–74 "Quellen im 1. Makkabäerbuch? Eine Entgegnung auf die Analyse von K.-D. Schunck." *JSJ* 5: 162–75.
1974   *Studien zu den poetischen Stücken im 1. Makkabäerbuch.* Würzburg: Echter-Verlag.

Neusner, Jacob
1972   "Josephus's Pharisees." Pp. 224–44 in *Ex orbe religionum: Studia Geo Widengren oblata,* vol. 1. Studies in the History of Religions 21. Leiden: Brill.

Nickelsburg, George W. E., Jr.
1971   "1 and 2 Maccabees — Same Story, Different Meaning." *CTM* 42: 515–26.
1972   *Resurrection, Immortality and Eternal Life in Intertestamental Judaism.* HTS 26. Cambridge, MA: Harvard University Press.

Nock, Arthur D.
1959   "Posidonius." *JRS* 49: 1–15. (= Pp. 853–76 in *Essays on Religion and the Ancient World.* Ed. Z. Stewart. Cambridge, MA: Harvard University Press, 1972).

North, Robert
1953   "Maccabean Sabbath Years." *Bib* 34: 501–15.

Pascal, Pierre
1965   *La prise de Jerusalem: Textes traduits du vieux russe et presentés.* Monaco: Rocher.

Pelletier, André, S.J.
1959   *Flavius Josèphe: Autobiographie.* Paris: Les belles lettres.
1962   *Flavius Josèphe adapteur de la lettre d'Aristée, une reaction atticisante contre le Koiné.* Etudes et commentaire 45. Paris: Klincksieck.
1967   *Philo Judaeus. In Flaccum.* Paris: Cerf.
1972   *Philo Judaeus. Legatio ad Gaium.* Paris: Cerf.

Penna, Angelo
1953   *Libri dei Maccabei.* Turin: Marietti.
1965   "Διαθήκη e συνθήκη nei libri dei Macabei." *Bib* 46: 149–80.

Petersen, H.
1958   "Real and Alleged Literary Projects of Josephus." *American Journal of Philology* 79: 259–74.

Philonenko, Marc
1956   "La notice du Josèphe slave sur les Esséniens." *Sem* 6: 69–73.

Pines, S.
1971   *An Arabic Version of the Testimonium Flavianum and Its Implications.* Jerusalem: Israel Academy of Sciences and Humanities.

Plöger, Otto
1955   "Die makkabäischen Burgen." *ZDPV* 71: 141–72.

| 1958 | "Die Feldzüge der Seleukiden gegen den Makkabäer Judas." *ZDPV* 74: 158–88. |

Pötscher, W.
1975   "Josephus Flavius. Antiquitates 18, 63f. (Sprachliche Form und thematischer Inhalt)." *Eranos* 73: 26–42.

Rajak, Tessa
1973   "Justus of Tiberius." *CQ* 23: 345–68.
1978   "Moses in Ethiopia: Legend and Literature." *JJS* 29: 111–22.
1983   *Josephus: The Historian and His Society*. London: Duckworth; Philadelphia: Fortress.

Reiling, J.
1971   "The use of ψευδοπροφήτης in the Septuagint, Philo and Josephus." *NovT* 13: 147–56.

Reiner, J.
1969–70   "The Original Hebrew Yosippon in the Chronicle of Jerachmeel." *JQR* 60: 128–46.

Renaud, B.
1961   "La loi et les lois dans les livres des Maccabées," *RB* 68: 39–67.

Rengstorf, Karl H.
1973–83   *A Complete Concordance to Flavius Josephus*. Leiden: Brill. Supplement, *Namenwörterbuch* by A. Schalit, 1968.

Ricciotti, Guiseppe
1960   *Flavio Guiseppe: La Guerre Guidaica*. Barcelona: Eler.

Richnow, W.
1967   "Untersuchungen zu Sprache und Stil des 2. Makkabäerbuches: Ein Beitrag zur hellenistischen Historiographie." Diss., Göttingen.

Rubinstein, A.
1957   "Observations on the Old Russian Version of Josephus' Wars." *JJS* 2: 329–48.

Sachs, Abraham J., and Donald J. Wiseman
1954   "A Babylonian King-List of the Hellenistic Period." *Iraq* 16: 202–12.

Saldarini, Anthony J.
1978   Review of J. Goldstein, *I Maccabees*. *JBL* 97: 288–89.

Sandmel, S. (see Thackeray, 1967)

Schalit, Abraham
1960   "The Letter of Antiochus III to Zeuxis regarding the Establishment of Military Colonies in Phrygia and Lydia." *JQR* 50: 289–318.
1965   "Evidence of an Aramaic Source in Josephus' Antiquities of the Jews." *ASTI* 4: 163–88.
1967   *Yosef ben Mattatyahu (Flavius Josephus), Qadmoniot ha-Yehudim.* 2d ed. Jerusalem: Mosad Bialik.
1968   See Rengstorf.
1972   *The Hellenistic Age: Political History of Jewish Palestine from 332 B.C.E. to 67 B.C.E.* World History of the Jewish People 1.6. New Brunswick, NJ: Rutgers University Press.

Schaller, Berndt
1963   "Hekataios von Abdera über die Juden: Zur Frage der Echtheit und der Datierung." *ZNW* 54: 15–31.

Schaumberger, Johannes B.
1955   "Die neue Seleukidenliste BM 35603 und die makkabäische Chrono-
            logie." *Bib* 36: 423–55.

Scheidweiler, F.
1950–51   "Sind die Interpolationen im altrussischen Josephus wertlos?" *ZNW*
            43: 155–78.

Schötz, Dionysius P.
1948   *Erstes und zweites Buch der Makkabäer.* Würzburg: Echter-Verlag.

Schreckenberg, Heinz
1968   *Bibliographie zu Flavius Josephus.* ALGHJ 1. Leiden: Brill.
1970   "Einige Vermutungen zum Josephustext." *Theokratia* 1: 76–87.
1972   *Die Flavius-Josephus-Tradition in Antike und Mittelalter.* ALGHJ
            5. Leiden: Brill.
1973   "Neue Beiträge zur Kritik des Josephustextes." *Theokratia* 2: 81–106.
1977   *Rezeptionsgeschichte und Textkritische Untersuchungen zu Flavius
            Josephus.* ALGHJ 10. Leiden: Brill.
1979   *Bibliographie zu Flavius Josephus: Supplementband mit Gesamt-
            register.* ALGHJ 14. Leiden: Brill.

Schubert, Kurt
1962   "Die Entwicklung der Auferstehungslehre von der nachexilischen
            bis zur frührabbinischen Zeit." *BZ* n.s. 6: 177–214.

Schunk, Klaus-Dietrich
1954   *Die Quellen des I. und II. Makkabäerbuches.* Halle: Niemeyer.

Schürer, Emil
1973,1979   *The History of the Jewish People in the Age of Jesus Christ.* New
            English version revised and edited by G. Vermes and F. Millar. 2
            vols. Edinburgh: T. & T. Clark.
1960   "Makkabäerbücher." *RGG*[3] 4: 620–22.
1980   *1. Makkabäerbuch.* JSHRZ 1.4. Gütersloh: Mohn.

Schwark, Jürgen
1973   "Matthäus der Schriftgelehrte und Josephus der Priester: Ein
            Vergleich." *Theokratia* 2:137–54.

Sherwin-White, A. N.
1972   "Philo and Avilius Flaccus: A Conundrum." *Latomus* 31: 820–28.

Shutt, R. J. H.
1961   *Studies in Josephus.* London: SPCK.

Smallwood, E. Mary
1961   *Philonis Alexandrini Legatio ad Gaium.* Leiden: Brill. 2d ed., 1970.

Smith, Morton
1956   "Palestinian Judaism in the First Century." Pp. 67–81 in *Israel: Its
            Role in Civilization.* Ed. M. Davis. New York: Harper.
1958   "The Description of the Essenes in Josephus and the Philosophou-
            mena." *HUCA* 29: 273–313.

Sobel, R. B.
1962   "Josephus' Conception of History in Relationship to the Pentateuch
            as a Source of Historical Data." Diss., Hebrew Union College.

Solomon, David
1970   "Philo's Use of γενάρχης in *In Flaccum.*" *JQR* 61: 119–31.

Sowers, Sidney
  1967   "On the Reinterpretation of Biblical History in Hellenistic Judaism."
            Pp. 18–25 in *Oikonomia, Heilsgeschichte als Thema der Theologie:
            Festschrift O. Cullman*. Ed. F. Christ. Hamburg-Bergstadt:
            Evangelische Verlag.

Stählin, Gustav
  1974   "Das Schicksal im Neuen Testament und bei Josephus." Pp. 319–43
            in Betz et al., eds.

Stearns, Wallace N.
  1908   *Fragments from Graeco-Jewish Writers*. Chicago: University of
            Chicago Press.

Stein, S.
  1954   "The Liturgy of Hanukkah and the First Two Books of the Macca-
            bees." *JJS* 5: 100–106, 148–55.

Stern, Menachem
  1960   "The Death of Onias III" (Hebrew). *Zion* 25: 1–16.
  1962   "Flavius Josephus' Method of Writing History" (Hebrew). Pp.
            22–28 in *Historia, Historionim ve Askolot*. Jerusalem: Israel His-
            torical Society.
  1974   *Greek and Latin Authors on Jews and Judaism*. Vol. 1, *From
            Herodotus to Plutarch*. Jerusalem: Israel Academy of Sciences and
            Humanities.

Tcherikover, Victor
  1956   "Jewish Apologetic Literature Reconsidered." *Eos* 48: 3: 169–93.
  1966   *Hellenistic Civilization and the Jews*. Trans. S. Applebaum.
            Philadelphia: Jewish Publication Society.

Thackeray, H. St. John
  1926–34   *Josephus*. LCL 1–5. Cambridge, MA: Harvard University Press;
            London: Heinemann.
  1967   *Josephus, the Man and the Historian*. New York: Ktav. With an
            introduction by S. Sandmel. Reprinted from the 1929 ed. (New
            York: Jewish Institute of Religion).

Thackeray, H. St. John, and Ralph Marcus
  1930–55   *A Lexicon to Josephus I–IV* (Α–ἐμφιλοχωρεῖν). Paris: Alexander
            Kohut Memorial Foundation.

Thoma, Clemens
  1969   "Die Weltanschauung des Flavius Josephus dargestellt an Hand
            seiner Schilderung des jüdischen Aufstandes gegen Rom (66–73 n.
            Chr.)." *Kairos* 11: 39–52.

Tiede, David
  1972   *The Charismatic Figure as Miracle Worker*. SBLDS 1. Missoula,
            MT: Scholars Press.

Timpe, D.
  1960   "Römische Geschichte bei Flavius Josephus." *Historia* 9: 474–502.

Ulrich, Eugene C.
  1978   *The Qumran Text of Samuel and Josephus*. HSM 19. Missoula, MT:
            Scholars Press.

Unnik, Willem C. van
1973 "An Attack on the Epicureans by Flavius Josephus." In *Romanitas et Christianitas: Festschrift H. Waszink*. Ed. W. den Boer. Amsterdam: North Holland.
1974a "Eine merkwürdige liturgische Aussage bei Josephus (Jos. Ant. 8, 111–113)." Pp. 362–69 in Betz et al., eds.
1974b "Josephus' Account of the Story of the Israel's Sin with Alien Women." Pp. 241–61 in *Travels in the World of the OT*. Ed. M. S. Heerma van Voss et al. Studia Semitica Neerlandica 16. Assen: Van Gorcum.
1978 *Flavius Josephus als historischer Schriftsteller*. Heidelberg: Schneider.

Wacholder, Ben-Zion
1962 *Nicolaus of Damascus*. Berkeley and Los Angeles: University of California Press.
1963 "Pseudo-Eupolemus' Two Greek Fragments on the Life of Abraham." *HUCA* 34: 83–113.
1968 "Biblical Chronology in the Hellenistic World Chronicles." *HTR* 61: 451–81.
1974 *Eupolemus: A Study of Judeo-Greek Literature*. Cincinnati, New York, Los Angeles, Jerusalem: Hebrew Union College– Jewish Institute of Religion.
1978 "The Letter from Judah Maccabee to Aristobulus: Is 2 Maccabees 1:10b–2:18 Authentic?" *HUCA* 49: 89–133.

Wächter, L.
1969 "Die unterschiedliche Haltung der Pharisäer, Sadduzäer und Essener zur Heimarmene nach dem Bericht des Josephus." *ZRGG* 21: 97–114.

Walter, Nicholas
1964 *Der Toraausleger Aristobulos*. TU 86. Berlin: Akademie-Verlag.
1965 "Zu Pseudo-Eupolemus." *Klio* 43/45: 282–90.
1966 "Zur Überlieferung einiger Reste früher jüdisch-hellenistischer Literatur bei Josephus, Clemens, und Euseb." Pp. 314–20 in *Studia Patristica*. TU 92. Berlin: Akademie-Verlag.
1976 *Fragmenta jüdisch-hellenistischer Historiker*. JSHRZ 1.2. Gütersloh: Mohn.
1980 *Fragmente jüdisch-hellenistischer Exegeten: Aristobulos, Demetrios, Aristeas*. JSHRZ 3.2. Gütersloh: Mohn.

Wibbing, Siegfried
1962 "Zur Topographie einzelner Schlachten des Judas Makkabäus." *ZDPV* 78: 159–70.

Williamson, Geoffrey A.
1959,1970 *Josephus, The Jewish War*. Harmondsworth and Baltimore: Penguin.
1964 *The World of Josephus*. London: Secker & Warburg.

Winter, Paul
1967–68 "Josephus on Jesus." *Journal of Historical Studies* 1: 289–302.

Yavetz, Zvi
1975 "Reflections on Titus and Josephus." *GRBS* 16: 411–32.

Zambelli, M.
   1965   "La composizione del secundo libro dei Maccabei e la nuova crono-
              logia di Antioco IV Epifane." Pp. 195–300 in *Miscellanea Greca e
              Romana*. Studi pubblicati dall' Instituto per la Storia Antica 16.
              Rome: Instituto per la storia antica.

Zeitlin, Solomon
   1962–78   *The Rise and Fall of the Judean State*. 3 vols. Philadelphia: Jewish
              Publication Society.
   1969   "A Survey of Jewish Historiography: From the Biblical Books to the
              Sefer ha-kabbalah, with special emphasis on Josephus." *JQR* 59:
              171–214.
   1978   "Josephus Flavius: A Biographical Essay." Pp. 385–417 in *The Rise
              and Fall of the Judaean State*, vol. 3. Philadelphia: Jewish Publica-
              tion Society.

Zeitlin, Solomon, and Sidney Tedesche
   1950   *The First Book of Maccabees*. Dropsie College Edition, Jewish
              Apocryphal Literature. New York: Harper.
   1954   *The Second Book of Maccabees*. Dropsie College Edition, Jewish
              Apocryphal Literature. New York: Harper.

14

APOCALYPTIC LITERATURE

John J. Collins

No aspect of Judaism in the Hellenistic period has received more extensive scholarly attention than the apocalyptic literature (see Schmidt; Barr; Coppens; Martin-Achard; Delcor, 1977a; Dexinger, 1977:3–94; Charlesworth: 46–52; Knibb, 1982; Koch and Schmidt; Hanson, ed.). The aim of this essay is to identify and clarify the central issues in the discussion. These will be considered under three main headings: (1) the scope of the literature; (2) the nature of the literature; and (3) its place in Judaism.

THE SCOPE OF THE LITERATURE

Much of the scholarly literature has been concerned with a rather vaguely defined phenomenon of "apocalyptic" rather than with specific texts (see the essays in Hellholm, ed., which range over a vast area of ancient religion). A significant advance was made by Klaus Koch's distinction between "apocalypse" as a literary type and "apocalyptic" as a historical movement (Koch, 1972). Subsequent English-language discussion has favored abandonment of "apocalyptic" as a noun and has distinguished between "apocalypse" as a literary genre, "apocalypticism" as a social ideology, and "apocalyptic eschatology" as a set of ideas and motifs that may be found also in other genres and social settings (Hanson, 1976a; Stone, 1976; Knibb, 1982).

Definitions of the Genre

Koch quite rightly insisted that the primary evidence for any discussion of apocalypticism is found in a corpus of texts that includes "first and foremost the book of Daniel, I Enoch, II Baruch, IV Ezra, the Apocalypse of Abraham and the Book of Revelation" (Koch, 1972:23). Koch offered only "a preliminary demonstration of the Apocalypse as a Literary Type" (reprinted in Hanson, ed.). A preliminary form-critical overview was also offered by P. Vielhauer. A more comprehensive survey of apocalyptic literature in Judaism, early Christianity, Gnosticism, and the Greco-Roman world was undertaken by the SBL Genres Project and published in *Semeia* 14 (Collins, ed.; the contributors were J. J. Collins, A. Yarbro Collins, F. T. Fallon, H. W. Attridge, and A. J. Saldarini). This survey arrived at the following definition of an apocalypse: "a genre of revelatory literature with a narrative framework, in which a revelation is mediated by an otherworldly being to a human recipient, disclosing a transcendent reality which is both temporal, insofar as it envisages eschatological salvation, and spatial insofar as it involves another, supernatural world." Within this genre thus broadly defined, subtypes can be distinguished. The most important distinction for the Jewish corpus is between "historical" apocalypses which do not have an otherworldly journey but include *ex eventu* prophecy of history culminating in an eschatological crisis, and the otherworldly journeys, where the spatial, rather than the temporal, aspect is prominent. According to this definition, the corpus of Jewish apocalypses may be divided as follows: (1) "historical" apocalypses: Daniel, Animal Apocalypse (*1 Enoch* 85–90), Apocalypse of Weeks (*1 Enoch* 93; 91:11–19), 4 Ezra, *2 Baruch, Jubilees;* (2) otherworldly journeys: Book of the Watchers, Astronomical Book and Similitudes in *1 Enoch; 2 Enoch; 3 Baruch; Testament of Abraham; Apocalypse of Abraham; Testament of Levi* 2–5; *Apocalypse of Zephaniah.* It is apparent that much traditional study of "apocalyptic" has been based on the "historical" apocalypses to the neglect of the otherworldly journeys, although there have recently been some attempts to reverse that trend (Gruenwald; Rowland). *Himmelfarb, Culianu*

This approach to the genre must be contrasted with others that have been advocated recently. On the one hand, E. P. Sanders (1983) proposes an "essentialist" definition. He agrees that apocalypses should be revelatory and that the form of the revelation should be supernatural. He argues, however, that "what is peculiar to the works which have traditionally been considered Palestinian Jewish apocalypses is the combination of revelation with the promise of restoration and reversal" (1983:456). Sanders can then explain the social function of the genre quite simply as literature of the oppressed. His definition, however, could equally well be taken to characterize the whole tradition of biblical prophecy and also political prophecy throughout the ancient Near East. It takes no account of the cosmological and mystical aspects of the apocalypses, which are especially prominent in otherworldly journeys. Sanders's definition is, no doubt, influenced by the limitation of his survey to works of Palestinian origin.

On the other hand, a number of scholars have argued for a purely formal definition that does not attempt to specify the content. So, for example, an apocalypse is "a revelation of heavenly mysteries" (Carmignac; Rowland; Stegemann). Such a definition is certainly accurate for the apocalypses, but it also covers a much broader range of revelatory literature. If one wished to give a more descriptive definition of the literature that has traditionally been regarded as apocalyptic, the question of eschatology inevitably arises. Although eschatology is certainly not the only concern of the apocalypses, it is nonetheless a defining characteristic that distinguishes apocalyptic from other revelatory literature. We should bear

Rowland:
"revelation of heavenly mysteries"
- but content ?

in mind, however, that eschatology may be either personal or public. Not all apocalypses are concerned with the end of the world or of an age. All apocalypses, however, have some concern for a judgment beyond this life, and this is the only kind of eschatology in some otherworldly journeys.

A quite different approach to the study of the genre has been advocated by D. Hellholm (1980, 1982), drawing heavily on text linguistics. Evaluation of his proposal must await the publication of the second volume of his dissertation. His published work, as of spring 1984, has not attempted to define a genre or a corpus, but is primarily concerned with establishing a scientific method for determining the function of a text. Hellholm insists on the importance of function in defining a genre, but unlike Sanders he is concerned with the literary or linguistic rather than the social or historical function (see also Hartman, 1983).

The importance of defining a genre is that it establishes a context for the interpretation of the individual texts by providing a backdrop that enables us to perceive both their conventional and their original aspects. The genre apocalypse is never the only relevant context for the apocalyptic literature. Historical setting provides quite a different kind of context. Even in literary terms, the apocalypses cannot be divorced from various categories of related literature—oracles, testaments, the Qumran scrolls, etc. Works such as *Testaments of the Twelve Patriarchs, Testament of Moses, Sibylline Oracles* or the Qumran *War Scroll* are "apocalyptic"in a qualified sense, insofar as they share some of the typical characteristics of the genre,[1] and are relevant to any discussion of apocalypticism. In view of the importance of this related literature too much weight should not be placed on the exact classification of borderline examples such as *Jubilees*, which is a rather unusual apocalypse and has equally strong affinities with other genres. The broader corpus of related material will be taken into account in the following discussion insofar as it bears on the nature of apocalyptic literature.

THE NATURE OF THE LITERATURE

The problem of genre leads us from the question of which writings are apocalyptic to the nature of this kind of writing, the expectations with which it should be read, and the methods and presuppositions that are appropriate for understanding it. The point at issue here is not only the precise definition of "apocalyptic" but, more fundamentally, the logic and conventions that govern those texts that are commonly called apocalyptic. We may distinguish two fundamentally different approaches to this problem: one that may be associated with the name of R. H. Charles, and the

[1] The inclusion of the *Testaments* and *Oracles* in Vol. 1 of *The Old Testament Pseudepigrapha* (Charlesworth, ed., 1983) must be welcomed, but the exclusion of *Jubilees* is unfortunate.

other with that of Hermann Gunkel. This is not, of course, to suggest that the approaches of these scholars were incompatible in every respect or that every subsequent scholar can be neatly aligned with one or the other. The works of these men, however, represent two divergent tendencies that underlie many scholarly disagreements.

R. H. Charles

The study of apocalyptic literature in the English-speaking world has to a great extent been influenced by R. H. Charles. His textual editions and annotated translations have remained standard reference works down to the present, and his knowledge of the material was undeniably vast. Yet such a sober critic as T. W. Manson could write that "there was a sense in which the language of Apocalyptic remained a foreign language to him. He could never be completely at home in the world of the Apocalyptists. And this made it impossible for him to achieve that perfect understanding which demands sympathy as well as knowledge" (cited in Barr: 32). Charles's lack of empathy with the material is apparent in two character-istics of his work. First, he tended to treat the texts as compendia of infor-mation and paid great attention to identifying historical allusions and extracting theological doctrines. By contrast he gave little attention to such matters as literary structure or mythological symbolism. The second char-acteristic is related to this. Since he assumed that the original documents presupposed a doctrinal consistency similar to his own and that the canons of style that governed them were similar to those of his own day, he posited interpolations and proposed emendations rather freely. So F. C. Burkitt wrote in his obituary of Charles: "If he came to have any respect for an ancient author he was unwilling to believe that such a person could have entertained conceptions which to Charles' trained and logical western mind were 'mutually exclusive,' and his favorite explanation was to posit interpolations and a multiplicity of sources, each of which may be sup-posed to have been written from a single and consistent point of view" (cited in Barr: 31).

The British Tradition

Of course, Charles was a child of his age. The principles of Well-hausenian literary/source criticism were still dominant in biblical studies when he wrote.[2] However, the underlying assumptions of this type of approach have continued to play a prominent role in the study of apoca-lyptic literature. In large part this has been due to the persistence of a British tradition that "has tended towards a clarity and simplicity,

---

[2] Although Charles shared the methodological assumptions of the Wellhausenian "literary critics" he did not share their negative evaluation of the apocalyptic literature (Hanson, 1976a:390–92).

and . . . has tended to lose from sight the essential problem of understanding the apocalyptic books as literary texts with their own strange form and language" (Barr: 31). In fact, the two most comprehensive and widely read books on "apocalyptic" in the last half century were by British authors—H. H. Rowley and D. S. Russell. Russell's book was for long the best comprehensive treatment available, although it has been rightly criticized at a number of points: the confusing list of characteristics (Hanson, 1975:6–7), the theory of corporate personality and the contrast of Greek and Hebrew thought (Barr: 33). However, as James Barr has pointed out, Rowley and Russell were characterized by the "reduction of the very enigmatic material to essentially simple questions" (32) and by the effort to take it as doctrine. (Note the systematic organization of Russell's book, with chapters on "the messianic kingdom," "life after death," etc.). It is also significant that Charles, Rowley, and Russell all sought the sources of apocalyptic language primarily in OT prophecy. Although prophecy may indeed be the single most important source on which the apocalyptists drew, the tendency to assimilate apocalyptic literature to the more familiar world of the prophet risks losing sight of its stronger mythological and cosmological components.

The Source-Critical Method

The source-critical aspect of Charles's legacy is embedded in the introductions to the various books in his edition of the pseudepigrapha. This approach has persisted in H. L. Ginsberg's *Studies in Daniel*, which identifies multiple sources even within individual verses, and again in the Anchor Bible commentary on Daniel by Hartman and Di Lella. (For a less extreme example see the work of A. F. J. Klijn on Syriac *Baruch*).

The problem with the source-critical method is obviously one of degree. No one will deny that it is sometimes possible to distinguish sources and to identify interpolations. We have learned, however, that the apocalyptic writings are far more tolerant of repetition and inconsistency than Charles and his collaborators suspected. Hasty recourse to source criticism may betray a failure to understand the coherence of a text on its own terms. Working assumptions should favor the unity of a document unless there is compelling evidence to the contrary. It will not do to excise a passage because the text would "run more smoothly" without it (Hartman and Di Lella: 145).

The Understanding of Symbolic Language

The methodological assumptions that posit sources and interpolations to maintain an ideal of consistency and style are frequently coupled with a lack of sympathy for symbolic narratives. The tendency of much historical scholarship has been to specify the referents of apocalyptic imagery in as unambiguous a manner as possible. This approach works well for a passage like Daniel 11, but often misses the element of mystery and allusiveness which is an important factor in these texts.

The idea that apocalyptic symbols are mere codes whose meaning can be exhausted by single referents is not uncommon. Norman Perrin argued that apocalyptic symbols were "steno-symbols": "This thing was Antiochus IV Epiphanes, that thing was Judas Maccabee, the other thing was the coming of the Romans and so on. But if this was the case, and it certainly was, then when the seer left the known facts of the past and present to express his expectation of the future his symbols remained 'steno-symbols' and his expectation concerned singular concrete historical events" (11). (Compare Hartman and Di Lella, who consider this supposed "uni-referential character" as a mark of the literary superiority of Daniel over his "second-rate imitators" in the pseudepigrapha). This view fails to account for the perennial ambiguity of some symbols (e.g., the "son of man"), for the fact that apocalypses often offer several different images of the future, or for the evocative power of allusions to ancient myths and traditions. (See further P. Ricoeur in Lacocque; Porter).

Scholars who have followed this approach have made many important contributions to text criticism, identification of historical references, and the compilation of relevent information. However, the tendency to reduce the apocalyptic material to clear and simple questions has generally been counterproductive for the appreciation of this literature.

H. Gunkel

Although the reduction of apocalyptic literature to clear and simple categories has been characteristic of much scholarship in the field, it has not gone unchallenged. Hermann Gunkel, who pioneered so many creative developments in biblical study, also pointed the way to a more satisfactory appreciation of the apocalypses (Gunkel, 1895, 1900; Schmidt: 195–204; Hanson, 1976b:393–96). Much of Gunkel's work on apocalyptic literature was directed to the recovery of traditional, and especially mythological, materials embedded in the apocalypses. On the one hand, this work suggested that the various seams detected by the so-called "literary" critics (e.g., when an interpretation ignores some elements in a vision) need not point to multiple authorship but only to the use of traditional material by a single author. In short, some authors who work with traditional material do not conform to the standards of consistency and coherence presupposed by Charles and Wellhausen, but may well allow loose ends and even contradictions to stand in their work. On the other hand, by pointing to the mythological roots of much apocalyptic imagery, Gunkel showed its symbolic and allusive character. Apocalyptic literature was not governed by the principles of Aristotelian logic, but was closer to the poetic nature of myth.

Compositional Techniques

Gunkel's critique of the principles of "literary" criticism was long neglected by students of apocalyptic literature, but has been repeatedly vindicated in recent study. The insight that the apocalypses did not aspire to conceptual consistency but could allow diverse formulations to complement each other is especially important. Scholars have long been aware that oral transmission involves compositional techniques quite different from those assumed by Charles and Wellhausen. It is doubtful whether oral transmission played a significant part in the formation of many apocalypses (witness the intensive scribal work of Qumran and the frequent choice of scribes as pseudonymous authors in the apocalypses). However, the principles of oral transmission at least provide a useful analogy for a type of composition that is not governed by logical consistency but makes use of repetitions and the juxtaposition of various formulations (Suter). From a distinctly literary perspective Earl Breech has drawn attention to the expressive function in repetition in 4 Ezra, which he compares to T. S. Eliot's technique in "The Waste Land" (cf. Thompson: 102–4). Closer, perhaps, to the idiom of the apocalypses is the analogy with the repetition of cycles in myths and the device of "tripling" in folklore (Collins, 1977a: 116–17). So the sevenfold "recapitulation of a basic pattern in the book of Revelation can be seen as a way of communicating the message of the book in an emphatic way while not identifying it exclusively with any one formulation" (Yarbro Collins, 1977a:32–44; cf. Gager: 49–57). The juxtaposition of visions and oracles that cover essentially the same material with varying imagery is a feature of a great number of apocalyptic writings—Daniel, the *Sibylline Oracles*, Similitudes of Enoch, 4 Ezra, *2 Baruch*, Revelation.[3] This fact can hardly be due to chance. Repetition is a common literary (and oral) convention in both ancient and modern times: compare the multiple dreams of Gilgamesh and Joseph. Recognition that such repetition is an intrinsic feature of apocalyptic writing provides a key to a new appreciation of that literature.

The Use of Mythology

The insight that the apocalypses are related to and draw on the mythology of the ancient Near East was preserved by writers of the Myth and Ritual school such as S. H. Hooke and especially by A. Bentzen and S. Mowinckel. In the English-speaking world it has been revived especially by

---

[3] Compare also the study of smaller repetitive patterns in *1 Enoch* 92–105 by Nickelsburg (1977a) and the structuralist study of *3 Baruch* by Picard.

P. D. Hanson, building on the work of F. M. Cross. It has also been the subject of a recent study by the French scholar M. Delcor (1977b). Gunkel had sought his mythological parallels in the Babylonian materials then available and subsequent scholars posited vast Persian influence, but more recent scholarship has looked to the Canaanite-Ugaritic myths. Although the discovery of mythic parallels to apocalyptic motifs and patterns has shed much light on the idiom of apocalyptic writings and much remains to be done in this area, the more important contribution of ancient mythology may be to illuminate the logic and manner of coherence of this type of literature.

The "Son of Man"

The range of problems here can be seen in the vast literature on the figure of the "Son of Man" (for a wide sample of views see the collection of essays in Pesch and Schnackenburg). C. Colpe's masterful review of the evidence has shown the untenability of the widely held Iranian derivation and the superiority of the Canaanite hypothesis. Thus, Mowinckel's discussion of the origin of the "Son of Man" imagery, which relies on Hellenistic-oriental syncretism ultimately derived from Iranian and Chaldean sources, is in need of revision. However, Mowinckel's appreciation of the mythic character of the "Son of Man" figure (contra M. P. Casey)[4] and the original distinction between this complex of motifs and those associated with the national messiah remain valid. The more serious defect in his presentation is the degree to which he regards "Son of Man" and "Messiah" as titles that represent basically uniform conceptions. It is by now widely agreed that "Son of Man" was not a title in intertestamental Judaism (Vermes). However, it is also clear that the idea of a heavenly savior figure was current and that this figure might be referred to in various ways and might be depicted with varying characteristics: the archangel Michael in Daniel and 1QM, Melchizedek in 11QMelch, the man from heaven in *Sib. Or.* 5, and the man from the sea in 4 Ezra 13. This multiform conception provides the natural context for the NT expectation of the Son of Man who will come on the clouds with his angels. It also provides the most plausible context for understanding the "one like a son of man" in Daniel 7 and "that son of man" in the Similitudes of Enoch (Lindars, 1975, 1976; Collins, 1977a: 144–46).[5]

---

[4] In his discussion of the Similitudes of Enoch, Casey correctly notes that "son of man" means simply "man," but he assumes that it must then refer to a human (Enoch) and does not take account of the frequency with which angelic or supernatural beings are described as "men" elsewhere in apocalyptic literature. A. Caquot, like Casey, argues that the "son of man" should be identified as Enoch throughout the Similitudes, but he shows a greater appreciation for the mythical traits of the figure.

[5] Glasson (1977) correctly notes the variety in Jewish eschatological formulations but fails to perceive any underlying coherence.

Multiform conception of heavenly savior

If we bear in mind that apocalypses, like myths, are concerned with patterns and impressions rather than with consistent doctrines and titles, the differences between the various formulations become less significant. What is important is the hope of salvation mediated by a supernatural, heavenly savior figure, which might be fulfilled in any of a number of ways. Mowinckel's distinction between Son of Man and Messiah is still useful, then, as a pointer to two types of expectation, but not to distinct titles or uniform conceptions. (The two types are increasingly woven together in later apocalypses; see Theisohn; U. Müller; Stone, 1968). The use of mythological parallels in the "Son of Man" debate does not permit the identification of a clearly defined figure, but it provides a key to understanding the nature of apocalyptic expectation in accordance with the more fluid logic of myths, which relies on multiplicity of images rather than on doctrinal clarity.

The Use of the OT

The importance of ancient mythology for understanding apocalyptic literature must not, of course, be thought to exclude other factors. There is no doubt that the interpretation of OT texts plays a significant part in apocalyptic compositions, as has been demonstrated especially by Lars Hartman (1966, 1976–77; also Nickelsburg, 1972). An equally important aspect of Hartman's work, however, concerns the identification of patterns of thought in these writings, and he readily admits that these should not necessarily be understood exclusively against an OT background. Rather, "it would seem to be realistic to expect a broad background to these texts, including a large number of factors" (1966:137). Exegesis of the OT can no more be treated as the sole key to apocalyptic literature than can ancient mythology. Both are important factors, which complement each other, as has been shown in recent work on *1 Enoch* (Hanson, 1977; Nickelsburg, 1977b). The significance of the tradition of scholarship descended from Gunkel is that it has shown that mythological parallels reveal a dimension of apocalyptic literature that is too often passed over by scholars who concentrate on the use of the OT.

Problems in the Quest for Traditional Sources

The interpretation of apocalyptic literature in terms of ancient myth is not, however, without its pitfalls. First, there is the temptation to confuse the quest for *sources* with the task of interpretation. The mythological elements are no more than building blocks. The meaning of any apocalypse must still be determined by examining its internal structure. Although this point is generally admitted in theory, the temptation remains in practice for scholars who have labored to trace the roots of imagery to rest their examination and leave the interpretation proper undone. This creates the misleading impression that apocalypticism is a derivative phenomenon that should be understood in terms of something other than itself—whether ancient mythology, prophecy, wisdom, or Hellenistic syncretism. In this respect the whole debate about the sources of "apocalyptic" is misdirected.

Second, there is the temptation to identify *one* tradition as the only or the essential source of apocalyptic imagery. However, if we recognize the autonomy of apocalypticism as a phenomenon in its own right, we must realize that it could draw its language from multiple sources. It is now clear that Canaanite mythology, filtered through the Israelite tradition, is far more important for apocalyptic imagery than previous generations had suspected. However, the central place of Canaanite imagery in Daniel 7 did not prevent the author from incorporating the Hellenistic schema of the four kingdoms, or from utilizing contemporary astrological ideas in Daniel 8 (Collins, 1977a:95–108). Again, although the importance of Persian influence was greatly exaggerated in the past, it cannot be dismissed entirely. The influence of Persian dualism on the Qumran scrolls is widely admitted (Shaked, followed by Frye, 1975; [contrast Frye, 1962] cf. Winston) and does not at all contradict the extensive influence of Israelite traditions on those documents (Collins, 1975a; von der Osten-Sacken, 1969a; Kobelski: 84–98). It would be foolhardy indeed to attempt to trace all apocalyptic imagery to a single tradition. In this respect the renewed emphasis on the Hellenistic environment of apocalypticism is especially important. The Hellenistic material is only one source of imagery among others, but it is also suggestive of the broad environment in which Jewish apocalypticism developed. It may therefore help to clarify the underlying questions of apocalypticism (Betz; Hengel, 1:181–96; K. Müller; Collins, 1975b; Smith, 1975; Yarbro Collins, 1977b).[6]

Third, we may note the widespread tendency to confuse the theological evaluation of apocalyptic literature with the historical identification of its sources. Frequently scholars who have assumed extensive Persian influence have assumed that apocalypticism is therefore unbiblical and theologically suspect (e.g., Murdock). This theological conclusion would not be warranted, even if the historical derivation were correct. It is now amply clear that much of the basic imagery of Yahwism was taken over from the environment (Cross, 1973). There is no solid theological reason why further borrowings should not occur. Conversely, apologetic attempts to affirm continuity with OT prophecy or more broadly with indigenous Palestinian or Northwest Semitic traditions are misplaced. The theological importance of apocalypticism depends on the intrinsic value of its perspective, not on the origin of its imagery or the locale where it developed.

---

[6] This emphasis on the Hellenistic-oriental environment should be distinguished from the attempt of Glasson (1961) to detect influence from Greek literature on the apocalypses. The relevant Hellenistic materials are discussed by H. W. Attridge in Collins, ed.: 159–86, and in the essays of Raphaël et al.; see also Betz.

Wisdom and the Apocalypses

These pitfalls are not peculiar to the attempts to derive apocalypticism from ancient mythology, but pertain to the quest for sources in all its forms. Too often valid insights into the nature of the phenomenon are hastily translated into genetic theories and are thereby distorted. The thesis of G. von Rad that apocalypticism derives from wisdom is a case in point (von Rad, 1965:315–30, 1972:263–83).[7] Von Rad correctly perceived that there are basic differences between apocalypticism and prophecy, despite their common interest in eschatology, so that the one cannot be simply perceived as an extension of the other. He also realized that apocalyptic revelation can be accurately described as a kind of wisdom (compare, from different perspectives, Hengel, 1:202–18; Smith, 1975; Luck). However, the thesis that apocalypticism therefore derives from wisdom neglects even more fundamental differences between OT wisdom and the apocalypses (von der Osten-Sacken, 1969b; compare Knibb, 1983a). The "wisdom" of Daniel is not the proverbial wisdom of Proverbs or Qoheleth[8] but rather the "mantic wisdom" which entails the interpretation of dreams and omens and which finds closer parallels in Mesopotamian divination than in OT wisdom (H. P. Müller, 1972, 1976; Collins, 1977a:67–93). The only Jewish wisdom book that has substantial affinities with the apocalypses is the late Wisdom of Solomon, where the points of contact are largely due to the common Hellenistic environment, and where influence by the apocalypses is also possible (Collins, 1977b).

Von Rad's attempt to establish a genetic connection between OT wisdom and apocalypticism has little to commend it, but it has nonetheless served a useful function in the recent discussion by directing attention to those aspects of apocalyptic literature which are not eschatological. Michael Stone (1976) has emphatically urged the importance of cosmological and other noneschatological material in the "lists of revealed things" in the apocalypses. Stone's sharp distinction between apocalypticism ("a certain pattern of ideas") and the apocalypses has heuristic value in highlighting the range of interests in the apocalypses, which goes far beyond what is usually called apocalypticism (Gruenwald; Willi-Plein; Rowland; and from a different perspective G. I. Davies). However, it is doubtful whether such a sharp distinction can be maintained. There is not at present a firm consensus on the "pattern of ideas" that constitutes apocalypticism. The interests of clarity would surely be best served if "apocalypticism" were defined by reference to the pattern of ideas found in the apocalypses

---

[7] A connection between wisdom and apocalyptic was proposed as early as 1857 by L. Noack (see Schmidt: 13–14).

[8] Gammie points out some features that are common to OT wisdom and the apocalyptic writings, but he does not show the significance of these features for either wisdom or the apocalypses.

(which also may be found in other literature besides). In short, if the pattern of ideas by which Klaus Koch (1972:24–30; cf. Stone, 1976:440) defines apocalypticism does not conform to what we find in the apocalypses, we may suggest that Koch's pattern needs revision rather than assume that we are dealing with diverse phenomena.

It may be that we need to distinguish different types of apocalypticism corresponding to the distinction between "historical apocalypses" and heavenly journeys. In any case, the eschatological/temporal aspects of the apocalypses cannot be cleanly divorced from the cosmological/spatial ones, since both recur persistently in the same works (Collins, 1979).

In summary, the attempt to recover the mythological and other sources of apocalyptic language has enriched our understanding of that language in many ways. The most important gains have concerned the idiom and allusions of the language, and the logic and manner of apocalyptic writings. However, the quest for sources has often distracted scholars from the inner coherence of apocalyptic literature in its own right.

THE PLACE OF APOCALYPTIC LITERATURE IN JUDAISM

The Historical Milieu

Just as scholarship has often tended to restrict the sources of apocalyptic literature to one tradition, so it has often tended to restrict the provenance of this literature to a single group within Judaism. Specifically, there has been widespread agreement that the earliest phase of the apocalyptic writings should be assigned to the Hasidim (Hengel, 1:175–80).[9] Despite its popularity, such a thesis seems far too simple (see Nickelsburg, 1983). Our evidence for the Hasidic movement is far too scanty to support such a hypothesis with any certainty (P. R. Davies, 1977). Further, the few statements we have in the books of Maccabees (1 Macc 2:42; 7:12–13; 2 Macc 14:6) represent the Hasidim as militant activists, even if they joined the Maccabees relatively late and were later eager to make peace. Despite the widespread assumption that the maskîlîm of Daniel 11 should be identified with these Hasidim, there is nothing in Daniel to suggest that the maskîlîm would have espoused militant action at all (Collins, 1977a:201–5). Again, the Essenes of Qumran are widely thought to be the heirs of the Hasidim (Cross, 1961). There is no doubt that the sect took a profound interest in apocalyptic literature. However, although many of the writings of the sect could be described as apocalyptic, there is no clear case of a work that is formally an apocalypse and was composed by the Qumran sect (see

[9] Delcor (1971:15–19; 1974) attributes Daniel to the Hasidim, but the other apocalyptic writings to the Essenes. So Daniel was canonized, but the others were not.

Stegemann; Carmignac). The Essenes cannot be regarded as the sole or primary carriers of apocalyptic literature, and their alleged relation to the Hasidim does not establish the latter as the authors of apocalypses. More serious, perhaps, than any of these considerations is the diversity in viewpoint that exists among the apocalypses themselves. The Animal Apocalypse (*1 Enoch* 85–90) shows an enthusiasm for the Maccabean revolt that is quite lacking in Daniel. Further, there is no apparent reason to assume that such Enochic works as the Book of the Watchers (*1 Enoch* 1–36) or the Book of the Heavenly Luminaries (*1 Enoch* 72–82) originated in the same circles as Daniel.

Scholars who regard the Hasidim as the originators of apocalyptic literature usually regard them as a group within Palestinian Judaism. Yet several scholars have noted the affinities of some of the earliest apocalypses with Babylonian tradition. The tales of Daniel 1–6 are set in Babylon, and Daniel and his friends are grouped with the Chaldean wise men (Collins 1977a:27–93). These features might most easily (though not necessarily) be explained by supposing that this stage of the Daniel tradition had developed in Babylon, although Daniel 7–12 was certainly composed in Palestine. (Note also Lambert's proposal that the genre of Daniel 11 be understood against the background of Babylonian political prophecy.) Several scholars have argued for Babylonian characteristics in *1 Enoch* 1–36 (Ludin Jansen; Grelot; VanderKam; cf. Stone, 1978, 1980). It is striking that the oldest sections of *1 Enoch* (the Book of the Watchers and the Astronomical Book) diverge more obviously from the biblical tradition than is the case with later apocalypses and also have the strongest parallels with Babylonian materials. (Note also Murphy-O'Connor's theory that the founders of the Qumran community returned from Babylon, although there is no clear positive evidence to support it. See the critique by Knibb, 1983b.) These considerations do not suggest a pan-Babylonian theory of the origins of apocalypticism and cannot be said to establish definitively the Babylonian origin of any of this literature. They do, however, demonstrate that <u>the common assumption that all the apocalyptic literature is Palestinian is open to question</u>. There is no a priori reason why a work like *1 Enoch* 1–36 should be assumed to be Palestinian unless a Palestinian origin can be proved.[10] It should of course be clear that a Babylonian provenance would not make any of this literature any less Jewish. Babylonian Jews stood in continuity with the biblical tradition as well as their Palestinian counterparts.

[10] The arguments advanced by Milik (25–26) for the Judean origin of *1 Enoch* 1–36 are unconvincing. Milik argues that the author was Judean "since he looks upon Jerusalem as the center of the earth, and the hill of the temple of Jerusalem as 'the sacred mountain' *par excellence*" (26:1–2). These considerations show only that the author was a Jew. A possible indication of Palestinian origin can be found in the localization of the descent of the Watchers and the vision of Enoch around Mount Hermon and Dan (chaps. 6 and 13), but its value is uncertain.

The possibility that the authors of some parts of *1 Enoch* and Daniel emerged from Babylonian Judaism is especially important since it involves some of the earliest apocalypses. Even apart from this possibility, apocalypticism cannot be considered a purely Palestinian phenomenon. There are at least a few apocalypses, none of them likely to be earlier than the turn of the era, which are generally believed to come from the Hellenistic (more specifically Egyptian) Diaspora. The most notable examples are *2 Enoch* and *3 Baruch* (Fischer: 37–84) but mention should also be made of the *Apocalypse of Zephaniah* and of the *Testament of Abraham*,which includes an apocalypse (chaps. 10–15 in recension A, chaps. 8–12 in recension B; see Collins, 1983). We should also note the wide distribution of Sybilline oracles, which are related to apocalypticism though not apocalypses in form. Here again there has been a tendency to restrict the provenance to one area—Egypt (e.g., Nikiprowetzky). However, the Sibylline books that have the most markedly apocalyptic character cannot be assigned to Egypt. The Jewish stratum in *Sib. Or.* 1/2 was most probably composed in Asia Minor about the turn of the era (Kurfess), and *Sib. Or.* 4 most probably originated in Syria or Palestine toward the end of the first century (Collins, 1974c). The Egyptian provenance of *Sib. Or.* 3 and 5 is generally accepted (Collins, 1974a; Nikiprowetzky).

Dating

Chronologically, this literature ranges from the third century B.C.E. to the beginning of the second century C.E. Milik (31) would push the date of the earliest sections of *1 Enoch* back even further, before the priestly redaction of Genesis, but this suggestion has been widely rejected. A date in the third century is more probable (Nickelsburg, 1977b:391; Stone 1978:484). Even so, the earliest sections of *1 Enoch* acquire considerable importance as evidence for a little-known period of Jewish history and as undisputed specimens of apocalyptic literature older than Daniel. Milik (89–124) has also proposed controversial datings for the Similitudes of Enoch and *2 (Slavonic) Enoch*,both of which he regards as late, Christian compositions. However, his argumentation rests on the absence of these documents from Qumran, and their supposed affinities with later Christian writings are no greater than those with intertestamental Jewish works. The only substantial arguments yet offered for the dating of either work still point to the period about the turn of the era for the Similitudes (Greenfield and Stone) and before 70 C.E. for *2 Enoch* (Greenfield; xviii). Disputes about the dating of other apocalyptic writings are less extreme. [11]

[11] The *Testament (Assumption) of Moses* is variously dated to the time of Antiochus Epiphanes or to the time after the death of Herod. See the discussion by Collins and Nickelsburg in Nickelsburg, ed., 1973:15–43. The later date is still held by Brandenburger. Nikiprowetzky (1970:195–225) dissents from the usual dating of *Sib. Or.* 3 to the second century

The apocalypses that can be more clearly dated are clustered in two groups around the Maccabean revolt and the aftermath of the first Jewish revolt. This is undoubtedly due to the fact that references to these great crises are more easily recognized than references to less prominent events. In any case, the apocalyptic literature clearly spans a period of more than three hundred years and extends to various geographical settings. Consequently, it seems rash to speak of "the apocalyptic movement" as if it were a continuous social phenomenon (Schreiner; Schmithals) or to attempt to relate it to a single party within Judaism. Although the Essenes of Qumran evidently treasured apocalyptic literature, there is also general agreement that two major apocalypses (4 Ezra and 2 Baruch) reflect a Pharisaic background (Bogaert; Harnisch). Eschatological and apocalyptic beliefs were widely known and held and not restricted by party lines (Dexinger, 1975).

We should also allow for some diversity in the kinds of groups that produced this literature. All the apocalypses would seem to be composed by SCRIBES scribes who had acquired considerable learning (however unscientific). Some (e.g., the Similitudes of Enoch) may have been produced by conventicles or sectarian groups, analogous to the Qumran community (see Vielhauer). Such a setting is much less likely in the case of Daniel or of 2 Baruch. Those who accepted apocalyptic revelations were not necessarily isolated from the rest of Jewish society.

Relation to Other Jewish Literature

Although apocalyptic literature cannot be assigned to a single party, the question arises concerning how it should be related to other strands of Judaism. Here two contrasting views have been proposed. On the one hand, D. Rössler argued for a sharp antithesis between apocalyptic and rabbinic Judaism, reflected in their differing attitudes to history and law. Rössler's position has been sharply criticized, and undoubtedly the contrast is overdrawn (Nissen; cf. Koch, 1972:41, 81–93). Rössler simplified his task considerably by leaving the Qumran scrolls out of consideration, since they show an intensive and detailed use of the law that does not conform to Rössler's generalizations about apocalypticism. The very fact that some apocalypses could be produced in Pharisaic circles should caution against so sharp a dichotomy. By contrast, E. P. Sanders has argued that the apocalyptic literature shares a common "pattern of religion" with rabbinic Judaism and indeed with all Palestinian Judaism from the time of Ben Sira. Sanders pursues his inquiry in terms of "how one gets 'in' and stays 'in,'" and the pattern he discerns is "covenantal nomism." Since he begins his study with the rabbinic literature (which is chronologically later), it is

---

B.C.E. and dates it to the time of Cleopatra. The complex debate over the dating of the *Testaments of the Twelve Patriarchs* lies outside the scope of this review.

difficult to avoid the suspicion that the apocalyptic literature is not being studied in its own right, but only checked for evidence of covenantal nomism. There is no doubt that such evidence can be found, especially at Qumran and in 4 Ezra and *2 Baruch*, but we may question whether covenantal nomism is always the central determining pattern (see Luck, who argues that the law is subordinated to apocalyptic wisdom in *1 Enoch* and 4 Ezra). Although Sanders's emphasis on the place of the law in apocalyptic literature is a welcome corrective to Rössler, his own treatment is also one-sided. Before the apocalyptic literature can be related to other strands of Judaism, its internal structure must be examined in its own right. Then the relative importance of individual elements such as law and eschatology can be seen in perspective, and both the distinctiveness of the apocalyptic world view and its continuity with other strands of Judaism can be appreciated. It is noteworthy that apocalyptic ideas never fully died out in Judaism and cannot have been totally alien to the rabbis (Scholem; W. D. Davies; Bloch; Saldarini; and especially Gruenwald; Rowland).

Theological Evaluation

Finally we must consider the theological evaluation of apocalyptic literature in recent study. The growth in appreciation of symbolic and mythological literature has generally led to a more positive assessment of the apocalypses. Apocalyptic imagery is less often viewed as idle speculation but is seen to express an interpretation of historical situations (often political crises) and to shape the human response to those situations (Silberman). In this respect, the existential interpretation of apocalypticism offered by Bultmann and Schmithals is noteworthy, even if it has not always done full justice to the allusiveness of the mythological symbolism. Martin Buber's sweeping condemnation of apocalyptic determinism and of the use of pseudonymity as an evasion of responsibility can now be seen as a mis-understanding of the function of apocalypses. Equally, the view that the apocalyptic use of history is directed only to a calculation of the end-time has been discredited (Hartman, 1976). Instead, the apocalyptic reviews of history serve to highlight the short period before the end, which is the actual time of the author, as a period of decision (Harnisch: 326; Collins, 1977c). The fact that the end is determined adds intensity to the call for decision, but the individual's choice is not determined (though Qumran may provide an exception). Even the occasional attempts to fix the date must be seen as attempts to heighten the realism of the expectation and the pressure to decide.

An alternative to the existential interpretation can be found in Klaus Koch's understanding of the use of history in Daniel (Koch, 1961; also Janssen; compare now Koch, 1978), which is in general conformity to the views of the Pannenberg school. [12] Koch finds in Daniel a teleological view of universal history that is moving toward a goal for both Israel and all humanity. The accuracy of such an understanding of Daniel is open to question (contrast Noth; Collins, 1977a:153–79). Koch's interpretation can be applied more easily to those apocalypses that include reviews of history than to those that do not (e.g., *1 Enoch* 1–36, *2 Enoch*, *3 Baruch*).

CONCLUSIONS AND PROSPECTS

The scholarship reviewed in this essay has dealt with the apocalyptic literature on a rather general level. One purpose of the study of the genre has been to refocus the discussion on a specific corpus of texts. An introduction to the apocalyptic literature which deals with each of the texts in turn can be found in Collins, 1984a (see also Nickelsburg, 1981a; Stone, 1984).

It is not possible here to review all the studies of individual texts in recent years. We should note, however, the progress that has been made in making this literature available. The publication of *The Old Testament Pseudepigrapha* (Charlesworth, ed., 1983, 1985) marks a great advance in this respect, especially since it contains a much more extensive collection of apocalyptic writings than the edition of R. H. Charles. Other major translation projects include the German series Jüdische Schriften aus hellenistisch-römischer Zeit and the British *Old Testament Apocrypha* edited by H. F. D. Sparks. Noteworthy editions of original texts include *Greek (3) Baruch* (Picard), the Armenian of 4 Ezra (Stone), and the Slavonic of *Apocalypse of Abraham* (Philonenko and Philonenko-Sayar). M. Knibb has published a single manuscript of *1 Enoch* with an apparatus and translation, but we still await a full critical edition. We also await an up-to-date edition of *2 Enoch*.

Past study of the apocalypses has often been hampered by the use of inappropriate "literary-critical" methods. This literature has seldom been studied in its own right but has more often been viewed as a "child" of prophecy or wisdom or as background to the NT. Future study must learn to appreciate the coherence of these documents as wholes in themselves. Study of the genre can provide a starting point, since it can guide our expectations by showing the patterns and conventions that are typical of this literature and focusing on the apocalyptic literature itself rather than on its sources. The canonical apocalypses, Daniel and Revelation, have often been distorted by exclusive reliance on biblical parallels and neglect of the pseudepigrapha. This tendency too can be corrected by the study of the

---

[12] The interpretation of apocalypticism by systematic theologians such as W. Pannenberg and J. Moltmann lies outside the scope of this review. An evaluation of apocalypticism from the viewpoint of process philosophy can be found in Beardslee.

genre. Much remains to be done in the form-criticism of this material, especially in the pseudepigrapha (see Collins, 1984b). Future study of the literary character of the apocalypses will undoubtedly be influenced increasingly by text linguistics (Hellholm; de Villiers). This development can contribute to greater precision, provided that "scientific" methods are not taken too rigidly or given dogmatic status.

This survey has paid little attention to sociological studies of apocalypticism. In fact, very little has been done in this area. The most important sociological studies of Jewish and early Christian apocalypticism (Hanson; Gager) fall outside the scope of this review. Rich comparative materials are available from anthropological studies (Wilson), but here again a word of caution is in order. Models derived from medieval peasant revolts or modern cargo cults cannot be assumed a priori to fit the phenomenon of Jewish apocalypticism. We are often hampered by lack of historical information about the setting of particular apocalypses. Indeed, some apocalypses seem to conceal their specific setting deliberately (Collins, 1982). The case of Qumran, where the extent of our information is exceptional, is in many ways anomalous as a millenarian movement (Isenberg). It is crucially important that sociological theories be controlled by a proper understanding of the literature in its own right and that settings not be invented to satisfy preconceived models (see Nickelsburg, 1983). Nonetheless, sociological study is an area wide open for exploration, where progress must be expected in the coming decade.

BIBLIOGRAPHY

Barr, J.
    1975   "Jewish Apocalyptic in Recent Scholarly Study." *BJRL* 58: 9–35.
Beardslee, W. A.
    1973   "Openness to the New in Apocalyptic and in Process Theology."
                Process Studies 3: 169–78.
Bentzen, A.
    1952   *Daniel.* HAT 19. 2d ed. Tübingen: Mohr-Siebeck.
Betz, H. D.
    1969   "On the Problem of the Religio-Historical Understanding of Apocalypticism." *JTC* 6: 134–56.
    1983   "The Problem of Apocalyptic Genre in Greek and Hellenistic Literature: 'The Case of the Oracle of Trophonius.'" Pp. 577–97 in Hellholm, ed.
Bloch, J.
    1952   *On the Apocalyptic in Judaism.* Philadelphia: Dropsie College.
Bogaert, P.
    1969   *Apocalypse de Baruch.* SC 144, 145. Paris: Cerf.
Brandenburger, E.
    1976   *Himmelfahrt Moses.* JSHRZ 5.2. Gütersloh: Mohn.
Breech, E.
    1973   "These Fragments I Have Shored Against My Ruins." *JBL* 92: 267–74.

Buber, M.
1957   "Prophecy, Apocalyptic and the Historical Hour." *Pointing the Way*. New York: Harper.

Bultmann, R.
1957   *History and Eschatology*. New York: Harper.

Caquot, A.
1977   "Remarques sur les chaps. 70 et 71 du livre éthiopien d'Hénoch." Pp. 111–22 in *Apocalypses et Théologie de l'Éspérance*. Ed. H. Monloubou. Paris: Cerf.

Carmignac, Jean
1983   "Description de phénomène de l'Apocalyptique dans L'Ancien Testament." Pp. 163–70 in Hellholm, ed.

Casey, M. P.
1976   "The Use of the Term 'Son of Man' in the Similitudes of Enoch." *JSJ* 7: 11–29.

Charles, R. H.
1913   *The Apocrypha and Pseudepigrapha of the Old Testament*. 2 vols. Oxford: Clarendon Press.

Charlesworth, J. H.
1976   *The Pseudepigrapha and Modern Research*. SBLSCS 7. Missoula, MT: Scholars Press.
1983   *The Old Testament Pseudepigrapha*. Vol. 1, *Apocalyptic Literature and Testaments*. Garden City, NY: Doubleday.
1985   *The Old Testament Pseudepigrapha*. Vol. 2, *Expansions of the "Old Testament" and Legends, Wisdom and Philosophical Literature, Prayers, Psalms, and Odes, Fragments of Lost Judeo-Hellenistic Works*. Garden City, NY: Doubleday.

Collins, J. J.
1974a   *The Sibylline Oracles of Egyptian Judaism*. SBLDS 13. Missoula, MT: Scholars Press.
1974b   "Apocalyptic Eschatology as the Transcendence of Death." *CBQ* 36: 21–43.
1974c   "The Place of the Fourth Sibyl in the Development of the Jewish Sibyllina." *JJS* 25: 366–80.
1975a   "The Mythology of Holy War in Daniel and the Qumran War Scroll." *VT* 25: 596–612.
1975b   "Jewish Apocalyptic against its Hellenistic Near Eastern Environment." *BASOR* 220: 27–36.
1977a   *The Apocalyptic Vision of the Book of Daniel*. HSM 16. Missoula, MT: Scholars Press.
1977b   "Cosmos and Salvation: Jewish Wisdom and Apocalyptic in the Hellenistic Age." *HR* 17: 121–42.
1977c   "Pseudonymity, Historical Reviews and the Genre of the Revelation of John." *CBQ* 39: 329–43.
1982   "The Apocalyptic Technique: Setting and Function in the Book of the Watchers." *CBQ* 44: 91–111.
1983   "The Genre Apocalypse in Hellenistic Judaism." Pp. 531–48 in Hellholm, ed.
1984a   *The Apocalyptic Imagination in Ancient Judaism*. New York: Crossroad.
1984b   *Daniel, with an Introduction to Apocalyptic Literature*. Forms of Old Testament Literature 20. Grand Rapids: Eerdmans.

Collins, J. J., ed.
1979   *Apocalypse: The Morphology of a Genre. Semeia* 14. Missoula, MT: Scholars Press.

Colpe, C.
1972   "Ho huios tou anthrōpou." *TDNT* 8: 400–430.

Coppens, J.
1976   "L'Apocalyptique: Son dossier, ses critères, ses eléments constitutifs, sa portée néotestamentaire." *ETL* 53: 1–23.

Cross, F. M.
1961   *The Ancient Library of Qumran and Modern Biblical Studies.* Rev. ed. Garden City, NY: Doubleday, Anchor Books.
1973   *Canaanite Myth and Hebrew Epic.* Cambridge, MA: Harvard University Press.

Davies, G. I.
1978   "Apocalyptic and Historiography." *JSOT* 5: 15–28.

Davies, P. R.
1977   "Hasidim in the Maccabean Period." *JJS* 28: 127–40.

Davies, W. D.
1962   "Apocalyptic and Pharisaism." Pp. 19–30 in *Christian Origins and Judaism.* Philadelphia: Westminster.

Delcor, M.
1971   *Le Livre de Daniel.* Paris: Gabalda.
1974   "Le milieu d'origine et le développement de l'apocalyptique juive." Pp. 101–17 in *La littérature juive entre Tenach et Mischna: Quelques problèmes.* Ed. W. C. van Unnik. RechBib 9. Leiden: Brill.
1977a   "Bilan des études sur l'apocalyptique." Pp. 27–42 in *Apocalypses et Théologie de l' Éspérance.* Ed. L. Monloubou. Paris: Cerf.
1977b   "Mythologie et apocalyptique." Pp. 143–78 in *Apocalypses et Théologie de l'Éspérance.* Ed. L. Monloubou. Paris: Cerf.

Dexinger, F.
1975   "Ein 'Messianisches Szenarium' als Gemeingut des Judentums in nachherodianischer Zeit?" *Kairos* 17: 249–78.
1977   *Henoch's Zehnwochenapokalypse und Offene Probleme der Apokalyptik.* Leiden: Brill.

Fischer, U.
1978   *Eschatologie und Jenseitserwartung im hellenistischen Diasporajudentum.* BZNW 44. Berlin: de Gruyter.

Frye, R. N.
1962   "Reitzenstein and Qumran Re-visited by an Iranian." *HTR* 55: 261–68.
1975   "Qumran and Iran: The State of Studies." Pp. 167–74 in *Christianity, Judaism and Other Greco-Roman Cults: Studies for Morton Smith at Sixty,* vol. 3. Ed. J. Neusner. SJLA 12. Leiden: Brill.

Gager, J. G.
1975   *Kingdom and Community.* Englewood Cliffs, NJ: Prentice-Hall.

Gammie, J. G.
1974   "Spatial and Ethical Dualism in Jewish Wisdom and Apocalyptic Literature." *JBL* 93: 356–85.

Ginsberg, H. L.
1948   *Studies in Daniel.* New York: Jewish Theological Seminary.

Glasson, T. F.
1961   *Greek Influence in Jewish Eschatology with Special Reference to the Apocalypses and Pseudepigrapha*. London: SPCK.
1977   "Schweitzer's Influence—Blessing or Bane." *JTS* 28: 289–302.

Greenfield, J. C.
1973   "Prolegomenon" in H. Odeberg, *3 Enoch or the Hebrew Book of Enoch*. New York: Ktav.

Greenfield, J. C., and M. E. Stone
1977   "The Enochic Pentateuch and the Date of the Similitudes." *HTR* 70: 51–66.

Grelot, P.
1958a   "La géographie mythique d'Hénoch et ses sources orientales." *RB* 65: 33–69.
1958b   "La Légende d'Hénoch dans les Apocryphes et dans la Bible." *RSR* 46: 5–26, 181–210.

Gruenwald, I.
1973   "Knowledge and Vision: Towards a Clarification of Two "Gnostic" Concepts in the Light of Their Alleged Origins." *Israel Oriental Studies* 3: 63–107.
1980   *Apocalyptic and Merkavah Mysticism*. Leiden: Brill.

Gunkel, H.
1895   *Schöpfung und Chaos in Urzeit und Endzeit*. Göttingen: Vandenhoeck & Ruprecht.
1900   "Das vierte Buch Ezra." Pp. 331–401 in *Die Apokryphen und Pseudepigraphen des Alten Testaments*, Vol. 2. Ed. E. Kautzsch. Tübingen: Mohr.

Hanson, P. D.
1971   "Jewish Apocalyptic against its Near Eastern Environment." *RB* 78: 39–40.
1975   *The Dawn of Apocalyptic*. Philadelphia: Fortress.
1976a   "Apocalypticism." *IDBSup*, 28–34.
1976b   "Prolegomena to the Study of Jewish Apocalyptic." Pp. 389–413 in *Magnalia Dei: The Mighty Acts of God: Essays on the Bible and Archaeology in Memory of G. Ernest Wright*. Ed. F. M. Cross, W. E. Lemke, and P. D. Miller, Jr. Garden City, NY: Doubleday.
1977   "Rebellion in Heaven, Azazel and Euhemeristic Heroes in 1 Enoch 6–11." *JBL* 96: 195–233.

Hanson, P. D., ed.
1983   *Visionaries and Their Apocalypses*. Issues in Religion and Theology 2. Philadelphia: Fortress.

Harnisch, W.
1969   *Verhängnis und Verheissung der Geschichte*. FRLANT 97. Göttingen: Vandenhoeck & Ruprecht.

Hartman, L.
1966   *Prophecy Interpreted*. ConBNT 1. Lund: Gleerup.
1976   "The Functions of the So-Called Apocalyptic Time-Tables." *NTS* 22: 1–14.
1976–77 "Comfort of the Scriptures—an Early Jewish Interpretation of Noah's Salvation, 1 En. 10:16–11:2." *SEÅ* 41–42: 87–96.
1979   *Asking for a Meaning: A Study of 1 Enoch 1–5*. ConBNT 12. Lund: Gleerup.

1983   "Survey of the Problem of Apocalyptic Genre." Pp. 329–43 in Hellholm, ed.

Hartman, L. F., and A. A. Di Lella
1978   *The Book of Daniel.* AB 23. Garden City, NY: Doubleday.

Hellholm, D.
1980   *Das Visionenbuch des Hermas als Apokalypse.* ConBNT 13.1. Lund: Gleerup.
1982   "The Problem of Apocalyptic Genre and the Apocalypse of John." Pp. 157–98 in *Society of Biblical Literature 1982 Seminar Papers.* Ed. K. H. Richards. Chico, CA: Scholars Press.

Hellholm, D., ed.
1983   *Apocalypticism in the Mediterranean World and the Near East: Proceedings of the International Colloquium on Apocalypticism, Uppsala, August 12–17, 1979.* Tübingen: Mohr-Siebeck.

Hengel, M.
1974   *Judaism and Hellenism: Studies in their Encounter in Palestine during the Early Hellenistic Period.* 2 vols. Trans. J. Bowden. Philadelphia: Fortress.

Himmelfarb, Martha
1983   *Tours of Hell: An Apocalyptic Form in Jewish and Christian Literature.* Philadelphia: University of Pennsylvania Press.

Hooke, S. H.
1935   "The Myth and Ritual Pattern in Jewish and Christian Apocalyptic." Pp. 213–33 in *The Labyrinth.* London: SPCK.

Isenberg, S. R.
1974   "Millenarianism in Greco-Roman Palestine." *Religion* 4: 26–46.

Janssen, E.
1971   *Das Gottesvolk und seine Geschichte.* Neukirchen-Vluyn: Erziehungsverein.

Klijn, A. F. J.
1976   *Die syrische Baruch-Apokalypse.* JSHRZ 5.2. Gütersloh: Mohn.

Knibb, M.
1976   "The Exile in the Intertestamental Period." *HeyJ* 17: 253–72.
1978   *The Ethiopic Book of Enoch.* 2 vols. Oxford: Clarendon Press.
1982   "Prophecy and the Emergence of the Jewish Apocalypses." In *Israel's Prophetic Tradition: Essays in Honour of Peter Ackroyd.* Ed. R. Coggins, A. Phillips, and M. Knibb. Cambridge: University Press.
1983a   "Apocalyptic and Wisdom in 4 Ezra." *JSJ* 13: 56–74.
1983b   "Exile in the Damascus Document," *JSOT* 25: 99–117.

Kobelski, P. J.
1981   *Melchizedek and Melchireša'.* CBQMS 10. Washington, DC: CBA.

Koch, K.
1961   "Spätisraelitisches Geschichtsdenken am Beispiel des Buches Daniel." *Historische Zeitschrift* 193: 1–32.
1972   *The Rediscovery of Apocalyptic.* SBT 2/22. Naperville, IL: Allenson.
1978   "Esras erste Vision: Weltzeiten und Weg des Höchsten." *BZ* 22: 46–75.

Koch, K., and J. M. Schmidt, eds.
1982   *Apokalyptik.* Darmstadt: Wissenschaftliche Buchgesellschaft.

Kurfess, A. M.
1941 "Oracula Sibyllina I/II." *ZNW* 40: 151–65.

Lacocque, A.
1976 *Le Livre de Daniel.* Commentaire de l'Ancien Testament XVb. Paris: Delachaux et Niestlé.

Lambert, W. G.
1978 *The Background of Jewish Apocalyptic.* London: Athlone.

Lindars, B.
1975 "Apocalyptic Myth and the Death of Christ." *BJRL* 57: 366–87.
1976 "Re-enter the Apocalyptic Son of Man." *NTS* 22: 52–72.

Luck, U.
1976 "Das Weltverständnis in der jüdischen Apokalyptik, dargestellt am äthiopischen Henoch und am 4 Ezra." *TLZ* 73: 283–305.

Ludin Jansen, H.
1939 *Die Henochgestalt.* Oslo: Dybwad.

Martin-Achard, R.
1977 "Essai d'évaluation théologique de l'apocalyptique juive." Pp. 262–75 in *Beiträge zur alttestamentlichen Theologie.* Ed. H. Donner, R. Hanhart, and R. Smend. Göttingen: Vandenhoeck & Ruprecht.

Milik, J. T., with M. Black
1976 *The Books of Enoch: Aramaic Fragments of Qumrân Cave 4.* Oxford: Clarendon Press.

Mowinckel, S.
1955 *He That Cometh.* Nashville: Abingdon.

Müller, H. P.
1972 "Mantische Weisheit und Apokalyptik." Pp. 268–93 in *Congress Volume: Uppsala, 1971.* VTSup 22. Leiden: Brill.
1976 "Märchen, Legenden und Enderwartung." *VT* 26: 338–50.

Müller, K.
1973 "Die Ansätze der Apokalyptik." Pp.31–42 in *Literatur und Religion des Frühjudentums.* Ed. J. Maier and J. Schreiner. Gütersloh: Mohn.

Müller, U. B.
1972 *Messias und Menschensohn in jüdischen Apokalypsen und in der Offenbarung des Johannes.* SNT 6. Gütersloh: Mohn.

Münchow, C.
1982 *Ethik und Eschatologie: Ein Beitrag zum Verständnis der früh-jüdischen Apokalyptik.* Göttingen: Vandenhoeck & Ruprecht.

Murdock. W.
1967 "History and Revelation in Jewish Apocalypticism." *Int* 21: 167–87.

Murphy-O'Connor, J.
1974 "The Essenes and their History." *RB* 81: 215–44.

Nickelsburg, G. W. E.
1972 *Resurrection, Immortality and Eternal Life in Intertestamental Judaism.* HTS 26. Cambridge, MA: Harvard University Press.
1977a "The Apocalyptic Message of 1 Enoch 92–105." *CBQ* 39: 309–28.
1977b "Apocalyptic and Myth in 1 Enoch 6–11." *JBL* 96: 383–405.
1981a *Jewish Literature Between the Bible and the Mishnah.* Philadelphia: Fortress.

1981b   "The Books of Enoch in Recent Research." *RSR* 7: 210–17.
1983   "Social Aspects of Palestinian Jewish Apocalypticism." Pp. 639–52
         in Hellholm, ed.

Nickelsburg, G. W. E., ed.
1973   *Studies on the Testament of Moses.* SBLSCS 4. Missoula, MT:
         Scholars Press.
1976   *Studies on the Testament of Abraham.* SBLSCS 6. Missoula, MT:
         Scholars Press.

Nikiprowetzky, V.
1970   *La troisième Sibylle.* The Hague: Mouton.
1972   "Reflexions sur quelques problèmes du quatrième et du cinquième
         livre des Oracles Sibyllins." *HUCA* 43: 29–76.

Nissen, A.
1967   "Tora und Geschichte in Spätjudentum." *NT* 9: 241–77.

Noth, M.
1967   "The Understanding of History in Old Testament Apocalyptic." Pp.
         194–214 in *The Laws in the Pentateuch and Other Essays.*
         Philadelphia: Fortress.

Osten-Sacken, P. von der
1969a   *Gott und Belial: Traditionsgeschichtliche Untersuchungen zum
         Dualismus in den Texten aus Qumran.* SUNT 6. Göttingen: Van-
         denhoeck & Ruprecht.
1969b   *Die Apokalyptik in ihrem Verhältnis zu Prophetie und Weisheit.*
         Theologische Existenz heute 157. Munich: Kaiser.

Perrin, N.
1974   "Eschatology and Hermeneutics: Reflections on Method in the
         Interpretation of the New Testament." *JBL* 93: 2–14.

Pesch, R., and R. Schnackenburg, eds.
1975   *Jesus und der Menschensohn: Für Anton Vögtle.* Freiburg: Herder.

Philonenko, M., and B. Philonenko-Sayar
1981   *L'Apocalypse d'Abraham: Introduction, texte slave, traduction et
         notes.* Semitica 31. Paris: Maisonneuve.

Picard, J.-C.
1967   *Apocalypsis Baruchi graece.* Leiden: Brill.
1970   "Observations sur l'Apocalypse Grecque de Baruch." *Sem* 20:
         77–103.

Porter, P. A.
1983   *Metaphors and Monsters: A Literary-critical Study of Daniel 7 and
         8.* ConBOT 20. Lund: Gleerup.

Rad, G. von
1965   *Theologie des Alten Testaments.* Vol. 2. 4th ed. Munich: Kaiser.
1972   *Wisdom in Israel.* Nashville: Abingdon.

Raphaël, F., et al.
1977   *L'Apocalyptique.* Etudes d'Histoire des Religions 3. Paris: Geuthner.

Rössler, D.
1960   *Gesetz und Geschichte.* WMANT 3. Neukirchen-Vluyn: Erzie-
         hungsverein.

Rowland, C.
1982   *The Open Heaven: A Study of Apocalyptic in Judaism and Chris-
         tianity.* New York: Crossroad.

Rowley, H. H.
1964   *The Relevance of Apocalyptic.* 3d ed. New York: Association.

Russell, D. S.
1964   *The Method and Message of Jewish Apocalyptic.* Philadelphia: Westminster.

Saldarini, A. J.
1975   "Apocalyptic and Rabbinic Literature." *CBQ* 37: 348–58.
1977   "The Uses of Apocalyptic in the Mishna and Tosepta." *CBQ* 39: 396–409.

Sanders, E. P.
1977   *Paul and Palestinian Judaism.* Philadelphia: Fortress.
1983   "The Genre of Palestinian Apocalypses." Pp. 447–59 in Hellholm, ed.

Schmidt, J. M.
1969   *Die jüdische Apokalyptik.* Neukirchen-Vluyn: Erziehungsverein.

Schmithals, W.
1975   *The Apocalyptic Movement: Introduction and Interpretation.* Trans. J. E. Steely. Nashville: Abingdon.

Scholem, G.
1971   *The Messianic Idea in Judaism.* New York: Schocken Books.

Schreiner, J.
1969   *Alttestamentlich-jüdische Apokalyptik.* Munich: Kösel.
1973   "Die apokalyptische Bewegung." Pp. 214–53 in *Literatur und Religion des Frühjudentums.* Ed. J. Maier and J. Schreiner. Gütersloh: Mohn.

Shaked, S.
1972   "Qumran and Iran: further considerations." *Israel Oriental Studies* 2: 443–446.

Silberman, L.
1974   "The Human Deed in a Time of Despair: The Ethics of Apocalyptic." Pp. 191–202 in *Essays in Old Testament Ethics.* Ed. J. L. Crenshaw and J. T. Willis. New York: Ktav.

Smith, J. Z.
1975   "Wisdom and Apocalyptic." Pp. 131–56 in *Religious Syncretism in Antiquity.* Ed. B. Pearson. Missoula, MT: Scholars Press.
1976   "A Pearl of Great Price and a Cargo of Yams: A Study in Situational Incongruity." *HR* 16: 1–19.

Sparks, H. F. D., ed.
1984   *The Old Testament Apocrypha.* Oxford: Clarendon Press.

Stegemann, Hartmut
1983   "Die Bedeutung der Qumranfunde für die Erforschung der Apokalyptic." Pp. 495–530 in Hellholm, ed.

Stone, M. E.
1968   "The Concept of the Messiah in 4 Ezra." Pp. 285–312 in *Religions in Antiquity: Essays in Memory of Erwin Ramsdell Goodenough.* Ed. J. Neusner. Supplements to *Numen* 14. Leiden: Brill.
1976   "Lists of Revealed Things in the Apocalyptic Literature." Pp. 414–52 in *Magnalia Dei: The Mighty Acts of God: Essays on the Bible and Archaeology in Memory of G. Ernest Wright.* Ed. F. M. Cross, W. E. Lemke, and P. D. Miller. Garden City, NY: Doubleday.

1978   "The Book of Enoch and Judaism in the Third Century." *CBQ* 40: 479–92.

1979   *The Armenian Version of IV Ezra.* University of Pennsylvania Armenian Texts and Studies 1. Missoula, MT: Scholars Press.

1980   *Scriptures, Sects and Visions.* Philadelphia: Fortress.

1983   "Coherence and Inconsistency in the Apocalypses: The Case of 'the End' in 4 Ezra." *JBL* 102: 229–43.

1984   "Apocalyptic Literature." Pp. 383–441 in *Jewish Writings of the Second Temple Period.* Ed. M. E. Stone. CRINT 2. Philadelphia: Fortress.

Suter, D. W.
1979   *Tradition and Composition in the Parables of Enoch.* SBLDS 47. Missoula, MT: Scholars Press.

Theisohn, J.
1975   *Der auserwählte Richter.* SUNT 12. Göttingen: Vandenhoeck & Ruprecht.

Thompson, A. L.
1977   *Responsibility for Evil in the Theodicy of IV Ezra.* SBLDS 29. Missoula, MT: Scholars Press.

VanderKam, J. C.
1984   *Enoch and the Growth of an Apocalyptic Tradition.* CBQMS 16. Washington, DC: CBA.

Vermes, G.
1967   "The Use of Bar-Nash/Bar Nasha in Jewish Aramaic." Pp. 310–30 in *An Aramaic Approach to the Gospels and Acts.* Ed. M. Black. Oxford: Clarendon Press.

Vielhauer, P.
1965   "Apocalypses and Related Subjects." Pp. 581–607 in *New Testament Apocrypha,* vol. 2. Ed. E. Hennecke and W. Schneemelcher. Philadelphia: Westminster.

Villiers, P. G. de, ed.
1983   *Studies in 1 Enoch and the New Testament.* Neotestamentica 17. Stellenbosch: New Testament Society of South Africa.

Willi-Plein, I.
1977   "Das Geheimnis der Apokalyptik." *VT* 27: 62–81.

Wilson, R. R.
1981   "From Prophecy to Apocalyptic: Reflections on the Shape of Israelite Religion." *Semeia* 21: 79–95.

Winston, D.
1966   "The Iranian Component in the Bible, Apocrypha and Qumran." *HR* 5: 183–216.

Yarbro Collins, A.
1977a   *The Combat Myth in the Book of Revelation.* HDR 9. Missoula, MT: Scholars Press.

1977b   "The History of Religions Approach to Apocalypticism and the 'Angel of the Waters' (Rev 16: 4–7)." *CBQ* 39: 367–81.

15

WISDOM LITERATURE

Burton L. Mack and Roland E. Murphy, O.Carm.

The article will review scholarship on the following writings: The Wisdom of Jesus ben Sira (Sirach), the wisdom poem in Baruch 3:9–4:4, the *Letter of Aristeas*, Aristobulus, the Wisdom of Solomon, Philo of Alexandria, the *Sentences* of Pseudo-Phocylides, and 4 Maccabees. These several writings have little in common and do not compose a corpus of literature either as a traditional collection or as manifestations of a single or coherent tradition of Jewish thought. They are taken together here as documents that, in one way or another, evidence early Judaism's encounter with Hellenic thought in the Hellenistic and early Roman eras. In this encounter, reflection upon Judaism's own traditions of wisdom occurred, and various attempts were made to image or conceptualize wisdom both as a mode and as an object of perception or thought. Such conceptualizations could be related to Hellenic philosophical categories and used to interpret other aspects of the Jewish religious tradition—its Torah, its cultus, its history, and its ethic.

To designate these writings as Jewish wisdom literature assumes some continuity with the wisdom literature of the Hebrew Bible. It should be noted, however, that even though it has been customary to speak of a wisdom tradition in Israel and Judaism, recent OT scholarship has become very cautious about the extent to which such a tradition can be delimited. The reasons for this have to do with the disparate nature of the three canonical books that have been classified as wisdom (Proverbs, Job, Qohelet); the difficulty of defining wisdom itself, either with regard to its content in thought or as a mode of thinking; the failure to locate a common setting for this literature, either in terms of a class of sages or in terms of social-cultural institutions; and the inability to delineate a development of wisdom language and thought, especially in relationship to the history of Israel and Judaism (Crenshaw). In spite of this circumstance of scholarship, however, it still appears possible to speak of an "intellectual tradition" in some broad sense, within which individual sages were enabled to collect and transmit a proverbial wisdom, reflect upon its assumptions about human experience and knowledge, and compose literatures that addressed the questions of the nature and adequacy of these assumptions. These assumptions concerned the trustworthiness of an ethico-religious ordering of the world and human affairs. The questions had to do with the limitations of human knowledge to grasp fully this ordering, especially when confronted by human suffering or experience which required theodicy. Thus, both Job and Qohelet can be placed in this tradition as sages who addressed this question. That such an intellectual tradition continued into the Hellenistic period as a constructive influence, however, is seen much more clearly in the wisdom of Ben Sira, where indebtedness to Israelite and Jewish wisdom is positively combined with Hellenistic thought in the interest of a theological conceptuality. It is Ben Sira's achievement, more than that of any other author, which enables us to envisage a continuity and development of wisdom language and thought from the Hebrew Bible into the period in which our literature is to be placed.

Continuity with the wisdom of the Hebrew Bible is evidenced by the continued use of speech forms common to that literature (von Rad): maxims (Sirach, *Letter of Aristeas*, Wisdom, Pseudo-Phocylides), riddles (*Letter of Aristeas*), autobiographical stylization (*Letter of Aristeas*, Wisdom, Philo), didactic poems (Sirach, Baruch, Wisdom, Pseudo-Phocylides), dialogue (*Letter of Aristeas*, 4 Maccabees), and hymns (Sirach, Baruch, Wisdom). Wisdom themes of creation and righteousness are present in some form in all of this literature. The old problem of the limits of (human) wisdom and the question of theodicy can be detected in Sirach, Baruch, Wisdom, and 4 Maccabees. Personification and abstraction of (the figure of) wisdom itself continued to be developed (Sirach, Baruch, Aristobulus, Wisdom, Philo).

But there are also significant differences to be noted. New literary forms are pressed into service: historiography (Sirach, Baruch, *Letter of Aristeas*, Wisdom, 4 Maccabees), commentary (Aristobulus, Philo), homily (Baruch, Philo, 4 Maccabees), discourse (*Letter of Aristeas*, Philo, 4 Maccabees), and apology (*Letter of Aristeas*, 4 Maccabees), to name a few. Wisdom forms of speech are combined with similar Hellenic genres (cf. riddle-chreia in *Letter of Aristeas*; proverb-maxim in Sirach and Pseudo-Phocylides), and wisdom itself comes to be understood in terms of Hellenistic conceptuality and mythology (cf. Stoic concepts in Sirach, *Letter of Aristeas*, Wisdom, Philo, 4 Maccabees; and Isis mythologumena in Sirach, Wisdom, and Philo).

In contrast to the skepticism of Job and Qohelet, this literature is characterized in general by the desire to affirm the availability of wisdom and to answer positively the question of theodicy. It does so by exploring both the noetic aspects of wisdom and the extent to which the forms of Jewish religious tradition might be understood to reflect a universal order of righteousness. Interpreted in this way were the Torah (Sirach, *Letter of Aristeas*, Aristobulus, Wisdom, Philo), the temple cultus (Sirach, Baruch, Aristobulus, Philo), Jewish ethical code (Sirach, *Letter of Aristeas*, Wisdom, Philo, 4 Maccabees), Israel's sacred history (Sirach, Wisdom, Philo,

4 Maccabees), and Israel's heroes of piety (Sirach, *Letter of Aristeas*, Wisdom, Philo, 4 Maccabees). Whether or not these attempts to claim a philosophical basis for Judaism of the Greco-Roman period are to be understood as constructive theology or as apologetic, a question about which scholars are not clear, they present strong evidence for a remarkable creativity in syncretistic discovery and the reinterpretation of given Jewish traditions.

BEN SIRA

One can rightly speak of a "renaissance" in Sirach studies in recent times (Marböck, 1976:1). This has followed a period of benign neglect which set in after the first flurry of excitement over the discovery and publication of large portions of the Hebrew text of Ben Sira, beginning with Solomon Schechter. The renewed interest was spurred by the development of studies in biblical wisdom literature, as well as by the appearance of fragments of the text among the Qumran discoveries.

Text

One reason for the neglect of Sirach is the state of the text, which is *sui generis*. After the first publications of the Cairo Geniza manuscripts by S. Schechter and others, more material was identified and published by J. Marcus and J. Schirmann (1957–58, 1959–60) and critically edited by A. A. Di Lella (1964). From Qumran came fragments of Sir 6:20–31 in stichometric arrangement, dating from the second half of the first century B.C.E. (Baillet), and Cave 11 yielded the poem in 51:13–20, 30 (J. A. Sanders, 1965, 1967). It seems to be the consensus that 11QPs^a provides the Hebrew original of the poem in Sirach 51, where it is extant, in contrast to the medieval Cairo Hebrew, which is perhaps a retroversion from the Syriac (J. A. Sanders, 1967:113). The detailed interpretation, particularly of the alleged eroticism, is subject to discussion (Skehan, 1971a; J. A. Sanders, 1974). Finally, Masada yielded twenty-six leather fragments dating from the first century B.C.E. (about 100 years after the book was written!), which contain Sir 39:27–32; 40:10–19c; 40:26–44:17 (Yadin; see the corrections in Strugnell). The edition of F. Vattioni is a convenient starting point for reconstructing the text, but much more laborious work, in the style of Skehan (1971b:124–31), H. P. Rüger, and O. Rickenbacher remains to be done. The concordance of D. Barthélemy and O. Rickenbacher is an invaluable tool for such work.

J. Ziegler published a critical edition of the Greek text, and he noted both the primitive form (the translation by Ben Sira's grandson in the late second century B.C.E.) and the later reworkings in the following century. The Old Latin in the Vulgate has been critically edited (Vulgate, 1964), but the Beuron *Vetus Latina* project has not yet reached Sirach. Similarly, the Leiden Peshitta project has not covered Sirach, but M. Winter's concordance (1976) is a beginning. In his study (1977) of the origins of the Syriac version he concludes that the first translation from Hebrew to Syriac was done by Ebionites no later than the early fourth century. Later in the same century it was revised by orthodox Christians who gave it the form in which it entered the Peshitta version.

A solid study of the interrelationship of the Greek version and its expansions and the relationship of these to the Hebrew has been done by C. Kearns (1969). At the present time it is helpful to speak of Hebrew I and II, and Greek I and II. Greek II is an expanded Greek text, based on later recensions of the Hebrew; it is witnessed to in certain Greek cursives (esp. Codex 248), and the Old Latin. Greek I (represented by the great uncials, such as *Vaticanus*) generally reflects the Hebrew text found in Qumran (11QPs^a) and Masada. Hebrew I and II are the respective *Vorlagen* of Greek I and II. These conclusions represent the current status of research into the text of Ecclesiasticus (Skehan, 1976).

Commentaries

At the present time there is no adequate commentary on Ecclesiasticus. Doubtless, the announced Anchor Bible commentary by A. A. Di Lella should remedy this situation. The commentaries published over the last forty years have been very uneven. Some are only brief exegetical notes accompanying a translation (Vaccari; Duesberg and Auvray; Alonso Schökel, 1968; Snaith). Others are more technical, but they are not adequately detailed (Spicq; Schilling; Hamp; Segal; Duesberg and Fransen; van den Born). This lack of commentaries results from the difficulty of the text, the length of the work, and its absence from the Hebrew Bible, but the renewal of interest in Sirach bodes well for the future.

The World of Sirach

It is all the more striking that numerous studies have appeared that deal with the historical background of Ben Sira's thought. The influence of Hellenistic thought upon him has been affirmed by several. R. Pautrel pointed out several influences that can be attributed to the Stoa. J. T. Sanders found Sirach open to Hellenistic thought, e.g., Theognis, "as long as it can be Judaized" (58). T. Middendorp has sharpened the issue. He claims that Sirach was written as a "school"-book in the Greek style, as its thematic treatment, in contrast to Proverbs, suggests (33–34). Ben Sira knew Greek and was acquainted with the sayings of Theognis, as Middendorp shows by about one hundred "possible" references to, or echoes of, Greek writers (13–24). About half of these are to Theognis, whom Ben Sira "probably" used, be it in a Greek chrestomathy. All in all, Middendorp has made a solid case for Greek influence upon Ben Sira and has established the fact that Ben Sira is not anti-Hellenistic (*pace* M. Hengel). But it is very difficult to provide sufficient evidence that Sirach put together a book for advanced education of his Hebrew students that would purportedly resemble a Greek "school"-book (one example of which has been preserved, dating from about 200 B.C.E.). On the other hand, Middendorp concurs with the traditional view of older authors that Sirach displays a marked dependence upon previous biblical works, especially Proverbs.

M. Hengel (followed by Maier: 43–59) takes a strong position on the "anti-Hellenism" of Ben Sira (1974:131–53), but his arguments are strained. One cannot seriously refer Ben Sira's words on pride and shame (Sir 10:6ff.) to the Tobiads (Hengel, 1974:150–51) or understand the words about false striving for wisdom (Sir 3:21–24) as being directed against the Greeks (Hengel, 1974:139). Hengel is vague about the dependence of Ben Sira on Greek thought; he acknowledges this for the Stoa, Theognis, and Euripides, but denies any real influence or direct literary dependence (in contrast to Middendorp: 33–34). There is a marked tendency to absolve Ben Sira of anti-Hellenism (Marböck; Middendorp); he had more positive goals, as we shall see. Although the prayer in chap. 36 can legitimately be interpreted as anti-Hellenistic, it remains an exception in the book. In fact, Middendorp denies Sirach's authorship of this prayer (125–32).

The discovery of the rich Qumran literature promoted comparisons between Ben Sira and the Essenes (Trinquet; Lehmann; Carmignac), and Carmignac has provided references to the biblical quotations found in both and also to similar formulas and themes. But there is nothing unusual in all this. More important, it has been pointed out that "it is only among the texts of unknown authorship that we encounter wisdom compositions," and that "while the Essene texts contain wisdom vocabulary and expressions, a concern for knowledge and instruction, and an ethical dualism characteristic of the wisdom literature, these elements are external to and superimposed upon the basically apocalyptic fabric of Qumran thought" (Lipscomb and Sanders: 280).

The Teaching of Sirach

Numerous studies within the last fifteen years have been given over to the interpretation of Ben Sira's teaching and theology. The detailed studies have been more successful than the massive summaries found, for example, in Hengel (1974) and E. P. Sanders. Hengel's summary is adequate when he indicates the main emphases of Sirach (divine retribution, purposefulness of creation, and the connection of wisdom with creation and Torah), but particular details about Sirach's anti-Hellenism are very tenuous. Although Sanders correctly claims that Ben Sira "presupposed the biblical view of the election of Israel and wrote within the context of the doctrine of the covenant" (330–31), his claim that the argument or theme of the book is "the dialectic between wisdom and law" (332) is too far-reaching. G. von Rad has successfully shown that Sirach interprets the law from the perspective of wisdom (246–47), and Marböck (1976) has bolstered this with a study of the key texts of 17:1–14 and 24:23. The Torah has become part of the universal wisdom of God which is established in creation; it is seen in the perspective of an all-embracing world law of God that dominates creation and history (1976:68). This orientation is not without biblical roots (Deut 4:6), but it was also triggered by Stoic views about *nomos* and wisdom (1976:20). One has the impression that the present is not the time for general characterizations of Ben Sira's thought. More study of the book, which has a tremendous variety of topics, is needed.

In this respect, the detailed studies have been rather fruitful. It is clear that Sirach should be exonerated from a "dead works-righteousness," as O. Kaiser has shown. The argument of D. Michaelis that Ecclesiasticus represents a humanism and a religious decline is off the mark (304). Several articles have dealt with Sirach's view of life after death (Hamp, 1950b; Fang; Dommershausen); it seems quite clear that the developed eschatology contained in the expanded Greek text and in the Old Latin does not represent Ben Sira's thought (Kearns: 549). The study of J. Haspecker singled out "fear of God" as a principle of literary unity in the work. This is less successful than his exposition of the meaning of the concept in terms of a personal relationship to God.

The problem of theodicy has caught the attention of J. Crenshaw (1975) and L. Prato. Crenshaw singles out two solutions contributed by Sirach to the problem of theodicy: the complementary parts in the universe, which provide for harmony, and the greater anxiety that God inflicts upon the guilty (1975:58). Prato presents a detailed study of seven passages pertinent to the problem of theodicy (33:7–15; 39:16–45; 42:15–43:33; 15:11–18:14; 40:1–17; 41:1–13). He has captured the style of reasoning employed by Ben Sira: the posing of the problem, the reply, the argument. In every argument Sirach has recourse to creation, and for two purposes: (1) to show how things were "at the beginning" and (2) to analyze the situation in terms of the functions assigned to things by the creator (385). Prato shows how Ben Sira has recourse to the original polarity in creation (Sir 33:15: things come in opposites). G. Maier (113–15) correctly recognizes an abiding tension in the doctrine of Ben Sira—a certain determinism on the one hand, and on the other a clear affirmation of the freedom of the will (see Sir 15:12–20)—and J. Hadot has underscored the freedom of the will in Sirach. Ben Sira's presentation of the human makeup (Sirach 17) has been analyzed by L. Alonso Schökel (1978) and J. de Fraine. M. Gilbert (1974) has attempted to absolve Ben Sira from misogynism (McKeating; Trenchard).

The "praise of the fathers" (chaps. 44–50) has been studied by T. Maertens, R. T. Siebeneck, and E. Jacob. The similarity to the genre *De viris illustribus* has been noted by many, and there is a general agreement that Sirach puts forth Israel's heroes as worthy of imitation for Jews in a Hellenistic world. G. von Rad emphasizes the change from the historical writing of the past. Instead of God and his actions, human activity comes to the forefront (257–58). P. Höffken explains the surprising silence about Ezra as a sign of a certain anti-Levitical bias (in contrast to the Chronicler).

Sirach 24 is generally recognized as a high point in Ben Sira's thought. P. Skehan (1979) has made a thorough study of its structure and provided a reconstruction of the original Hebrew. Other literary studies were made by H. Conzelmann and Gilbert (1974). Conzelmann assessed 24:3–7 in terms of *Religionsgeschichte* and pointed out the similarity to the Isis aretalogies (these verses would be "a song to Isis, practically taken over word for word, and lightly touched up only in one or two places" [228]). Gilbert stressed the association of *homichlē* ("mist") in 24:3 with the *ʿēd* of Gen 2:6 and the relationship between 24:23 concerning law/wisdom and Deut 4:6 (see also Marböck, 1971:95). Marböck has rightly set Sirach 24 in the broader context of the several explicit discussions of wisdom in Sirach (1:1–10; 4:11–19; 14:20–15:10; 6:18–37; 38:24–39:11; 51:13–30). This makes clear the theological understanding of wisdom in Sirach; she is not a hypostasis or a demiurge, but "a poetic personification for God's intimate activity and for his personal summons" (Marböck, 1971:130). Theological wisdom is a new way in which Israel understands herself, since the election is now taken up into wisdom with the identity of wisdom and law. At the same time, wisdom achieves a unity between creation and Israel's history (1971:68–74, 131).

The Future of Ben Sira Scholarship

There is a continuing need for text-critical analysis because of the peculiarities in the transmission of the text. Little has been done about the literary features, such as meter (Mowinckel) and composition (Fuss). One may expect synthetic presentations of Sirach's thought along the lines of the initial studies that have been noted. Unfortunately, little as yet is known about the life setting of Ben Sira and his "school" (Sir 51:23). However, the last twenty years have marked a resurgence in the study of this book which will doubtless continue.

THE WISDOM POEM IN BARUCH 3:9–4:4

This passage was a favorite among the Greek and Latin fathers, who interpreted 3:38 as a reference to the incarnation of Jesus Christ (there is no evidence that it is a Christian interpolation). In contrast, there have been few recent studies of the passage or even of the entire book. Brief commentaries to accompany a translation have been produced by H. Schneider, A. Gelin, A. H. J. Gunneweg, and L. Alonso Schökel. There are lengthier works by V. Hamp (1950a), A. Penna, B. Wambacq, and C. A. Moore. J. Battistone has written a dissertation on the literary and the theological background of the wisdom poem. D. Burke has reconstructed and analyzed the original Hebrew text of Bar 3:9–5:9.

Baruch has been preserved in Greek as the primary text, but there is good reason to think that most (certainly 1:1–3:8), if not all, was written originally in Hebrew. A critical edition of the Greek text has been published by J. Ziegler, and E. Tov has provided a reconstruction of the Hebrew of 1:1–3:8. The work attributed to Jeremiah's scribe is short but composite, and at least three parts have been recognized: 1:1–3:8 (cf. Dan 9:9–19 for 1:15–2:19); 3:9–4:4; 4:5–5:9 (cf. *Psalms of Solomon* 11 for 4:30–5:6). One cannot be precise about the dating of the several parts, but theories range from about 200 B.C.E. to the first half of the first century C.E.

The wisdom poem is notably similar to Job 28. However, it is given a peculiar literary setting by means of an introduction: why is Israel as one who is dead, in exile? Answer: she has abandoned the spring of wisdom. Hence, Israel is invited to learn where wisdom is (3:9–14). Battistone (26–27), following Wambacq, judges that 3:10–13 is probably a later addition. It is reasonable to regard it as a deliberately contrived setting. The poem itself concentrates on the same question as Job 28: who knows where wisdom lives? The answer is, of course, no one (3:15–31)—except God, who has given her to Israel (3:32–38). In 4:1 wisdom is explicitly identified with the Torah, as in Sir 24:23. Finally, reverting to the introductory lines, the author of the work invites "Jacob" to take hold of wisdom. Jacob's distress will then be ended.

Several new things appear in this poem, even if the theme of the inaccessibility of wisdom is an old one. First, there is the application of the wisdom poem to salvation history, and v. 27 makes a clear connection between election and wisdom. Second, although Israel had always recognized wisdom as being an international possession, now it is denied to non-Israelites (vv. 16–23), because it is identified with the Torah. The traditional theme of inaccessibility has yielded to accessibility in the Torah. If one were to sketch a trajectory of personified wisdom in Jewish tradition, this poem fits after Job 28 and Sirach 24 (see Le Moyne: 732, for a comparison with Sirach).

THE LETTER OF ARISTEAS

Complete bibliographies on this work are offered by G. Delling and J. H. Charlesworth, and S. Jellicoe has a valuable summary of recent studies. Here we shall limit ourselves to the discussions of the Septuagint and Aristeas.

P. Kahle interpreted the letter as propaganda in favor of a new revision of the Greek Torah, and thus he attacked the thesis of P. de Lagarde that the Septuagint could be traced back to one prototype in the pre-Christian period. For other reasons (mainly because of Qumran discoveries) than the ambiguous section 30 of the *Letter*, it appears that Kahle was wrong. The present trend (Bickerman; Gooding; Howard; Zuntz) is to recognize that section 30 refers to poorly copied Hebrew manuscripts extant in Egypt and not to previous translations of the Law.

The fictional character of the description of the translation of the Torah is recognized by all, but the general purpose of the letter is disputed. Propaganda it is. Generally, this seems to be directed toward pagan authorities, seeking their appreciation for Judaism and Jewish law. However, Howard, anticipated in some respects by V. Tcherikover, has argued that it is an apology directed against Palestinian Judaism by Diaspora Jews who wanted to vindicate the translation of the Law. Zuntz (1959a) has studied some of the sources that must have been behind the composition. The most recent critical translations have been done by N. H. Meisner and A. Pelletier. Meisner expresses the view that the banquet scene does not contain Israelite wisdom material (41).

ARISTOBULUS

N. Walter (1964) has demonstrated the authenticity of the fragments and given an impressive interpretation of the function of allegorization in Aristobulus, the earliest witness to this development in Alexandria. Hengel found explicit in Aristobulus the identification of wisdom with the Stoic Logos, an identification which he saw implicitly at work in Sirach (1974:168). Charlesworth summarized as follows (81): "[He] combined Pythagorean, Platonic, and Stoic thought with Jewish ideas, especially those characteristic of Proverbs, Ben Sira, the Wisdom of Solomon, Pseudo-Phocylides, and 4 Maccabees." It does appear possible to place Aristobulus in the tradition of wisdom. He cites Prov 8:22 to support the interpretation of the *hebdomad* in Gen 2:1-4a as the source of all light; he uses the metaphor of "following her" to find rest; and he describes Moses as having both wisdom and divine spirit. One might argue, too, for the correlation of wisdom and Logos, since the *hebdomad* is taken to be symbolic of both. What is far from clear is the extent to which wisdom reflection on the Torah may have played a role in the view of the Pentateuch that called for such allegorization. There is in Aristobulus a freedom to cite Greek authors alongside Moses in support of his express intent to argue for the transcendence and power of the one God. And he rationalizes the need for interpretation in order to come to true and philosophical (*physichos*) ideas about God. Thus, the status of the Pentateuch itself, both as source and as authority for the true conceptions is unclear. Nor is the intention of the exegetical endeavor—whether apologetic or theologically constructive—clear. Nevertheless, the combination of wisdom terminology, a theology of

creation, corresponding philosophical conceptuality, and allegorical interpretation of the Pentateuch in the interest of a philosophically defensible
ethical theism is impressive evidence for a constructive theology along
wisdom lines. The new developments would be the explication of wisdom's
order in philosophical terms, and the quest for the reflection of this order
in the Pentateuch itself. Both of these concerns are clearly in evidence in
the Wisdom of Solomon and in Philo.

THE WISDOM OF SOLOMON

Literary Analysis

The publication of the critical edition of the Greek text in 1962
(Ziegler) stimulated an already rich and long tradition of scholarship on the
Wisdom of Solomon. Those who first studied the literary structure of
Wisdom were able to work with the Swete edition, and A. G. Wright
(1967a) preferred Swete because of its versification. Skehan (1945) attempted a reconstruction of the text essentially by expanding MS B from
1108 to 1120 *stichoi* in the interest of a stichometric theory according to
which chaps. 1–10 and chaps. 11–19 originally consisted of 560 *stichoi*
each. Wright (1965, 1967b) combined this thesis with J. M. Reese's discovery of the *inclusio* in Wisdom (1965) to argue for patterns of units of
composition which he found to be those of concentric symmetry in the form
abcb'a' (Wisdom 1–6; 7–8; 13–15), parallel symmetry (chap. 9), and linear
sequencing of repetition (chap. 10) and development (chaps. 11–19).
Wright supported his thesis of compositional units by a study of the relationships of the number of verses per section which he found to reflect the
proportional ratio of the so-called golden section (1967a).

In 1970, Reese built upon these beginnings, though without taking up
Wright's theory of numerical patterns, and produced a major work on the
influences of Hellenistic language, conceptuality, style, and literary genre
in Wisdom. His main contribution to the study of the literary composition
of the book was probably the rhetorical analysis, which took up older
scholarship in this area, contributed new findings, and presented a unified
thesis for the composition and intention of the book. Wisdom as a whole
was found to be a *protrepic*, which combines as smaller units the following
genres: diatribe (1:1–6:11; 6:16–20; 11:15–15:19), aporia (6:12–16; 6:21–
10:21), sorites (6:17–20), and syncrisis (11:1–14; 16:1–19:22). The unity of
the book was supported by a study of "flashbacks" and themes. Reese concluded that the author of this piece of educational literature ". . . was evidently a teacher in one of the Jewish centers of learning in Alexandria, well
acquainted with contemporary culture and committed to demonstrating
the relevance of the principles of Judaism to the future intellectual leaders
of his people" (1970:151).

It should be noted that the unity of the book has found strong support in Reese's analysis of its composition and that its intention, setting, and mode of argumentation have been clarified to some extent by his analysis of its rhetorical genre. But the question of meaning stubbornly remains after all, and it is not really furthered in Reese's summary statements, for example: ". . . to enable the future intellectual leaders of his people to develop a positive attitude toward their actual situation" (148), or ". . . to show the relation between their sacred history and the growth of the entire human race" (150). This question—that is, the question of meaning—has been engaged at a deeper level by the literary analysis of M. Gilbert.

In his article of 1970 and his monograph of 1973 Gilbert combined rhetorical and structuralist methods in an analysis of two textual units (1970: Wisdom 9; 1973: Wisdom 13–15), exploring their principles of composition and thought in relation both to Greek and to biblical analogues. He was able to elucidate the artistic skill with which the author related biblical and Hellenistic themes and language forms in the interest of the creation of a new expression which recast the ideas and modes of argumentation of each tradition to achieve a statement of significant theological consequence. He found Wisdom 13–15 to be a whole that is structured concentrically by theme in the pattern abcb'a', coming to focus on 14:21, where the polemic against idolatry (central theme) is related to the question of the knowledge of God (central theological concern). Indebted to Hellenistic *topoi* which reject or rationalize idols and animals as symbols of the gods, the theological point or polemic is inexplicable until one sees its roots in Jewish traditions and its function in the book of Wisdom as a theological statement that clarifies the position of Judaism vis à vis paganism in the Hellenistic milieu. In Gilbert's work the analysis of literary structure and composition was capable of taking up the questions of sources and systems of thought as well as explorations of the dimension of scriptural hermeneutic that was involved. It is an excellent study and stands as the finest achievement yet in the area of the literary-compositional analysis of Wisdom.

Sources of Its Religious Thought

Hellenistic Philosophy

Scholarly concern to place Wisdom in the traditions of Hellenistic philosophical and religious thought—a concern to which many fine works of the earlier periods were devoted—has continued to be very strong throughout the postwar period. Articles that explore sources of particular themes include Dupont-Sommer (immortality of the soul and astrological mysticism); Finan; Gill (description of Dionysiac rites); and Sweet (theory of miracles). Mention should also be made of the study by Vellas (1961), though it was not available for review, and of the fact that most monographs dealing with a theme, such as that of Gilbert (1973), have found it necessary to trace and evaluate the Hellenistic sources.

The state of scholarship in this area in general can be assessed by a review of the works of Larcher, Reese (1970), and Winston. Larcher's comprehensive study of the literary-historical relations of Wisdom with biblical, Jewish, Greek, and Christian literatures presented an exhaustive collection of the literary, linguistic, and semantic parallels that pertain, as well as a critical summary of scholarship on the direction and nature of the influence indicated. Since he organized the book by classification of the extra-Wisdom corpora and did not include an index to passages in Wisdom, it is difficult to use as a general resource for exegesis. But the study itself is first-rate at the level of *Motivgeschichte*, and Larcher came to some important conclusions regarding sources. In regard to the sources for Greek philosophical thought, he rejected earlier attempts to determine particular authors (such as Posidonius) or schools (such as Stoic) in favor of Hellenistic manuals or epitomes of philosophical traditions produced in the eclectic Alexandrian milieu. In keeping with his long-standing interest in the French tradition, Larcher gave special attention to the idea of the immortality of the soul, which he found to be a Greek concept, though qualified in Wisdom by means of its dependence upon one's righteousness, and the concept of wisdom itself, for which Larcher found only echoes in Greek speculation.

Reese's work was not as exhaustive as Larcher's, but he did expand upon Larcher's collection of Hellenistic literatures from which lines of influence might be drawn. Especially important in this regard were found to be the kingship tracts as sources for Wisdom's anthropological imagery, the Hellenistic Isis aretalogies as sources for the configuration of Wisdom, and the works of Philodemus as offering new and helpful parallels to the terminology and conceptuality of the immortality of the soul. In the 1979 commentary by Winston the question of the relationship to Hellenistic philosophical thought was approached in two ways. The notes of the commentary are replete with extensive references to the literature of the philosophical traditions, and in the introduction the "religious ideas" of Wisdom are discussed in such a way as to place them firmly within the traditions of Greek philosophy. Considerable attention was given to the ideas of the preexistence, immortality, and eschatology of the soul, the idea of wisdom, and the problem of determinism and the freedom of the will. It is clear that Winston understands many of these ideas and problems to be rooted in Jewish tradition as well, but he did not discuss the phenomenon of double source as a syncretistic or hermeneutical moment of significance.

Special note should be made of the work of Reese and of Mack (1973) on the relation of Wisdom 6–9 and the Isis aretalogies. Both have documented the extent to which the aretalogies provide close parallels to the description of Wisdom. Reese has done this to show another example of

Hellenistic influence, whereas Mack has applied his study to illustrate the way in which the wisdom tradition continued to be open to these sources for its metaphors in Isis mythology. The question of the relation of Isis mythology to the Hellenistic philosophical conceptuality in Wisdom has not yet been explored adequately.

Biblical and Jewish Sources

The quest to place Wisdom in the traditions of Judaism of the Second Temple period has not been pursued as aggressively, nor with as clear a focus, as that for its Hellenistic philosophical placement. On the one hand, Wisdom was simply accepted as a product of (Hellenistic) Judaism and therefore one did not need to prove Jewish influence; on the other hand, the conception of "sources" and traditions in this direction was more vague and therefore more difficult to apply in research. There has been significant work, nonetheless, on three fronts: the extent to which Wisdom knew and used the Septuagint; the relation of Wisdom to literature of the Second Temple period, especially apocalyptic writings and literature from Qumran; and the relation of Wisdom to a wisdom tradition of theology.

Skehan (1940, 1948), Wevers, and Larcher have all explored the extent to which citations of, allusions to, and use of the language of the Septuagint may be documented in Wisdom. Here the question has not yet been placed as a problem in understanding the hermeneutic involved, but important findings have resulted. Larcher has summarized this effort and noted, for instance, that Wisdom used a Greek text with similarities to Symmachus (see Fichtner, 1938) and Theodotion; that among the books of the Septuagint there is a marked preference for Genesis, Second and Third Isaiah, Proverbs, and Psalms; and that the manner of reference is quite free, both in regard to citation of the text itself and in regard to its interpretation.

The designation by Fichtner (1938:8) of Wisdom as "apocalyptic wisdom" was based on studying the descriptions of the persecution and (cosmic-destiny) vindication of Israel (Wisdom 11–19) and the *Dikaios* (Wisdom 1–5) using language reminiscent of apocalyptic texts. Fichtner (1937:124–26) pointed to *1 Enoch* 91–105. Since the Qumran discoveries there have been several attempts to trace the sources of Wisdom's eschatology to that literature (Grelot, 1958, 1961; Dubarle, 1953; Delcor; Philonenko). Larcher has summed up the discussion with a detailed analysis of the similarities that scholars had suggested (103–29). He concluded that, since there are a number of significant parallels and since the motifs of violence and persecution do reflect a Palestinian rather than an Alexandrian situation, it is possible that the author of Wisdom worked with some literature from Qumran "directly or indirectly" (127). However, because of significant differences, the difficulty of proving specific literary relationships, and the recasting of views of eschatology that takes place in Wisdom, his conclusion must remain hypothetical.

A third area of investigation with regard to placing Wisdom in Jewish traditions of literature and thought has to do with its relation to the wisdom tradition itself. Scholars working in the OT wisdom literature have frequently suggested a line of development through Sirach to Wisdom (e.g., Rylaarsdam; von Rad; Marböck; Crenshaw, 1976:25), but few have taken up the question for special investigation. Mack attempted to work out a typology of the mythological configurations of Wisdom (hidden–transcendent; near–immanent; once near–now retreated) which functioned as theological categories. Mack suggested that, in Wisdom, the dialectic of wisdom as immanent and transcendent, together with the identification of wisdom and *pneuma*, enabled a new theology of revelation. He argued also that the pattern of destiny for the *Dikaios* (Wisdom 1–5), "Solomon" (6–9), the series of patriarchs (10), and Israel as *laos* (11–19) could be understood as developments of wisdom mythology and theology that had focused on the problem of the nature and destiny of Israel. Mention should also be made in this regard of the very important study by Nickelsburg, who was able to show that the "story of the persecution and exaltation of the righteous man" in Wisdom 2, 4–5 was a form of an old wisdom story that had entered the Isaianic tradition (Isaiah 14, 52–53), was reshaped (exaltation became vindication) in the Maccabean traditions, and could be traced through developments in Qumran and the apocalyptic literature. The importance of Nickelsburg's thesis for Wisdom is that it makes possible a way to begin to understand the interrelationships of the Isaianic and apocalyptic influences on Wisdom 1–5 as developments of a genre and concern that had their origin in wisdom thought itself. An excellent recent article by Collins explores the extent to which both the Wisdom of Solomon and Jewish apocalyptic shared "the conviction that the experience of God and even eschatology is mediated through the cosmic order" (138). This shared conviction about the significance of knowing the structure of the world, though prepared for by earlier Semitic views of creation, Collins found to be a product of the Hellenistic environment in which both apocalyptic and conceptualized wisdom developed.

System of Thought and Theology

In 1964, D. Georgi noted that "a serious effort to grasp the self-understanding of Wisdom was not to be found in the entire corpus of secondary literature" (269 n. 30). The failure is due no doubt to the preoccupation of scholarship with questions of composition and sources, which needed to be worked out first. But it is also due to the extremely difficult problem of understanding the Hellenistic-Jewish mode of language and conception of the world and of history. There has been a long tradition of French scholarship devoted to the theological thought of Wisdom, but it has approached the book as a source for the theology of the church and has concentrated on the extent to which Wisdom reflects the ideas of original sin, the immortality of the soul, and wisdom as the spirit of revelation (Dubarle, 1956, 1964a, 1964b; Beauchamp; Drouet; Lacon; Larcher: chaps. 4 and 5). Even Reese concluded his study of Hellenistic influence by discussing how Greek conceptuality allowed the author to "develop biblical themes that had an appeal to Hellenistic readers. . . . [He] universalizes the picture of God's cure for men and stresses the destiny of each man to an incorruptible state of eternal friendship with God" (156).

The older German scholarship understood Wisdom as a document of Hellenistic-Jewish propaganda and mission. In 1954, P. Dalbert discussed this literature as a class and emphasized its three cardinal convictions—monotheism, spiritual revelation, and the election of Israel. There is now less certainty about the apologetic and missionary intention of this literature, but Dalbert's finding with regard to the centers of theological concern remains valid. The question is how to understand the language form and intention of its conceptuality.

Georgi's essay broke new ground in several respects. He saw that Wisdom was working out of the wisdom tradition and its concern for theodicy. In the context of new experiences of persecution, the concern with affirming God's justice in creation eventuated in a form of dualism in which the dynamic aspects of the real world of Wisdom were seen to be separated from the world of empirical experience. The moment of salvation as vindication was now located in the destiny of the righteous one whose early death and exaltation transferred the arena of theodicy into the real world of God's eternal purposes. What the function of this imagery might have been for Jews living in the empirical world was less clearly addressed by Georgi, but by placing it in the context of the wisdom tradition he made it possible to see clearly the problem that was being addressed. Mack emphasized the way in which the pattern of destiny related wisdom mythology and the exodus story and argued that the figures of the righteous ones in all sections of the book functioned as representations of a corporate conception of Israel in the interest of Jewish identity. The problem of the relationship of wisdom mythology to Greek conceptuality in Wisdom was not addressed here, except at the point of seeing the extent to which the employment of certain concepts (e.g., *pneuma*) "explicated" the intentions of the older mythopoetic language of wisdom itself (1973:64).

Mention should also be made of the summary statement of Wisdom's "biblical theology" which Gilbert (1973) was able to make as a conclusion to his study of Wisdom 13–15. His approach to the text had put him in touch with a moment of creative composition in which biblical and Hellenistic traditions of literature and thought could not be isolated for consideration without destroying the new meaning. The new meaning lay precisely in the reinterpretation both of the biblical and of the Hellenistic views on idols, and it achieved a powerful theological understanding of the nature of idolatry as the expression of human achievement and quest for security which frustrates acknowledgment of the transcendent power of God. If one were to relate this finding to the question of the theological concern of the book as a whole, it might not be too much to say that Gilbert has studied what most scholars have called a digression and has shown it to be of central significance for the purpose of the whole. It is not unimportant that this amazing study was achieved by paying attention to the function of the biblical "reminiscences" in the composition and the nature of the language as poetry.

Wisdom and Interpretation

Scholarship on Wisdom has always been interested in its relation to the Hebrew Bible and has collected a sizable list of references under the rubrics of citation of, allusion to, and source of its religious language and ideas. Advancement beyond these rubrics has been very difficult to achieve, however, mainly because a disciplined approach to the question of comparative midrash and hermeneutic has been lacking. Nevertheless, small beginnings at significant observations have been made, evidenced at first by studies that have concentrated on the question of the selection of OT texts in Wisdom and the extent to which they are employed. Here should be mentioned Skehan's works on the references to Isaiah (1940) and the Psalms (1948), G. Ziener's study of the use of scripture in Wisdom, and Larcher's summary (86–103). Larcher's conclusion about Wisdom's preference for Genesis, Isaiah, and the wisdom literature is an important finding in itself. He noted further that the Isaianic material was heavy in Wisdom 1–5; that, in addition to sapiential language in Wisdom 6–9, Wisdom 9 was working with 1 Kings 3; and that Wisdom 11–19 interwove themes from the Genesis account to achieve a kind of midrash on the exodus story. One should add the obvious interpretation of the patriarchal narratives of Genesis in chap. 10. Taken together, the evidence points to a serious reflection on the scriptures and calls for investigation of the methods and principles of hermeneutic involved. Most have been content to note an anthological style of selection with its enhancement of the resulting language as "religious." But in 1957, M. J. Suggs made the creative suggestion that Wisdom 2:10–5 was a homily based on the fourth servant song. The subsequent studies of Georgi and Nickelsburg have qualified this thesis somewhat by pointing to an Isaianic (exegetical) tradition that Wisdom took up for its own literary purposes. Nevertheless, the exegetical nature of that tradition is clear, and the question of the hermeneutical intention of Wisdom 2:10–5 remains. Reese has rejected Suggs's thesis on the basis of what he understood to be the passage's Greek literary form and didactic intention (113). Reese argued also against the long-standing designation of Wisdom 11–19 as a "midrash" on the basis that it does not provide a "commentary" on the text in "some orderly fashion" (1970:98). His resistance to the question of the hermeneutical aspects of Wisdom illustrates the poverty of that tradition of scholarship which has looked only for the system of Hellenistic-philosophical ideas in Wisdom. Again it is Gilbert who pointed the way to a more appropriate placing of the question in the interest of a more adequate grasp of its "biblical theology." The next task will be an exploration of the hermeneutic that could achieve such a theology.

Date and Provenance

There is no consensus about dating, though recent studies have tended to argue for the Augustan age rather than an earlier date, and Winston has suggested the reign of Caligula (38-41 c.e.) as the most probable. Occasionally Syria has been proposed as a place (Georgi and earlier scholars), but most scholars continue to assume Alexandrian provenance.

PHILO OF ALEXANDRIA

E. Hilgert's bibliography of scholarship on Philo in the postwar period contains over 850 entries. The selection of studies for the present article is limited to major works and studies that, in the opinion of the reviewer, enable an assessment of the present state of scholarship and its trends. It will not be possible here, for instance, to discuss a rich literature on the importance of the Philonic witness for reconstructing the history of Hellenistic philosophy, Jewish and Roman history, for NT exegetical studies, and the influence of Alexandrian Judaism on the early Christian fathers. There are three introductions to Philo: Daniélou; Goodenough, 1962; Sandmel, 1979. Reviews of the scholarship from different perspectives may be found in Thyen, 1955a; Hamerton-Kelly, 1972; and Mack, 1984. The period has witnessed two conferences on Philo, one in Lyon in 1966 (Centre National) and one in Alexandria in 1963 (Daumas). Three collaborative projects have emerged. The Lyon group, under the direction of C. Mondésert, has produced a French translation-edition of the corpus, which contains the Greek text, some critical-exegetical notes, and introductions to each treatise. It constitutes the most notable achievement of the period, contributes to questions of philological, source and literary criticism, and in some cases creatively takes up the question of the hermeneutical significance of the allegory and the commentary form. It has also produced the scholarly discussions from which the new directions have emerged, as is evidenced by other published work of many of its contributors. A second project is under way at the Institute for Antiquity and Christianity, Claremont, to explore exegetical traditions in Philo—a project that grew out of the earlier work of the Philo Institute at McCormick Theological Seminary, Chicago

(Mack, 1974–75). A third project at the Center for Hermeneutical Studies, Berkeley, is producing a commentary on *De gigantibus* and *Quod Deus immutabilis sit*. The Philadelphia Seminar on Christian Origins has collaborated (1978–79) on a study of W. Bousset's 1915 thesis of exegetical school traditions in Alexandria.

Literary Analysis

Texts and Translations

The principal edition of the text by L. Cohn and P. Wendland (1896–1930) was reprinted in 1962. The Loeb and French editions for translation have made only minor changes in the printed text and offered discussions of variations and emendations in the notes. Text criticism in our period has appeared only in the form of brief articles and notes on specific problems. An index of the corpus has finally appeared (Mayer), though without including the Greek fragments on the *Quaestiones*. A critical edition of the ancient Latin translation of the Armenian text of the *Quaestiones* has been published by F. Petit. The preparation of the Greek fragments at the Institutum Judaicum, Münster, by James Royse, is very close to completion. The Philo Institute at McCormick is collecting microfilms of the Armenian corpus, and Abraham Terian's critical edition of the Armenian text of *De animalibus* has recently appeared. In addition to the French translation project, which is now complete except for the *Quaestiones*, the final volumes both of the Loeb and of the German translation series have appeared. A few Hebrew translations have appeared.

Literary Sources

The older quest for Philo's literary sources in a documentary sense has not been pursued vigorously in the postwar period. This is probably due in part to the failure of many studies to establish much more than probable dependence in matters of form or content on the basis of similarity to generally comparable Hellenistic examples. But the studies of A. H. Chroust and W. Lameere should be mentioned as indications that the quest has not ended. The question of Philo's Septuagint text is unresolved (see Katz; Howard).

Literary Composition

The history of Philonic scholarship is not distinguished for its work in literary criticism. Philo has been read mainly by philosophers and theologians, who have looked for his ideas instead of noting his literary activity. Nevertheless, some advance beyond the older satisfaction with the designation "diatribe" can be noted and needs to be supported. One development has been the introduction of "homily" as a description of the particular

form of the diatribe style in Philo (Thyen, 1955b; Borgen, 1965). Another
has been the expansion of the investigation to include other Hellenistic
rhetorical genres that may have influenced Philo's compositions (Michel;
Hamerton-Kelly, 1976). A third approach has been suggested in the work
of Cazeaux, namely, structuralist (1965). It is indicative of the scholarship
that the commentary form itself has not been investigated seriously in
comparison with Hellenistic commentaries on Homer and the *Timaeus*,
though these are frequently cited as analogues (Borgen, 1976–77).

The Sources of his Religious Thought

The history of scholarship on Philo has been determined largely by
two questions: (1) What were the sources of his religious thought? (2) What
are the components and structure of his own system of thought? Three
major works stand at the beginning of the period under discussion, representing three scholarly traditions that have taken different positions with
respect to these questions. Goodenough (1935) sought the sources of Philo's
thought in the Hellenistic mystery religions and made the attempt to reconstruct a Jewish mystery religion in Alexandria that interpreted and celebrated the Torah as revelation of the sacred order available in the mystery.
W. Völker (1938) reacted vigorously against this interpretation and offered
an explanation of Philo as a theologian of the biblical tradition who
employed the categories of Hellenistic philosophy and religion in the
interest of confronting the Hellenistic world with the ideas of the Jewish
faith. H. A. Wolfson acknowledged Philo's loyalty to the principles of
Jewish faith but saw Philo's concern and contribution to the history of ideas
to be the construction of a system of religious philosophy for which he was
indebted primarily to the Greek school traditions, among which the
Platonic was found to be the most decisive. In the period under discussion
each of these three positions has been qualified in significant ways, even
though the problem that they illustrate—of finding Philo's place in relation
to the sources of his religious thought—remains the fundamental question.

Hellenic and Hellenistic Philosophy

The period has been marked by studies that have concentrated upon
particular aspects of Philo's philosophical terminology and conceptuality.
Illustrations are the works of F. W. Eltester on *Eikon*, A. Wlosok on the
ascent-vision, M. Harl and U. Früchtel on cosmologies. The tendency has
been to substantiate Wolfson's placing of Philo predominantly within the
tradition of Platonic thought, and this has been supported by scholarship
on the history of Middle Platonism, which has increasingly come to see
Philo as a reflection of, and therefore a source for, the reconstruction of
Middle Platonism in Alexandria (Krämer; Theiler; Dillon). But these
studies have also made clear the extent to which Philo cannot be viewed

merely as a Platonist, that is, a philosopher whose major concern was to take a position vis à vis the classical philosophical schools in the interest of constructing a new coherent system.

The most important study in this area is that of Früchtel, who was able to show Philo's indebtedness to a variety of conflicting Hellenistic cosmologies, which he could use because he understood them as intending a single truth about the ordering of the cosmos by God. Whereas Früchtel saw this assumption of the oneness of philosophical truth in all school traditions as a reflection of the philosophical situation in Alexandria in general, Harl argued for an essentially religious imagination at work, which saw God's power in the world according to oriental models. Both emphasized the function of the philosophical traditions for the hermeneutical enterprise and thus pointed toward the convergence of this line of scholarship with the question of Philo as interpreter of Jewish traditions.

Hellenistic Mystery Religions

Goodenough's thesis has been qualified by further studies of Philo's mythological metaphors which have not found it necessary to posit a mystery religion as a source. Greek mythology can frequently be traced to literary traditions rather than to literal mysteries (e.g., Méasson; Menard); and Mack has argued that the Isis mythologoumena, which were so basic to Goodenough's thesis, can be understood as metaphors of wisdom that intend a theological explanation of Jewish traditions rather than their transformation into a mystery religion.

Jewish Sources

Halakah. At the beginning of the period under discussion the question of Philo's relationship to Judaism focused on comparative halakah. Goodenough (1929) and I. Heinemann (1932) had argued for a unique Alexandrian halakic tradition. S. Belkin (1940) challenged this in the interest of placing Philo in close contact with Pharisaic traditions in Palestine. This debate has not been continued vigorously, nor has it been resolved. For an excellent recent review, see Hecht.

Haggadah. In contrast to the above, there has been considerable research in the area of haggadic traditions. Most of these studies have focused on specific figures and themes, for example, Borgen, 1965 (on manna); Meeks (on Moses); and Sandmel, 1971 (on Abraham). Belkin, too, has turned again and again to the study of comparative midrash to argue for common traditions reflected in Philo and the Palestinian rabbinic midrashim. But the attempt to determine Philo's place within the Jewish traditions of the Second Temple period on the basis of comparative haggadah has not found a way to account for the similarities in the face of marked

differences in interpretive intention. Sandmel spoke of distinct "religios-
ities" and the creative personality of Philo as an author (1971:199). Borgen
discussed the relationship of the haggadah to homiletic composition, but
did not ask about the origination of the haggadah itself. Nevertheless, this
work as a whole does begin to point to the moment of scriptural interpretation as the matrix for haggadic traditions and thus joins in the call for
investigation of the various hermeneutical principles and methods that
may be involved.

Theological and exegetical traditions. Older works that investigated
the possibility of pre-Philonic exegetical traditions reflected in the corpus—
for example, a stoicizing allegory of Adam and Eve as *Nous* and *Aisthesis*
(Bousset), an ethical allegory on etymologies (Stein), a Stoic-Cynic interpretation of the festivals (Heinemann)—have not received much discussion
(Mack, 1984). But there are several major works that have made the
attempt to trace Jewish theological (and exegetical) traditions upon which
Philo may have drawn. H. Hegermann was able to show that a great deal
of the material in Philo that deals with the high priest's robes, the temple,
and the Sinai story reflects a coherent symbolical interpretation of Jewish
cult as cosmic mystery. His thesis was that these interpretations belonged
to a pre-Philonic Jewish tradition that he traced from an original cosmic
symbolism, through a Logos allegorization, to its use as a metaphor in
Philo in the service of ethical instruction. H. F. Weiss showed that Philo's
conception of the Logos as mediator of creation was a development of
earlier Jewish views of wisdom. The work of Laporte (1972) showed the
extent to which Philo was indebted to a tradition of Jewish piety for his
fundamentally religious concern expressed in the notions of grace and
thanksgiving. Mack argued for an understanding of Philo as a wisdom
theologian by tracing the pattern of wisdom configurations from the wisdom tradition into Philo, where they converged with Platonic thought and
Logos speculation. Taken together, these studies point to the probability
of vigorous Jewish theological activity in Alexandria before Philo's time.
With them, the question has been raised concerning the social setting(s) for
such activity and Philo's place within it.

Schools in Alexandria. R. A. Culpepper has summarized the discussion of the question of Jewish schools in Alexandria. The evidence includes
Philo's theological and exegetical activity, and the strong probability of a
rather long tradition of such activity in Jewish and Christian circles in
Alexandria. But the precise manner in which the synagogue may have
functioned as a school, as well as its relation to the Hellenistic schools
which Philo himself must have attended, is not clearly understood. The
difficulty of finding clarity here is illustrated in the discussion of Conley's

paper on "General Education" at the Center for Hermeneutical Studies in Berkeley (1975).

Patterns and Systems of Thought

Conceptual Systems

A commonplace in reviews of the scholarship on Philo has been to distinguish between those who attribute to him a coherent system of thought and those who see him merely as a collector of disparate *topoi* for practical and pedagogical purposes. The chief representative of the first group in the period under discussion is Wolfson, who, in spite of the "peculiar literary form in which the works of Philo are written," worked out the "systematic structure of his thought" (1945:vi–vii). This he found to be a religious philosophy whose systematization was achieved by integrating the scriptural presuppositions of faith with the Hellenic philosophies of reason. Wolfson reconstructed this new philosophy as a coherent system of conceptualities of God, the world, humanity, epistemology, and ethics. His study stands as the greatest achievement of the period by a single scholar, respected as an important and constructive work in the history of ideas. But its significance for the history of Philonic scholarship is extremely difficult to assess. His thesis about Philo's position with regard to the traditional philosophic schools has not been accepted by Dillon (182), and his creation of a new philosophy on the model of philosophy as the servant of scripture has been criticized by Winston (in Conley: 18–20). But more telling is the fact that Philonic scholarship has simply failed to engage Wolfson's work, choosing to regard it mainly as a monument to a tradition of scholarship, not as a charter for the new directions that scholarship must take. The new directions have turned, rather, to the "peculiar literary form" of the commentary as the clue to Philo's structure of thought.

The book by Maddalena is the only other attempt in the period under discussion at a reconstruction of a system of thought in Philo, in this case a theology of grace and salvation. Its reflection of Christian theological concerns will hinder its integration into the recent scholarship.

Patterns of Metaphor

Another characteristic of Philonic scholarship, related to interest in the systematic aspects of his thought, has been the repeated finding of major metaphors that appear to function as structuring devices according to some scheme of contrasts and stages. The single most important major metaphor has been the imagery of the path or way. Windisch, Pascher, Völker, and Mack all saw the path with its two stages as an organizing principle of Philonic thought that could be related on the one hand to his cosmology with its two orders, and on the other to the process of allegorization itself with its movement from the (literal) text to its significance.

Goodenough (1935) saw the stages in terms of the two mysteries, and Mendelson saw them in terms of the two educational stages. Mack argued that the narrative of the exodus had been identified with the way of wisdom and has been interpreted according to its pattern of stages, that is, discipline and fulfillment. In these studies a structuring principle of thought, exegesis, and composition has been seen that is not philosophical but hermeneutical.

Philo as Biblical Interpreter

The clear tendency in the period under discussion has been the increasing awareness that Philo must be read primarily as an interpreter of scripture. To understand the intention of his language and the composition of his commentaries one must discover the principles that govern his hermeneutic.

Allegory

The traditional view was that Philo simply took over the method of Hellenistic allegorization of (especially) Homer and used it (arbitrarily) to win from the scriptures a reflection of Greek philosophy and ethics. Its purpose was apologetic (see Pépin: 231–42). In 1969, I. Christiansen, working in the tradition of Wolfson and Früchtel, sought to clarify the technique by which the Platonist Philo actually derived a philosophical concept from the scriptural text. She argued that the diaeretic technique of ordering reality, which for Plato began with the world of ideas, was applied by Philo to the words of scripture taken as symbols. The symbolic equivalent was won by discovering a diaeretic scheme that could relate the scriptural term and a symbol, usually as subdivisions of a more general category that could assume both and guarantee their equivalence. The categories themselves were found to be the ten Aristotelian categories for the attributes of existing things. Thus, the allegorical technique may be described, according to Christiansen, as the scholastic means by which the words of the scripture could be taken as symbols for a world of existent phenomena ordered diaeretically.

This extremely important attempt to investigate the hermeneutical principle of Philonic allegory did not move beyond the conception of Philo as a systematic philosopher and cannot account for his religious and ethical concerns, nor for a great deal of symbolic and allegorical interpretation which appears not to illustrate the principle. But the asking of the question and the discovery of the importance of a diaeretic pattern of exegetical thought at all marked a significant moment in Philonic scholarship. Because of Christiansen's work it will no longer be possible to avoid the question of hermeneutical principle involved in the allegories.

The Commentaries as Systems

In 1977, Nikiprowetzky published a 1974 dissertation in which he could show that many of the enduring problems in Philonic research could be resolved in principle if it were acknowledged that Philo's essential concern was with a religious interpretation of the Torah and that his employment of conceptual systems was determined by that concern. He did not engage the question of the logic or method of allegorization directly, but he did lay the foundation for such an investigation by showing clearly the presuppositions for the allegorical enterprise. These were found to be the series of identifications of wisdom, the law of Moses, and the law of nature, as well as the series of distinctions between Greek philosophy, wisdom, and the practical wisdom of life according to the law of Moses. He went on to argue for the unity of the allegorical and expositional series of commentaries, indicating that the Pentateuch itself was the structuring principle of the series and calling for the investigation of the modes of interpretation by which Philo could transform the narrative of the Pentateuch into a pattern for the way to spiritual and intellectual wisdom.

The Types of Exegetical Activity

Studies are now under way that ask about the various methods of scriptural interpretation evidenced in the commentaries. Hamerton-Kelly (1976) and Cazeaux (1979–80) have investigated the composition and structure of treatises as hermeneutical methods. The Philo Project at Claremont is investigating the possibility of a typology of exegetical methods in Philo including the anti-anthropomorphic apology, the encomium, symbol identification, reasoned allegory, development of a theme, and the literal interpretation of the text. If clarity can be won on the question of Philo's hermeneutic it may be possible for scholarship to return to the question of Philo's place both in the history of Alexandrian Judaism and in the history of Hellenistic philosophy with a more precise understanding of his own intention.

Summary

The *status quaestionis* in scholarship on the Wisdom of Solomon and Philo is therefore to be seen in the convergence of the many lines of investigation on the question of hermeneutic. The creativity of the assimilation of Greek conceptuality in the interest of Jewish theological concerns; the possibility of seeing those concerns as developments within a tradition of wisdom thought; the correlations of wisdom patterns of thought, mythology, and narrative with the scriptures; the forms of literary composition as midrash and commentary; the setting in a synagogue-related school—all demand a recognition of the essentially constructive aspects of a syncretism that intended not only an understanding of the scriptures as Greek philosophy but also an interpretation of scripture in terms of Jewish theological traditions, which, to be sure, could be open to the new Greek thought as an aid to conceptualization. To understand the creativity of such a synthesis and the extent to which scripture, tradition, and Hellenistic ethos were all both interpreted and interpreting is the focus of the new quest.

PSEUDO-PHOCYLIDES

Text and Bibliography

A critical edition of the text, which is extant in several Greek manuscripts, was published in the Teubner series by Young in 1961. Bibliographies have been compiled by Delling (1975:56), Charlesworth (1976: 173–75) and van der Horst. A thorough review of the history of scholarship on Pseudo-Phocylides is given in the introduction to van der Horst's publication of the text with translation and commentary. This work is the most extensive study of Pseudo-Phocylides to date, complete with a rich selection of parallels from both Greek and Jewish sources, and makes several fine contributions toward the resolution of critical questions.

Authorship, Date, and Provenance

There is now considerable consensus that Pseudo-Phocylides is of Jewish authorship (Crouch, Charlesworth, van der Horst). This consensus has been difficult to reach because the writing does not include explicit reference to specifically Jewish codes or concerns (see below under "Purpose"). The evidence is given, however, in the summaries of the decalogue and Leviticus 19, as well as in the parallels to ethical and gnomic material in the Pentateuch and wisdom literature of the OT (LXX) which have been combined with Hellenic gnomic material. Analogous selections of universalized Jewish ethic have been noted in Josephus (*Ag. Ap.* 2.190–219) and Philo (*Hypothetica* 7.1–9). There, too, combination with Hellenistic (Stoic) ethical commonplaces has occurred (Crouch). The pseudonym has been explained by van der Horst as an expression of intention to claim for Jewish wisdom-ethic a correlation with the best of the Hellenic tradition of wise and useful advice. Phocylides' popularity and fame as a poet of didactic and gnomic wisdom could account for the ascription of this material to him (see also Hengel).

The openness to the gnomology of the Greek tradition, supported by a study of the incidence of Hellenistic vocabulary, indicates a dating of 50 B.C.E.–100 C.E. with possible provenance in Alexandria (van der Horst).

Genre and Content

The writing combines aspects of aphoristic wisdom, didactic poetry, and gnomological collection. It is written in dactylic hexameter and shows evidence of a Hesiodic-Ionic dialect, this in keeping with Hellenic modes of didactic poetry (van der Horst). Over one half of the material has clear parallels in the Greek gnomological traditions, and most lines can be shown to have both Greek and Jewish parallels. There is no *parallelismus membrorum*, and the preponderance of ethical maxims leaves little room for reflective instruction. There appears to be some arrangement according to topics such as justice, moderation, labor, marriage, and sexual codes. With the exception of a section on death and the afterlife there is no inclusion of philosophical or theological teaching to undergird the ethic. But the writing appears to presuppose an ethical monotheism that assumes that humans can lead their lives in accordance with the divine intention for them. Jewish concerns are reflected in the statements about care for the needy and helpless, the treatment of a stranger, and the severity of the sexual ethic. But there is no inclusion of specifically Jewish codes (e.g., sabbath, circumcision, ritual purity), and the whole is cast in terms of a universalized ethic that reflects commonplaces of the Hellenic and Hellenistic ethical traditions (e.g., Stoic [so Crouch]).

Purpose

There is no consensus on the intention of the writing. Its lack of explicit allusion to Judaism seems to preclude the older view of apologetic or missionary purpose. Van der Horst proposes that it could have provided an intra-Jewish apologetic by showing that Jewish ethic was in agreement with Hellenic ideals. More intriguing, however, is an alternative suggestion by him that it may have been intended for use in the education of Jewish children. He cites the analogy of the use of gnomological material in the Hellenistic school and its twofold purpose—the learning of letters and the inculcation of ethos. As it stands, the writing is an extremely interesting and important document of Jewish-Hellenic syncreticism which was achievable on the basis of wisdom modes of speech and thought. Van der Horst calls it a "didactic poem with a content which may be called gnomic Wisdom" (80).

4 MACCABEES

Text and Bibliography

The text has been published by Rahlfs in his *Septuaginta* and reprinted by Hadas. Bibliography on the scholarship has been published by Hadas, Delling, and Charlesworth. To these should be added the study by Breitenstein and that by Williams.

Contents, Genre, and Sources

The writing contains an account of the martyrdom of Eleazar and of the seven brothers and their mother under Antiochus Epiphanes. By means of an introduction, conclusion, and other interwoven material this account is put forth as proof of the philosophical theme that reason is master of the passions. It is the correlation of these two kinds of material that marks the uniqueness of the writing and presents the scholar with an array of difficult questions.

There is considerable consensus about the author's skilled employment of a wide range of Greek compositional and rhetorical devices. These include the introduction of a theme, the casting of the martyrs as examples, the development of the accounts as encomiums, the use of speeches for characterization, and a concluding exhortation. A full complement of common tropes and rhetorical conventions used in the writing has been documented by Breitenstein. Most scholars have called the writing a diatribe because of its express intention to argue for a statement of truth (Lebram; Hadas; Charlesworth; Williams; and earlier scholars). But the preponderance of encomiastic and paradigmatic material relative to the characterization of the martyrs has led some to consider forms of the panegyric as well (see the next section).

Debated is whether 4 Maccabees is dependent on 2 Maccabees as a source for the martyrologies or whether it has used a source common to them both, perhaps the accounts of Jason of Cyrene to which 2 Maccabees refers. Hadas has argued strongly for dependence on 2 Maccabees, and Breitenstein has shown the extent to which the material in 2 Maccabees has been expanded in 4 Maccabees, especially by means of *ēthopoiia*, that is, characterization by construction of speeches. This employment of a common literary compositional device may be sufficient to account for the differences between the two writings.

The search for a source for the philosophical position of 4 Maccabees from among the traditional Hellenic and Hellenistic schools has moved away from a general reference to Stoicism found in earlier studies. Hadas noted the Platonic aspects of 4 Maccabees' dependence upon the Socratic tradition (*Gorgias*), and Breitenstein has shown the extremely eclectic nature of the author's use of Hellenistic philosophical commonplaces. He has argued that the author has no coherent philosophical position and that he has used hearsay philosophical conceptuality to enhance an ethic that remains essentially Jewish.

There are several tensions and inconsistencies that result from these findings. One has to do with the correlation of the martyrologies with the theme itself, since the martyrdoms exemplify obedience to the Torah and endurance rather than the mastery of passions by reason (Charlesworth). Another has to do with the author's understanding of reason as determined essentially by piety (Breitenstein). A third has to do with the introduction of piety itself as (the chief) virtue that is able to master the passions, an idea that would hardly commend itself to non-Jewish readers (Breitenstein). As it appears, then, the author has used Hellenistic philosophical common-places in the interest of an exhortation to Torah obedience. The precise function of the appeal to Hellenistic conceptuality is yet to be determined.

In another respect the writing has been seen to be very significant in the development of Jewish and Christian martyrology. Especially impor-tant is the idea of the effectiveness of the deaths of the martyrs for the people as a whole. Williams has argued that this idea is a result of creative syncretism, dependent upon the Hellenic heroic and Socratic traditions of the noble death. It is significant that the writing does not contain any reflection about the causes for persecution or the reasons for the efficacy of martyrdom. It is accepted as having paradigmatic power and consequence for the historical circumstance of the people.

Date, Purpose, and Provenance

A traditional late dating into the early second century C.E. has been argued recently by Breitenstein, mainly on the basis of the occurrence of Atticisms (denied by E. Norden and earlier scholars). But Hadas has argued for a dating about 40 C.E. on the basis of internal evidence, purpose, and the appropriateness of historical occasion. He was preceded in this dating by Bickerman and has been supported by Williams. Both Hadas and Williams think that the panegyric aspects of the writing indicate the strong possibility of oral delivery at a commemoration of the martyrs in Antioch. Breitenstein regards the lack of convincing philosophical argumentation as evidence against its appropriateness for such an address. But its purpose as exhortation to steadfastness in obedience to the law (Hadas; Williams) appears to leave open this possibility. Although Antiochian provenance has not been proved, it now appears, following Hadas's argumentation, the strongest probability. Whether as diatribe or as panegyric, the writing is evidence of an openness to Hellenistic literature and thought by a Jew whose ultimate loyalties continued to be determined by Torah obedience and its piety. Hadas has argued that this piety is less exclusivistic in claim than many have thought, showing that the issue of eating swine's flesh, for example, is significant ultimately as a symbol of idolatry and that the rationale for religion in the book as a whole is not out of keeping with Jewish participation in the Hellenistic *oikoumenē* of the early Roman period. The extent to which developments in Jewish wisdom could have enabled such a posture has not been explored.

BIBLIOGRAPHY

Alonso Schökel, Luis
　　1968　　*Proverbios y Ecclesiastico.* Madrid: Ediciones Cristiandad.
　　1976　　"Baruc." Pp. 125–65 in *Los Libros Sagrados* 18. Madrid: Ediciones Cristiandad.

1978 "The Vision of Man in Sirach 16:24–17:14." Pp. 235–45 in *Israelite Wisdom: Theological and Literary Essays in Honor of Samuel Terrien*. Ed. J. G. Gammie. Missoula, MT: Scholars Press.

Arnaldez, Roger, Claude Mondésert, and Jean Pouilloux, eds.
1961– *Les ouevres de Philon d'Alexandrie*. Paris: Cerf.

Baillet, Maurice, Józef Milik, and Roland de Vaux
1962 *Les "Petites Grottes" de Qumran*. DJD 3. Oxford: Clarendon Press.

Barthélemy, Jean-Dominique, and Otto Rickenbacher
1973 *Konkordanz zum hebräischen Sirach*. Göttingen: Vandenhoeck & Ruprecht.

Battistone, Joseph John
1968 "An Examination of the Literary and Theological Background of the Wisdom Passage of the Book of Baruch." Diss., Duke University.

Bauckmann, Ernst Günter
1960 "Die Proverbien und die Sprüche des Jesus Sirach." *ZAW* 72: 33–63.

Beaucamp, Évode
1957 *Sous la main de Dieu II: La Sagesse et le destin des élus*. Paris: Fleurus.

Beauchamp, Paul
1964 "Le salut corporel des justes et la conclusion du livre de la Sagesse." *Bib* 45: 491–526.

Belkin, Samuel
1940 *Philo and the Oral Law*. Cambridge, MA: Harvard University Press.

Bickerman, Elias
1944 "The Colophon of the Greek Book of Esther." *JBL* 63: 339–62.
1945 "The Date of Fourth Maccabees." Pp. 105–12 in *Louis Ginzberg Jubilee Volume*. New York: American Academy for Jewish Research.

Borgen, Peder
1965 *Bread from Heaven: An Exegetical Study of the Concept of Manna in the Gospel of John and the Writings of Philo*. NovTSup 10. Leiden: Brill.
1976–77 "*Quaestiones et Solutiones:* Some Observations on the Form of Philo's Exegesis." *Studia Philonica* 4: 1–15.

Born, Adrianus van den
1968 *Wijsheid van Jesus Sirach (Ecclesiasticus)*. De Boeken van het Oude Testament 8/5. Roermond: Romen.

Bousset, Wilhelm
1915 *Jüdisch-christlicher Schulbetrieb in Alexandria und Rom*. FRLANT 4. Göttingen: Vandenhoeck & Ruprecht.

Breitenstein, Urs
1976 *Beobachtungen zu Sprache, Stil und Gedankengut des vierten Makkabäerbuchs*. Basel/Stuttgart: Schwabc.

Burke, D.
1982 *The Poetry of Baruch*. SBLSCS 10. Chico, CA: Scholars Press.

Caquot, André
1966 "Ben Sira et le messianisme." *Sem* 16: 43–68.

Carmignac, Jean
1961 "Les rapports entre l'Ecclésiastique et Qumran." *RevQ* 3: 209–18.

Cazeaux, Jacques
1965 "Introduction." Pp. 15–80 in *De Migratione Abrahami*. Ed. Jacques Cazeaux. *Les oeuvres de Philon d'Alexandrie* 14. Paris: Cerf.
1979–80 "Système implicite dans l'exégèse de Philon: Un exemple: le *De praemiis*." *Studia Philonica* 6: 3–36.

Centre National de la Recherche Scientifique
1967 *Philon d'Alexandre: Lyon 11–15 Septembre 1966*. Colloques nationaux du Centre national de la recherche scientifique. Paris: Editions du Centre National de la Recherche Scientifique.

Charlesworth, James H.
1976 *The Pseudepigrapha and Modern Research*. SBLSCS 7. Missoula, MT: Scholars Press.

Christiansen, Irmgard
1969 *Die Technik der allegorischen Auslegungswissenschaft bei Philon von Alexandrien*. Beiträge zur Geschichte der biblischen Hermeneutik 7. Tübingen: Mohr-Siebeck.

Chroust, Anton Hermann
1971 "A Fragment of Aristotle's On Philosophy: Some Remarks about Philo of Alexandria, *De Aeternitate Mundi* Q 8, 41." *Wiener Studien*, N.F. 8 (87): 15–19.
1974 "A Fragment of Aristotle's On Philosophy in Philo of Alexandria *De Opificio Mundi* I.7." *Divus Thomas* 77: 224–35.

Cohn, Leopold, and Paul Wendland, eds.
1896–1930 *Philonis Alexandrini Opera quae Supersunt I–VII*. Berlin: de Gruyter. Reprinted 1962.

Collins, John J.
1977 "Cosmos and Salvation: Jewish Wisdom and Apocalyptic in the Hellenistic Age." *HR* 17: 121–42.

Conley, Thomas
1975 *"General Education" in Philo of Alexandria*. Colloquy 15. Berkeley: Center for Hermeneutical Studies.

Conzelmann, Hans
1964 "Die Mutter der Weisheit." Pp. 225–34 in *Zeit und Geschichte: Dankesgabe an Rudolf Bultmann zum 80. Geburtstag*. Ed. E. Dinkler. Tübingen: Mohr-Siebeck.

Crenshaw, James L.
1975 "The Problem of Theodicy in Sirach: On Human Bondage." *JBL* 94: 47–64.
1976 "Prolegomenon." Pp. 1–60 in *Studies in Ancient Israelite Literature*. Ed. James L. Crenshaw. New York: Ktav.

Crouch, James E.
1972 *The Origin and Intention of the Colossian Haustafel*. FRLANT 109. Göttingen: Vandenhoeck & Ruprecht.

Culpepper, R. Alan
1975 *The Johannine School*. SBLDS 26. Missoula, MT: Scholars Press.

Dalbert, Peter
1954   *Die Theologie der hellenistisch-jüdischen Missionsliteratur unter Ausschluss von Philo und Josephus.* Theologische Forschung 4. Hamburg-Volksdorf: Reich.

Daniélou, Jean
1958   *Philon d'Alexandrie.* Paris: Fayard.

Daumas, François
1964   "Philon d'Alexandrie et le problème des Thérapeutes." *Compte rendu et commentaire de la conférence donnée le 12 décembre 1963 au siége de la Y.M.C.A. sous les auspices de la Société archaéologique d'Alexandrie.* Conferences 1. Alexandrie.

de Fraine, Jean
1950   "Het loflied op de menselijke waardigheid in Eccli 17, 1–14." *Bijdragen* 11: 10–23.

Delcor, Matthias
1955   "L'immortalité de l'âme dans le Livre de la Sagesse et dans les documents de Qumrân." *NRT* 77: 614–30.

Delling, Gerhard
1975   *Bibliographie zur jüdisch-hellenistischen und intertestamentarischen Literatur 1900–1970.* TU 106. 2d ed. Berlin: Akademie.

Desecar, Alejandro J.
1970   *La sabiduría y la necedad en Sirac 21–22.* Pontificium Athenaeum Antonianum: Theses ad Lauream 199. Rome: Edizioni Francescane.

Di Lella, Alexander A.
1964   "The Recently Identified Leaves of Sirach in Hebrew." *Bib* 45: 153–67.
1966   *The Hebrew Text of Sirach.* The Hague: Mouton.

Dillon, John
1977   *The Middle Platonists 80 B.C. to A.D. 220.* Ithaca, NY: Cornell University Press.

Dommershausen, Werner
1973   "Zum Vergeltungsdenken des Ben Sira." Pp. 37–43 in *Wort und Geschichte: Festschrift für Karl Elliger zum 70. Geburtstag.* Ed. H. Gese and H. P. Rüger. AOAT 18. Kevelaer: Butzon & Bercker.

Drouet, Jacques
1966   *Le Livre de la Sagesse.* Paris: Mame.

Dubarle, André Marie
1953   "Une source du livre de la Sagesse?" *RSPT* 37: 424–43.
1956   "Le péché originel dans les livre sapientiaux." *RevThom* 56: 597–619.
1964a   *The Biblical Doctrine of Original Sin.* New York: Herder.
1964b   "La tentation diabolique dans le Livre de la Sagesse (2,24)." Pp. 187–95 in *Mélanges Eugéne Tisserant I.* Studi e Testi 231. Vatican City: Biblioteca Apostolica Vaticana.

Duesberg, Hilaire, and Paul Auvray
1953   *Le livre de l'Ecclésiastique.* Paris: Cerf.

Duesberg, Hilaire, and Irénée Fransen
1966   *Ecclesiastico. La sacra Bibbia.* Turin and Rome: Marietti.

Dupont-Sommer, André
1949   "De l'immortalité dans la 'Sagesse de Salomon.'" *Revue des études grecques* 62: 80–87.

Eltester, Friedrich Wilhelm
1958   *Eikon im Neuen Testament.* BZNW 23. Berlin: Töpelmann.

Fang Che-Young, M.
1963   "Ben Sira de novissimis hominum." *VD* 41: 21–38.

Fichtner, Johannes
1937   "Die Stellung der Sapientia Salomonis in der Literatur und Geistesgeschichte ihrer Zeit." *ZNW* 36: 113–32.
1938   *Weisheit Salomos.* HNT 2/6. Tübingen: Mohr-Siebeck.

Finan, Thomas
1960   "Hellenistic Humanism in the Book of Wisdom." *ITQ* 27: 30–48.

Früchtel, Ursula
1968   *Die kosmologischen Vorstellungen bei Philo von Alexandrien: Ein Beitrag zur Geschichte der Genesis-Exegese.* ALGHJ 2. Leiden: Brill.

Fuss, Werner
1963   "Tradition und Komposition im Buche Jesus Sirach." *TLZ* 88: 948–49.

Gelin, Albert
1959   *Le livre de Baruch.* 2d ed. Paris: Cerf.

Georgi, Dieter
1964   "Der vorpaulinische Hymnus Phil 2, 6-11." Pp. 263–93 in *Zeit und Geschichte: Dankesgabe an Rudolf Bultmann zum 80. Geburtstag.* Ed. E. Dinkler. Tübingen: Mohr-Siebeck.

Gilbert, Maurice
1970   "La structure de la prière de Salomon (Sg 9)." *Bib* 51: 301–31.
1973   *La critique des dieux dans le Livre de la Sagesse.* AnBib 53. Rome: Biblical Institute Press.
1974   "L'éloge de la Sagesse (Siracide 24)." *RTL* 5: 326–48.
1976   "Ben Sira et la femme." *RTL* 7: 426–42.

Gill, David
1965   "The Greek Sources of Wisdom 12. 3-7." *VT* 15: 383–86.

Goodenough, Erwin R.
1929   *The Jurisprudence of the Jewish Courts of Egypt.* New Haven: Yale University Press. Reprinted, Amsterdam: Philo, 1968.
1935   *By Light, Light: The Mystic Gospel of Hellenistic Judaism.* New Haven: Yale University Press.
1962   *An Introduction to Philo Judaeus.* London: Blackwell.

Gooding, D. W.
1963   "Aristeas and Septuagint Origins." *VT* 13:357–79.

Grelot, Pierre
1958   "L'eschatologie des Esséniens et le Livre d'Hénoch." *RevQ* 1: 119–20.
1961   "L'eschatologie de la Sagesse et les apocalypses juives." Pp. 165–78 in *À la Rencontre de Dieu: Mémorial Albert Gelin.* Bibliotheque de la faculté catholique de théologie de Lyon 8. Le Puy: Xavier Mappus.

Gunneweg, Antonius H. J.
 1975   *Das Buch Baruch.* JSHRZ 3.2. Gütersloh: Mohn.

Hadas, Moses
 1953   *The Third and Fourth Books of Maccabees.* New York: Harper.

Hadot, Jean
 1970   *Penchant mauvais et volonté libre dans la Sagesse de Ben Sira (l'Ecclésiastique).* Brussels: Presses Universitaires.

Hamerton-Kelly, Robert G.
 1972   "Sources and Traditions in Philo Judaeus: Prolegomena to an Analysis of His Writings." *Studia Philonica* 1: 3–26.
 1976   "Some Techniques of Composition in Philo's Allegorical Commentary with Special Reference to *De Agricultura.*" Pp. 45–56 in *Jews, Greeks and Christians: Religious Cultures in Late Antiquity.* Ed. R. Hamerton-Kelly and R. Scroggs. SJLA 21. Leiden: Brill.

Hamp, Vinzenz
 1950a   *Baruch.* Echter-Bibel 11. Würzburg: Echter-Verlag.
 1950b   "Zukunft und Jenseits im Buche Sirach." In *Alttestamentliche Studien. Friedrich Nötscher zum 60. Geburtstag gewidmet.* Ed. H. Junker and J. Botterweck. BBB 1. Bonn: Hanstein.
 1954   *Sirach.* Echter Bibel 13. Würzburg: Echter-Verlag.

Harl, Marguerite
 1967   "Cosmologie grecque et representations juives dans l'oeuvre de Philon d'Alexandrie." Pp. 189–205 in *Philon d'Alexandrie: Lyon 11–15 Septembre 1966.* Colloques nationaux du Centre National de la Recherche Scientifique. Paris: Editions du Centre National de la Recherche Scientifique.

Hartman, Louis F.
 1961   "Sirach in Hebrew and Greek." *CBQ* 23: 443–51.

Haspecker, Josef
 1967   *Gottesfurcht bei Jesus Sirach.* AnBib 30. Rome: Pontifical Biblical Institute.

Hecht, Richard
 1979   "Preliminary Issues in the Analysis of Philo's *De Specialibus Legibus.*" *Studia Philonica* 5: 1–56.

Hegermann, Harald
 1961   *Die Vorstellung vom Schöpfungsmittler im hellenistischen Judentum und Urchristentum.* TU 82. Berlin: Akademie.

Heinemann, Isaak
 1932   *Philons griechische und jüdische Bildung.* Reprint, Hildesheim: Olms, 1962.

Hengel, Martin
 1972   "Anonymität, Pseudepigraphie und 'literarische Fälschung' in der jüdisch-hellenistischen Literatur." Pp. 232–308 in *Pseudepigrapha I: Pseudopythagorica, Lettres de Platon, Littérature pseudépigraphe juive.* Entretiens sur l'antiquité classique 18. Ed. K. von Fritz. Geneva: Fondation Hardt.
 1974   *Judaism and Hellenism: Studies in their Encounter in Palestine during the Early Hellenistic Period.* 2 vols. Trans. J. Bowden. Philadelphia: Fortress.

Hilgert, Earle
 1984 "Bibliographia Philoniana 1935–1975." Pp. 47–97 in *ANRW* 2.21.1. Ed. W. Haase. Berlin and New York: de Gruyter.

Höffken, Peter
 1975 "Warum schwieg Jesus Sirach über Ezra?" *ZAW* 87: 184–202.

van der Horst, P. W.
 1978 *The Sentences of Pseudo-Phocylides*. SVTP 4. Leiden: Brill.

Howard, George E.
 1971 "The Letter of Aristeas and Diaspora Judaism." *JTS* 22: 337–48.
 1973 "The 'Aberrant' Text of Philo's Quotations Reconsidered." *HUCA* 44: 197–209.

Jacob, Edmond
 1957 "L'histoire d'Israel vue par Ben Sira." Pp. 288–94 in *Mélanges bibliques André Robert*. Paris: Bloud & Gay.
 1978 "Wisdom and Religion in Sirach." Pp. 247–60 in *Israelite Wisdom: Theology and Literary Essays in Honor of Samuel Terrien*. Ed. J. G. Gammie. Missoula, MT: Scholars Press.

Jellicoe, Sidney
 1968 *The Septuagint and Modern Study*. Oxford: Oxford University Press.

Kahle, Paul
 1959 *The Cairo Geniza*. 2d ed. Oxford: Blackwell.

Kaiser, Otto
 1958 "Die Begründung der Sittlichkeit im Buche Jesus Sirach." *ZTK* 55: 51–63.

Katz, Peter
 1950 *Philo's Bible: The Aberrant Text of Bible Quotations in Some Philonic Writings and its Place in the Textual History of the Greek Bible*. Cambridge: University Press.

Kearns, Conleth
 1969 "Ecclesiasticus or the Wisdom of Jesus the Son of Sirach." Pp. 541–62 in *A New Catholic Commentary on Holy Scripture*. London: Nelson.

Klijn, A. F. J.
 1964/65 "The Letter of Aristeas and the Greek Translation of the Pentateuch." *NTS* 11: 154–58.

Krämer, Hans Joachim
 1964 *Der Ursprung der Geistmetaphysik: Untersuchungen zur Geschichte des Platonismus zwischen Platon und Plotin*. Amsterdam: Schippers.

Lacon, F. M., and J. G. Gourbillon
 1966 "La Sagesse, une source d'immortalité." *Évangile* 61: 22–32.

Lameere, W.
 1951 "Sur un passage de Philon d'Alexandrie (*De Plantatione* 1–6)." *Mnemosyne* 4a, Ser. 4: 73–80.

Laporte, Jean
 1972 *La doctrine eucharistique chez Philon d'Alexandrie*. Théologie historique 16. Paris: Beauchesne.

Larcher, Chrysostome
 1969 *Études sur le Livre de la Sagesse*. Paris: Gabalda.

Lebram, J. C. H.
1974   "Die literarische Form des vierten Makkabäerbuches." *VC* 28: 81–96.

Lehmann, Manfred R.
1961–62   "Ben Sira and the Qumran Literature." *RevQ* 3: 103–16.

Le Moyne, Jean
1972   "Baruch, le livre." *DBSup*, vol. 8, cols. 724–36.

Lipscomb, W. Loundes, and James Alvin Sanders
1978   "Wisdom at Qumran." Pp. 277–85 in *Israelite Wisdom: Theological and Literary Essays in Honor of Samuel Terrien.* Ed. J. G. Gammie. Missoula, MT: Scholars Press.

Mack, Burton Lee
1973   *Logos und Sophia: Untersuchungen zur Weisheitstheologie im hellenistischen Judentum.* SUNT 10. Göttingen: Vandenhoeck & Ruprecht.
1974–75   "Exegetical Traditions in Alexandrian Judaism: A Program for the Analysis of the Philonic Corpus." *Studia Philonica* 3: 71–112.
1984   "Philo Judaeus and Exegetical Traditions in Alexandria." Pp. 227–71 in *ANRW* 2.21.1. Ed. W. Haase. Berlin and New York: de Gruyter.

McKeating, Henry
1973   "Jesus Ben Sira's Attitude to Women." *ExpTim* 85: 85–87.

Maddalena, Antonio
1970   *Filone Alessandrino.* Biblioteca de filosofia saggi 2. Milan: Mursia.

Maertens, Thierry
1956   *L'Eloge des Pères (Ecclésiastique XLIV–L).* Bruges: Desclée de Brouwer.

Maier, Gerhard
1971   *Mensch und freier Wille nach den jüdischen Religionsparteien zwischen Ben Sira und Paulus.* WUNT 12. Tübingen: Mohr-Siebeck.

Marböck, Johann
1971   *Weisheit im Wandel.* BBB 37. Bonn: Hanstein.
1976   "Gesetz und Weisheit: Zum Verständnis des Gesetzes bei Jesus ben Sira." *BZ* 20: 1–21.

Marcus, Joseph
1930–31   "A Fifth Ms. of Ben Sira." *JQR* 21: 223–40.

Mayer, Günter
1974   *Index Philoneus.* Berlin: de Gruyter.

Méasson, Anita
1966   "Le *De Sacrificiis, Abelis et Caini* de Philon d'Alexandrie." *Bulletin de l'Association Guillaume Budé* 4: 309–16.

Meeks, Wayne A.
1967   *The Prophet-King, Moses Traditions and the Johannine Christology.* Leiden: Brill.

Meisner, Norbert Hans
1973   "Aristeasbrief." Pp. 35–87 in JSHRZ 2.1. Gütersloh: Mohn.

Ménard, Jacques E.
1968   "Le Mythe de Dionysos Zagreus chez Philon." *RevScRel* 42: 339–45.

Mendelson, Alan
1971   "Encyclical Education in Philo of Alexandria." Diss., University of Chicago.

Michaelis, Dieter
1958   "Das Buch Jesus Sirach als typischer Ausdruck für das Gottesverhältnis des nachalttestamentlichen Menschen." *TLZ* 83: 601–8.

Michel, M. Alain
1964   "Quelques aspects de la rhétorique chez Philon." *Compte rendu et commentaire de la conférence donnée le 12 décembre 1963 au siége de la Y.M.C.A. sous les auspices de la Société archaéologique d'Alexandrie.* Conferences 1. Alexandrie.

Middendorp, Theophil
1973   *Die Stellung Jesu Ben Siras zwischen Judentum und Hellenismus.* Leiden: Brill.

Moore, Carey A.
1977   "I Baruch." Pp. 255–316 in *Daniel, Esther, and Jeremiah: The Additions.* AB 44. Garden City, NY: Doubleday.

Mowinckel, Sigmund
1955   "Die Metrik bei Jesus Sirach." *ST* 9: 137–55.

Nickelsburg, George W. E., Jr.
1972   *Resurrection, Immortality and Eternal Life in Intertestamental Judaism.* HTS 26. Cambridge, MA: Harvard University Press.

Nikiprowetzky, Valentin
1977   *Le commentaire de l'écriture chez Philon d'Alexandrie.* ALGHJ 11. Leiden: Brill.

Pascher, Joseph
1931   Η ΒΑΣΙΛΙΚΗ ΟΔΟΣ: *Der Königsweg zu Wiedergeburt und Vergottung bei Philon von Alexandreia.* Studien zur Geschichte und Kultur des Altertums 17. 3–4. Paderborn: Schöningh.

Pautrel, Raymond
1963   "Ben Sira et le Stoicisme," *RSR* 51: 535–49.

Pelletier, André
1962   *Lettre d'Aristée à Philocrate.* SC 89. Paris: Cerf.

Penna, Angelo
1956   *Baruch.* La Sacra Bibbia. Rome: Marietti.

Pépin, Jean
1958   *Mythe et Allégorie: Les origines grecques et les contestations judéo-chrétiennes.* Paris: Aubier.

Petit, Françoise
1973   *L'ancienne version latine des Questions sur la Genèse de Philon d'Alexandrie. I: Edition critique. II: Commentaire.* TU 113, 114. Berlin: Akademie-Verlag.

Philonenko, Marc
1958   "Le Maître de justice et la Sagesse de Salomon." *TZ* 14: 81–88.

Prato, Gian Luigi
1975   *Il problema della teodicea in Ben Sira.* AnBib 65. Rome: Pontifical Biblical Institute.

Rad, Gerhard von
    1970   *Weisheit in Israel.* Neukirchen-Vluyn: Neukirchener Verlag.
              English trans.: *Wisdom in Israel.* Trans. James D. Martin. Nash-
              ville: Abingdon, 1972.

Reese, James M.
    1965   "Plan and Structure in the Book of Wisdom." *CBQ* 27: 391–99.
    1970   *Hellenistic Influences on the Book of Wisdom and its Consequences.*
              AnBib 41. Rome: Biblical Institute Press.

Rickenbacher, Otto
    1973   *Weisheitsperikopen bei Ben Sira.* OBO 1. Göttingen: Vandenhoeck
              & Ruprecht.

Rüger, Hans Peter
    1970   *Text und Textform im hebräischen Sirach.* BZAW 112. Berlin:
              Töpelmann.

Rylaarsdam, J. Coert
    1946   *Revelation in Jewish Wisdom Literature.* Chicago: University of
              Chicago Press.

Sanders, Ed Parrish
    1977   *Paul and Palestinian Judaism.* Philadelphia: Fortress.

Sanders, J. A.
    1965   *The Psalms Scroll of Qumrân Cave 11 (11QPsᵃ).* DJD 4. Oxford:
              Clarendon Press.
    1967   *The Dead Sea Psalms Scroll.* Ithaca, NY: Cornell University Press.
    1971   "The Sirach 51 Acrostic." Pp. 429–38 in *Hommages à André
              Dupont-Sommer.* Paris: Adrien-Maisonneuve.
    1974   "The Qumran Psalms Scroll (11QPsᵃ) Reviewed." Pp. 79–99 in *On
              Language, Culture and Religion: In Honor of Eugene A. Nida.* Ed.
              M. Black and W. W. Smalley. The Hague: Mouton.

Sanders, J. T.
    1983   *Ben Sira and Demotic Wisdom.* Chico, CA: Scholars Press.

Sandmel, Samuel
    1971   *Philo's Place in Judaism: A Study of Conceptions of Abraham in
              Jewish Literature.* Augmented Edition. New York: Ktav. First pub-
              lished *HUCA* 25: 209–37; 26: 151–332. First reprint, Cincinnati:
              Hebrew Union College Press, 1956.
    1979   *Philo of Alexandria: An Introduction.* Oxford: University Press.

Schilling, Othmar
    1956   *Das Buch Jesus Sirach.* Herders Bibelkommentar 7.2. Freiburg:
              Herder.

Schirmann, J.
    1957-58   "A New Leaf from the Hebrew Ecclesiasticus." *Tarbiz* 27: 440–43.
    1959-60   "Some Additional Leaves from Ecclesiasticus." *Tarbiz* 29: 125–34.

Schneider, Heinrich
    1954   "Baruch." Pp. 133–62 in *Herders Bibelkommentar.* Freiburg:
              Herder.

Segal, Moshe Zvi
    1959   *Seper Ben Sira' Ha-Salem.* 2d ed. Jerusalem: Bialik Institute.

Siebeneck, Robert T.
    1959   "May their bones return to life! — Sirach's Praise of the Fathers."
              CBQ 21: 411–28.

Skehan, Patrick W.
1940 "Isaias and the Teaching of the Book of Wisdom." *CBQ* 2: 289–99.
1945 "The Text and Structure of the Book of Wisdom." *Traditio* 3: 1–12.
1948 "Borrowings from the Psalms in the Book of Wisdom." *CBQ* 10: 384–97.
1971a "The Acrostic Poem in Sirach 51:13–30." *HTR* 64: 387–400.
1971b *Studies in Israelite Poetry and Wisdom.* CBQMS 1. Washington, DC: CBA.
1976 "Ecclesiasticus." *IDBSup*, 250–51.
1979 "Structures in Poems on Wisdom: Proverbs 8 and Sirach 24." *CBQ* 41: 365–79.

Snaith, John G.
1974 *Ecclesiasticus.* CBC. Cambridge: University Press.

Spicq, Ceslaus
1951 "L'Ecclésiastique." Pp. 529–841 in *La Sainte Bible*, vol. 6. Ed. L. Pirot and A. Clamer. Paris: Letouzey.

Stein, Edmund
1929 *Die allegorische Exegese des Philo aus Alexandria.* BZAW 51. Giessen: Töpelmann.

Strugnell, John
1969 "Notes and Queries on 'The Ben Sira Scroll from Masada.'" Pp. 109–19 in *W. F. Albright Volume.* Ed. A. Malamat. Eretz-Israel 9. Jerusalem: Israel Exploration Society.

Suggs, M. Jack
1957 "Wisdom of Solomon 2:10–5: A Homily Based on the Fourth Servant Song." *JBL* 76: 26–33.

Sweet, J. P. M.
1965 "The Theory of Miracles in the Wisdom of Solomon." Pp. 113–26 in *Miracles, Cambridge Studies in their Philosophy and History.* Ed. C. F. D. Moule. London: Mowbray.

Tcherikover, Victor
1958 "The Ideology of the Letter of Aristeas." *HTR* 51: 59–85.

Theiler, Willy
1965 "Philo von Alexandria und der Beginn des Kaiserzeitliche Platonismus." Pp. 199–218 in *Parusia: Festgabe für Johannes Hirschberger.* Ed. K. Flasch. Frankfurt am Main: Minerva. Reprinted in his *Untersuchungen zur antiken Literatur*, 484–501. Berlin: de Gruyter, 1970.

Thyen, Hartwig
1955a "Die Probleme der neueren Philo-Forschung." *TRu* N.F. 23: 230–46.
1955b *Der Stil der jüdisch-hellenistischen Homilie.* FRLANT N.F. 47. Göttingen: Vandenhoeck & Ruprecht.

Tov, Emanuel
1975 *The Book of Baruch also called I Baruch (Greek and Hebrew): Edited, Reconstructed and Translated.* SBLTT 8, Pseudepigrapha, 6. Missoula, MT: Scholars Press.

Trenchard, W.
1982 *Ben Sira's View of Women: A Literary Analysis.* Chico, CA: Scholars Press.

Trinquet, Joseph
1951 "Les Lines 'sadocites' de l'Écrit de Damas, des Manuscrits de la Mer Morte et de l'Ecclésiastique." *VT* 1: 287–92.

Vaccari, Alberto
1949 "Ecclesiastico." Pp. 177–289 in *La Sacra Bibbia*, 5.2. Florence: A. Salani.

Vattioni, Francesco
1968 *Ecclesiastico: Testo ebraico con apparato critico e versioni greca, latina e siriaca*. Pubbicazioni del Seminario de Semitistica, Testi 1. Naples: Istituto Orientale di Napoli.

Vellas, Basileios M.
1961 Ἡ ἐπίδρασις τῆς Ἑλληνικῆς Φιλοσοφίας ἐπὶ τοῦ Βιβλίου τῆς Σοφίας Σολομῶντος. [The Influence of Greek Philosophy on the Book of Wisdom.] Athens.

Völker, Walther
1938 *Fortschritt und Vollendung bei Philo von Alexandrien*. TU 49.1. Leipzig: Hinrichs.

Vulgate
1964 *Biblia Sacra juxta latinam vulgatam versionem: liber Hiesu Filii Sirach*, vol. 12. Rome: Typis Polyglottis Vaticanis.

Walter, Nikolaus
1964 *Der Thoraausleger Aristobulos*. TU 86. Berlin: Akademie-Verlag.

Wambacq, Bernard N.
1957 *Jeremias, Klaagliederen, Baruch, Brief van Jeremias*. De Boeken van het Oude Testament. Roermond: Romen & Zonen.

Weiss, Hans Friedrich
1966 *Untersuchungen zur Kosmologie des hellenistischen und palästinischen Judentums*. TU 97. Berlin: Akademie-Verlag.

Wevers, John W.
1961 *The Way of the Righteous: Psalms and the Book of Wisdom*. Philadelphia: Westminster.

Whybray, R. N.
1974 *The Intellectual Tradition in the Old Testament*. BZAW 135. Berlin: de Gruyter.

Williams, S. K.
1975 *Jesus' Death as Saving Event: The Background and Origin of a Concept*. HDR 2. Missoula, MT: Scholars Press.

Windisch, Hans
1909 *Die Frömmigkeit Philos und ihre Bedeutung für das Christentum*. Leipzig: Hinrichs.

Winston, David
1979 *Wisdom of Solomon*. AB 43. Garden City, NY: Doubleday.

Winter, Michael M.
1976 *A Concordance to the Peshitta Version of Ben Sira*. Monographs of the Peshitta Institute 2. Leiden: Brill.
1977 "The Origins of Ben Sira in Syriac." *VT* 27: 237–53, 494–507.

Wlosok, Antony
1960 *Laktanz und die philosophische Gnosis*. Abhandlungen der Akademie der Wissenschaften. Heidelberg: Winter.

Wolfson, Harry Austryn
 1945   *Philo, Foundations of Religious Philosophy in Judaism, Christianity and Islam.* 2 vols. Cambridge, MA: Harvard University Press.
Wright, Addison G.
 1965   "The Structure of Wisdom 11-19." *CBQ* 27: 28–34.
 1967a   "Numerical Patterns in the Book of Wisdom." *CBQ* 29: 524–38.
 1967b   "The Structure of the Book of Wisdom." *Bib* 48: 165–84.
Yadin, Yigael
 1965   *The Ben Sira Scroll from Masada.* Jerusalem: Israel Exploration Society.
Young, D., ed.
 1971   *Theognis, Ps-Pythagoras, Ps-Phocylides, Chares, Anonymi Aulodia, Fragm. Teliambicum.* Leipzig: Teubner.
Ziegler, Joseph, ed.
 1957   *Jeremias, Baruch, Threni, Epistula Ieremiae.* Septuaginta. Vetus Testamentum Graecum auctoritate Societatis Gottingensis editum 15. Göttingen: Vandenhoeck & Ruprecht.
 1962   *Sapientia Salomonis.* Septuaginta. Vetus Testamentum Graecum auctoritate Societatis Gottingensis editum 12.1. Göttingen: Vandenhoeck & Ruprecht.
 1965   *Sapientia Jesu Filii Sirach.* Septuaginta. Vetus Testamentum Graecum auctoritate Societatis Gottingensis editum 12.2. Göttingen: Vandenhoeck & Ruprecht.
Ziener, Georg
 1957   "Die Verwendung der Schrift im Buch der Weisheit." *TTZ* 66: 138–52.
Zuntz, Günther
 1959a   "Aristeas Studies I: The Seven Banquets." *JSS* 4: 21–36.
 1959b   "Aristeas Studies II: Aristeas on the Translation of the Torah." *JSS* 4: 109–26.

16
JEWISH HYMNS, ODES, AND PRAYERS
(ca. 167 B.C.E.–135 C.E.)

James H. Charlesworth

One hundred years ago we knew very little about Jewish hymns, odes, and prayers composed during the period of early Judaism. Since then we have been overwhelmed by the quantity of recovered material and it enables us to recognize that the Jews of this period produced an abundance of liturgical compositions, which provided a contemporary tone and perspective to services wherever Jews would worship collectively or alone. For example, in 1880 only one early Jewish hymnbook had been recovered, the *Psalms of Solomon* (*editio princeps* in 1626). Since then other hymnbooks have been recognized or discovered: the Hellenistic Synagogal Prayers (in the *Apostolic Constitutions*), the *Hodayoth* (1QH), and the *Odes of Solomon*. No handbook or synthesis is available as an introduction to this area of historical study. Research has been limited almost always to one prayer or one hymnic composition, with only a few references to compositions contemporaneous with it. Certainly we have no comprehensive survey of early Jewish hymns and prayers comparable to J. Heinemann's *Prayer in the Talmud*. S. Talmon (265) has accurately observed that for the most part recent scholarly research on "institutionalized prayer in Israel" has focused on historical and philological questions, "on the textual criticism of individual prayers and the reconstruction of their original forms."

Few of the extant early Jewish hymns and prayers have been analyzed and examined with the sophisticated methods developed in the study of the Psalter, and this procedure must precede any synthesis of research on them. Hence, we cannot speak of schools of scholars or of chronological phases of research. What can be attempted now is a brief report on the significant developments since 1945 in the study of hymns, prayers, and liturgies in intertestamental Judaism. The first part of this chapter will be a succinct descriptive review; the second will be an evaluative critique.

REVIEW

Caveats should introduce the report. It is obvious that many of the cardinal distinctions that once were thought to represent the categorical separation of early Judaism from early Christianity have eroded. In the

411

light of this recognition G. Vermes has called for a historical approach to early Judaism that would abolish "the age-old distinction between the New Testament and its Jewish background." He claims that the NT is "but a fraction of the literary legacy of first-century Judaism" (Vermes, 1980:13). There can be no question that early Christians could have (and did) compose hymns and prayers that contained no peculiarly "Christian" concept or word (see, e.g., R. A. Kraft). We have not yet been able to agree on a definition of "Judaism" prior to 200 c.e. (see Neusner, 1980). The ambiguity of our categories "Jewish" and "Christian" and the recognition that many early Jewish Christians considered themselves fully Jewish indicate that it is wise to include for consideration compositions by a Christian who was profoundly influenced by Jewish theology and employed Jewish perceptions, expressions, and forms (Charlesworth, 1982). Hence, among the hymnbooks we have included the *Odes of Solomon*, which, from the time of their discovery until the present, some distinguished scholars have considered to be Jewish.

The vast amount of liturgical material now available from early Judaism and the new methodology now employed by scholars seriously date almost all attempts at a synthesis. Hence, the works by H. L. Jansen (1937) and N. B. Johnson (1948) should not be seen as reliable surveys.

Each of the hymnbooks is discussed in the following way: After brief prefatory comments each is assessed in terms of the debates over the original language, date, and provenance. Subsequently the characteristic theological features or ideas are summarized.

The Hymnbooks

The movement from private instantaneous prayers to formalized, sometimes cultic, prayers was accompanied both by injunctions not "to make any prayer a fixed form" (*m. Abot* 2:13) and by the appearance of communal fixed prayers and hymns (Heinemann, 1977:14–15) and even hymnbooks that were apparently intended to supplement—certainly not to replace—the Psalter (see, e.g., Holm-Nielsen, 1955, 1960b). Impressive progress has already been made toward the publication of reliable critical texts and translations of these hymnbooks and other documents that contain numerous hymns and prayers. Likewise, significant progress has been made toward a better understanding of the original language, date, and, at times, provenance of the respective writings. In particular: (1) Various scholars have published significant studies on each of the aforementioned hymnbooks (1QH, *Pss. Sol.*, Hell. Syn. Pr., *Odes Sol.*) and on the "Supplement" to the Psalter, Psalms 151–55. (2) Christian scholars, especially, have examined intensely the hymns and prayers embedded in the canonical NT and have argued for the pre-Christian Jewish character of many of them. (3) Jewish scholars have similarly scrutinized the prayers in rabbinic literature and isolated the existence of some proto-rabbinic prayers.

Hodayoth

Many hymns and prayers were discovered among the Dead Sea Scrolls (see Baillet; Moraldi). Here only a brief summary of the major consensuses among scholars will suffice; our focus will be solely upon the Qumran community's hymnbook, the *Hodayoth*, which was discovered in Cave 1 in the spring of 1947 and was edited with photographs by E. L. Sukenik (1955). This hymnbook (frequently called the *Thanksgiving Hymns* because of the formula "I thank you, O Lord") contains thirty-four (Morawe), thirty-two (Licht, 1957; Dupont-Sommer, 1962; Mansoor) or nineteen hymns or psalms (Holm-Nielsen, 1960a)—depending upon how one divides the poetic compositions. The hymnbook must predate the first century B.C.E. because the script of 1QH is Herodian (ca. 30 B.C.E. to 70 C.E.; see S. A. Birnbaum; Avigad: 72f., 76f.). As a result, the compositions are usually dated (Delcor, 1962:38) from the middle of the second century B.C.E. to the early decades of the first century C.E.

Soon after the publication of the *editio princeps* numerous scholars (Sukenik; Michaud; cf. Dupont-Sommer, 1962:100, 1977:15–18) argued that the founder of the community, the Teacher of Righteousness, had composed the hymns. Licht (1957:25–26) and others (Mansoor: 45; Bardtke, 1956, 1956–57) rejected this argument. In search of the author or authors of these hymns scholars focused upon the use of the first-person pronoun in the *Hodayoth*. S. Holm-Nielsen (1960a:329–31) suggested that the "I" represents the collective solidarity of the Qumran community. A. Dupont-Sommer argued that "I" always represents an individual person, "who must be the Teacher of Righteousness" (1962:200). It is more probable that the "I" reflects the personal experiences of the Teacher of Righteousness in some hymns but that in other passages it represents the collective consciousness of the Qumran community (Milik: 40, 74). This insight was researched by G. Morawe, who showed that the *Hodayoth* collection contains more than one *Gattung* and was not composed by one person. This idea was developed by G. Jeremias (1963) and P. Schulz with regard to the hymns of the Teacher of Righteousness, and by J. Becker and H.-W. Kuhn with regard to the hymns of the community.

The language of the *Hodayoth* is heavily influenced by biblical Hebrew, Aramaic, postbiblical Hebrew, and Samaritan Hebrew (Licht, 1957; Delcor, 1962; Mansoor). Unlike the later *Psalms of Solomon* and *Odes of Solomon*, the poetic forms are a mixture of the Psalter's *parallelismus membrorum* (C. F. Kraft), usually synonymous (Licht, 1957; Mansoor: 23–25), often with extreme disparity in the length of the lines and with no structured meter (Licht, 1957; C. F. Kraft; Mansoor; Holm-Nielsen, 1960a; but on prosody in the *Hodayoth* see Ehlen). Scholars have discerned three *Gattungen* in the *Hodayoth:* the Thanksgiving Song (*Danklied;* Mowinckel; Morawe; Delcor, 1962; Schulz) the Hymn (*hymnischen Bekenntnislied;* Morawe; Schulz), and the Didactic Psalm (*Lehrpsalm;* Schulz: 3). The hymnbook was obviously used liturgically in the cult ceremonies at Qumran (Holm-Nielsen, 1960a:332–48; H.-W. Kuhn, 1966; Aune), certainly in the daily celebration (with the angels) to God of the cosmic dimension of the sanctification of time (1QH 12:3–9; see Mansoor, 1961:49) and probably in the yearly renewal of the covenant (see 1QS 1:16–2:25a; Murphy-O'Connor, 1969). These hymns have been thought to be "mystical" (Dupont-Sommer, 1962:199, 1977:7) and to stress the fundamental importance of salvation and knowledge (Vermes, 1978: 56). Holm-Nielsen (1960a) and Delcor (1962) have shown cumulatively that the *Hodayoth* are frequently similar to other compositions, especially the Lucan hymns, the Five More "Davidic" Psalms, the *Psalms of Solomon*, and the *Odes of Solomon*. Parallels with the *Odes* are impressive (Charlesworth, 1972); both hymnbooks celebrate the present experience of a "realized" eschatology (clearly demonstrated for 1QH by H.-W. Kuhn, 1966; see also Nickelsburg) and frequently employ the paradise motif (as in the *Pss. Sol.*) to express the conception that the eschatological end (*Endzeit*) is portrayed in light of the beginning of time (*Urzeit*) as a restored creation (*restitutio principii;* see Aune: 37–42).

Considerable progress has been made in the attempt to understand the *Hodayoth*. Some issues debated in the study of other hymnbooks are impressively solved. First, there can be no doubt that the *Hoyadoth* were composed originally in their extant language, Hebrew. Second, they predate the destruction of the temple in 70 c.e. Third, they were all—or almost all—composed at Qumran. Fourth, the *Hodayoth* contain numerous ideas, some of which probably express the personal sufferings of the founder of the Qumran community when he was persecuted by the Wicked Priest and forced to live exiled in the desert, and others of which preserve the community's collective consciousness of being the elect and holy ones who live near the end of time.

The Supplement to the Psalter:
Five More "Davidic" Psalms

In Hebrew the Davidic Psalter contains 150 psalms; in Greek (and in some Syriac manuscripts) it has 151. Almost one hundred years ago W. Wright drew attention to and translated five apocryphal psalms in Syriac (now called Psalms 151–155). The significance and early date of these psalms became clear with the discovery of three (Psalms 151a–151b, 154, 155) in the Dead Sea Psalms Scroll (11QPs[a]; see J. A. Sanders, 1965,

1967). These three psalms are certainly earlier than the Qumran Psalms Scroll, which dates from the first half of the first century C.E. (J. A. Sanders, 1965; Strugnell, 1965). Some specialists claim that one or more of these psalms were composed by the Essenes (Philonenko, 1959; Delcor, 1962; Dupont-Sommer, 1964). Others argue that the evidence will not support this identification (J. A. Sanders, 1967:108; van der Woude: 35). M. Hengel links these psalms with the Hasidim (1: 80, 176–78).

The style is clearly imitative of the Psalter. In contrast to the *Hodayoth* but similar to the *Odes of Solomon*, the parallel lines are of roughly uniform length and usually constructed in synonymous parallelism. The appearance of "apocryphal" psalms within the Davidic Psalter suggested to M. H. Goshen-Gottstein and P. Skehan that the Dead Sea Psalms Scroll is a sectarian version of the canonical Psalter, but this phenomenon seems to reveal that (at least in some Jewish circles) the Psalter was not set, closed, and canonized prior to the first century C.E. (J. A. Sanders, 1965, 1967).

The original language of Psalms 151a–151b, 154, and 155 is certainly Hebrew (Strugnell, 1966; Charlesworth and Sanders); the original language of Psalm 152 is possibly Hebrew (Strugnell, 1966:259; Charlesworth and Sanders), and that of Psalm 153 is perhaps Hebrew (Charlesworth and Sanders; contrast Strugnell, 1966:259). The date of these compositions varies: Psalm 151 may date from as early as the third century B.C.E. (Cross: 70). Psalms 154 and 155 apparently date from the second century B.C.E. to the early first century C.E., and Psalms 152 and 153 are difficult to date (Charlesworth and Sanders). The provenance of composition for these hymns is uncertain, but it is clear that all were not composed at Qumran— and perhaps none were written there. Psalms 151a–151b, 152 and 153 are pseudepigraphically composed with David in mind and celebrate how he rendered glory to the Lord (151a), defeated the Philistine (151b), the lion and the wolf (152, 153). Psalm 154, anonymous in Hebrew but attributed to Hezekiah in the Syriac, is a hymn of praise to God. Psalm 155 is a petition and praise for deliverance.

Psalms of Solomon

The *Psalms of Solomon* consist of eighteen hymns (or psalms) composed and presumably recited by Jews around the turn of the common era. Near the beginning of this century there was a consensus that these hymns are Pharisaic (Wellhausen: 112–20; Ryle and James: xliv–lii; Gray: 630). Some scholars today continue to affirm a Pharisaic origin (Black: 777; Schüpphaus: 158); others correctly warn that they should not be linked with the Pharisees (O'Dell; R. B. Wright, 1972; E. P. Sanders: 388), the Essenes (Holm-Nielsen, 1968), or any particular sectarian group (Winter, 1962; Rappaport). The Greek and Syriac derive ultimately from Hebrew, which is certainly the original language (Wellhausen; Ryle and James;

Gray; K. G. Kuhn, 1937; Delcor, 1973: cols. 221–25; Holm-Nielsen,
1970). Trafton has shown that the Syriac and the Greek texts are important
and that in some passages the Syriac may derive directly from the lost
Hebrew. There is wide agreement that they date from the middle or latter
half of the first century B.C.E. (Gray: 627–30; Delcor, 1973: col. 235;
Schüpphaus: 157–58; R. B. Wright, 1985; contrast Holm-Nielsen [1977],
who dates them to the second century B.C.E.) The provenance of these
psalms is Palestinian; they probably were composed in or near Jerusalem
(Denis: 60–69; R. B. Wright, 1972:150; Schüpphaus: 158).

Like the *Odes of Solomon*, but in contrast to the *Hodayoth*, they are
composed in the style of the Psalter and continue the poetic norm of
parallelismus membrorum, transforming some of the older *Gattungen*
(Jansen; Delcor, 1973: cols. 228–29). Schüpphaus (154–58) has argued
recently that the theme of these psalms is the righteousness of God and his
help in difficulties and that they reflect the Pharisaic divine service of
Jerusalem synagogues near the end of the first century B.C.E. Other characteristics of these psalms should be mentioned: the belief in the resurrection for those who fear God (3:16; 13:9; see Nickelsburg: 131–34), the
pervasive claim that Israel is in covenant with God (9:16–19; 10:5; 17:7;
see Jaubert: 256; E. P. Sanders: 387–409), the celebration over the death
of Pompey (2:24–35; see Gray: 627–30; Delcor, 1973: cols. 233–35), and
a *locus classicus* for Jewish messianism (17:4–51; 18:1–14; see Charlesworth, 1979:197–99). Striking parallels between the *Psalms of Solomon*
and the hymns in the first two chapters of the Gospel of Luke have been
discussed by Ryle and James (1891) and Viteau (1911; see below).

Hellenistic Synagogal Prayers

The other hymnbooks discussed in this section have received more
attention than the Hellenistic Synagogal Prayers, which are unknown to
many scholars, even to specialists in early Judaism. Yet, scattered throughout the Christian liturgy of books 7 and 8 of the *Apostolic Constitutions* are
at least sixteen prayers that are most likely originally Jewish (Fiensy).

The first scholar to publicize the existence of remnants of Jewish
synagogal prayers in this major Christian writing was K. Kohler (1893,
1903). Apparently unfamiliar with Kohler's insight, W. Bousset (1915)
claimed that the *Apostolic Constitutions* preserved Jewish prayers derived
from Diaspora Judaism. Less than a decade later, Kohler, unfamiliar with
Bousset's publication—a phenomenon all too prevalent in the study of the
hymns and prayers of early Judaism—developed his idea that the *Apostolic
Constitutions* incorporated originally Jewish "Essene prayers" that were
"Christianized by verbal changes or additions" (Kohler, 1924: 410).
Although ignorant of Kohler's pioneering publications, E. R. Goodenough
was introduced to Bousset's study by A. D. Nock. Goodenough became

thoroughly persuaded by Bousset's arguments and utilized these Jewish prayers to demonstrate the existence of a "mystic Judaism" that is similar and prior to the thought of Philo of Alexandria who can be understood only in light of this "Jewish Mystery." Although Kohler's theory of Essene origin should now be rejected in light of our vastly increased knowledge of the Essenes, and although Goodenough's hypothesis should be isolated for separate examination (see Sandmel), it is becoming increasingly apparent (see Charlesworth, 1980; Fiensy and Darnell, 1981; Fiensy) that Jewish prayers, now interpolated and redacted (with deletions) by Christians, are incorporated in books 7 and 8 of the *Apostolic Constitutions*.

Research on these allegedly Jewish prayers is in its infancy. Their number, provenance, and date have not yet been adequately examined. The publication by Darnell and the monograph by Fiensy will direct scholars' attention to these Jewish prayers, which are frequently similar to the Seven Benedictions and to the *Kiddush* for Sabbath Eve (see Birnbaum: 189–90); this and subsequent research will help us better understand their origin, character, and form (which seems to be another example of development of the Psalter's synonymous and synthetic parallelism).

Odes of Solomon

The original forty-two hymns (or odes) are preserved, except for the second and portions of the third and perhaps first. These odes are Christian (Emerton, 1977; Chadwick; Charlesworth, 1978; Baarda; Murray), although some scholars (Testuz; cf. Gruenwald) claim that they are Jewish (an old view, which goes back to Harnack; and Menzies). They are closely aligned with many of the early Jewish hymns already mentioned, and the Christian (or Jewish-Christian) who composed them was probably influenced by the images and thoughts contained in the Dead Sea Scrolls, especially the *Hodayoth* (Carmignac, 1961, 1963; Charlesworth, 1970, 1972; Licht, 1971; Gruenwald). Three positions recently have been defended regarding the original language of the *Odes:* Hebrew (Carmignac, 1963), Greek (Testuz: 57; Klijn, 1965; Philonenko, 1962), and Syriac (Vööbus, 1962; Gibson; Emerton, 1967; Charlesworth, 1978). The *Odes* were most likely composed near 100 c.e. (Charlesworth, 1976) or in the early second century (Ehlers; Vööbus, 1971), but surely not as late as the first half of the third century (Drijvers, 1978, 1979). Although they may come from in or near Antioch (Harris and Mingana: 2:69; Charlesworth, 1976a, 1976b), their provenance is not clear.

The odist's thoughts and images are strikingly similar to those of the author and editors of the Gospel of John (Bultmann, 1971; Metzger, 1955; Charlesworth, 1972; Charlesworth and Culpepper; contrast Barrett). They are not gnostic (Charlesworth, 1969; Chadwick; Vööbus, 1971; Murray; contrast Rudolph) but contain ideas, images, and emphases that were systematically developed and redefined by gnostics. As stated above, the *Odes* continue the style of the Psalter, and the thought is presented in parallel lines. These hymns were most likely used in public services (Charlesworth, 1976b, 1978)—perhaps even in the community (or "school") in which the Gospel of John was written and edited (see Charlesworth and Culpepper). The pervasive tone is an expression of joy because of the present experience of salvation, eternal life (as at Qumran and in the *Psalms of Solomon* expressed through the paradise motif), and divine love (see Charlesworth, 1976b; Terzoli; Aune: 166–94). The thesis of J. H. Bernard that the *Odes* were used in baptismal services has been accepted in a modified form by some scholars (Schille; Murray).

Possibly Jewish Prayers and Hymns in the New Testament

Significant developments in the study of the NT will be discussed in the third volume of this trilogy (also see Charlesworth, 1982). Our attention here will be solely upon Jewish hymns and prayers inherited by early Christians and incorporated into the NT (see Deichgräber; Schille; Rese; J. T. Sanders; Wengst). Hence, the pre-Pauline Christological hymns, for example, in Colossians (1:15–20) and Philippians (2:6–11) will not be discussed, although Paul, who is clearly a Christian, still considered himself a Jew (Gal 2:15; Rom 11:1–2; 2 Cor 11:22).

Most important, of course, is the Jewish prayer that Jesus of Nazareth reputedly taught to his disciples (Luke 11:1; cf. Matt 5:1), which "displays all of the characteristics of Jewish private prayer" (Heinemann, 1978:88). Although we do not possess the prayer supposedly taught by John the Baptist to his disciples (see Luke 11:1), we do have three distinct versions of the Lord's Prayer (Luke 11:1–4; Matt 6:9–13; *Didache* 8). Some have claimed that the evangelists created this prayer (van Tilborg; Goulder, 1963, 1974), but most scholars have been persuaded—and I think correctly—that it (or most of it) is genuine Jesus tradition (Carmignac, 1969; J. Jeremias; Brown, 1965; Noack; Harner). J. Jeremias has argued that generally Luke preserves the original length, and Matthew the original wording. Jesus' prayer was certainly spoken and perhaps first composed in Aramaic (see J. Jeremias: 93). The prayer is constructed especially in Matthew according to *parallelismus membrorum*. It is frequently similar to other early Jewish prayers in Aramaic, especially the Qaddish (see below), and in Hebrew, notably Psalm 155 (esp. vv 11–12). According to *Didache* 8:3 the prayer was to be said "three times a day"; the parallel to the other Jewish "prayers," especially the *Shema* (see Harner: 69–70) and Eighteen Benedictions (see K. G. Kuhn, 1950), is impressive. As with these "prayers," the Lord's Prayer was soon included in worship services, first probably as a model for prayer (see Matt 6:9) and then as a prayer with an added conclusion. Our earliest clear evidence for the liturgical use of the Lord's Prayer is either the *Didache* (ca. early second century) or the twenty-fourth catechetical lecture by Cyril of Jerusalem (ca. 315–386).

Other pre-Christian Jewish prayers may be preserved in the New Testament. Numerous specialists, especially Winter (1954–1955; also earlier scholars like K. Bornhäuser; H. Gunkel, S. Mowinckel, and F. Spitta; contrast, e.g., Benoit; Brown, 1977), have argued that the Magnificat, the Benedictus, the Gloria in Excelsis, and the Nunc Dimittis preserved in the first two chapters of Luke are totally or in part originally Jewish. Ryle and James (xci–xcii) and Viteau (146–48) pointed to numerous significant parallels between the Magnificat and Benedictus and the *Psalms of Solomon*.

Bultmann (1923, 1971) argued that behind John 1:1–18 lies an originally Jewish hymn, which is strikingly similar to the *Odes of Solomon*. His arguments have been challenged or rejected by many scholars (see esp. de Ausejo; Schattenmann: 29; Brown, 1966, 1:20; J. T. Sanders). The hymns in Revelation are seen as originally Jewish by J. M. Ford (21, 79–80, 316), but a more persuasive case for Christian authorship has been presented in a detailed study by K. P. Jörns (see also Delling; Deichgräber; Kroll; Wengst).

Proto-Rabbinic Prayers

L. Finkelstein (1938, 1942–43) demonstrated to many scholars that parts of the Passover Haggadah antedated the present era and are possibly "pre-Maccabean" documents. I. Elbogen, E. Schürer (1897–98), G. F. Moore, J. Neusner (1971, 2:41, 49; 1979b:111–13), E. E. Urbach (1975, 1:400–402), J. Heinemann and J. J. Petuchowski (15–28), L. A. Hoffman, and other scholars have shown that the *Shema* (Deut 6:4; the liturgy included the reading of Deut 6:4–9; 11:13–21; Num 15:37–41, plus beginning and closing benedictions), although not a prayer in the strict sense because "it is God's word addressed to man" (Petuchowski, 1978:48), was liturgically recited long before the fall of Jerusalem. Before the beginning of the present era Jews religiously recited the *Shema* in the evening and in the morning (*m. Ber.* 1:1–3:5); the houses of Hillel and Shammai debated the proper way to recite it (see Neusner, 1971, 2:41, 49).

Recently specialists in rabbinics have been more concerned than their forebears about the date of rabbinic traditions. J. Neusner (e.g., 1971) has certainly been the most prominent leader and the most prolific writer in this endeavor, but J. Heinemann (1977) has demonstrated the importance of approaching Jewish liturgy using form-critical analysis (see also Spanier, 1934, 1936, 1937, 1939; Finkelstein, 1925–26). At least five prayers are very early, certainly proto-rabbinic: the Grace after Meals, the *'Ahabāh Rabbāh* (With Abounding Love), the *'Alenu lĕšabbeaḥ* Prayer (It is our duty to praise), the *Qaddish* (Magnified and sanctified . . .), and the *Tefillah* (*Shemoneh 'Esreh* or Eighteen Benedictions).

The Hebrew text and English translation of the 'Amidah (עמידה) are presented conveniently by Heinemann (1977:70–72, 288–89), who asserts that its original form(s) "goes back to the ancient ḥᵃbûrāh meals" (1977:3). This liturgical formula for grace after meals clearly predates the fall of Jerusalem in 70 C.E. (see Heinemann and Petuchowski: 89–90; moreover, grace is mentioned in *Jub*. 22:6 and *Letter of Aristeas* 184–85; see also *m. Ber*. 3:4; 6:5).

The Hebrew text and English translation of the 'Ahabāh Rabbāh are found in P. Birnbaum (73–74). Heinemann (1977:129, 174) traces the original form(s) of this benediction to the period before the destruction of Jerusalem; it was recited by the priests (see *m. Tamid* 5:1).

The Hebrew text and English translation of the 'Alenu lĕšabbeaḥ (עלינו לשבח) are printed in P. Birnbaum (135–38; see Heinemann, 1977:271). This prayer clearly predates 70 C.E. since it "was composed against the background of the Temple service" (Heinemann, 1977:273; so also *EncJud* 2: col. 557). Heinemann (1977:270–73) has demonstrated that this prayer has "all the formal elements of the Bêt Midrāš pattern" and should be considered a *Bêt-midrāš* prayer.

The Hebrew text and English translation of the *Qaddish* (קדיש) are published in P. Birnbaum (45–48; cf. Heinemann and Petuchowski: 81–84). The simple form of the eschatological hopes for the establishment of the kingdom of God and the absence of any allusion to the destruction of the Temple may indicate that this prayer predates 70 C.E. (*EncJud* 10: col. 661). However, the *Qaddish* was probably not "a part of the congregational service during the Mishnaic period" (Heinemann, 1977:25). It was originally recited at the conclusion of the public sermon (Heinemann, 1977:25, 266, 301). Like the 'Alenu lĕšabbeaḥ, it is another classic example of the *Bêt-midrāš* prayers (Heinemann, 1977:256–75, 280). It is strikingly similar to the Lord's Prayer (de Sola, 1964:112), and both may "spring from the same source and are at home in one and the same world of belief" (Graubard: 62).

The most famous of the proto-rabbinic prayers ("the Prayer" in Talmudic sources), of course, is the Eighteen Benedictions (the *Tefillah* or *Shemoneh 'Esreh*). The common Hebrew text and translation are found in P. Birnbaum (81–98); Schechter's English translation of the Cairo Genizah fragment (which is the old Palestinian rite) is reprinted in Heinemann (1977:26–29; see also Heinemann and Petuchowski: 33–36). There is little doubt that this prayer *par excellence*, which according to the Mishnah is to be recited in the morning, afternoon, and evening (*m. Ber*. 2:4–5:5), was redacted at Jamnia (Yavneh) under the direction of Rabban Gamaliel II and that the original forms (it circulated orally in more than one form) antedate "the destruction of the Temple by a considerable period of time" (Heinemann, 1977:22; Heinemann in *EncJud* 2: cols. 839–40; Le Déaut,

1977:37; Elbogen: 28–29; Elbogen, Kohler, and Finkelstein in Petuchowski, ed.). The Eighteen Benedictions is similar in numerous ways to the Lord's Prayer (Heinemann, 1978:86). In support of Elbogen's (41–42) and Spanier's (1939) argument that with liturgical texts that once circulated orally it is unwise to search for an "original" text, Heinemann (1977:43–44) rejects Finkelstein's (1925–26), Grant's, and K. G. Kuhn's (1950) claim or assumption that the Eighteen Benedictions originally existed in one standard text. Heinemann amasses impressive evidence to support the claim that this prayer, as well as others, originally did not receive standardization (1977:45–52).

Urbach (1980) argues against the consensus date for the insertion of the *Birkat ha-Minim* ("Let the Christians and *mynym* perish in a moment . . .") to the twelfth benediction of the *Tefillah*, which—according to most recent publications (e.g., Davies: 272–77)—is attributed to the time of Rabban Gamaliel II (ca. 85 c.e.). Urbach claims that this benediction prior to 70 contained a curse against the *pryshym*, those leaving the community, and that this curse later was directed against the *mynym*, which did not include the Christians but denoted the heretics. Eventually, after the Bar Kokhba revolt, Christians were included in the curse, "and to emphasize their inclusion the נוצרים are mentioned explicitly" (Urbach, 1980; see also Urbach, 1975, 1:401).

SUMMARY

This brief report attempts to survey the results of the most fruitful recent research regarding the early hymnbooks, the possibly Jewish prayers and hymns in the New Testament, and the proto-rabbinic prayers. The progress and quality of analytical research are impressive, and the origins of these hymns and prayers have been clarified considerably.

If one is to speak of a scholarly consensus, it would seem to be the growing recognition of the importance of such hymns and prayers not only as a significant witness to forms of Jewish piety and liturgy around the turn of the era but also as a major source for understanding Jesus and his earliest followers, as well as the nomenclature, style, and form of the earliest Christian hymns and prayers now preserved in the New Testament and related literature. Grant argued convincingly that "the study of the ancient Jewish liturgy is of paramount importance" for "the proper understanding of the New Testament" (60). There is also a growing consensus today that research on these compositions must be freed from the attempt to align them with the Essenes, the Pharisees, or any other sectarian group (e.g., Smith, 1956; Schürer, ed., 1979); from the misleading and anachronistic attempt to separate them into Hellenistic or Palestinian provenances; and from the assumption that early Judaism was ordered by a dominant orthodoxy.

It is clear that from the earliest times emphasis was upon personal and instantaneous prayer (Heinemann, 1977:37–51; Le Déaut, 1977:69–70). Although an emphasis upon the spontaneous nature of authentic prayer continued after 70 (see *m Ber.* 4:4 and *m. 'Abot* 2:13), fixed prayers did begin to develop prior to the destruction of the Temple and during the period of early Judaism (Heinemann, 1977:15; Heinemann and Petuchowski: 31; Le Déaut, 1977). Talmon focuses upon this development, but he correctly cautions that we do not presently know the "precise beginning of institutionalized prayer in Judaism" (265–84). The development is clear, but unfortunately it has been discussed with little, if any, reference to the hymnbooks described above.

CRITIQUE

Research upon early Jewish hymns, odes, and prayers has been characteristically analytical, focusing generally upon manuscript study and the higher critical issues of language, date, and provenance. Relatively little, if any, research has been directed to the questions of genre, form criticism, the relation of a composition's poetic style (*parallelismus membrorum*, rhythm, meter) to the Davidic Psalter, the similarities among the numerous hymns, odes, and prayers, and their use and function in the cult, synagogue *ḥăbûrâ* meals, *Bêt-midrāš*, and even the Temple. Heinemann's monumental publication (1977) is a singular exception.

We remain ignorant of the social and religious settings of most of the extant hymns and prayers (see Jansen). We do not know why some hymns and prayers are in prose (e.g., Bar 1:15–3:8) and others in poetry (e.g., *Pss. Sol.*), and why and to what extent wisdom motifs are dominant in late hymns and prayers (e.g., the poem in praise of Wisdom in Bar 3:9–4:4; see C. A. Moore; 295–304). We need to know more about the historical background of these compositions and to explore the theology of the shared themes. We need to examine why many of the Jewish apocalypses are intermittently punctuated by hymns and prayers.

Publications have tended to be atomistic. Focus has customarily been narrowed to one (or a few) hymn(s) or a single hymnbook with scarcely any attention to the other extant data. For example, too frequently an article titled "Qumran Hymns" will discuss only the *Hodayoth*, and another article similarly titled will barely mention this collection. Jansen's monograph of 1937 is seriously out-dated and includes only the following early Jewish documents: 1, 2, 3 Maccabees, Tobit, Judith, Prayer of Manasseh, Prayer of Azariah, Song of the Three Young Men, Esther, Baruch, Ben Sira, Wisdom of Solomon, *Psalms of Solomon*, and *2 Baruch*. No one has yet attempted to write the history of liturgy in early Judaism.

To assist preparations for this desideratum—and with the hope that for the bicentennial celebrations of the SBL some future person may report its existence and receptions—the following prolegomenous comments are offered.

The Jewish hymns and prayers need to be discussed in the context of the history of religions. G. F. Moore correctly noted that Jewish prayers are unique in that they do not request material possessions or luxuries (also Martin: 14–23). Certainly the documents discussed herein will prove to be classified within B. Tylor's (455–56) "higher" levels of culture. If the "true nature of a religion is most clearly revealed by what men seek from God in it" (G. F. Moore: 2:213), then it is clear that the early Jews neither created an efficacious God (*pace* L. Feuerbach) nor evidenced tendencies toward a *deus ex machina*. Rather they often adhered to traditions regardless of rewards or punishments (see Dan 3:18; 2 Macc 6:27–28). Some later Jews, however, using these and other early traditions, attempted to manipulate God through magical formulas (Simon: 399–404; Goodenough, 1953:161; Urbach, 1975:97–134).

Although early Jewish writers emphasized the remoteness of God, they habitually punctuated their compositions with prayers in which God's presence is affirmed (see the list below). He hears prayers and answers them (*T. 12 Patr.*, esp. *T. Jos.* 10:1–2; *2 Bar.* 48:25–43 [esp. v. 26]; *Par. Jer.* 6:15; cf. Pseudo-Philo *Liber Antiquitatum Biblicarum* (*LAB*) 51; Sir 35:17; *m. Ber.* 4:4; and the fifteenth of the Eighteen Benedictions). The responsiveness of God is illustrated in the well-known traditions regarding the "heroes of prayer": Akiba, Hanina ben Dosa, and Ḥoni. God's historical acts demonstrated the valid assumption of his continuing mercy (see *Prayer of Manasseh*, Charlesworth, 1985). There is abundant evidence to warrant the conclusion that many Jews, rejoicing in God's benevolence and the joy of the law, felt constrained—even in amazingly trying periods—at all times to praise the creator and covenanter (see *Letter of Aristeas* 197; Tob 4:19; 1QS 10:9–17; cf. *Odes Sol.* 16). The cosmic and calendrical dimension of praise is palpable (see *Jubilees, 1 Enoch*, 1QH). According to the late, Christian portions of the *Ascension of Isaiah*, the quality of angelic singing improves as one ascends, and according to the (Christian?) *Testament of Adam*, the hours of the day and night are filled with praises to God by all his creatures.

Within many of the pseudepigrapha there are hundreds of hymns and prayers. For example, Pseudo-Philo obviously felt impelled—for reasons still unknown to us—to rewrite "the Bible" (see Harrington, chap. 11 above), so that the narrative was expanded with poetic compositions. He added at least four psalms (Lament of Seila, *LAB* 40:5–7; Psalms of David, *LAB* 59:4; 60:2–3; Hymn of Deborah, *LAB* 32:1–17) and twelve prayers (of Moses, *LAB* 12:8–9; 19:8–9; 19:14–16; of Joshua, *LAB* 21:2–5; of Kenaz, *LAB* 25:6; 27:7; 28:5; of Jael, *LAB* 31:5, 7; of "the people," *LAB* 39:7; of Samson's parents, *LAB* 42:2, 5; of Anna, *LAB* 50:4; 51:3–6).

Recognizing that many early Jewish hymns and prayers are now lost (see *T. Job* 49:3; 50:3), we should include in a survey of them *at least* the following compositions:

A. *Early Jewish Hymns*
  1. Hymns of Joshua ben Sira (Sir 51:1–12; 51:13–30; 39:12–35)
  2. The psalms in 1 Maccabees (3:50–53)
  3. Psalms 151–155 (Supplement to the Psalter)
  4. Qumran non-Masoretic psalms (11QPs a-e)
  5. *Hodayoth* (Qumran hymnbook)
  6. Other Qumran hymns (1QS 10–11; 1QM 10:8–12:16; 13:7–14:1)
  7. Hymns from Qumran, probably not Essene (e.g., 4QŠirŠabb)
  8. Psalm in Baruch (1:15–3:8)
  9. The Song of the Three Young Men
 10. Judith's Song of Thanksgiving (Jdt 16:1–17)
 11. Hymn to Wisdom (Wis 7:22–8:1)
 12. *Psalms of Solomon* (hymnbook)
 13. Psalms in Pseudo-Philo (see above)
 14. Hymns in the *T. Job* (25:1–7b; 32:1a–12c; 43:2b–13b; 53:1b–4)
 15. Psalm of Taxo (*T. Mos.* 10:1–10)
 16. Psalms in *2 Baruch* (10:6–19; 11:1–7; 14:8–10; 35:2–5; 75:1–8)

B. *Early Nonrabbinic Jewish Prayers*
  1. Prayer of Joshua ben Sira (Sir 36:1–17)
  2. Prayer of Enoch (*1 Enoch* 84:1–6)
  3. Prayer of Judas Maccabeus and the Priests (1 Macc 4:30–33)
  4. Prayers in 2 Maccabees (1:24–29; 15:22–24)
  5. Prayers in 3 Maccabees (2:2–20; 6:2–15)
  6. Prayers in *Jubilees* (1:19–21; 5:24–26; 12:2–5; 15:6–8; *et passim*)
  7. Prayer of Azariah
  8. Prayers in Tobit (Tob 3:2–6; 3:11–15a; 8:5–8; 13:1–18)
  9. Prayer of Judith (Jdt 9:2–14)
 10. Prayers of Esther and Mordecai (Add Esth 14:3–19; 13:9–19)
 11. Prayer of Manasseh
 12. Prayer of Solomon (Wis 9:1–18)
 13. Prayer of Jesus (Matt 6; Luke 11; *Didache* 8)
 14. Prayers in Pseudo-Philo (see above)
 15. Prayer of Asenath (*Joseph and Asenath* 12–13)
 16. Laments and Prayers of Ezra (esp. Confessio Esdrae, 4 Ezra 8:20–36)
 17. Prayers in *2 Baruch* (38:1–4; 48:2–24; 54:1–22)
 18. Prayers in *Paraleipomena Jeremiou* (esp. 6:6–10; 6:12–14; 9:3–6)
 19. Prayer of Joseph
 20. Prayer of Jacob
 21. Zephaniah's Prayers (*Apoc. Zeph.* 9:1–10; 12:5–10)

22. Hellenistic Synagogal Prayers (*Apos. Const.* 7–8, a hymnbook)
23. Prayers in the targumim; e.g., Tamar (Gen 38:25); Moses (Deut 32:50), Abraham (Gen 22)

C. *Proto-Rabbinic Prayers and Synagogue Litanies*
   1. *'Amîdāh* (Standing Prayer)
   2. *Šemôneh 'Eśreh* or *Tefillāh* (Eighteen Benedictions)
   3. *'Ahabāh Rabbāh* (With Abounding Love)
   4. *'Alênû lĕšabbeaḥ* (It is our duty to praise . . .)
   5. *Qaddîš* (Magnified and sanctified . . .)
   6. Grace after Meals

D. *Other Early Possibly Jewish or Jewish-Christian Hymns and Prayers*
   1. Magnificat, Benedictus, Gloria in Excelsis, Nunc Dimittis (Luke 1–2)
   2. Hymns in Paul (Col 1:15–20; Phil 2:6–11)
   3. Hymns in Revelation
   4. John 1:1–18
   5. *Odes of Solomon* (hymnbook)
   6. Hymn in Ignatius (*Eph.* 19:2–3)
   7. Hymn of the Pearl (*Acts Thom.* 108–113)
   8. Hermes' Hymn of Rebirth (*C.H.* XIII)
   9. Hermetic Prayer of Thanksgiving (CG VI, 7)
   10. Hymn of the First Stele of Seth (CG VII,5)
   11. The Mandean Hymnbook (late)
   12. The Manichaean Psalmbook (late)

CONCLUSION

These hymns and prayers need to be examined in light of the psalms and prayers in the late canonical documents, namely, the psalm in Dan 2:20–23 and Psalm 110, and the prayers in Dan 2:4–19, Ezra 9:6–15, and Neh 1:5–11. The abundance of the data should be evaluated in light of the fact that the earliest prayers were not written down, following the principle that "they who write down prayers are as they who burn the Torah" (*b. Šab.* 115b; see Elbogen in Petuchowski, ed.).

New Testament scholars must put aside the old view that Jewish liturgy in Jesus' time was cold and concretized. Schürer (1897–98, Div. 2, vol. 2:115–25) was in error when he claimed that in early Judaism prayer "was bound in the fetters of a rigid mechanism" and that the *Shema* and *Shemoneh 'Esreh* were "degraded to an external function" (115). The editors of the "New Schürer" have wisely rewritten this section "from a historical rather than a theological vantage point" (Schürer, ed., 1979:464). Jewish prayers and hymns were frequently warm, alive, and personal. Even for the apocalyptists, prayers and hymns provided intimate interlocution with God. Codified laws for *some* Jews did lead to a myopic, legalistic religion; to others they ordered time and cosmos, regularizing stimuli for prayer, praise, and the experience of God's oneness with and presence in creation (see, e.g., Kadushin; E. P. Sanders).

BIBLIOGRAPHY

Aune, D. E.
1972   *The Cultic Setting of Realized Eschatology in Early Christianity.*
            NovTSup 28. Leiden: Brill.

Ausejo, S. de
1956   "¿Es un himno a Christo el prologo de San Juan?" *EstBib* 15:
            223-77, 381-427.

Avigad, N.
1958   "The Palaeography of the Dead Sea Scrolls and Related Docu-
            ments." Pp. 56-87 in *Aspects of the Dead Sea Scrolls.* Ed. C. Rabin
            and Y. Yadin. Scripta Hierosolymitana 4. Jerusalem: Magnes Press.

Baarda, T.
1975   "Het Uitbreiden van mijn Handen is zijn Teken." Pp. 245-59 in
            Loven en Geloven: Festschrift voor Prof. Dr. N. H. Ridderbos.
            Amsterdam: Bolland.

Baillet, M.
1962   "Psaumes, hymnes, cantiques et prières dans les manuscrits de
            Qumran." Pp. 339-405 in *Le Psautier: Ses origines, ses problèmes
            littéraires, son influence.* Ed. R. De Langhe. Orientalia et Biblica
            Lovaniensia 4. Louvain: Institut Orientaliste.

Bardtke, H.
1956   "Considérations sur les Cantiques de Qumran." *RB* 63: 220-33.
1956-57   "Das Ich des Meisters in den Hodajoth von Qumran." *Wissenschaft-
            liche Zeitschrift der Karl-Marx-Universität Leipzig* 6: 93-104.

Barrett, C. K.
1978   *The Gospel According to St. John: An Introduction with Commen-
            tary and Notes on the Greek Text.* 2d ed. Philadelphia: West-
            minster; see esp. pp. 65, 112-13, 507.

Becker, J.
1964   *Das Heil Gottes: Heils- und Sündenbegriffe in den Qumrantexten
            und im Neuen Testament.* SUNT 3. Göttingen: Vandenhoeck &
            Ruprecht.

Benoit, P.
1956-57   "L'enfance de Jean-Baptiste selon Luc I." *NTS* 3: 169-94.

Bernard, J. H.
1912   *The Odes of Solomon.* TS 8.3. Cambridge: University Press.

Birnbaum, P.
1949   *Daily Prayer Book: Ha-Siddur Ha-Shalem.* New York: Hebrew
            Publishing Company.

Birnbaum, S. A.
1952   "The Date of the Hymns Scroll." *PEQ* 84: 94-103.

Black, M.
1962   "Pharisees." *IDB* 3. 774–81.
Bousset, W.
1915   "Eine jüdische Gebetssammlung im siebenten Buch der apostolischen Konstitutionen." Reprint, pp. 231–86 in *Religionsgeschichtliche Studien: Aufsätze zur Religionsgeschichte des Hellenistischen Zeitalters.* NovTSup 50. Leiden: Brill, 1979.
Brocke, M., and J. J. Petuchowski, eds.
1978   *The Lord's Prayer and Jewish Liturgy.* New York: Seabury.
Brown, R. E.
1965   "The Pater Noster as an Eschatological Prayer." In *New Testament Essays.* New York: Doubleday.
1966   *The Gospel According to John.* 2 vols. AB 29, 29A. Garden City, NY: Doubleday.
1977   *The Birth of the Messiah: A Commentary on the Infancy Narratives in Matthew and Luke.* Garden City, NY: Doubleday.
Bultmann, R.
1923   "Der religionsgeschichtliche Hintergrund des Prologs zum Johannes-Evangelium." Pp. 1–26 in *Eucharisterion: Festschrift für Hermann Gunkel,* vol. 2. Ed. H. Schmidt. FRLANT 36.2. Göttingen: Vandenhoeck & Ruprecht.
1971   *The Gospel of John: A Commentary.* Trans. G. R. Beasley-Murray. Oxford: Blackwell.
Burrows, M.
1958   *More Light on the Dead Sea Scrolls.* New York: Viking.
Carmignac, J.
1961   "Les affinités qumrâniennes de la onzième Ode de Salomon." *RevQ* 3: 71–102.
1963   "Un qumrânien converti au christianisme: L'auteur des Odes de Salomon." Pp. 75–108 in *Qumran-Probleme.* Ed. H. Bardtke. Deutsche Akademie der Wissenschaften zu Berlin 42. Berlin: Akademie-Verlag.
1969   *Recherches sur le "Notre Père."* Paris: Letouzey & Ané.
Chadwick, H.
1970   "Some Reflections on the Character and Theology of the Odes of Solomon." In *Kyriakon: Festschrift Johannes Quasten.* Ed. P. Granfield and J. A. Jungmann. Münster: Aschendorff.
Charles, R. H., ed.
1913   *APOT.*
Charlesworth, J. H.
1969   "The Odes of Solomon—Not Gnostic." *CBQ* 31: 357–69.
1970   "Les Odes de Salomon et les manuscrits de la mer morte." *RB* 77: 522–49.
1972   "Qumran, John and the Odes of Solomon." In *John and Qumran.* Ed. J. H. Charlesworth. London: Chapman.
1973   *The Odes of Solomon.* Oxford: Clarendon Press. Corrected reprint, SBLTT; Pseudepigrapha Series 7. Missoula, MT: Scholars Press, 1977.
1976a   *The Pseudepigrapha and Modern Research.* SBLSCS 7. Missoula, MT: Scholars Press.

1976b   "Odes of Solomon." *IDBSup*, 637–38.
1979   "The Concept of the Messiah in the Pseudepigrapha." Pp. 188–218
           in *ANRW* 2.19.1. Ed. W. Haase. Berlin and New York: de Gruyter.
1980   "Christian and Jewish Self-Definition in Light of the Christian
           Additions to the Apocryphal Writings." In *Judaism from the Mac-
           cabees to the Mid-Third Century*. Ed. E. P. Sanders and A. I.
           Baumgarten. Philadelphia: Fortress.
1982   "A Prolegomenon to a New Study of the Jewish Background of the
           Hymns and Prayers in the New Testament." In *Essays in Honour of
           Yigael Yadin*. Ed. G. Vermes and J. Neusner. Oxford: Oxford
           Centre for Postgraduate Hebrew Studies (= *JJS* 33: 1–21).
1985   "Prayer of Manasseh." Pp. 625–37 in Charlesworth, ed., 1985.

Charlesworth, J. H., ed.
1983   *OTP*. Vol. 1. *Apocalyptic Literature and Testaments*.
1985   *OTP*. Vol. 2. *Expansions of the "Old Testament" and Legends,
           Wisdom and Philosophical Literature, Prayers, Psalms, and Odes,
           Fragments of Lost Judeo-Hellenistic Works*.

Charlesworth, J. H., and R. A. Culpepper
1973   "The Odes of Solomon and the Gospel of John." *CBQ* 35: 298–322.

Charlesworth, J. H., with J. A. Sanders
1985   "More Psalms of David." Pp. 609–24 in Charlesworth, ed., 1985.

Cross, F. M.
1978   "David, Orpheus, and Psalm 151:3–4." *BASOR* 231: 69–71.

Davies, W. D.
1966   *The Setting of the Sermon on the Mount*. Cambridge: University
           Press.

Deichgräber, R.
1967   *Gotteshymnus und Christushymnus in der frühen Christenheit:
           Untersuchungen zu Form, Sprache und Stil der frühchristlichen
           Hymnen*. SUNT 5. Göttingen: Vandenhoeck & Ruprecht.

Delcor, M.
1962   *Les Hymnes de Qumran (Hodayot)*. Paris: Letouzey et Ané.
1963   "Salomón, Salmos de." *Enciclopedia de la Biblia*. Ed. J. A.
           Gutiérrez-Larraya. Barcelona: Garriga. Vol. 6, col. 401.
1973   "Psaumes de Salomon." *DBSup* 48: 214–45.

Delcor, M., ed.
1978   *Qumrân: Sa piété, sa théologie et son milieu*. BETL 46. Paris and
           Gembloux: Duculot. Leuven: University Press.

Delling, G.
1959   "Zum gottesdienstlichen Stil der Johannesapokalypse." *NovT* 3:
           107–37.

Denis, A.-M.
1970   *Introduction aux pseudépigraphes grecs d'Ancien Testament*.
           SVTP 1. Leiden: Brill.

Drijvers, H. J. W.
1978   "Die Oden Salomos und die Polemik mit den Markioniten im
           Syrischen Christentum." Pp. 39–55 in OCA 205. Rome: Pontificium
           Institutum Orientalium Studiorum.
1979   "Kerygma und Logos in den Oden Salomos dargestellt am Beispiel
           der 23. Ode." In *Kerygma und Logos: Festschrift für Carl An-
           dresen*. Ed. A. M. Ritter. Göttingen: Vandenhoeck & Ruprecht.

Dupont-Sommer, A.
1962   *The Essene Writings from Qumran.* Trans. G. Vermes. New York: Meridian Books.
1964   "Le psaume CLI dans 11QPs^a et la problème de son origine essénienne." *Sem* 14: 25–62.
1977   *Trente années de recherches sur les manuscrits de la mer morte (1947–1977).* Paris: Institut de France.

Ehlen, Arlis J.
1970   "The Poetic Structure of a Hodayah from Qumran: An Analysis of Grammatical, Semantic, and Auditory Correspondence in 1QH 3:19–36." Diss., Harvard University. Summarized in *HTR* 63 (1970) 516.

Ehlers, B.
1970   "Kann das Thomasevangelium aus Edessa Stammen? Ein Beitrag zur Frühgeschichte des Christentums in Edessa." *NovT* 12: 284–317.

Elbogen, I.
1931   *Der jüdische Gottesdienst in seiner geschichtlichen Entwicklung.* 3d ed. Frankfurt: Kauffmann.

Emerton, J. A.
1967   "Some Problems of Text and Language in the Odes of Solomon." *JTS* n.s. 18: 372–406.
1977   "Notes on Some Passages in the Odes of Solomon." *JTS* n.s. 28: 507–19.

EncJud
1971   "Alenu," 2: 557; "Kaddish," 10: 661.

Fiensy, D. A.
1985   *Prayers Alleged to be Jewish: An Examination of the* Constitutiones Apostolorum. Brown Judaic Studies 65. Chico, CA: Scholars Press.

Fiensy, D. A., and D. Darnell
1985   "Hellenistic Synagogal Prayers." Pp. 671–97 in Charlesworth, ed., 1985.

Finkelstein, L.
1925–26 "The Development of the Amidah." *JQR* n.s. 16: 1–43, 127–70.
1938   "The Oldest Midrash: Pre-Rabbinic Ideals and Teachings in the Passover Haggadah." *HTR* 31: 291–317. Reprinted in Finkelstein, 1972.
1940   *The Pharisees: The Sociological Background of Their Faith.* 2 vols. Philadelphia: Jewish Publication Society.
1942–43 "Pre-Maccabean Documents in the Passover Haggadah." *HTR* 35: 291–332; 36: 1–38. Reprinted in Finkelstein, 1972.
1972   *Pharisaism in the Making: Selected Essays.* New York: Ktav.

Ford, J. M.
1975   *Revelation.* AB 38. Garden City, NY: Doubleday.

Gibson, J. C. L.
1965   "From Qumran to Edessa: Or the Aramaic Speaking Church Before and After 70 A.D." *New College Bulletin* 2: 9–19. Reprinted in *ALUOS* 5 (1963–1965) 24–39.

Goodenough, E. R.
1935   *By Light, Light: The Mystic Gospel of Hellenistic Judaism.* New Haven: Yale University Press.

1953   *Jewish Symbols in the Greco-Roman Period*, vol. 2. Princeton:
            Princeton University Press.

Goshen-Gottstein, M. H.
1966   "The Psalms Scroll (11QPsª): A Problem of Canon and Text."
            Textus 5: 22–33.

Goulder, M. D.
1963   "The Composition of the Lord's Prayer." *JTS* n.s. 14: 32–45.
1974   *Midrash and Lection in Matthew*. London: SPCK.

Grant, F. C.
1953   "Modern Study of the Jewish Liturgy." *ZAW* 65: 59–77.

Graubard, B.
1978   "The Kaddish Prayer." Pp. 59–72 in *The Lord's Prayer and Jewish
            Liturgy*. Ed. J. J. Petuchowski and M. Brocke. New York: Seabury.

Gray, G. B.
1913   "The Psalms of Solomon." *APOT* 2: 625–52.

Gruenwald, I.
1973   "Knowledge and Vision: Towards a Clarification of Two 'Gnostic'
            Concepts in the Light of Their Alleged Origins." *Israel Oriental
            Studies* 3: 63–107.

Gutmann, J., ed.
1975   *The Synagogue: Studies in Origins, Archaeology and Architecture*.
            New York: Ktav.

Harnack, A. von
1910   *Ein jüdisch-christliches Psalmbuch aus dem ersten Jahrhundert*.
            Aus dem Syrischen übersetzt von Johannes Flemming, bearbeitet
            und herausgegeben von Adolf Harnack. TU 35.4. Leipzig: Hinrichs.

Harner, P. B.
1975   *Understanding the Lord's Prayer*. Philadelphia: Fortress.

Harrington, D. J., J. Cazeaux, C. Perrot, P.-M. Bogaert, eds.
1976   *Pseudo-Philon: Les Antiquités Bibliques*. 2 vols. SC 229, 230. Paris:
            Cerf.

Harris, J. R., and A. Mingana
1916–20   *The Odes and Psalms of Solomon*. 2 vols. Manchester: University
            Press; London and New York: Longmans, Green.

Heinemann, J.
1977   *Prayer in the Talmud: Forms and Patterns*. SJ 9. Berlin and New
            York: de Gruyter.
1978   "The Background of Jesus' Prayer in the Jewish Liturgical Tradi-
            tion." Pp. 81–89 in *The Lord's Prayer and Jewish Liturgy*. Ed. J. J.
            Petuchowski and M. Brocke. New York: Seabury.

Heinemann, J., and J. J. Petuchowski, eds.
1975   *Literature of the Synagogue*. New York: Behrman.

Hengel, M.
1974   *Judaism and Hellenism: Studies in their Encounter in Palestine
            during the Early Hellenistic Period*. 2 vols. Trans. J. Bowden. Phil-
            adelphia: Fortress.

Hennecke, E.
1924   *Neutestamentliche Apokryphen*. 2d ed. Tübingen: Mohr-Siebeck.

1959-64   *Neutestamentliche Apokryphen in deutscher Übersetzung.* 3d ed.
           Ed. W. Schneemelcher. 2 vols. Tübingen: Mohr-Siebeck.

Hoffman, L. A.
1979   *The Canonization of the Synagogue Service.* UNDCSJCA 4. Notre
           Dame and London: University of Notre Dame Press.

Holm-Nielsen, S.
1955   "Den gammeltestamentlige salmetradition." *DTT* 18: 135–48,
           193–215.
1960a   *Hodayot: Psalms from Qumran.* ATDan 2. Aarhus: Universitets-
           forlaget.
1960b   "The Importance of Late Jewish Psalmody for the Understanding of
           Old Testament Psalmodic Tradition." *ST* 13: 1–53.
1970   "Salomos Salmer." Pp. 548–95 in *De Gammeltestamentlige Pseud-
           epigrapher,* vol. 5. Ed. E. Hammershaimb et al. Copenhagen: Gad.
1977   *Die Psalmen Salomos.* JSHRZ 4.2. Gütersloh: Mohn.

Jansen, H. L.
1937   *Die spätjüdische Psalmendichtung, ihr Entstehungskreis und ihr
           "Sitz im Leben": Eine literaturgeschichtlich-soziologische Unter-
           suchung.* Skrifter utgitt av det Norske Videnskaps-Akademi i Oslo,
           II. Historisk-Filosofisk Klasse, 1937. No. 3. Oslo: Dybwad.

Jaubert, A.
1963   *La notion d'alliance dans le judaïsme aux abords de l'ère chrétienne.*
           Patristica Sorbonensia 6. Paris: Seuil.

Jeremias, G.
1963   *Der Lehrer der Gerechtigkeit.* SUNT 2. Göttingen: Vandenhoeck &
           Ruprecht.

Jeremias, J.
1967   *The Prayers of Jesus.* SBT 2/6. London: SCM. Reprint, Philadelphia:
           Fortress, 1978.

Johnson, N. B.
1948   *Prayer in the Apocrypha and Pseudepigrapha: A Study of the Jewish
           Concept of God.* SBLMS 2. Philadelphia: SBL.

Jörns, K.-P.
1971   *Das hymnische Evangelium: Untersuchungen zu Aufbau, Funktion
           und Herkunft der hymnischen Stücke in der Johannesoffenbarung.*
           SNT 5. Gütersloh: Mohn.

Kadushin, M.
1972   *The Rabbinic Mind.* 3d ed. Appendix by S. Greenberg. New York:
           Bloch.

Klijn, A. F. J.
1965   "The Influence of Jewish Theology on the Odes of Solomon and the
           Acts of Thomas." *Aspects du judéo-christianisme: Colloque de
           Strasbourg 23–25 avril 1964.* Paris: Presses universitaires de France.

Kohler, K.
1893   "Über die Ursprünge und Grundformen der synagogalen Liturgie:
           Eine Studie." *MGWJ* N.F. 1: 441–51, 489–97.
1903   "Didascalia." *The Jewish Encyclopedia.* 4: 588–95. New York and
           London: Funk & Wagnalls.
1924   "The Essene Version of the Seven Benedictions as Preserved in the
           VII Book of the Apostolic Constitutions." *HUCA* 1: 410–25.

Kraft, C. F.
1957   "Poetical Structure in the Qumran Thanksgiving Psalms." *BR* 2:
        1-18.

Kraft, R. A.
1975   "The Multiform Jewish Heritage of Early Christianity." Pp.
        174-99 in *Christianity, Judaism and Other Greco-Roman Cults: Studies for
        Morton Smith at Sixty*, vol. 3. Ed. J. Neusner. SJLA 12. Leiden:
        Brill.

Kroll, J.
1968   *Die christliche Hymnodik bis zu Klemens von Alexandreia.* 2d ed.
        Darmstadt: Wissenschaftliche Buchgesellschaft.

Kuhn, H.-W.
1966   *Enderwartung und gegenwärtiges Heil: Untersuchungen zu den
        Gemeindeliedern von Qumran.* SUNT 4. Göttingen: Vandenhoeck
        & Ruprecht.

Kuhn, K. G.
1937   *Die älteste Textgestalt der Psalmen Salomos insbesondere auf
        Grund der syrischen Übersetzung neu untersucht, Mit einer Be-
        arbeitung und Übersetzung der Psalmen Salomos 13-17.* BWANT
        4.21. Stuttgart: Kohlhammer.
1950   *Achtzehngebet und Vaterunser und der Reim.* Tübingen: Mohr-
        Siebeck.

Le Déaut, R., A. Jaubert, and K. Hruby
1977   *The Spirituality of Judaism.* Trans. P. Barrett. Religious Experience
        Series 11. St. Meinrad, IN: Abbey Press.

Licht, J.
1957   *The Thanksgiving Scroll.* Jerusalem: Bialik Institute (Hebrew).
1971   "Solomon, Odes of." *EncJud* 15: 114-15.

Mach, R.
1957   *Der Zaddik in Talmud und Midrasch.* Leiden: Brill.

Mansoor, M.
1961   *The Thanksgiving Hymns.* STDJ 3. Grand Rapids: Eerdmans.

Martin, B.
1968   *Prayer in Judaism.* New York: Basic Books.

Menzies, A.
1910   "The Odes of Solomon." *Interpreter* [London] 7: 7-22.

Metzger, B. M.
1955   "Odes of Solomon." Pp. 811-12 in *Twentieth Century Encyclopedia
        of Religious Knowledge, Supplement.* Vol. 2. Ed. L. A. Loetscher.
        Grand Rapids: Baker.
1957   *An Introduction to the Apocrypha.* New York: Oxford University
        Press.

Michaud, H.
1956   "Le Maître de la Justice d'après les hymnes de Qumran." *Bulletin
        de la faculté libre de théologie protestante de Paris* 19: 67-77.

Milik, J. T.
1959   *Ten Years of Discovery in the Wilderness of Judaea.* Trans. J.
        Strugnell. SBT 26. London: SCM.

Moore, C. A.
1977   *Daniel, Esther, and Jeremiah: The Additions. A New Translation with Introduction and Commentary.* AB 44. Garden City, NY: Doubleday.

Moore, G. F.
1927-30   *Judaism in the First Centuries of the Christian Era: The Age of the Tannaim.* 3 vols. Cambridge, MA: Harvard University Press.

Moraldi, L.
1971   *I manoscritti di Qumrān.* Turin: Unione Tipografico-Editrice Torinese. (See esp. pp. 327-494.)

Morawe, G.
1960   *Aufbau und Abgrenzung der Loblieder von Qumrân: Studien zur gattungsgeschichtlichen Einordnung der Hodajôth.* Theologische Arbeiten 16. Berlin: Evangelische Verlagsanstalt.

Mowinckel, S.
1956   "Some Remarks on Hodayoth 39 (V, 5-20)." *JBL* 75: 265-76.

Murphy-O'Connor, J.
1969   "La genése littéraire de la Règle de la Communauté." *RB* 76: 528-49.

Murray, R.
1975   *Symbols of Church and Kingdom: A Study in Early Syriac Tradition.* Cambridge: University Press.

Neusner, J.
1971   *The Rabbinic Traditions About the Pharisees Before 70.* 3 vols. Leiden: Brill.
1979a   "The Formation of Rabbinic Judaism: Yavneh (Jamnia) from A.D. 70 to 100." Pp. 3-42 in *ANRW* 2.19.2. Ed. W. Haase. Berlin and New York: de Gruyter.
1979b   *From Politics to Piety: The Emergence of Pharisaic Judaism.* 2d ed. New York: Ktav.
1980   "'Judaism' After Moore: A Programmatic Statement." *JJS* 31: 141-56.

Nickelsburg, G. W. E., Jr.
1972   *Resurrection, Immortality and Eternal Life in Intertestamental Judaism.* HTS 26. Cambridge, MA: Harvard University Press.

Noack, B.
1969   *Om Fadervor.* Copenhagen: Gad.

O'Dell, J.
1961   "The Religious Background of the Psalms of Solomon (Re-evaluated in the Light of the Qumran Texts)." *RevQ* 3: 241-57.

Petuchowski, J. J.
1972   *Understanding Jewish Prayer.* New York: Ktav.
1978   "The Liturgy of the Synagogue." Pp. 45-57 in *The Lord's Prayer and Jewish Liturgy.* Ed. J. J. Petuchowski and M. Brocke. New York: Seabury.

Petuchowski, J. J., ed.
1970   *Contributions to the Scientific Study of Jewish Liturgy.* New York: Ktav.

Philonenko, M.
1959   "L'origine essénienne des cinq psaumes syriaques de David." *Sem* 9: 35–48.
1962   "Conjecture sur un verset de la onzième Ode de Salomon." *ZNW* 53: 264.

Rappaport, U.
1971   "Solomon, Psalms of." *EncJud* 15: 115–16.

Rese, M.
1970   "Formeln und Lieder im Neuen Testament: Einige notwendige Anmerkungen." *Verkündigung und Forschung* (Beihefte zu *Evangelische Theologie*) 15: 75–95.

Rudolph, K.
1964   "War der Verfasser der Oden Salomos ein 'Qumran-Christ'? Ein Beitrag zur Diskussion um die Anfänge der Gnosis." *RevQ* 4: 523–55.

Ryle, H. E., and M. R. James
1891   *Psalmoi Solomōntos: Psalms of the Pharisees Commonly Called the Psalms of Solomon.* Cambridge: University Press.

Sanders, E. P.
1977   *Paul and Palestinian Judaism: A Comparison of Patterns of Religion.* Philadelphia: Fortress.

Sanders, J. A.
1965   *The Psalms Scroll of Qumrân Cave 11 (11QPsᵃ).* DJD 4. Oxford: Clarendon Press.
1967   *The Dead Sea Psalms Scroll.* Ithaca, NY: Cornell University Press.

Sanders, J. T.
1971   *The New Testament Christological Hymns: Their Historical Religious Background.* SNTSMS 15. Cambridge: University Press.

Sandmel, S.
1979   "Goodenough on Philo." Pp. 140–141 in *Philo of Alexandria: An Introduction.* New York: Oxford University Press.

Schattenmann, J.
1965   *Studien zum neutestamentlichen Prosahymnus.* Munich: Beck.

Schille, G.
1965   *Frühchristliche Hymnen.* Berlin: Evangelische Verlagsanstalt.

Schulz, P.
1974   *Der Autoritätsanspruch des Lehrers der Gerechtigkeit in Qumran.* Meisenheim am Glan: Hain.

Schüpphaus, J.
1977   *Die Psalmen Salomos.* ALGHJ 7. Leiden: Brill.

Schürer, E.
1897–98   *A History of the Jewish People in the Time of Jesus Christ.* Trans. J. MacPherson, S. Taylor, and P. Christie. 6 vols. Edinburgh: T. & T. Clark.
1973–   *The History of the Jewish People in the Age of Jesus Christ, 175 B.C.–A.D. 135).* New English version revised and edited by G. Vermes, F. Millar, and M. Black. 3 vols. Edinburgh: T. & T. Clark.

Simon, M.
1948   *Verus Israel: Étude sur les relations entre chrétiens et juifs dans l'empire romain (135–425).* Paris: Boccard. [+ Suppl., 1966]

Skehan P.
1973 "A Liturgical Complex in 11QPs^a." *CBQ* 35: 195–205.

Smith, M.
1956 "Palestinian Judaism in the First Century." Pp. 67–81 in *Israel: Its Role in Civilization*. Ed. M. Davis. New York: Harper.

Sola Pool, D. de
1964 *The Kaddish*. 3d ed. Jerusalem and New York: Sivan Press.

Spanier, A.
1934 "Zur Formengeschichte des altjüdischen Gebetes." *MGWJ* 77: 438–47.
1936 "Stilkritisches zum jüdischen Gebet." *MGWJ* 80: 339–50.
1937 "Die erste Benediktion des Achtzehngebets." *MGWJ* 81: 71–76.
1939 "Dubletten in Gebetstexten." *MGWJ* 83: 142–49.

Strugnell, J.
1965 "More Psalms of David." *CBQ* 27: 207–16.
1966 "Notes on the Text and Transmission of the Apocryphal Psalms 151, 154 (= Syr. II) and 155 (= Syr. III)." *HTR* 59: 257–81.

Sukenik, E.L.
1955 *The Dead Sea Scrolls of the Hebrew University*. Ed. N. Avigad and Y. Yadin. Jerusalem: Hebrew University and Magnes Press.

Talmon, S.
1978 "The Emergence of Institutionalized Prayer in Israel in the Light of the Qumran Literature." Pp. 265–84 in *Qumrân: Sa piété, sa théologie et son milieu*. Ed. M. Delcor. BETL 46. Paris and Gembloux: Duculot. Leuven: University Press.

Terzoli, R.
1972 "Le Odi di Salomone." In *Il Tema della Beatitudine nei Patri Siri*. Rome: Morcelliana.

Testuz, M., ed.
1959 *Papyrus Bodmer VII–IX*. Cologne and Geneva: Bibliothèque Bodmer.

Thompson, L. L.
1968 "The Form and Function of Hymns in the New Testament: A Study in Cultic History." Ph.D. diss., University of Chicago.
1969 "Cult and Eschatology in the Apocalypse of John." *JR* 49: 330–50.

Tilborg, S. van
1972 "A Form-Criticism of the Lord's Prayer." *NovT* 14: 94–105.

Trafton, J. L.
1985 *The Syriac Version of the Psalms of Solomon: A Critical Evaluation*. SBLSCS 11. Atlanta, GA: Scholars Press.

Tylor, E. B.
1871 *Religion in Primitive Culture*. New York: Harper & Brothers, 1958. [This volume is part II of *Primitive Culture*, which appeared in 1871.]

Urbach, E. E.
1975 *The Sages: Their Concepts and Beliefs*. 2 vols. Trans. I. Abrahams. Jerusalem: Magnes Press.

1980   "Self-Isolation or Self-Affirmation in Judaism: Theory and Practice in the First Three Centuries." In *Judaism from the Maccabees to the Mid-Third Century.* Ed. E. P. Sanders and A. I. Baumgarten. Philadelphia: Fortress.

Vermes, G.
1980   "Jewish Studies and New Testament Interpretation." *JJS* 31: 1–17.

Vermes, G., with P. Vermes
1978   *The Dead Sea Scrolls: Qumran in Perspective.* Cleveland, OH: Collins.

Viteau, J.
1911   *Les Psaumes de Salomon.* Paris: Letouzey et Ané.

Vööbus, A.
1962   "Neues Licht zur Frage der Originalsprache der Oden Salomos." *Muséon* 75: 275–90.
1971   "Solomon, Odes of." *Encylopaedia Britannica* 20: 878.

Wellhausen, J.
1874   *Die Pharisäer und die Sadducäer: Eine Untersuchung zur inneren jüdischen Geschichte.* Greifswald: Bamberg.

Wengst, K.
1972   *Christologische Formeln und Lieder des Urchristentums.* Gütersloh: Mohn.

Winter, P.
1954–55   "Magnificat and Benedictus—Maccabean Psalms?" *BJRL* 37: 328–47.
1962   "Psalms of Solomon." *IDB* 3: 958–60.

Woude, A. S. van der
1974   *Die fünf syrischen Psalmen.* JSHRZ 4.1. Gütersloh: Mohn.

Wright, R. B.
1972   "The Psalms of Solomon, the Pharisees and the Essenes." Pp. 136–54 in *1972 Proceedings: International Organization for Septuagint and Cognate Studies and the Society of Biblical Literature Pseudepigrapha Seminar.* Ed. R. A. Kraft. SBLSCS 2. Missoula, MT: SBL.
1985   "Psalms of Solomon." Pp. 639–70 in Charlesworth, ed., 1985.

Wright, W.
1887   "Some Apocryphal Psalms in Syriac." *Proceedings of the Society of Biblical Archaeology* 9: 257–66.

17
RECONSTRUCTIONS OF
RABBINIC JUDAISM

Anthony J. Saldarini

Critical study of rabbinic Judaism was already practiced during the nineteenth century in some traditional Jewish educational institutions (Yeshivot), rabbinical seminaries, and European universities in the approach that has come to be known as *Wissenschaft des Judentums*. Between the Second World War and 1980, the year of the Society of Biblical Literature's centennial, heirs of this approach at Israeli universities, in American departments of religious and Judaic studies, and among Christian New Testament scholars who became extraordinarily aware of the importance of Judaism for understanding the New Testament have built upon, advanced, and often questioned the methods and results bequeathed to them. In the following pages the work of major scholars and the studies done on central problems connected with early rabbinic Judaism and depending on evidence from talmudic sources will be reviewed. Attention will be focused on the analytic methods used on different types of texts, upon awareness of critical problems, on the extremely difficult problem of dating the sources, and on the proper use of these materials for understanding history and the development of thought within rabbinic Judaism. Special attention will be given to the development of rabbinic Judaism from earlier forms of Judaism in the Second Temple period. For the explicit uses to which rabbinic Judaism has been put in the interpretation of the NT, readers are referred to the chapter "Judaism and the New Testament," *The New Testament and its Modern Interpreters* (1987). In the same chapter the Christian tendency to interpret rabbinic Judaism in a pejorative fashion as legalistic and decadent is also addressed.

The very term "rabbinic Judaism" is problematic and subject to serious misunderstanding. G. F. Moore (1927-30) characterized rabbinic Judaism as "normative" Judaism, and the influence of the Talmuds within Judaism from the first few centuries until the present has often led to an anachronistic portrayal of Maccabean Judaism as essentially identical to talmudic Judaism. The Dead Sea Scrolls and further detailed research on the apocrypha, the pseudepigrapha, and other early sources as well as archaeological finds have convinced scholars of the diversity within Judaism (at least) before the destruction of the Temple in 70 C.E. In addition, evidence for rabbinic Judaism is derived from collections that date from 200 C.E. and later. Stories, anecdotes, halakic and historical statements may also be suspected of anachronism or distortion by later experience and have become increasingly uncertain as sources for the reconstruction of *early* rabbinic Judaism. It is very likely that the antecedents of Mishna, Midrash, the schools, and the rabbis were very different from their later mature progeny and that they underwent a complex development in varied social and historical settings and in response to important human and theological needs and tendencies. These antecedents are masked by the tendency of later sources to treat all statements and interpretations as part of a dialectically related whole rather than a series of historically related stages. Consequently, "rabbinic Judaism" is used as a convenient designation whose meaning and limitations will be demonstrated in the course of this review.

First, the rabbinic sources, especially Mishna and Midrash, will be examined through the eyes of contemporary research on them. The fundamental interpretation of these sources and the contribution they make to our understanding of Judaism are being radically affected by methods previously used on the Bible such as form and redaction criticism. These and other approaches frequently must be modified before they can appropriately be used in the study of rabbinic literature, but the results obtained from such studies have produced striking contributions and have also left nagging questions.

Second, three categories of studies that draw materials primarily from rabbinic literature will be examined: biography, history, and rabbinic "thought." Under history, the description of the Pharisees will be given special consideration. In no instance can the complete bibliography be reviewed, but major authors and major publications will be evaluated for their contributions to the broad outline of our understanding of Judaism and for the promise that their methods of interpretation offer for future study in the respective fields.

SOURCES

The sources most directly relevant for the study of rabbinic Judaism are the Mishna, Tosefta, Palestinian and Babylonian Talmuds, Targums, and midrashic collections compiled from talmudic times until the Middle Ages. J. Townsend lists all the texts and editions. A fine review of recent study on this literature has been published in French by G. Stemberger. Work of methodological significance on the Mishna, Tosefta, and Midrash will be reviewed in some detail below. Work on the Targums and Talmuds will be noted much more briefly in the hope that the issues raised in the discussion of Mishna and Midrash will be seen as similarly applicable to the essential problems of the other literature.

The difficulties of using the rabbinic sources for understanding the history of Judaism deserve to be noted from the outset. Most reconstructions of rabbinic Judaism have woven together stories and sayings concerning figures and institutions to create a coherent account of the origin of Rabbinism, which is placed somewhere between the exile and the Maccabean war. Critical difficulties arose because of paucity of source materials, inconsistencies among the sources, variant versions of stories and sayings, including attribution of sayings and incidents to different figures, and the late date of some post-talmudic collections which contained significant amounts of otherwise attractive haggadic (nonlegal) material. Attempts were made to overcome these difficulties by studying the manuscripts to recover more reliable texts, comparing versions of stories to find the "original" or "most reliable" form (usually considered to be the least elaborate or least confused), using historical criteria to assess probability, appealing to consistency to resolve contradictions among the sources, and assigning halakic and institutional variations to different stages of development in the tradition. Although halakot attributed to the "pairs" and to the "men of the Great Assembly" are few, it has been assumed that the core of rabbinic teaching, custom, and procedure existed at least among the Pharisees from the mid-second century B.C.E. Stories of dubious historical value were labeled legendary and the attribution of some teachings and institutions to early periods was recognized as anachronistic. But, in general, the rabbinic Judaism of the Mishna was seen as the core of Judaism as it developed from the postexilic period; sayings, teachings, and narratives attributed to or recounted about the (later) rabbis were accepted as reliable data for historical reconstruction of *early* rabbinic Judaism.

The interpretations of rabbinic literature used to support this generally accepted reconstruction of rabbinic Judaism are now regarded with increasing skepticism. The use of methods analogous to form, tradition, and redaction criticism in biblical study has made clear that Mishna, Talmud, and Midrash have undergone extremely complex processes of transmission and redaction and that the literary forms, contents, and even information we have before us may represent the concerns and views of late centuries rather than those of the pre-70 C.E. period. Though no one has postulated complete discontinuity, the gap between the first century and the later redactions of various rabbinic collections leaves ample room for uncertainty. Materials concerning earlier centuries can no longer be lifted from later collections and designated as accurate accounts of events and attitudes in a distant period. More careful and extensive attention must be given to the exact formal patterns used, to the contexts that may have modified the accounts and teachings, and to the redactional structure and tendencies of whole collections. Though such a programmatic statement is easily enunciated, its execution necessarily transforms the work of the historian and the theologian into a slow, cautious, and painstaking review of the sources and it injects a large dose of uncertainty into the consensus of the last hundred years.

Before elaborating on the work being done in this area, we must note that rabbinic Judaism, which has often been studied in isolation and treated as the center of Judaism, must now be studied in relation to the many other streams of Jewish thought and practice, especially those existing before the destruction of the Temple. Greek-speaking Jews in the Diaspora (such as Philo and Josephus), Samaritans, Essenes, and the still obscure groups who authored the pseudepigrapha must take their place alongside rabbinic Judaism, as can be seen from other chapters in this volume. Palestinian Judaism itself was deeply influenced by Hellenism (see S. Lieberman, 1942, 1950, 1974; Fischel, ed.; Fischel; see also the discussions of M. Hengel and M. Smith above, chap. 2). There is growing recognition that the Pharisaic schools, institutions, and even teachings may be modeled on Hellenistic religious associations and philosophical schools (Rivkin, 1978:242–43; Mantel, 1967). Recent work on apocalypses and apocalypticism has shown how integral apocalyptic thought was to Judaism (see chap. 14 above), and the work of G. Scholem on mysticism (1941, 1965), along with more recent work by I. Gruenwald (1974), Arnold Goldberg (1973), and P. Schäfer (1977), has made it clear that mysticism not only has a place in rabbinic Judaism but also has deep, though hidden, roots there (see also Saldarini, 1979a). Vigorous research taking place in other areas of Jewish studies and any reconstruction of Judaism in the early centuries will be complete only if account is given of all these tendencies and movements within Judaism.

Though the materials contained in Midrashim, the Mishna, Targums, and the Talmuds are often studied under the headings of halakah and haggadah, these categories are too broad and themselves encompass a variety of literary forms. We shall try to examine the extant documents and explore their redactional form and the different materials contained in them.

Mishna

The Mishna, along with its appendix, the Tosefta, is the earliest and most important source for understanding rabbinic Judaism in its early phases. The Mishna is also extremely difficult to use as a historical source because it does not tell us directly how it came into existence or what its purpose was. The traditional picture, derived from comments scattered throughout rabbinic literature and especially the Letter of Sherira Gaon (tenth century), holds that the oral law began to develop sometime between Ezra and the second century B.C.E., though the form and content of that law are much disputed. According to this view various rabbis had their own collections of Mishna until Akiba and Meir arranged and collected these bodies of teachings in a systematic way. Rabbi Judah the Prince, also known simply as "Rabbi," around 200 C.E., finally edited the authoritative collection of the Mishna. There has been much dispute over whether he mainly collected, edited, or authored the Mishna, and whether he meant it as a collection, a law code, or a textbook. The work of many scholars has been based on spotty and late accounts which must be augmented by hypotheses that are often based on phenomena found in some texts but are not characteristic of the whole of Mishna.

There have been several recent efforts to explain the origins and nature of the Mishna. Each of these scholars treats the Mishna as an entity, sometimes with reference to, but not in subordination to, the Talmuds, and each attempts to support his theories with data found in the text of the Mishna rather than on later accounts about what supposedly happened in the second century. A convenient critical review of these and other recent publications can be found in *The Modern Study of the Mishnah*, edited by J. Neusner (1973c).

J. N. Epstein still dominates study of the Mishna through his *Introduction to the Text of the Mishna* (1948) and his *Introductions to Tannaitic Literature* (1957). Epstein pursues a fundamentally literary- and source-critical analysis of the Mishna. Through an analysis of manuscripts, quotations in the Talmuds, commentaries and exegetical comments in the Talmuds, he proves that the text of the Mishna was not fixed in 200, but subsequently underwent many alterations for a variety of reasons. Furthermore, the teachings of the early Amoraim (third and fourth centuries C.E.) show that they did not accept the Mishna as final and authoritative but argued against it and tried to assign anonymous laws to earlier authorities in an attempt to limit the greater authority assigned to anonymous teachings. Later amoraic authorities tried to harmonize contradictory positions, sometimes by changing the text. This sophisticated criticism of legal variants in manuscript and tradition and tracing of post-mishnaic developments has been carried on with great success by D. Weiss Halivni (1968, 1975) and demonstrates that the Mishna as we have it cannot simply be dated to 200 nor treated as a fixed and fully accepted core of the rabbinic tradition from its inception.

Epstein does think that Judah the Prince meant the Mishna as a law code, that he drew on earlier collections which are not embedded in the Mishna, and that he altered his sources (against C. Albeck) in order to shape them into a code. He argues his position with extensive reference to evidence internal to the Mishna. One may ask, however, whether the groups of materials found there are from earlier sources or are redactional. Epstein accepts the often-attested position that Akiba first gave order to a multiplicity of earlier teachings. This may be so, but it is still unclear exactly what he had to work with and what he did. The teachings attributed to Akiba in the Mishna went through at least two generations of editing prior to Rabbi's work, and though Epstein gathers important data and lays down some fundamental analyses, he does not totally explain the nature and purpose of the Mishna.

C. Albeck has also carried out detailed source analyses of the Mishna (1923, 1959). He concludes that Judah the Prince was the only redactor of the Mishna and that he did not intend it as a law code nor did he draw upon previous authoritative decisions of the rabbinic court. Rather, he quoted verbatim from previous collections without changing anything. He was interested in collecting the teachings of the rabbis, not promulgating them. The anonymous teachings were already anonymous in his sources; different versions of a teaching are to be assigned to different schools, and the sources Rabbi drew on derived from various circles and teachers. Albeck's thesis has the advantage of simplicity. He need not hypothesize several stages of development, and he need not harmonize all rough spots and halakic tensions in the Mishna. The Mishna is simply a collection. However, Albeck must presuppose intense activity carried on in a variety of schools for which we have no direct evidence. He must also suppose that Judah the Prince changed nothing—and this without being able to show precisely Judah's goal in collecting this material.

Abraham Goldberg (1958–59), a student of Albeck, accepts Albeck's understanding of Mishna as a collection, but stresses the legal content as a way of disentangling strata and understanding the historical development of halakah. He understands Rabbi's purpose to have been pedagogical: Rabbi wished to record and relate the views of all the students of Akiba, who interpreted his mishna in various ways, and he wished to teach, suggest or imply the maximum number of views in the minimum space. Rabbi also arranged teachings according to similarity of words, ease of explanation, and other criteria. Goldberg's careful analyses of certain passages are helpful and illuminating to the study of the Mishna, but the unraveling of legal traditions is not by itself a sufficient basis for history. In addition, not all the complexities in the organization of the Mishna are explained by the hypothesis that it is a textbook, though this thesis may contain some truth (see also Abraham Goldberg, 1955, 1976).

In a brief treatment of Mishna in the *Encyclopedia Judaica* (1971), E. E. Urbach stresses the varied origins of the materials in the Mishna, concluding that some come from Second Temple times, some from decisions of the rabbinical court, some from different schools, etc. Urbach evaluates the language used in various tractates and subsections, the authorities cited, and halakic development. Though his attention to detail is sometimes helpful, many of Urbach's criteria are very subjective and at their base rest upon an acceptance of talmudic accounts of earlier days and mishnaic attributions as reliable historical records. But mishnaic accounts are a literary form and can only be related to history with great caution (Arnold Goldberg, 1974).

J. Neusner has devoted a massive effort to interpreting the Mishna as an independent text and understanding the system and world view that underlie the complex and often confusing laws that make up the bulk of the text. He has produced a commentary on the sixth order, *Purities*, in twenty-two volumes (1974–1977), on the fifth, *Holy Things*, in six volumes (1978–1980), on the third, *Women*, in five volumes (1980), on the second, *Appointed Times* (1981–1983), and on the fourth, *Damages* (1983–85). Several of his students are doing the first order, *Agriculture*. The commentary includes a translation of both Mishna and Tosefta and, where relevant, of other sources (e.g., *Sifra* for the treatise *Negaim*), and each tractate and order is followed by a thorough analysis of its literary characteristics and systematic organization. It should be noted that Neusner finds that Tosefta is exactly what its name implies, additions to the Mishna in the form of further comments, supplementary and independent material. The major aid to the study of Tosefta is the text and commentary by S. Lieberman, partially complete (1955–); see also a translation by J. Neusner (1977–1980) of the second through sixth orders.

Neusner has more consciously and consistently applied historical-critical, form-critical and redaction-critical methodology to the Mishna than previous scholars and has more thoroughly challenged the traditional picture of how the Mishna developed. He began by attempting to discern the development of forms in the Mishna in order to understand the transmission and development of the law, but he found that the Mishna shows no evidence of developing forms and gained its present form from its final redactor, Rabbi Judah the Prince. Neusner does not deny that there may have been and even probably were earlier collections and a very lively development of the law; but we cannot discern this from the formal literary characteristics of the Mishna, which has been transformed into a tightly integrated whole. Neusner then turned to the content of the Mishna, to its ideas, rules, and principles and their logical relationship to one another. He found that logically prior rules or steps in the complex of laws are never attributed to later authorities. The attributions in the Mishna are consistent with the logical relationships among the laws. Furthermore, logical steps in the development of laws in various tractates can be assigned to various periods during the late first and second century (Jamnia, Usha, Rabbi), and certain basic attitudes or principles seem to antedate the destruction of the Temple in 70 and to be presumed by all developments in mishnaic law. We do not have the formulations of these earlier generations, nor do we know the context in which they taught the laws, but we do know the substance of what was accepted and taught.

Neusner does not claim to be writing a history of rabbinic Judaism or a history of the schools of thought, but only a history of the law itself, a history of how the ideas developed. He is probably correct in seeing much of the Mishna as deriving from what we today would call intellectual circles. Yet even a history of ideas cannot be derived from the Mishna with certainty. The consistency among the authorities could be redactional. Stages in the argument for certain laws and the dependence of some laws on others do not necessarily indicate successive generations. Though this may be true in some instances, it may be explained by other causes elsewhere (Saldarini, 1977:268–69; Schäfer, 1978:5–6; Green, 1973:231). Neusner has certainly shown the profound structure of the Mishna, which can appear to be a mere jumble of laws; but the establishment of its historical development on the basis of its logical development remains hypothetical. The history of Jewish law may be accomplished in part by a correlation of Mishna with evidence in the Gospels, Josephus, Qumran, etc. Neusner has contributed to this ongoing area of research by the comparisons he makes in many parts of his commentary and by his synthesis of the whole.

Neusner does show very successfully the nature of the final form of the Mishna, and the synthetic studies he has done for each tractate and order, based on his detailed commentary, have begun to fill out the world view, or better, conceptual world of the editors of the Mishna. Certain concepts, problems, interests, and even images were central for these framers of the Mishna in its final form, and from an examination of the sweep of these items some grasp can be gained of how they saw themselves and their world. Still many questions remain. For example, why did the order on *Purities* receive no further elaboration in the Talmud and little stress in Jewish life (except for *Niddah*)? Neusner suggests that it was experience with the loss of the Temple, but the full implications of what lies before us remain to be worked out. Since the Mishna is logically consistent and subtly organized, as Neusner has shown in his redactional studies, why did the framers of the Mishna choose to relegate that structure to the background, leave many operating principles unstated, and insist that the student learn the detailed and intricate maze of the law? Such questions will find answers with the help of anthropology, sociology, and intellectual history.

Neusner has also addressed a number of other questions in his study of Mishna (1975). He has found that some orders and tractates are based on scripture or merely repeat scriptural law with further detail worked out, for example, the fifth order, *Holy Things* (1979b). Other orders, such as *Purities*, have their own basic generative concepts not based on scripture, but generating the agenda and particulars of various tractates (1978b). *Sifra* on the matters taken up in *Negaim* serves the function of connecting the Mishna to scripture after the fact. Many of Neusner's conclusions contain material helpful for relating Midrash to Mishna and speculating on the old and perhaps insoluble question concerning their origins and original relationship to each other. Finally, the studies of Neusner, Epstein, and others necessitate a change in the idea of oral Torah, probably a third-century concept (Schäfer, 1978:153–97), and oral transmission of traditions, a more complex process than previously thought.

Midrash

Because of the complexity of the midrashic collections as well as the variety of nonrabbinic sources that interpret scripture, a vigorous debate has arisen over the nature and definition of midrash. R. Bloch (1955, 1957) understood midrash as a set of attitudes and a process that resulted in various interpretations of scripture with related purposes. Her view has been supported by Le Déaut and with modifications by Vermes (1970) and J. A. Sanders. Midrash relates both to the text and to the situation of the interpreter; its main purpose is to make the text clear and relevant to the audience in the interpreter's time. Consequently, comments may be stimulated by the difficulties and peculiarities of the text that require explanation or, more often, by the interests, questions, and needs of the audience. Midrash renders the text contemporary in each age and is the process that gives continuity and life to the tradition. When reading midrash one can speak of a midrashic mode of thought or approach to the tradition and to life itself. This way of thought is discernible in and productive of attempts to update the tradition, whether they are formal commentaries or rewriting of earlier traditions. This midrashic perspective can already be found in OT glosses. Chronicles and Josephus's *Antiquities* are midrashic rewritings of the Bible.

This broad definition of midrash as a way of thought, a process, and a literary product has prompted a more formal definition of midrash as a literary genre by A. Wright (1967) and G. Porton (1979). Both understand the genre midrash to consist of formal commentary on scripture. Wright works from the classical rabbinic forms and uses them as a criterion for judging earlier products in relation to midrash. Porton defines midrash more generally as "a type of literature, oral or written, which has its starting point in a fixed, canonical text, considered the revealed word of God by the midrashist and his audience, and in which this original verse is explicitly cited or clearly alluded to" (112). The emphasis on canon and revelation identifies midrash as a religious literature and differentiates it from other kinds of interpretation of texts (with which it still has much in common). The emphasis on the original verse gives shape to midrash as a genre and ties it to a concrete origin in relation to a text. Porton's definition provides a stable starting point in the works that are before us and avoids the all-inclusive and vague scope of midrash defined as a process or way of thought. It allows Porton to emphasize the many forms of scriptural interpretation and the unique qualities of rabbinic midrash, which probably took shape after 70 c.e., and the role in biblical interpretation probably played by the priests before the destruction of the Temple.

Porton's definition of midrash does not deal with its purpose and its desired effect on its audience. Statements concerning purpose are more hypothetical and inferential than observations concerning literary form, yet they must be attempted. All the authors cited above find multiple purposes in midrash and variations in form and content according to the needs and orientation of the group producing the midrash. The goals of midrash are, by definition, tied to the development of biblical interpretation in the tradition and the motives that produced the interpretations. Since both purpose and development are so controversial and hard to establish, Porton's literary definition is probably the most satisfactory, with the strong proviso that any adequate analysis of a midrash must attempt to uncover the purpose of the work and its concrete place in the tradition.

One final note: Though midrash has come to be used for any interpretation of Scripture, its use would be better restricted to rabbinic midrash or to those works that closely resemble rabbinic midrash. All reuse of earlier tradition should be understood under the category of development of tradition. The titles given to the Psalms, the composition of Second Isaiah, the production of Chronicles, and the introduction of "glosses" into the biblical texts all involve interaction with earlier traditions. When a canonical text can be discerned as playing a crucial role in what is written and is viewed as a fixed point that may be explained but not ignored, then we should speak of the broad category of biblical interpretation. It is noteworthy that the Jewish tradition from about the second century B.C.E. is impelled to interact in many ways with an authoritative, canonical text, substantially fixed in that century (Leiman). The forms that this interaction take vary tremendously (Targum, pesher, rewritten Bible, renewed prophecy, Midrash, story, etc.), but the ultimate interaction with scripture is constant. These forms must be analyzed and related to one another, and it is not particularly helpful when they are all lumped together under one definition or even under a single typology that can be designated "midrash."

The so-called halakic midrashim are collections of comments relevant to certain sections of Exodus through Deuteronomy, and arranged in sequence according to the biblical verses. Though the commentaries are usually designated as exegetical, they omit many parts of these books and wander far from the verse under discussion. Though they are called halakic, they contain large amounts of haggadic material. Study of these midrashim as well as the *Midrash Rabbah* on the Pentateuch and the five scrolls demands application of a number of different techniques and a comparison with the whole range of rabbinic literature. The standard introduction, which especially relates this material to the Talmud, is that of J. N. Epstein (1957). See also C. Albeck (1969) and E. Z. Melamed. Text, sources, development of traditions, and redaction are all taken into account for those sections studied.

Redaction and Form Criticism of the Midrash

After World War II, form criticism and especially redaction criticism have strongly affected biblical studies, and their effect has also been felt in the study of rabbinic literature. Methods have been modified, and results differ because of the particular nature of the sources. Earlier work comparing various midrashic works and variant forms of traditions had given attention to the literary interactions among the sources, to the technical terminology used in different midrashim, and to the purposes of individual midrashim. In recent years more emphasis has been placed on the final, composite nature of midrashim, and a recent article by Arnold Goldberg (1977a) stresses the redactional context as the foundation for interpretation of midrash (and by extension for all of rabbinic literature). Such an approach has allowed P. Schäfer (1976) to elucidate the structure and meaning of the *Mekilta* to Exod 20:2. The use of traditional materials and the themes uniting them in the *parasha* provide definitional context and prompt Schäfer to theorize that this unit took shape around the end of the second century.

The homiletical midrashim, *Leviticus Rabba,* and the *Pesiktas* have been a center of interest for those doing literary, formal, and redactional analysis of midrash. J. Heinemann (1969/71) and L. Silberman have both shown the complex and sophisticated structures that bind together the varied materials in each chapter. W. Braude, in the introductions to his translations of *Pesikta Rabbati* (1968) and *Pesikta de Rab Kahana* (1975) has briefly described the structure of each chapter; see also the study of *Pesikta Rabbati* 20 by K. E. Grözinger and of *Pesikta Rabbati* 35 by Arnold Goldberg (1977b). Further brief analyses and examples of these forms can be found in J. Heinemann (1970, 1982), and in Heinemann and Petuchowski. Earlier studies of the proems in the homiletical midrashim have been complemented by the form-critical analysis of proems by J. Heinemann (1971), who suggests that the proems were brief sermons preceding the readings during the morning Sabbath service. Such studies offer hope that the bulk of the corpus of homiletical literature may be analyzed and compared with other sources in rabbinic literature to show the resultant meaning of the traditions as they have come down to us and to give us a glimpse of the process and stages that led to the final products.

W. S. Towner has written a comprehensive study of one limited form, the enumeration form, which succeeds in demonstrating the various functions of the form and the probable stages of development within the tradition. Lists initiated by a statement of the number of items in the list and a description of the kind of items in the list are common in many cultures, and Towner is able to use this comparative material to establish the characteristics of the proverbial list. This list survives in rabbinic literature, but it gradually assimilates with and is dominated by the exegetical list, which uses a scriptural proof text to support each item. The thirty-six examples of this form found in *Mekilta de Rabbi Ishmael* along with their parallels provide a limited but representative sample that exhibits six categories of lists differentiated according to function; for example, texts united by a key word (*Stichwort*) or by legal analogy. A series of such studies would probably give a broad and precise insight into the concerns and tactics of the rabbinic commentators and the literary forms they created to communicate their message.

Some attention has been given to the techniques, interests, and purposes found in the haggadah. Isaac Heinemann studied haggadic materials in the midrashim, Talmuds, etc., under the general categories "creative historiography" and "creative philology." He pointed out the types of interpretations and the range of story and embellishment characteristic of this sort of work. His book is filled with valuable information, but it is weakened by the fact that it treats "the haggadah" as a unified whole. Heinemann does not give serious consideration to differences among documents and periods, nor does he plot out historical development of traditions. Rather he suggests that a way of thought underlies the haggadah and he seeks to elucidate its presuppositions and procedures. He does compare rabbinic haggadah with other Jewish and non-Jewish literature. He concludes that the union of description and explanation in rabbinic haggadah makes it unique in Jewish literature (chap. 15), but he fails to speak to the objection that haggadah is not an independent literature nor a unified composition. It is a very loose classification of materials varied in themselves and scattered in many contexts. Individual techniques and traditions gathered under the name haggadah and in composite collections must be compared with like material and compositions elsewhere in ancient literature.

Joseph Heinemann's *Aggadot and Their History* (1974) is more satisfactory in that it approaches the haggadah as a series of traditions that have developed over time which cannot be understood satisfactorily without reference to their complex history. He chooses a number of concrete traditions to illustrate critical problems and different methods for penetrating the haggadah. He compares different versions, treats Targums and *Pirke de Rabbi Eliezer* as special cases, investigates the relationship of some haggadot to history and to their polemical intent and explains their origin in oral tradition. Heinemann tends to date the Targums relatively early, a position held by many but increasingly subject to serious question; in particular instances he does argue for the early date of a given tradition with sophistication and care. Though work on individual documents is sorely needed and the origins of haggadah remain obscure, Heinemann's methods are a definite improvement over previous approaches. Likewise, the work of G. Vermes has advanced the study of traditions in Judaism. Vermes (1961) began with targumic traditions but compared them to all the sources within Judaism and Christianity. His further work (1975) has shed light on

methods and motives for interpreting scripture and the growth and influence of traditions in Judaism. Other studies of the targumic materials are
listed in the bibliographies by B. Grossfeld (1972, 1977).

Rabbinic stories contained in the haggadah are increasingly being
studied through the prism of structuralism and hermeneutical theory. D.
Ben-Amos approached a number of talmudic stories using the type of structural analysis (especially the formalism of V. Propp) common in folklore
studies. Treating genre as "a general framework which limits the possible
patterns of the plot," he examines five: legend, tall tale, fable, exemplum,
and riddling tale. Legend, for example, has three narrative constituents—
intrusion, mediation, and outcome—which may be combined in various
ways. Though Ben-Amos tries to arrive at a purely formal description of
genre without reference to content, he does depend on general motifs in his
choice of stories since legends must involve the natural and supernatural.
Ben-Amos notes correctly that such analysis must precede questions concerning historicity since unstructured and nonrecurrent information is more
likely to be true than stereotyped and expected characterization and plot.

J. Fraenkel (1978) has used the hermeneutic theories of E. Betti,
H. G. Gadamer, and E. Hirsch in order to show that many haggadic
stories are literary creations and are not intended to give historical information. The structure of the stories and the details of their development
are highlighted to demonstrate that the authors are expressing their own
world view, rather than reporting events in the past. Fraenkel's effort is
especially welcome since he relates his method to the larger and increasingly
important field of hermeneutic theory.

The larger cultural context of the ancient world can be seen in the
influence of Hellenistic forms and rules on rabbinic literature. The works
of H. Fischel (1973, 1977) show how Hellenistic literary forms and rhetorical devices have influenced rabbinic literature. The two well-known
articles of D. Daube (1949, 1953) show how the exegetical rules of Hillel
have a relationship to procedures used in Hellenistic literature. Some
scholars doubt that there is a direct literary dependence on Greek literature
(Jacobs) and suggest that Jewish exegetical procedures may have developed
independently or more likely are indirectly related by means of the general
cultural influence of Hellenism after Alexander. The seven rules of Hillel
and the thirteen rules of Rabbi Ishmael are impossible to date with certainty
to Hillel and Ishmael, and they are probably post factum formulations of
exegetical procedures long in use. Further influence of the Hellenistic environment on the haggadah has been elucidated by E. Halevi (1963, 1972).
His studies contain a wealth of material, but his historical evaluation of the
material is generally uncritical.

Liturgy, though not part of midrash and haggadah, has benefited
greatly from critical study of forms and traditions. J. Heinemann (1962;
rev. ed. 1964; 1977) demonstrated convincingly that the fundamental

prayers of the Siddur cannot be traced back to an "original" form, as was attempted by Finkelstein and others, but that the written forms of the prayers reflect varied, independent, and equally authoritative versions of the prayers derived from separate oral traditions. Since the *Sitz im Leben* of the synagogue prayers is known, it had only to be correctly evaluated by Heinemann to be of decisive importance for establishing the nature of synagogue prayers. For a review of other scholars leading up to Heinemann, see Sarason (1978), and for a collection of classic studies see Petuchowski. Of special interest is the problem of the triennial cycle. Though W. Bacher and J. Mann previously argued for a fixed cycle that can be established from manuscripts and midrashim, J. Heinemann (1963–64, 1968) has argued that the shape of the sections and the days when they were read varied with time and place, much like the prayers.

The Talmuds

Only a few remarks can be devoted here to the immensely important talmudic corpus. Literature relevant to the Palestinian Talmud has been reviewed by B. Bokser (1979) and literature relevant to the Babylonian Talmud by D. Goodblatt. The methods used and the results achieved by major talmudic scholars of the last century have been summarized and criticized in a volume edited by J. Neusner (1970b). Work on a critical edition of the Babylonian Talmud has been begun (1972–) by the Complete Israeli Talmud Institute of the Rab Herzog Foundation, but its task of collating the many manuscripts, fragments, readings in commentaries and early printed editions and producing a critical edition will require extensive work. Because the talmudic corpora consist of collected literature, there probably was no single talmudic "original text" (*Urtext*) and so critical editions must take into account various traditions and recensions. The lack of satisfactory critical editions, which are crucial to understanding the materials, also impedes the study of the dialects of Hebrew and Aramaic contained in these documents. Though great progress has been made, especially in editing transcriptions of many manuscripts and of some tractates and midrashim and the close study of some inscriptions and other literature, many manuscripts have been affected by changes in idiom and morphology and, what is even more important, by the introduction of certain technical terms by later copyists. Basic research in this area continues with a steady stream of useful tools.

The Babylonian Talmud has been studied especially through the prisms of literary criticism and historical criticism and in the last few decades this work has been carried on in increasingly sophisticated ways that recognize the developmental and fluid nature of the traditions compiled in the various collections. Form criticism and redaction criticism, adapted to the peculiarities of the sources and often called by other names, have had an effect on the work done by A. Weiss, D. Weiss Halivni (1968, 1975), C. Albeck (1969), and J. N. Epstein. The results of these studies on the sources are only gradually filtering into the writing of rabbinic history. It should also be noted that a wealth of studies elucidates the realia of the Talmuds (commerce, medicine, geography) as well as cross-cultural influences and the later traditional commentaries.

BIOGRAPHY

Modern scholars have asked of rabbinic literature questions that its authors were not interested in answering. We shall review three areas in which such questions have been asked: biography, history and rabbinic thought or theology. Numerous works have been published that collect the sayings by and anecdotes about individual rabbis. A. Hyman on the Tannaim and Amoraim (1936) is a standard reference work, I. Konovitz has published a series of volumes collecting the materials on individual Tannaim such as Akiba. Many "biographies" have ordered the events and sayings associated with rabbis into a coherent structure or a topical selection with evidence drawn from the history of the period to provide a more or less probable setting for the figure. N. N. Glatzer did this in a brief treatment of Hillel, as did J. Podro for Joshua ben Hananiah. One is introduced to the rabbinic sources in a pleasing way, but no historically probable conclusions are established. L. Finkelstein wrote a more elaborate and ambitious biography of Akiba, in which he placed Akiba within his overall interpretation of the development of rabbinic traditions and society. Finkelstein must still give hypothetical order and meaning to many disconnected incidents and sayings of Akiba. Moreover, his controlling thesis that conflict between rural and urban groups was the matrix for the development of rabbinic society and law has been often refuted and generally rejected. The power and attraction that his portrait of Akiba achieves rests not upon the sources but on Finkelstein's own hypothesis of social dynamics.

Jacob Neusner wrote a biography of Johanan ben Zakkai (1962), in which he followed the general procedures used in previous biographies. A revision of this work in 1970 found Neusner acknowledging the ambiguity of the sources and turning toward a study of the traditions themselves not only for the little they yield about Johanan but also for the picture they give us of those who passed on and used traditions about Johanan (1970a). Neusner found, however, that Johanan's corpus was too narrow and many traditions too late for a comprehensive and reliable analysis, so he turned to Eliezer ben Hyrcanus (1973a). He identified the more reliable traditions by attestations, that is, teachings attributed to a named rabbi which are then quoted, modified, or contradicted in substance or wording by a named sage of the same or next generation. The second sage attests to (by presuming the existence of) the teaching of the first sage and the second sage is close enough in time to the first sage to know what the first taught and to be prevented from falsifying it. (This same method is used in his earlier work on Pharisees, mentioned below.) Even though we lack Eliezer's own formulations and his own context for teaching the law, because of later editing of all sources, his legal agenda includes interest in Temple Law and priestly duties and in rationalizing and liberalizing some pharisaic rules. These teachings, drawn from Mishna-Tosefta, the earliest and most reliable source, show no emphasis on Torah nor adherence to any of the schools. These legal tendencies contradict the biographical and exegetical traditions associated with Eliezer in the Talmuds and Midrashim, which portray him as very conservative, Shammaite, and at odds with the authorities. Biographical and exegetical traditions are excluded from the Mishna and Tosefta by their very nature, and since they are in later sources and not attested, they are less reliable, according to Neusner's criteria. Still, these traditions need more intensive study according to the methods outlined in the section on Midrash above, so that their true import will become clear. Neusner's emphasis on the centrality of the legal traditions for sketching what we know of rabbinic figures and his discovery of how thoroughly these traditions had been edited and integrated into their present sources led him to turn from the study of biography to that of Mishna and Tosefta, outlined above.

Neusner's insights that the study of rabbinic "biography" must really consist of analysis of traditions and must focus on the legal corpus, not the biographical anecdotes, have been carried further by several of his students with interesting and varied results both for biography and for the study of Mishna and Midrash. Like Neusner they have analyzed the whole corpus of a teacher, or at least a distinct part of it, rather than choosing anecdotes to be strung together. G. Porton (1976–82) has discovered that Ishmael's teachings do not support the traditional view that he was the founder of a distinct school of exegesis opposed to that of Akiba. C. Primus's study of Akiba's agricultural laws shows that the Mishna on agriculture does not depend on Akiba's teachings as their core, except in two tractates. Consequently, there is no support for the traditional view that Akiba's ordering of the Mishna is the foundation of its final redaction. J. Gereboff on Tarfon, W. Green on Joshua ben Hananiah (1980), T. Zahavy on Eleazar ben Azariah, and S. Kanter on Rabban Gamaliel II have all shown that each figure is portrayed as having special teachings and interests in Mishna. These figures are presented consistently in the legal materials, and this presentation may reflect history. However, we do not know what prompted each to teach as he did, nor do we have the complete teachings of any one of them or a real insight into any one's world view. They were used by the redactors of the traditions to fulfill a certain function in the tradition. This use of figures in the tradition can be seen even more clearly with the minor figures studied in *Persons and Institutions in Early Rabbinic Judaism*, ed. W. S. Green (1977).

One other major conclusion has been reached by most of these studies. The legal materials found in Mishna and Tosefta do not bear the marks of the conflicts among the rabbis that are recounted in biographical anecdotes contained in the Talmuds and Midrashim, for example, alleged hostility toward Gamaliel. R. Goldenberg (1978), who studied Meir, a mid-second-century figure, found that his teachings on Sabbath law do not stand alone but are integrated into disputes, and that Meir is presented as a protagonist in the working out of the law. Consequently, the attribution of what belongs to Meir and exactly what he taught is very unreliable. Sources often disagree on whether Meir or another taught certain laws and on which position Meir took. The work of the redactors relies very heavily on the teachings of all the rabbis. One small window on premishnaic traditions may be opened by the teachings of Jose the Galilean. J. Lightstone's study (1979) of this small corpus of teachings shows that Jose's traditions have not been completely assimilated into mishnaic forms and context and may show something of the sources used by Mishna.

The methodological difficulties attendant upon the study of a single rabbi have been perceptively reviewed by W. Green (1978), who is pessimistic about learning anything that is historically valid. Biography in the usual sense of the term is impossible, and even intellectual history of a single rabbi may be premature, given the molding of various figures into the tradition by later editors. Green begins to pursue the reasons why those handing on a very homogenous tradition insisted on using the names of sages in the passing on of traditions. He also asks what role pseudepigraphy played in the tradition. Further illumination can be expected in the study of biographical anecdotes from methods drawn from literary criticism and folklore (e.g., Fraenkel, 1971; Kagan; Noy) as well as the study of rhetorical *topoi* and proverbial forms in the Greco-Roman world by H. Fischel and others. Some progress has been made in understanding the purposes for which various stories were told and the historical core that may be beneath them. Saldarini (1975) and Schäfer (1979) have both pointed out the function of Johanan's escape from Jerusalem as a foundation story for the rabbinic school at Jamnia, and Schäfer has done a very sophisticated analysis of what may be accepted as historical in the accounts about Johanan. Kagan complements this analysis by showing how the biblical verses have helped generate the story. Goldenberg (1972) showed the polemical issues motivating the stories of Gamaliel's deposition. Schäfer (1978) has done an exhaustive study of the traditions connecting Akiba to the Bar Kokhba War and has demonstrated that they actually tell us very little about Akiba's involvement (if any) in the events. Schäfer's work may be contrasted with M. Herr's equation of historical verisimilitude with historical probability in his study of the dialogues of the sages with Roman dignitaries, or S.

Safrai's general acceptance of the historicity of biographical anecdotes in the Talmuds (1971). Though results are often meager, a sober and critical evaluation of the rabbinic sources about the rabbis is beginning to take shape.

HISTORY

The authors to be reviewed here have made extensive use of rabbinic sources to write the history of tannaitic and talmudic times. Attention will be restricted to authors who have done comprehensive work in this area, and comments will focus on their general approach and method. A large number of institutions, events, and persons remain obscure or controversial in historical analysis and cannot be treated in detail here.

G. Alon (sometimes spelled Allon in English) was a student of the famous talmudic scholar J. N. Epstein and was dean of Israeli rabbinic historians. Alon's history of talmudic times was published posthumously from his papers (1954–56), and his many essays were collected into two volumes (1957–58). Thoroughly learned in both rabbinic and Greek sources, Alon especially examined the social, political, and economic relationships implied by the rabbinic texts. He was acute in gathering varied and conflicting sources and working out the most probable explanation for what had been handed down. His work lacks consistent criteria for deciding which texts are more accurate or more probable in their contents, and he pays insufficient attention to redactional processes to be fully satisfying. His thesis that Judea was not crushed in 70 c.e. but retained substantial independence until 135 has been influential. His contention that Jamnia was used as a prison camp for Jews and that the Romans tried to break the Jewish people, as well as his often polemical and emotional descriptions of the Romans, betrays a tendentiousness derived from the events during and after World War II. Despite these shortcomings Alon's work is a standard reference for those studying early rabbinic history.

S. Zeitlin, who was the most prolific and comprehensive American historian of rabbinic Judaism in his generation, published a three-volume history of the Second Temple period (1962, 1967, 1978), four volumes of essays (1973–78), and numerous other books and articles. He read a wide variety of ancient sources and brought massive learning to their interpretation; however, he was idiosyncratic in many of his views, often polemical in tone, and not attentive enough to the views of others. His comments on the sources are often acute and illuminating, but just as often he overinterpreted them. His method for assessing the reliability of documents was not consistent; often the presence of *some* late expressions caused him to date whole documents late without reference to questions of redaction, revisions, and additions. His history makes coherent sense out of disparate sources in an attractive way, but he often took rabbinic texts too much at face value. Zeitlin's work is best consulted with caution.

A. Guttmann (1970) wrote a survey of the rabbinic leaders and teachings from the Great Sanhedrin to Judah the Prince. His perspective and sources are derived from the older *Wissenschaft des Judentums* approach; his work serves as a convenient summary of that stream of research, but his discussion is badly dated. (See also his essays, 1976.) Guttmann gathers relevant texts, takes them at face value, and reviews the usual controversies concerning their interpretation. He treats halakic controversies but does not critically evaluate his sources in terms of date, development, and reliability.

S. Safrai is the most prominent contemporary Israeli historian. He has written books on the Second Temple (1959) and the pilgrimage feasts (1965) and numerous articles and chapters on various subjects in rabbinic history. He is best known in English for his editing and contributions to the first two volumes of CRINT (1974, 1976). In volume 1, chapter 1, Safrai reviews the nature of the Hebrew and Aramaic sources to be used in studying the history of the first century. He treats rabbinic sources, but not Qumran, nor those apocrypha and pseudepigrapha originally written in Hebrew or Aramaic. Safrai holds that the Mishna doubtless contains early sources from the Second Temple period, and he treats the Mishna as generally accurate in its historical data and as reflective of earlier times. Safrai pictures the Mishna as a product of constantly growing tradition and as derived from popular discussion and practice rather than from scholastic argument in the second century.

In volume 2, in the chapter on the "Home," Safrai draws on Mishna and Tosefta to characterize the first century. He does distinguish some talmudic sources as being too late to be reliable for the first century, but he cites sayings from the Babylonian Talmud to describe Palestine without taking into account their context in the Talmud. No allowance is made for development of or variations in local customs; and, most surprising, Safrai describes typical houses and their contents, including ceramic vessels, without reference to archaeology. Likewise, in treating the Temple he says, "The main source of knowledge concerning the Temple service and an understanding of the status and role of the Temple in the life of the community during the final generations of its existence is the Tannaitic literature, especially the Mishnah" (1975:282). Safrai's work leads the reader into the world implied by rabbinic literature, but greater rigor must be used in the analysis of the sources to achieve results reliable for the first century.

G. Vermes and F. Millar have published two of a projected three-volume revision of E. Schürer's classic, *The History of the Jewish People in the Age of Jesus Christ* (1973, 1979). Volume 1 treats the history of the period in reliance mostly upon nonrabbinic sources. Volume 2 covers the

institutions and sects of Judaism and uses rabbinic sources more extensively, often in conjunction with Greek and other Hebrew and Aramaic
sources. As a handbook, the revised Schürer is characterized by concise and
clear statements of major positions, a sane discussion of reasonable alter-
natives, and bibliographical materials for all major positions. In the section
on Temple and priesthood (#24) the Mishna is extensively used to indicate
the historical situation before the destruction of the Temple. Section #25
on Torah scholarship uses 'Abot and other parts of the Mishna as data for
describing the scribes and attitudes toward law before 70. Both of these
sections are plagued with the methodological uncertainties mentioned in
regard to previous authors. In treating the Pharisees (#26) and the sanhedrin (#23.3) the editors draw upon Josephus and the New Testament as
well as on rabbinic sources, and the clash of texts leads to various modifications of views found in rabbinic literature. The Pharisees are mainly
described on the basis of a sophisticated analysis of Josephus. The editors
do not accept as likely the rabbinic view that Pharisees headed the sanhedrin before 70 (#25) and they opt for the one sanhedrin theory on the basis
of the Greek sources (see also Safrai, 1978:69), contrary to Büchler,
Hoenig, Mantel, 1961; and Rivkin, 1975, who hypothesize two sanhedrins
in order to resolve the contradictions between rabbinic texts and Greek
texts. The editors suggest, quite reasonably, that the scattered references
to the sanhedrin in rabbinic literature are not reliable. Though no great
breakthroughs are made in the revised Schürer, it is generally balanced and
useful.

M. Avi-Yonah wrote a history of the Jews of Palestine from Bar
Kokhba to the Arab conquest; it was published in Hebrew (1946), German
(1962), and English (1976) with various revisions and adaptations. Avi-
Yonah was a classical historian, expert in Jewish art and architecture as
well as in Palestinian archaeology and geography. He was familiar with
talmudic literature and related it to broad movements in the Roman
Empire, Christianity, and Judaism. Scattered comments in rabbinic literature are used as illustrations of political and social realities known elsewhere
in Roman history. Even with support from external sources, Avi-Yonah's
use of rabbinic literature pays too little attention to context and accepts
statements too uncritically to inspire confidence. In addition, what he
describes as a third-century crisis in Palestine should be interpreted rather
as a symptom of general stress in the empire (Goodman). His treatment is
now somewhat dated and should be used with caution.

J. Neusner more recently wrote a five-volume history of the Jews in
Babylonia (1965–70) and he summarized some of his results in a popular
volume (1972). Neusner set out to write a complete, sequential history of
the Jews in Babylon, not just a review of halakic developments and controversies recorded in the Talmud. Both the talmudic sources and the general
sources for Parthian and Persian history leave many issues obscure. Neusner

proceeds with proper caution, trying to isolate historical causes and generating probable hypotheses to explain events and literary records. He asks religious, political, and social questions together and inductively builds a description of Judaism as a religion in its relation to society. But the talmudic sources are very difficult to assess historically, and Neusner is constantly driven to weigh one group of materials against another and to note contextual and redactional characteristics that may affect meaning. The severe difficulties and unsolved ambiguities that frustrated Neusner moved him toward his work in the seventies, which uses more sophisticated methodology.

In summary, the rabbinic sources provide a treacherous but necessary foundation for anyone writing Jewish history. Thoroughly edited and sifted, the Mishna and Talmud give us little that can be firmly assigned to the first or even the second century. The interests and purposes manifested in this literature are so different from those of modern historians that any reconstruction must be founded on sophisticated methods and must remain properly hypothetical.

The Pharisees

Because the New Testament speaks so negatively of the Pharisees, their nature, origins, teachings, and history have been controversial for generations. All the evidence concerning them demands critical interpretation. Rabbinic literature is subject to all the difficulties in interpretation noted above; Josephus presents the Pharisees in the mode of a philosophical school, to further his own ends; the NT is polemical and must be used with extreme caution. The classic studies by Lauterbach and R. T. Herford are still cited frequently; the identification of the Pharisees with urban, middle-class society by L. Ginsberg and more explicitly by Finkelstein, though rejected in the form presented, still makes its presence felt in descriptions (see Black; works by L. Baeck, I. Abrahams, and H. Loewe remain fundamental). These earlier writings are conveniently reviewed by R. Marcus. More recently major hypotheses based on the sources have been advanced by E. Rivkin, J. Bowker, and J. Neusner (see the following paragraphs).

E. Rivkin examined the rabbinic sources that mention the *perushim* in a major article (1969–70) that has formed the core of his book (1978) and numerous other essays. A convenient summary of his position may be found in *IDBSup* (1976). Rivkin follows sound method in treating the three major sources thoroughly. With M. Smith (1956) Rivkin correctly notes the Hellenistic characteristics of the Pharasaic movement (1978:242–43), but he does not sufficiently allow for Josephus's own thesis and post-70 date in his general conclusions (1978:278ff.). In his treatment of the Gospels he notes correctly that scribes and Pharisees are not precisely distinguished, and he suggests that scribes were originally cited and that Pharisees were added

later. Mention should also be made of the thesis of M. Cook, which draws
similar conclusions but is marred by an outdated source analysis of Mark.
Rivkin's analysis of the Gospels concentrates too much on vocabulary while
ignoring redactional history (1978:270–71). He takes Matthew to be a
reflection of the pre-70 situation and interprets the leadership status of the
Pharisees in John as evidence that the Pharisees ruled the synagogues before
70. The last twenty years of NT studies will not allow such conclusions
based on a simple reading of the texts.

Rivkin's analysis of the rabbinic evidence is his most detailed and
imaginative contribution. Rivkin separates into several groups the passages
that mention Pharisees and finds that the passages in which the Pharisees
are contrasted with the Sadducees are not polemical attacks but reliable
accounts of what the Pharisees truly were. What can be done with these
texts, Rivkin does. However, he treats them as all of equal historical validity and then correlates them with one another out of context to produce a
description of the Pharisees. He does not take into account later use or even
production of these passages, and consequently his conclusions are not
historically reliable on their own (see the critique in Lightstone, 1975.)
Rivkin recognizes that a historian must generate a complete picture of a
period or movement insofar as probable inferences can be made from the
evidence (see an analysis of his method in Ellenson). Rivkin concludes that
the Pharisees were mainly a scholarly group who wrested control over
much of Jewish life from the established authorities. They developed an
internalized approach to the law and truly led an internal revolution
within Judaism in that the interpretation of scripture, customs, and values
of Jewish life were transformed. Rivkin correctly recognizes how "untradi-
tional" the Pharisees were and how far they moved from the way of living
Judaism and following the Bible which preceded them. His thesis of inter-
nalization is broadly acceptable in that the Pharisees did create their own
world, but his interpretation of many texts to support this thesis suffers
from a tendency to take everything said as historically accurate and to
ignore the long evolution of the rabbinic collections that have come down
to us. Despite these criticisms, Rivkin's work is a major effort that, along
with Neusner's below, must be taken with great seriousness.

J. Bowker has provided in English translation a handy collection of
sources mentioning the Pharisees. In a lengthy introduction he proposes
that the Pharisees should be understood as part of a larger intellectual
movement which he calls the "hakhamic" movement, after the Hebrew
designation of the sages as "hakhamim." Like Rivkin (and Baeck before
him), Bowker notes the pejorative use of the word Pharisee. These Pharisees (perushim) were extreme representatives of a broad movement within
the Jewish community attempting to make Torah more concrete in everyday life. The older scribes also become part of the hakhamic movement as
did other groups. Bowker's hypothesis is all-inclusive but too general and

uncontrolled. His conclusion that the Pharisees are a scholar class agrees with that of Rivkin, but Bowker does not provide a detailed and controlled analysis to support his thesis.

J. Neusner published a three-volume study of the Pharisees (1971) and a popularization of this work (1973b) as well as a number of articles, including a recent statement on methodology from a later perspective (1977; see also the reviews by Saldarini, 1973, 1977). Neusner does not turn to the relatively few passages that mention the Pharisees, but to the large corpus of tradition that is attributed to the Pharisaic teachers and to the schools of Hillel and Shammai. Neusner presents his evidence pericope by pericope, analyzing each for its structure, forms, and reliability in context. He develops the criterion of "attestations" (see "Biography" above). With his study on the Pharisees, Neusner begins doing in earnest for early rabbinic Judaism what form criticism did for the NT. (We have already noted that subsequent work led him to redaction criticism and to the study of whole books rather than disparate sources.) Neusner found that forms became consistent in the corpus of Hillel and the two schools, and so he suggested that rabbinic traditions as we know them came into existence during the first century. Since then his work with the Mishna has made him more skeptical of this conclusion and more appreciative of the formative role played by the redactors at the end of the second century.

Neusner's increasingly sophisticated and critical analysis of the sources in the course of his writings has shown how difficult it is to draw firm conclusions about the Pharisees or any early rabbinic figure. In his study of the Pharisees, he shows that both the attested rabbinic traditions and the Gospel data depict the Pharisees as having a primary interest in tithing, ritual purity, and Sabbath laws. These interests are consistent with a sect that emphasizes table fellowship. Interest in civil law and Temple regulations is conspicuously absent, and so Neusner concludes that stories about the Pharisees dominating the Temple worship and life of the people are later characterizations retrojected into the first century. In a way broadly similar to Rivkin, Neusner shows that the Pharisees extended rules that were originally confined to the priests and Temple to the whole population and so created a new "world" of ideas and practice. Not until after the destruction of the Temple, however, did the Pharisees become dominant as they and other groups were transmuted into the rabbis. Neusner also indicates that passages which try to reconstruct the history of the Pharisees before 70 date from the Ushan period in the latter half of the second century and thus are not generally reliable as unbiased accounts.

Recent research on the Pharisees has made them more obscure and difficult to describe. Each of the sources (rabbinic literature, NT, and Josephus) is hedged with critical problems and even the critical minimum that Neusner attempts to provide is beset with unanswered questions. Why did this group turn to teaching attributed to named authorities? What is the role of oral tradition in the development of their teachings? (See Schäfer, 1978:153–97.) From which social class and political stream did the Pharisees come? Did they have authority over the people? How is the group depicted by Josephus in the second and first centuries B.C.E. to be related to the first-century group only vaguely visible in the Gospels and rabbinic traditions? Rivkin, Bowker, and Neusner along with earlier scholars have suggested some answers to these questions, but no position is without grave uncertainties, and there is even less consensus now than previously.

RABBINIC THOUGHT

The Mishna, Talmud, and Midrash demand endless mastery of detail and enormous recall before a scholar can be called expert. Their principles of organization and central themes differ sharply from the categories and interests of most twentieth-century readers. Modern scholars, under the influence of Western philosophy and theology, have made various attempts to systematize rabbinic thought and develop a rabbinic theology that would parallel Western (Christian) theology and attract modern readers. In 1909, S. Schechter published a series of essays on selected topics with the prudent title *Some Aspects of Rabbinic Theology.* Schechter quotes copiously from the sources to give his readers a sense of various concepts, like sin, kingdom, Torah, Israel, etc., as they are elucidated in rabbinic literature. K. Kohler (1910; revised English translation 1918) presented Judaism as a system of faith under the title *Jewish Theology Systematically and Historically Considered.* As a leader of the Reform deeply influenced by rationalism and other intellectual currents of his day, Kohler tried to move from the historical development of Orthodoxy to a modern interpretation based on the essence of Judaism. G. F. Moore (1927–30), in his justly famous three-volume study, presented rabbinic Judaism more historically, but he too saw it as a single "normative" system. These books, along with the more limited studies of Büchler, Marmorstein, and others, are still consulted and can provide valuable data and insights. However, new problems and approaches demand a more critical and cautious approach.

M. Kadushin developed a distinctive conceptual approach in a series of four books (1932, 1938, 1952, 1964). In the first two, he did a thorough study of *Seder Eliahu;* his concentration on one work, albeit a late one, has the clear methodological advantages that he must speak to every part of the work and that his results can claim as their base a limited whole that has its own structure, purpose, and coherence. He found that the many topics treated in this work are based upon four organically related concepts, which are all intrinsic to the literature: God's loving kindness, God's justice, Torah, and Israel. Kadushin does not say that everything in *Seder Eliahu* is derived logically or rigidly from these concepts; rather, the various concepts found in the book are related to one another in a living, changing, but definite, way. Kadushin is very aware of the hermeneutical task he has undertaken, and he theorizes about it explicitly. Since *Seder Eliahu* has undergone a process of development and editing, we would wish today that his study were more conscious of redactional and literary issues as a basis for his conceptual approach. His stress on flexibility of the concepts is good, but he often imposes more order than is there. His description of the relationship among concepts as organic is helpful, but more relating of this approach to a historical approach would give more controlled conclusions. In two later books, Kadushin applies his conclusions to all of rabbinic literature. This expansion of his method rests upon the similarity of themes in rabbinic literature, but it loses the precision and firm foundation provided by analysis of a concrete work or collection.

E. E. Urbach's *The Sages: Their Concepts and Beliefs* (1969; Eng. trans. 1975) is the major recent study of rabbinic thought. Urbach brings immense erudition and a broad grasp of rabbinic literature to his task. He discusses all the major passages for the topics he takes up: God, his attributes and titles, creation, angels, humanity, providence, law, commandments, sin, mercy, reward and punishment, Israel as the elect, redemption, and messiah. He also has a long section on the history of the sages. He refers to manuscript variants, philological arguments, and the halakic tradition. He traces the development of ideas first in the tannaitic and then in the amoraic texts. He sometimes gives attention to the circumstances in which an idea arose, and he admits that there is no single, completely coherent system of rabbinic thought. Urbach's synthesis and summary of rabbinic thought, like Moore's before him, must surely function as a standard reference in the field.

Urbach's project is plagued with several difficulties, despite its substantial achievement. The categories under which he organizes rabbinic thought are drawn from Western theology and philosophy. Rather than doing a history of the development of rabbinic thought, he fundamentally harmonizes conflicting texts, this despite some attempts to show historical development (see Schäfer, 1978:8). Often he seeks a psychological explanation for contradictory statements by the sage, without considering such factors as later editing. Urbach does not consistently attend to the context, form, and redactional characteristics of the thousands of passages to which he refers. In general, attribution of a saying to a sage is taken as historical without due regard for the difficulties involved in demonstrating this. Urbach sees most of the texts he examines as parts of a unified whole, rabbinic thought, without seriously considering that some sayings and ideas may be idiosyncratic or very late and derivative. Finally, the organization of his chapters is often not clear, consisting of a series of topics and exegeses of texts and problems. The reader learns much, but even on Urbach's own terms does not get a clear sense of a unified rabbinic world view, its development and thought. Despite these criticisms, Urbach's book is an important study, which gathers together many of the results achieved by traditional talmudic study, derived from classical philological and literary techniques.

A series of studies of themes in rabbinic literature have emerged from German universities with positive results. Arnold Goldberg has done a massive study of the Shekinah (1969). His student Peter Schäfer has written on the Holy Spirit (1972) and on rivalry between angels and humans (1975). Peter Kuhn has studied God's lowering of himself (1968) and God's mourning and lamentation (1978). Others, in addition, have chosen themes less prominent in rabbinic literature but important for NT study, for example, A. Nissen on the love commandments. Each of these studies presents a thorough exegesis of each text pertinent to the theme. The studies on Shekinah and Holy Spirit choose their passages because the thematic word appears in them; the others must gather passages that have the idea or relationship being studied. The analyses of the texts are lengthy and require patience, but they preserve the authors from facile generalizations based on three or four supposedly "key" texts. The analyses show the actual range of meaning of a term or substance of an idea by showing its relationships to other terms and ideas in rabbinic literature and by showing the contexts in which it occurs.

The results achieved by these studies are helpful but limited. Since rabbinic literature is filled with pregnant terms that are not defined or explained and with unfamiliar ideas that are often important, these studies help to uncover the basic meaning of the texts. They also help the scholar to grasp the assumptions and connotations of the rabbinic world view, and in some instances they show the changes in emphasis and understanding from the biblical to the rabbinic corpus. The limits and difficulties of this kind of study are numerous and generally recognized by the scholars listed above. As noted, the original contexts for many statements are unknown, and the historical development of ideas is unclear. Definitions and descriptions culled from such materials often remain modern and are not necessarily characteristic of the thought world of the rabbis being studied. Many of the themes being investigated are not the main point of the passages studied, and we can know their meaning only by inference. Finally, statements about these themes are scattered throughout rabbinic literature and do not form a coherent body of teaching. It is very hard to distinguish an idiosyncratic teaching from a generally accepted idea. Despite these obstacles and the critically cautious results reached by these scholars, thematic studies are one tool for understanding the complex collections that make up rabbinic literature.

J. Neusner, drawing upon his commentary on the Mishna, has described the type of Judaism implicit in the Mishna and outlined the structure underlying its mass of details (1981). Neusner shows that the authors of Mishna chose from scripture those topics which they decided were pertinent and expounded them using all known relevant passages in scripture. But they ranged far beyond scripture, questioning and distinguishing numerous theoretical and practical implications of simple principles and statements. The framers of the Mishna created their own intellectual world by analogy with the altar, Temple, and land. This world, characterized by sanctity, separateness, and life in a fuller and more real sense ignores politics, history, the traditions that prevailed in postbiblical times, and even the concrete groups (priests, scribes, and householders) whose concerns are reflected in the Mishna. Rather, Mishna concentrates on what effect humans may have on the world, especially by the intention with which they do sacred actions. It urges its readers to transcend the world, time, and history, and by its demand that the reader master excessive detail and its refusal to state principle simply and patently it requires that its readers enter into its world and its patterns of speech, assimilating what it has to say rather than dominating it. Neusner has used mishnaic categories in his reconstruction of mishnaic thought and has asked questions drawn from the history of religion and anthropology. His work gives a fresh and independent view of Mishna which must be assimilated by the scholarly community.

A debate over the proper method to be used in studying rabbinic thought has recently arisen. Neusner has criticized the traditional method used in Urbach's *The Sages*, while recognizing its positive contribution (1976, 1979a), and the method used by E. P. Sanders in his *Paul and Palestinian Judaism*. Neusner's review article (1978a), as well as Saldarini's review (1979b), has been answered by Sanders (1980). In these reviews and in another article (1977) Neusner has set out his program for elucidating rabbinic and especially mishnaic literature. P. Schäfer (1978:1-12) has also commented productively on the questions raised by these articles. The central questions are the following: What is the proper source to use for determining rabbinic thought or theology? What kind of descriptive method should be used? What kind of historical conclusions can be reached?

Neusner notes very properly that the earliest dated source that we have is the Mishna, along with its supplement the Tosefta. Consequently, he concludes that any valid description of early rabbinic, tannaitic thought must be based on the Mishna and must focus on the subjects that the sages thought important: purities, sacrifices, festivals, etc. Sanders has suggested in reply that the topics covered in the Midrash, though absent from the Mishna, are presumed there and are crucial to the rabbinic way of thought; for example, election and repentance. Schäfer notes that both Neusner's studies of the teachings of individual rabbis and his own thematic studies introduce questions not native to the rabbinic documents, and both produce valid results. Though Neusner is undoubtedly correct that the Mishna is of crucial importance for knowing the mind of the rabbis, all the more so because the categories and interests found there are so foreign to the modern period, the midrashic collections and other works must also be used to complete the picture since we cannot assume that the concerns of Mishna *alone* were central. Midrash must be subjected to critical scrutiny, and Mishna, though more difficult to use, must serve as a major foundation for any future synthesis of rabbinic thought.

Many of the studies reviewed here have been criticized for taking fragments of rabbinic literature out of context and melding them into a historical or conceptual whole. What is needed now is a holistic description of rabbinic thought. Sanders has attempted such a description for the themes usually associated with the theological category soteriology. Neusner has criticized Sanders's effort while affirming the principle that whole systems of thought and belief should be investigated. In addition, since all of the rabbinic documents are collections of earlier traditions that have undergone extensive editing, it is essential that scholars deal with whole documents or at least larger literary units within the collections and subject them to redactional and literary criticism before using parts of them for reconstruction of certain historical periods. Each collection most probably has its own emphases and ethos, and these must be discerned before parts of the documents can be used for other purposes.

Will study of this type lead to valid historical conclusions concerning the development of rabbinic thought and also of the rabbinic schools, institutions, etc.? It should be clear that critically demonstrated historical results are squeezed from rabbinic literature very slowly. Rabbinic literature does not address historical concerns directly. Neusner, in his commentary on the Mishna and in other works, discerns what is logically early and late and concludes that what is assumed by the whole system is most probably early. He also theorizes about the concerns and perspectives that produced the magnificent intellectual structure of Mishna. Neusner argues cautiously and refers constantly to data that his studies have established. Yet his hypotheses are still problematic, since the transition from the logic of the Mishna to the history of its development is very uncertain (Saldarini, 1977:268–69; Schäfer, 1978:4–6). The reconstruction of the social world and historical/political situation that produced the Mishna may be impossible, though the question continues to confront us. What may be achievable is the description of the conceptual and intellectual world constructed by and to some extent implied by various rabbinic documents like the Mishna and various midrashim.

POSTSCRIPT (1984)

Since this chapter was essentially completed in early 1980 for the centennial of the Society of Biblical Literature, research into rabbinic Judaism has continued at a rapid pace. This postscript will not attempt to bring the chapter completely up to date, but only to note major trends and publications that complement the main text. More detailed reviews of recent work on rabbinic literature may be found in Horbury (1980) and Bokser (1983).

Some introductory and general works that may help orient the reader are a history of Judaism from Alexander to the Arabs by P. Schäfer (1983) and a revised and expanded German version of H. L. Strack's *Introduction to the Talmud and Midrash* (1982). Another introduction to ancient Jewish literature by R. Musaph-Andriesse contains outdated historical and literary positions which mar its simple review of the contents of rabbinic literature.

Jacob Neusner's almost completely published translation of and commentary on the Mishna (see main text) has been supplemented by a number of articles collected in *Method and Meaning in Ancient Judaism* (3 vols., 1979–80) and *Formative Judaism* (3 vols., 1982–83). Neusner has carried his studies forward with a translation of and brief commentary on the Palestinian Talmud (1982–). Though Neusner's translation has been severely criticized (Lieberman, 1984), it is a preliminary translation and the first into English. It should be used for initial orientation and as a preliminary interpretation of the whole text. Its presence should encourage a wide variety of scholars to approach the Palestinian Talmud and engage in a variety of specialized studies. Neusner's own study of the Palestinian Talmud as a whole (1983a) attempts to deduce the final authors' views of both the law and their society. Neusner does not attempt to write history from the Talmud, but to see how the authors adapted and reinterpreted the Mishna and saw their own world. From the unified voice of the final text of the Talmud Neusner argues that the authors dealt with questions of certainty, authority, salvation, Torah, and the role of the rabbi as holy man. Neusner's elucidation of the Palestinian Talmud as a whole document is methodologically correct, and his interpretation highlights some of the main ideas of the document. The complexity of the Palestinian Talmud's transmission and the composite nature of the final product may allow further literary and historical studies to describe more surely the world of the third to fifth centuries.

The study of midrash has continued in numerous articles devoted to the literary and historical analysis of discrete sections of the midrashic collections as literary wholes. It becomes more and more apparent that some units of midrashic literature received a thorough and sophisticated final redaction and that the redactors subtly revealed their outlook and goals, even though hypotheses about the historical settings of midrashic passages remain very uncertain. Two recent essays by Sarason (1981b) and Fraade (1983) have set forth programmatic arguments for the necessity of thorough and comprehensive studies of this type with attention to the development of midrashic traditions in variant forms within the rabbinic corpus. G. Porton (1981) has refined his analysis of the problem of defining midrash presented in his 1979 essay and has defended his definition of midrash as "a type of literature, oral or written, which stands in direct relationship to a fixed, canonical text, considered to be the authoritative and the revealed word of God by the midrashist and his audience, and in which this canonical text is explicitly cited or clearly alluded to" (62). J. Neusner (1983b) has provided a general introduction to midrash with textual examples and has argued that midrashic collections must be studied as wholes. His own work on *Genesis Rabba* indicates that the whole midrash is made up of four categories of comments which parallel those found in the Palestinian Talmud: close exegesis of a law or verse, amplification of a law or verse, expansion on the problems or themes in the law or verse, and, finally, less unified anthologies of scriptural verses on a topic associated with the law or verse. The presence of these four categories in both the Talmud and *Genesis Rabba* suggests that both stem from the same period and intellectual circles. However, the categories are very abstract, and other aspects of the texts need to be studied before definitive and complete conclusions can be reached. In addition, studies of midrashic collections as whole literary works must first determine whether they are indeed unified literary works in any real sense, with a consistent agenda and a perspective from which they address the agenda. In other words, it is not yet clear whether midrashic collections are texts or merely compilations of traditional material without significant organizing principles.

To the studies of Jewish liturgy mentioned in the body of the chapter should be added an additional review of developments in the study of the liturgy by R. Sarason (1981a), a major study of the synagogue service by L. Hoffman (1979), and a complete study of the development of Passover traditions in the Mishna and Seder by B. Bokser (1984).

Many studies of the history of the rabbinic period have appeared in recent years. Most utilize a wide range of Greco-Roman, Jewish, and archaeological sources and fall outside the purvue of this review. Of those which use rabbinic sources extensively, P. Schäfer's study of the Bar Kokhba War (1981a) may be singled out for its rigorous method and sophisticated interpretation of the rabbinic sources. S. Applebaum's study of the Jews in Cyrene and of the revolt under Trajan in 115–117 (1979), and A. Oppenheimer's study of the Am Ha-aretz (1977) are both flawed by simple acceptance of rabbinic dicta as historical statements and a lack of coherent theory and method to guide the study and conclusions. A. I. Baumgarten (1983) attempts to reconcile Greek and rabbinic sources concerning the Pharisees by suggesting that the name Pharisees refers to their reputation as "specifiers" of the law. The collection of essays edited by E. P. Sanders, *Jewish and Christian Self-Definition* (Vol. 2, 1981), contains several articles that relate rabbinic sources to the Greco-Roman world and Christianity, especially the excellent article by R. Kimelman, which shows that the Birkat

Ha-Minim did not signal a sharp break between Judaism and Christianity in the late first or early second century.

Study of the Hekhalot and Merkabah literature has intensified in recent years, and relationships have been established with rabbinic and apocalyptic literature. Modern study of this mystical literature was founded by G. Scholem in two fundamental studies (1941, 1960) which rendered this literature accessible to scholars and set out lines of interpretation. A very useful introduction to the literature as a whole has been written by I. Gruenwald (1980). D. Halperin (1980) has examined the rabbinic texts concerning Merkabah mysticism and argued that the tradition concerns exegesis of key texts rather than mystical experiences. The rabbis feared the popular enthusiasm and possible excesses that greeted the exegesis of Ezekiel 1. I. Chernus (1982) has shown that many midrashic passages reflect the vocabulary and images of mystical literature and may reflect covert involvement with or criticism of mystical trends. P. Schäfer (1981b) has published several versions of the Hekhalot literature in a synoptic arrangement which points out the fluidity and variety in the tradition and makes possible an adequate literary study of the manuscript texts.

BIBLIOGRAPHY

Albeck, C.
    1923   *Untersuchungen über die Redaktion der Mischna*. Berlin: Schvet-schke.
    1959   *Mābô' lā-Mišnâ* (Introduction to the Mishnah). Jerusalem: Bialik Institute. Tel Aviv: Dvir.
    1969   *Mābô' la-Talmûdîm* (Introduction to the Talmuds). Tel-Aviv: Dvir.

Alon, G.
    1954-56   *Tôlĕdôt ha-Yĕhûdîm bĕ'Ereṣ Yiśrā'ēl bitqûpat ha-Mišnâ wĕha-Talmûd* (The History of the Jews in Israel during the Period of the Mishna and Talmud). Israel: Hakkibbutz Hameuchad. A revised and edited English version has begun to appear: *The Jews in Their Land in the Talmudic Age 70-640 C.E.* Vol. 1. Jerusalem: Magnes Press, 1980.
    1957-58   *Mehqārîm bĕ-Tôlĕdôt Yiśrā'ēl*. 2 vols. Israel: Hakkibbutz Hameuchad. Trans. by I. Abrahams in an abridged form: *Jews, Judaism and the Classical World: Studies in Jewish History in the Times of the Second Temple*. Jerusalem: Magnes Press, 1977.

Applebaum, S.
    1979   *Jews and Greeks in Ancient Cyrene*. SJLA 28. Leiden: Brill.

Avi-Yonah, M.
    1946   *Biyyĕmê Roma Û-Bîzā'ntîyôn*. Jerusalem: Bialik Institute. German trans.: *Geschichte der Juden im Zeitalter der Talmud*. Berlin: de Gruyter, 1962. English trans. from German: *The Jews of Palestine: A Political History from the Bar Kokhba War to the Arab Conquest*. New York: Schocken Books, 1976.

Baumgarten, A.
1983   "The Name of the Pharisees." *JBL* 102: 411–28.

Bavier, R.
1972   "Judaism in New Testament Times." Pp. 7–34 in *The Study of Judaism: Bibliographic Essays*. New York: Anti-Defamation League.

Ben-Amos, D.
1967   "Narrative Forms in the Haggadah: Structural Analysis." Ph.D. diss., Indiana University. Ann Arbor: University Microfilms.

Black, M.
1962   "Pharisees." *IDB* 3: 774–81.

Bloch, R.
1955   "Note méthodologique pour l'étude de la littérature rabbinique." *RSR* 43: 194–227. Trans. W. S. Green and W. J. Sullivan: "Methodological Note for the Study of Rabbinic Literature." Pp. 51–75 in Green, ed.
1957   "Midrash." *DBSup* 5: 1263–81. Trans. M. H. Callaway: pp. 29–50 in Green, ed.

Bokser, B.
1979   "The Palestinian Talmud." Pp. 139–256 in *ANRW* 2.19.2. Ed. W. Haase. Berlin and New York: de Gruyter. Reprinted, pp. 1–119 in *The Study of Ancient Judaism*, vol. 2. Ed. J. Neusner. New York: Ktav, 1981.
1983   "Recent Developments in the Study of Judaism. 70–200 C.E." *Second Century* 3: 1–68.
1984   *The Origins of the Seder: The Passover Rite and Early Rabbinic Judaism*. Berkeley: University of California Press.

Bowker, J.
1973   *Jesus and the Pharisees*. Cambridge: University Press.

Braude, W.
1968   *Pesikta Rabbati*. 2 vols. New Haven and London: Yale University Press.

Braude, W., and I. Kapstein
1975   *Pesikta de-Rav Kahana*. Philadelphia: Jewish Publication Society.

Büchler, A.
1902   *Das Synedrion in Jerusalem und das Grosse Bet Din in der Quaderkammer der Jerusalemischen Tempels*. Vienna: Hölder.

Chernus, I.
1982   *Mysticism in Rabbinic Judaism: Studies in the History of Midrash*. Berlin and NewYork: de Gruyter.

Cook, M.
1978   *Mark's Treatment of the Jewish Leaders*. NovTSup 51. Leiden: Brill.

Daube, D.
1949   "Rabbinic Methods of Interpretation and Hellenistic Rhetoric." *HUCA* 32: 239–63.
1953   "Alexandrian Methods of Interpretation and the Rabbis." Pp. 27–44 in *Festschrift Hans Lewald*. Basel: Helbing & Lichtenhahn.

Ellenson, D.
1975   "Ellis Rivkin and the Problems of Pharisaic History: A Study in
          Historiography." *JAAR* 43: 787–802.

Epstein, J. N.
1948   *Mābô' le-Nusah ha-Mišnâ* (Introduction to the Text of the Mishna).
          Jerusalem: Magnes Press. Tel Aviv: Dvir.
1957   *Měbô'ôt lě-siprût ha-Tannā'îm* (Introductions to the Literature of
          the Tannaim). Jerusalem: Magnes Press. Tel-Aviv: Dvir.

Finkelstein, L.
1936   *Akiba: Scholar, Saint and Martyr.* Philadelphia: Jewish Publication
          Society.

Fischel, H.
1973   *Rabbinic Literature and Greco-Roman Philosophy: A Study of Epi-
          curea and Rhetorica in Early Midrashic Writings.* SPB 21. Leiden:
          Brill.

Fischel, H., ed.
1977   *Essays in Greco-Roman and Related Talmudic Literature.* New
          York: Ktav.

Fraade, S.
1983   "Sifre Deuteronomy 26 (ad Deut. 3:23): How Conscious the Com-
          position?" *HUCA* 54: 245–301.

Fraenkel, J.
1971   "Bible Verses Quoted in the Tales of the Sages." Pp. 80–99 in Heine-
          mann and Noy, eds.
1978   "Šě'ēlôt Hermenûtyôt Běheqer Sîppûr hā-'Aggādâ" (Hermeneutic
          Problems in the Study of the Aggadic Narrative). *Tarbiz* 47: 139–72.

Gereboff, J.
1979   *Rabbi Tarfon: The Tradition, the Man, and Early Rabbinic
          Judaism.* Brown Judaic Studies 7. Missoula, MT: Scholars Press.

Glatzer, N.
1956   *Hillel the Elder: The Emergence of Classical Judaism.* New York:
          Bnai Brith.

Goldberg, Abraham
1955   *Masseket 'Ōhālôt* (The Mishnah Treatise Ohalot). Jerusalem:
          Magnes Press.
1958–59   "Darkô šel R. Yěhûdâ Hā-Nāśî' běsiddûr ha-Mišnâ" (The Method of
          Judah the Patriarch in the Arrangement of the Mishnah). *Tarbiz*
          28: 260–69.
1976   *Pērûš la-Mišnâ Masseket Šabbāt* (Commentary to the Mishnah:
          Shabbat). Jerusalem: Jewish Theological Seminary.

Goldberg, Arnold
1969   *Untersuchungen über die Vorstellung von der Schekhinah in der
          frühen Rabbinischen Literatur — Talmud und Midrasch.* SJ 5.
          Berlin: de Gruyter.
1973   "Der Vortrag des Ma'ase Merkawa: Eine Vermutung zur frühen
          Merkawamystik." *Judaica* 29: 4–23.
1974   "Form und Funktion des Ma'ase in der Mischna." *Frankfurter
          Jüdische Beiträge.* 2: 1–38.

1977a "Entwurf einer formanalytischer Methode für die Exegese der rabbinischen Traditionsliteratur." *Frankfurter Jüdische Beiträge* 5: 1–41.

1977b *Ich komme und wohne in deiner Mitte: Eine rabbinische Homilie zu Sach. 2, 14 (PesR 35)*. Frankfurter Jüdische Studien 3. Frankfurt am Main: Gesellschaft zur Forderung Jud. St.

Goldenberg, R.

1972 "The Deposition of Rabban Gamaliel II: An Examination of the Sources." *JJS* 23: 167–90.

1978 *The Sabbath Law of Rabbi Meir*. Brown Judaic Studies 6. Missoula, MT: Scholars Press.

Goldin, J.

1965 "Judaism." Pp. 191–228 in *A Reader's Guide to the Great Religions*. Ed. Charles Adams. New York: Free Press.

Goodblatt, D.

1979 "The Babylonian Talmud." Pp. 257–336 in *ANRW* 2.19.2. Ed. W. Haase. Berlin and New York: de Gruyter.

Goodman, M.

1977 Review of M. Avi-Yonah, *The Jews of Palestine. JJS* 28: 85–88.

Green, W.

1973 "Abraham Goldberg." Pp. 225–41 in *The Modern Study of the Mishnah*. Ed. J. Neusner. SPB 23. Leiden: Brill.

1977 *Persons and Institutions in Early Rabbinic Judaism*. Brown Judaic Studies 3. Missoula, MT: Scholars Press.

1978 "What's in a Name—The Problematic of Rabbinic 'Biography.'" Pp. 77–96 in Green, ed.

1980 *The Traditions of Joshua ben Hananiah*, part 1. Leiden: Brill.

Green, W., ed.

1978 *Approaches to Ancient Judaism: Theory and Practice*. Brown Judaic Studies 1. Missoula, MT: Scholars Press.

Grossfeld, B.

1972, 1977 *A Bibliography of Targum Literature*. Bibliographa Judaica 38. 2 vols. Cincinnati: Hebrew Union College. New York: Ktav.

Grözinger, K. E.

1976 *Ich bin der Herr, dein Gott: Eine rabbinische Homilie zum Ersten Gebot (PesR 20)*. Frankfurter Jüdische Studien 2. Bern and Frankfurt am Main: Lang.

Gruenwald, I.

1974 "The Jewish Esoteric Literature in the Time of the Mishnah and Talmud." *Immanuel* 4: 37–46.

1980 *Apocalyptic and Merkavah Mysticism*. Leiden: Brill.

Guttmann, A.

1970 *Rabbinic Judaism in the Making: A Chapter in the History of the Halakhah from Ezra to Judah I*. Detroit, MI: Wayne State University Press.

1976 *Studies in Rabbinic Judaism*. New York: Ktav.

Halevi (Hallewy), E.

1963 *Sa'ărê hā-'Aggādâ* (On the Nature of the Aggadah). Tel Aviv: Armoni.

1972 *'Ôlāmâ šel hā-'Aggādâ* (The World of Aggadah). Tel Aviv: Dvir.

Halperin, D.
1980   *The Merkabah in Rabbinic Literature*. New Haven, CT: American
          Oriental Society.
Heinemann, I.
1954   *Darkê ha-'Aggādâ* (The Ways of Haggada). Jerusalem: Magnes
          Press.
Heinemann, J.
1963–64   "Ha-Mahăzōr hā-'Atlat Šannatî wĕ-Lûah ha-Šānâ" (The Triennial
          Cycle and Calendar). *Tarbiz* 33: 362–68.
1968   "The Triennial Lectionary Cycle." *JJS* 19: 41–48.
1969/71   " 'Ommānût Haqômpôzîsiyya Bĕmidraš Wayyiqrā' Rabbā' " (The
          Art of Composition in Leviticus Rabba). *Ha-Sifrut* 2: 808–34. Ab-
          breviated English version: "Profile of a Midrash: The Art of Com-
          position in Leviticus Rabba." *JAAR* 39 (1971) 141–50.
1970   *Ha-Dĕrāšôt ba-Ṣibbûr Bitqûpat ha-Talmûd* (Expositions in the
          Community during the Talmudic Period). Jerusalem: Bialik
          Institute.
1971   "The Proem in the Aggadic Midrashim: A Form-Critical Study."
          Pp. 100–122 in Heinemann and Noy, eds.
1974   *'Aggādôt we-Tôlĕdôtêhen* (Haggodot and Their History). Jerusa-
          lem: Keter.
1977   *Prayer in the Talmud: Forms and Patterns*. Trans. by R. Sarason.
          SJ 9. Berlin and New York: de Gruyter. Translation of *Ha-Tĕfillâ
          Bitĕqûfat ha-Tannā'îm wĕ-hā-'Amôrā'îm*. Jerusalem: Magnes Press,
          1964 (original ed., 1962)
1982   "A Homily on Jeremiah and the Fall of Jerusalem." Pp. 106–27 in
          The Biblical Mosaic: Changing Perspectives. Ed. E. Rothman and
          R. Polzin. Semeia Supplement. Missoula, MT: Scholars Press.

Heinemann, J., and D. Noy, eds.
1971   *Studies in Aggadah and Folk Lore*. Scripta Hierosolymitana 22.
          Jerusalem: Magnes Press.

Heinemann, J., and J. Petuchowski, eds.
1975   *Literature of the Synagogue*. New York: Behrman.

Herr, M.
1971   "The Historical Significance of the Dialogues between Jewish Sages
          and Roman Dignitaries." Pp. 123–50 in Heinemann and Noy, eds.

Hoenig, S.
1953   *The Great Sanhedrin*. New York: Bloch.

Hoffman, L. A.
1979   *The Canonization of the Synagogue Service*. UNDCSJCA 4. Notre
          Dame and London: University of Notre Dame Press.

Horbury, W.
1980   "Keeping Up with Recent Studies. V. Rabbinics." *ExpTim* 91:
          233–40.

Hyman, A.
1936   *Seper Tōlĕdôt Tannā'îm wĕ-'Amôrā'îm* (The History of the Tan-
          naim and Amoraim). Jerusalem: Kiryah Neemanah.

Institute for the Complete Israeli Talmud, Jerusalem
1972–   *The Babylonian Talmud. Tractate Ketuboth*. 2 vols. Ed. M. Hersh-
          ler. 1972, 1977. *Tractate Sotah*. Ed. A. Liss. 1979.

Jacobs, L.
1971   "Hermeneutics." *EncJud* 8: cols. 366–72.

Kadushin, M.
1932   *The Theology of Seder Eliahu (Rabba and Zuta)*. New York: Bloch.
1938   *Organic Thinking: A Study in Rabbinic Thought*. New York: Jewish
            Theological Seminary.
1952   *The Rabbinic Mind*. New York: Jewish Theological Seminary.
1964   *Worship and Ethics: A Study in Rabbinic Judaism*. Evanston, IL:
            Northwestern University Press.

Kagan, Z.
1971   "Divergent Tendencies and Their Literary Moulding in the Agga-
            dah." Pp. 151–70 in Heinemann and Noy, eds.

Kanter, S.
1977   *Legal Traditions of Rabban Gamaliel II*. SJLA 8. Leiden: Brill.

Kohler, K.
1918   *Jewish Theology Systematically and Historically Considered*.
            Reprint, New York: Ktav, 1968. Revised from *Grundriss einer syste-
            matischen Theologie des Judentums auf geschichtlicher Grundlage*.
            Leipzig: Fock, 1910.

Konovitz, I.
1965   *Rabbi 'Aqîbâ* (Rabbi Akiba: Collected Sayings in Halakah and
            Aggadah in the Talmudic Literature). Jerusalem: Mossad Harav
            Kook.

Kuhn, P.
1968   *Gottes Selbsterniedrigung in der Theologie der Rabbinen*. SANT
            17. Munich: Kösel.
1978   *Gottes Trauer und Klage in der Rabbinischen Überlieferung
            (Talmud und Midrasch)*. AGJU 13. Leiden: Brill.

Le Déaut, R.
1969   "A propos d'une définition du midrash." *Bib* 50: 395–413. Trans.
            Mary Howard, "Apropos a Definition of Midrash." *Int* 25 (1971)
            259–82.

Leiman, S. Z.
1976   *The Canonization of Hebrew Scripture: The Talmudic and Mid-
            rashic Evidence*. Hamden, CT: Archon Books.

Lieberman, S.
1942   *Greek in Jewish Palestine: Studies in the Life and Manners of Jewish
            Palestine in the II–IV Centuries C.E.* 2d ed. New York: Feldheim,
            1965.
1950   *Hellenism in Jewish Palestine: Studies in the Literary Transmission
            of Beliefs and Manners of Palestine in the 1 Century B.C.E.–IV
            Century C.E.* New York: Jewish Theological Seminary. 2d im-
            proved ed., 1962.
1955–   *Tosefta and Tosefta Ki-Fshutah*. New York: Jewish Theological
            Seminary.
1974   *Texts and Studies*. New York: Ktav.
1984   "A Tragedy or Comedy?" *JAOS* 104: 315–19.

Lightstone, J.
  1975   "Sadducees vs. Pharisees." Pp. 206–21 in *Christianity, Judaism and Other Greco-Roman Cults: Studies for Morton Smith at Sixty*, vol. 3. Ed. J. Neusner. Leiden: Brill.
  1979   *Yose the Galilean: I, Traditions in Mishnah-Tosefta.* SJLA 31. Leiden: Brill.

Mantel, H.
  1961   *Studies in the History of the Sanhedrin.* Cambridge, MA: Harvard University Press.
  1967   "The Nature of the Great Synagogue." *HTR* 60: 69–91.

Marcus, R.
  1952   "The Pharisees in the Light of Modern Scholarship." *JR* 32: 153–64.

Melamed, E. Z.
  1973   *Pirqê Mābô' lě-Siprût ha-Talmûd* (An Introduction to the Talmudic Literature). Jerusalem: Dvir.

Moore, G. F.
  1927–30   *Judaism in the First Centuries of the Christian Era: The Age of the Tannaim.* 3 vols. Cambridge, MA: Harvard University Press.

Musaph-Andriesse, R.
  1982   *From Torah to Kabbalah: A Basic Introduction to the Writings of Judaism.* New York: Oxford University Press.

Neusner, J.
  1962   *A Life of Rabban Yohanan ben Zakkai ca. 1–80 C.E.* SPB 6. Leiden: Brill. Rev. ed., 1970.
  1965–70 *A History of the Jews in Babylonia.* 5 vols. Leiden: Brill.
  1970a   *Development of a Legend: Studies on the Traditions Concerning Yohanan ben Zakkai.* SPB 16. Leiden: Brill.
  1971   *The Rabbinic Traditions About the Pharisees Before 70.* 3 vols. Leiden: Brill.
  1972   *There We Sat Down: Talmudic Judaism in the Making.* Nashville: Abingdon.
  1973a   *Eliezer ben Hyrcanus: The Tradition and the Man.* 2 vols. Leiden: Brill.
  1973b   *From Politics to Piety: The Emergence of Pharisaic Judaism.* Englewood Cliffs, NJ: Prentice-Hall.
  1974–77 *A History of the Mishnaic Law of Purities.* 22 parts. SJLA 6. Leiden: Brill.
  1975   *Early Rabbinic Judaism: Historical Studies in Religion, Literature, and Art.* Leiden: Brill.
  1976   "The Teaching of the Rabbis: Approaches Old and New." *JJS* 27: 23–35.
  1977   "The History of Earlier Rabbinic Judaism: Some New Approaches." *HR* 16: 216–36.
  1977–80 *The Tosefta Translated From the Hebrew.* 5 vols. New York: Ktav.
  1978a   "Comparing Judaisms." *HR* 18: 177–91.
  1978b   "From Scripture to Mishnah: The Origins of Tractate Middah." *JJS* 29: 135–48.
  1978–80 *A History of the Mishnaic Law of Holy Things.* 5 parts. SJLA 30. Leiden: Brill.

1979a   "The Formation of Rabbinic Judaism: Yavneh (Jamnia) from A.D. 70 to 100." Pp. 3–42 in *ANRW* 2.19.2. Ed. W. Haase. Berlin and New York: de Gruyter.

1979b   "From Scripture to Mishnah: The Origin of Mishnah's Fifth Division." *JBL* 98: 269–83.

1979–80   *Method and Meaning in Ancient Judaism.* 3 vols. Brown Judaic Studies 10, 15, 16. Missoula, MT: Scholars Press.

1980   *The History of the Mishnaic Law of Women.* 5 vols. Leiden: Brill.

1981   *Judaism: The Evidence of the Mishnah.* Chicago: University of Chicago Press.

1981–83   *The History of the Mishnaic Law of Appointed Times.* 5 vols. Leiden: Brill.

1982–83   *Formative Judaism.* 3 vols. Brown Judaic Studies 37, 41, 46. Chico, CA: Scholars Press.

1982–   *The Talmud of the Land of Israel: A Preliminary Translation and Explanation.* Chicago: University of Chicago Press. 35 vols. projected.

1983–85   *The History of the Mishnaic Law of Damages.* 5 vols. Leiden: Brill.

1983a   *Judaism in Society: The Evidence of the Yerushalmi. Toward the Natural History of a Religion.* Chicago: University of Chicago Press.

1983b   *Midrash in Context: Exegesis in Formative Judaism.* Philadelphia: Fortress.

Neusner, J., ed.

1970b   *The Formation of the Babylonian Talmud: Studies in the Achievements of Late Nineteenth and Twentieth Century Historical and Literary-Critical Research.* SPB 17. Leiden: Brill.

1973c   *The Modern Study of the Mishnah.* SPB 23. Leiden: Brill.

Nissen, A.

1974   *Gott und der Nächste im Antiken Judentum.* Tübingen: Mohr-Siebeck.

Noy, D.

1971   "The Jewish Versions of the 'Animal Languages' Folktale (AT670)—A Typological—Structural Study." Pp. 171–208 in Heinemann and Noy, eds.

Oppenheimer, A.

1977   *The 'Am Ha-Aretz: A Study in the Social History of the Jewish People in the Hellenistic-Roman Period.* Leiden: Brill.

Petuchowski, J., ed.

1970   *Contributions to the Scientific Study of Jewish Liturgy.* New York: Ktav.

Podro, J.

1959   *The Last Pharisee: The Life and Times of Rabbi Joshua ben Hananyah.* London: Vallentine.

Porton, G.

1976–82   *The Traditions of Rabbi Ishmael.* Parts 1–4. SJLA 19. Leiden: Brill.

1979   "Midrash: Palestinian Jews and the Hebrew Bible in the Greco-Roman Period." Pp. 103–38 in *ANRW* 2.19.2. Ed. W. Haase. Berlin and New York: de Gruyter.

1981   "Defining Midrash." Pp. 55–92 in *The Study of Ancient Judaism:* vol. 1, *Mishnah, Midrash, Siddur.* Ed. J. Neusner. New York: Ktav.

Primus, C.
1977   *Aqiva's Contribution to the Law of Zera'im.* SJLA 22. Leiden: Brill.

Rivkin, E.
1969–70   "Defining the Pharisees: The Tannaitic Sources." *HUCA* 40–41: 205–49.
1975   "Beth Din, Boulē, Sanhedrin: A Tragedy of Errors." *HUCA* 46: 181–99.
1976   "Pharisees." *IDBSup,* 657–63.
1978   *A Hidden Revolution: The Pharisees' Search for the Kingdom Within.* Nashville: Abingdon.

Safrai, S.
1959   *Ha-Miqdāš Bitqûpat Ha-Bayyit ha-Šēnî* (The Temple in the Second Temple Period). Jerusalem: The Jewish Agency.
1965   *Hā-'Āliyyâ Lāregel Bîmê Bayyit Šēnî* (Pilgrimage at the Time of the Second Temple). Tel Aviv: Am Hassefer.
1971   "Tales of the Sages in the Palestinian Tradition and the Babylonian Talmud." Pp. 209–32 in Heinemann and Noy, eds.
1975   "The Temple and the Divine Service." Pp. 284–337 in *The World History of the Jewish People.* First Series: *Ancient Times.* Vol. 7, *The Herodian Period.* Ed. M. Avi-Yonah. New Brunswick, NJ: Rutgers University Press.
1978   *Das jüdische Volk im Zeitalter des zweiten Tempels.* Neukirchen-Vluyn: Neukirchener Verlag.

Safrai, S., and M. Stern, eds.
1974,   *The Jewish People in the First Century: Historical Geography,*
1976   *Political History, Social, Cultural and Religious Life and Institutions.* 2 vols. CRINT, Section 1, vols. 1, 2. Philadelphia: Fortress.

Saldarini, A.
1973   Review of J. Neusner, *The Rabbinic Traditions About the Pharisees Before 70. CBQ* 35: 258–61.
1975   "Johanan ben Zakkai's Escape from Jerusalem: Origin and Development of A Rabbinic Story." *JSJ* 6: 189–204.
1977   "'Form Criticism' of Rabbinic Literature." JBL 96: 257–74.
1979a   "Apocalypses and 'Apocalyptic' in Rabbinic Literature and Mysticism." *Semeia* 14: 187–205.
1979b   Review of E. P. Sanders, *Paul and Palestinian Judaism. JBL* 98: 299–303.

Sanders, E. P.
1980   "Puzzling Out Rabbinic Judaism." Pp. 65–79 in Green, ed.

Sanders, E. P., et al.
1981   *Jewish and Christian Self-Definition.* Vol. 2, *Aspects of Judaism in the Greco-Roman Period.* Philadelphia: Fortress.

Sanders, J. A.
1972   *Torah and Canon.* Philadelphia: Fortress. Reprinted with minor revisions, 1974.

Sarason, R.
1978   "On the Use of Method in the Modern Study of Jewish Liturgy." Pp. 97–172 in Green, ed. Reprinted, pp. 107–79 in *The Study of Ancient Judaism:* vol. 1, *Mishnah, Midrash, Siddur.* Ed. J. Neusner. New York: Ktav, 1981.

1979   *A History of the Mishnaic Law of Agriculture: Section Three, A
              Study of Tractate Demai. Part One: Commentary.* SJLA 27.
              Leiden: Brill.
1981a   "Recent Developments in the Study of Jewish Liturgy." Pp.
              180–87 in *The Study of Ancient Judaism:* vol. 1, *Mishnah, Midrash, Siddur.*
              Ed. J. Neusner. New York: Ktav.
1981b   "Toward a New Agendum for the Study of Rabbinic Midrashic
              Literature." Pp. 55–73 in *Studies in Aggadah, Targum, and Jewish
              Liturgy in Memory of Joseph Heinemann.* Ed. J. J. Petuchowski et
              al. Jerusalem: Magnes Press and Hebrew Union College.

Schäfer, P.
1972   *Die Vorstellung vom heiligen Geist in der rabbinischen Literatur.*
              SANT 28. Munich: Kösel.
1975   *Rivalität zwischen Engeln und Menschen: Untersuchungen zur rab-
              binischen Engelvorstellung.* SJ 8. Berlin and New York: de Gruyter.
1976   "Israel und die Völker der Welt: Zur Auslegung von Mekhilta de
              Rabbi Yishma'el, bahodesh Yitro 5." *Frankfurter Jüdische Beiträge*
              4: 32–62.
1977   "Prolegomena zu einer kritischen Edition und Analyse der Merkava
              Rabba." *Frankfurter Jüdische Beiträge* 5: 65–99.
1978   *Studien zur Geschichte und Theologie des rabbinischen Judentums.*
              AGJU 15. Leiden: Brill.
1979   "Die Flucht Johanan b. Zakkais aus Jerusalem und die Gründung
              des 'Lehrhauses' in Jabne." Pp. 43–101 in *ANRW* 2.19.2. Ed. W.
              Haase. Berlin and New York: de Gruyter.
1981a   *Der Bar Kokhba-Aufstand.* Tübingen: Mohr-Siebeck.
1981b   *Synopse zur Hekhalot-Literatur.* TSAJ 2. Tübingen: Mohr-Siebeck.
1983   *Geschichte der Juden in der Antike: Die Juden Palästinas von
              Alexander dem Grossen bis zur arabischen Eroberung.* Stuttgart:
              Katholisches Bibelwerk. Neukirchen-Vluyn: Neukirchener Verlag.

Schechter, S.
1909   *Some Aspects of Rabbinic Theology.* New York: Macmillan.

Scholem, G.
1941   *Major Trends in Jewish Mysticism.* Jerusalem: Schocken. Rev. ed.
              New York: Schocken Books, 1946.
1965   *Jewish Gnosticism, Merkabah Mysticism and Talmudic Tradition.*
              2d ed. New York: Jewish Theological Seminary.

Schürer, E.
1973–   *The History of the Jewish People in the Age of Jesus Christ,
              175 B.C.–A.D. 135.* 3 vols. New English version revised and edited
              by G. Vermes, F. Millar, and M. Black. Edinburgh: T. & T. Clark.

Silberman, L.
1982   "Toward a Rhetoric of Midrash: A Preliminary Account." Pp. 15–29
              in *The Biblical Mosaic: Changing Perspectives.* Ed. E. Rothman
              and R. Polzin. Semeia Supplement. Missoula, MT: Scholars Press.

Smith, M.
1956   "Palestinian Judaism in the First Century." Pp. 67–81 in *Israel: Its
              Role in Civilization.* Ed. M. Davis. New York: Harper.

Stemberger, G.
1975   "La recherche rabbinique depuis Strack." *RHPR* 55: 543–74.

Strack, H. L., and G. Stemberger
1982   *Einleitung in Talmud und Midrasch*. 7th rev. ed. Munich: Beck.

Towner, W. S.
1973   *The Rabbinic "Enumeration of Scriptural Examples": A Study of a Rabbinic Pattern of Discourse with Special Reference to Mekhilta d'R. Ishmael*. SPB 22. Leiden: Brill.

Townsend, J.
1972   "Rabbinic Sources." Pp. 35–80 in *The Study of Judaism: Bibliographic Essays*. New York: Anti-Defamation League.

Urbach, E. E.
1969   *Hazal: Pirqê 'Ĕmûnôt wĕ-Dēʿôt*. Jerusalem: Magnes Press. Trans. I. Abrahams, *The Sages: Their Concepts and Beliefs*. Jerusalem: Magnes Press, 1975.
1971   "Mishnah." *EncJud* 12: cols. 93–109.

Vermes, G.
1961   *Scripture and Tradition in Judaism: Haggadic Studies*. SPB 4. Leiden: Brill. 2d ed., 1973.
1970   "Bible and Midrash: Early Old Testament Exegesis." Pp. 199–231 in *The Cambridge History of the Bible*, vol. 1. Ed. P. R. Ackroyd and G. F. Evans. Cambridge: University Press.
1975   *Post Biblical Jewish Studies*. SJLA 8. Leiden: Brill.

Weiss, A.
1943   *Hithāwût HaTalmûd Bĕšelēmutô* (The Babylonian Talmud as a Literary Unit: Its Place of Origin, Development and Final Redaction). New York: Kohut Foundation.

Weiss Halivni, D.
1968, 1975   *Mĕqôrôt û-Mĕsôrôt* (Sources and Traditions). Vol. 1, Jerusalem: Bialik Institute; Tel Aviv: Dvir. Vol. 2, Jerusalem: Jewish Theological Seminary.

Wright, A.
1967   *The Literary Genre Midrash*. Staten Island, NY: Alba House.

Zahavy, T.
1977   *The Traditions of Eleazar ben Azariah*. Brown Judaic Studies 2. Missoula, MT: Scholars Press.

Zeitlin, S.
1962–78   *The Rise and Fall of the Judaean State: A Political, Social, and Religious History of the Second Commonwealth*. 3 vols. Philadelphia: Jewish Publication Society.
1973–78   *Studies in the Early History of Judaism*. 4 vols. New York: Ktav.

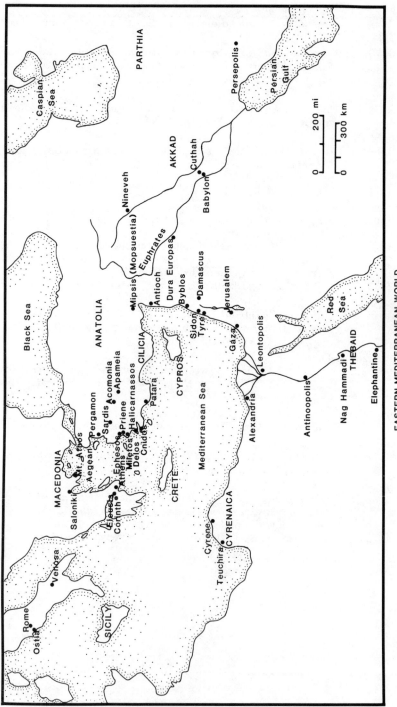

EASTERN MEDITERRANEAN WORLD

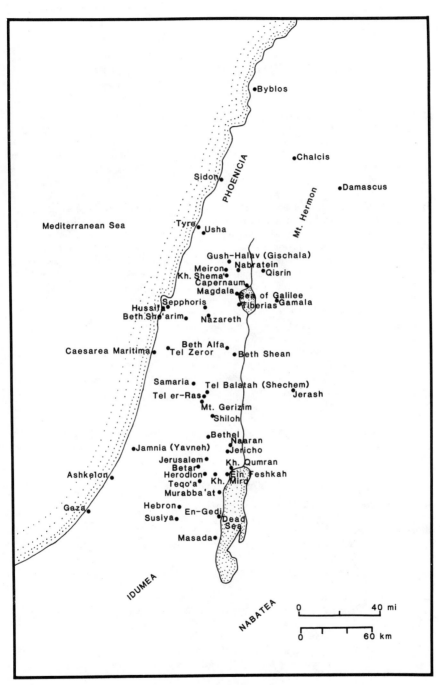

•Byblos

•Chalcis

Sidon•   •Damascus

PHOENICIA

Mt. Hermon

Mediterranean Sea   Tyre•
                                •Usha

                          Gush-Halav (Gischala)
                          •Nabratein
                    Meiron•   •Qisrin
                    Kh. Shema'
                        Capernaum•
                    Magdala• Sea of Galilee
            Hussifa•Sepphoris• •Tiberias•Gamala
        Beth She'arim•   •Nazareth

                    Beth Alfa•
Caesarea Maritima• •Tel Zeror   •Beth Shean

            Samaria•   Tel Balatah (Shechem)
        Tel er-Ras•   •Jerash
                Mt. Gerizim
                •Shiloh

                    •Bethel
Jamnia (Yavneh)•   •Naaran
                      •Jericho
        Jerusalem•   Kh. Qumran•
            Betar•
Ashkelon•   Herodion• •Ein Feshkah
        Teqo'a•   Kh. Mird•
        Murabba'at•

        Hebron•
Gaza•   Susiya• •En-Gedi Dead
                        Sea
            Masada•

IDUMEA

NABATEA   0   40 mi

                    0   60 km

SYRO-PALESTINIAN SITES

BIBLIOGRAPHIES AND TEXT EDITIONS
FOR EARLY JEWISH SOURCE MATERIALS

The primary focus of this appendix is on editions and studies of the apocrypha and pseudepigrapha, but we have also included references to some other bibliographical aids for the user's convenience. There are, of course, various other general sources to which one may turn for bibliographical assistance, such as bibliographic periodicals (e.g., *Biblica/Elenchus Bibliographicus, OT Abstracts, NT Abstracts, Ephemerides Theologicae Lovanienses*), encyclopedia articles, "state of the question" anthologies (e.g., CRINT, *ANRW, Semeia* 14 [Collins, 1979], the present volume), collected introductions to the texts (e.g., in *OTA, AOT, JSHRZ*), and survey works such as those mentioned in the Introduction (e.g., Reicke; Gowan; Nickelsburg, 1981; Collins; the new Schürer). For consistency, we have included here only those individual publications primarily and expressly devoted to bibliographic listings.

Recent decades have seen the publication of numerous new editions of early Jewish texts and some new translations based on unpublished text-critical work. Two series are especially noteworthy: The Göttingen Septuagint is a long-term project to produce critical editions of the pertinent Greek materials, which include, of course, the Greek apocrypha, of which ten volumes (plus "Psalms with Odes") have now appeared (see chap. 9). In the Pseudepigrapha Section of SBL Texts and Translations Series, edited under the auspices of the Pseudepigrapha Group of the SBL, thirteen volumes have now been published (usually with text and facing English translation). New translations of the apocrypha have also appeared in many modern translations of the Bible, in English and other languages. New translations of the pseudepigrapha include those in the two volumes of *OTP* (ed. Charlesworth), the single-volumed *AOT* (ed. Sparks), and the series of JSHRZ (ed. Kümmel). The following list does not normally cite translations from within these collections, nor have we included every work discussed in these collections, since some of them seem to be much later in date. Finally, we have not attempted to cover the possibly early Jewish materials now being culled from the Nag Hammadi Coptic codices (e.g., *ParaShem, ApocAdam, 3StSeth, Zost, Allog, Mar, Nor*; see RelSRev 8 [1982]).

GENERAL BIBLIOGRAPHIES

Brock, Sebastian, Charles T. Fritsch, and Sidney Jellicoe
    1973   *A Classified Bibliography of the Septuagint*. Leiden: Brill.
Burchard, Christoph
    1957   *Bibliographie zu den Handschriften vom Totem Meer*. BZAW 76. Berlin: Töpelmann.
    1965   *Bibliographie zu den Handschriften vom Totem Meer*. BZAW 89. Berlin: Töpelmann.
Charlesworth, James H.
    1981   The Pseudepigrapha and Modern Research, with a Supplement. SBLSCS 7S. Chico, CA: Scholars Press.
Delling, Gerhard, with Malwine Mayser
    1975   *Bibliographie zur jüdisch-hellenistischen und intertestamentarischen Literatur, 1900–1970*. TU 106/2. Berlin: Akademie-Verlag.

Denis, Albert-Marie
 1970   *Introduction aux Pseudépigraphes Greces d'Ancien Testament.* Leiden: Brill.
Feldman, Louis H.
 1962   *Scholarship on Philo and Josephus (1937–1962).* Studies in Judaica. New York: Yeshiva. [Reprinted from *Classical World* 54–55 (1960–62).]
Fitzmyer, Joseph A.
 1975   *The Dead Sea Scrolls: Major Publications and Tools for Study.* SBLSBS 8. Missoula, MT: Scholars Press.
Grossfeld, Bernard
 1972–77   *A Bibliography of Targum Literature.* Bibliographa Judaica 38. 2 vols. Cincinnati/New York: Hebrew Union College/Ktav.
Hilgert, Earle
 1984   "Bibliographia Philoniana 1935–1975." Pp. 47–97 in *ANRW* 2.21.1. Ed. W. Haase. Berlin: de Gruyter.
Jongeling, Bastiaan
 1971   *A Classified Bibliography of the Finds in the Desert of Judah 1958–1969.* STDJ 7. Leiden: Brill.
Kraemer, Ross S.
 1983   "Bibliography: Women in the Religions of the Greco-Roman World." *RelSRev* 9: 127–39.
La Sor, William S.
 1958   *Bibliography of the Dead Sea Scrolls.* Fuller Theological Seminary Bibliography Series 2. Pasadena: Fuller Theological Seminary.
Manns, Frederic
 1979   *Bibliographie du Judeo-Christianisme.* Studium Biblicum Franciscanum, Analecta B. Jerusalem: Franciscan Printing Press.
Marcus, Ralph
 1946–47   "A Select Bibliography (1920–1945) of the Jews in the Hellenistic-Roman Period." *PAAJR* 16: 91–181.
Schreckenberg, Heinz
 1968   *Bibliographie zu Flavius Josephus.* ALGHJ 1. Leiden: Brill.
 1979   *Bibliographie zu Flavius Josephus. Supplementband mit Gesamtregister.* ALGHJ 14. Leiden: Brill.
Townsend, John T.
 1972   "Rabbinic Sources." Pp. 35–80 in *The Study of Judaism: Bibliographic Essays.* New York: Anti-Defamation League.
Vogel, E. K.
 1971   "Bibliography of Holy Land Sites." *HUCA* 42: 1–96.
Yizhar, M.
 1967   "Bibliography of Hebrew Publications on the Dead Sea Scrolls, 1948–1964." *HTS* 23.

INDIVIDUAL TEXTS OF THE APOCRYPHA AND PSEUDEPIGRAPHA

Bibliography for the individual works of the apocrypha and pseudepigrapha is cited by abbreviations in smaller type at the end of each entry. The following abbreviations are used:

Charlesworth = Charlesworth, James H. *The Pseudepigrapha and Modern Research, With a Supplement.* SBLCS 7S. Chico, CA: Scholars Press, 1981.
 Delling = Delling, Gerhard. *Bibliographie zur jüdisch-hellenistischen und intertestamentarischen Literatur, 1900–1970.* TU 106.2. Berlin: Akademie-Verlag, 1975.

Denis = Denis, Albert-Marie. *Introduction aux Pseudépigraphes Grecs d'Ancien Testament*. Leiden: Brill, 1970.
CRINT = Stone, Michael E., ed. *Jewish Writings of the Second Temple Period: The Literature of the Jewish People in the Period of the Second Temple and the Talmud*, vol. 2. CRINT, section 2. Assen: Van Gorcum; Philadelphia: Fortress, 1984.
Nickelsburg = Nickelsburg, George W. E. *Jewish Literature Between the Bible and the Mishnah: A Historical and Literary Introduction*. Philadelphia: Fortress, 1981.

In addition the reader should consult the two volumes of *OTP.*

• *Abraham, Apocalypse of*
Rubinkiewicz, R. "L'Apocalypse d'Abraham en slave:Édition critique du texte, introduction, traduction et commentaire." PhD. diss., Rome, 1977.
Charlesworth, 68–69; 269–70; Delling, 163–64.

• *Abraham, Testament of*
Stone, Michael E. *The Testament of Abraham*. SBLTT 2; Pseudepigrapha Series 2. Missoula, MT: Scholars Press, 1972. (Reproduction of James's 1892 Greek texts of long and short recensions, with revised, facing translation.)
Schmidt, Francis. "Le Testament d'Abraham: Introduction, édition de la recension courte, traduction et notes." 2 vols. Diss., University of Strasbourg, 1971. (Edition of the best manuscript (E) of the Greek version of the short recension.)
Cooper, Donald S., and Harry B. Weber. "The Church Slavonic Testament of Abraham." Pp. 301–26 in *Studies on the Testament of Abraham*, ed. Nickelsburg. (Introduction, translation with critical apparatus.)
Charlesworth, 70–72; 270–71; Delling, 166–67; Denis, 31–39; Nickelsburg, ed., *Studies on the Testament of Abraham*, 9–22. (Annotated bibliographies of major works and reviews of recent translations and commentaries.)

• *Adam and Eve, Life of* (and *Apocalypse of Moses*)
Nagel, M. "La Vie grecque d'Adam et d'Eve (Apocalypse de Moïse)." Diss., University of Strassbourg, 1972. (Greek texts and concordance.)
Charlesworth, 74–75; 159–60; 273; 296; Denis, 3–14; CRINT, 153–54.

• *Ahiqar*
Lindenberger, James M. *The Aramaic Proverbs of Ahiqar*. Baltimore: Johns Hopkins University Press, 1983. (Text, translation, and commentary on Aramaic.)
Charlesworth, 75–77; 273; Denis, 201–14; Lindenberger, 319–37.

• *Aristeas, Letter of*
Hadas, Moses. *Aristeas to Philocrates*. JAL. New York: Harper, 1951. (Greek text and facing translation.)
Charlesworth, 78–80; 274; Delling, 97–98; Denis, 105–10.

• 1 Baruch
Tov, Emanuel. *The Book of Baruch also called 1 Baruch*. SBLTT 8. Missoula, MT: Scholars Press, 1975. (Hebrew retroversion of 1:1–3:8 with facing translation of Hebrew and Greek of 3:9ff.)
Delling, 140; CRINT, 155–56.

• *2 Baruch* (Syriac)
Dedering, S. *Apocalypse of Baruch*. Peshitta Institute, part IV, fasc. 3. Leiden: Brill, 1973. (Syriac text of chaps. 1–77.)
Charlesworth, 83–86; 275; Delling, 162–63; Denis, 182–86; CRINT, 439.

• *3 Baruch* (Greek)
Picard, J.-C. *Apocalypsis Baruchi Graece*. PVTG 2. Leiden: Brill, 1967.
Charlesworth, 86–87; 275; Delling, 163; Denis, 79–84; Nickelsburg, 309.

• *4 Baruch* = *Jeremiou, Paraleipomena*

• Daniel, Additions to
Ziegler, Joseph. *Susanna, Daniel, Bel et Draco*. Septuaginta, Vetus Testamentum Graecum
16.2. Göttingen: Vandenhoeck & Ruprecht, 1954.)
Delling, 148; CRINT, 156.

• *Elijah, Apocalypse of*
Pietersma, Albert, and Susan Turner Comstock with Harold W. Attridge. *The Apocalypse of
Elijah, based on P. Chester Beatty 2018*. SBLTT 19; Pseudepigrapha Series 9. Chico, CA:
Scholars Press, 1981. (Introduction, Coptic text, and facing translation, photoreproduction.)

• *Elijah, Books of*
Stone, Michael E., and John Strugnell. *The Books of Elijah, Parts 1–2*. SBLTT 18;
Pseudepigrapha Series 8. Missoula, MT: Scholars Press, 1979. (Introduction, texts, and fac-
ing translations.)

• *1 Enoch* (Ethiopic)
Knibb, Michael A. *The Ethiopic Book of Enoch: A New Edition in Light of the Aramaic Dead
Sea Fragments*. Oxford and New York: Oxford University Press, 1978. (Introduction, photo-
reproduction of MS p, translation of p with reference to Aramaic fragments and Greek.)
Black, Matthew. *Apocalypsis Henochi graece*. PVTG 3. Leiden: Brill, 1970. (Reedition of
Greek texts.)
Milik, J. T. *The Books of Enoch: Aramaic Fragments of Qumrân Cave 4*. (Oxford: Clarendon
Press, 1976. (Publication of all Qumran Aramaic fragments [except some MSS of Astronomical
Book and Book of Giants], translation, and commentary.)
Charlesworth, 98–103; 278–83; Delling, 157–59; Denis, 15–30; CRINT, 439; Nickelsburg, G. W. E. "The
Books of Enoch in Recent Research." *RelSRev* 7 (1981) 210–17; Suter, David W. "Weighed in the Balance:
The Similitudes of Enoch in Recent Discussion." *RelSRev* 7 (1981) 217–21.

• *2 Enoch* (Slavonic)
Vaillant, A. *Le Livre des Secrets d'Hénoch*. Paris: Institut d'études slaves, 1952. (Slavonic text
with facing French translation.)
Charlesworth, 103–6; 283; Delling, 160; Nickelsburg, 193; CRINT, 439.

• *3 Enoch* (Hebrew)
Odeberg, H. *3 Enoch or the Hebrew Book of Enoch*. Cambridge: University Press, 1928.
Reprint, with prolegomenon by J. C. Greenfield, New York: Ktav, 1973.
Charlesworth, 106–7; 283.

• Esther, Additions to
Hanhart, Robert. *Esther*. Septuaginta, Vetus Testamentum Graecum 8.3. Göttingen:
Vandenhoeck & Ruprecht, 1966.
Delling, 147–48; CRINT, 155.

• Eupolemus
Denis, A.-M. *Fragmenta pseudepigraphorum quae supersunt graeca*, 179–86. PVTG 3.
Leiden: Brill, 1970.
Charlesworth, 107–8; Denis, 252–55.

• Pseudo-Eupolemus
Denis, A.-M. *Fragmenta pseudepigraphorum quae supersunt graeca*, 197ff. PVTG 3. Leiden:
Brill, 1970.
Charlesworth, 77–78; 108; 273.

• Ezekiel the Tragedian
Holladay, Carl R. *Fragments from Hellenistic Jewish Authors: Volume II.* SBLTT; Pseudepigrapha Series. Chico, CA: Scholars Press)
Charlesworth, 110–11; 284; Delling, 55; Denis, 273–76; CRINT, 154–55.

• 4 Ezra
Stone, Michael E. *The Armenian Version of IV Ezra.* University of Pennsylvania Armenian Texts and Studies 1. Missoula, MT: Scholars Press, 1979. (Critical edition with facing translation.)
Charlesworth, 111–16; 284–86; Delling, 160–62; Denis, 194–200.

• *Isaiah, Martyrdom of (Ascension)*
Charlesworth, 125–30; 289–90; Delling, 166; Denis, 170–76.

• Jeremiah, Letter of
Ziegler, Joseph. *Jeremias, Baruch, Threni, Epistula Jeremiae,* 494–504. Septuaginta, Vetus Testamentum Graecum 15. Göttingen: Vandenhoeck & Ruprecht, 1957.
Delling, 140; CRINT, 156.

• *Jeremiou, Paraleipomena*
Kraft, Robert A., and A.-E. Purintun. *Paraleipomena Jeremiou.* SBLTT 1; Pseudepigrapha Series 1. Missoula, MT: SBL, 1972.
Charlesworth, 88–91; 275–76; Delling, 171; Denis, 70–78; CRINT, 86; Kraft and Purintun, *Paraleipomena,* 7–10. (Annotated bibliography.)

• *Job, Testament of*
Brock, S. P. *Testamentum Iobi.* PVTG 2. Leiden: Brill, 1967.
Kraft, Robert A. *The Testament of Job.* SBLTT 5; Pseudepigrapha Series 4. Missoula, MT: Scholars Press, 1974.
Charlesworth, 134–36; 291; Denis, 100–104; CRINT, 355; Spittler, Russell, in Kraft, *Testament of Job,* 17–20. (Annotated bibliography.)

• *Joseph and Aseneth*
Philonenko, M. *Joseph et Asénath.* SPB 13. Leiden: Brill, 1968.
Burchard, Christoph. "Ein vorläufiger Text von Joseph und Asenath." *Dielheimer Blätter zum Alten Testament* 14 (1979) 2–53.
Charlesworth, 137–40; 291–92; Delling, 95–97; Denis, 40–48; CRINT, 86.

• *Joseph, Prayer of*
Denis, A.-M. *Fragmenta pseudepigraphorum quae supersunt graeca,* 61ff. PVTG 3. Leiden: Brill, 1970.
Charlesworth, 140–42; 293; Denis, 125–27.

• *Jubilees*
VanderKam, James C. *Textual and Historical Studies in the Book of Jubilees.* HSM 14. Missoula, MT: Scholars Press, 1977. (Reconstruction of Qumran Hebrew fragments.)
Charlesworth, 143–47; 293–95; Delling, 172–74; Denis, 150–62; CRINT, 152–53.

• Judith
Hanhart, Robert. *Iudith.* Septuaginta, Vetus Testamentum Graecum 8.4. Göttingen: Vandenhoeck & Ruprecht, 1979.
Delling, 136–37; CRINT, 84–85.

• *Liber Antiquitatum Biblicarum (LAB)*
Harrington, D. J. *Pseudo-Philon: Les Antiquités Bibliques. Tome I: Introduction et texts critiques, traduction.* SC 229. Paris: Cerf, 1976. (Introduction, critical text, and French translation.)

Idem. *The Hebrew Fragments of Pseudo-Philo.* SBLTT 3; Pseudepigrapha Series 3. Missoula, MT: SBL, 1974.
Charlesworth, 170–73; 298; Delling, 174–75; CRINT, 153.

• 1 Maccabees
Kappler, Werner. *Maccabaeorum liber I.* Septuaginta, Vetus Testamentum Graecum 9.1. Göttingen: Vandenhoeck & Ruprecht, 1936.
Delling, 141–46; Nickelsburg, 159; CRINT, 184.

• 2 Maccabees
Kappler, Werner, and Robert Hanhart. *Maccabaeorum liber II.* Septuaginta, Vetus Testamentum Graecum 9.2. Göttingen: Vandenhoeck & Ruprecht, 1959.
Delling, 141–46; Nickelsburg, 159; CRINT, 184.

• 3 Maccabees
Hanhart, Robert. *Maccabaeorum liber III.* Septuaginta, Vetus Testamentum Graecum 9.3. Göttingen: Vandenhoeck & Ruprecht, 1960.
Hadas, Moses. *The Third and Fourth Books of Maccabees.* JAL. New York: Harper, 1953. (Text with facing translation.)
Charlesworth, 149–51; 295; Delling, 146–47; CRINT, 87.

• 4 Maccabees
Hadas, Moses. *The Third and Fourth Books of Maccabees.* JAL. New York: Harper, 1953. (Text with facing translation.)
Charlesworth, 151–53; 295–96; Delling, 95; CRINT, 323.

• Manasseh, Prayer of
Charlesworth, 156–58; 296; Delling, 149; Denis, 177–81.

• *Moses, Assumption of*
Denis, A.-M. *Fragmenta pseudepigraphorum quae supersunt graeca*, 63–67. PVTG 3. Leiden: Brill, 1970. (Greek.)
Charlesworth, 160–66; 297; Delling, 164–65; Denis, 128–41; Nickelsburg, 99; 229.

• Philo the Epic Poet
Holladay, Carl R. *Fragments from Hellenistic Jewish Authors: Volume II.* SBLTT; Pseudepigrapha Series. Chico: CA: Scholars Press.
Charlesworth, 168–69; Denis, 270–71; CRINT, 154.

• *Prophets, Lives of the (Vitae Prophetarum)*
Torrey, Charles C. *The Lives of the Prophets: Greek Text and Translation.* JBL Monograph Series 1. Philadelphia, SBL, 1946.
Charlesworth, 175–77; Delling, 172; Nickelsburg; CRINT, 56–60.

• *Psalm 151* and Other Psalms Not in the Hebrew Canon
Sanders, James A. *The Psalms Scroll of Qumrân Cave 11 (11QPsª).* DJD 4. Oxford: Clarendon, 1965.
Charlesworth, 202–209; Delling; Nickelsburg; CRINT, 558–60.

• Pseudo-Phocylides
Horst, P. W. van der. *The Sentences of Pseudo-Phocylides: With Introduction and Commentary.* SVTP 4. Leiden: Brill, 1978. (Text, translation, and commentary.)
Charlesworth, 173–75; 298–99; Delling, 56; Denis, 215–19.

• *Rechabites, History of*
Charlesworth, J. H. *The History of the Rechabites: Volume I: The Greek Recension.* SBLTT 17; Pseudepigrapha Series 10. Chico, CA: Scholars Press, 1982. (Introduction, text, and facing translation.)

• *Sibylline Oracles*

Collins, John J. *OTP* 1: 325. (Translation of all fourteen books and fragments.)

Charlesworth, 184–88; 300–301; Delling, 155–56; Denis, 111–22; Nickelsburg, 192.

• Sirach

Ziegler, Joseph. *Sapientia Iesu Filii Sirach.* Septuaginta, Vetus Testamentum Graecum 12.2. Göttingen: Vandenhoeck & Ruprecht, 1965.

Delling, 131–36; Nickelsburg, 69; CRINT, 322–23.

• *Solomon, Odes of*

Charlesworth, J. H. *The Odes of Solomon: The Syriac Texts.* SBLTT 13; Pseudepigrapha Series 7. Missoula, MT: Scholars Press, 1977.

Charlesworth, 189–94; 301–3.

• *Solomon, Psalms of*

Trafton, Joseph L. *The Syriac Version of the Psalms of Solomon: A Critical Evaluation.* SBLSCS 11. Atlanta, GA: Scholars Press, 1985.

Charlesworth, 195–97; 303–4; Delling, 175–76; Denis, 60–69; Schüpphaus, Joachim. *Die Psalmen Salomos: Ein Zeugnis jerusalemer Theologie und Frömmigkeit in der Mitte des vorchristlichen Jahrhunderts,* 159–63. Leiden: Brill, 1976.

• Solomon, Wisdom of

Ziegler, Joseph. *Sapientia Solomonis.* Septuaginta, Vetus Testamentum Graecum 12.1. Göttingen: Vandenhoeck & Ruprecht, 1962.

Delling, 125–31; Nickelsburg, 193; CRINT, 323.

• Tobit

Hanhart, Robert. *Tobit.* Septuaginta, Vetus Testamentum Graecum 8.5. Göttingen: Vandenhoeck & Ruprecht, 1983.

Delling, 137–38; CRINT, 84.

• *Twelve Patriarchs, Testaments of*

Jonge, M. de. *Testamenta XII Patriarcharum.* PVTG 1. Leiden: Brill, 1964. (*Editio minor,* based on MS b.)

Idem. *The Testaments of the Twelve Patriarchs.* PVTG 1.2. Leiden: Brill, 1978. (Critical edition.)

Stone, Michael E. *The Testament of Levi.* Jerusalem: St. James Press, 1969. (Critical edition of the Armenian version.)

Idem. *The Armenian Version of the Testament of Joseph.* SBLTT 6; Pseudepigrapha Series 5. Missoula, MT: Scholars Press, 1975. (Critical edition with facing translation.)

Charlesworth, 211–20; 305–7; Delling, 167–71; Denis, 49–59; Nickelsburg, 273.

• *Zephaniah, Apocalypse of*

Houghton, H. P. "The Coptic Apocalypse." *Aegyptus* 39 (1959) 43–67, 177–210.

Charlesworth, 220–23; Delling; Nickelsburg.

INDEX OF MODERN AUTHORS

Abel, Felix-Marie, 33, 36, 51, 316-17, 319-22, 329
Abercrombie, J., 231
Abrahams, I., 457
Adam, Alfred, 125, 144
Adinolfi, M., 318, 329
Aharoni, Yohanan, 120, 144
Aland, Kurt, 136, 144, 158, 168, 224, 232
Albeck, C., 441-42, 446, 451, 467
Albright, William Foxwell, 86, 92, 95, 121, 123, 142, 144, 175
Aleksandrov, G. S., 37, 51
Alföldy, Geza, 46, 51
Allegro, John M., 121, 134-35, 144
Allen, Leslie C., 227, 229, 232
Allon, Gedalyahu. See Alon
Alon, Gedalyahu, 36-37, 45, 50, 52, 454, 467
Alonso Schökel, Luis, 303, 305, 374, 376-77, 398-99
Aly, Zaki, 160, 168
Amstutz, J., 274, 279
Applebaum, Shimon, 43-44, 52, 104, 113, 189, 200, 202, 466-67
Aquila, F. Dell', 188, 202
Arendt, Hannah, 100, 113
Arenhoevel, Diego, 317-18, 320, 322, 329
Arnaldez, Roger, 399
Aschermann, P. H., 273, 279
Attridge, Harold W., 245-46, 255, 326-27, 329, 345, 354
Audet, Jean-Paul, 124, 144
Aune, D. E., 414, 418, 426
Ausejo, S. de, 419, 426
Auvray, Paul, 374, 401
Avigad, Nahman, 123, 144, 166-68, 181-82, 194-95, 198, 202-3, 413, 426
Avi-Yonah, Michael, 6, 33, 36-37, 39, 45, 52, 59, 73, 175, 178, 182, 185, 203, 205, 456, 467
Aymard, A., 320, 329

Baarda, T., 417, 426
Baars, W., 223-24, 232
Bacher, W., 450
Baeck, L., 457-58
Baer, Yitzhaq, 49, 52
Bagatti, B., 166, 168, 198, 203
Baillet, Maurice, 121, 132-33, 136-37, 144, 270, 279, 373, 399, 412, 426

Baltzer, Klaus, 16, 26, 260, 262-64, 273, 276, 279
Bammel, Ernst, 328-29
Bar-Adon, Pessah, 120, 124, 144-45
Barag, D., 212, 214, 219
Bardtke, Hans, 124, 126, 128, 130-32, 135, 145, 247, 255, 413, 426
Bardy, G., 325, 329
Barish, David A., 328-29
Baron, Salo Wittmayer, 33, 46, 48, 52, 61, 66, 69, 73
Barr, James, 26, 197, 203, 226-27, 229, 232, 345, 348-49, 362
Barrett, C. K., 417, 426
Bartelmus, R., 62, 73
Barthélemy, Dominique, 120-21, 137, 145, 159, 168, 224, 229-32, 373, 399
Bartlett, John R., 316, 329
Battifol, Pierre, 290, 305
Battistone, Joseph John, 378, 399
Bauckmann, Ernst Günter, 399
Bauernfeind, Otto, 324, 326, 337
Baum, Gregory, 101, 113
Baumbach, G., 66-67, 73
Baumgarten, A., 466, 468
Baumgarten, J., 64, 74
Baumgartner, Walter, 300, 305
Bavier, R., 468
Beardslee, W. A., 361-62
Beaucamp, Evode, 385, 399
Beauchamp, Paul, 399
Becker, Jürgen, 127, 129, 130-32, 139, 145, 260, 263, 268-71, 273-76, 279, 413, 426
Behm, J., 259, 261, 279
Beit Arye, M., 163, 169
Belkin, Samuel, 390, 399
Bell, A. A., Jr., 328-29
Bellet, Paulinus M., 317, 322, 330
Ben-Amos, Dan, 449, 468
Bengtson, Hermann, 42, 52
Benoit, Pierre, 121, 136, 145, 164-65, 169, 419, 426
Ben-Sasson, Haim Hillel, 33, 52
Bentzen, Aage, 351, 362
Bernard, J. H., 418, 426
Bertram, Georg, 226
Betti, E., 449
Betz, Hans Dieter, 354, 362
Betz, Otto, 250, 255, 327, 330
Bickerman, Elias J., 5, 11, 26, 41, 57-58, 60, 74, 88, 95, 106, 113, 201, 203, 225, 232, 275, 279, 314, 319-21, 326, 330, 379, 398-99

Birnbaum, P., 417, 420, 426
Birnbaum, Solomon A., 123, 145, 413, 426
Black, Matthew, 5, 30, 36, 60-61, 69, 74, 137-38, 145, 151, 283, 325, 330, 367, 415, 427, 457, 468
Blake, Ian, 124, 145
Blatt, Franz, 325, 330
Blenkinsopp, J., 327, 330
Bloch, J., 360, 362
Bloch, Renée, 242, 255, 445, 468
Blumenkranz, B., 103-4, 113
Bocher, Otto, 327, 330
Bodine, Walter R., 232
Bogaert, Pierre-Maurice, 294-95, 305, 359, 362
Bokser, B., 450, 465-66, 468
Borg, M., 72, 74
Borgen, Peder, 389-91, 399
Born, Adrianus van den, 374, 399
Bornhäuser, K., 419
Bousset, Wilhelm, 3, 20, 26, 35, 52, 388, 391, 399, 416, 427
Bowker, J., 60, 67-69, 74, 457-60, 468
Bowman, John, 82, 84, 88, 92-96
Brandenburger, E., 277, 279, 358, 362
Brandon, S. G. F., 72, 74, 325, 331
Braude, W., 447, 468
Braun, François-M., 138, 145
Breech, Earl, 7, 26, 351, 362
Breitenstein, Urs, 396-99
Briessmann, Adalbert, 325, 331
Bright, John, 36, 52
Brock, Sebastian P., 163, 169, 223, 227-28, 231, 233, 277, 279
Brocke, M., 427
Brooke, Gerald, 251, 255
Brooten, Bernadette, 14, 26
Broshi, Magen, 140, 145, 182
Brown, Raymond E., 248, 255, 418-19, 427
Brownlee, William H., 124, 135, 140, 142, 146, 251, 255, 317, 320, 331
Bruce, F. F., 326, 331
Brull, Nehemiah, 301, 305
Bruneau, Philippe, 185, 200, 203
Buber, M., 360, 363
Buchanan, George W., 92, 96, 140, 146
Büchler, Adolph, 50, 52, 456, 460, 468
Bulhart, V., 325, 331

Bull, R. J., 86, 89, 90, 96
Bultmann, Rudolf, 262, 265, 360, 363, 417, 419, 427
Bunge, Jochen-Gabriel, 42, 52, 320-22, 331
Burchard, Christoph, 64, 74, 119, 124, 146, 271, 279, 290, 291-92, 305-6, 325, 331
Burgmann, Hans, 140-41, 146
Burke, D., 378, 399
Burkitt, F. C., 348
Burrows, Millar, 130, 134, 146, 427
Burton, D., 123, 146
Busto Saiz, José Ramon, 232-33, 301, 306
Butler, Harry A., 124, 146

Caird, George B., 227, 233
Caldwell, T., 82, 96
Campbell, Edward F., 86, 89-90, 96
Caquot, Andre, 136, 146, 255, 293, 306, 352, 363, 399
Carmignac, Jean, 126, 130-33, 135, 139-41, 146, 248, 256, 346, 357, 363, 375, 400, 417-18, 427
Casey, M. P., 352, 363
Cassuto-Salzmann, Milka, 175, 203
Cavallin, H. C. C., 19, 27
Cazeaux, Jacques, 389, 394, 400
Chadwick, H., 417, 427
Charles, Robert H., 3, 6, 20, 27, 127, 146, 243, 256, 268-72, 274, 277, 279, 293, 347-51, 361, 363, 427
Charlesworth, James H., 3, 27, 130, 137-40, 142, 147, 233, 279, 290, 312-13, 331, 345, 347, 361, 363, 378-79, 395-97, 400, 414-18, 427-28
Chernus, I., 467-68
Chiat, M. J. S., 180, 198, 203
Chiesa, Bruno, 158, 169
Christiansen, Irmgard, 393, 400
Chroust, Anton Hermann, 388, 400
Coggins, R. J., 63, 74, 86-91, 93, 96
Cohen, Jeremy, 107, 113
Cohen, Naomi G., 326, 331
Cohen, Shaye J. D., 38, 44, 53, 140, 147, 321, 328, 331
Cohn, Leopold, 388, 400
Colafemmina, C., 188, 203
Collins, A. Yarbro. See Yarbro Collins
Collins, John J., 5, 27, 43, 53, 58, 61-62, 74, 252-53, 256, 264, 267, 276-80, 288-89, 306, 345, 351-52, 354-58, 360-64, 384, 400
Collomp, P., 326, 331
Colpe, C., 352, 364
Colson, F. H., 323, 331

Conder, Claude R., 175, 203
Conley, Thomas, 391-92, 400
Conzelmann, Hans, 377, 400
Cook, M. J., 60, 71, 73-74, 458, 468
Coote, Margaret P., 303, 306
Coppens, Joseph, 138, 147, 345, 364
Corbo, V., 179, 204
Cortès, E., 259, 262, 264, 280
Cothenet, E., 125, 127, 147
Craghan, John F., 306
Craven, Toni, 303, 305-6
Crenshaw, James L., 371, 376, 384, 400
Cross, Frank Moore, 63-65, 74-75, 86-87, 90, 96, 121, 123-24, 126, 128, 135, 142, 147, 164, 169, 198, 204, 228-29, 231-33, 240-41, 253, 256, 352, 354, 356, 364, 415, 428
Crouch, James E., 395-96, 400
Crown, A. D., 82, 93, 95-96
Cullmann, Oscar, 92, 96
Culpepper, R. Alan, 391, 400, 417-18, 428
Cumont, Franz, 184

Dagut, M. B., 319, 332
Dalbert, Peter, 312, 313, 332, 385, 401
Dancy, John C., 75, 302-3, 306, 316, 332
Daniel, Suzanne, 226-27, 233
Daniélou, Jean, 387, 401
Darnell, D., 417, 429
Daube, David, 59, 75, 325, 332, 449, 468
Daumas, François, 65, 75, 252, 256, 387, 401
Dautzenberg, Gerhard, 252, 256
Davenport, Gene L., 244, 256
Davies, Alan T., 99, 100, 102, 113
Davies, G. I., 355, 364
Davies, Philip R., 61, 75, 128, 132-33, 137, 141-43, 147, 356, 364
Davies, W. D., 59, 62, 67, 69, 75, 360, 364, 421, 428
Davis, M. C., 158, 169
de Ausejo. See Ausejo de Fraine, Jean, 376, 401
Deichgräber, Reinhard, 132, 147, 418-19, 428
Deininger, Jürgen, 45, 53
de Jonge, M. See Jonge, M. de
de Lagarde, P. See Lagarde
De Lange, Nicholas R. M., 160, 170
De Langhe, Robert, 120
Delcor, Mathias, 89, 97, 126, 128, 130, 132, 134-35, 147, 276, 277-78, 280, 287-89, 292, 303, 304, 306, 345, 352, 356, 364, 383, 401, 413-16, 428

Delehaye, Hippolyte, 39, 53
Dell'Aquila, F. See Aquila
Delling, Gerhard, 201, 204, 246, 256, 295, 306, 312, 324, 327, 332, 378, 395-96, 401, 419, 428
del Medico, H. E., 128, 148
Denis, Albert-Marie, 5, 27, 126-27, 129, 148, 169, 312-13, 332, 416, 428
Derenbourg, Josephe, 39, 53
Desecar, Alejandro J., 401
Deselaers, Paul, 296-99, 305-6
de Sola. See Sola Pool
Dever, William G., 8, 27, 175, 204
Dexinger, F., 345, 359, 364
Díaz Estefan, F., 164, 169
Díez Macho, A., 158, 161, 169, 171, 179
Díez Merino, Luis, 158, 169
Di Lella, Alexander, 163, 169, 349-50, 373-74, 401
Dillon, John, 389, 392, 401
Dommershausen, Werner, 376, 401
Doran, Robert, 321-22, 332
Dothan, Moshe, 180, 204
Downing, F. Gerald, 246, 256, 326, 332
Drijvers, H. J. W., 417, 428
Driver, Godfrey Rolles, 122, 124, 148
Drouet, Jacques, 385, 401
Dubarle, André M., 302, 304, 306, 325, 328, 332, 383, 385, 401
Duesberg, Hilaire, 374, 401
Duhaime, Jean, 129, 133, 148
Dunand, Françoise, 160, 169
Dupont-Sommer, André, 124-25, 129-30, 132, 148, 268-69, 280, 381, 402, 413-15, 429
Durry, M., 325, 332
Dyson, Stephen L., 43, 44, 53

Eckardt. A. Roy, 99, 113
Eddy, S. K., 43, 53
Efroymson, David P., 102-4, 113
Ehlen, Arlis J., 414, 429
Ehlers, B., 417, 429
Eissfeldt, Otto, 293, 307
Ek, S., 326, 332
Elbogen, I., 419, 421, 425, 429
Ellenson, D., 458, 469
Elliger, Karl, 251-52, 256
Eltester, Friedrich Wilhelm, 280, 389, 402
Emerton, J. A., 417, 429
Endrös, Hermann, 329, 333
Enslin, Morton S., 302, 307
Ephron, Yehoshua, 36, 39, 53
Eppel, R., 276, 280
Eppstein, V., 67, 75
Epstein, J. N., 441, 444, 446, 451, 454, 469
Estrada, David, 136, 148

Fallon, F. T., 345
Fang Che-Young, M., 376, 402
Farmer, William R., 57, 75, 327, 333
Farrer, A., 261, 280
Fascher, E., 265, 280
Favoloro, G., 317
Fee, Gordon D., 136, 148
Feldman, Louis H., 246, 256, 324-26, 328, 333
Fenz, Augustinus K., 301, 307
Fernández Marcos, Natalio, 223, 233
Feuerbach, L., 423
Fichtner, Johannes, 383, 402
Fiensy, D. A., 417, 429
Figueras, P., 198, 204
Finan, Thomas, 381, 402
Finkel, A., 57, 60, 69-70, 75
Finkelstein, Louis, 49, 53, 419, 421, 429, 450-51, 457, 469
Finney, Paul C., 194, 204
Fiorenza, Elisabeth Schüssler. See Schüssler Fiorenza
Fischel, Henry A., 59, 75, 267, 280, 294, 307, 440, 449, 453, 469
Fischer, Bonifatius, 224, 233
Fischer, Ulrich, 198, 204, 358, 364
Fishburne, Charles W., 289, 307
Fitzmyer, Joseph A., 12, 27, 64-65, 75, 119-20, 124-26, 134, 136-38, 142, 148, 158, 166, 169, 197, 204, 228, 233, 242, 245, 247, 256, 270, 280
Floriani Squarciapino, M., 187, 200, 204
Flusser, David, 138, 280, 293-94, 325, 333
Foakes Jackson, Frederick J., 325, 333
Foerster, G., 204
Foerster, W., 6, 27
Ford, J. M., 92, 97, 419, 429
Fraade, S., 465, 469
Fraenkel, J., 449, 453, 469
Franco, F., 164, 169
Frankfort, T., 328, 333
Fransen, Irénée, 374, 401
Franxman, Thomas W., 245, 256, 326, 334
Freed, E. D., 92, 97
Freedman, David Noel, 121
Freudenthal, Jacob, 312, 334
Frey, Jean-Baptiste, 166, 185, 188, 198, 200, 204
Freyne, Sean, 183, 197, 204, 328, 334
Fritsch, Charles T., 223, 233
Fritz, K., 265, 280
Früchtel, Ursula, 389-90, 393, 402
Frye, R. N., 354, 364
Fuchs, Harald, 43, 53

Fuks, Alexander, 107-8, 113, 166-67, 172
Fuss, Werner, 377, 402

Gadamer, H. G., 449
Gagé, Jean, 46, 53
Gager, John, 46, 53, 108, 114, 315, 334, 351, 362, 364
Gammie, J. G., 335, 364
Garnet, Paul, 136, 148
Gärtner, B., 64-65, 75
Garzetti, Albino, 42, 53
Gaster, Moses, 84, 87, 92, 97, 269, 280
Gaston, Lloyd, 99, 102-3, 114
Gehman, Henry S., 226, 233
Gelin, Albert, 377, 402
Gelzer, M., 328, 334
Geoltrain, P., 65-66, 75-76
Georgi, Dieter, 312, 334, 384-87, 402
Gereboff, J., 452, 469
Gibbert, J., 334
Gibson, J. C. L., 417, 429
Gil, Luis, 322, 334, 381
Gilbert, Maurice, 376-77, 381-82, 385-87, 402
Gill, David, 402
Ginsberg, H. L., 349, 364
Ginzberg, Louis, 126, 142, 148, 457
Giovannini, Adalberto, 320, 334
Glasson, T. F., 297, 307, 352, 354, 365
Glatzer, N., 451, 469
Glock, C. Y., 103, 114
Goldberg, Abraham, 442, 469
Goldberg, Arnold, 440, 442, 447, 462, 469-70
Goldenberg, Robert, 112, 114, 453, 470
Goldin, J., 470
Goldstein, Jonathan A., 42, 53, 61, 66, 76, 316-18, 320-22, 334
Goodblatt, D., 450, 470
Goodenough, Erwin R., 176, 184-85, 187, 194, 200, 205, 213, 219, 387, 389-90, 393, 402, 416-17, 423, 429
Gooding, David W., 225, 229, 233-34, 379, 402
Goodman, M., 456, 470
Goppelt, L., 100, 114
Goshen-Gottstein, Moshe H., 224, 228, 229, 234, 415, 429
Gottstein, M. H., 125, 148
Goulder, M. D., 418, 430
Gourbillon, J. G., 404
Gowan, Donald E., 6, 27, 33, 53
Grabe, J. E., 268, 280
Grant, F. C., 421, 430
Grant, Robert M., 46, 53
Graubard, B., 420, 430
Gray, G. B., 415, 416, 430
Grayson, A. K., 167, 169

Green, W. S., 72, 76, 444, 452-53, 470
Greenfield, Jonas C., 12, 27-28, 138, 149, 164, 170, 280, 358, 365
Grelot, Pierre, 357, 365, 383, 402
Gressmann, Hugo, 3, 20, 26
Grintz, Y., 299, 302, 304, 307. See also Grinz
Grinz, Yehoshua M., 125, 149. See also Grintz
Groh, D., 179, 208
Grossfeld, B., 449, 470
Grözinger, K. E., 447, 470
Gruenwald, I., 346, 355, 360, 365, 417, 430, 440, 467, 470
Guérin, Victor, 175, 205
Guilbert, P., 129, 149
Gunkel, Hermann, 348, 350-53, 365, 419
Gunneweg, Antonius H. J., 377, 403
Gutman, Yehoshua, 312, 315, 334
Gutmann, Joseph, 178-79, 184, 190, 205, 430
Guttmann, A., 57, 60-61, 67-69, 71, 76, 455, 470

Haacker, Klaus, 326, 334
Haag, Ernst, 303, 307
Haas, Lee, 242, 256
Habicht, Christian, 316, 320-23, 334
Hachlili, R., 166, 170, 181, 193, 198, 205
Hadas, Moses, 57-58, 60, 76, 396-98, 403
Hadot, Jean, 376, 403
Haelst, J. van, 158, 170, 224, 234
Hahn, I., 327, 334
Halevi (Hallewy), E., 449, 470
Halivni, D. Weiss. See Weiss Halivni
Halperin, D., 467, 471
Hamerton-Kelly, Robert G., 387, 389, 394, 403
Hammershaimb, Erling, 293-94, 307
Hamp, Vinzenz, 374, 376, 378, 403
Hanfmann, G. M. A., 184, 191, 205
Hanhart, Robert, 223, 224, 234, 316-17, 319-20, 334-35
Hanson, Paul D., 43, 53, 61-62, 76, 345, 349-50, 352-53, 362, 365
Harding, G. Lankester, 119, 123, 149
Hare, D. R. A., 99, 102-3, 114
Harl, Marguerite, 389-90, 403
Harnack, A., 417, 430
Harner, P. B., 418, 430
Harnisch, W., 359-60, 365
Harrelson, W., 275, 280

Harrington, Daniel J., 12, 27, 99, 114, 166, 169, 197, 204, 241, 257, 423, 430
Harris, J. R., 294-95, 307, 417, 430
Hartman, Lars, 347, 360, 365-66
Hartman, Louis F., 349-50, 366, 403
Haspecker, Josef, 376, 403
Hata, Gohei, 326, 335
Hayes, John H., 33, 53
Hecht, Richard, 390, 403
Hegermann, Harald, 391, 403
Heinemann, Isaak, 102, 108, 114, 390-91, 403, 448, 471
Heinemann, Joseph, 411-12, 418-22, 430, 447-50, 471
Hellholm, David, 8, 27, 345, 347, 362, 366
Hengel, Martin, 6, 10, 27, 33, 43-44, 54, 57-58, 60-62, 72, 76, 105-6, 114, 142, 149, 186, 197, 200, 205, 265, 280-81, 314-15, 320-21, 327, 335, 354-56, 366, 375, 379, 395, 403, 415, 430, 440
Hennecke, E., 430
Herford, R. T., 457
Herr, M., 453, 471
Hilgert, Earle, 387, 404
Hill, David, 227, 234
Hill, G. F., 214, 219
Hillers, Delbert R., 12
Himmelfarb, Martha, 23, 27, 366
Hirsch, E., 449
Höcherl, Alfons, 325, 335
Hoenig, S., 456, 471
Höffken, Peter, 377, 404
Hoffman, Lawrence A., 205, 419, 430, 466, 471
Holladay, Carl, 326, 335
Hollander, H. W., 276, 281
Holm-Nielsen, Svend, 130, 149, 412-16, 431
Holtz, T., 292, 307
Hooke, S. H., 351, 366
Hopkins, C., 184, 206
Hopkins, Keith, 39, 54
Hopkins, Simon, 163, 170
Horbury, W., 465, 471
Horgan, Maurya P., 135, 247, 257
Horst, P. W. van der, 395, 396, 404
Howard, George E., 103, 114, 223, 234, 379, 388, 404
Huet, Gedeon, 300, 307
Hultgård, A., 268, 271, 275-76, 281
Hunkin, J. W., 271, 281
Hunzinger, C.-H., 121, 132, 149
Hüttenmeister, F., 180, 193, 198, 206
Hyman, A., 451, 471
Hyvärinen, Kyösti, 234

Isaac, Jules, 100-102, 104, 114
Isbell, Charles D., 164, 170
Isenberg, S. R., 362, 366
Isser, S. J., 82, 90, 93-95, 97
Iwry, Samuel, 126-27, 142, 149

Jacob, Edmond, 376, 404
Jacobs, L., 449, 472
Jacoby, Felix, 312, 335
Jacques, Xavier, 224, 234
James, M. R., 276-77, 281, 415-16, 419, 434
Jansen, H. L., 412, 416, 422, 431
Janssen, Enno, 277-78, 281, 287-89, 307, 360, 366
Janzen, J. Gerald, 159, 170, 229, 234
Jaubert, Annie, 137, 149, 281, 327, 416, 431
Jellicoe, Sidney, 223, 227, 233-34, 378, 404
Jeremias, Gert, 130-31, 139-41, 149, 413, 431
Jeremias, Joachim, 6, 27, 37, 48, 54, 60, 66-70, 76, 281, 290, 292, 307, 418, 431
Jervell, Jacob, 272, 281, 326
Johnson, N. B., 412, 431
Jones, A. H. M., 48, 54
Jonge, H. J. de, 5, 271-72
Jonge, M. de, 27, 138, 147, 154, 260, 268-73, 276, 281, 327, 335
Jongeling, Bastiaan, 64, 76, 119, 149
Jörns, K.-P., 419, 431
Juster, Jean, 102, 114
Justus, Bernard, 326, 335

Kadman, L., 214, 219
Kadushin, M., 426, 431, 460-61, 472
Kagan, Z., 453, 472
Kahle, Paul E., 158, 225, 234, 378-79, 404
Kaiser, Otto, 376, 404
Kanael, B., 212, 214, 219
Kanter, S., 452, 472
Kaplan, J., 166, 170
Kappler, Werner, 223, 316, 335
Kapstein, I., 468
Käsemann, E., 281
Katz, Peter, 223, 229, 234, 316, 335, 388, 404
Kaufman, Stephen A., 12, 164, 170
Kautzsch, Emil, 3, 6, 27, 268, 282
Kearns, Conleth, 374, 376, 404
Kee, H. C., 264, 268, 275-76, 282
Kellermann, Ulrich, 322, 336
Kennard, J. Spencer, 39, 45, 54
Kiechle, Franz, 320, 336
Kilpatrick, George D., 290, 307, 316, 336
Kimelman, R., 466
Kindler, A., 191, 206, 212-13, 215, 219

Kingdon, H. P., 72, 76
Kippenberg, H. G., 48, 54, 63, 76, 82, 86, 88, 90, 93-94, 97
Kitchener, H. H., 175, 203
Kittel, Gerhard, 200-201, 206, 226, 234
Klausner, J., 72, 76
Klein, Charlotte, 10, 28, 104, 115
Klein, M. L., 161, 170
Klein, Ralph W., 86, 90, 97, 235, 241, 257
Klein, S., 198, 206
Klijn, A. F. J., 349, 366, 404, 417, 431
Klinzing, Georg, 129, 149
Kloner, A., 206
Knibb, Michael A., 5, 127, 138-40, 142, 149, 345, 355, 357, 361, 366
Knight, Douglas A., 4, 28
Kobelski, P. J., 354, 366
Koch, K., 345, 356, 359-61, 366
Kochavi, Moshe, 179, 206
Koenig, John, 99, 115
Koester, Helmut, 328, 336
Koffmahn, Elisabeth, 165, 170
Kohl, H., 177, 206
Kohler, K., 265, 282, 416-17, 421, 431, 460, 472
Kolenkow, A. B., 260-61, 263-64, 266-67, 273, 276-77, 282, 288-89, 307-8
Konovitz, I., 451, 472
Korteweg, T., 282
Kovacs, B. W., 62, 76
Kraabel, A. Thomas, 6, 28, 104, 115, 176-77, 183-88, 191-92, 194, 201, 206, 208
Kraeling, C. H., 184, 200, 206
Kraemer, Ross S., 8, 14, 28
Kraft, C. F., 413-14, 431
Kraft, Robert A., 6-7, 9, 13, 22-23, 28, 159, 170, 224-25, 227, 231, 235, 277, 282, 287, 294, 308, 412, 432
Krämer, Hans Joachim, 389, 404
Krauss, S., 195, 206
Kreissig, Heinz, 42, 44, 48, 54, 320, 336
Kroll, J., 200, 419, 432
Küchler, M., 282
Kuhn, Heinz-Wolfgang, 130-31, 149, 413-14, 432
Kuhn, Karl Georg, 127, 129-30, 135, 138, 142-43, 150, 269, 282, 292, 308, 416, 418, 421, 432
Kuhn, Peter, 462, 472
Kümmel, Werner Georg, 3, 28
Kurfess, A. M., 358, 367
Kutscher, Eduard Y., 12, 28, 159, 170, 244, 257

Lacheman, Ernest R., 122, 150
Lacocque, A., 350, 367
Lacon, F. M., 385, 404

Lagarde, P. de, 225, 378
Lambert, W. G., 357, 367
Lameere, W., 388, 404
Lane, E., 201, 207
Laperrousaz, E. M., 64-65, 76, 119, 124, 135, 150, 277, 282
Laporte, Jean, 391, 404
Laqueur, R., 328, 336
Larcher, Chrysostome, 382, 383, 385-86, 404
Larraya, J. A. G., 324, 336
La Sor, William S., 64, 77, 119, 150
Lauterbach, J., 457
Leaney, A. R. C., 33, 129, 150
Lebram, J. C. H., 299, 308, 315, 319, 336, 397, 405
Le Déaut, R., 420, 422, 432, 445, 472
Lee, John A. L., 226-27, 235
Lefèvre, A., 317, 336
Lehmann, Manfred R., 135, 150, 375, 405
Leiman, S. Z., 446, 472
Leivestad, Ragnar, 138, 150
Le Moyne, J., 66-69, 77, 378, 405
Leon, H. J., 188, 194, 200, 207
Levi, Israel, 126, 150
Levine, Baruch A., 136-37, 150
Levine, L. I., 104, 115, 176, 178-79, 190, 199, 207
Lévy, Isidore, 321, 323, 336
Lewis, David M., 166, 170, 200
Licht, Jacob, 244, 257, 277, 282, 413-14, 417, 432
Lichtenberger, Hans, 143, 150
Lieberman, Saul, 11, 28, 42, 54, 58-59, 77, 440, 443, 465, 472
Liebermann-Frankfort, Thérese, 320, 336
Lifshitz, Baruch, 120, 150, 159, 162, 166, 170, 172, 181, 185, 188, 195, 198, 200, 207, 209
Lightstone, J., 453, 458, 473
Liljeblad, Sven, 297, 308
Lindars, B., 352, 367
Lindblom, J., 61, 77
Lindner, Helgo, 325-27, 336
Lipscomb, W. Loundes, 375, 405
Liver, J., 269, 282
Loewe, H., 457
Loewenstamm, Samuel E., 289, 308
Loewenstein, R. L., 103, 115
Loffreda, Stanislao, 178, 207
Lohmeyer, E., 282
Lovsky, F., 103, 105, 115
Luck, U., 355, 360, 367
Ludin Jansen, H., 357, 367

McCullough, W. S., 164, 171
Macdonald, John, 82, 84, 87, 91, 97
McEleney, Neil J., 317, 320, 336
Mach, R., 432
McHardy, W. D., 159, 171

Mack, Burton Lee, 382-85, 387-88, 390-93, 405
McKeating, Henry, 376, 405
MacKenzie, Roderick A. F., 300-301, 308
MacMullen, Ramsay, 44, 46, 54
MacRae, George W., 327, 336
Maddalena, Antonio, 392, 405
Maertens, Thierry, 376, 405
Maier, Gerhard, 375-76, 405
Maier, Johann, 129, 136, 150
Mancini, Ignazio, 196, 207
Mann, J., 450
Manns, Frederic, 196, 207
Mano-Zissi, Djordje, 186
Manson, T. W., 348
Mansoor, M., 66-67, 69, 71, 77, 413-14, 432
Mantel, Hugo, 39, 45, 54, 440, 456, 473
Maoz, T., 179, 207
Maraval, P., 163, 171
Marböck, Johann, 373, 375-77, 384, 405
Marcus, Joseph, 373, 405
Marcus, Ralph, 6, 11, 28, 60-61, 69, 77, 86, 97, 324-25, 337, 341, 457, 473
Margalioth, M., 163, 171
Margolis, M. L., 224, 229
Marmorstein, A., 460
Martin, B., 423, 432
Martin, Raymond A., 224, 226, 235, 274, 277, 282-83, 288, 300, 308
Martin-Achard, R., 345, 367
Mayer, Günter, 388, 405
Mayer, Reinhold, 325, 337
Mazar, Benjamin, 124, 150, 175, 181-82, 194-95, 198, 207
Mearns, Christopher L., 138, 150
Méasson, Anita, 390, 405
Meeks, Wayne A., 92, 97, 103-4, 115, 390, 405
Meisner, Norbert Hans, 379, 405
Mejía, J., 320, 337
Melamed, E. Z., 326, 337, 446, 473
Ménard, Jacques E., 390, 337
Mendelson, Alan, 393, 406
Menzies, A., 417, 432
Mercati, Giovanni, 160, 171
Mertens, Alfred, 252, 257
Meshcherskii, N. A., 325, 337
Meshorer, Y., 211-16, 219
Metzger, Bruce, 316, 337, 417, 432
Meyer, R., 60-61, 66-67, 69-71, 77, 107
Meyers, Carol, 178, 208
Meyers, Eric M., 176-81, 188, 197, 207-8
Michaelis, Dieter, 376, 406
Michaud, H., 413, 432
Michel, H. J., 261, 263, 267, 283
Michel, M. Alain, 389, 406

Michel, Otto, 324, 326-27, 337
Middendorp, Theophil, 374-75, 406
Mikolásek, A., 91, 97
Mildenberg, L., 211, 215, 219
Milgrom, Jacob, 136, 150, 244, 257
Milik, Józef T., 5, 120-21, 123-24, 126, 128, 135, 137-39, 142, 151, 163, 165-66, 168-69, 171, 198, 203, 269-70, 283, 296, 298-99, 308, 357-58, 367, 399, 413, 432
Millar, Fergus, 5, 30, 33, 38-40, 125-26, 141, 166, 198, 455
Miller, J. Maxwell, 33, 53
Mingana, A., 417, 430
Moe, D., 187, 208
Moehring, Horst R., 326, 337
Molin, G., 130, 151
Mölleken, Wolfgang, 320, 337
Möller, Christa, 325, 337
Momigliano, Arnoldo, 320-22, 337
Mommsen, Theodor, 34
Mondésert, Claude, 387, 399
Monsengwo Pasinya, Laurent, 227, 235
Montgomery, James, 84, 91, 93, 97
Moore, Carey A., 299-302, 308, 378, 406, 422, 432
Moore, George Foot, 3, 10, 28, 102, 104, 115, 419, 423, 433, 437, 460-61, 473
Moraldi, Luigi, 135, 151, 413, 433
Morawe, G., 130, 151, 413-14, 433
Mørkholm, Otto, 320, 338
Mowinckel, S., 351-53, 367, 377, 406, 414, 419, 433
Mras, Karl, 325, 338
Müller, H. P., 355, 367
Muller, Helmut, 320, 334
Müller, K., 354, 367
Müller, U. B., 353, 367
Münchow, C., 367
Munck, J., 261-63, 283
Murdock, W., 354, 367
Murphy-O'Connor, Jerome, 64-65, 73, 77, 126-29, 136, 138, 140-43, 151-52, 357, 367, 414, 433
Murray, Robert, 104, 115, 417-18, 433
Musaph-Andriesse, R., 465, 473
Mussies, G., 198, 208

Naveh, Joseph, 12, 28, 166-67, 171, 198-99, 208
Negev, Abraham, 166, 171
Netzer, E., 178, 181, 205, 208
Neuhaus, Gunter O., 317, 338

Neusner, Jacob, 38, 49, 59, 69-73, 77, 104, 115, 141, 152, 184, 190-91, 196, 202, 208, 327, 338, 412, 419, 433, 441, 443-44, 450-52, 456-57, 459-60, 462-66, 473-74
Nicholl, G. R., 124, 155
Nickelsburg, George W. E., 5, 8, 14-15, 19, 24, 28-29, 61-62, 77, 137-39, 142-43, 152, 243-46, 257, 276-78, 283, 288-95, 297-305, 308, 317, 322, 338, 351, 353, 356, 358, 361-62, 367-68, 384, 386, 406, 414, 416, 433
Niditch, Susan, 294, 308
Nikiprowetzky, V., 358, 368, 394, 406
Nissen, A., 359, 368, 462, 474
Noack, B., 355, 418, 433
Nock, Arthur D., 315, 338, 416
Noja, S., 82
Norden, E., 398
Nordheim, E. von, 259, 262, 273, 283
North, Robert, 124, 152, 320, 338
Noth, Martin, 36, 54, 361, 368
Noy, D., 453, 471, 474
Nuñes Carreira, J., 304-8

O'Callaghan, Jose, 136, 152
O'Connell, Kevin, 231, 235
O'Dell, J., 415, 433
Oppenheim, A. Leo, 253, 257
Oppenheimer, Aharon, 50, 54, 68, 70-71, 78, 466, 474
Orlinsky, Harry M., 223, 227, 229, 235
Ory, G., 64, 78, 125, 152
Osten-Sacken, Peter von der, 129, 133, 152, 354-55, 368
Otzen, B., 138, 152, 269, 283
Ovadiah, A., 179, 198, 208

Paeslack, Meinhard, 227, 235
Parker, Pierson, 136, 152
Parkes, James, 102, 115
Pascal, Pierre, 325, 338
Pascher, Joseph, 392, 406
Patte, Daniel, 242, 257
Paul, André, 142, 152
Pautrel, Raymond, 374, 406
Pelletier, André, 324, 326, 328, 338, 379, 406
Penna, Angelo, 316, 318, 338, 378, 406
Pépin, Jean, 393, 406
Perrin, Norman, 350, 368
Perrot, Charles, 120, 153, 242, 245, 257
Pervo, Richard I., 291, 309
Pesch, R., 352, 368
Peters, Melvin K. H., 224, 235
Petersen, H., 326, 338
Petit, Françoise, 388, 406

Petuchowski, J. J., 419-22, 425, 427, 430, 433, 447, 450, 471, 474
Pfeiffer, Robert H., 6, 29, 299-304, 309
Philonenko, Marc, 138, 153, 268-69, 276, 283, 290-93, 309, 325, 338, 361, 368, 383, 406, 415, 417, 433
Philonenko-Sayar, B., 361, 368
Picard, J.-C., 351, 368
Pietersma, Albert, 163, 224, 235
Pines, S., 328, 338
Plöger, Otto, 14, 29, 61-62, 78, 300-301, 309, 320, 338-39
Plassart, A., 185
Ploeg, J. P. M. van der, 121, 132, 135-36, 153
Podro, J., 451, 474
Poehlmann, W., 186, 200, 209
Poole, J. B., 146
Porter, P. A., 350, 368
Porton, Gary G., 59, 65, 78, 242, 257, 445-46, 452, 465, 474
Poswick, F., 224
Pötscher, W., 328, 339
Pouilloux, Jean, 399
Pouilly, Jean, 129, 153
Prato, Gian Luigi, 376, 406
Priebatsch, H. Y., 304, 309
Priest, J., 277, 284
Primus, C., 452, 475
Propp, V., 449
Pummer, Reinhard, 82, 97
Purintun, Ann-Elizabeth, 294, 308
Purvis. James D., 63, 78, 82, 86, 88-90, 92, 94, 97, 100

Qedar, S. H., 212, 219
Qimron, A., 136, 153

Rabin, Chaim, 50, 54, 124, 126, 153, 209, 227, 236
Rabinowitz, I., 125, 127, 140, 153, 200
Rabinowitz, L., 142, 153, 377
Rad, G. von, 262, 355, 368, 372, 376, 384, 407
Rahlfs, A., 171, 223, 396
Rahmani, L. Y., 198, 209
Rajak, Tessa, 325, 328, 339
Rapallo, Umberto, 226, 236
Raphaël, F., 354, 368
Rappaport, U., 212, 219, 415, 434
Reed, R., 146
Reeg, G., 180, 193, 198, 206
Reese, James M., 380, 382, 385-87, 407
Reicke, Bo, 6, 29, 33, 36, 54, 86, 97
Reider, Joseph, 122, 153, 232, 236
Reifenberg, A., 214, 219
Reiling, J., 327, 339

Reinach, T., 29, 102, 105, 115
Reiner, J., 325, 339
Renaud, B., 318, 339
Rengstorf, K. H., 274, 284, 324-25, 339
Repo, Eero, 227, 236
Rese, M., 418, 434
Revell, E. J., 171
Rhoads, David M., 43, 54, 277, 284
Ricciotti, Giuseppe, 36, 324, 339
Richardson, Peter, 103-4, 115
Richnow, W., 321-22, 339
Rickenbacher, Otto, 373, 399, 407
Ricoeur, P., 265, 350
Riessler, Paul, 3, 29
Rivkin, Ellis, 39, 55, 59-60, 68-69, 71, 78, 141, 153, 440, 456-60, 475
Robert, L., 167, 171, 185, 198, 200-201, 209
Roberts, Colin H., 136, 153, 160, 171
Robinson, Edward, 175
Robinson, S. E., 284
Rokeah, David, 164, 171
Ros, Jan, 226, 236
Rosen, H. B., 12, 29
Rössler, D., 359-60, 368
Rostovtzeff, Michael, 46, 55
Roth, Cecil, 72, 78, 124-25, 153
Roth, Wolfgang M. W., 302, 309
Rowland, C., 61, 78, 346, 355, 360, 368
Rowley, Harold H., 63, 78, 84-85, 87, 98, 121, 125, 134, 140, 154, 349, 369
Royse, James, 388
Rubinstein, A., 325, 339
Rudolph, K., 417, 434
Ruether, Rosemary, 99, 101-4, 115-16
Rüger, Hans Peter, 160, 171, 373, 407
Ruppert, Lothar, 297, 309
Russell, D. S., 5-6, 29, 33, 36, 55, 61, 78, 349, 369
Rylaarsdam, J. Coert, 384, 407
Ryle, H. E., 415-16, 419, 434

Sachs, Abraham J., 167, 171, 319, 339
Safrai, Shmuel, 28-29, 55, 197-98, 209, 454-56, 475
Saldarini, Anthony J., 62, 78, 321, 339, 345, 360, 369, 440, 444, 453, 459, 463-64, 475
Sanders, E. P., 10, 16, 20-21, 29, 78, 104, 284, 287-89, 309, 346, 359-60, 369, 375, 407, 415-16, 426, 434, 463-64, 466, 475
Sanders, J. A., 64, 78, 121, 266, 373, 375, 405, 407, 414-15, 428, 434, 445, 475

Lagarde, P. de, 225, 378
Lambert, W. G., 357, 367
Lameere, W., 388, 404
Lane, E., 201, 207
Laperrousaz, E. M., 64-65, 76, 119, 124, 135, 150, 277, 282
Laporte, Jean, 391, 404
Laqueur, R., 328, 336
Larcher, Chrysostome, 382, 383, 385-86, 404
Larraya, J. A. G., 324, 336
La Sor, William S., 64, 77, 119, 150
Lauterbach, J., 457
Leaney, A. R. C., 33, 129, 150
Lebram, J. C. H., 299, 308, 315, 319, 336, 397, 405
Le Déaut, R., 420, 422, 432, 445, 472
Lee, John A. L., 226-27, 235
Lefèvre, A., 317, 336
Lehmann, Manfred R., 135, 150, 375, 405
Leiman, S. Z., 446, 472
Leivestad, Ragnar, 138, 150
Le Moyne, J., 66-69, 77, 378, 405
Leon, H. J., 188, 194, 200, 207
Levi, Israel, 126, 150
Levine, Baruch A., 136-37, 150
Levine, L. I., 104, 115, 176, 178-79, 190, 199, 207
Lévy, Isidore, 321, 323, 336
Lewis, David M., 166, 170, 200
Licht, Jacob, 244, 257, 277, 282, 413-14, 417, 432
Lichtenberger, Hans, 143, 150
Lieberman, Saul, 11, 28, 42, 54, 58-59, 77, 440, 443, 465, 472
Liebermann-Frankfort, Thérèse, 320, 336
Lifshitz, Baruch, 120, 150, 159, 162, 166, 170, 172, 181, 185, 188, 195, 198, 200, 207, 209
Lightstone, J., 453, 458, 473
Liljeblad, Sven, 297, 308
Lindars, B., 352, 367
Lindblom, J., 61, 77
Lindner, Helgo, 325-27, 336
Lipscomb, W. Loundes, 375, 405
Liver, J., 269, 282
Loewe, H., 457
Loewenstamm, Samuel E., 289, 308
Loewenstein, R. L., 103, 115
Loffreda, Stanislao, 178, 207
Lohmeyer, E., 282
Lovsky, F., 103, 105, 115
Luck, U., 355, 360, 367
Ludin Jansen, H., 357, 367

McCullough, W. S., 164, 171
Macdonald, John, 82, 84, 87, 91, 97
McEleney, Neil J., 317, 320, 336
Mach, R., 432
McHardy, W. D., 159, 171

Mack, Burton Lee, 382-85, 387-88, 390-93, 405
McKeating, Henry, 376, 405
MacKenzie, Roderick A. F., 300-301, 308
MacMullen, Ramsay, 44, 46, 54
MacRae, George W., 327, 336
Maddalena, Antonio, 392, 405
Maertens, Thierry, 376, 405
Maier, Gerhard, 375-76, 405
Maier, Johann, 129, 136, 150
Mancini, Ignazio, 196, 207
Mann, J., 450
Manns, Frederic, 196, 207
Mano-Zissi, Djordje, 186
Manson, T. W., 348
Mansoor, M., 66-67, 69, 71, 77, 413-14, 432
Mantel, Hugo, 39, 45, 54, 440, 456, 473
Maoz, T., 179, 207
Maraval, P., 163, 171
Marböck, Johann, 373, 375-77, 384, 405
Marcus, Joseph, 373, 405
Marcus, Ralph, 6, 11, 28, 60-61, 69, 77, 86, 97, 324-25, 337, 341, 457, 473
Margalioth, M., 163, 171
Margolis, M. L., 224, 229
Marmorstein, A., 460
Martin, B., 423, 432
Martin, Raymond A., 224, 226, 235, 274, 277, 282-83, 288, 300, 308
Martin-Achard, R., 345, 367
Mayer, Günter, 388, 405
Mayer, Reinhold, 325, 337
Mazar, Benjamin, 124, 150, 175, 181-82, 194-95, 198, 207
Mearns, Christopher L., 138, 150
Méasson, Anita, 390, 405
Meeks, Wayne A., 92, 97, 103-4, 115, 390, 405
Meisner, Norbert Hans, 379, 405
Mejía, J., 320, 337
Melamed, E. Z., 326, 337, 446, 473
Ménard, Jacques E., 390, 337
Mendelson, Alan, 393, 406
Menzies, A., 417, 432
Mercati, Giovanni, 160, 171
Mertens, Alfred, 252, 257
Meshcherskii, N. A., 325, 337
Meshorer, Y., 211-16, 219
Metzger, Bruce, 316, 337, 417, 432
Meyer, R., 60-61, 66-67, 69-71, 77, 107
Meyers, Carol, 178, 208
Meyers, Eric M., 176-81, 188, 197, 207-8
Michaelis, Dieter, 376, 406
Michaud, H., 413, 432
Michel, H. J., 261, 263, 267, 283
Michel, M. Alain, 389, 406

Michel, Otto, 324, 326-27, 337
Middendorp, Theophil, 374-75, 406
Mikolásek, A., 91, 97
Mildenberg, L., 211, 215, 219
Milgrom, Jacob, 136, 150, 244, 257
Milik, Józef T., 5, 120-21, 123-24, 126, 128, 135, 137-39, 142, 151, 163, 165-66, 168-69, 171, 198, 203, 269-70, 283, 296, 298-99, 308, 357-58, 367, 399, 413, 432
Millar, Fergus, 5, 30, 33, 38-40, 125-26, 141, 166, 198, 455
Miller, J. Maxwell, 33, 53
Mingana, A., 417, 430
Moe, D., 187, 208
Moehring, Horst R., 326, 337
Molin, G., 130, 151
Mölleken, Wolfgang, 320, 337
Möller, Christa, 325, 337
Momigliano, Arnoldo, 320-22, 337
Mommsen, Theodor, 34
Mondésert, Claude, 387, 399
Monsengwo Pasinya, Laurent, 227, 235
Montgomery, James, 84, 91, 93, 97
Moore, Carey A., 299-302, 308, 378, 406, 422, 432
Moore, George Foot, 3, 10, 28, 102, 104, 115, 419, 423, 433, 437, 460-61, 473
Moraldi, Luigi, 135, 151, 413, 433
Morawe, G., 130, 151, 413-14, 433
Mørkholm, Otto, 320, 338
Mowinckel, S., 351-53, 367, 377, 406, 414, 419, 433
Mras, Karl, 325, 338
Müller, H. P., 355, 367
Muller, Helmut, 320, 334
Müller, K., 354, 367
Müller, U. B., 353, 367
Münchow, C., 367
Munck, J., 261-63, 283
Murdock, W., 354, 367
Murphy-O'Connor, Jerome, 64-65, 73, 77, 126-29, 136, 138, 140-43, 151-52, 357, 367, 414, 433
Murray, Robert, 104, 115, 417-18, 433
Musaph-Andriesse, R., 465, 473
Mussies, G., 198, 208

Naveh, Joseph, 12, 28, 166-67, 171, 198-99, 208
Negev, Abraham, 166, 171
Netzer, E., 178, 181, 205, 208
Neuhaus, Gunter O., 317, 338

Sanders, J. T., 374, 407, 418-19, 434
Sandmel, Samuel, 60-61, 67, 78, 325, 339, 387, 390-91, 407, 417, 434
Sänger, Dieter, 292, 309
Santos, Elmaro Camilo dos, 224, 236
Sarason, R., 450, 465-66, 475-76
Saunders, Ernest W., 4, 29, 196, 209
Sayler, Gwendolyn B., 8, 29
Schäfer, Peter, 33, 326, 334, 440, 444, 447, 453, 460-67, 476
Schalit, Abraham, 6, 29, 33, 55, 91, 98, 320, 324, 325, 339
Schaller, Berndt, 276-77, 284, 315, 339
Schattenmann, J., 419, 434
Schaumberger, Johannes B., 319, 340
Schechter, Solomon, 373, 420, 460, 476
Scheidweiler, F., 325, 340
Schenker, Adrian, 160, 172, 232, 236
Schiby, J., 162, 170
Schiffman, Lawrence H., 126, 154
Schille, G., 418, 434
Schilling, Othmar, 374, 407
Schirmann, J., 373, 407
Schlatter, A., 317
Schmidt, Francis, 260, 266, 278, 284, 287-89, 309
Schmidt, J. M., 345, 350, 355, 366, 369
Schmithals, W., 61-62, 79, 359-60, 369
Schmitt, Armin, 300-301, 310
Schnackenburg, R., 259, 261, 284, 352, 368
Schnapp, F., 268, 284
Schneider, Heinrich, 377, 407
Scholem, G., 193, 360, 369, 440, 467, 476
Schönfeld. H. G., 79
Schötz, Dionysius P., 316, 340
Schrader, H., 189, 210
Schreckenberg, Heinz, 324-25, 340
Schreiner, J., 61, 79, 359, 369
Schubert, Kurt, 322, 340
Schulz, Paul, 137, 154, 413-14, 434
Schunck, Klaus-Dietrich, 316-17, 319-22, 340
Schüpphaus, Joakim, 300-301, 310, 415-16, 434
Schürer, Emil, 3, 5, 10, 20, 29, 33-39, 41, 46, 48, 55, 125-26, 141, 154, 166, 172, 198, 209, 276-77, 284, 325-26, 328, 340, 419, 421, 425, 434, 455-56, 476
Schüssler Fiorenza, Elisabeth, 14, 27

Schwabe, Moshe, 166, 172, 181, 195, 198, 209
Schwark, Jürgen, 325, 340
Scobie, Charles H. H., 92, 98
Seager, A. R., 184, 191, 209
Seager, Robin, 41, 55
Seeligmann, Isaac L., 223, 227, 229, 236
Segal, M. H., 127, 142, 154
Segal, Moshe Zvi, 374, 407
Sellers, Ovid R., 123, 154
Sevenster, J. N., 103, 105, 106, 108, 116
Shaked, S., 354, 369
Shanks, H., 179, 209
Sharpe, John L., 246, 257
Sherwin-White, A. N., 324, 340
Shutt, R. J. H., 326, 340
Siebeneck, Robert T., 376, 407
Silberman, L., 360, 369, 447, 476
Silva, Moises, 227, 236
Simon, Marcel, 13, 29, 59, 61, 71, 79, 92, 98, 100-104, 116, 423, 434
Skeat, Theodore C., 158, 167, 172
Skehan, Patrick W., 86, 98, 121, 123, 125, 133, 137, 154, 225, 228, 236, 302-3, 310, 373-74, 377, 380, 383, 386, 408, 415, 434
Slingerland, H. D., 268-69, 272, 284
Sloyan, Gerard S., 99, 116
Smallwood, E. Mary, 33, 41, 55, 108, 116, 324, 340
Smelik, K. A. D., 164, 172
Smith, Edgar W., Jr., 292, 310
Smith, J. Z., 354-55, 369
Smith, Morton, 6, 9, 29, 43, 55, 57, 59, 66, 69, 71-73, 79, 111, 116, 125, 154, 184, 209, 265, 284, 325, 327, 340, 421, 434, 440, 457, 476
Snaith, John G., 374, 408
Sobel, R. B., 326, 340
Soisalon-Soininen, Ilmari, 227, 236
Sola Pool, D. de, 420, 435
Sollamo, R., 227, 236
Soloff, R. A., 127, 154
Solomon, David, 324, 340
Sowers, Sidney, 326, 341
Spaer, A., 212, 220
Spanier, A., 419, 421, 435
Sparks, H. F. D., 3, 29, 361, 369
Sperber, Alexander, 225, 236
Spicq, Ceslaus, 374, 408
Spijkerman, A., 213, 220
Spiro, Abram, 92, 98
Spitta, F., 419
Spittler, R., 263, 276, 284
Stählin, Gustav, 327, 341
Starcky, Jean, 121, 139, 140, 154, 270, 316-17, 319-22, 329
Stark, R., 103, 114

Stauffer, E., 259, 261, 284
Stearns, Wallace N., 341
Steck, Odil H., 294, 310
Stegemann, Hartmut, 127, 130-31, 134, 140-41, 154, 346, 357, 369
Stein, Edmund, 391, 408
Stein, S., 320, 341
Stemberger, G., 438, 476-77
Stendahl, Krister, 103-4, 116
Stern, Menahem, 5, 29, 43, 48, 55, 72-73, 79, 105-6, 108, 111, 116, 197-98, 209, 315, 320, 326, 341
Stichel, Rainer, 162, 172
Stillwell, R., 183, 209
Stone, Michael E., 3, 9, 18, 30, 62, 79, 138, 149, 271, 277, 280, 284-85, 293-95, 310, 345, 353, 355-58, 361, 365, 369-70
Strack, H. L., 465, 477
Strange, J. F., 176-79, 181, 197, 208-9
Strugnell, John, 120-21, 130, 134, 154, 263-64, 373, 408, 415, 435
Stutchbury, H. E., 124, 155
Suggs, M. Jack, 386, 408
Sukenik, E. L., 119, 130, 155, 175, 185, 210-11, 220, 413, 435
Sundberg, A. C., 16, 30, 66-68, 79
Sussman, Ya'aqov, 50, 55, 167, 172
Suter, David W., 10, 30, 138, 155, 351, 370
Sweet, J. P. M., 381, 408
Swete, H. B., 223, 380

Tal, Abraham, 162, 172
Talmon, Shemaryahu, 64, 75, 228, 233, 236, 411, 422, 435
Tcherikover, Victor, 33, 36-37, 39, 42, 45, 55, 57-58, 61, 79, 106-8, 113-14, 116, 167, 172, 312, 323, 341, 379, 408
Tedesche, Sidney, 61, 79, 316, 343
Teicher, J. L., 124, 155
Teixidor, J., 197
Terian, Abraham, 388
Terzoli, R., 418, 435
Testa, E., 166, 172, 196, 210
Testuz, M., 417, 435
Thackeray, H. St. John, 324-25, 341
Theiler, Willy, 389, 408
Theisohn, J., 353, 370
Theissen, Gerd, 46, 55
Thiele, Walter, 236
Thiering, Barbara E., 140, 155
Thoma, Clemens, 79, 327, 341
Thomas, J., 263, 267, 274-75, 285, 296, 310
Thompson, A. L., 351, 370
Thompson, L. L., 435

Thompson, Stith, 297, 300, 303, 305, 310
Thyen, Hartwig, 387, 389, 408
Tiede, David, 326, 341
Tilborg, S. van, 418, 435
Timpe, D., 326, 341
Tov, Emanuel, 22, 125, 162, 172, 224-29, 231, 235-37, 378, 408
Towner, W. S., 447, 477
Townsend, John, 103, 116, 477
Trafton, J. L., 416, 435
Trenchard, W., 376, 408
Treu, K., 200, 210
Trever, John C., 119, 121, 123, 155
Trinquet, Joseph, 375, 409
Tucker, Gene M., 4, 28
Turdeaunu, E., 285
Turner, E. G., 37, 56
Turner, Nigel, 226, 232, 236-37, 277, 285, 288, 310
Tylor, E. B., 423, 435

Ulrich, Eugene Charles, 121, 159, 172, 228-29, 231, 237, 241, 257, 326, 341
Unnik, Willem C. van, 326, 342
Urbach, Ephraim E., 49, 50, 56, 419, 421, 423, 435, 442, 461-63, 477
Urban, A. C., 136, 155
Urman, D., 176, 179, 210

Vaccari, Alberto, 374, 409
van Haelst, J. See Haelst
van den Born, Adrianus. See Born
VanderKam, James C., 137, 142, 155, 241, 243, 258, 357, 370
van der Horst, P. W., See Horst
Vattioni, Francesco, 373, 409
Vaux, Roland de, 119-25, 135, 155, 165, 169, 399
Vellas, Basileios M., 381, 409
Venetz, Hermann-Josef, 231, 237
Vergote, J., 226, 237
Vermes, Geza, 5, 30, 33, 38-39, 64-66, 79-80, 119, 125-26, 140-42, 155, 166, 198, 239, 251, 258, 352, 370, 412, 414, 435, 445, 448, 455, 477

Vermes, Pamela, 155, 435
Vielhauer, P., 345, 359, 370
Villiers, P. G. de, 362, 370
Viteau, J., 416, 419, 435
Vleeming, S. P., 167, 172
Vogel, E. K., 210
Völker, Walther, 389, 392, 409
Vööbus, Arthur, 104, 116, 161, 172, 224, 237, 417, 436
Wacholder, Ben-Zion, 89, 98, 313-17, 326, 342
Wächter, L., 342
Waldbaum, J. C., 184, 205
Walter, N., 312-13, 315-16, 342, 379, 409
Walters, Peter, 237
Wambacq, Bernard N., 378, 409
Watzinger, C., 177, 206
Weinert, Frank D., 142, 155
Weis, P. R., 122, 155
Weise, M., 129, 156
Weiss, A., 451, 477
Weiss, Hans Friedrich, 80, 391, 409
Weiss Halivni, D., 441, 451, 477
Wellhausen, J., 350-51, 415, 436
Wendland, Paul, 388, 400
Wengst, K., 418-19, 436
Wernberg-Møller, P., 129, 156
Wertheimer, S. A., 163, 172
Wesselius, J. W., 167, 172
West, S., 290-91, 310
Westerholm, S., 60, 71, 80
Wevers, John W., 161, 223-25, 229, 234, 237, 383, 409
White, William, 136, 148
Whybray, R. N., 409
Wibbing, Siegfried, 320, 342
Wiegand, T., 189, 210
Wikgren, Allen, 296-97, 299, 310
Wilde, R., 100, 116
Wilken, Robert L., 103-4, 115-16, 184, 210
Will, Edouard, 42-43, 56
Williams, S. K., 396-98, 409
Williamson, Geoffrey A., 324-25, 342
Willi-Plein, I., 355, 370
Wills, Lawrence, 137, 156
Wilson, Andrew M., 137, 156

Wilson, R. R., 362, 370
Windisch, Hans, 392, 409
Winston, David, 354, 370, 382, 392, 409
Winter, Michael M., 374, 409
Winter, Paul, 328, 342, 415, 419, 436
Wiseman, Donald J., 167, 171, 319, 339
Wiseman, James R., 186, 210
Wlosok, Antony, 389, 409
Wolfson, Harry Austryn, 389, 392-93, 410
Woude, A. S. van der, 121, 137-38, 140, 156, 269, 285, 415, 436
Wright, Addison G., 242, 258, 380, 410, 448, 477
Wright. G. E., 63, 80, 86-87, 89-90, 98, 175
Wright, G. R. H., 120, 156
Wright, R. B., 415-16, 436
Wright, W., 414, 436

Yadin, Yigael, 120, 132, 136, 156, 165-66, 173, 182, 210, 244, 258, 373, 410
Yahalom, Joseph, 161, 173
Yankelevitch, Refael, 51, 56
Yarbro Collins, Adela, 277, 285, 345, 351, 354, 370
Yavetz, Zvi, 325, 342
Yeivin, S., 178, 205
Yizhar, M., 64, 80
Young, D., 395, 410

Zahavy, T., 452, 477
Zambelli, M., 319, 323, 343
Zauzich, K.-T., 167, 173
Zeitlin, Solomon, 61, 66, 69, 71, 79-80, 122, 156, 303-4, 307, 310, 316-17, 319, 325, 343, 454-55, 477
Zenger, Erich, 302-4, 310
Ziegler, Joseph, 223, 227-28, 237, 310, 373, 378, 380, 410
Ziener, Georg, 386, 410
Zimmermann, Frank, 296-99, 301, 310
Zuntz, Günther, 379, 410